NEW PERSPECTIVES
ON THE AMERICAN PAST

1877 TO THE PRESENT

NEW PERSPECTIVES
ON THE AMERICAN PAST

VOLUME II   1877 TO THE PRESENT

edited by   STANLEY N. KATZ
STANLEY I. KUTLER
The University of Wisconsin

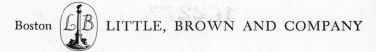

Boston LITTLE, BROWN AND COMPANY

Contents

II   MODERN POLITICAL TRENDS

III MODERN SOCIAL AND ECONOMIC TRENDS

IV WORLD POLICY IN THE TWENTIETH CENTURY: MYTH AND REALITY

Introduction

Historians traditionally have found it difficult to describe their work systematically. Until the late nineteenth century, practically everyone accepted the idea that history was a literary art, subject to aesthetic canons of judgment. But with the work of Leopold von Ranke and the other "scientific" historians who appeared at the end of the last century, new standards for research and writing came into vogue. History was conceived of as subject to precise definition and verification — for the first time, historians became professional men. When examined carefully, however, it is evident that the methodology of the early scientific historians consisted merely of the application of rigid testing to evidence in a manner analogous to the work of linguistic scholars. There was little that was conceptually distinctive in their attack upon the sources, and they were interested primarily in the political and military questions that had always been the substance of the craft.

The German historical school exerted the greatest influence in shaping the work of American historians at the beginning of the twentieth century. Universities throughout the United States adopted the seminar system of teaching and the Germanic method of rigorous research. The result was a tremendous step forward in our understanding of the American past. As doctoral dissertations were produced at Johns Hopkins, Harvard, Wisconsin, and other great universities, a more detailed and dispassionate picture of the development of the United States began to emerge. No longer were pious affirmations of national accomplishments and literary *tours de force* sufficient to command respect. Social and economic institutions, in particular, were analyzed logically and in detail, and most of the chauvinistic myths cultivated by nineteenth-century historians were discarded. Still, for all their descriptive and corrective attempts, historians had not developed many new analytical tools. For the most part, their histories were merely more painstakingly researched and less obviously self-serving.

Coincidentally with the emergence of scientific history, however, were other and more important intellectual events — in particular, the appearance of the social sciences as distinct and legitimate fields of intellectual effort. Psychology, sociology, and economics all date, in their modern garb, from this period. They had in common a desire to account systematically for human behavior, although in doing so they frequently — as in the work of Freud — resorted to non-rational explanations. As the social sciences became increasingly professionalized and sophisticated, they developed a wide range of techniques, both empirical and intuitive, for investigating human activity. They were also, and this is more important from our point of view, truly scientific in their attitude — they sought to discover the general laws that govern the operation of natural phenomena. For the social scientist, empirical data, however derived, were important only insofar as they enabled him to make statements about individual and group behavior that expressed universal truths.

Until fairly recently — rarely before the Second World War — historians seldom accepted the standards of the social scientists. They prided themselves upon their accuracy, and they occasionally talked about historical laws, but they were not as a rule interested in using historical data in order to establish behavioral generalizations. They were concerned with particular and isolated problems rather than with the rules suggested by repeated problems. History remained, for the most part, a humane and literary discipline provincial in its isolation from other disciplines.

During the past twenty years or so, however, there has appeared a generation of historians who have recognized the importance and application of social science techniques to their own work. They believe that historical data can be employed in the same fashion as experimental data in the establishment of laws of social behavior, and that historians must develop rigorous research methods and standards of proof. This movement toward amalgamation with the social sciences has had an impact upon methodology in three ways. It has evoked an interest in quantification in the search for scientifically measurable historical data. It has, in a somewhat related fashion, led to a behavioral approach at the expense of the study of thought and other less obviously behavioral phenomena. And, finally, social scientific history is characterized by its primary concern with conceptualization, since social historians are less interested in describing isolated historical events than in verifying hypotheses about conduct. In short, where traditional history is primarily descriptive, the new history is oriented toward the establishment of behavioral laws.

Historians have certain obvious liabilities as scientists. They cannot, in any real sense, design and perform experiments. The subjects of their investigation are, for the most part, dead and no longer capable of responding to inquiry. They deal with very limited quantities and types of evidence, and their evidence is frequently not easily adaptable to systematic analysis, quantitative or otherwise.

In spite of these difficulties, historians are increasingly interested in broadening the scope of their effort in the direction of the more rigorous social sciences. Some are becoming extremely adept in the use of quantification and computer techniques, and their work is sufficiently sophisticated so that they call themselves "cliometricians." Economic history has, for obvious reasons, gone farthest down the road of machine analysis. Other historians have begun to "retool" themselves in the techniques of the social sciences. African historians, among others, employ the tools of anthropologists. Social historians are becoming increasingly interested in the possibilities of demographic analysis. The motivational and behavioral discoveries of the psychologist are of obvious interest to anyone who tries to explain why men acted as they did in the past. And, in a more general sense, many historians have become more optimistic about the conceptual possibilities of their craft. They are determined to move beyond description and particularism to the investigation of behavioral — and other — rules. At the very least, the impact of the social sciences has been to make all historians question the character and relevance of their time-honored practices.

Most of the essays in these volumes reflect the new viewpoints, although they are keyed to the traditional topical and chronological subjects of American history. We have not selected articles to demonstrate (often artificial) historiographical debates; instead our selections are designed to illuminate familiar problems with sophisticated conceptualization and analysis. We are aware that some problems are not covered, sometimes because of space limitations, but often because of a scarcity of materials. The essays are reprinted *in toto*, including full citations.

Our selections are varied. Some are explicitly social scientific, and indeed many are written by non-historians. Others are written in almost total isolation from the new techniques. They are all, however, distinguished at least by their conceptual orientation; specifically, they are directed toward establishing generalizations that go beyond their immediate subject matter. Thus there are essays that utilize quantification techniques, demography, comparative history, model-building for analogizing, and derivative concepts of behavior. While some of the essays are largely descriptive, they, too, have a purpose that transcends the relation of a particular and limited body of data.

History, like most other academic disciplines, is under tremendous pressure to be relevant. The conventional recital of facts, names, dates, and the arbitrary structuring of topics and periods — all fitted into neat, but isolated, compartments — simply lacks meaning for many of today's students. Making history relevant, of course, need not involve history as propaganda or result in a promiscuous use of the past to "prove" the validity of a present viewpoint. Nor are there necessarily great lessons from the past that can be applied to the present or the future. But a comprehension of human behavior at given points and under certain conditions affords insight into similar contemporary experiences. Many of the authors included in these volumes would doubtless be amused or chagrined to discover the common company we have set them in, but we believe that they are all similar in the freshness of their approaches to the ancient problem of understanding man's past. They present a variety of perspectives on the American past, but they share something in their ambition to make it relevant to the present.

NEW PERSPECTIVES
ON THE AMERICAN PAST

1877 TO THE PRESENT

ECONOMIC AND SOCIAL CHANGE 1877–1933: IMPACT AND RESPONSE

I

The Beginnings
of "Big Business"
in American Industry

ALFRED D. CHANDLER, JR.

*The accounts of business history during the late nineteenth
century have been dominated by a long controversy surrounding the character and accomplishments of the leading entrepreneurs. Some have envisioned them as "robber barons,"
piratical, avaricious, ruthless men, motivated by an insatiable
drive for profits and power. This view developed from grievances against trusts and monopolies and gained widespread
currency during the Depression of the 1930's. For others,
these entrepreneurs were "captains of industry," innovative,
bold men whose accomplishments led to the full flowering of
the American economy. The underlying assumption of both
points of view is economist Joseph A. Shumpeter's dictum
that the innovative entrepreneur was the agent for dynamic
change. Business historian Alfred D. Chandler, Jr., accepts
the second view, but he is concerned not so much with the
personalities as with their environment, opportunities, and
responses. The great entrepreneurial achievement of the time
was not technological but organizational; it was the creation
of the vertically integrated American corporation. For Chandler, big business primarily developed to fulfill a need for the
large-scale manufacture and delivery of goods that was demanded by the rapid growth of a national and urban market
that, in turn, was created by the development of the national
railroad system. Thus Chandler emphasizes business history as
the response to changing conditions and opportunities within
an environmental, rather than a personal, framework.*

Criteria for Selection and Analysis

The historian, by the very nature of his task, must be concerned with
change. What made for change? Why did it come when it did, and in
the way it did? These are characteristically historians' questions. For the
student of American business history, these basic questions can be put a

Reprinted by permission of the publisher from the *Business History Review*,
XXXIII (Spring 1959), pp. 1–30. Copyright 1959.

little more precisely. What in the American past has given businessmen the opportunity or created the need for them to change what they were doing or the way they were doing it? In other words, what stimulated them to develop new products, new markets, new sources of raw materials, new ways of procuring, processing, or marketing the goods they handled? What encouraged them to find new methods of financing, new ways of managing or organizing their businesses? What turned them to altering their relations with their working force, their customers and competitors, and with the larger American public?

The question of what constitutes the dynamic factors in American business history, dynamic in the sense of stimulating change and innovation, can be more clearly defined if the country's land, natural resources, and cultural patterns are taken as given. Land and resources were the raw materials with which the businessmen had to work, and the cultural attitudes and values helped set the legal and ethical rules of the game they had to play. Within this cultural and geographic environment a number of historical developments appear to have stimulated change. These provide a framework around which historical data can be compiled and analyzed.

The following major dynamic forces are visible in the American business economy since 1815: the western expansion of population; the construction and initial operation of the national railroad network; the development of a national and increasingly urban market; the application of two new sources of power: the internal combustion engine and electricity, to industry and transportation; and the systematic application of the natural and physical sciences, particularly chemistry and physics, to industry through the institutionalizing of research and development activities.

The first, the westward expansion, appears to have provided the primary impetus, except possibly in New England, to business innovation in the years from 1815 to about 1850; the building of the railroads appears to have been the major factor from the 1850's to the late 1870's; the growth of the national and urban market from the 1880's until a little after 1900; the coming of electricity and the internal combustion engine from the early 1900's to the 1920's; and, finally, the growth of systematic and institutionalized research and development since the 1920's.

These five factors are essentially aspects of fundamental population changes and technological advances. There were, of course, other factors that encouraged business innovation and change. The coming of the new machines and mechanical devices may have been a more important stimulant to innovation in New England than the growth of her markets and sources of supply in the expanding South and West. Wars usually precipitated change. The business cycle, flow of capital, government policy and legislation all played a significant part in business innovation. But such political and financial developments appear to have intensified or delayed the more basic changes encouraged initially by fundamental population shifts and technological achievements.

The purpose of making such a list is, however, not to argue that one development was more dynamic than the other. Nor are these five factors to be considered as "causes" for change; nor are they "theses" to be argued as representing reality, nor "theories" to provide an over-all explanation of change or possibly of predicting change. They are, rather, a framework on which historical information can be tied and inter-related. They provide a consistent basis upon which meaningful questions can be asked of the data.

This framework and these questions are, it should be emphasized, concerned only with fundamental changes and innovation in the business economy. They do not deal with the day-to-day activities to which businessmen must devote nearly all of their time. They are not concerned with the continuous adaptation to the constant variations of the market, sources of supply, availability of capital, and technological developments. Nor do they consider why some businesses and businessmen responded quickly and creatively to the basic population and technological changes and others did not. But an understanding of the continuous response and adjustment would seem to require first an awareness of the meaning of the more fundamental or "discontinuous" changes.

Since historical compilation and analysis must be selective, it is impossible to undertake any historical study without some criteria either implicit or explicit for selection. Further study and analysis, by indicating the defects of this approach and framework, will suggest more satisfactory ones. In the process, an analysis and interpretation of change in the American business past should come a little nearer to reality.

The purpose of this article then is, by using the framework of basic, dynamic forces, to look a little more closely at the years that witnessed the beginnings of big business in American industry. What types of changes came during these years in the ways of marketing, purchasing, processing, and in the forms of business organization? Why did these changes come when they did in the way they did? Was the growth of the national market a major prerequisite for such innovation and change? If not, what then was? How did these innovations relate to the growth of the railroad network or the coming of electricity and the internal combustion engine?

In addition to secondary works on this period, the data used in seeking answers to these questions have been annual and other corporation reports, government documents, articles in periodicals, histories, and biographies concerning the 50 largest industrial companies in the country in 1909. Nearly all these companies, listed in Table 1, had their beginnings in the last years of the nineteenth century.

TABLE 1

The Fifty
Largest Industrials *

Consumers' Goods Companies

Agricultural Processing	Extractive	Manufacturing
3. Am. Tobacco	2. Standard Oil	4. Int'l. Harvester
8. Armour & Co.	26. Va.-Carolina Chem.	10. U.S. Rubber
9. American Sugar	35. American Agri. Chem.	12. Singer Mfg. Co.
13. Swift & Co.		
30. Nat'l. Biscuit		
33. Distillers' Securities		
50. United Fruit		

Producers' Goods Companies

Agricultural Processing	Extractive	Manufacturing
6. Central Leather	1. U.S. Steel	7. Pullman
18. Corn Products Co.	5. Amalgamated	15. Gen. Elec.
21. Am. Woolens	(Anaconda) Copper	16. Am. Car & Foundry
	11. Am. Smelting &	19. Am. Can
	Refining	22. Westinghouse
	14. Pittsburgh Coal	24. DuPont
	17. Colo. Fuel & Iron	29. Am. Locomotive
	20. Lackawanna	36. Allis-Chalmers
	23. Consolidation Coal	44. Int. Steam Pump
	25. Republic Steel	46. Western Electric
	27. Int'l. Paper	47. Baldwin Locomo-
	28. Bethlehem Steel	tive Works
	31. Cambria Steel	
	32. Associated Oil	
	34. Calumet & Hecla	
	37. Crucible Steel	
	38. Lake Superior Corp.	
	39. U.S. Smelting & Ref.	
	40. United Copper	
	41. National Lead	
	42. Phelps Dodge	
	43. Lehigh Coal	
	45. Jones & Laughlin	
	48. Am. Writing Paper	
	49. Copper Range	

* Numbers indicate relative size according to 1909 assets.

Major Changes in American Industry at the End of the Nineteenth Century

Between the depression of the 1870's and the beginning of the twentieth century, American industry underwent a significant transformation. In the 1870's, the major industries serviced an agrarian economy. Except for a few companies equipping the rapidly expanding railroad network, the leading industrial firms processed agricultural products and provided farmers with food and clothing. These firms tended to be small, and bought their raw materials and sold their finished goods locally. Where they manufactured for a market more than a few miles away from the factory, they bought and sold through commissioned agents who handled the business of several other similar firms.

By the beginning of the twentieth century, many more companies were making producers' goods, to be used in industry rather than on the farm or by the ultimate consumer. Most of the major industries had become dominated by a few large enterprises. These great industrial corporations no longer purchased and sold through agents, but had their own nation-wide buying and marketing organizations. Many, primarily those in the extractive industries, had come to control their own raw materials. In other words, the business economy had become industrial. Major industries were dominated by a few firms that had become great, vertically integrated, centralized enterprises.

In the terms of the economist and sociologist a significant sector of American industry had become bureaucratic, in the sense that business decisions were made within large hierarchical structures. Externally, oligopoly was prevalent, the decision-makers being as much concerned with the actions of the few other large firms in the industry as with over-all changes in markets, sources of supplies, and technological improvements.

These basic changes came only after the railroads had created a national market. The railroad network, in turn, had grown swiftly primarily because of the near desperate requirements for efficient transportation created by the movement of population westward after 1815.[1] Except for the Atlantic seaboard between Boston and Washington, the construction of the American railroads was stimulated almost wholly by the demand for better transportation to move crops, to bring farmers supplies, and to open up new territories to commercial agriculture.

By greatly expanding the scope of the agrarian economy, the railroads quickened the growth of the older commercial centers, such as New York, Philadelphia, Cincinnati, Cleveland, and St. Louis, and helped create new cities like Chicago, Indianapolis, Atlanta, Kansas City, Dallas, and the Twin Cities. This rapid urban expansion intensified the demand for the products of the older consumer goods industries — particularly those which processed the crops of the farmer and planter into food, stimulants, and clothing.

At the same time, railroad construction developed the first large market

[1] The factors stimulating the growth of the American railroad network and the impact of the earlier construction and operation of this network on the American business economy and business institutions is suggested in Chandler, *Henry Varnum Poor — Business Editor, Analyst, and Reformer* (Cambridge, 1956), especially chaps. 4, 6–9.

in this country for producers' goods. Except for the making of relatively few textile machines, steamboat engines, and ordnance, the iron and non-ferrous manufacturers had before 1850 concentrated on providing metals and simple tools for merchants and farmers. Even textile machinery was usually made by the cloth manufacturers themselves. However, by 1860, only a decade after beginning America's first major railroad construction boom, railroad companies had already replaced the blacksmiths as the primary market for iron products, and had become far and away the most important market for the heavy engineering industries. By then, too, the locomotive was competing with the Connecticut brass industry as a major consumer of copper. More than this, the railroads, with their huge capital outlay, their fixed operating costs, the large size of their labor and management force, and the technical complexity of their operations, pioneered in the new ways of oligopolistic competition and large-scale, professionalized, bureaucratized management.

The new nation-wide market created by the construction of the railroad network became an increasingly urban one. From 1850 on, if not before, urban areas were growing more rapidly than rural ones. In the four decades from 1840 to 1880 the proportion of urban population rose from 11 per cent to 28 per cent of the total population, or about 4 per cent a decade. In the two decades from 1880 to 1900 it grew from 28 per cent to 40 per cent or an increase of 6 per cent a decade. Was this new urban and national market, then, the primary stimulant for business innovation and change, and for the coming of big business to American industry?

Changes in the Consumers' Goods Industries

The industries first to become dominated by great business enterprises were those making consumer goods, the majority of which were processed from products grown on the farm and sold in the urban markets. Consolidation and centralization in the consumers' goods industries were well under way by 1893. The unit that appeared was one which integrated within a single business organization the major economic processes: production or purchasing of raw materials, manufacturing, distribution, and finance.

Such vertically integrated organizations came in two quite different ways. Where the product tended to be somewhat new in kind and especially fitted for the urban market, its makers created their businesses by first building large marketing and then purchasing organizations. This technique appears to have been true of the manufacturers or distributors of fresh meat, cigarettes, high-grade flour, bananas, harvesters, sewing machines, and typewriters. Where the products were established staple items, horizontal combination tended to precede vertical integration. In the sugar, salt, leather, whiskey, glucose, starch, biscuit, kerosene, fertilizer, and rubber industries a large number of small manufacturers first combined into large business units and then created their marketing and buying organizations. For a number of reasons the makers of the newer types of products found the older outlets less satisfactory and felt more of a need for direct marketing than did the manufacturers of the long-established goods.

Integration via the Creation of Marketing Organization. The story of the changes and the possible reasons behind them can be more clearly understood by examining briefly the experience of a few innovating firms. First, consider the experience of companies that grew large through the creation of a nation-wide marketing and distributing organization. Here the story of Gustavus F. Swift and his brother Edwin is a significant one. Gustavus F. Swift, an Easterner, came relatively late to the Chicago meat-packing business. Possibly because he was from Massachusetts, he appreciated the potential market for fresh western meat in the eastern cities.[2] For after the Civil War, Boston, New York, Philadelphia, and other cities were rapidly outrunning their local meat supply. At the same time, great herds of cattle were gathering on the western plains. Swift saw the possibilities of connecting the new market with the new source of supply by the use of the refrigerated railroad car. In 1878, shortly after his first experimental shipment of refrigerated meat, he formed a partnership with his younger brother, Edwin, to market fresh western meat in the eastern cities.

For the next decade, Swift struggled hard to carry out his plans, the essence of which was the creation, during the 1880's, of the nation-wide distributing and marketing organization built around a network of branch houses. Each "house" had its storage plant and its own marketing organization. The latter included outlets in major towns and cities, often managed by Swift's own salaried representatives. In marketing the product, Swift had to break down, through advertising and other means, the prejudices against eating meat killed more than a thousand miles away and many weeks earlier. At the same time he had to combat boycotts of local butchers and the concerted efforts of the National Butchers' Protective Association to prevent the sale of his meat in the urban markets.

To make effective use of the branch house network, the company soon began to market products other than beef. The "full line" soon came to

[2] Swift's story as outlined in Louis F. Swift in collaboration with Arthur Van Vlissingen, *The Yankee of the Yards — the Biography of Gustavus Franklin Swift* (New York, 1928). The United States Bureau of Corporations, *Report of the Commissioner of Corporations on the Beef Industry, March 3, 1905* (Washington, 1905), is excellent on the internal operations and external activities of the large meat-packing firms. There is additional information in the later three-volume *Report of the Federal Trade Commission on the Meat Packing Industry* (Washington, 1918–1919). R. A. Clemen, *The American Livestock and Meat Industry* (New York, 1923) has some useful background data.

include lamb, mutton, pork, and, some time later, poultry, eggs, and dairy products. The growing distributing organization soon demanded an increase in supply. So between 1888 and 1892, the Swifts set up meat-packing establishments in Kansas City, Omaha, and St. Louis, and, after the depression of the 1890's, three more in St. Joseph, St. Paul, and Ft. Worth. At the same time, the company systematized the buying of its cattle and other products at the stockyards. In the 1890's, too, Swift began a concerted effort to make more profitable use of by-products.

Before the end of the 1890's, then, Swift had effectively fashioned a great, vertically integrated organization. The major departments — marketing, processing, purchasing, and accounting — were all tightly controlled from the central office in Chicago. A report of the Commissioner of Corporations published in 1905 makes clear the reason for such control: [3]

> Differences in quality of animals and of their products are so great that the closest supervision of the Central Office is necessary to enforce the exercise of skill and sound judgement on the part of the agents who buy the stock, and the agents who sell the meat. With this object, the branches of the Selling and Accounting Department of those packing companies which have charge of the purchasing, killing, and dressing and selling of fresh meat, are organized in the most extensive and thorough manner. The Central Office is in constant telegraphic correspondence with the distributing houses, with a view to adjusting the supply of meat and the price as nearly as possible to the demand.

As this statement suggests, the other meat packers followed Swift's example. To compete effectively, Armour, Morris, Cudahy, and Schwarzschild & Sulzberger had to build up similar integrated organizations. Those that did not follow the Swift model were destined to remain small local companies. Thus by the middle of the 1890's, the meat-packing industry, with the rapid growth of these great vertically integrated firms had become oligopolistic (the "Big Five" had the major share of the market) and bureaucratic; each of the five had its many departments and several levels of management.

This story has parallels in other industries processing agricultural products. In tobacco, James B. Duke was the first to appreciate the growing market for the cigarette, a new product which was sold almost wholly in the cities.[4] However, after he had applied machinery to the manufacture of cigarettes, production soon outran supply. Duke then concentrated on

---

[3] *Report of Commissioner of Corporations on the Beef Industry*, p. 21.

[4] Some information on James B. Duke and the American Tobacco Company can be found in John W. Jenkins, *James B. Duke, Master Builder* (New York, 1927), chaps. 5–7, 10. More useful was the United States Bureau of Corporations, *Report of the Commissioner of Corporations on the Tobacco Industry* (Washington, 1909).

expanding the market through extensive advertising and the creation of a national and then world-wide selling organization. In 1884, he left Durham, North Carolina, for New York City, where he set up factories, sales, and administrative offices. New York was closer to his major urban markets, and was the more logical place to manage an international advertising campaign than Durham. While he was building his marketing department, Duke was also creating the network of warehouses and buyers in the tobacco-growing areas of the country.

In 1890, he merged his company with five smaller competitors in the cigarette business to form the American Tobacco Company. By 1895 the activities of these firms had been consolidated into the manufacturing, marketing, purchasing, and finance departments of the single operating structure Duke had earlier fashioned. Duke next undertook development of a full line by handling all types of smoking and chewing tobacco. By the end of the century, his company completely dominated the tobacco business. Only two other firms, R. J. Reynolds & Company and P. Lorillard & Company had been able to build up comparable vertically integrated organizations. When they merged with American Tobacco they continued to retain their separate operating organizations. When the 1911 antitrust decree split these and other units off from the American company, the tobacco industry had become, like the meat-packing business, oligopolistic, and its dominant firms bureaucratic.

What Duke and Swift did for their industries, James S. Bell of the Washburn-Crosby Company did during these same years in the making and selling of high-grade flour to the urban bakeries and housewives, and Andrew J. Preston achieved in growing, transporting, and selling another new product for the urban market, the banana.[5] Like Swift and Duke, both these men made their major innovations in marketing, and then went on to create large-scale, departmentalized, vertically integrated structures.

The innovators in new consumer durables followed much the same pattern. Both Cyrus McCormick, pioneer harvester manufacturer, and William Clark, the business brains of the Singer Sewing Machine Company, first sold through commissioned agents. Clark soon discovered that salaried men, working out of branch offices, could more effectively and at less cost display, demonstrate, and service sewing machines than could the agents.[6] Just as important, the branch offices were able to provide the customer with essential credit. McCormick, while retaining the dealer to

[5] The story of Bell is outlined in James Gray, *Business Without Boundary, the Story of General Mills* (Minneapolis, 1954), and of Preston in Charles M. Wilson, *Empire in Green and Gold* (New York, 1947).

[6] The early Singer Sewing Machine experience is well analyzed in Andrew B. Jack, "The Channels of Distribution for an Innovation: the Sewing Machine Industry in America, 1860–1865," *Explorations in Entrepreneurial History*, Vol. IX (Feb., 1957), pp. 113–141.

handle the final sales, came to appreciate the need for a strong selling and distributing organization, with warehouses, servicing facilities, and a large salaried force, to stand behind the dealer.[7] So in the years following the Civil War, both McCormick and Singer Sewing Machine Company concentrated on building up national and then world-wide marketing departments. As they purchased their raw materials from a few industrial companies rather than from a mass of farmers, their purchasing departments were smaller, and required less attention than those in the firms processing farmers' products. But the net result was the creation of a very similar type of organization.

Integration via Horizontal Combination. In those industries making more standard goods, the creation of marketing organizations usually followed large-scale combinations of a number of small manufacturing firms. For these small firms, the coming of the railroad had in many cases enlarged their markets but simultaneously brought them for the first time into competition with many other companies. Most of these firms appear to have expanded production in order to take advantage of the new markets. As a result, their industries became plagued with overproduction and excess capacity; that is, continued production at full capacity threatened to drop prices below the cost of production. So in the 1880's and early 1890's, many small manufacturers in the leather, sugar, salt, distilling and other corn products, linseed and cotton oil, biscuit, petroleum, fertilizer and rubber boot and glove industries, joined in large horizontal combinations.

In most of these industries, combination was followed by consolidation and vertical integration, and the pattern was comparatively consistent. First, the new combinations concentrated their manufacturing activities in locations more advantageously situated to meet the new growing urban demands. Next they systematized and standardized their manufacturing processes. Then, except in the case of sugar and corn products (glucose and starch), the combinations began to build large distributing and smaller purchasing departments. In so doing, many dropped their initial efforts to buy out competitors or to drive them out of business by price-cutting. Instead they concentrated on the creation of a more efficient flow from the producers of their raw materials to the ultimate consumer, and of the development and maintenance of markets through brand names and advertising. Since the large majority of these combinations began as regional groupings, most industries came to have more than one great firm. Only oil, sugar, and corn products remained long dominated by a single company. By World War I, partly because of the dissolutions under the Sherman Act, these industries had also become oligopolistic, and their leading firms vertically integrated.

[7] William T. Hutchinson, *Cyrus Hall McCormick* (New York, 1935), Vol. II, pp. 704–712.

Specific illustrations help to make these generalizations more precise. The best-known is the story of the oil industry, but equally illustrative is the experience of the leading distilling, baking, and rubber companies.

The first permanent combination in the whiskey industry came in 1887 when a large number of Midwestern distillers, operating more than 80 small plants, formed the Distillers' and Cattle Feeders' Trust.[8] Like other trusts, it adopted the more satisfactory legal form of a holding company shortly after New Jersey in 1889 passed the general incorporation law for holding companies. The major efforts of the Distillers Company were, first, to concentrate production in a relatively few plants. By 1895 only 21 were operating. The managers maintained that the large volume per plant permitted by such concentration would mean lower costs, and also that the location of few plants more advantageously in relation to supply and marketing would still reduce expenses further. However, the company kept the price of whiskey up, and since the cost of setting up a distillery was small, it soon had competition from small local plants. The company's answer was to purchase the new competitors and to cut prices. This strategy proved so expensive that the enterprise was unable to survive the depression of the 1890's.

Shortly before going into receivership in 1896, the Distillers Company had begun to think more about marketing. In 1895, it had planned to spend a million dollars to build up a distributing and selling organization in the urban East — the company's largest market. In 1898, through the purchase of the Standard Distilling & Distributing Company and the Spirits Distributing Company, it did acquire a marketing organization based in New York City. In 1903, the marketing and manufacturing units were combined into a single operating organization under the direction of the Distillers Securities Company. At the same time, the company's president announced plans to concentrate on the development of brand names and specialties, particularly through advertising and packaging.[9] By the early years of the twentieth century, then, the Distillers Company had become a vertically integrated, departmentalized, centralized operating organization, competing in the modern manner, more through advertising and product differentiation than price.

[8] The major sources of information on combination and consolidation in the distilling industry are Jeremiah W. Jenks, "The Development of the Whiskey Trust," *Political Science Quarterly*, Vol. IV (June, 1889), pp. 296–319; J. W. Jenks and W. E. Clark, *The Trust Problem* (rev. ed.; New York, 1917), pp. 141–149. The annual reports of the Distilling and Cattle Feeding Company and its various successors provide some useful additional data, as does the Industrial Commission, *Preliminary Report on Trusts and Industrial Combinations* (Washington, 1900), Vol. I, pp. 74–89, 167–259, 813–848, and Victor S. Clark, *History of Manufactures in the United States* (New York, 1929), Vol. II, pp. 505–506. Changes in taxes on liquors also affected the company's policies in the early 1890's.

[9] *Annual Report of the President of the Distillers Securities Company* for 1903.

The experience of the biscuit industry is even more explicit. The National Biscuit Company came into being in 1898 as a merger of three regional combinations: the New York Biscuit Company formed in 1890, the American Biscuit and Manufacturing Company, and the United States Biscuit Company founded a little later.[10] Its initial objective was to control price and production, but as in the case of the Distillers Company, this strategy proved too expensive. The Annual Report for 1901 suggests why National Biscuit shifted its basic policies: [11]

> This Company is four years old and it may be of interest to shortly review its history. . . . When the Company started, it was an aggregation of plants. It is now an organized business. When we look back over the four years, we find that a radical change has been wrought in our methods of business. In the past, the managers of large merchandising corporations have found it necessary, for success, to control or limit competition. So when this company started, it was thought that we must control competition, and that to do this we must either fight competition or buy it. The first meant a ruinous war of prices, and a great loss of profit; the second, a constantly increasing capitalization. Experience soon proved to us that, instead of bringing success, either of those courses, if persevered in, must bring disaster. This led us to reflect whether it was necessary to control competition. . . . we soon satisfied ourselves that within the Company itself we must look for success.
>
> We turned our attention and bent our energies to improving the internal management of our business, to getting full benefit from purchasing our raw materials in large quantities, to economizing the expenses of manufacture, to systematizing and rendering more effective our selling department; and above all things and before all things to improve the quality of our goods and the condition in which they should reach the customer.
>
> It became the settled policy of this Company to buy out no competition. . . .

In concentrating on distribution, the company first changed its policy from selling in bulk to wholesalers to marketing small packages to retailers. It developed the various "Uneeda Biscuit" brands, which immediately became popular. "The next point," the same Annual Report continued,

[10] The information on National Biscuit comes largely from its annual reports.
[11] *Annual Report of the National Biscuit Company for the Year Ending December, 1901,* January 3, 1902. References to centralizing of manufacturing facilities appear in several early annual reports. As this was written before Theodore Roosevelt had started to make the Sherman Act an effective antitrust instrument and Ida Tarbell and other journalists had begun to make "muck raking" of big business popular and profitable, the Biscuit Company's shift in policy could hardly have been the result of the pressure of public opinion or the threat of government action.

"was to reach the customer. Thinking we had something that the customer wanted, we had to advise the customer of its existence. We did this by extensive advertising." This new packaging and advertising not only quickly created a profitable business, but also required the building of a sizable marketing organization. Since flour could be quickly and easily purchased in quantity from large milling firms, the purchasing requirements were less complex, and so the company needed a smaller purchasing organization. On the other hand, it spent much energy after 1901 in improving plant layout and manufacturing processes in order to cut production costs and to improve and standardize quality. Throughout the first decade of its history, National Biscuit continued the policy of "centralizing" manufacturing operations, particularly in its great New York and Chicago plants.

In the rubber boot, shoe, and glove industries, the story is much the same. Expansion of manufacturing facilities and increasing competition as early as 1874, led to the formation, by several leading firms, of the Associated Rubber Shoe Companies — an organization for setting price and production schedules through its board of directors.[12] This company continued until 1886. Its successor, the Rubber Boot and Shoe Company, which lasted only a year, attempted, besides controlling prices and production, to handle marketing, which had always been done by commissioned agents. After five years of uncontrolled competition, four of the five firms that had organized the selling company again combined, this time with the assistance of a large rubber importer, Charles A. Flint. The resulting United States Rubber Company came, by 1898, to control 75 per cent of the nation's rubber boot, shoe, and glove output.

At first the new company remained a decentralized holding company. Each constituent company retained its corporate identity with much freedom of action, including the purchasing of raw materials and the selling of finished products, which was done, as before, through jobbers. The central office's concern was primarily with controlling price and production schedules. Very soon, however, the company began, in the words of the 1896 Annual Report, a policy of "perfecting consolidation of purchasing, selling, and manufacturing." [13] This was to be accomplished in four ways. First, as the 1895 Annual Report had pointed out, the managers agreed "so far as practicable, to consolidate the purchasing of all

[12] The background for the creation of the United States Rubber Company can be found in Nancy P. Norton, "Industrial Pioneer: the Goodyear Metallic Rubber Shoe Company" (Ph.D. thesis, Radcliffe College, 1950), Constance McL. Green, *History of Naugatuck, Connecticut* (New Haven, 1948), pp. 126–131, 193–194, and Clark, *History of Manufactures*, Vol. II, pp. 479–481, Vol. III, pp. 235–237. The company's annual reports provide most of the information on its activities.

[13] *The Fifth Annual Report of the United States Rubber Company, March 31, 1897,* pp. 6–7.

supplies of raw materials for the various manufacturies into one single buying agency, believing that the purchase of large quantities of goods can be made at more advantageous figures than the buying of small isolated lots." [14] The second new "general policy" was "to undertake to reduce the number of brands of goods manufactured, and to consolidate the manufacturing of the remaining brands in those factories which have demonstrated superior facilities for production or advantageous labor conditions. This course was for the purpose of utilizing the most efficient instruments of production and closing those that were inefficient and unprofitable." The third policy was to consolidate sales through the formation of a "Selling Department," which was to handle all goods made by the constituent companies in order to achieve "economy in the distribution expense." Selling was now to be handled by a central office in the New York City headquarters, with branch offices throughout the United States and Europe. Of the three great new departments, actually manufacturing was the slowest to be fully consolidated and centralized. Finally, the treasurer's office at headquarters began to obtain accurate data on profit and loss through the institution of uniform, centralized cost accounting.

Thus United States Rubber, National Biscuit, and the Distillers Securities Company soon came to have organizational structures paralleling those of Swift and American Tobacco. By the first decade of the twentieth century, the leading firms in many consumers' goods industries had become departmentalized and centralized. This was the organizational concomitant to vertical integration. Each major function, manufacturing, sales, purchasing, and finance, became managed by a single and separate department head, usually a vice president, who, assisted by a director or a manager, had full authority and responsibility for the activities of his unit. These departmental chiefs, with the president, coordinated and evaluated the work of the different functional units, and made policy for the company as a whole. In coordinating, appraising, and policy-making, the president and the vice presidents in charge of departments came to rely more and more on the accounting and statistical information, usually provided by the finance department, on costs, output, purchases, and sales.

Changes in the Producers' Goods Industries

Bureaucracy and oligopoly came to the producers' goods industries somewhat later than to those making products for the mass market. Until the depression of the 1890's, most of the combinations and consolidations had been in the consumers' goods industries. After that, the major changes came in those industries selling to other businesses and industrialists. The reason for the time difference seems to be that the city took a little longer

[14] This and the following quotations are from the *Fourth Annual Report of the United States Rubber Company, May 25, 1896*, pp. 4–5, 7–8.

to become a major market for producers' goods. Throughout the 1880's, railroad construction and operation continued to take the larger share of the output of steel, copper, power machinery, explosives, and other heavy industries. Then in the 1890's, as railroad construction declined the rapidly growing American cities became the primary market. The insatiable demand for urban lighting, communication, heat, power, transportation, water, sewerage, and other services directly and indirectly took ever growing quantities of electric lighting apparatus, telephones, copper wire, newsprint, streetcars, coal, and iron, steel, copper, and lead piping, structures and fixtures; while the constantly expanding urban construction created new calls on the power machinery and explosives as well as the metals industries. Carnegie's decision in 1887 to shift the Homestead Works, the nation's largest and most modern steel plant, from rails to structures, symbolized the coming change in the market.[15]

Also the new combinations and consolidations in the consumers' goods industries increased the demand for producers' products in the urban areas. Standard Oil, American Tobacco, Swift and other meat packers, McCormick's Harvesting Machinery and other farm implement firms, American Sugar, Singer Sewing Machine, and many other great consumer goods companies concentrated their production in or near major cities, particularly New York and Chicago.

The changes after 1897 differed from the earlier ones not only in types of industries in which they occurred but also in the way they were promoted and financed. Combinations and vertical integration in the consumer goods industries before 1897 had been almost all engineered and financed by the manufacturers themselves, so the stock control remained in the hands of the industrialists. After 1897, however, outside funds and often outside promoters, who were usually Wall Street financiers, played an increasingly significant role in industrial combination and consolidation. The change reflected a new attitude of investor and financier who controlled capital toward the value of industrial securities.[16] Before the depression of the 1890's investment and speculation had been overwhelmingly in railroad stocks and bonds. The institutionalizing of the American

---

[15] Clark, *History of Manufactures*, Vol. II, chap. 19.

[16] The story of the shift from rails to industrials as acceptable investments is told in Thomas R. Navin and Marian V. Sears, "The Rise of the Market for Industrial Securities, 1887–1902," *Business History Review*, Vol. XIX (June, 1955), pp. 105–138. Government securities were, of course, important in the years before 1850 and during and after the Civil War, but in the late 1870's and 1880's as in the 1850's, railroads dominated the American security exchanges. As Navin and Sears point out, some coal and mining firms were traded on the New York Exchange, but the only manufacturing securities, outside of those of the Pullman Company, were some textile stocks traded on the local Boston Exchange. The connections between the railroad expansion and the beginnings of modern Wall Street are described in detail in Chandler, *Poor*, chap. 4.

security market in Wall Street had come, in fact, as a response to the needs for financing the first great railroad boom in the 1850's.

The railroads, however, had made a poor showing financially in the middle years of the 1890's when one-third of the nation's trackage went through receivership and financial reorganization. The dividend records of some of the new large industrial corporations, on the other hand, proved unexpectedly satisfactory. Moreover, railroad construction was slowing, and the major financial and administrative reorganizations of the 1890's had pretty well stabilized the industry. So there was less demand for investment bankers and brokers to market new issues of railroad securities.

Industrials were obviously the coming field, and by 1898 there was a rush in Wall Street to get in on this new business. The sudden availability of funds stimulated, and undoubtedly overstimulated, industrial combination. Many of the mergers in the years after 1897 came more from the desire of financiers for promotional profits, and because combination had become the thing to do, and less from the special needs and opportunities in the several industries. Moreover, as the financiers and promoters began to provide funds for mergers and expansion, they began to acquire, for the first time, the same type of control over industrial corporations that they had enjoyed in railroads since the 1850's.

The changes in the producers' goods industries were essentially like those in the consumer goods firms before the depression. Only after 1897 the changes came more rapidly, partly because of Wall Street pressures; and the differences that did develop between the two types of industries reflected the basic differences in the nature of their businesses. Like the companies making consumer goods, those manufacturing items for producers set up nation-wide and often world-wide marketing and distributing organizations, consolidated production into a relatively few large plants and fashioned purchasing departments. Because they had fewer customers, their sales departments tended to be smaller than those in firms selling to the mass market. On the other hand, they were more concerned with obtaining control over the sources of their supply than were most of the consumer goods companies.

Here a distinction can be made between the manufacturers who made semi-finished products from raw materials taken from the ground, and those who made finished goods from semi-finished products. The former, producing a uniform product for a few large industrial customers, developed only small sales departments and concentrated on obtaining control of raw materials, and often of the means of transporting such materials from mine to market. The latter, selling a larger variety of products and ones that often required servicing and financing, had much larger marketing and distributing organizations. These makers of finished goods, except for a brief period around 1900, rarely attempted to control their raw materials or their semi-finished steel and other metal supplies. They did, however, in the years after 1900, begin to buy or set up plants making parts and components that went into the construction of their finished products.

Except in steel, integration usually followed combination in the producers' goods industries. And for both makers of semi-finished and finished goods, integration became more of a defensive strategy than it was in the consumers' goods industries processing agricultural products. In the latter the manufacturers had an assured supply of raw materials from the output of the nation's millions of farms. In the former, on the other hand, they had to consider the threatening possibility of an outsider obtaining complete control of raw materials or supplies.

Integration and Combination in the Extractive Industries. By the early twentieth century nearly all the companies making semi-finished product goods controlled the mining of their own raw materials. The industries in which they operated can, therefore, be considered as extractive. This was also true of two consumers' goods industries: oil and fertilizer. The experience of these two provides a good introduction to the motives for integration and the role it played in the coming of "big business" in steel, copper, paper, explosives and other businesses producing semi-finished goods.

In both the oil and fertilizer industries, control over raw materials came well after combination and consolidation of groups of small manufacturing firms. The Standard Oil Trust, after its formation in 1882, consolidated its manufacturing activities and then created a domestic marketing organization. Only in the late 1880's, when the new Indiana field began to be developed and the older Pennsylvania ones began to decline, did the Trust consider going into the production of crude oil. Both Allan Nevins in his biography of John D. Rockefeller and the Hidys in their history of Standard Oil agree that the need to be assured of a steady supply of crude oil was the major reason for the move into production.[17] Other reasons, the Hidys indicate, were a fear that the producers might combine and so control supplies, and the desire of the pipeline subsidiaries to keep their facilities operating at full capacity. Although neither Nevins nor the Hidys suggest that the desire to obtain a more efficient flow of oil from the well to the distributor was a motive for this integration, both describe the committees and staff units that were formed at the central office at 26 Broadway to assure more effective coordination between production, refining, and marketing.

What little evidence there is suggests somewhat the same story in the fertilizer industry. Shortly after its organization in the mid-1890's, the Virginia-Carolina Chemical Company, a merger of many small southern

[17] Ralph W. Hidy and Muriel E. Hidy, *Pioneering in Big Business, 1882–1911* (New York, 1955), pp. 176–188. Allan Nevins, *Study in Power, John D. Rockefeller, Industrialist and Philanthropist* (New York, 1953), Vol. II, pp. 1–3. Nevins adds that another reason for the move into production was "partly to limit the number of active wells and reduce the overproduction of crude oil," Vol. II, p. 2, but he gives no documentation for this statement.

fertilizer firms, began, apparently for the same defensive reasons, to purchase phosphate mines. Quickly its major competitor, the American Agricultural Chemical Company, a similar combination of small northeastern companies formed in 1893, responded by making its own purchases of mines. As the latter company explained in a later annual report: "The growth of the business, as well as the fact that available phosphate properties were being fast taken up, indicated that it was the part of wisdom to make additional provision for the future, and accordingly . . . available phosphate properties were purchased, and the necessary plants were erected and equipped, so the company now has in hand a supply of phosphate rock which will satisfy its growing demand for 60 years and upwards." [18] However, neither of these companies appeared to have set up organizational devices to guide the flow of materials from mine to plant to market; nor did the managers of a third large integrated fertilizer company, the International Agricultural Corporation, formed in 1909.

Defensive motives were certainly significant in the changes in the steel industry. Here the story can be most briefly described by focusing on the history of the industry's leader, the Carnegie Steel Company.[19] That company's chairman, Henry C. Frick, had in the early 1890's consolidated and rationalized the several Carnegie manufacturing properties in and about Pittsburgh into an integrated whole. At the same time, he systematized and departmentalized its purchasing, engineering, and marketing activities. The fashioning of a sales department became more necessary since the shift from rails to structures had enlarged the number of the company's customers.

Then in 1896 the Carnegie company made a massive purchase of ore lands when it joined with Henry W. Oliver to buy out the Rockefeller holdings in the Mesabi Range. As Allan Nevins points out, the depression of the 1890's had worked a rapid transformation in the recently discovered Mesabi region.[20] By 1896, the ore fields had become dominated by three great interests: the Oliver Mining Company, the Minnesota Mining Company, and Rockefeller's Consolidated Iron Mines. A fourth, James J. Hill's Great Northern Railroad, was just entering the field. Frick's purchases,

[18] *Annual Report of the American Agricultural Chemical Company*, August 14, 1907, also the same company's *Annual Report* dated August 25, 1902. In addition to the annual reports of the two companies, Clark, *History of Manufactures*, Vol. III, pp. 289–291, provides information. There is a brief summary of the story of the International Agricultural Corporation in Williams Haynes, *American Chemical Industry* — *A History* (New York, 1945), Vol. III, p. 173.

[19] The information on the Carnegie Steel Company is taken from Burton J. Hendrick, *The Life of Andrew Carnegie*, 2 vols. (New York, 1932), George Harvey, *Henry Clay Frick, the Man* (New York, 1928), James H. Bridge, *The Inside Story of the Carnegie Steel Company* (New York, 1903).

[20] Nevins, *Rockefeller*, Vol. II, p. 252.

therefore, gave the Carnegie company an assured supply of cheap ore, as well as providing it with a fleet of ore ships. Next, Frick and Carnegie bought and rebuilt a railroad from Lake Erie to Pittsburgh to carry the new supplies to the mills.

Yet the steel company's managers did little to coordinate systematically the mining, shipping, and manufacturing units in their industrial empire. These activities did not become departments controlled from one central office but remained completely separate companies under independent managements, whose contact with one another was through negotiated contracts. This was the same sort of relation that existed between the Frick Coke Company and Carnegie Steel from the time Frick had joined Carnegie in 1889. If the Carnegie company's strategy had been to provide a more effective flow of materials as well as to assure itself of not being caught without a supply of ore and the means to transport it, then Frick and Carnegie would have created some sort of central coordinating office.

The steel industry responded quickly to the Carnegie purchases.[21] In 1898, Chicago's Illinois Steel Company, with capital supplied by J. P. Morgan & Company, joined the Lorain Steel Company (with plants on Lake Erie and in Johnstown, Pennsylvania) to purchase the Minnesota Mining Company, a fleet of ore boats, and railroads in the Mesabi and Chicago areas. Again, little attempt was made to coordinate mining and shipping with manufacturing and marketing. In the same year, many iron and steel firms in Ohio and Pennsylvania merged to form the Republic and National Steel Companies. Shortly thereafter, a similar combination in the Sault Sainte Marie area became the Consolidated Lake Superior Company. These three new mergers began at once to set up their marketing organizations and to obtain control by lease and purchase of raw materials and transportation facilities. In 1900, several small firms making high-grade steel did much the same thing by the formation of the Crucible Steel Company of America. In these same years, the larger, established steel companies, like Lackawanna, Cambria, and Jones & Laughlin ob-

[21] The experience of the other steel firms comes primarily from their annual reports and from prospectuses and other reports in the Corporation Records Division of Baker Library. A company publication, *J & L — The Growth of an American Business* (Pittsburgh, 1953) has some additional information on that company. Also, books listed in footnote 26 on the United States Steel Corporation have something on these companies. Two other steel companies listed in Table 1 made major changes somewhat before and after the period immediately following 1898. One, the Colorado Fuel & Iron Co., established in 1892, quickly became an integrated steel company in the Colorado area. The Bethlehem Steel Corporation was formed in 1904 when Charles F. Schwab, formerly of the Carnegie company and the United States Steel Corporation, reorganized the finances, corporate structure, and administrative organization of the bankrupt United States Shipbuilding Company.

tained control of more supplies of ore, coke, and limestone and simultaneously reorganized their manufacturing and marketing organizations. Like Carnegie and Federal, they at first made little effort to bring their mining and coke operations under the direct control of the central office.

In copper, defensive motives for integration appear to have been somewhat less significant. In the 1890's, mining, smelting and refining were combined on a large scale. During the 'eighties the railroad had opened up many western mining areas, particularly in Montana and Arizona; a little later the new electrical and telephone businesses greatly increased the demand for copper. Mining firms like Anaconda, Calumet & Hecla, and Phelps Dodge moved into smelting and refining, while the Guggenheims' Philadelphia Smelting & Refining Company began to buy mining properties.[22] In the copper industry, the high cost of ore shipment meant that smelting and — after the introduction of the electrolytic process in the early 1890's — even refining could be done more cheaply close to the mines. Of the large copper firms, only Calumet & Hecla and the Guggenheims set up refineries in the East before 1898, and both made use of direct water transportation.

After 1898, several large mergers occurred in the nonferrous metals industries. Nearly all were initially promoted by eastern financiers. Of these, the most important were Amalgamated Copper, engineered by H. H. Rogers of Standard Oil and Marcus Daly of Anaconda, the American Smelting and Refining Company which the Guggenheims came to control, and United Copper promoted by F. Augustus Heinze. United Copper remained little more than a holding company. Amalgamated set up a subsidiary to operate a large refinery at Perth Amboy and another, the United Metals Selling Company, with headquarters in New York City, to market the products of its mining and processing subsidiaries. The holding company's central offices in New York remained small and apparently did comparatively little to coordinate the activities of its several operating companies. The Guggenheims formed a much tighter organization with direct headquarters control of the company's mining, shipping, smelting and marketing departments. On the whole, there appears to have been somewhat closer coordination between mining and processing in the large copper than in the major steel companies.

Lowering of costs through more effective coordination appears to have been a major motive for consolidation and combination in three other businesses whose raw materials came from the ground: explosives, paper, and coal.[23] The mergers that created the Pittsburgh Coal Company in

[22] Information on the mining companies came from their annual reports and from Isaac P. Marcosson's two books, *Magic Metal — the Story of the American Smelting and Refining Company* (New York, 1949), and *Anaconda* (New York, 1957), also Clark, *History of Manufactures*, Vol. II, pp. 368–369.

[23] The story of the leading explosives, paper, salt and coal companies comes from annual reports and also from Charles E. Beachley, *History of the Consolida-*

1899 and greatly enlarged the Consolidation Coal Company in 1903 were followed by a reorganization and consolidation of mining properties and then by the creation of large marketing departments which operated throughout most of the country. The merger of close to 30 paper companies, forming the International Paper Company in 1899, was followed first by consolidation and reorganization of the manufacturing plants, next by the formation of a national marketing organization with headquarters in New York City, and then by the purchase of large tracts of timber in Maine and Canada. These three activities were departmentalized under vice presidents and controlled from the New York office. In all these cases, the central office was responsible for the flow of materials from mine or forest to the customer or retailer.

The explosive industries underwent a comparable sweeping change in 1902 and 1903. Since the 1870's, price and production schedules had been decided by the industry's Gunpowder Trade Association, and almost from its beginning, that Association had been controlled by one firm, the E. I. DuPont de Nemours & Company. However, the member concerns had retained their own corporate identities and managements. In 1902, the DuPonts bought out a large number of these independent companies through exchanges of stock, and then consolidated them into a single centralized organization. In the process, plants were shut down, others enlarged, and new ones built. A nation-wide selling organization was created, and centralized accounting, purchasing, engineering and traffic departments formed. Once the new organization was completed, then the company's executives obtained control of their raw materials through the purchase of nitrate mines and deposits in Chile.

Except possibly in paper, the control of price and production does not appear to have been a major motive for the initial combinations in the extractive industries making producers' goods. In steel before 1901, and in nonferrous metals and coal, there were several combinations, but none acquired as much as 20 per cent of the market. Nor is there any evidence that the creators of the different mergers, while they were forming their organizations, were arranging with one another to set over-all price and production schedules. In explosives, control of competition could not have been a significant reason for the 1902 changes since the DuPont company had enjoyed such control since the 1870's. In coal and explosives, and

---

tion Coal Company 1864–1934 (New York, 1934), George H. Love, An Exciting Century in Coal (New York, 1955), the company-written, The International Paper Company, 1898–1948 (n.p., 1948), William S. Dutton, DuPont — One Hundred and Forty Years (New York, 1940), and U.S. v. E. I. DuPont de Nemours & Company et al. in Circuit Court of the United States for the District of Delaware, #280 in Equity (1909), Defendants' Record Testimony, Vol. I, and for the paper industry, Clark, History of Manufactures, Vol. III, pp. 245–252. The American Writing Paper Company, though less successful, had many parallels to International Paper.

possibly in copper, the major motive for combination, consolidation, and the integration of supply with the manufacturing and marketing processes seems to have been an expectation of lowered costs through the creation of a national distributing organization, the consolidation of manufacturing activities, and the effective coordination of the different industrial processes by one central office. In steel and possibly copper, the desire for an assured supply of raw materials appears to have been more significant in encouraging combination and integration.

Changes and Integration in the Finished Producers' Goods Industries. Control of price and production was, on the other hand, much more of an obvious motive for combination and resulting consolidation in the industries manufacturing finished products or machinery from the semi-finished materials produced by the extractive firms. Concern over supply, however, was also a cause for change, for after 1898 the users of steel, copper, coal, and other semi-finished materials felt threatened by the growing number of combinations among their suppliers. In any case, between 1898 and 1900 there was a wave of mergers in these industries, largely Wall Street financed, which led to the formation of American Tin Plate, American Wire & Steel, American Steel Hoop, National Tube, American Bridge, American Sheet Metal, Shelby Steel Tube, American Can, National Enameling & Stamping Company and a number of other combinations among steel-fabricating firms.[24] At the same time, there were many amalgamations in the power machinery and implement businesses, such as American Car & Foundry, American Locomotive, Allis-Chalmers, International Steam Pump, and International Harvester. The largest combination among the copper users, the American Brass Company, came a little later, in 1903, after the Guggenheims, Rogers, and Heinze had completed the major copper mergers.

Nearly all these combinations quickly consolidated their constituent companies into a single operating organization. Manufacturing facilities were unified and systematized, over-all accounting procedures instituted, and national and often world-wide distributing organizations formed. Many set up central traffic and purchasing departments; some even began to assure themselves control over supply by building up their own rolling mills and blast furnaces. As American Wire & Steel and National Tube began to make their own steel, they cancelled contracts with Carnegie and other semi-finished steel producers. This development, in turn, led Carnegie to develop plans for fabricating his own finished products.[25]

The resulting threat of overcapacity and price-cutting led to the forma-

[24] The best brief summary of these mergers and the formation of the United States Steel Corporation is in Eliot Jones, *The Trust Problem in the United States* (New York, 1924), pp. 189–200. The companies' annual reports and prospectuses provide additional material.

[25] Hendrick, *Carnegie*, Vol. II, pp. 116–119.

tion of the United States Steel Corporation.[26] This giant merger, which included Carnegie, Federal and National Steel, and the first six of the fabricating companies listed above, continued on as a combination. Although the activities of the various subsidiaries were re-formed and redefined, there was no consolidation. United States Steel remained a holding company only, and the central office at 72 Broadway did comparatively little to coordinate the operations of its many subsidiary companies.

After 1901, the fabricators and the machinery manufacturers made little attempt to produce their own steel or copper. Nor did the makers of semi-finished products try, for some years to come, to do their own fabricating. Possibly the metal users realized that even with the formation of United States Steel they were fairly certain of alternative sources of supply. Also they may have found that once they had combined they had enough bargaining power to assure themselves of a supply of steel and other materials more cheaply than they could make it themselves.

While such firms no longer sought to control their basic materials, many, particularly the machinery makers like General Electric, Westinghouse, American Car & Foundry, International Harvester and, a little later, General Motors, began to purchase or set up subsidiaries or departments to make parts and components.[27] Here again the motive was essentially defensive. Since much of their manufacturing had now become mainly assembling, they wanted to be sure to have a supply of parts available at all times. The lack of a vital part could temporarily shut down a plant. However, they expected to take only a portion of the output; a major share was sold to outsiders. One outstanding exception to this pattern was Henry Ford. He came to control his raw materials as well as his parts and components, and rarely sold such parts to outside companies. But Ford's insistence on having a completely integrated organization from mine to market, concentrated largely in one huge plant, proved to be one of the most costly mistakes in American business history.

Control of parts and accessory units led to a diversification of the types of products these manufacturing companies made and sold. Such diversification brought, over time, important changes in business organization. Even more significant for stimulating product diversification was the new "full line" strategy adopted by a number of these recently consolidated concerns. Such a policy, initiated largely to help assure the maximum use of the new departments, encouraged technological as well as organizational change.

[26] The beginnings and the operation of the United States Steel Corporation are outlined in Abraham Berglund, *The United States Steel Corporation: A Study of Growth and Combination in the Iron and Steel Industry* (New York, 1907), Arundel Cotter, *The Authentic History of the United States Steel Corporation* (New York, 1916), Ida M. Tarbell, *The Life of Elbert H. Gary, the Story of Steel* (New York, 1925).

[27] This generalization is based on the annual reports of the several companies.

. Pioneers in developing "full lines" in the producers' goods industries were the two great electrical companies: General Electric and Westinghouse. Unlike almost any other of the leading American industrial companies in 1900, these two had begun as research and development rather than manufacturing organizations. Because of their origins, they had the skilled personnel and the necessary equipment to move, in the mid-1890's, from making lighting equipment alone to manufacturing many lines of electric traction and power machinery products.[28] Allis-Chalmers, International Steam Pump, and American Locomotive began, shortly after their formation and subsequent consolidations, to develop new lines using electric and gasoline engines.[29] International Harvester, building up a number of farm implement lines, also started to experiment with the use of the gasoline engine for machinery on the farm. In this same first decade of the twentieth century, rubber, explosive, and chemical companies began to turn to industrial chemistry in their search to develop broader lines of products.

Continuing diversification came, however, largely in industries where science, particularly chemistry and physics, could be most easily applied. And it was in these industries, and in those which were directly affected by the coming of two new sources of power, electricity and the internal combustion engine, that the major innovations in American industry came after 1900. The chemical, automotive, power machinery, rubber, and petroleum industries led the way to the development of new processes and products, new ways of internal organization and new techniques of external competition as the new century unfolded. The metals industries and those processing agricultural goods have, on the other hand, changed relatively little since the beginning of the century. In these industries, the same firms make much the same products, use much the same processes, and compete in much the same manner in the 1950's as they did in the 1900's. For them the greatest period of change came in the last decade of the nineteenth century.

Conclusion: The Basic Innovations

The middle of the first decade of the new century might be said to mark the end of an era. By 1903, the great merger movement was almost over,

[28] As is well described in Harold C. Passer, *The Electrical Manufacturers* (Cambridge, 1953).

[29] The development of new lines by Allis-Chalmers, International Steam Pump, and American Locomotive is mentioned in their annual reports in the first decade of the twentieth century. International Harvester's similar "full line" policies are described in Cyrus McCormick, *The Century of the Reaper* (New York, 1931), chaps. 6–9, and United States Bureau of Corporations, *The International Harvester Co., March 3, 1913* (Washington, 1913), especially pp. 156–158.

and by then the metals industries and those processing agricultural products had developed patterns of internal organization and external competition which were to remain. In those years, too, leading chemical, electrical, rubber, power machinery and implement companies had initiated their "full line" policy, and had instituted the earliest formal research and development departments created in this country. In this decade also, electricity was becoming for the first time a significant source of industrial power, and the automobile was just beginning to revolutionize American transportation. From 1903 on, the new generators of power and the new technologies appear to have become the dominant stimuli to innovation in American industry, and such innovations were primarily those which created new products and processes. Changes in organizational methods and marketing techniques were largely responses to technological advances.

This seems much less true of the changes during the 20 to 25 years before 1903. In that period, the basic innovations were more in the creation of new forms of organization and new ways of marketing. The great modern corporation, carrying on the major industrial processes, namely, purchasing, and often production of materials and parts, manufacturing, marketing, and finance — all within the same organizational structure — had its beginnings in that period. Such organizations hardly existed, outside of the railroads, before the 1880's. By 1900 they had become the basic business unit in American industry.

Each of these major processes became managed by a corporate department, and all were coordinated and supervised from a central office. Of the departments, marketing was the most significant. The creation of nationwide distributing and selling organizations was the initial step in the growth of many large consumer goods companies. Mergers in both the consumer and producer goods industries were almost always followed by the formation of a centralized sales department.

The consolidation of plants under a single manufacturing department usually accompanied or followed the formation of a national marketing organization. The creation of such a manufacturing department normally meant the concentration of production in fewer and larger plants, and such consolidation probably lowered unit costs and increased output per worker. The creation of such a department in turn led to the setting up of central traffic, purchasing, and often engineering organizations. Large-scale buying, more rational routing of raw materials and finished products, more systematic plant lay-out, and plant location in relation to materials and markets probably lowered costs still further. Certainly the creators of these organizations believed that it did. In the extractive and machinery industries integration went one step further. Here the motives for controlling raw materials or parts and components were defensive as well as designed to cut costs through providing a more efficient flow of materials from mine to market.

These great national industrial organizations required a large market to provide the volume necessary to support the increased overhead costs. Also, to be profitable, they needed careful coordination between the different functional departments. This coordination required a steady flow of accurate data on costs, sales, and on all purchasing, manufacturing, and marketing activities. As a result, the comptroller's office became an increasingly important department. In fact, one of the first moves after a combination by merger or purchase was to institute more effective and detailed accounting procedures. Also, the leading entrepreneurs of the period, men like Rockefeller, Carnegie, Swift, Duke, Preston, Clark, and the DuPonts, had to become, as had the railroad executives of an earlier generation, experts in reading and interpreting business statistics.

Consolidation and departmentalization meant that the leading industrial corporations became operating rather than holding companies, in the sense that the officers and managers of the companies were directly concerned with operating activities. In fact, of the 50 companies with the largest assets in 1909, only United States Steel, Amalgamated Copper, and one or two other copper companies remained purely holding companies. In most others, the central office included the heads of the major functional departments, usually the president, vice presidents, and sometimes a chairman of the board and one or two representatives of financial interests. These men made major policy and administrative decisions and evaluated the performance of the departments and the corporation as a whole. In the extractive industries a few companies, like Standard Oil (N.J.) and some of the metals companies, were partly holding and partly operating companies. At Standard Oil nearly all important decisions were made in the central headquarters, at 26 Broadway, which housed not only the presidents of the subsidiaries but the powerful policy formulating and coordinating committees.[30] But in some of the metals companies, the subsidiaries producing and transporting raw materials retained a large degree of autonomy.

The coming of the large vertically integrated, centralized, functionally departmentalized industrial organization altered the internal and external situations in which and about which business decisions were made. Information about markets, supplies, and operating performances as well as suggestions for action often had to come up through the several levels of the departmental hierarchies, while decisions and suggestions based on this data had to be transmitted down the same ladder for implementation. Executives on each level became increasingly specialists in one function — in sales, production, purchasing, or finance — and most remained in one department and so handled one function only for the major part of their business careers. Only he who climbed to the very top of the departmental ladder had a chance to see his own company as a single operating unit.

[30] Hidys, *Pioneering in Big Business*, chap. 3 and pp. 323–388.

Where a company's markets, sources of raw materials, and manufacturing processes remained relatively stable, as was true in the metals industries and in those processing agricultural goods, the nature of the business executive's work became increasingly routine and administrative.

When the internal situation had become bureaucratic, the external one tended to be oligopolistic. Vertical integration by one manufacturer forced others to follow. Thus, in a very short time, many American industries became dominated by a few large firms, with the smaller ones handling local and more specialized aspects of the business. Occasionally industries · like oil, tobacco, and sugar, came to be controlled by one company, but in most cases legal action by the federal government in the years after 1900 turned monopolistic industries into oligopolistic ones.

Costs, rather than interfirm competition, began to determine prices. With better information on costs, supplies, and market conditions, the companies were able to determine price quite accurately on the basis of the desired return on investment. The managers of the different major companies had little to gain by cutting prices below an acceptable profit margin. On the other hand, if one firm set its prices excessively high, the other firms could increase their share of the market by selling at a lower price and still maintain a profit. They would, however, rarely cut to the point where this margin was eliminated. As a result, after 1900, price leadership, price umbrellas, and other evidences of oligopolistic competition became common in many American industries. To increase their share of the market and to improve their profit position, the large corporations therefore concerned themselves less with price and concentrated more on obtaining new customers by advertising, brand names, and product differentiations; on cutting costs through further improvement and integration of the manufacturing, marketing, and buying processes; and on developing more diversified lines of products.

The coming of the large vertically integrated corporation changed more than just the practices of American industrialists and their industries. The effect on the merchant, particularly the wholesaler, and on the financier, especially the investment banker, has been suggested here. The relation between the growth of these great industrial units and the rise of labor unions has often been pointed out. Certainly the regulation of the large corporation became one of the major political issues of these years, and the devices created to carry out such a regulation were significant innovations in American constitutional, legal, and political institutions. But an examination of such effects is beyond the scope of this paper.

Reasons for the Basic Innovations. One question remains to be reviewed. Why did the vertically integrated corporation come when it did, and in the way it did? The creation by nearly all the large firms of nationwide selling and distributing organizations indicates the importance of the national market. It was necessary that the market be an increasingly urban one. The city took the largest share of the goods manufactured by the processors of agricultural products. The city, too, with its demands for construction materials, lighting, heating and many other facilities, provided the major market for the metals and other producers' goods industries after railroad construction slowed. Without the rapidly growing urban market there would have been little need and little opportunity for the coming of big business in American industry. And such a market could hardly have existed before the completion of a nation-wide railroad network.

What other reasons might there have been for the swift growth of the great industrial corporation? What about foreign markets? In some industries, particularly oil, the overseas trade may have been an important factor. However, in most businesses the domestic customers took the lion's share of the output, and in nearly all of them the move abroad appears to have come after the creation of the large corporation, and after such corporations had fashioned their domestic marketing organization.

What about the investor looking for profitable investments, and the promoter seeking new promotions? Financiers and promoters certainly had an impact on the changes after 1897, but again they seem primarily to have taken advantage of what had already proved successful. The industrialists themselves, rather than the financiers, initiated most of the major changes in business organization. Availability of capital and cooperation with the financier figured much less prominently in these industrial combinations and consolidations than had been the case with the earlier construction of the railroads and with the financing of the Civil War.

What about technological changes? Actually, except for electricity, the major innovations in the metals industries seem to have come before or after the years under study here. Most of the technological improvements in the agricultural processing industries appear to have been made to meet the demands of the new urban market. The great technological innovations that accompanied the development of electricity, the internal combustion engine, and industrial chemistry did have their beginning in these years, and were, indeed, to have a fundamental impact on the American business economy. Yet this impact was not to be really felt until after 1900.

What about entrepreneurial talent? Certainly the best-known entrepreneurs of this period were those who helped to create the large industrial corporation. If, as Joseph A. Schumpeter suggests, "The defining characteristic [of the entrepreneur and his function] is simply the doing of new things, and doing things that are already done, in a new way (innovation)," Rockefeller, Carnegie, Frick, Swift, Duke, McCormick, the DuPonts, the Guggenheims, Coffin of General Electric, Preston of United Fruit, and Clark of Singer Sewing Machine were all major innovators of their time.[31] And their innovations were not in technology, but rather in organization and in marketing. "Doing a new thing," is, to Schumpeter a "creative response" to a new situation, and the situation to which these innovators responded appears to have been the rise of the national urban market.

There must be an emphasis here on the words "seem" and "appear." The framework used is a preliminary one and the data itself, based on readily available printed material rather than on business records are hardly as detailed or accurate as could be desired. More data, more precise and explicit questions, and other types and ranges of questions will modify the generalizations suggested here. For the moment, however, I would like to suggest, if only to encourage the raising of questions and the further compilation and analysis of data, that *the* major innovation in the American economy between the 1880's and the turn of the century was the creation of the great corporations in American industry. This innovation, as I have tried to show, was a response to the growth of a national and increasingly urban market that was created by the building of a national railroad network — the dynamic force in the economy in the quarter century before 1880. After 1900 the newly modified methods of interfirm and intrafirm administration remained relatively unchanged (as did the location of major markets and sources of raw materials) except in those industries directly affected by new sources of power and the systematic application of science to industry. In the twentieth century electricity, the internal combustion engine, and systematic, institutionalized research and development took the place of the national urban market as the dynamic factor in the American industrial economy.[32]

[31] Joseph A. Schumpeter, "The Creative Response in Economic History," *Journal of Economic History*, Vol. VII (May, 1947), p. 151, and also his *Theory of Economic Development*, trans. Redvers Opie (Cambridge, 1934), pp. 74–94.

[32] This point has only been considered briefly here, but has been developed at some length in my "Development, Diversification, and Decentralization," in Ralph E. Freeman, ed., *Post-War Economic Trends in the United States* (New York, 1960).

"The Weakened Spring of Government": A Study in Nineteenth-Century American History

WALLACE D. FARNHAM

No discussion of the process of economic development and change can exclude the role of government. The traditional picture of the government-business relationship in the late nineteenth century is rather one-sided and emphasizes the overwhelming influence of the business community that served to immunize it from regulatory reactions by government. Thus we generally view government as having operated under an evil spell and the "people," in turn, as stymied. In short, the assumption is that there was nothing basically wrong with the body politic or its institutions. But Wallace D. Farnham, a historian at the University of Illinois, finds political malaise and a flawed political system during the late nineteenth century. Farnham's analysis proceeds from a traditional model of what government should do. First, it must govern: that is, it must maintain order and guarantee justice, impartially and detached from the exclusive concerns of private interests. Second, government must ensure and assist in the production of wealth: that is, it must stimulate the release of creative energy so that its constituents might gain material security and comfort. Farnham focuses on the relationship of the Union Pacific Railroad to the federal government in order to contrast this model with prevailing practices of government. The record everywhere was one of deficiency, neglect, and failure on the part of the government to fulfill its primary responsibility of governing. But Farnham finds the source of the flaw not in corruption or influence, but rather in the national consciousness. Governmental neglect and irresolution, he contends, stemmed from prevailing concepts of government, which demanded privileges without restraints, subsidies without controls — a government, in brief, that would foster the "production of wealth," but would not re-

*press the ensuing excesses and abuses. How can Farnham's
essay be applied to understanding the governmental response,
or lack of it, to other developments of the nineteenth century?*

The Union Pacific, as everyone knows, was a railroad company that
secured vast wealth from the government and wasted it in riotous living.[1]
In time its profligate ways were discovered, and an angry nation sentenced
the culprit to the perpetual flames of hostility and investigation. To this
judgment of contemporaries, historians have added little, and chronicles
of the robber barons and the "great barbecue" commonly start with the
story of the Union Pacific.[2] One cannot help seeing, however, that the
verdict is one-sided. It notices only the conduct of the company and
the company's alleged success in corrupting the government. But what of
the conduct of the government and its effects upon the company? Congress passed various laws, which were executed in at least certain obvious
respects. Are the manner of passing the laws and the details of executing
them without consequence? This can be true only if we are sure that the
government was at all times efficient and impartial, its actions straightforward and predictable. The government of the United States was supposedly a disinterested sovereign, writing and executing law for the public
good. In practice it was probably less than this, but we have seldom
reckoned seriously with this probability. We are in fact so accustomed to
assuming that American political society was basically sound that the
intrusion of a blatant defect is accounted an abnormality.[3] In such fashion
we commonly dispose of the Union Pacific's rascalities and of a regrettable
handful of episodes contemporary with it. A closer study of the grinding
of the wheels of government illumines these events by suggesting that
they were more typical than otherwise, that they were in fact symptoms of
a deeper and more pervasive ailment.

The most promising kind of inquiry is the microscopic one that a case
study permits. The government's relations with the Union Pacific provide

Reprinted by permission of the author from the *American Historical Review*,
LXVIII (April 1963), pp. 662–680.

[1] The evidence for some of the statements is too voluminous for citation, and
the footnotes are often only suggestive of its character. Unfortunately the archives
of the Union Pacific Railroad Company have not been open to me.

[2] A recent exception is Robert William Fogel, *The Union Pacific Railroad; A
Case in Premature Enterprise* (Baltimore, 1960).

[3] For a vigorous statement of this idea, see Bernard Weisberger, "The Dark
and Bloody Ground of Reconstruction Historiography," *Journal of Southern
History*, XXV (Nov. 1959), 427–47.

a case that is suitable and rewarding. The Union Pacific stood in more intimate relation to the government than almost any other private person or group in the nineteenth century; thus the connections between the two are more than usually instructive. Scrutiny of these relations during the tumultuous years from 1862 to 1873 suggests that the actions of the government had much to do with the troubles of the company and that, in fact, the government hardly governed at all, in any technical sense, where the Union Pacific was concerned. What was true for the Union Pacific may have been true for others, and we may at least conjecture about what can be learned from similar inquiries into other appropriate subjects.

One who reads the debates in Congress relating to the Pacific railroads encounters a number of persistent themes. Members from states adjacent to the road wrangled interminably; some few members objected doggedly but vainly to the efforts of private interests; and a majority in both houses were absent or silent. After several days of fruitless protest during the debates in 1862 Justin Morrill complained to the House:

> I have been somewhat astonished that a matter of so great importance as this bill should claim so small a share of the attention of the House. . . . Here is a measure in which the Government is about to embark, involving the expenditure of hundreds of millions of dollars, and yet amendments are offered and voted in, according to the will of the gentlemen having charge of the measure, without the slightest apparent interest or attention upon the part of a majority of the House as to their character or effect.[4]

In 1864 the various companies building the Pacific railroad called upon Congress for a larger subsidy, and for other changes in the law. By this time the Union Pacific had come into the hands of a clever Wall Street operator named Thomas C. Durant, and eminent railroad men sent up storm warnings. J. Edgar Thomson and William B. Ogden advised leading congressmen that the project was in danger, and one of the New York Central's officers demanded, of all things, that the government take over the enterprise.[5] In the face of these alarms Congress declined to impose new restraints and, instead, reduced the government's lien from a first to a second mortgage. When the House passed the bill, 41 per cent

---

[4] *Congressional Globe*, 37 Cong., 2 sess., 1947 (May 5, 1862). For a full discussion of the Act of 1862, see Wallace D. Farnham, "The Pacific Railroad Act of 1862," *Nebraska History*, XLIII (Sept. 1962), 141–67.

[5] J. Edgar Thomson to Thaddeus Stevens, Jan. 26, 1864, Thaddeus Stevens Papers, Manuscript Division, Library of Congress; memo by William B. Ogden, Apr. 26, 1864, J. F. D. Lanier to John Sherman, Apr. 27, 1864, John Sherman Papers, Manuscript Division, Library of Congress; J. V. L. Pruyn, *Congressional Globe*, 38 Cong., 1 sess., 3149 (June 21, 1862).

of the members were absent; the Senate accepted the second mortgage without debate and without a roll call vote.[6]

The congressman who complained during the debates that "we are asked to confer everything upon this company and to receive nothing at their hands" had a strong case.[7] The government held a second mortgage to secure its loan, but many congressmen regarded the loan as a gift. The President of the United States would appoint one-fourth of the Union Pacific's directors, but they were a minority without special powers. The companies were bound to construct a "first class railroad," but the law failed to define a "first class railroad." A board of government commissioners would have to approve each section of the road before the subsidies were released, but this safeguard was as futile as a government director said it was:

> Even if the Commissioners have nerve enough to reject an imperfectly built Road, yet, the work being done it cannot be undone to any great extent. . . . If you wish a building erected in substantial and perfect manner you must control the materials and workmanship as it progresses, rather than rely upon a condemnation of the work and a legal controversy after it is finished.[8]

Congress might "alter, amend, or repeal" the acts, but most lawyers thought the acts a contract with the companies, and few were disposed to tamper with contracts. Clearly Congress had preserved its record of "delay, indifference, partisanship, and reluctance to provide the [administrators] the resources for effective work." [9] The nation might later make a hobby of scolding the Union Pacific, but the people's representatives had framed a charter of privileges, not an instrument of restraint.

For the most part the laws were executed in the spirit in which they had been written. Congress provided neither money nor machinery for administering them, and the task fell chiefly to the Secretary of the Interior. One of the Secretaries concerned, John P. Usher, held stock in one of the Pacific railroad companies and was personally associated with some of its promoters.[10] Of all of them only Secretary Harlan displayed much independence or energy. In the spring of 1865 Harlan created an "Engineer Office" in his department, entrusted it with the supervision of the Pacific railroads, and installed at its head one of the army's ablest engineers, Lieutenant Colonel James H. Simpson. Simpson took his

[6] *Ibid.*, 3267 (June 25, 1864), 3458–59 (July 1, 1864).

[7] *Ibid.*, 3022 (June 16, 1864).

[8] J. L. Williams to James Harlan, Aug. 17, 1865, Railroad Package 242, Records of the Office of the Secretary of the Interior, National Archives [hereafter cited as Railroad Package, with appropriate number].

[9] Leonard D. White, *The Jacksonians: A Study in Administrative History, 1829–1861* (New York, 1954), 162.

[10] Elmo R. Richardson and Alan W. Farley, *John Palmer Usher, Lincoln's Secretary of the Interior* (Lawrence, Kan., 1960), 24–26, 51–62.

work seriously and threatened to save both government and companies their subsequent embarrassment, but his office vanished before the railroads had laid much track.[11] A Congress bent on retrenchment dismissed the Engineers Office as a frill, and Orville Browning, Harlan's successor, saw no reason to protest.

Except under Harlan and Simpson, faulty execution of the law was everywhere the rule. Two or three of the government's directors were able and diligent, but they chanced to be engineers rather than businessmen and seldom inquired into company finance.[12] As watchdogs for the government they accomplished little, owing to their lack of authority and to indifference in the Interior Department. More often than not the job was a sinecure, a politician's prize. As one of them confessed, "I never solicited this place, and it has been given to me rather as a testimonial of my political consistency, than on account of any other value there is in it, and it is on this account that I am desirous of retaining it." [13] The inspecting commissioners, meanwhile, were turning in useless reports. The reports were usually prepared by company clerks rather than by the commissioners, and often they were signed before the inspection took place. With a few exceptions, each read precisely like all the others, save for its digits. Commissioners reported forty-three times on sections of the Union Pacific, and only in the first and last of these did they suggest even minor defects, despite the fact that when the last rail was laid parts of the road would scarcely bear a locomotive, and a special examination showed that nearly seven million dollars must be spent to make the road acceptable.[14] Until the company's rivals started whispering in his ear Secretary Browning endorsed these reports mechanically and passed them along to President Johnson, who regularly approved them. In effect, the government encouraged the company to build carelessly. In other matters, too, Browning seldom acted without prodding from the company or its rivals. He apparently took no steps to deal with ineffective subordinates or to have Congress correct faults in the laws. Like Congress, Browning and

[11] See *Report of Lt. Col. James H. Simpson to James Harlan*, Nov. 23, 1865 (Washington, D.C., 1865).

[12] See, e.g., the report of Springer Harbaugh to Harlan, July 20, 1865, Railroad Package 241.

[13] George Ashmun to Andrew Johnson, Sept. 21, 1867, Records of the Office of the Secretary of the Interior, Appointments Division, Government Directors Union Pacific Railway Company, National Archives.

[14] The reports of the government commissioners, endorsed by the Secretary of the Interior and the President, are filed in Railroad Packages 342–44. For comments on the commissioners' proceedings, see Huntington to Mark Hopkins, July 8, 1868, *Letters from Collis P. Huntington to Mark Hopkins, Leland Stanford, Charles Crocker, and E. B. Crocker* (New York, 1892) [hereafter cited as *Huntington Letters*]; Lewis Levey to Durant, Feb. 8, 1868, Leonard Collection, State University of Iowa Library, I, 3, 26; Frank Denver to Browning, June 8, 1868, Railroad Package 36.

his colleagues should have been inspired to vigilance, for by 1869 the files of the Interior Department held disquieting reports about the Union Pacific. The reports seem not to have been noticed.[15] Altogether, the government's conduct was a blend of neglect and irresolution, and one finds nearly as many conscientious persons in company offices as in Washington. In these circumstances the early history of the Union Pacific would probably have been little happier if the government had built it as nervous congressmen proposed in 1864.

There was no lack of activity under the Pacific Railway Acts, but the activity issued from the clamor of private interests rather than from the energy of impartial officers. In the hands of a passive government the statutes took on whatever meaning interested persons chose for them. The defects in government gave rise to the lobby, in these circumstances a necessity as well as an opportunity. Apathy in office tempted the company to extend its powers; the same apathy exposed it to loss of its rights and to the pressures of its rivals. Finding itself at the mercy of an unreliable government, each company felt obliged to send agents to Washington to collect its bounties and to protect itself against the hostile maneuvers of others. In this manner the halls of Congress and the executive departments became annexes to the market place. The law became a tool and government a servant, used or ignored as suited the convenience of interested parties. The executive of another railroad later described the tactic: " 'Let us ask the Commissioners to enforce the law when its violation by others hurts us.' " [16] It was hard to predict which feature of the law would next become the vehicle for some private undertaking. The provision requiring the company to keep its stock subscription books open was ignored until Jim Fisk persuaded Judge George G. Barnard to insist upon it.[17] Few people seemed to care whether the Union Pacific built a "first class railroad" as required by law until the Central Pacific set out to embarrass the company and delay its workmen.[18] The citizens of Omaha rejoiced in the progress of the road until it seemed to threaten them, whereupon they at once clamored for "a thorough investigation of Pacific

[15] See J. L. Williams to Harlan, May 30, 1865, ibid., 240; C. A. Trowbridge to Harlan, Aug. 19, 1865, ibid., 242.

[16] C. E. Perkins to H. Stone, Jan. 9, 1889, quoted in Thomas C. Cochran, Railroad Leaders, 1845–1890 (Cambridge, Mass., 1953), 198.

[17] James Fisk, Jr., v. Union Pacific Railroad Company and others, City and County of New York Supreme Court, July 2, 1868.

[18] Secretary Browning's first inquiry into the quality of UP construction came three days after Huntington had written him complaining about UP work with the object, he wrote Hopkins, of embarrassing the UP. (See Huntington to Hopkins, June 8, 1868, Huntington Letters; Huntington to Browning, June 10, 1868, Railroad Package 36; Browning to J. L. Williams and J. S. Rollins, June 13, 1868, Pacific Railroad Letterbook No. 2, Records of the Office of the Secretary of the Interior, National Archives.) There is much subsequent evidence that the Central Pacific was behind the periodic investigations of UP construction.

RR matters by next congress." [19] Later, in 1878, the president of the rival Atchison, Topeka and Santa Fe directed his agent in Washington to press for legislative curbs on the Union Pacific's finances — curbs that, by mere chance, would make it a less dangerous competitor.[20] Law enforcement also varied with the interests of the company, which naturally pressed more zealously for the payment of subsidies than for careful inspection of its track. Even the factional wars inside the Union Pacific reverberated in Washington, as rival groups sought shelter and advantage from the law.[21] The company's activity in Washington mushroomed with the natural increase of its internal and external problems, until in the early 1870's its lobbyists were groping their way through a dozen tangled disputes.[22] At that point the company's fortunes depended largely upon the course of events in Washington. Profits, the price of securities, and relations with competitors were as much political as business problems. The line dividing private from public business faded, and government passed by default into private hands.

The conversion of public officials into spokesmen for a private program was generally not difficult. There was no tradition of public service, no professional governing group. In the debates of Congress and the conduct of executives a man's attitude toward the Pacific railroad varied with his place of residence, business interests, and personal friendships. As a senator in 1862, Browning announced that he must oppose the Pacific railway unless the road were to connect with the line serving his home town. Thaddeus Stevens would not vote for it unless the companies were compelled to use American iron.[23] Collis P. Huntington obtained favors from the Interior Department through Browning's recent law partner, Thomas Ewing, Jr., and Grenville Dodge prevailed upon Grant's close friend and aid, John Rawlins, for advantage for the Union Pacific.[24] Many congressmen, government directors, and other officials were indebted to one or another company for contracts, land, stock, or help in elections.[25]

[19] N. P. Dodge to Dodge, May 26, 1865, Grenville M. Dodge Papers, box 10, Iowa State Department of History and Archives, Des Moines.

[20] Thomas Nickerson to J. Sterling Morton, Apr. 16, 1878, J. Sterling Morton Papers, Nebraska State Historical Society.

[21] See, e.g., B. M. Boyer to Durant, Jan. 4, 1868, Leonard Collection, I, 3, 32.

[22] General Dodge recalled the company's contests in Washington in 1870 and 1871 in a letter to Sidney Dillon, Aug. 17, 1874, Dodge Papers, box 382.

[23] *Congressional Globe*, 37 Cong., 2 sess., 2812 (June 19, 1862), 1909 (May 1, 1862).

[24] Huntington to Hopkins, June 8, June 10, 1868, *Huntington Letters*; E. S. Parker, for J. A. Rawlins, to G. M. Dodge, Feb. 26, 1869, Dodge Papers, box 156.

[25] For example: L. D. M. Sweat to Durant, May 6, 1864, Leonard Collection, I, 3, 32; C. T. Sherman to Durant, Nov. 29, 1866, *ibid.*, 3, 26; G. W. Frost to G. M. Dodge, Jan. 19, 1869, Dodge Papers, box 156; Huntington to Charles Crocker, Feb. 21, 1868, and Huntington to Hopkins, Oct 23, 1868, *Huntington Letters*.

The most costly bit of lobbying doubtless occurred in passing the act of 1864; as one agent reported, "To meet all of our engagements, in both Senate and House, it will require not short of 400 Bonds and at least $25,000 in money." [26] Altogether, "conflicts of interest" were common enough that Oakes Ames's celebrated favors to congressmen lack significance.

Nor did the companies need to take much initiative in securing co-operation in Washington. Men in all branches of government sought an annual pass. Those who had been promised cash and bonds in 1864 pursued their rewards importunately.[27] Army officers stationed in Union Pacific towns complained that they had been slighted in the distribution of town lots.[28] The Pacific railroad seemed to many congressmen a part of the loaves and fishes of patronage, and they sought both jobs and passes for their constituents. Vice-President Schuyler Colfax wanted some fifty passes from Huntington, who confessed that "as he is President of the Senate and can help or hurt us much I have not refused him yet, but think I shall be compelled to." James G. Blaine called repeatedly for favors, writing on one occasion that "I will be personally obliged" if a pass were sent to a Mrs. Marble, adding, "What about the chance for young Stinson. My protege for whom I asked a place in yr ticket Dept?" [29] Favors aside, some congressmen came to rely upon interested parties for advice in the discharge of their duties. One senator complained after a losing vote for the Union Pacific that he had "had no posting" and "had to work in the Dark." [30] Another, respected for his independence, observed to the president of the Burlington road that "those who are disposed to be friendly to you do not know how to act, because they are ignorant of what you have concluded is the true policy of your companies & there is no one here to enlighten them." [31] In various ways, it appears, public officials made up for their reluctance to govern with a willingness, even eagerness, to abandon the public interest, and contending parties had only the straightforward task of outbidding and outmaneuvering each other.

To follow convention we should be saying that weak government resulted from private pressures. The sight of this convention's standing on

[26] J. B. Stewart to Durant, July 3, 1864, Leonard Collection, III, 3, 14.

[27] Stewart to Durant, Nov. 22, 1864, *ibid.*

[28] Lieutenant Colonel H. R. Mizner to Dodge, May 13, 1868, Dodge Papers, box 15; Brevet Major General John Gibbon to Dodge, June 22, 1868, *ibid.*, box 154.

[29] Huntington to Leland Stanford, Apr. 30, 1869, *Huntington Letters*; Blaine to Dodge, June 27, 1869, Dodge Papers, box 158; see also, as examples of others, Senator J. M. Howard to Durant, Dec. 27, 1868, Leonard Collection, III, 3, 21; Senator George H. Williams to Durant, May 25, 1869, *ibid.*, 3, 2.

[30] S. J. Kirkwood to Dodge, July 13, 1866, Dodge Papers, box 151.

[31] James W. Grimes to James F. Joy, Jan. 14, 1867, James F. Joy Papers, Burton Historical Collections, Detroit Public Library.

its head may cause some disquiet. Doubtless cause and effect became tangled at an early stage, and a long progression ensued. Yet it is difficult to blame the lobbies for indifference and absenteeism in Congress, for the inertia of administrative officers when they were left alone, and for the willingness of so many of them to be pressured. We know from the writings of Leonard White, Earl Pomeroy, and others that ineffective government was the rule rather than the exception for much of the nineteenth century,[32] and we may be sure that inept officers sat behind many a door through which few lobbyists had ever passed.

That the frailty of American government went beyond the Pacific Railway Acts, that it had an existence of its own apart from the lobby, is the more certain from other facets of the history of the Union Pacific. The company depended upon the government for more than its charter and a subsidy. Like the citizens of the nation, it required order, stability, and protection for its property. The road made its way through regions that were subject to federal authority, and the company was entitled to expect the government to bring order to the West before summoning its citizens to build a railroad there. The company discovered very soon that this had not been done. Except in eastern Nebraska and parts of Utah, Indian violence was common and civil government unknown. It fell to the company, therefore, to bring order to a vast region. Federal instruments lay at hand, slightly used, in the army and the system of territorial government. Seizing these instruments, the company subdued and organized its domains.

Any careful government would have had the Indians in hand before the first locomotive appeared on the Platte. Many of the Indians were quite out of hand, however, and each rail that went down gave them a fresh grievance. Meanwhile, thousands of people trailed the railroad and its costly properties into a region devoid of effective civil government. Seeking protection for their property against a boisterous population, the company's officers turned naturally to the army. If they seemed to call for special favors it was only proper for, they observed, theirs was substantially a government enterprise. They won their case easily, as General Grant seemed to imply.

> Now that Government has assumed the obligation to guarantee the bonds of the Pacific Railroad, it becomes a matter of great pecuniary interest to see it completed as soon as possible. Every protection practicable should be given by the military.[33]

[32] White, *Jacksonians*, and *The Republican Era, 1869–1901* (New York, 1958); Earl S. Pomeroy, *The Territories and the United States, 1861–1900* (Philadelphia, 1947).

[33] U. S. Grant to W. T. Sherman, Jan. 26, 1867, Dodge Papers, box 152. General Sherman's interest in assisting the Union Pacific is discussed at length in R. G. Athearn, *William Tecumseh Sherman and the Settlement of the West* (Norman, Okla., 1956).

To restrain both Indians and whites the army was virtually loaned to the Union Pacific, and Grenville Dodge became almost *de facto* commander of the Department of the Platte.[34] Old, scattered posts were abandoned and new ones built along the railroad, while most of the troops found themselves posted to guard the company's surveyors, workmen, stations, or bridges. At the company's request detachments went out to quell riots, bounce whiskey traders from construction camps, and even to corral rioting laborers at a company coal mine.[35] The company had particular difficulty with "squatters" on its town sites. This was a delicate matter, for the company was selling lots in towns to which it had as yet no title, and the "squatters" offered a brisk challenge. But Dodge supplied choice lots to army officers, who found it possible to uphold the company's claims.[36]

As a police force the army was convenient but impermanent, and the company hastened to sponsor more conventional forms of government. The energy with which it created and managed the machinery of territorial government is most evident in Wyoming. In 1867 and 1868 the company prevailed upon Congress to split off Wyoming from Dakota Territory.[37] For some years thereafter the new territory consisted chiefly of Union Pacific towns and property, and the thinnest of lines separated company from government. Territorial officers called so regularly upon Dodge that his office in Council Bluffs was probably the most eligible site for the capital of Wyoming. As the chief justice of the territory admitted, "We most earnestly desire your concurrence and cooperation in all things pertaining to our young Territory and its welfare for we well know how much you can aid us." [38] The company did not always prevail among the bickering political factions, but its rebuffs had a way of turning up in Washington, where an objectionable law might be repealed or an officer

[34] See, e.g., General Order No. 18, Department of the Platte, Apr. 29, 1867, Records of United States Army Commands, National Archives; and Brevet Major H. G. Litchfield to O. P. Hurford, Omaha, May 29, 1867, Letters Sent, Department of the Platte, *ibid.*,

[35] For discussion of the labor dispute, see Major General C. C. Augur to Adjutant General, May 6, 1871, *ibid.*; for an illustration of general police duty, see Lieutenant M. L. Brand to Captain Arthur McArthur, July 7, 1868, Letters Sent, Ft. Bridger, Records of Army Commands, National Archives.

[36] Dodge's management of the town sites is described in letters to Sidney Dillon, Aug. 17, 1874, Dodge Papers, box 382, and to William E. Chandler, July 18, 1874, William E. Chandler Papers, Manuscript Division, Library of Congress. The extent to which army officers received lots in Laramie can be seen in W. G. Bent to Durant, May 4, 1868, Leonard Collection, I, 1, 22.

[37] J. B. Chaffee to John Evans, Nov. 30, 1867, John Evans Collection, box 9, Colorado State Archives; Minute Book of House of Representatives, Committee on Territories, 1868, Legislative Branch, National Archives.

[38] J. H. Howe to Dodge, Dec. 27, 1869, Dodge Papers, box 16; for other examples, see Governor J. A. Campbell to Dodge, May 20, 1869, *ibid.*; Campbell to Dodge, July 20, 1870, *ibid.*, box 17; Church Howe to Dodge, Oct. 30, 1871, *ibid.*, box 18.

threatened with removal.[39] When the editor of a Wyoming newspaper wrote that "It is of more vital importance to us who is Superintendent of the Road, than who is President of the United States," [40] he paid homage to a feudal lord who ruled in the absence of a weak sovereign.

We have only to remember as well that the railroad served as regional land agent to conclude that it was the Union Pacific rather than the government that subdued, organized, and settled its portion of the West. The company learned, as the Mormons had before them and others did later, that the semiarid West was hospitable only to those with authority and large resources. The government had yet to learn this lesson, or at any rate to profit from it, and so the Union Pacific seized the government's unused powers and ruled in its place. In the West as in Washington the government failed to govern, and private interests of necessity stepped into the breach. The Union Pacific supplied only ex parte government, to be sure, and if for a time this seemed better than nothing, it would in due course be resented. As rival interests gained strength in its territory, the company would become only one faction among many, and its affairs would be as troubled in the West as they were in Washington.

That the government neglected its duties is clear enough. It had nonetheless delivered its subsidy into the company's vaults, filling out its strange gift of pain and pleasure. What, we may ask, were the results? One of the results, obviously, was a railroad. As the first transcontinental the Union Pacific faced a distressing array of hazards and uncertainties, and without a handsome subsidy it would not have been built for some time. From the subsidy the nation got a railroad and the company its existence. Having admitted what is obvious, however, we are left with the suspicion that the results of this collaboration depended less upon the amount of the subsidy than upon the conduct of the government. The subsidy was a product of weakness rather than of generosity, and its value was diminished as a result. The terms of the bargain were unduly costly to both sides; by its ineptitude the government nearly vitiated its own contribution. Congress failed to inquire with any care into the costs of building on the central route, with the result that the subsidy was overlarge. The government bonds, and the company bonds they helped to create, should have built the road. The land grant was almost superfluous so far as construction was concerned. It may have brought prestige, but it yielded no cash until the last days of construction when the land-grant

[39] In the spring of 1870, for example, the company induced Congress to repeal laws of Wyoming Territory obnoxious to the company. During the same season, the company persuaded President Grant and the Attorney General to threaten one of the Wyoming Supreme Court justices with removal if a pending case were decided against the company. For illustrations of company activity in these matters, see Ames to Dodge, May 4, May 21, 1870, U. H. Painter to Dodge, May 18, 1870, Dodge Papers, box 160; Painter to Dodge, May 9, 1870, *ibid.*, box 17.
[40] Laramie *Daily Sentinel*, Oct. 5, 1870.

bonds were released.[41] Even the bond subsidy would have been excessive if the nature of the route had been known at the outset and construction had been managed properly. It would have been still more excessive if the government had provided an orderly setting for the company's activities. Private business has need "of a calculable legal system and of administration in terms of formal rules," as Max Weber observed.[42] The government's failure to provide this security worked a discount on the value of its subsidy to the Union Pacific. Thus while the nation wasted its resources the company was lured by its excessive wealth into policies that nearly proved its undoing.

Whatever the effects of the size of the subsidy, its mere existence plunged the Union Pacific into the muddy waters of American government. There it discovered both hazards and opportunities. This was the government by faction of which James Madison had warned, and according to Madison government by faction ends in "instability, injustice, and confusion." [43] That this happened with the Pacific railroads is certain. The government being what it was, one could never be really sure that the law, or its application, would not soon be changed, or that it would be enforced at all. We see vividly the chances for mischief in one of the campaigns of Collis P. Huntington, a master in the use of docile government for private advantage. The Central Pacific hoped to exclude the Union Pacific from the Salt Lake Valley, but in the summer of 1868 the Central Pacific was losing the race of the tracklayers. They could not win, Huntington decided, "unless it is done in Washington," [44] and he gave battle accordingly. It was a campaign of sparkling audacity, a blend of bribery and quiet pressure, cartographic sleight of hand, and tireless effort. His chief weapon was the law: every possible legal restraint was to be thrust upon the enemy. The sudden enforcement of the law baffled the Union Pacific, understandably enough, but it managed to fight back with similar methods. Chaos prevailed, and the Union Pacific nearly collapsed in the financial crisis that resulted. On the Johnson administration's last day in office Huntington roared out of Washington with the right to build to Ogden and part of the subsidy for the task, though his company was still 175 miles from the town while the enemy was even then nearing its outskirts. "This was the biggest fight I ever had in Washington," he

[41] The consequences of ignorance concerning the nature of the route were noted in the Senate in 1869 by Senator William Stewart (Nevada), April 5, and by Senator John Sherman (Ohio), April 6. (*Congressional Globe*, 41 Cong., 1 sess., 504, 545.) The decision to sell the land-grant bonds was made by the Union Pacific board of directors, April 9, 1869. (See extracts from the minutes, Leonard Collection, I, 2, 33.)

[42] Max Weber, *The Protestant Ethic and the Spirit of Capitalism*, tr. Talcott Parsons (New York, 1958), 25.

[43] *The Federalist*, ed. Benjamin F. Wright (Cambridge, Mass., 1961), 129.

[44] Huntington to Stanford, June 26, 1868, *Huntington Letters*.

crowed, "and it cost a considerable sum, but I thought it of so much importance that I should have put it through at a much higher price if it had been necessary." [45] Next day the Grant administration took over and with it a rising Union Pacific influence, but Huntington's masterful lobbying could not be undone, and the Central Pacific went to Ogden. He had induced pliable officials to revive dormant sections of the law. Creating just the "instability, injustice, and confusion" that Madison had predicted, he won a business victory with the weapons of government.

After the road was finished the subsidy became a heavy liability for the company, quite apart from the legal indebtedness it created. Many officers of the firm must have cursed a form of "help" that exposed the company to incessant public scrutiny and assault and to the uncertainties of the government's procedure, and opened to its rivals in business a covert avenue of attack. In years of fierce business competition and rising hostility toward railroads there could be few worse fates for a railroad company than to be conspicuously indebted to the government. The embarrassments of which Charles Francis Adams complained to the Pacific Railway Commission in 1887 flowed in no small measure from the company's peculiar connection with the government.[46] It is hard to concur in the recent verdict of a distinguished commentator on Madison's essay that "the rivalry of groups and interests, religious, political, or economic, reformist or reactionary, does serve to help in preventing the kind of oppression and instability feared by Publius." [47] When Huntington and the Union Pacific quarreled in Washington, instability and a kind of oppression were the chief results, as they were in the subsequent storms that a frail government allowed to flourish. It is no surprise that the Union Pacific found in the government a generous patron but an inconstant ruler. Confusion and uncertainty were costly and vexing and constituted a liability of no mean dimensions.[48]

[45] Huntington to Hopkins, Mar. 5, 1869, *ibid*. The voluminous documentation of this episode is scattered through the *Huntington Letters*, *The Diary of Orville Hickman Browning, 1850–1881*, ed. T. C. Pease and J. G. Randall (2 vols., New York, 1925–31), the Railroad Packages of the Interior Department, and the Dodge Papers. After trying in vain to have the action set aside, the Union Pacific was compelled to make an agreement with the Central Pacific on April 9, 1869, recognizing Huntington's victory. (For a discussion of the UP's plight, see Dodge to Oliver Ames, Apr. 19, 1869, Dodge Papers, box 337.) On April 10 Congress adopted a joint resolution ratifying the agreement between the companies.

[46] The subject is a recurring one in testimony before the commission; see especially Adams' testimony, *Senate Executive Document*, 50 Cong., 1 sess., No. 51, 982–99.

[47] Wright, introd. to *The Federalist*, 40.

[48] Professor Edward C. Kirkland has suggested that dislike of uncertainty was one of the chief sources of businessmen's suspicion of governmental activity. (E. C. Kirkland, *Dream and Thought in the Business Community, 1860–1900* [Ithaca, N.Y., 1956], 115.)

Whatever the hazards its ties with government created, the Union Pacific was neither innocent nor ineffective in its·own use of those ties. In the early 1870's, especially, it gained much for itself by operating in Washington. The connections with government brought other, subtler benefits as well. The company lured investors with a notice that "the Union Pacific Railroad is in fact, a Government work, built under the supervision of Government officers, and to a large extent with Government money." [49] To those who complained that its road was poorly built it retorted that the government's inspectors had found otherwise.[50] Without its special claim upon the government's protection the company might have failed to save its western interests from plunder. Governmental directors who held "correct" views were sent to Washington to give "impartial" testimony, while critics might expect to be told that their assaults damaged the government's investment in the road.[51] General Dodge, the company's ambassador to the United States, became expert in such matters, and in 1874 he counseled Jay Gould, then new to the company, to have congressional inquisitors "call upon the Gov't Directors for an opinion in this case — upon the effect of this action upon the Gov't lien." [52] The government's skirts obviously gave shelter through many storms, and the company used them freely.

Whether, on balance, the company gained or lost from its connection with the government is hard to decide. It gained its existence, but it suffered the losses that must come when government neglects its powers. The government was not unlike the indulgent parent whose child becomes delinquent. The company's officers acted unwisely at times in construction and finance, but a reckless and supine government opened for them a smooth road to irresponsibility. The company's lobby in Washington was busy and powerful and at times unethical, but the more honorable paths all led to extinction, or so it might easily have seemed. The company discarded the rule book of the democratic philosophers, but so did its rivals, and, indeed, so did the government. Though the company enjoyed large powers and many liberties, they were the powers and liberties of the jungle — so troubled and insecure that the company would in the long run have been better off under a government that wrote and executed law with a firm, impartial hand.

The company's position in no way excuses its actions, but it does help to explain them and to assign responsibility more accurately. The government was hardly the author of all of the ills of the Union Pacific, at least

[49] Union Pacific Railroad Company, *Progress of Their Road West from Omaha, Nebraska, across the Continent* (New York, 1867), 23.

[50] Oliver Ames to Browning, Aug. 21, 1868, Railroad Package 251.

[51] For example: minutes of UP board (extract), Jan. 3, 1867, and government directors to Browning, Jan. 10, 1867, Railroad Package 248; government directors to Secretary of the Interior, Mar. 11, 1869, *ibid.*, 254.

[52] Dodge to Gould, June 4, 1874, Dodge Papers, box 382.

not directly. The nature of the project, the character of its leaders, the feuds inside the company and the assaults from without, the momentous disorders and distractions of the 1860's, and other troubles compounded the problems of the Union Pacific and ordained that it should be at best a precarious venture. Yet in even the most private of these afflictions the government was involved, for it was the direct and deliberate creator of the company and at all times had a hand in its affairs, while its failure to govern tended to aggravate the problems of which it was not the source. At very least the government was an accomplice in trouble, offering the setting and sometimes the tools wanted by men whose private interests collided or whose public virtues were frail. Was it to some extent also the author of such troubles? Not often, perhaps, for at least there could not be lobbying or corruption unless private citizens were willing to engage in these practices. Yet the condition of the government made them so easy as to be almost inevitable, while under some circumstances the government appears chiefly responsible. In 1864, for example, reputable railroad men like J. Edgar Thomson left it to Congress to decide whether the Union Pacific should be run by themselves or by adventurers like Durant.[53] Congress chose Durant. Amply warned, it had the power to choose, and it chose the crooked rather than the straight path. Was the government also the chief author of the "education" of Charles Francis Adams, Jr., that model of probity who after two years at the helm of the Union Pacific could bring himself to give out instructions like these?

> I want you to go to Washington at once, and fix things up so far as [William B.] Allison and [James F.] Wilson, the two Iowa Senators, are concerned. You know just how the resolve of the Iowa legislature as respects the Pacific railroad funding bill came to be passed. It was done, without any consideration whatever on the part of the legislature, at the request of certain parties in Council Bluffs, who thought they had grievances against us, and who wished to use this thing as a club over our heads. . . . arrange with Allison and Wilson so that any opposition they offer shall be merely formal.[54]

Whether an upright man was being unhinged by the "club over our heads" in a weak government or whether his latent qualities were just emerging is probably impossible to say. Perhaps such episodes are exceptional. Perhaps the government was more commonly accomplice than

[53] This is the main point of the letters from Thomson and others cited in note 5, above. They urged that along with the amendments needed to make the project more practicable, Congress require that the board of directors be reorganized. They also showed interest in an enlarged influence for the government in the project.

[54] Adams to Dodge, May 7, 1886, Dodge Papers, box 164. Edward C. Kirkland discusses Adams' predicament in "Divide and Ruin," *Mississippi Valley Historical Review*, XLIII (June 1956), 3–17, esp. 11–12; he quotes this letter more briefly, though its date is misprinted.

author in the troubles of the Union Pacific. In either case it was by no means wholly responsible, but its share in the responsibility was a sizable one.

The early fortunes of the Union Pacific, and the story of the "robber barons," are in great part questions of government and of the conditions that shape a particular government. To say that the government created the robber barons is to utter at least part of the truth. If the United States in the Gilded Age contained ambitious men with elastic principles, and if it presented these men with temptation, this was not so very unusual. The arresting fact for the historian, the key to understanding the subject, is the shelter and encouragement afforded these children of Adam. If the managers of the Union Pacific were at times wayward in their actions we must say so, but we must say also that much of this would not have occurred, and we should hear very little of the rest if the government had properly discharged its ancient duty, the duty to govern impartially, to maintain order and justice, and to curb the Adam in its citizens.

We have lately heard much talk about the role of government in American history, a discussion rising at first from the desire to learn whether governments had in the nineteenth century followed the policies of laissez faire of which orators were wont to speak. Able scholars have found new ways of looking at a subject that is in many respects quite old. It has been no trouble to show that the kind of program William Graham Sumner desired was nowhere in force.[55] Amid this new knowledge and wisdom, however, a few ambiguities and contradictions survive. We may read, often in a single book, of government's odious deals with robber barons on the one hand and its wholesome aid to private citizens on the other, leaving us wondering wherein lies the difference between the tycoon and his unrebuked cousin. We have painstaking accounts of government's partnership in "mixed" enterprises, but alongside them we must place Leonard White's portraits of a government too inept to share usefully in any substantial venture. Historians of the West describe a government whose vigor was indispensable to that region, building roads and priming the pump with contracts and salaries;[56] yet they show that the same government was an incorrigible bungler that presided weakly over territorial government, Indian affairs, and the distribution of lands.[57]

[55] A recent summary of parts of this inquiry is in Carter Goodrich, *Government Promotion of American Canals and Railroads, 1800–1890* (New York, 1960).
[56] William H. Goetzmann, *Army Exploration in the American West, 1803–1863* (New Haven, Conn., 1959); Athearn, *William Tecumseh Sherman;* Howard R. Lamar, *Dakota Territory, 1861–1889: A Study of Frontier Politics* (New Haven, Conn., 1956).
[57] See Pomeroy, *Territories;* Mary E. Young, "The Creek Frauds: A Study in Conscience and Corruption," *Mississippi Valley Historical Review,* XLII (Dec.

At a much deeper level, two of the ablest commentators on the American past reach conclusions that seem wholly unmarriageable: David Potter writes of "the constant endeavor of government to make the economic abundance of the nation accessible to the public"; [58] yet David Donald describes a "gradual erosion of all authority" that would put such reasoned and deliberate programs in the realm of things not possible.[59] What policies, if there were any policies, can we discern in this muddled picture? Were governments corrupt or benevolent, strong or weak, vigorous or inert? Apparently we shall have no answers until we discover some new formula that accommodates these warring facts, or, perhaps, new questions to ask of the facts.

The contours of a solution rise from the pages of a remarkable book that is not new, M. I. Ostrogorski's *Democracy and the Organization of Political Parties*. What tasks did the people assign to government? What kinds of duties did they ask it to discharge? Ostrogorski answers with a distinction of which Americans have been too little aware. "The notion of the moral objects of the State grew dim in the public mind, the State was asked only to ensure or assist the production of wealth." [60] The "moral objects" of government presumably have at their heart the guarantee of justice, a guarantee whose execution demands a reservoir of power and authority, detached from private interests and directed in the first instance toward the creation of an orderly community. Whatever else it may do, a government must first of all govern. If it does not do this, it can hardly do anything else very effectively. If it fails to maintain order and justice and to use its powers with reasonable detachment and impartiality, then its efforts to "assist the production of wealth" will be partisan and confused. In reminding us of this, Ostrogorski left a tool that is invaluable in exploring the government's connection with the Union Pacific and its place in nineteenth-century history.

In its dealings with the Union Pacific the United States government tried to perform the second of these tasks while it shirked the first. It subsidized, but it did not rule. The subsidy was faulty in design, therefore, because it was more a result of pressures than of policies. It was perilous to its "beneficiaries" and chaotic in its results because the government persistently failed to govern. What was labeled corruption was a result rather than a cause of the defects in the government, a mere symptom of a more pervasive flaw. What the world has called policies were nothing

---

1955), 411–37; John B. Rae, "Commissioner Sparks and the Railroad Land Grants," *ibid.*, XXV (Sept. 1938), 211–30; Paul W. Gates, *Fifty Million Acres; Conflicts over Kansas Land Policy, 1854–1890* (Ithaca, N.Y., 1954).

[58] David Potter, *People of Plenty* (Chicago, 1954), 123.

[59] David Donald, *Lincoln Reconsidered: Essays on the Civil War Era* (2d ed., New York, 1961), 228.

[60] M. I. Ostrogorski, *Democracy and the Organization of Political Parties* (2 vols., London, 1902), II, 577.

of the kind, as a rule, but only a rationale for the more palatable results of weakness.

That the experience of the Union Pacific has a wider application seems likely enough. Indeed, it offers a tool for cutting through some of the ambiguities and contradictions that we have noticed. The government's peculiar blend of weakness and vigor in the West, for example, had nothing anomalous or contradictory about it. The "vigor" is misleading, for it was the vigor of private citizens acting for private ends through a weak government. The government's failure to govern could thus lead at the same time to a lack of control in the West and to lucrative subsidies for the region. Other contradictions vanish as easily as this one. An inept government could obviously take plunges into "mixed" enterprises; this is precisely what happened in the case of the Union Pacific. It could help an enterprise with one law and hinder it with another or with feeble enforcement of the first one. More generally, the government might be afflicted by a "gradual erosion of all authority," as Donald contends, and still seem to try "to make the economic abundance of the nation accessible to the public," as Potter asserts. For the erosion of authority did not carry with it the erosion of powers, as Donald might seem to imply. It meant only that the powers were not used by the government, and that "policies," such as the one Potter describes, were private rather than public in origin. Ostrogorski's conclusion is a compelling one:

> From one end of the scale to the other, the constituted authorities are unequal to their duty; they prove incapable of ensuring the protection of the general interest, or even place the power which has been entrusted to them by the community at the disposal of private interests. The spring of government is weakened or warped everywhere.[61]

What caused the spring to weaken is a question of great interest and meaning. It is also a question that we cannot answer in these pages. Only a persistent inquiry into the attitude of the citizens toward government will yield a full answer. For surely the prime sources of a so persistent a trait of government are more plausibly sought in the mass of citizens than in scattered groups of conspiring rascals. We may well ask anew whether the people were genuinely reconciled to having a government of laws rather than of men, and, indeed, whether they were even reconciled to having any sort of government worthy of the name. The answer is likely to go well beyond Ostrogorski's doctrine of political parties and the caucus. That it will extend to the deepest roots of democracy in America is altogether probable, and we may at the end find elements of what Donald has called "an excess of democracy." [62]

Nor can we speak with much more assurance about the effects of this

[61] *Ibid.*, 550.
[62] Donald, *Lincoln Reconsidered*, 209–35.

weakened spring. Leonard White sketched the outlines of a government that was ineffective for much of the nineteenth century, but his volumes are only exploratory, as he himself warned, and he made little effort to probe the consequences of the conditions he found. The path to understanding in this matter seems likely to lead us through a great many inspections of the detailed operations of government in every branch of its activities. If we are to understand the obvious and formal acts of government better than we do, we must have minute-by-minute investigations of their origin and operations. We shall have to discard the habit of taking largely for granted the operations of an office or of a statute and make way for the truism that the text of a law is about as revealing as the exposed part of an iceberg.

With the experience of the Union Pacific before us, we may venture a forecast of the results of such inquiries. Surely we will decide that it is usually irrelevant to ask what policies the government pursued in any matter, and whether or not it exhibited a laissez faire attitude toward business. That it did not stand aloof from business is clear. But even when it seemed to, it was not so much a government of limited powers, based on notions of laissez faire, as a government that failed to use the powers it had.[63] As one military commander explained, "The people scattered through the territories are expected to themselves organize so as to protect their own lives and property." [64] Or, as a Secretary of War once wrote about Indian affairs, "there appears to have been scarcely any other rule to guide the Officers and agents in the discharge of their functions, . . . than their own several notions of justice and policy." [65] The task of governing was left to private enterprise or a social compact, the use of which is a venerable part of American political behavior. Following this custom, the Union Pacific created its own law. But when the citizens of Omaha, the officers of the Central Pacific, and the speculators in Wall Street each in turn followed suit, the law of the social compact was found to resemble closely the law of the jungle. Corruption and robber barons were only the most fascinating results, the creations of an ungoverned people. But it is idle to look for conscious and deliberate policies in a jungle of this kind, and it is just as idle to assume that the execution of a

[63] For comparative studies indicating that the Canadian West was governed more successfully than the American, see William J. Trimble, *The Mining Advance into the Inland Empire* (Madison, Wis., 1914), 187–247; Paul F. Sharp, *Whoop-up Country: The Canadian-American West, 1865–1885* (Minneapolis, 1955).

[64] Brevet Major General John Gibbon to Colonel H. A. Morrow, Aug. 26, 1868, Department of the Platte, Rocky Mountain District, Letters Sent, Records of Army Commands, National Archives.

[65] Secretary of War P. B. Porter to Lewis Cass, July 28, 1828, in *Territorial Papers of the United States,* ed. C. E. Carter (25 vols., Washington, D.C., 1934–   ), XI, 1195.

law reflected in any rational way the avowed purpose or the contents of the law.

That the effects of a "weakened spring of government" — to return to Ostrogorski's admirable metaphor — were potentially enormous needs no demonstration. In all likelihood it was a central cause of the troubled history of the West, and of the orgies of the Gilded Age, as in fact the experience of the Union Pacific plainly suggests. Whether it also produced the Civil War, as Donald asserts, is less obviously true. We may safely conclude, though, that the spring was almost as weak before the war as after, and that in this respect as in others [66] the war wrought fewer changes than it is now fashionable to believe. The same line of inquiry may turn up fresh understanding of the recurring crusades for political reform, those fervent but largely futile campaigns to repair the faults of democracy by making it more democratic. But whatever the result of these and similar investigations, we are left with the near certainty that Americans in the nineteenth century asked the impossible of their government. In requiring that it subsidize without governing, that it transfer the nation's resources into their hands without ensuring justice and order,[67] they made it certain that the "spring of government" would be weakened and warped. This basic flaw in the nation's political society became a central fact in the early history of the Union Pacific. Perhaps the study of kindred subjects with this theme in mind will permit us to decide that it was a central fact in the history of the United States in the last century.

[66] See Thomas C. Cochran, "Did the Civil War Retard Industrialization?" *Mississippi Valley Historical Review*, XLVIII (Sept. 1961), 197–210.

[67] For an interesting statement of this theme, from the standpoint of legal history, see James Willard Hurst, *Law and the Conditions of Freedom in the Nineteenth-Century United States* (Madison, Wis., 1956).

Migration from Europe Overseas in the Nineteenth and Twentieth Centuries

FRANK THISTLETHWAITE

The subject of immigration naturally has attracted a great deal of attention from American historians. After all, we are a nation of immigrants. But almost without exception, the approach has been peculiarly nationalistic. Historians have stressed who came, where they came from, when, what attracted them, and what they did in the United States after they arrived. The process of settlement and acculturation, as far back as the establishment of the Jamestown, Plymouth, and Massachusetts Bay colonies in the seventeenth century, has been the chief area of interest of historical and sociological investigations. The emphasis, then, has been on the consequences, rather than the causes, of migration, and almost exclusively within the context of the American experience. But in the essay below, Frank Thistlethwaite, a British historian long concerned with "Atlantic" history, analyzes the problem of migration in its intercontinental setting. Employing techniques and data from the social sciences, Thistlethwaite turns from the "pull" considerations of migration history, that is from the factors attracting migrants, to the "push" considerations, that is the motives, drives, and immediate experiences stimulating migration. From this, we can understand better that, whatever the attractions of the New World, the process of migration acquired momentum within Europe itself, formed by impulses that were local in origin. In what ways does Thistlethwaite's analysis of the forces underlying migration offer new insights into the problems of settlement and acculturation?

A generation has elapsed since the late Marcus Lee Hansen, the father of modern historical scholarship in migration, first set the field for meaning-

Reprinted by permission of the publishers, Almquist & Wiksell (Stockholm) from XIe Congrès International des Sciences Historiques, Stockholm, 1960. *Rapports, V:Histoire Contemporaine.*

ful investigation.[1] The questions posed by Hansen in his famous article published in 1927 largely remain unanswered and continue to haunt the student of migration. Five years after the Hansen paper a committee of the American Historical Association merely re-phrased them; [2] and as recently as 1956 the latest commentator has little further progress to report. Dr. Richard Haskett's "introductory" bibliography for the history of American immigration (1607–1955), to which it will not be possible to do justice in this *rapport*, runs to about two hundred pages of close print: yet in his prefatory essay he can hardly do more than proliferate the questions which are implicit in Hansen's seminal paper; and he concludes that

> the chief effect of a generation of professional study has been a recognition of the awesome task confronting anyone who attempts to master the subject of emigration.[3]

As candid students we must endorse both the awesome character of the job before us and the inconclusive nature of the results hitherto achieved.

Why is this so? An attempt to answer this question is relevant not only to historiography but also to the present state of migration studies.

The study of modern migration has its origin not in Europe, the continent of emigration, but in what came to be overwhelmingly the most important country of immigration, the United States. This is scarcely surprising in view of the intimate connection which exists between migration and the American experience. Migration is central to American national tradition. The influx of diverse European, African and Asiatic strains induced a self-consciousness about ethnic origins, the juxtaposition of minorities and concern for the effect of ethnic mixture upon the national character and institutions which is unique in modern history. The attitude of American publicists and scholars towards this controversial subject at the turn of the 20th century when the inpouring of millions of "new" immigrants presented urgent social problems was contentious and in part wildly ethnocentric; yet it was in a true sense sociological. It is no accident that the adopted home of the struggling science of sociology came to be the United States, and its chief stimulus has been the immigrant problem.[4]

[1] M. L. Hansen, "The History of American Immigration as a Field for Research," *American Historical Review*, Vol. XXXII, 1926–27.

[2] American Historical Association, Committee on the Planning of Research; *Historical Scholarship in America: Needs and Opportunities* (New York, 1932).

[3] R. C. Haskett, "Problems and Prospects in the History of American Immigration," in W. E. Schmidt, C. B. Lavell and R. C. Haskett (eds.), *A report on World Population Migrations as related to the United States of America* (Washington, D.C., 1956), p. 48.

[4] See C. Wright Mills, *The Sociological Imagination* (New York, 1959), pp. 90–91.

One must also bear in mind that the study of migration originated with the social scientists, as more narrowly defined, and not with the historians. Investigations resulting from the concern of social reformers at the "new" immigration provided the first comprehensive and systematic evidence for historical research into immigration. The publication of the forty-one volumes of the United States Immigration Commission Report in 1911 was accompanied and followed by a spate of studies of different ethnic, immigrant groups. Only later did historians like McMaster and Channing begin to show that the historical craft had assimilated both the subject matter and the disciplined approach of social science in this respect.

Some of this literature is of limited use as historical evidence owing to the partisan spirit in which it was written. This is particularly the case with the highly-coloured pseudo-historical writing of the filio-pietists, usually of the older immigrant stocks, who were quick to assert the positive contribution of their Scotch–Irish, German, Irish or Scandinavian fellow-citizens to American culture.[5] More useful, though often pessimistic enough to provide ammunition for the restrictionists, were studies of a more sociological nature, usually of the new immigrants, such as that by Foerster on the Italians and those by Fairchild and Burgess on the Greeks, which, together with that by Babcock on the Scandinavians, are of continuing usefulness.[6] Between the Wars filio-pietist and sociological approaches each resulted in a flood of periodical literature of mixed quality, and in a few major works of scholarship of which Blegen's work on the Norwegian migration might be allowed to represent the filio-pietist tradition and Handlin's work on Boston's immigrants, the sociological.[7] Each is the end-product of a long process of refinement and sophistication peculiar to American scholarship in which the sociological and the narrative–historical have grown closer to mutual advantage. In particular the Handlin achievement represents a blending of the historical and the sociological approaches of immense value to the study of migration. I shall return to this later.

There are, however, limitations to the American achievement. Naturally enough, in view of the original impetus to migration studies in the United

[5] Notorious examples are H. J. Ford, *The Scotch–Irish in America*, 1915; A. B. Faust, *The German Element in the United States*, 1909. A. O. Fonkalsrud, *Scandinavians as a Social Force in America*, 1913; G. T. Flom, *A History of Norwegian Immigration to the United States from the Earliest Beginning down to the Year 1848*, 1909. In this connection see the comments of E. N. Saveth, *American Historians and European Immigrants*, 1948, p. 216.

[6] R. F. Foerster, *Italian Emigration of Our Times*, 1919; H. P. Fairchild, *Greek Immigration to the United States*, 1911; Thomas Burgess, *Greeks in America*, 1913; K. C. Babcock, *The Scandinavian Element in the United States*, 1914.

[7] T. C. Blegen, *Norwegian Migration to America 1820–1860*, 1931; Oscar Handlin, *Boston's Immigrants*, 1941.

States, American scholars have been overwhelmingly pre-occupied with one phase, and one phase only, of the migration process: that of immigration. The term "immigrant" is said to have been coined in 1789 by Samuel Morse as an Americanism essential to describe someone whom language had hitherto universally described as an "emigrant"; [8] and it was in the nature of things that American tradition and, when it came to recognize migration as a legitimate field of study, American historical scholarship should assume the same point of view and, taking the migrant's departure very much for granted, should concentrate upon his destination. Settlement, assimilation and, more recently, acculturation: these have been the central, urgent issues for American historians and sociologists alike.

As a result it has been the consequences and not the causes of migration which have received most attention; and, moreover, the consequences in the receiving, not the sending country. The causes, if not exactly taken for granted, have been given more perfunctory investigation. It is a long time since a scholar could assert that the reason why the French did not emigrate was because they had liberal institutions and leave it at that; [9] and American scholars are no longer guilty of succumbing to what the State Department demographer calls "the American stereotype of the hungry denizen of the old world casting an envious eye on the wealth and opportunities of the new"; [10] yet there are few with the detachment to ask the question posed of immigrants long ago by Foerster: "Has the game for them been worth the candle?" [11]

One of the few is Professor Oscar Handlin whose powerfully written study of *The Uprooted* manages to communicate a much deeper insight into immigrant experience than anyone has hitherto achieved.[12] To convey the immigrant experience as tragic as well as epic has exalted rather than diminished the moral experience of migration and has forced it upon the attention of general historians as one of the great historical themes. Yet even Professor Handlin is not entirely innocent of the American limitations. It has been pointed out that "what emerges is a mystical projection of the 'peasant' conditioned through fifteen hundred years in Europe to passive and pathetic acceptance of his unhappy lot" before

[8] M. M. Mathews, A *Dictionary of Americanisms on Historical Principles*, 1951, Vol. I, p. 863.

[9] T. W. Page, "The Causes of the Earlier European Immigration," *Journal of Political Economy*, Vol. CXIX (Oct. 1911).

[10] Dudley Kirk, "Demographic Trends in Europe," *Annals of the American Academy of Political and Social Science*, 1949, p. 46.

[11] Foerster, *op. cit.*, p. 374.

[12] Oscar Handlin, *The Uprooted: The Epic Study of the Great Migrations that made the American People* (Boston 1951); an autobiographical study, equally valid and powerful is Alfred Kazin's A *Walker in the City* (London, 1952).

being uprooted and transplanted willy-nilly to the American scene.[13] I shall return later to this characteristically American stereotype of "the peasant" which, along with "feudalism" and "the customary society," makes a romantic backdrop to the realistic drama of immigrant adjustment in America. Suffice it here to say that this touch of unreality in Handlin's work derives from the immigrant — or American — centredness of it. Europe is given, so to speak, taken for granted as necessary background: only the immigrant is real; and the result is that the historic experience of migration, as a totality from the first intimation of dislodgement at home to ultimate reconciliation or defeat abroad, is frustrated. Recent American scholarship has wonderfully enriched our knowledge of immigrant adjustment; but there still appears to be a salt-water curtain inhibiting understanding of European origins.

The great, though not the only, exception to this judgement is Marcus Lee Hansen himself. Hansen's work [14] was the result not only of painstaking researches in European archives and newspapers but of long brooding upon the complete process of migration; and the discerning reader may find in his closely-woven writing not merely all the important questions but suggestive leads of the kind that Americans delight to call "insights." For Hansen the history of emigration had almost universal implications and it is regrettable that he did not live long enough to complete a general history of the subject.[15] He could have made it the central theme for a history of the American people which would have been more lasting, because more profound, than that of Frederick Jackson Turner; for settlers were emigrants before they settled and migration has more than the wilderness to do with American character and institutions. Yet in the search for a history of migration Hansen was destined to be a Moses not because he died young, but because, despite his masterly diagnosis of the emigration fever as it touched neighbourhood after neighbourhood across Europe, he only concerned himself with migrants who had one special destination: the United States. His history would have been American, not universal. This is the final limitation of American scholarship in migration. Even in so fine a mind as Hansen's there is always the presumption that the ultimate objective of overseas migration from Europe is North America and even, because so much Canadian immigration was transient, the United States.

> During the century, therefore, it may be said that America was a
> huge magnet of varying intensity, drawing the people of Europe from

[13] Vera Shlakman, review of Handlin, *op. cit., Journal of Economic History*, XIII, 1953, pp. 242–243.

[14] Marcus Lee Hansen, *The Atlantic Migration, 1607–1860*, 1940; *The Immigrant in American History*, 1941; *The Mingling of the Canadian and American Peoples*, 1940.

[15] Saveth, *op. cit.*, pp. 222–223.

those regions where conditions made them mobile and from which transportation provided a path. American conditions determined the duration and height of the waves, European, the particular source.[16]

Now one must face the fact that of the fifty-five million Europeans who emigrated overseas between 1821 and 1924 thirty-three million or three-fifths went to the United States: [17] and yet an argument of this paper is that to treat 19th, and still more, 20th-century overseas migration as an essay in the peopling of the United States may provide a false perspective. As will be argued below the process was much more complex than the transatlantic movement would imply. Viewing the phenomenon of migration as a whole the United States destination, though a powerful "magnet," may be a less significant factor than American scholars have assumed; and it may be that in concentrating so much upon the "American fever" we have got off on the wrong foot and that this may be one reason for the slow progress of scholarship in the migration field.

Should this hypothesis prove correct, Europeans have themselves, not the Americans, to blame for it. If American efforts have been limited largely to "domestic" aspects of the subject European efforts have hardly had any results at all, even in those aspects of the subject which are domestic to us. We see mere flashes of welcome light in an otherwise dark continent.

The treatment of modern migration by European historians is a remarkable example of the blinkers which traditional ways of looking at the past impose on the historical imagination. The removal overseas of some fifty-five million Europeans in the century before American restriction is one of the more remarkable phenomena of modern times; and yet it appears to have made little if any impact upon the writers of general European history. The reasons for this are no doubt bound up with the fact that European history has been the history of nations and, from this point of view, overseas migration is essentially negative. Supra-national in manifestation, it represents a drain or loss to the nation which cannot easily be assessed. For example, the British Isles contributed by far the largest proportion of emigrants, about 19 million; [18] yet even taking into account the fact that this includes an important proportion of Irish, it is surprising how little notice English historians take of the fact. The volume of the standard Oxford History of England which covers the 1880's, a decade when the rate of British (and largely English) emigration, at six persons per thousand population, was almost as high as that of Scandinavia, contains two laconic references to the figures without interpreta-

---

[16] Hansen, *The Immigrant in American History*, p. 192.

[17] Imre Ferenczi, "An Historical Study of Migration Statistics," *International Labour Review*, XX, 1929.

[18] W. F. Willcox (ed.), *International Migrations* (New York, 1931), Vol. I, p. 85.

tion; [19] and a few general and meagre references to emigration in the standard social history of England, where, if anywhere, one would expect the subject to be properly handled, give the totally erroneous impression that most British emigrants in the 19th century went to the British colonies.[20] To the national historian emigration appears to be an embarrassing subject, best ignored.

Yet, if it is plausible, by concentrating upon the phenomena of agrarian upheaval, industrialization and urbanization, to by-pass the *causes* of emigration and to dismiss emigrants as so much inconsequential wastage, one might think that the *consequences* of an important bloodletting of population through emigration would not be so easy to ignore. It was once again an American, W. R. Shepherd, who, in a famous article as long ago as 1919, asserted that

> the possibilities of investigation suggested by a survey of the process by which the world at large has become Europeanized are neither so moral nor so interesting and important as those involved in a study of the reaction of its expansion upon the life and thought of Europe itself.[21]

But in 1932 that Committee of the American Historical Association was still touting the field as virgin territory,[22] and as recently as 1952 a United Nations report lamented the paucity of studies of the social effects of emigration on the home country.[23] In particular the effects of emigration on a country where the *rate* of emigration to total population has been as high as, say, in Scandinavia (700 per 100,000) must have been so great as to determine to a degree the course of national development. Indeed, as long ago as 1913 the great Swedish demographer Sundbärg said

> to discuss 'Swedish emigration' is the same as to discuss 'Sweden'; there is hardly a single political, social or economic problem in our country which has not been conditioned, directly or indirectly, by the phenomenon of emigration.[24]

Yet this does not yet appear to have been attempted; [25] and, despite the

[19] R. C. K. Ensor, *England 1870–1914* (Oxford, 1936), pp. 271, 500.

[20] G. M. Trevelyan, *English Social History*, 1942, e.g., pp. 473–475, 547.

[21] W. R. Shepherd, "The Expansion of Europe," *Political Science Quarterly*, XXXIV, 1919.

[22] American Historical Association, *Historical Scholarship in America: Needs and Opportunities* (New York, 1932), p. 76.

[23] United Nations, *Determinants and Consequences of Population Trends* (New York, 1952), p. 299.

[24] *Emigrationsutredningen: Betänkande i Utvandringsfrågan* (Stockholm, 1913), p. 660.

[25] B. J. Hovde, "Effects of Emigration upon Scandinavia," *Journal of Modern History*, Vol. VI, 1934, p. 254.

brilliant efforts of Professor Koht and Mrs. Semmingsen this would also appear to be the case in Norway.[26]

This is not to imply that there has not been good, even brilliant mono-graphic work of recent years: the point I am making is that it is still a comparatively neglected field, that it is a field dominated by American, not European, scholarship and that the best hope of a new advance is to take a new look at the subject *as a whole* from a different point of view; from neither the continent of origin nor from the principal country of reception; we should try to think neither of emigrants nor immigrants, but of migrants, and to treat the process of migration as a complete sequence of experiences whereby the individual moves from one social identity to another. This paper attempts to suggest ways of re-directing inquiries along these lines.

One group of students who have habitually studied migrants rather than immigrants or emigrants are the demographers. I have already re-ferred to the extent to which the historical study of migration has in the past leant upon the social scientists. The findings of demographers, econo-mists and sociologists are no substitute for historical research; yet it is once again the case, as it was fifty years ago, that the social scientists are setting the pace and historians have much to learn from the advances they have made. One reason for this is the elusiveness of the usually anonymous individual migrant compared with other subjects of historical research, so that special reliance must be placed upon the evidence of the statistics.

The first point to be made is that their handling of statistics has at last given us the orders of magnitude of the problems concerned. Migration statistics have been a notoriously intractable problem, discussed at confer-ence after conference of the International Statistical Institute since 1891, at the International Conference on Emigration and Immigration at Rome (1924), and the International Parliamentary Commercial Conference at Rio in 1927. The International Labour Organization in 1947 considered migration statistics "still very imperfect and incapable of serving as a basis for international comparisons," [27] an opinion re-iterated by the United Nations Department of Social Affairs and the World Population Conference of 1954.[28]

The gaps and discrepancies between the various types of statistical evi-dence — from ports, frontiers, passenger lists and passports — each of

[26] See T. C. Blegen, *op. cit.*, p. 326, for the failure to understand the impor-tance of emigration on the Thrane movement.

[27] International Labour Office, *First Report of the International Labour Or-ganization to the United Nations* (Geneva, 1947), "Reports," Vol. I, Chapter XI.

[28] United Nations, Dept. of Social Affairs, *Problems of Migration Statistics* (New York, 1949), p. 41; *Proceedings of the World Population Conference,* 1954, "Papers," Vol. II, p. 761.

which vary from country to country and in time-scale are notorious; [29] it has sometimes been more convenient to make up rough estimates of migration based upon natural increase rather than rely on the emigration statistics and much historical research still remains to be done.[30] Yet the famous survey undertaken on American initiative for the International Labour Office by Ferenczi and Willcox in 1931 did, as the authors claimed, enable the historical study of migration to be "taken up on new bases." [31] Since 1931 historians have had at their disposal at least the broad orders of magnitude of overseas migration between continents, countries and even districts, of return migration, and of cyclical fluctuations; and in relation to particular countries such as Sweden and the United States, where population statistics have been especially well developed, there is buried away a wealth of occupational and other information about migrants which demographers are beginning to bring to light but which historians have hardly yet taken into account.[32] In short, the demographers have given us a sense of proportion which makes some of the earlier narrative writing, revealing as it is, often obsolescent. We know statistics are dangerous; the contributors to *World Migrations* for instance, were quick to point out that figures cannot determine motives; [33] but at least they are a guide to the sensitive areas of investigation.

The statistical evidence would on the surface appear to justify the "American-centredness" of the older historians. In the century before restriction 33 million of the 55 million emigrants from Europe went to the United States; and the power of Hansen's magnet is revealed by the attraction thither rather than to the British Empire of perhaps 60 per cent of British emigrants.[34] Surely this is justification for the assumption that the history of migration is virtually the history of American immigration? Yet the more one qualifies this crude figure the more complex does the picture begin to look and the less prominent, in many respects, does the United States begin to appear.

In the first place, it is estimated that perhaps a third of United States immigrants re-emigrated, thereby considerably reducing the intensity of

[29] Imre Ferenczi, "An Historical Study of Migration Statistics," *International Labour Review*, Vol. XX, 1929, p. 359.

[30] United Nations, *Problems of Migration Statistics*, p. 3.

[31] Ferenczi, *op. cit.*, p. 384.

[32] See especially the work of Professors E. P. Hutchinson, S. Kuznets and Dorothy Thomas of the United States and Professor Brinley Thomas of the United Kingdom; see below, pp. 70–72.

[33] Willcox, *op. cit.*, Vol. II, pp. 291, 341.

[34] Willcox, *op. cit.*, Vol. I, p. 101; the British percentage to the United States excludes migration into Canada, much of it transient, on its way south. In the second half of the 19th century between 61 per cent and 72 per cent of British emigrants sailed for the United States (W. A. Carruthers, *Emigration from the British Isles* [London, 1929], Appendix II, p. 308).

the immigrant impact; [35] yet between the First and the Second World
Wars, the residue of the great trans-oceanic migration left some twenty
million persons in overseas countries who were born in Europe, of whom
about 12 million were to be found in the United States, the same proportion as the crude figure.[36]

In the second place there were other receiving countries in the western
hemisphere with a volume of immigration *relatively* more significant than
the United States: Argentina with 5.4 million, Brazil with 3.8 million and
Canada with 4.5 million.[37] If one takes *intensity* of immigration, a more
significant criterion than the crude absolute figure, one finds that Argentina has had the largest number of immigrants in proportion to population
and that Canada occupies as a rule a higher place than the United States.
In the decade 1901–1910 the rates per hundred thousand were: United
States just over 1000, Canada 1500, Argentina 3000.[38] It would seem,
therefore, from these proportions that the South American countries, and
especially Argentina, might be of even greater importance than the United
States to one concerned strictly with the impact of immigrants upon the
receiving country. Further, the South American differs from the North
American experience in the comparatively limited number of ethnic
groups from whom the immigrants were recruited. Before 1900, when
more Italians went to Brazil than to the United States,[39] they provided
up to 70 per cent of immigrants into Argentina and up to 63 per cent into
Brazil; [40] in the generation after 1895 one-eighth of the population of
Argentina was Italian; [41] and in 1910 they comprised a third of the population of the Brazilian State of Sao Paulo.[42] Such a concentration of one
culture group presents an interesting contrast from the situation in North
America; for example, by dominating both the building trade and the profession of architecture the Italians have given an Italian character to the
cities of South America, an immigrant influence without parallel in the
United States. Certainly the South American, as well as the Canadian,

[35] The estimate is a projection backwards from figures for the period after 1907
when returns for re-emigration first became available; Willcox, *op. cit.*, Vol. II,
p. 89, table 17; A. M. Carr-Saunders, *World Population* (Oxford, 1936), p. 49;
J. Isaac, "International Migration and European Trends," *International Labour
Review*, LXVI, 1952, p. 188.

[36] Dudley Kirk, *Europe's Population in the Interwar Years* (Princeton, Office
of Population Research, Princeton University, 1946), p. 90.

[37] Each country with a comparative re-migration; the figures cover the period
1821–1924 (Ferenczi, *Historical Study*, pp. 374–375).

[38] Willcox, *op. cit.*, Vol. I, p. 210; Dorothy S. Thomas, "International Migration," in Philip M. Hauser (ed.), *Population and World Politics*, 1958, p. 141.

[39] Foerster, *op. cit.*, pp. 279, 320.

[40] Ferenczi, *op. cit.*, p. 379.

[41] Foerster, *op. cit.*, pp. 229, 275.

[42] *Ibid.*, p. 289.

experience is of the greatest importance for any comparative study of migration and here, also, is a field ripe for research. We need to know very much more, not only about the relation, sometimes oscillating, between migrant flows to South and to North America but about the different ways immigrants from the same ethnic stock adjusted to their respective communities.

However, even this appears a formal and limited problem as one explores further the implications of the statistics. For instance, I have mentioned that the repatriation rate for the United States may have been over 30 per cent; for Argentina it was as high as 53 per cent.[43] It is clear that in South, even more than in North, America and for an important fraction of individuals, migration was temporary and transitory. We know that this proportion varied greatly between periods — it was at its greatest during the height of the "new" industrial immigration to the United States — and between ethnic groups — between 1908 and 1923 the repatriation rate was as high as 86–89 per cent for Balkan peoples and as low as 11 per cent for the Irish and 5 per cent for Jews.[44] The rate of naturalization was equally variable: for example, for the southern Italians who had qualified for United States citizenship less than a sixth had become citizens at the time of the U.S. Immigration Commission.[45] Whatever else the experience may have meant, migration often did not mean settlement and "acculturation."

Unfortunately, we know comparatively little about this important aspect of the history of oceanic migration.[46] What was the rate of velocity of re-migration? What was the proportion of "repeaters" moving to and from the country of emigration, the proportion of "wanderers" moving from one receiving country to another? What was the experience of remigrants who returned permanently to their country of birth? These areas of exploration are almost the further face of the moon; but what we can glean from qualitative sources suggests a configuration of great interest and complexity.

To begin with, it is clear that a significant proportion of the re-migrants were "repeaters," who made a regular practice of temporary migration. In 1904, 10 per cent of Italian immigrants entering the U.S. had been there before.[47] Migrants in several of the important ethnic groups were seasonal

[43] Ferenczi, *op. cit.*, p. 380; whereas the U.S. figure is an estimate projected backwards from 1907, the first year of repatriation returns, the Argentina figure is based upon returns over the entire period 1857–1924.

[44] *Ibid.*, p. 380; there is a rough correlation between repatriation rates and the proportion of males to females, e.g., a high proportion of 96 per cent males among the Greeks and a low proportion (52 per cent) among Jews (Fairchild, *op. cit.*, p. 112; Willcox, *op. cit.*, Vol. II, pp. 506–507).

[45] Foerster, *op. cit.*, pp. 273, 400.

[46] The term "oceanic migration" is used to exclude migration across the Mediterranean Sea.

[47] *Ibid.*, p. 36.

workers who hired themselves out on alternate shores of the ocean. The *golondrina* (swallow) was a peasant who left Italy in November after harvest for the flax and wheat fields of northern Cordoba and Santa Fe; between December and April he harvested corn in southern Cordoba and Buenos Aires, and in May he returned to Piedmont for the spring planting. This great seasonal movement differed only in the remarkable ocean ferry from the flux of Mexican harvesters through the wheat fields of Montana and California.[48] The building workers who departed from Venetia for the United States each March and returned in October to repeat their migration the following spring, had further to travel but a less complicated routine than the English house-painters who pursued their trade to the United States in the spring, to Scotland in the summer before English families went north and to England in the autumn while the shooting season was still in progress.[49] The miner who returned to Scotland to idle the winter through on dollars earned in summer in an Appalachian coal-seam, risked finding his underground pitch queered by a peasant earning dollars to buy land in his native Polish village.[50] The mule-spinner who shuttled between Bolton, Lancashire, and Fall River, Massachusetts, found himself replaced by a French-Canadian who hoped to return with a little laid by to the Province of Quebec.[51] This restlessness sometimes impelled the migrant to travel from one receiving country to another, like the Italian cobbler in Pennsylvania who had worked for several years in Brazil, or the father of Charles Forte, the London-born caterer, who had been an Italian steel worker in Pittsburgh where he had understood the importance of the soda fountain.[52] Before the First World War between five and ten thousand Italian immigrants entered the United States each year from other countries than Italy.[53] Such birds of passage provide as yet only partial information concerning the complex migration patterns of the Atlantic in the 19th and early 20th centuries. Yet as one authority puts it:

> It is possible that if records of such movements were to be gathered they would reveal an amazing frequency of proletariat globe-trotting, a frequency unequalled by the upper-class traveller of the richer countries.[54]

If, like good ornithologists, we persevere in "ringing" birds of passage,

[48] Foerster, *op. cit.*, pp. 47, 243–244.
[49] Foerster, *op. cit.*, p. 37; R. T. Berthoff, *British Immigrants in Industrial America* (Cambridge, Mass., 1955), p. 82.
[50] Berthoff, *op. cit.*, p. 52; Andrew Roy, *A History of the Coal Miners of the United States*, pp. 41–2; W. L. Thomas, and F. W. Znaniecki, *The Polish Peasant in Europe and America* (Chicago, 1918–20), Vol. I, p. 192.
[51] Hansen, *The Mingling of the Canadian and American Peoples*, pp. 165–166.
[52] Foerster, *op. cit.*, p. 21; *The Observer*, Aug. 3, 1959.
[53] Foerster, *op. cit.*, p. 21.
[54] Foerster, *op. cit.*, p. 37.

we begin to find that the migration pattern is even more complicated. It has to take into account, not merely a one-way movement from Europe overseas nor a reciprocal movement between country of origin and country of reception, nor even between countries of reception, but an extensive migration within the Mediterranean basin and Europe itself.

The British potter in East Liverpool, Ohio, who had worked for years at a time in Holland and France before reaching the United States, the Irish immigrant in a Rhode Island spinning mill who had learnt his trade in Lancashire, the Jewish tailor or cigar-maker who had learnt *his* trade in the East End of London as a bird of passage from Russian Poland,[55] all these are tell-tale evidence that the movements of 19th-century migration may have been powerfully attracted to the New World but acquired momentum within Europe itself. The waves of migration surging across to the Americas in ever-widening circles were formed by impulses which were local and had originally quite neighbourly affects. Take the Mediterranean for instance. The Italian *mediero* or *arrendatio* who pioneered the wheatfields of Argentina and the coffee plantations of Brazil was the compatriot of the Sicilian or Calabrian colonist on a less remote wheat frontier only six hours journey from Palermo in Tunis.[56] The Greeks who, after having tried the Transvaal, followed the Italians to both South and North America, had already provided Bulgaria and Rumania with general labourers and Turkey and Egypt with merchants and petty traders.[57] Italians helped build the Panama Canal; but their compatriots had already worked on its Suez exemplar.[58] In the early stages most of this Italian emigration had Europe or North Africa as its destination, though the proportions shifted from 82 per cent to Europe and North Africa in 1876 to 36 per cent in 1913; between 1876 and 1926, whereas 8.9 million Italians went to the Americas, as many as 7.5 million were content to move within Europe and the Mediterranean.[59]

As the foregoing figures imply, we are dealing with an intra-European as well as a trans-oceanic phenomenon. While Calabrian labourers were working on the Suez Canal, artisans from Lombardy and Piedmont were building tunnels and railways in Switzerland and France. There were over a quarter of a million Italians in France by 1886 and nearly half a million in 1911, roughly a third of the Italian-born population in the United States.[60] The emergence of France as one of the major countries of immigration is a neglected fact of migration history. France's slow and lagging

[55] F. Thistlethwaite, "The Atlantic Migration of the Pottery Industry," *Economic History Review*, 2nd Series, Vol. XI, 1958, p. 270; Berthoff, *op. cit.*, p. 33.

[56] Foerster, *op. cit.*, pp. 215–216.

[57] Fairchild, *op. cit.*, pp. 75–78.

[58] Foerster, *op. cit.*, p. 21.

[59] Willcox, *op. cit.*, Vol. II, p. 450; 1876 marks the first attempt, by Carpi, at a statistical coverage.

[60] Foerster, *op. cit.*, pp. 129–130.

industrialization attracted not only Italian labourers, but Poles, Belgians and, later, Spaniards to the extent of about two million by the 1920's when France became the second most important and, after the United States Restriction Acts, *the* most important country of immigration in the world.[61] By 1931 there were in France over 900,000 Italians, over 500,000 Poles, over 330,000 Spaniards and over 300,000 Belgians. German industrialization attracted an even more intensive, though shorter-lived immigration after 1890, chiefly from Austria-Hungary and Italy.[62]

Again, it is difficult to distinguish emigration from migration within countries. Speaking of the southern Italians who moved north in such large numbers, Foerster wrote: "Emigration is in some respects more of a kind with the extraordinary internal migration of Italy than with the trans-oceanic movement," [63] and the experience of the Irish who migrated to Lancashire, the Scots to Birmingham and the South Welsh to London differed only in degree from that of their neighbours who migrated to Boston, Toronto and Scranton respectively. Each move involved uprooting and in varying degrees the development of the migrant mentality.

In short, trans-oceanic migration was only one aspect of a bewilderingly complex pattern of tidal currents which carried not merely Norwegian settlers to Minnesota homesteads and Irish immigrants to New York tenements, but Polish peasants to *and from* East German estates, Appalachian coalmines and Silesian steelworks, Italian labourers to and from Chicago, Illinois, and Homécourt, France, Italian hotel workers to and from Lausanne, Nice and Rio de Janeiro, Scotsmen to and from London and Buenos Aires and Spaniards to and from Marseilles and Santos. We are a long way from a simple case of "America fever." [64]

Next, if we look more closely at the *origins* of migrants, we do not discover what both the gross statistics and the stereotypes of the older historiography might lead one to expect, that is to say, an undifferentiated, mass movement of "peasants" or indeed "artisans" thronging towards immigrant ports from vaguely conceived "countries of origin" like "Italy," "Germany," or even "Poland" or "Ireland." Even discounting the obvious fact that such terms were, for most of the period, inept labels for geographical expressions or political provinces, the picture is false. Seen through a magnifying glass, this undifferentiated mass surface breaks down into a honeycomb of innumerable particular cells, districts, villages, towns, each with an individual reaction or lack of it to the pull of migration. This is not simply a question of Scottish Highlanders emigrating in a body to Upper Canada, Rhinelanders to Wisconsin, Swedes to Montana, northern Italians to France and Argentina, southern Italians to the

---

[61] Dudley Kirk, *Europe's Population in the Inter-War Years*, pp. 100, 105.
[62] *Ibid.*, pp. 97–104.
[63] Foerster, *op. cit.*, p. 19.
[64] Thomas and Znaniecki, *op. cit.*, Vol. I, p. 168; Foerster, *op. cit.*, p. 21.

United States, though these elementary distinctions are important. We only come to the secret sources of the movement if we work to a finer tolerance. We must talk, not of Wales, but of Portmadoc or Swansea, not of North or South Italy, but of Venetia Giulia, Friuli, Basilicata and Calabria, not of Greece, or even the Peloponnese, but of Tripolis, Sparta and Megalopolis, not of Lancashire but of Darwin or Blackburn, not of Norway but of Kristian and North Bergenhus. There were villages in the Peloponnese, Basilicata and Friuli where boys grew up expecting to emigrate:[65] there were sections of New York where immigrants from individual Italian districts occupied separate streets, with often mutual hostility.[66] Only when we examine such districts and townships, and trace the fortunes of their native sons, do we begin to understand the true anatomy of migration. As Hansen well recognized, "at any given moment the phenomenon of emigration is characterized, not by the nation as a whole, but by a comparatively restricted part of it, and when again it makes its appearance, though the participants are still listed as Germans or Italians, their origin was distinct." [67]

Intimately connected with particular districts are particular occupations, an acquaintance with which will dispose once and for all of the stereotype of an undifferentiated "peasant" mass. One of the most striking features of successive analyses of the foreign-born in the United States since 1911 is the extent to which different ethnic groups have adhered to particular trades.[68] Although this was partly the consequence of job opportunities, it was often related to work conditions in the home country. Thus unskilled southern Italians worked on construction and heavy industry in the United States; but they also congregated in certain specific, self-employed occupations. The Italians, and after them the Greeks, who followed a similar pattern, established their first "toe-hold," so to speak, in American cities as bootblacks. A few dollars earned in this way on the street permitted an outlay on a fruit or ice-cream barrow and ultimately an opening by way of ice-cream parlours and florists into the restaurant and hotel trade.[69] Four-fifths of the emigrants from Laurenzana, in Basilicata, became bootblacks in America.[70]

Such a concentration was partly due to a follow-the-leader instinct which was exploited by the Italian or Greek *padroni* who recruited youths from their home districts under informal and often sweated-labour contracts. However, the *padroni* in the United States were able to do this because the system was already well established, both in southern Italy and

[65] Fairchild, *op. cit.*, p. 87; Foerster, *op. cit.*, pp. 123–4, 145.
[66] *Ibid.*, p. 393.
[67] Hansen, *The Immigrant in American History*, pp. 191–2.
[68] See E. P. Hutchinson, *Immigrants and Their Children 1850–1950* (New York, 1956), passim.
[69] *Ibid.*, pp. 338–339, Appendix, Table A, 2a; Fairchild, *op. cit.*, pp. 127, 165 and Appendix, Table 15, p. 161; Foerster, *op. cit.*, p. 147.
[70] Foerster, *op. cit.*, p. 417.

in Greece. It was the practice in the poverty-stricken pastoral district of the Peloponnese to send a boy of ten or twelve away to the cities of Greece or Turkey to earn money for his parents, often in brutal conditions, as a bootblack or in a coffee-house or grocery store; and it was from here that the *padroni* often recruited them for the United States.[71]

This was low-grade work which anyone from the fields could do. However, "peasant" emigrants were not limited to such occupations. The Italian was the largest of such migrations; yet of those who settled in Argentina during the wheat boom of 1876 to 1897, at least a third were not farmers but craftsmen, including those masons, carpenters, quarrymen, gardeners, brick workers and plasterers who gave South American cities their Italian manner, and the Genoese shipmasters, navigators and sailors who ran the coastal shipping of the River Plate.[72] And there was a similar concentration of craftsmen in the United States.[73] Here too the pattern was set before migrants crossed the Atlantic in any numbers. An important element in the Italian migration to Switzerland, France and later to Germany were skilled tradesmen especially from Friuli, the greatest single source of Italian emigrants, where the élite of the population came increasingly to think in terms of temporary migration. Scores of thousands of workmen kept a winter habitat in Venetia who could not have found permanent work there and who had never expected to be other than emigrants.[74] Boys in Friuli were deliberately trained as stonecutters or carpenters to take advantage of the demand for these skills in France, just as boys in Caserta or Basilicata were recruited by direct arrangement with their fathers for the Lyons glass industry.[75] The connection between migration and a trade was often close, and it was, moreover, already well established in Europe before the attraction of America began to be felt.

In discussing the skilled migrant we have so far been concerned with the village craftsman who was easily absorbed into the comparatively primitive economies of an agricultural frontier. The subject acquires a heightened significance when one examines the role of the migrant technician in the industrialization of countries of immigration. The dissemination of technology through the migration of technicians is an aspect of migration history which deserves a great deal of further study: and it is here that the student of British emigration has a special contribution to make. British industrial leadership, capital, commerce and trade routes combined to encourage an unprecedented emigration of British technicians who, in country after country, provided the essential *cadre* of skills for industrialization. In the case of new countries, such as the United States in the 19th and Canada or Australia in the 20th century, the role of the British technician was so important that industrialization itself may

[71] Fairchild, *op. cit.*, pp. 174–5.
[72] Foerster, *op. cit.*, p. 255.
[73] Hutchinson, *loc. cit.*
[74] Foerster, *op. cit.*, pp. 123–4.
[75] *Ibid.*, p. 145.

be conceived as an aspect of migration history. However, even in old-established economies that role was considerable; and although there is a temptation to concentrate on the spectacular case of the United States, here, as in other aspects of migration history, we are dealing with a phenomenon which is best treated internationally. Men used to practising a specialized trade took advantage of demand and cheaper transport to pursue it all over the world. Cornish miners hired themselves out wherever there was a need for their skill and provided the first, aristocratic generation of mine captains in the lead, tin and copper mines not only of Illinois and Michigan, but of Bolivia, the Rand and Broken Hill, sometimes moving from continent to continent in the single-minded pursuit of their esoteric craft.[76] Textile operatives from the Pennines built and worked the looms of France and Belgium at the time when Slater, the Scholfields and their successors were building and working the mills of New England; Welsh and English foundrymen and furnacemen performed a similar office for the iron trade not only in Pennsylvania but in France and Russia; [77] Staffordshire potters also worked in France and Russia as well as mastering the problems of New World clays; [78] English and Scots engineers built and operated railways in almost every quarter of the globe *except* the United States, from Belgium to New Zealand, India to Argentina; and so on, throughout most of the range of 19th-century industrial technique; and if we knew more about them, it is possible that the resulting British communities in Fall River, Massachusetts, or East Liverpool, Ohio, would be found to bear more relation to the British communities in, say, Buenos Aires, Charenton and Montreal, than to other hyphenated American communities in the United States.[79]

The study of the migration of technicians in fact often provides a clue to identifiable communities (and through communities to individuals) which is often lacking in the study of the inchoate ethnic mass, but which is essential if we are to learn anything worth while about motives, causes, adjustment, indeed anything at all about the true nature of the migrant *experience*. Skill acts, as it were, as a radioactive tracer in the blood stream of migration and, as I have argued elsewhere, we would do well to develop

[76] Berthoff, *op. cit.*, Chapter 4; John Rowe, "Cornish Emigrants and America," *Bulletin of the British Association for American Studies*, No. 8, 1950.

[77] W. O. Henderson, *Britain and Industrial Europe, 1750–1870* (Liverpool, 1954), Chapters 2 and 3; Berthoff, *op. cit.*, Chapter 5.

[78] Thistlethwaite, *loc. cit.*

[79] Unfortunately, owing to a surprising absence of British filio-pietists, very little is known about the British communities abroad, even in the United States, where, contrary to the normal assumption, "hyphenated" American communities were as characteristic of the British as of other ethnic groups; an exceptional study is L. G. Reynolds, *The British Immigrant: His Economic and Social Adjustment in Canada* (Toronto, 1935).

the study of it as an instrumental technique.[80] Enough is known, for example, about British technicians in the United States, for the student with the right kind of eye to suggest answers to most of the big questions.

The migration of British technicians has a distinctive character. One can discern successive phases: first the migration of the carriers, of creative innovators, in textiles, iron and steel, pottery and mining, who introduced the new technology; then, on their heels the scores and hundreds of skilled operatives who were to provide the mule spinners, machine makers, foundrymen and miners, some only seasonal migrants, some settling into communities of British folk ways and craft loyalties and organizing labour unions; then there was the third phase when improved machinery and American production methods reduced the scope for skilled labour and increased the number of jobs which could be handled by cheaper, unskilled and more docile workers recruited from more recent immigrant stocks from Ireland, French Canada and eastern Europe. As this happened the British element moved upwards into supervisory or managerial positions, and apart for an occasional specialist, the migration of technicians came to an end. The many illuminated facets of this sequence would take us far beyond the limits of this paper.[81] Suffice it to state that it had characteristics which were repeated in industry after industry from the Lancashire cotton spinners of 1800 to the Welsh tinplaters of the 1890's; and although one would like to be able to compare such migration to the United States with that to, say, Canada or Australia, both of which are still in progress, the evidence at hand already provides important clues about the wider implications of transatlantic migration.

The migration of tradesmen calls attention to the economic aspects of the subject. Although it is a truism that 19th-century emigration was predominantly economic in motivation, in the older conceptual framework the actual economic determinants were very vaguely formulated. One was presented with a laundry list of "push" and "pull" factors which were then left in the background owing to a preoccupation with the cultural and political considerations involved in assimilation. A knowledge of artisan migration is a good way to achieve a greater definition. In the first place, it was determined by trade routes and, as far as North America was concerned, trade routes from the British Isles. The fact that emigrants were essentially valuable bulk cargo for unused shipping space in raw cotton or timber ships on the return voyage is a basic fact which is only beginning to receive the attention it deserves.[82] The fortunes of shipping

[80] Thistlethwaite, *loc. cit.*; see also O. Handlin, "International Migration and the Acquisition of New Skills," in B. F. Hoselitz (ed.), *The Progress of Underdeveloped Areas* (Chicago, 1952).

[81] Thistlethwaite, *The Anglo-American Connection in the Early 19th Century* (Philadelphia, 1959), pp. 29–33.

[82] See Maldwyn Jones, *The Role of the United Kingdom in the Transatlantic Emigrant Trade 1815–1875* (unpublished dissertation, Oxford, 1956).

companies from Cunard and Austro-American to the modern Greek lines
have been based upon emigrants; the trade remained long in British hands
and to some extent continued to pass through British ports long after the
recruiting grounds had moved to central and eastern Europe. The trade in
emigrants was a development of that largely Anglo-American trade which
brought America and north-west Europe together into a single Atlantic
economy.

The concept of an Atlantic economy, like that of an Atlantic history
itself, is of comparatively recent origin; [83] but is of first importance in understanding Western history in the 19th century. The term is justified
because it describes, not merely a condition of international trade, but one
in which there was such freedom of movement for the factors of production, that we can hardly distinguish the two principal countries concerned,
Britain and the United States, as separate, closed economies. The Atlantic
economy was concerned with exploiting the grasslands of North America
by means of European capital and labour in the interests of cheaper cotton and wheat for Europe and overseas markets for European manufactures. The migration of the twin factors of capital investment and labour
was the key to it and emigrants were essential to its operation. [84] The precise way in which this mechanism worked is still a matter for research and
controversy. As far as emigration is concerned, the first attempt to refine
the old crude assumptions about the push mechanism of over-population
and exploitation in Europe and the pull mechanism of American opportunity was made by American economists — and here again one must
notice the initiative of Americans and of non-historians — as a by-
product of research into the operations of the business cycle some thirty
years ago. Jerome found a direct correlation between fluctuations in immigration into the United States and the short-term American business cycle,
and, later, Kuznets and Rubin established three long swings in net immigration between 1870 and 1945 which tended to follow swings in income
per head. [85]

These statistical estimates are, however, of only limited usefulness to
historians of migration; the emphasis on "pull" factors leaves much out of
account and is open to the suspicion of American-centredness. However,
a more ambitious, but in the long run, more satisfactory attempt at a
theory relating the flow of migration to other economic activity is that

---

[83] See Brinley Thomas, *Migration and Economic Growth: A Study of Great
Britain and the Atlantic Economy* (Cambridge, 1954); H. Hale Bellott, "Atlantic
History," *History*, Vol. XXXI (March, 1946).

[84] For a sketch of the system as it affected emigration see Thistlethwaite, *op.
cit.*, Chapter I.

[85] H. Jerome, *Migration and Business Cycles* (New York, 1926); S. Kuznets
and E. Rubin, *Immigration and the Foreign Born* (Occasional Paper 46, National
Bureau of Economic Research, 1954).

recently put forward by Brinley Thomas.[86] In his study of Great Britain and the Atlantic economy Thomas set out to show that the rhythms of economic growth in the United States and the United Kingdom were closely related to the course of migration between the two countries. Briefly he found that there was an inverse relation between home investment and the level of income in Britain, on the one hand, and emigration and capital exports, on the other; a positive relationship between immigration, investment and income in the United States and, correspondingly, disharmony between the rates of economic growth on the eastern and the western sides of the Atlantic. Despite the controversial nature of some of Thomas's statistical data, his work represents a major advance for the student of emigration. In the first place he found no simple correlation between upswings in American business and in immigration: before about 1870 the upswing in business activity tended to come after an upswing in immigration, the inference being that, at least for this period, migration was impelled more by "push" factors in Europe than "pull" factors in the United States; but more important, in concentrating upon the Atlantic economy he develops a two-country theory which is more complex but more helpful to the historian than the single-country theories of American-centredness which had preceded it. He demonstrates that the mechanism is at least a two-way process and can only be understood by taking into account conditions in both country of origin and country of destination, as well as the whole complex of interacting factors, of which labour was only one, contributing to the economic development of the North Atlantic basin.[87]

The Thomas approach opens possibilities of relating emigration to the dynamics of economic growth on a more universal scale: for though he produces valuable corroborative evidence for Sweden and the British Dominions, the United Kingdom and the United States remain the focus of his interest. One can conceive a time when a development of his technique will enable us to understand much that is obscure about the mechanisms of migration, not merely in the North Atlantic basin but in other theatres, as well as the complex of connections among them.

Thomas also sharpens our focus about problems of phasing. The Atlantic economy was only a phase of economic development and carried within itself the seeds of its dissolution. The ease of movement which brought farmers to grow wheat on the prairies brought artisans to exploit minerals and markets and establish modern industry on the western shores of the Atlantic. As it developed from colonial to metropolitan status, the American economy ceased to be dependent upon European capital, labour or skills. The difficult adjustments facing the Atlantic basin as a result

[86] Brinley Thomas, *op. cit.*, passim.
[87] See also Dorothy Thomas, in Hauser, *op. cit.*, p. 159.

of the emergence of the United States as a great Power are a logical consequence of the transcendence of the old Atlantic economy; and there is no doubt that the difficulty of those adjustments has been enhanced, as Thomas points out, by the inadequacy of United States policies between the two Wars, compared with the British attitude towards the emigration of capital and labour in the great liberal era of the 19th century. As far as the labour side of the question is concerned, it may be that the drastic restrictionist policies of the United States between 1917 and 1924, together with those of South America, had important effects on the course of events in the late 1920's and 1930's. The contribution of restriction to the "stagnation" of the American economy during the depression of the 1930's, a widely held conviction among economists at the time, needs further investigation; as well as its alleged effects on over-crowding in Europe such as the deflection of Italian emigration to Mussolini's North African empire. The investigation of the effects of large-scale emigration upon European countries is a difficult historical problem, though even here an American scholar like Dr. Schrier has done pioneer work for Ireland on the basis of the materials of the Irish Folklore Commission; [88] but it might be illuminated by studies of the effects of restriction and this is one of the many problems hitherto neglected by European students.

However, it seems clear that whatever the short-term problems of restriction, the long cycle of mass emigration from Europe was coming to an end between the Wars.[89] That cycle was determined by the settlement of the great unoccupied grasslands outside Europe, part of a greater cycle which colonized, not merely Australia, Argentina and North America, but the Indus Valley, Siberia, Inner Mongolia and Manchukuo.[90] By 1930 the limits of effective settlement were approaching even in Australia where so much of the interior, by known agricultural standards, remains desert. Already by the turn of the 20th century the centrifugal tendencies of European migration were counter-balanced by centripetal tendencies.

The greatest migrations were not to the grasslands, but to the concentrations of coal and iron where industries were being established. Between 1870 and 1914 there was a net migration of even American natives from the farms to the mines, factories and cities of Appalachia and the Rockies; and more European immigrants found a living in American industry than on prairie homesteads. The peak of the great cycle, the so-called "new" immigration, may profitably be thought of as a rural-urban migration which happened to be trans-oceanic rather than local in character; and while some Italians, Poles and Ukrainians were moving to Pittsburgh or

[88] Arnold Schrier, *Ireland and the American Emigration* (Minneapolis, 1958), passim.

[89] W. D. Forsyth, *The Myth of the Open Spaces* (Melbourne, 1942), passim.

[90] I. Bowman, *The Limits of Land Settlement* (New York, 1937), passim.; Forsyth, *op. cit.*, p. 13.

Chicago, others were swelling the immigrant populations of France and Germany in Le Creuzot, the Ruhr and Silesia. By 1927 European migrants to European destinations outnumbered those to trans-oceanic destinations; [91] and France had become the most important country of immigration in the world. In the 1930's for the first time in modern history Europe gained population through net in-migration.[92]

Moreover, there are signs that this trans-oceanic migration was slackening even before American restriction. For example, the intensity of emigration — or the international mobility of labour — that is to say, migrants per thousand of population, had declined well before 1914 both in countries of emigration and in the United States; [93] and the shutting down on the United States intake did not lead to any corresponding diversion to other countries.[94]

In fact at the outbreak of the Second World War it already looked as if the great cycle had come to an end and students of emigration would have to deal with a purely historical problem with little contemporary relevance. "The peopling of other continents from Europe is probably a passing phenomenon." [95] Postwar experience has not seriously modified this view. Europe still has its black spots for rural over-population, notably southern Italy and Greece and no doubt other Balkan countries; and there has been an interesting case of emigration fever in the Netherlands; [96] but in general there is no great pressure to emigrate in Europe; and while rates of economic growth in some of the traditional receiving countries, especially Australia and Canada, have been accompanied by a demand for immigrants, and although Australia was for a time absorbing them at a record rate, the movement has settled down to more modest and selective proportions. An international conference of economists were in fairly general agreement in 1955 that a renewal of large-scale emigration was neither likely nor relevant to the problems of the under-developed countries of the mid-20th century which, unlike the virgin grasslands of the 19th, are already over-populated.[97]

In short, a consideration of the phasing of overseas migration both places it within a limited time-scale and reduces its significance in relation to intra-European migration. These proportions are foreshortened still

[91] Forsyth, op. cit., pp. 14–16.

[92] Kirk, Europe's Population, pp. 83–88.

[93] Willcox, International Migrations, Vol. II, pp. 244, 290, 335; Hennig Ravnholt, "A Quantitative Concept of the International Mobility of Population and its Application to certain European Countries in the period 1851–1935," "Proceedings, International Population Congress (Paris, 1937); Forsyth, op. cit., pp. 7, 8.

[94] Kirk, Europe's Population, p. 86.

[95] Kirk, "Demographic Trends" in Annals, loc. cit., p. 96; see Forsyth, op. cit., passim.

[96] See pp. 78–79.

[97] Brinley Thomas, ed., Economics of International Migration (London, 1958), passim.

further if one examines the orders of magnitude of European population as a whole. At the same time as Europe was providing up to sixty million emigrants for overseas countries, the Continent was increasing its own numbers so greatly that its proportion of world population rose from 20.7 per cent in 1802 to 25.2 per cent: [98] and it is as well to remember that in no decade has emigration drawn off more than 40 per cent of Europe's natural increase.[99] In other words, the centripetal tendencies which kept people at home were at least as strong as the centrifugal tendencies which sent them abroad. If we accept this fact and look at "the great dispersion," not as the dominant demographic factor of the 19th century, but as a subordinate feature of demographic trends within Europe, a very different and more interesting picture begins to emerge. Instead of Europeans taking flight to the Americas and Australasia we see Europeans themselves colonizing. By using their labour, capital and know-how to exploit the foodstuffs and raw materials of virgin lands, Europeans made it possible not only to feed an ever-growing population at home, but to industrialize their continent; as population emigrated so did it multiply and concentrate at home in the regions of coal and iron. Moreover once the outward movement of population had gone far enough to ensure adequate supplies of essential raw materials, it began to slacken and the mobile element in the population migrated, not overseas, but into the urban-industrial complex of western Europe itself. In the end this tendency became the dominant one and, as Forsyth put it, the "areas of concentration" replaced the "great open spaces" as magnets of migration.[100] The great overseas migration, therefore, is in a very broad sense to be treated as a major, but subordinate, aspect of European population growth and European industrialization. We are, again, a long way from the America fever.

In other words, this new angle of vision for which I am arguing shifts the focus from frontier to metropolis, from "pull" to "push" factors, and especially to those demographic influences which Brinley Thomas suggests may have been the dynamic element in Atlantic growth.[101] The inner secrets of emigration are to be sought in the working of those two "revolutions" which are so inter-connected, the demographic and the industrial.[102]

There is no space to enter into the notorious complexities of the demographic revolution. It looks, however, as if a reduction in death rates without a compensating reduction in birth rates led to a rise in the rate of natural increase, beginning in north-west Europe and moving east and south, as communities became affected by medical and dietary advances. This increase, though compensated for by new and nutritious foods, espe-

[98] Carr-Saunders, *op. cit.*, p. 42.

[99] Dudley Kirk, "Survey of Recent Overseas Migration," Vol. II, *Proceedings, World Population Conference*, 1954, p. 97.

[100] Forsyth, *op. cit.*, pp. 16–17; J. Isaac, "International Migration and European Trends," *International Labour Review*, LXVI, 1957, pp. 186–191.

[101] See pp. 70–71 above.

[102] Kirk, "Demographic Trends," *loc. cit.*, p. 48.

cially the potato, brought the rural population to the margin of subsistence.[103] The result was a latent propensity to emigrate which transformed
itself sometimes, though by no means invariably, into actual emigration,
not only at times of catastrophe caused by the failure of the potato crop,
but as transport and communication to the ports and overseas made this
possible. In country after country, beginning with Ireland and ending with
Italy and Greece, there is a direct correlation between rates of emigration
and rates of natural increase twenty years previously, which represents the
migration of the surplus proportion of a larger age group at the point
when it was ready to enter the labour market. In the case of Norway, for
example, two major upward swings in emigration, in the late 1830's and
the late 1860's, occurred when there was a disproportionately large age
group between 20 and 30.[104] This is confirmed by the overwhelmingly
youthful character of emigrants; between 86 and 95 per cent of immigrants into the United States during the period for which figures are available were under forty years; and in the early 20th century two-thirds of
British emigrants were under thirty-one.[105] Manifestations of the Malthusian devil appeared in country after country across Europe irrespective
of rural social structure, laws of inheritance, land tenure, the condition of
agriculture or the policies of landlords.[106]

However, rural overcrowding did not in itself result in mass emigration
as the condition of Ireland in the 1830's or Greece in the 1890's showed.
There had to be three further conditions which Hansen defines as *freedom*, *desire* and *means* to move; [107] and it is in the operation of these
conditions that the ultimate secrets of migration are to be found.

The *means* to move are easiest to define; but the roads and railways,
canals and steamships, posts and telegraphs, banks and travel agencies, by
means of which the emigrant travelled, were themselves the product of
forces which were breaking up the self-contained existence of rural Europe, and providing the peasant with both the *freedom* to move, negative
as in the abolition of serfdom, positive as in opportunities for employment,
and the *desire* to move resulting from widening horizons, and contracting
opportunities at home. Emigration was, in fact, intimately connected with
that quickening of communications, markets, commerce and capital which,
in the 1840's and 1850's in Scandinavia, the 1880's and 1890's in Italy,
was the first phase of the establishment of a modern economy.[108] This

[103] This increase came at a time when, in some instances, labour-saving techniques were cutting the demand for farm labourers.
[104] Ravnholt, *loc. cit.*; United Nations, *Population Trends*, pp. 117–118;
Blegen, *op.* cit., Vol. I, pp. 165–166.
[105] Forsyth, *op. cit.*, p. 45; the preponderance of males is also marked.
[106] Kirk, *Europe's Population*, pp. 148–149.
[107] Hansen, *The Immigrant in American History*, p. 192.
[108] For Norway see Blegen, *op. cit.*, Vol. I, p. 354; for Sweden, Dorothy
Thomas, *Social and Economic Aspects of Swedish Migration 1750 to 1930* (New
York, 1941), passim.

erosion of the customary community by commercial forces was an essential pre-condition to migration; it caused a revolutionary increase in social mobility which both job and travel opportunities transformed into a propensity to migrate. Migration was, in fact, an aspect of social mobility.

This propensity had differing effects in different periods and countrysides. It might, as in the case of the Irish in 1846, result in a catastrophic, direct, oceanic emigration; or, with the Poles in Germany, it might be largely European in its ramifications or even, as with the London Welsh, internal and local. The point is that overseas migration was only one, though the most important, result of a revolutionary increase in social mobility which had the effect of creating large numbers prepared to travel in search of jobs. In the first instance it was only where there were no suitable jobs close at hand that the young man was impelled to look overseas and take what appeared to be the once-for-all step of alienation and become an emigrant. Later, when the habit became established by emigrant letters and remittances, it might persist long after there were jobs at home; but despite such lags, all the evidence goes to show that Europeans in general emigrated in large numbers while there were no opportunities in the home country and ceased to do so when opportunities once again existed. For some people those opportunities were never to come again, as in the case of those Jewish traders and clothing workers who lost their function in Tzarist Russia and had to seek an outlet in New York,[109] or the Scottish handloom weavers, or the southern Italians and Greeks, whose emigration was shut off at its height by American restriction and who were to contribute to the rural under-employment or concealed unemployment of the present times. But in the principal countries of western and central Europe those opportunities did come, in the form of work in mines, factories and offices.

The connection of migration with industrialization and urbanization (the two cannot be separated) was as close as with the Malthusian devil. Now it is true that Lombard peasants farmed in Argentina and Swedish *statare* in Montana; and that a growing proportion of British emigrants to the United States in the 1880's and 1890's were skilled technicians moving from one industrial area to another. But, by and large, the great migrations after 1890 were from farm to factory, from village to city, whether this meant from Iowa to Chicago, Silesia to Pittsburgh or Piedmont to Buenos Aires.[110] To the country people of the Norwegian fjords a fellow countryman on his way to embark was already an "American"; [111] and even after the Second World War "Americanization" was a synonym for

[109] Willcox, Vol. II, *op. cit.*, pp. 515–517.

[110] Even the later urban emigrants from Norway were very largely rural migrants who had sojourned a while in the towns. Ingrid Gaustad Semmingsen, *Studies and Records* (Norwegian-American Historical Association), Northfield, Minn., II, pp. 78–80.

[111] Blegen, *op. cit.*, Vol. 2, p. 3.

"urbanization" in an immigrant Norwegian community which was attempting to preserve its Lutheran integrity in rural Wisconsin.[112]

However, the dynamic forces which created the propensity to emigrate in time fostered those industries which, by providing employment, made emigration no longer imperative. At this point oceanic migration began to diminish. Industrial Britain was already absorbing most of the potential yeoman emigrants of England by 1850 and many potential Irish emigrants to America from 1900. Norwegian timber and Swedish mining began in the 1870's to make inroads into Scandinavian emigration, the course of which was thenceforward determined by the pulls of American employment and the uneven progress of Scandinavian industrialization, until it petered out on the eve of the First World War.[113] The most spectacular case is that of Germany, where the emigration peak had already been passed for the west and south-west by the 1850's and for the country as a whole by the mid-1880's with the onset of heavy industrialization in that decade.[114] Nor was employment the only aspect of industrialization-urbanization to lessen the attractiveness of emigration. Cheap meats and grains from overseas increased real wages; with the growing number of white-collar occupations, urban life became more attractive; the emergence of the concept of State welfare, with public education, unemployment and old-age insurance offset the old fear of military service; a new sense of nationalism, which was the ultimate and potent compensation for the peasant's loss of identity in his village, led to State action against emigration; and finally, the reduction in the birth-rate, the absence of which alongside low death-rates had started the demographic revolution, reduced that pressure on population which had been the latent condition of emigration and eventually was to depress population rates below the level of replacement.[115] Thus the great oceanic migrations of the 19th and early 20th centuries occurred in a transitional phase of European development between the break-down of the old rural societies and the onset of modern industrialism.[116]

Economically, that phase was concerned with the widening of markets, commerce and finance; but I am not trying to suggest that the resulting social mobility, of which emigration was only one aspect, was a simple effect of economic causes. Only in the impossible world of economic

[112] Peter Munch, "Social Adjustment among Wisconsin Norwegians," *American Sociological Review*, 1949.

[113] Dorothy Thomas, *Swedish Migration*, pp. 169, 304–305; A. J. Youngson, "The Acceleration of Economic Progress in Sweden, 1850–1880," in *Possibilities of Economic Progress* (Cambridge, 1959), pp. 176–177; Blegen, *op. cit.*, Vol. II, p. 456.

[114] Kirk, *Annals*, pp. 53–54; Wilcox, Vol. II, p. 244.

[115] Kirk, *op. cit.*, pp. 83–88.

[116] See Isaac, "International Migration and European Trends," *loc. cit.*, pp. 186–191; Kirk, *Europe's Population*, pp. 148–149; *ibid.*, "Demographic Trends," *loc. cit.*, pp. 53–54.

abstractions could Hansen's *desire* to move be conceived of as mere economic opportunity; commercialization, like an enhanced social mobility, was a result as well as a cause of the dissolution of the customary rural community; and the search for the inner secrets of emigration, as of population growth, leads to a consideration of the many unknowns which hedge round this breakdown.[117] It is beyond the scope of this paper to do more than indicate the rough dimensions of this, the penultimate problem in the field of emigration.

The gulf which may exist between *freedom* and *means*, on the one hand, and *desire*, on the other, is strikingly illustrated by the Netherlands. Even in 1870 the rate of increase of the Dutch population was greater than that of any other country in north-west Europe and unlike those other countries showed hardly any decline down to the present. Yet there was very little emigration until the end of the Second World War. The increase was absorbed at home into a society which was resistant to change. As one Netherlands authority puts it: "The 19th Century ended only in 1930 in the Netherlands." [118] The efforts of the Netherlands Government since 1945 to encourage systematic emigration to Canada in order to syphon off an expected surplus population have met with least response precisely in those parts of the south-east where the cumulative effects of population growth had produced heavy and chronic rural under-employment; this is a district of small family farms, orthodox and conservative in religion and politics, with strong ties binding the individual to his family and to the local community which he only reluctantly leaves. "Evidently, when judging the need for emigration, the demographers and economists apply standards whose validity the agrarian population has not yet recognised." [119]

This is an extreme example, chosen because of its full modern documentation, of almost total resistance on the part of a community to emigration, even where the economic inducements are apparently overwhelming. It is not suggested that this is typical, but the degrees of cohesion, of homogeneity and the comparative rigidities in the structure in the local community which it illustrates are important to understanding the great 19th-century migrations. Where there was no emigration, it looks as if there was probably a highly stable social situation, whatever its comparative lack of prosperity. Where there was emigration, there was likely to be a degree of social instability which prompted elements in the population

---

[117] Thomas and Znaniecki, *op. cit.*, Vol. I, pp. 204–205, Vol. II, p. 1499; P. Hauser, "Present Status and Prospects of Research in Population," *American Sociological Review*, XIII (August, 1948), p. 380.

[118] E. E. Hofstee, in Brinley Thomas, ed., *Economics of International Migration*, pp. 105–106.

[119] G. H. L. Zeegers, "Some Sociographic Aspects of Emigration from the Netherlands," in *Proceedings of the World Population Conference, 1954, Papers*, Vol. II, pp. 297–298.

to take steps to protect or better their status. Emigrants, more concerned with status than job opportunity, were driven to seek it abroad because of despair at preserving or improving it at home. We might expect to find causes of emigration, therefore, in a social situation which was unstable, but contained rigidities threatening inherited status or impending advancement.

With present knowledge it is impossible to substantiate so general a hypothesis. Certainly the study of social history has not reached a point in my country where much that is useful may be said in its favour. However, the evidence for Scandinavia seems more promising, because it is less complex, because of the excellence of demographic statistics, especially for Sweden, and their use by authorities like Professors Dorothy Thomas and Arne Skaug and because of the outstanding work of historians like Professor Blegen and Professor Semmingsen.[120]

To begin with, emigrants were overwhelmingly youthful; a very high proportion were young men of the landless and labouring classes whom one would expect to form the surplus population; and in addition they included an important contribution from the independent land-owning class in the persons of younger sons denied an inheritance by the process of overpopulation and subdivision. But the situation was characterized by a spirit of revolt which went far beyond the natural consequences of rural under-employment and restless youth. "A transformation of values had taken place among the country youth," wrote Mrs. Semmingsen, of the Norwegians: "Many of them refused to remain in the home community any longer." [121] "Forth will I! Forth," sang Björnson, "I will be crushed and consumed if I stay." [122]

Here at last, the cautiously statistical approach of this paper enters upon that more familiar historical country concerned with individual values and motives. This spirit of revolt was more than the frustration of lack-land youth; it infected others who were beginning to chafe at a situation in which a small privileged class kept a tight hold on government, the church and the professions and resisted or neglected demands and opportunities for a broader social order. In Mrs. Semmingsen's words, there was a "more conscious self-assertion," instead of a "dull hopeless spirit." [123]

It was no accident of history that the "Sloopers" whose voyage in the *Restauration* in 1825 heralded the large-scale Norwegian emigration to America, were Dissenters seeking refuge from an intolerant State Church; nor that they should have been members of the Society of Friends, con-

120 D. S. Thomas, *Social and Economic Aspects of Swedish Migration 1750–1930* (New York, 1941); *Betänkande*, passim; Arne Skaug, *Migration from Norway*; Blegen, *op. cit.*, Ingrid Gaustad Semmingsen, *Norwegian Emigration to America during the Nineteenth Century*, passim.
121 Semmingsen, *Studies and Records*, 2, p. 76.
122 Quoted in Blegen, *op. cit.*, Vol. 2, p. 468.
123 Semmingsen, *Studies and Records*, 2, p. 76.

verted by Quaker missionaries from England. For the emigrant stream to
the United States from Norway and Sweden, as from England, contained
a marked Dissenting element disproportionately great both in numbers
and in leadership. The phenomenon deserves comparative study.[124]

Moreover, it was not simply a matter of Janssonists or Haugeans fleeing
their respective Conventicle Acts or English Nonconformist farmers fleeing religious tithes, still less of Mormons from all three countries seeking
the promised land. Dissenters of whatever persuasion from Evangelical
"enthusiasts" to Unitarians developed towards institutional orthodoxy an
attitude of criticism and withdrawal which led them to resist not merely
the church Establishment but what in England has been recently called
the governing "establishment" of politics and the professions. This made
them natural leaders for emigrants, who, in Blegen's words, were "always
non-conformist in some sense." [125] Among emigrants, in fact, the Dissenter
was the archetypal personality. The affinity of Dissent with emigration
was especially marked in relation to the United States, where republican
institutions and the separation of church from state exerted a positive influence not only on emigrants but on European domestic politics.[126] For,
where it did not culminate in emigration, this dissenting spirit found expression in radical politics, as in the case of the Haugeans who "sharpened
the issue of the *bønder* with officialdom" and "blazed the trail of popular
agitation" in Norway.[127] If universal suffrage had been granted in Sweden
in 1880, many subsequent emigrants might not have left.[128] Radicals were
ultimately to reform those institutions and practices from which emigration was a reaction and even to throw their weight in favour of emigrant
restriction. The relation of the labour movement to emigration in its various phases, in Scandinavia as in Britain, was an aspect of these changing
tensions.

With Dissent in this broad sense we are dealing with a phenomenon
which, ubiquitous in its 19th-century form, almost transcends social history. The ultimate problem of emigration is one of individual psychology.
Not all oppressed *bønder*, landless sons, workless labourers or Evangelical
clergy chose the emigrant course. The choice, or the line of least resistance, for many was to stay at home, to adjust, to conform, even though

[124] See Florence E. Janson, *The Background to Swedish Immigration*, 1840–
1930 (Chicago, 1931), pp. 167–196; Franklin D. Scott, "The Causes and Consequences of Emigration in Sweden," *The Chronicle of the American-Swedish
Historical Foundation* (Spring, 1955); Blegen, *op. cit.*, Vol. I, pp. 27–36, 159–
160; Thistlethwaite, *op. cit.*, Chapters 1 and 3.
[125] Blegen, *op. cit.*, Vol. I, p. 56.
[126] H. Koht, *The American Spirit in Europe* (Philadelphia, 1949), passim;
Thistlethwaite, *op. cit.*, Chapter 2; G. D. Lillibridge, *Beacon of Freedom: the
Impact of American Democracy upon Britain 1830–70* (Philadelphia, 1954),
passim.
[127] Blegen, *op. cit.*, Vol. I, pp. 162–163.
[128] *Betänkande*, p. 836.

this might mean bearing the strains of radical politics. The contrast in temperament between he for whom the moral choice is to stay put and he for whom it is "to get out from under" or, as the Americans say "to go someplace else," is central to the study of emigration, just as it is to an understanding of the perennial tensions between American and European cultures. With the emigrant we are studying the effects on the human being of choosing the one rather than the other of these two alternatives. Emigration is undoubtedly the more momentous. One does not have to be familiar with the harrowing conditions of 19th-century emigration to be aware that it was a disturbing experience even where little was at stake; and where, as in the characteristic case, it meant uprooting from a traditional rural culture and transplanting thousands of ocean miles to a modern, urban, industrial community, it could be traumatic. The effects of such an experience upon the human psyche lie perhaps beyond the powers of the historian to assess and fully to understand. Yet Oscar Handlin has made a not unsuccessful attempt to do so and Florian Znaniecki, in his phenomenal study of the Polish peasant in Europe and America, based upon his work for the Emigrants Protective Society in Warsaw between 1911 and 1914, has provided historians with an enormous volume of pertinently chosen evidence bearing upon what this paper defined earlier as the "complete sequence of experiences whereby the individual moves from one social identity to another." [129] Znaniecki's work is sociological, not historical; but we need more scholars both prepared to assemble emigrant letters and other data on a comprehensive scale, and with the mental power to address themselves to this, the ultimate problem of emigration.[130] Only by such means will it be possible to achieve what this paper set out to discuss, namely, an understanding not merely of uprooting as profound as that which American scholarship has given us of acculturation, but of the complete experience of migration from one society to another such as Hansen set out to achieve for the North Atlantic. It will be an achievement of the highest order; no less than a study of liberty in a modern setting.

[129] Thomas and Znaniecki, *op. cit.*, Vol. I, passim; see pp. 58–59 above.

[130] That important bodies of emigrant letters may still be uncovered has been proved by the results of an advertising campaign in England, the results of which it is hoped will shortly be edited and published by Dr. Charlotte Erickson of the London School of Economics.

Origins of Immigration Restriction, 1882–1897: A Social Analysis

JOHN HIGHAM

From 1607 onward the flow of migration to America was steadily advanced both by considerations in the Old World and encouragement and inducements in the New. By the nineteenth century, the demands of industrialization had led to active labor recruitment. Railroads and steamship lines employed agents throughout Europe to advertise the glories and opportunities awaiting those who migrated to the United States. But in the last decades of the century, there developed a perceptible change in American attitudes toward immigration, a change that within a few decades led to a dramatic reversal of the traditional policy of unlimited immigration and to the imposition of nationality quotas. John Higham, a historian at the University of Michigan, explores the reasons for this attitude shift within the framework of contemporary social and economic change. He examines such obvious influences as the fear of a continuous supply of cheap workers glutting the labor market, xenophobia, and religious prejudice. But he finds that in many ways these considerations were often episodic or isolated in their impact. Higham contends instead that social unrest, generated by class-conscious immigrants steeped in European traditions, offers a more pervasive explanation for the sudden interest in restriction. He measures the fears of social instability and dislocation within the context of significant changes in American society and the economy. How did these changes affect the nation's capacity to absorb and re-direct discontent? In another essay below, Stanley Coben applies psychological and anthropological concepts of nativism to the Red Scare of 1919–1920. How would these ideas enrich or alter Higham's study?

At no period in American national history has immigration from Europe been so strongly encouraged and so fervently blessed as in the 1860's

Reprinted by permission of the publisher from the *Mississippi Valley Historical Review*, XXXIX (June 1952), pp. 77–88. Copyright by the Organization of American Historians.

and early 1870's. During these years the federal government, two thirds of the states, and innumerable business organizations raided Europe's manpower.[1] Exuberant patriots rejoiced at the trans-Atlantic influx,[2] and few indeed opposed it. Yet a very few years saw a very great change. A campaign to reduce immigration replaced the campaign to increase it; friendliness turned into fright. Beginning with the law of 1882, which established federal supervision of immigration and excluded certain groups unable to support themselves, the restriction movement blossomed into a formidable and even violent crusade in the late eighties and nineties. It reached its crest in the winter of 1896–1897, when only the stubbornness of Grover Cleveland prevented the enactment of a drastic test to stop the entry of illiterates. Thereafter the drive subsided abruptly, but it left a legacy of tensions, policies, and ideas which a later generation abundantly exploited.

To explain the formative stage in the restriction of European immigration, one might employ several methods. Most broadly, one might attempt a cultural approach, appraising the clash of native and immigrant folkways and illuminating the American experience by contrast with the traditions and behavior of other nations.[3] Most specifically, one might examine the tangled interlocking of particular events and ideas within the restriction movement. The second procedure could profitably direct attention to struggles for partisan political advantage, to the activities of important individuals, or to the appearance of new antiforeign concepts.[4] The present essay follows a course somewhere between these two general methods, less adventurous perhaps than the first, less precise than the second. The object here is to establish — in summary fashion — the connections between the nativist upsurge and certain large, concurrent changes in American society. This stressing of the functional context neither does

[1] Merle Curti and Kendall Birr, "The Immigrant and the American Image in Europe, 1860–1914," *Mississippi Valley Historical Review* (Cedar Rapids), XXXVII (September, 1950), 204–11; Maurice G. Baxter, "Encouragement of Immigration to the Middle West during the Era of the Civil War," *Indiana Magazine of History* (Bloomington), XLVI (March, 1950), 25–38. A thorough compilation of federal and state legislation is contained in Reports of the Immigration Commission, "Immigration Legislation," *Senate Documents*, No. 758, 61 Cong., 3 Sess. Since the regulation of Chinese immigration was regarded at the time as a wholly different issue, it does not enter into the present discussion.

[2] Kirk H. Porter (ed.), *National Party Platforms* (New York, 1924), 82–83; New York *Tribune Extra*, July 4, 1876, pp. 9, 38; William T. Harris, "On the Relation of Education to the Individual, to Society, and to the State," *Wisconsin Journal of Education* (Madison), IV (January, 1874), 1.

[3] Ralph Linton, "Nativistic Movements," *American Anthropologist* (Washington, New York, Lancaster, Menasha), XLV (April–June, 1943), 230–40; Elin Anderson, *We Americans: A Study of Cleavage in an American City* (Cambridge, 1937).

[4] Elmer C. Sandmeyer, *The Anti-Chinese Movement in California*, University of Illinois *Studies in the Social Sciences* (Urbana), XXIV (1939); Carl F. Wittke, *German-Americans and the World War* (*with Special Emphasis on Ohio's German-Language Press*) (Columbus, 1936).

justice to the weight of persistent traditions nor does it clarify the totality of immediate circumstance. But whatever may have been the cultural heritages behind immigration restriction, they were catalyzed by a new social situation. And whatever political maneuvers of intellectual ferment may have contributed, they worked within a framework of social change.

Of the general mutations in late nineteenth-century America, four had a special relevance to the rise of the restriction movement. The first of these to play a measurable part in the organized campaign was the development of a confused but many-pronged reform movement aimed at solving the problems of an urban, industrial society. A second transformation came with the so-called "new immigration," the flow of peasant and ghetto peoples from Italy, Austria-Hungary, the Balkans, and Russia, which began increasing rapidly in the early 1880's. Thirdly, the Roman Catholic Church experienced an unusual surge of strength and activity during the same years. Finally, the period from 1885 to 1897 was one of drastic social and economic dislocations — an epoch in which anger and misery raised a frightening challenge to the historic promise of a fluid society. Each of these factors entered into the making and shaping of the immigration restriction movement. In one aspect it was a reform effort, in another an expression of ethnic antipathy. In still another, it represented a response to anti-Catholic sentiment. And it was also a reaction to fears and frustrations generated by class conflict and economic collapse. None of these causes operated independently, but they had diverse and unequal impacts and deserve separate consideration.

The first general immigration law in 1882 demonstrated the early influence of humanitarian and reform impulses in launching the restriction movement. For many years relief agencies in eastern cities had been more or less constantly concerned at the strain which impoverished and disorganized immigrants imposed upon their own financial resources and upon the life of the community.[5] The charity groups had more philanthropic than reformist zeal, but many of them did hope for social improvement through public action. They began to lobby for federal supervision and regulation of immigration in 1876, after the Supreme Court forbade the states to collect an immigrant welfare fund from shipowners. Six years later the charity officials won their fight, although the statute was less restrictive than they had hoped it might be.[6]

[5] L. L. Bernard and Jessie Bernard, *Origins of American Sociology: The Social Science Movement in the United States* (New York, 1943), 530–40; Edith Abbott, *Historical Aspects of the Immigration Problem; Select Documents* (Chicago, 1926), 345, 651–56.

[6] New York *Tribune*, January 19, 1878, p. 8, January 25, 1878, p. 1; *Proceedings of the Conference of Charities*, 1876 (Albany, 1876), 162–70; *Proceedings of the Eighth Annual Conference of Charities and Correction*, 1881 (Boston, 1881), 217–27; *Proceedings of the National Conference of Charities and Cor-*

The emergence of other groups with broader conceptions of social responsibility and a larger interest in public control quickened the restriction movement. To various types of reformers, restriction seemed a relatively easy and painless way of invoking national authority to combat corruption, squalor, and injustice. Was not the immigrant a demoralized tool of privilege? Edmund James said so as early as 1883,[7] and the progressive-minded economists who joined him in founding the American Economic Association offered a prize of $150 for the best essay on "The Evil Effects of Unrestricted Immigration." [8] Following Josiah Strong, many spokesmen of the Social Gospel took a similar view.[9] The rising municipal reform movement felt a special alarm over the boss-ridden immigrant vote and produced in Abram S. Hewitt the most colorful nativist of the 1880's.[10]

While middle-class critics of laissez faire lent dignity to restrictionism, organized labor put pressure behind it. Through the Knights of Labor unionization was recovering in the early eighties from the debacle of the previous decade; but unemployment and immigration were increasing too. Vaguely class-conscious in outlook, the Knights held corporate wealth responsible for the tightening job market. Accordingly, they opened an

rection, 1890 (Boston, 1890), 279; Cong. Record, 47 Cong., 1 Sess., 5106–13, 5415. For background, see Frank J. Bruno, Trends in Social Work as Reflected in the Proceedings of the National Conference of Social Work, 1874–1946 (New York, 1948).

[7] John J. Lalor (ed.), Cyclopaedia of Political Science, Political Economy, and of the Political History of the United States, 3 vols. (Chicago, 1881–1884), II, 89–90.

[8] Richard T. Ely, "Scrapbook: American Economic Association, 1885–1906" (State Historical Society of Wisconsin, Madison), 27, 32.

[9] Josiah Strong, Our Country: Its Possible Future and Its Present Crisis (New York, 1885), 30–46; Samuel L. Loomis, Modern Cities and Their Religious Problems (New York, 1887), 67–100; William D. P. Bliss, The Encyclopedia of Social Reform (New York, 1897), 714; Wilbur F. Crafts, superintendent of the Reform Bureau, to Grover Cleveland, February 18, 1897, Grover Cleveland Papers (Manuscripts Division, Library of Congress).

[10] Allan Nevins, Abram S. Hewitt: with Some Account of Peter Cooper (New York, 1935), 512–16; Nation (New York), LII (April 16, 1891), 312; Charles E. Norton (ed.), Orations and Addresses of George William Curtis, 3 vols. (New York, 1894), III, 78–79. The degradation and misery of immigrant lives in tenement houses were first spread fully before the public by Jacob A. Riis, How the Other Half Lives (New York, 1890), but the conditions he described were not new. A quarter of a century before Riis wrote, the slum areas of some of the leading cities were already crowded with abject immigrant residents; yet their condition attracted little comment. It seems evident, therefore, that the restriction movement stemmed immediately from a rising concern over urban problems and only indirectly from an objective change in urban conditions. For descriptions of mid-century immigrant slums, see Oscar Handlin, Boston's Immigrants, 1790–1865: A Study in Acculturation (Cambridge, 1941), 93–127; Robert Ernst, Immigrant Life in New York City, 1825–1863 (New York, 1949), 37–60.

assault, not on immigration itself, but on the importation of European labor by American employers.[11] This attack led to the second step in federal restriction, the contract labor law of 1885, which expressed the Knights' conviction that undesirable immigration was almost entirely provoked by scheming capitalists.[12] Other unions drew the same distinction between voluntary and induced immigration. For seven years after 1885 the principal labor spokesmen rebuffed all pleas for a general limitation on immigration. The American Federation of Labor rejected the literacy test as late as 1896.[13] They did so partly because of an idealistic belief in the international solidarity of the working class and partly because an extremely large proportion of union members were themselves foreign-born.[14] These factors limited the role of organized labor in the early restriction movement more than historians have usually believed.

Neither middle-class nor working-class reformers had a preponderant effect on the nativist crusade as a whole, but their attitudes point to another of its aspects. Very often the arguments for restriction as a technique of social improvement revealed a sharp contempt for the new immigration from southern and eastern Europe. Many reformers were also race-conscious. Indeed, the first concentrated attack on the new immigrants came from labor leaders during the campaign for the contract labor law. Since employers apparently introduced the first appreciable Slovakian and Italian settlements into the mining and industrial centers of western Pennsylvania in the early eighties, union officials concluded that this new immigration was an entirely unnatural one — a product of corporate greed. In this context hatred of the strange newcomers seemed very natural. Identifying southern Europeans with contract labor, the

---

[11] *Journal of United Labor* (Washington), X (September 26, 1889), 2; *Journal of the Knights of Labor* (Washington), XII (December 31, 1891), 1.

[12] *Cong. Record*, 48 Cong., 1 Sess., 5349; 2 Sess., 1785; Terence V. Powderly, *Thirty Years of Labor* (Columbus, 1889), 442–47.

[13] *Report of Proceedings of the Sixteenth Annual Convention of the American Federation of Labor, 1896* (Bloomington, Ill., 1905), 81–82; "Testimony Taken by the Select Committee of the House of Representatives to Inquire into the Alleged Violation of the Laws Prohibiting the Importation of Contract Laborers, Paupers, Convicts, and Other Classes," *House Miscellaneous Documents*, No. 572, 50 Cong., 1 Sess., 392, 399; "Report of the Select Committee on Immigration and Naturalization," *House Reports*, No. 3472, 51 Cong., 2 Sess., 706–709; Porter (ed.), *National Party Platforms*, 155. The Knights of Labor swung over to a general restrictionist position in 1892. *Proceedings of the General Assembly of the Knights of Labor, 1892* (Philadelphia, 1892), 4, 86.

[14] Powderly, *Thirty Years of Labor*, 429; Boston Central Labor Union to Cleveland, February 9, 1897, Cleveland Papers; *Report of Proceedings of the Seventeenth Annual Convention of the American Federation of Labor, 1897* (Bloomington, Ill., 1905), 88–91; Isaac A. Hourwich, *Immigration and Labor; The Economic Aspects of European Immigration to the United States* (2nd ed., New York, 1922), 330–33, 552.

unions fell to reviling the people along with the system.[15] In the next few years this ethnic animosity infected a number of liberal intellectuals. The economist Edward Bemis concocted the idea of a literacy test in 1887 as a means of discriminating against southern and eastern Europeans.[16]

By 1890 abhorrence of the new immigration was spreading to wider circles.[17] Exactly why many Americans singled out these peoples for special dislike is not entirely clear. For one thing, their very newness meant that they had fewer powerful friends and less influence than longer established groups; it also meant that they could provide a target for both the old immigration and the old stock. For another thing, the new immigrants submitted to particularly primitive living conditions — a fact which, in itself, affronted the competitive, material values of the period. Thus the Italians, who had a lower standard of living than any of the other prominent nationalities, also experienced more prejudice than any of the others.[18] Some West Coast nativists thought that the Italians were no less degraded than the Chinese.[19]

Whatever the reasons for the particular distrust of the new immigration, we should not overestimate this aspect of the late nineteenth-century restriction movement. Antipathy to southern and eastern Europeans did channel support to the plan for a literacy test, but that antipathy did not dominate the movement as a whole. If it had done so, one might expect to find a close correlation between the size of the new immigration and the intensity of xenophobia. The two trends arose simultaneously in the 1880's, but they soon parted company. From 1893 through 1895 immigration from southern and eastern Europe decreased sharply while the campaign for restriction surged ahead with increasing power. Not

[15] *Cong. Record*, 48 Cong., 1 Sess., 5349–50; "To Prohibit the Importation of Foreign Contract Labor into the United States," *House Reports*, No. 444, 48 Cong., 1 Sess., 8–9.

[16] Edward W. Bemis, "Restriction of Immigration," *Andover Review* (Boston), IX (March, 1888), 263. See also Richmond Mayo-Smith, *Emigration and Immigration; A Study in Social Science* (New York, 1890), 132–35; Riis, *How the Other Half Lives*, 27, 106–107; Arthur Mann, "Frank Parsons: The Professor as Crusader," *Mississippi Valley Historical Review*, XXXVII (December, 1950), 483.

[17] Henry C. Lodge, "Lynch Law and Unrestricted Immigration," *North American Review* (Boston, New York), CLII (May, 1891), 611–12; *Public Opinion* (Washington), X (January 10, 1891), 325; Boston *Post*, April 14, 1891.

[18] *House Miscellaneous Documents*, No. 572, 50 Cong., 1 Sess., 208–14, 215–16; George J. Manson, "The 'Foreign Element' in New York City," *Harper's Weekly* (New York), XXXIV (October 18, 1890), 817. For another index to — and element in — the hatred of Italians, see the record of lynchings compiled in John B. Moore, *A Digest of International Law*, 8 vols. (Washington, 1906), VI, 837–49.

[19] "Chinese Immigration," *House Reports*, No. 4048, 51 Cong., 2 Sess., 1–5, 44, 55.

until the turn of the century did the new immigration begin to skyrocket, yet this was the very time when opposition died to a whisper.[20] Furthermore, restrictionists often showed little discrimination in choosing adversaries. An extensive examination of congressional debates and hearings, magazine articles, newspaper editorials, and the publications of nativist and other organizations indicates that a general dislike of *all foreigners* was much more pervasive than the specific dislike of the new nationalities.[21] Actually, the new immigration stands out in hindsight more sharply than it did at the time. As late as 1900, 74 per cent of the European-born population of the United States derived from accustomed sources.[22] With vast numbers of old immigrants still conspicuous and partially unassimilated, antiforeignism prevailed over ethnic distinctions.

Clearly, other factors entered into the making of this generalized antiforeign sentiment. Some of it arose out of a third change in the American scene — a revival of religious conflict. With the meeting of the Third Plenary Council in 1884, the Roman Catholic Church in the United States entered upon one of its most vigorous decades, a period which brought twenty new dioceses, many parochial schools, the establishment of the Catholic University of America, and the appointment of the first Apostolic Delegate to the United States. Also, the Council's decrees strengthened the Catholic school policy and led to new pressure for state aid to parochial education.[23] These advances touched off a wave of Protestant hysteria. The few existing nativist societies expanded rapidly in the late eighties, and many new ones appeared.[24] Like similar Protestant groups in earlier periods, these organizations were antiforeign as well as anti-Catholic. Since the Roman hierarchy followed the leadership of the

[20] United States Bureau of the Census, *Historical Statistics of the United States: 1789–1945* (Washington, 1949), 33–34. For evidence of the rise and fall of restriction sentiment, see n. 39 and n. 41. It should be noted, however, that a sudden surge of Italian immigration in 1896 contributed to the congressional passage of the literacy test in that year. Bliss, *Encyclopedia of Social Reform*, 714; New York *Tribune*, April 24, 1896, p. 3.

[21] Evidences of this indiscriminate restriction sentiment are too numerous to cite, but for examples see Rena M. Atchison, *Un-American Immigration: Its Present Effects and Future Perils* (Chicago, 1894); *Literary Digest* (New York), II (April 18, 1891), 693; Robert DeCourcy Ward, "Immigration Clippings, 1891–94" (Widener Library, Harvard University, Cambridge).

[22] United States Bureau of the Census, *Historical Statistics*, 32. A leading proponent of the literacy test came mournfully to the same conclusion. Prescott F. Hall, "Present Status of Immigration Restriction," *Gunton's Magazine* (New York), XVIII (April, 1900), 308.

[23] Gerald Shaughnessy, *Has the Immigrant Kept the Faith? A Study of Immigration and Catholic Growth in the United States, 1790–1920* (New York, 1925), 166; Daniel F. Reilly, *The School Controversy (1891–1893)* (Washington, 1943), 31–46.

[24] Albert C. Stevens, *The Cyclopaedia of Fraternities* (New York, 1899), 290–327.

Vatican, anti-Catholic crusaders regarded the Church as alien and sub-versive. Since it recruited members chiefly from immigration, most re-ligious nativists joined the restriction movement. Another connection between anti-Catholic and antiforeign fears arose out of the conditions of municipal politics; in the eyes of alarmed Protestants the growing power of Irish Catholics in city government seemed an additional reason to slam the national gates. During this period Protestant agitators paid back-handed tribute to the importance of the Irish in ecclesiastical and political affairs by continuing to hurl more abuse at them than at any other nationality.[25] It is significant that the American Protective Association, which absorbed most of the other anti-Catholic societies in the early nineties, showed almost no interest in the new immigration and had little part in the campaign for the literacy test.

This fact in itself suggests that the impact of anti-Catholicism on the restriction movement was hardly decisive. The passion of midwestern Protestants, who armed to meet a rumored papal uprising in 1893, soon spent itself in empty fury. The immigration restriction bill introduced by William A. Linton, chief A.P.A. spokesman in Congress, never got out of committee.[26] The A.P.A. itself began to decline in 1894,[27] two years be-fore the restriction movement reached its crest. Indeed, anti-Catholicism throughout this period lacked the respectability which it had previously enjoyed. No outstanding political leader identified himself with it, as Rutherford B. Hayes had done in 1875, and even many Protestant min-isters urged a reduction of immigration without mentioning its de-nominational character.[28]

Xenophobia in late nineteenth-century America had a more potent source than religion or racism or reform. In its largest aspect it issued from a crisis in the whole American social order. From the mid-eighties to the mid-nineties a society already uneasy at the emergence of the first great trusts felt the shock of fierce industrial unrest. Americans had long believed that their land of mobility and opportunity was immune to the class conflicts of Europe. The railroad strikes of 1877 passed too quickly to do serious damage to their faith. But the labor upheaval that began in 1885 ushered in a decade of massive and recurrent discontent. Alarmed at these new class antagonisms, unwilling to recognize them as indigenous,

[25] Ibid.; A. P. A. Magazine (San Francisco), I (June, 1895), 89; Alvin P. Stauffer, Jr., "Anti-Catholicism in American Politics, 1865–1900" (Ph.D. dis-sertation, Harvard University, 1933), 18–19, 93–108.

[26] A. P. A. Magazine, I (July, 1895), 170; Index to the Cong. Record, 53 Cong., 3 Sess., H. R. 8774.

[27] Stauffer, "Anti-Catholicism in American Politics," 374–75.

[28] Charles R. Williams (ed.), Diary and Letters of Rutherford Birchard Hayes, 5 vols. (Columbus, 1922–1926), III, 274–90; Rev. B. W. Williams, "Our Attitude Toward Foreigners," American Magazine of Civics (New York), VIII (January, 1896), 65–66; Public Opinion, XIV (February 25, 1893), 585; XV (June 10, 1893), 222.

and unready to deal with them as such, many Americans surrendered to the conviction that they came from abroad. The equation between immigration and unrest seemed confirmed by the riot which occurred at Haymarket Square in Chicago in 1886. Coming as it did at the height of the huge eight-hour strikes, the bombing at Chicago struck panic from coast to coast over the threat of foreign-born anarchists. No other single incident did so much to provoke restriction sentiment. For years the memory of Haymarket and the dread of imported anarchy haunted the American consciousness. No general stereotype of the immigrant prevailed more widely than that of a lawless creature, given over to violence and disorder. Scores of conservative politicians, newspaper editors, educators, popular writers, and Protestant clergymen labeled the immigrant as peculiarly susceptible to anarchism.[29] Many blamed all of the major strikes of the period on foreign influence, and the composition of the trade unions gave specious credibility to the charge.[30]

In short, fears for social stability and the projection of those fears upon the immigrant became almost a common denominator of the restriction movement. Of all major restrictionist groups, only organized labor did not connect immigration with unrest; and even here a patrician organization like the Order of Railway Conductors, which favored cooperation with management, denounced immigration as the chief cause of current labor troubles.[31] Middle-class reformers saw the immigrant as both an author of revolution and an agent of reaction.[32] Opponents of Catholicism and of the new immigration often reacted in a similar way. The A.P.A. and other Protestant societies deplored the use of the strike and proposed antiforeign measures as a solution to class conflict.[33] The first full-length anti-Semitic

[29] *Public Opinion*, I (May 15, 1886), 83–86; III (April 30, 1887), 49; XV (June 10, 1893), 222; clippings from Boston *Journal*, July, 1894, Ward, "Immigration Clippings," 31, 38; *Proceedings of the National Conference of Charities and Correction*, 1887 (Boston, 1887), 203–205; *The Poems of Thomas Bailey Aldrich*, 2 vols. (Boston, n.d.), II, 72; John H. Denison, "The Survival of the American Type," *Atlantic Monthly* (Boston), LXXV (January, 1895), 26.

[30] T. N. Carver, "Immigration and the Labor Problem," *American Journal of Politics* (New York), III (July, 1893), 80–81; H. H. Boyesen, "Immigration," *National Perils and Opportunities* (New York, 1887), 67; National Educational Association, *Journal of Proceedings, and Addresses*, 1888 (Topeka, 1888), 145–47; *Public Opinion*, V (August 25, 1888), 432; XIII (August 6, 1892), 426.

[31] *Railway Conductor's Monthly* (Elmira, Cedar Rapids), V (December, 1888), 613; *Railway Conductor* (Cedar Rapids), XI (April, 1894), 189.

[32] *Publications of the Immigration Restriction League*, No. 1 (Boston, 1894); William H. Tolman, *Municipal Reform Movements in the United States* (New York, 1895), 103; Strong, *Our Country*, 43; Mayo-Smith, *Emigration and Immigration*, 88; Atchison, *Un-American Immigration*, *passim*.

[33] *A.P.A. Magazine*, I (July, 1895), 173–74; *American Standard* (San Francisco), I (May 25, 1889), 1; *Council Chat: A Journal Devoted to the Jr. O.U.A.M. and Kindred Orders* (Wilkes-Barre), I (November, 1890), 539.

tract written in the United States, the work of a Greek immigrant in
1888, described the strike as a peculiarly Jewish idea and John D. Rockefeller as a representative of the Jewish monopoly.[34] At a more august social
level the fear of the foreign-bred discontent contributed powerfully to
the mushroom growth of hereditary patriotic societies in the early nineties. Many of the new societies followed the lead of the Sons of the
American Revolution in dedicating themselves to saving the country from
insurrectionary immigrants.[35] The same concern contributed powerfully
to a shift of business opinion toward a restrictionist position. By the late
1880's large numbers of American business leaders were turning to immigration restriction as a weapon against strikes, lawlessness, and other disorders.[36]

The specter of unrest would not have looked so frightening to Americans if they had preserved intact their old confidence in the capacity of
their civilization to liberate men automatically from the restraints of fixed
class and enforced poverty. But changes in American conditions seemed
now to narrow the horizon of opportunity and compound the menace of
discontent. The year after Haymarket the agricultural frontier collapsed.
Simultaneously, alarm over the dwindling of the public domain became
widespread. Here was another reason for reducing immigration. As early
as 1883 Henry George warned that the immigrant tide was becoming
dangerous because the safety valve of western land was closing. After
1886 many newspapers expressed similar fears.[37] In the midst of more

[34] [Telemachus T. Timayenis], The Original Mr. Jacobs: A Startling Exposé
(New York, 1888), 283–85, 295. This is the earliest indigenous book of this
character in the Library of Congress, the New York Public Library, and the Jewish Theological Seminary of America. It is mentioned in Leonard A. Greenberg,
"Some American Anti-Semitic Publications of the Late 19th Century," Publications of the American Jewish Historical Society (Philadelphia), XXXVII (1947),
421–25.

[35] Proceedings of the Second Annual Congress of the Sons of the American
Revolution, 1891 (New York, n.d.), 8; American Monthly Magazine (Washing-
ton), XXVI (May, 1905), 407; Society of Colonial Wars, Constitution and
By-Laws, Membership (New York, 1893), 53; American Historical Register and
Monthly Gazette of the Patriotic-Hereditary Societies of the United States of
America (Philadelphia), II (June, 1895), 1069.

[36] Commercial and Financial Chronicle (New York), LI (September 13,
1890), 316–17; Bradstreet's: A Journal of Trade, Finance and Public Economy
(New York), XIII (June 5, 1886), 369; Proceedings of the Twenty-First Annual
Meeting of the National Board of Trade, 1892 (Boston), 126–28, 272–73; Wisconsin Bureau of Labor and Industrial Statistics, Second Biennial Report, 1885–
1886 (Madison, 1886), 416–21, 428–30.

[37] Henry George, Social Problems (reprint, New York, 1886), 39–46, 161–62;
Public Opinion, III (April 30, 1887), 50; III (May 14, 1887), 98–99; IX (May
24, 1890), 151; XXII (February 25, 1897), 231–32. See also John Swinton,
Striking for Life: Labor's Side of the Labor Question (Philadelphia[?], 1894),
53–54.

concrete troubles, western farmers shared in the general anxiety over pressure of immigration on the remaining land supply.[38] Then in 1893 economic distress spread throughout the whole country. In the next three years the contraction of employment and business activity added an urgency to the nation's claustrophobia. While restriction proposals as harsh as total prohibition received a hearing, an organized campaign for the literacy test developed.[39] To this plan Congress gave its first and overwhelming approval in 1896.[40]

Then suddenly the fears and frustrations of the Cleveland period dissolved, and the restriction crusade faded with them. Beginning in 1897 a tide of prosperity washed over the country's domestic troubles; soon the intoxication of war and imperialism added further impetus to the revival of national self-confidence. As the tensions of the nineties relaxed, much of the interest in restricting immigration disappeared.[41]

The downfall of nativism at the close of the century emphasizes again its function as an outlet for the baffled discontents of the preceding years. For the social historian those discontents supply the central key to the origins of immigration restriction. But surely this key will not unlock the whole problem. A balanced view will encompass the many-sidedness and complexity of the situation from which restriction arose. It grew in a climate of social crisis, but its roots extended into reform, into religion, and into immigration itself.

[38] For an example, see Ed Brown to Henry Baldwin, February 13, 1888, Henry Baldwin Papers (Manuscript Division, New York Public Library). See also *Western Rural and American Stockman* (Chicago), XXX (April 23, 1892), 263.

[39] For symptoms of the quickening of the restriction movement by economic depression, see Office of Commissioner-General of Immigration, *Report of the Immigration Investigating Commission to the Honorable the Secretary of the Treasury* (Washington, 1895), 127–51; *Cong. Record*, 54 Cong., 1 Sess., 1028, 5421, 5425–26. The literacy test was first endorsed by a congressional committee in 1893. *Ibid.*, 52 Cong., 2 Sess., 901.

[40] *Cong. Record*, 54 Cong., 1 Sess., 5485; 2 Sess., 246.

[41] For indications of a sharp fall of interest in immigration, see Hall, "Present Status of Immigration Restriction," *Gunton's Magazine*, XVIII (April, 1900), 305–307; *Nation*, LXIX (October 19, 1899), 293–94; A. P. C. Griffin, *List of Books (with References to Periodicals) on Immigration* (Washington, 1907), 59–61.

The Last Days of "Texan" Abilene: A Study in Community Conflict on the Farmer's Frontier

ROBERT R. DYKSTRA

Significant social and economic change is usually accompanied by conflict. The conflict need not be violent in terms of human life, but generally it leads to power struggles, group clashes, and ultimately, social destruction or dislocation. The competition between canals and the new railroads in the 1830's is a classic example. In the essay below, Robert R. Dykstra, a social historian at the University of Iowa, focuses on the experiences of a typical "cattle town" of the late nineteenth century that found itself in conflict over the desirability of an important enterprise. Dykstra utilizes sociological theories of community conflict to examine the roots of change and the dynamics of political interaction and leadership. Although his study is confined to the Abilene experience, Dykstra offers interesting insights into patterns of change and "reformist" movements. He clearly traces the convergence of numerous, sometimes diverse, economic impulses with moral forces. Thus in Abilene, local real estate interests, farmers in surrounding areas, and urban anti-vice elements combined to bar the Texas cattlemen. The harmony of divergent groups responding to different stimuli is by no means unique. A similar example can be found in the twentieth-century drive against child labor that only succeeded when Northern manufacturers, faced with growing Southern competition, allied with social workers and labor unions to secure federal legislation.

In 1867, on the very brink of its boom as the first of the famous Kansas "cowtowns," Abilene was but a dreary handful of log and earthen huts,

Reprinted by permission with minor revisions approved by the author from *Agricultural History*, XXXIV (July 1960), pp. 107–119.

flanked on the south by a string of bottomland farmsteads which functioned, like others in the county, at little better than a subsistence level. Four years later the visitors crowding Abilene's dusty streets noted over 100 frame dwellings, a courthouse, a school, four substantial hotels, a wide choice of taverns, at least three restaurants, a mammoth livery stable, two lumber yards, a theater, a tinshop, as well as a blacksmith's, and retail establishments dealing in hardware, furniture, farm machinery, footwear, groceries, jewelry and firearms, besides numerous outlets for clothing, dry goods and general merchandise. From outlying Dickinson County, farm products of all types poured into Abilene to feed a consumer market so immense it could not be met locally, and a scattering of new frame farmhouses testified to a measure of rural wealth. The community's phenomenal prosperity in 1871 was the obvious result of its flourishing commerce in Texas cattle. Yet, the following spring, Abilene and vicinity exiled the lucrative cattle-trading industry with a hostile vote, and thereupon became just another struggling little rural community like countless others on the trans-Mississippi frontier, economically much as it had been before its great transformation.[1]

Local historians, strangely enough, record the expulsion of Abilene's cattle trade only in the most casual manner.[2] But in reality, was not a change with such important consequences attended by sharp conflict, as sociological theory would suggest? [3] The answer provides an interesting insight into the dynamics of political interaction and leadership in an important, and not wholly unrepresentative, frontier community.

Joseph G. McCoy's own account of how he impulsively launched Abilene as a cattle center is well-known.[4] In two years Abilene was indeed the cattle-trade capital of the West. Yet, its peculiar industry was not without local enemies from the start. Dickinson County rural settlers, especially, feared "Spanish fever," to which the rugged longhorns were practically immune, but which usually proved fatal to domestic stock.[5] In

---

[1] "Community" is used throughout as synonymous with the sociologist's definition of "rural community," i.e., a village and its rural service area. See Dwight Sanderson and Robert A. Polson, *Rural Community Organization* (New York, 1939), 8.

[2] See J. B. Edwards, *Early Days in Abilene* ([Abilene, 1940]), 11 (contents originally published in 1896), and [William G. Cutler, ed.,] *History of the State of Kansas* (Chicago, 1883), 688.

[3] For an early study calling attention to the connection between impending change and community social conflict see The Inquiry, *Community Conflict* (New York, 1929). Briefly, the reasoning behind its analysis is that any proposal to change the status quo in a given community invariably gives rise to those who favor and those who oppose the change. Hence, conflict ensues.

[4] Joseph G. McCoy, *Historic Sketches of the Cattle Trade of the West and Southwest* (Kansas City, 1874).

[5] This was also widely known as "Texas fever." For a comprehensive discussion

1867 McCoy was able to stifle this opposition by bribing local officials and promising settlers an immediate market for farm produce.[6] The following year he arranged reimbursement for local stock lost through Spanish fever.[7] In 1869 an indemnifying bond in the amount of $20,000 was executed to protect settlers against damages.[8] And always prosperity itself was a convincing argument for continued encouragement of the trade.

The second of Abilene's major entrepreneurs, the young man around whom anti-cattle sentiment eventually coalesced, was well-established in town by this time. The heir of a prosperous upstate New Yorker, Theodore C. Henry, arrived in Abilene in December, 1867. He spent his first winter writing advertising copy for a local land speculator, then himself purchased about 550 acres adjoining the town and began to see that the best profits lay in a combination of real estate and politics.[9] By September, 1869, he commanded sufficient stature to be appointed to the provisional city council of the newly-incorporated Abilene along with cattleman Joe McCoy, one James B. Shane and two others.[10]

Shane, who preceded both McCoy and Henry to Abilene, was a land speculator as well as Dickinson County clerk.[11] In 1868 he was agent for the 200,000-odd acres of Dickinson real estate opened to settlers by the Kansas Pacific Railroad.[12] In 1869 he and Henry became partners.[13] A partially disabled veteran, Shane probably managed the office while Henry did the actual selling. "Henry was right in his element," recalled one informant, "it was *His* chance. I presume he was responsible for more farm sales in 1868–69 & 70 & 71 than all the others combined — Henry was a Hustler. . . ."[14] The firm of Shane & Henry, Real Estate Brokers, also

see T. R. Havins, "Texas Fever," *Southwestern Historical Quarterly,* 52:147–162 (July, 1948).

[6] McCoy, *Historic Sketches,* 63–65; Newton Blair to Gov. Samuel J. Crawford, Oct. 7, 1867, Governors' Correspondence, Kansas State Historical Society, Topeka.

[7] McCoy, *Historic Sketches,* 150; Charles F. Gross to J. B. Edwards, April 13, 1922, J. B. Edwards Papers, Kansas State Historical Society; Leavenworth *Times and Conservative,* June 25, 1869.

[8] *Ibid.*

[9] Abilene *Gazette,* Feb. 25, 1881; T. C. Henry, *An Address to the Old Settlers Re-Union at Enterprise, Kansas, October 9, 1902* (n.p., n.d.), 1; T. C. Henry, "The Story of a Fenceless Winter-Wheat Field," *Transactions of the Kansas State Historical Society,* 9:502, ftn. 1, 503 (1905–1906).

[10] *City of Abilene Ordinance Book, 1869–1874,* microfilm, Kansas State Historical Society, 3–4.

[11] *Dickinson County Commissioners' Journal, 1861–1883,* microfilm, Kansas State Historical Society, 49–50.

[12] Lawrence *Kansas Daily Tribune,* June 23, 1868.

[13] Henry, "Story of a Wheat Field," 502, ftn. 1.

[14] Gross to Edwards, April 13, 1922.

included a secret partner, apparently S. A. Burroughs, a local lawyer.[15] The trio's stature and influence reached a peak in the fall of 1869 when Shane was elected county treasurer and Henry became county recorder; Burroughs won the position of county attorney the following year to complete their triumph.[16]

The year 1870 was more to Abilene than just another cattle-shipping season. The activities of Henry and his associates reflected the fact that rural settlement on a large scale was at last under way in the county. Real estate boomed. Joe McCoy, the foremost Abilene entrepreneur, on the other hand, was now burdened with debt because of failure to collect fees owed him by the railroad. Forced to dispose of his extensive land holdings, McCoy had no trouble finding purchasers, among whom was T. C. Henry. The principal buyer, however, was an Illinois speculator named Jacob Augustine.[17]

As characterized many years later, Augustine "had been a man of large means, but in an evil hour went security on notes for friends for large amounts. He had these notes to pay and it left him without means." Determined to recoup his losses on the frontier, he arrived in Abilene with limited resources.[18] But as McCoy wryly certified, Augustine found him "in a selling humor," and was not long in closing a deal.[19] Apparently Augustine bought $3,000 worth of townsite property on 30 days' time, "then returned east to find the money." C. H. Lebold, a wealthy young man in Tuscarawas County, Ohio, where Augustine had lived for many years, provided the capital in exchange for a half-interest in the acquisition.[20]

Upon becoming owners of Abilene real estate, Augustine and Lebold strove to stimulate investment in and emigration to Abilene and its hinterlands. Vear P. Wilson, editor of the *Tuscarawas Chronicle*, agreed to

---

[15] Shane was Henry's overt partner, but Henry mentions two partners, both county officers, in his "Story of a Wheat Field," 503. The identification of Burroughs as the secret partner admittedly is on circumstantial evidence. Henry says all three were elected twice to county office. He and Shane were elected and re-elected in 1869 an 1871, Burroughs in 1870 and 1872. Each held other offices, as Henry contends. Henry bought out Shane's interest in the business in 1872, and a year later bought out Augustine and Lebold, his competitors. Burroughs retired to a farm in June, 1873, but this is the only evidence that by this time he, as the other partner, had also sold out as Henry states. See *Dickinson Commissioners' Journal*, 103, 144–145, 187–188, 250; Abilene *Chronicle*, June 20, 1872; Abilene *Dickinson County Chronicle*, April 3, 1873; Enterprise *Kansas Gazette*, May 19, 1876.

[16] *Dickinson Commissioners' Journal*, 103, 144–145.

[17] Ralph P. Bieber, Introduction to McCoy's *Historic Sketches* (Glendale, Calif., 1940), 64.

[18] Adolph Roenigk, ed., *Pioneer History of Kansas* ([Lincoln, Kansas], 1933), 32.

[19] McCoy, *Historic Sketches*, 229.

[20] Roenigk, *Pioneer History*, 32–33.

undertake the formation and leadership of a colony of rural emigrants. The main body of the "Buckeye Colony," as it came to be called, arrived in Dickinson County in the spring of 1870. Wilson himself was rushed in beforehand to participate in an unexpected county seat contest with nearby Detroit. Wilson hurriedly produced an issue of the new Abilene *Chronicle* on February 12, just three days before the crucial plebiscite.[21] Land speculators generally felt that possessing a county seat guaranteed rising real estate values. Probably due most to the timely appearance of the *Chronicle*, Abilene retained the courthouse by a slim margin of 23 votes.[22]

With this threat to future prosperity dispelled, Augustine and Lebold, with Wilson perhaps a secret partner, opened the National Union Land Office.[23] Lebold was in charge; the elder partner did not locate in Abilene until late in 1871. The new firm's relationship with the land agency operated by T. C. Henry and his partners was mutually accommodating. In April, 1870, the *Chronicle* carried the first half-page spread by Shane & Henry, and throughout the next two years their ad and a similar one by Lebold's agency co-existed, sometimes in adjoining columns. Late in the year the paper observed that the two firms, sharing a booming market, were now the only ones in town.[24] Although Lebold's agency seems to have monopolized the sale of town lots, both firms advertised quantities of farms and farmlands, thus sharing a powerful interest in an increased rural immigration.[25] The owners of the two land offices were also active in the political realm. On April 25, in the election of citizens to replace Abilene's provisional council, Henry, Shane, and a local grocer were returned to office, while Lebold replaced Joe McCoy. The new council re-elected Henry as provisional mayor.[26] In the November elections Burroughs became county attorney, while V. P. Wilson won the county's probate judgeship.[27]

21 The first issue of the *Chronicle* was an election "extra." The first regular issue was published Feb. 25. Copies of these two are not extant. The March 3 issue is the first included in the Kansas State Historical Society's microfilm reproduction of the *Chronicle* files from 1870 through 1872.

22 *Dickinson Commissioners' Journal*, 110. Following the defeat of Detroit in the final county seat war, most of its businessmen deserted it. See *Dickinson County Historical Sketches* (3 vols.), Kansas State Historical Society, 1:117.

23 In November, 1870, Wilson was announced as a member of the firm, but was silently dropped from its advertisement six months later. See Abilene *Chronicle*, Nov. 3, 1870, through May 4, 1871.

24 *Ibid.*, Dec. 8, 1870.

25 For the most specific division-of-interest statement see Gross to Edwards, March 31, 1925.

26 See Abilene *Chronicle*, April 21, 1870, for announcement of the election. The results can only be deduced from the membership of the council that met after June 4, 1870. See *City of Abilene Minute Book, 1870–1876*, microfilm, Kansas State Historical Society, 29 ff.

27 *Dickinson Commissioners' Journal*, 144–145.

Throughout the year 1870, the newspaper reported immigrant arrivals. Abilene's cattle trade was not without its blessings for the new Dickinson settler. Texas drovers often gave settlers the calves from their herds, which usually were killed as nuisances.[28] Texas cows, sold cheaply for butchering as well as milking, often helped settlers get through their first winter in the county.[29] The herds of longhorns also mitigated the upland settlers' fuel situation.[30] More important, the transient demand for farm produce that Joe McCoy predicted in 1867 was now a major economic reality in Dickinson County, a market so great that produce was shipped in by rail to help meet the demand.[31] In September, 1870, the *Chronicle* quoted a corn-grower living north of town as asserting that Abilene was "fast becoming a first-class market for farm products as well as cattle." [32] Many of the original bottomland farmers, in fact, viewed the settlement of the rural uplands with alarm, foreseeing the eventual extinction of pasturage for Texas cattle and the county's loss of the cattle trade and its demand. As old-timers along Chapman Creek declared, the homestead law would be the ruination of the area.[33]

Settlement of the uplands intruded a more immediate factor into the problem of the cattle trade. For the new upland settler, the fear of Spanish fever was eclipsed by a fear of trampled crops. The old streambed settlers had small, fertile fields that could be fenced if necessary with bottomland timber. The treeless upland claims, however, could be fenced only with purchased materials and great labor. By 1870, James Bell, a comparatively wealthy farmer, had fenced his entire acreage with posts and boards, but only at a cost of $1,200.[34] The next year homesteader Peter Oleson fenced a couple of acres with posts and wire, but lacking the money for staples, had laboriously to pierce each post to receive the strands.[35] As barbed wire was yet to be invented, the only practical solution appeared to lie in a "herd law" which termed every livestock owner responsible for all damage to others by reason of his stock running at large, practically obliging him to herd his animals. With a herd law in force, therefore, fencing became unnecessary. In February, 1870, the Kansas legislators passed the first herd law provisions for six Kansas counties.[36] T. C. Henry, giving the main address at the first Dickinson County fair in October of

[28] J. Marvin Hunter, ed., *The Trail Drivers of Texas* (2nd ed. rev., Nashville, 1925), 860; *Kansas Daily Tribune*, Aug. 8, 1869.

[29] *Dickinson Historical Sketches*, 2:49.

[30] Hunter, *Trail Drivers*, 435–436.

[31] Edwards, *Early Days in Abilene*, 8.

[32] Abilene *Chronicle*, Sept. 1, 1870.

[33] Edwards, *Early Days in Abilene*, 8; unidentified news article in *Dickinson County Clippings* (4 vols.), Kansas State Historical Society, 2:283.

[34] Abilene *Chronicle*, May 12, 1870.

[35] *Dickinson Historical Sketches*, 1:27.

[36] *Laws of the State of Kansas*, 1870, 236–238.

that year, demanded a herd law for Dickinson. In fact, said Henry, the entire cattle trade soon must go. His point was crystal clear —

> When the time comes that these thousands and hundreds of thousands of cattle that are annually pouring in upon us, retard the development of our county by deterring its settlement and cultivation — rather than contributing to its advancement, as perhaps they have done heretofore, then their presence should no longer be encouraged or tolerated here. Possibly I am mistaken, but my conviction is, that that time is very near at hand.[37]

Henry's call for abolishing the cattle trade in Dickinson County was a turning point, but at first glance the Abilene *Chronicle* appears to have overlooked it. Actually, the newspaper was committed to being a promotional medium for stimulating immigration and capital investment, and thus approached any controversial question with extreme caution. No word against the Texas cattle trade, except that contained in the text of Henry's speech, entered its columns in 1870; for public consumption the industry remained "One of the Most Important Interests of the Country." [38]

Editor Wilson cautiously opened the year 1871 on a new note, however. Allegedly from one of the county's oldest settlers, a letter to the editor published in mid-January complained bitterly of high county taxes which, except for bridge taxes, it argued, sprang from expensive county law-enforcement machinery made necessary by Abilene's cattle trade. This trade, furthermore, "A. F." concluded, benefited only a minority of actual county residents, contributed no taxes and brought with it increased taxation, crime and "demoralizing influences." Wilson's comment on the letter was tentative. He welcomed a "temperate discussion of subjects relating to the general welfare of the people, of which the cattle trade is not the least important," and was willing to print a few communications arguing its pros and cons.[39]

In the next issue Wilson noted that "As our readers well know, we are in favor of the cattle trade. . . . While we have hitherto advocated the trade, we have refused to publish anything, until last week, against it. . . ." A number of replies to "A. F." had been received, one of which was printed. This writer argued that if the cattle trade closed down, so would local business. "The citizens of Dickinson county who are becoming enriched by the cattle trade," he declared, "prays [sic] for its continuance." [40] A rebuttal by "A. F.," printed without comment by Wilson, repeated that most of the profits of the trade went to non-residents and asserted

---

[37] Abilene *Chronicle*, Nov. 10, 1870.
[38] Headline in *ibid.*, Sept. 22, 1870.
[39] *Ibid.*, Jan. 12, 1871.
[40] "Defendant" in *ibid.*, Jan. 19, 1871.

that Abilene's major return was simply a reputation as "the meanest hole in the State." He demanded that a herd law which, in effect, would abolish the trade in Dickinson be put to a vote in the forthcoming county elections, and predicted a three-to-one margin of victory.[41] Editor Wilson now realized that he had opened a Pandora's box that threatened the paper's whole tone of social harmony and optimism. Only two more weeks remained, he announced in February, for presentation of letters discussing the issue. A communication followed which asserted that the cattle trade was acceptable to most settlers as long as drovers kept their herds away from homesteads and that lawlessness, on the other hand, was the result of *"bad whiskey"* served out to Texans by "these miserable *leeches* on society (saloon keepers). . . ." The writer recommended either a stiff tax on taverns to support the costs of law-enforcement or else the suppression of such establishments.[42] More comprehensive was a lengthy letter signed "Ibex." The writer, who was probably Joe McCoy, compared the "obscure" Abilene of 1867 with the Abilene of 1871. Among other benefits, he claimed, the trade had conferred upon the area a $100,000 a week banking business, full employment and a farmers' market for grain, garden, poultry and dairy products. If taxes had increased, so had the ability to pay them. As for immorality, that was a problem faced by any burgeoning commercial center. Anyone in the county, "Ibex" concluded,

> who has ability to transact business without a guardian can, if he so desires, make money out of the cattle trade. — And by a proper effort of the law-abiding men, good order can be maintained and lawlessness suppressed, and immorality of every description so regulated that even the over-tender sensibilities of "A. F." may not be offended.[43]

In spite of the fact that two weeks remained for submission of cattle trade letters, Wilson published no more. But events in Topeka, where the state legislature was meeting, assured that the issue would rise again. Taking its cue from the 1870 session, the legislators passed "An Act to provide for a herd law in the counties herein named," among which was Dickinson. These counties were to be exempted for five years from an act of 1868 which required that fields be fenced. Instead, a settler need only plow a furrow one rod wide entirely around his land in order to collect damages from the owner of any trespassing stock. The only requirement

---

[41] *Ibid.*, Jan. 26, 1871.

[42] "Equal Rights" in *ibid.*, Feb. 2, 1871.

[43] *Ibid.* George L. Cushman, "Abilene, First of the Kansas Cow Towns," *Kansas Historical Quarterly*, 9:257, ftn. 81 (Aug., 1940), observes that "Ibex" was probably McCoy because the description of 1867 Abilene in the letter closely resembles the description in McCoy's *Historic Sketches*, 44. Also lending this impression is the fact that "Ibex" implored readers to consider the money spent by the person who originally obtained the cattle trade for Abilene.

for local enactment was that a county plebiscite approve the herd law in April, 1871.[44]

Because Wilson had clamped the lid on the cattle-trade controversy, the vote on the herd law was attended with little fanfare in the *Chronicle*. The prediction by "A. F." of a decisive defeat of the cattle trade was grossly inaccurate. The herd law was disapproved by a 123-vote margin, carrying only four of the 14 county precincts. Yet, due primarily to the heavy margins against Abilene's cattle trade registered in both her sister settlements of Detroit and Solomon City, the herd law won nearly 41 per cent of the votes. The new upland settlers of Buckeye Precinct also went heavily against the trade, as did those of Upper Chapman Creek.[45] The law's failure may have surprised Editor Wilson and others, but the *Chronicle* failed to comment.[46]

Within Abilene itself, meanwhile, the cattle-trade controversy encompassed another issue. In March, 1871, Abilene prepared to organize as a city of the third class. Elections of officials were scheduled for April 3, and the intervening month witnessed a sharp campaign for municipal office.[47] Emerging from his involuntary retirement, Joe McCoy spent much of March in Junction City where his suit against the Kansas Pacific for payment of fees owed him was at last being heard.[48] At the end of March he returned triumphant, and obviously decided to run for mayor to capture the best possible position from which to defend his cattle trade from critics. Henry Hazlett, a political nonentity, was McCoy's opponent. C. H. Lebold almost entered the race, but for some reason decided against it, perhaps because he felt his chances were not good enough at that time. The problem of handling social immorality attending the cattle trade was the major campaign issue, with all candidates apparently declaring for regulation. In the elections held the day before the herd law voting, McCoy was winner by a substantial majority. Emerging as the new city council, each like the mayor elected to one-year terms, were Samuel Carpenter, a merchant, Dr. Lucius Boudinot, S. A. Burroughs of the Shane & Henry firm, and two others.[49]

Dissension sabotaged the harmony of the new council almost immediately, primarily over a tavern license fee. Taking the extreme position, Burroughs advocated a $500 fee as a means of paying all municipal ex-

[44] *Laws of Kansas,* 1871, 208–211. The *Chronicle* of March 23, 1871, printed the text of the law on its front page.

[45] *Dickinson Commissioners' Journal,* 157–164. The *Journal* mistakenly notes defeat of the law by only 66 votes.

[46] The paper observed only that "From what we can learn the herd law was defeated on last Tuesday, in this county." See Abilene *Chronicle,* April 6, 1871.

[47] *Ibid.* The *Chronicle* issues of March 16 and 30, which must have contained information on the election, are not extant.

[48] McCoy, *Historic Sketches,* ed. Bieber, 279, ftn. 331.

[49] Edwards, *Early Days in Abilene,* 6; Abilene *Chronicle,* April 6, 1871; *Abilene Minute Book,* 51.

penses. When it became clear, however, that Mayor McCoy was set on imposing a general tax on all businesses, Burroughs switched to the $100 low-fee proposal of Boudinot and Carpenter, vindictively opposing the Mayor's moderate $200 position.[50] An impasse was thus reached, and to break it a day or two later, McCoy approached Boudinot and Carpenter individually and advised that if they would support the $200 fee, any friends of theirs who were tavernkeepers would have to pay only $100. The difference, he explained, would be made up by means of a covert taxation of gamblers and prostitutes by the city marshal, J. B. ("Wild Bill") Hickok. He added that he planned to have Burroughs absent from the next council meeting on some pretext so that the rest of them could "shove the thing through. . . ."[51] The two refused McCoy's offer and at the next meeting tendered their resignations rather than vote at all on the tavern fee.[52] The meeting, implied the *Chronicle*, "broke up . . . in a row." Editor Wilson, self-appointed keeper of the public conscience, observed grimly that certain persons were "trying to force their own selfish or pet measures upon the people." [53] He meant Joe McCoy.

At the infamous meeting of May 8, Boudinot and Carpenter withdrew, their resignations having been accepted. As they stalked from the council chamber Burroughs joined them, withdrawing a quorum. Marshal Hickok was ordered to bring him back, but no sooner had this been accomplished than he bolted again. Hickok this time brought Burroughs in on his shoulder and stood guard while the council transacted further business.[54]

The dramatic incident soon became statewide gossip. At the state capital McCoy commissioned the noted artist Henry Worrall to get up a comic drawing of the incident.[55] Three days later the Topeka *Commonwealth* announced that "At McMeekin's is a fine engraving . . . of Wild Bill 'toting' on his shoulder the refractory and absconding councilman of Abilene. Knight has photographed it, and copies can be obtained at the Riverside." [56] In Abilene Editor Wilson was furious, charging that McCoy personally commissioned the sketch and was sending prints "all over the country to be hawked about and laughed at as a standing disgrace to his own town." [57] Indeed, less than a month afterward a diarist viewing Abilene from his train window heard that

> the council of Abeline [sic] were to decide some very important
> measure, at an appointed time, the majority of whom, wishing to

[50] *Ibid.*, 58–62; Abilene *Chronicle*, May 18, 1871; Edwards, *Early Days in Abilene*, 7.
[51] Abilene *Chronicle*, May 18, 1871.
[52] *Abilene Minute Book*, 63.
[53] Abilene *Chronicle*, May 4, 1871.
[54] *Abilene Minute Book*, 64; Edwards, *Early Days in Abilene*, 7–8.
[55] Topeka *Kansas Daily Commonwealth*, May 10, 1871.
[56] *Ibid.*, May 11, 1871.
[57] Abilene *Chronicle*, May 18, 1871.

shirk their duty in regard to the question, did not put in an appearance, consequently there was not a quorum present. Wild Bill being
equal to any emergency, went out into the Gambling houses and
saloons, and carried members of the council on his back, until he
had got a quorum. . . .[58]

Such repercussion of McCoy's little joke caused the *Chronicle* to abandon its policy of circumspection regarding controversial issues. Wilson
declared total war on the mayor. Seven separate items in the May 18 edition assaulted McCoy and his policy of "high [municipal] salaries, high
taxes and high foolishness." A major item was a signed statement by
Boudinot and Carpenter describing McCoy's clumsy attempt to influence
their voting on the tavern tax. Backed by Wilson, these two subsequently
ran for their old council positions on Burroughs' low-expenditure, low-tax
platform, calling for modification of the general business tax and a $100
tavern fee. They were re-elected and, assisted by Burroughs, obtained passage of these reforms.[59] But no sooner had these measures been enacted
than the prostitution aspect of the cattle trade became a major community issue.

In the spring of 1871, the prostitutes who annually serviced the transient
Texans returned to Abilene in greater numbers than ever before. Respectable ladies of Abilene were treated politely by the Texans while visiting
the business district to do their shopping, but the brilliantly-dressed prostitutes who paraded Texas Street, often drunk, were sometimes insult-
ing.[60] To aggravate matters, a brothel was located practically next door to
the schoolhouse.[61] On May 27 a petition signed by over 100 ladies was
presented to the city council demanding that it suppress prostitution.[62]
On June 13 two new candidates were elected to council vacancies due to
new resignations. These men ran on an anti-prostitution platform, but
Editor Wilson was skeptical. "We heard of no other issue being made
than the question of allowing disreputable houses to be run in town," he
observed. "The bagnios did not stand a ghost of a chance, the vote being
almost unanimous against them." [63]

The newspaper suddenly joined the anti-prostitute campaign, however,
when Mayor McCoy, after a good deal of thought, came up with a solution of sorts to the problem. The presence of the Texans, he felt, demanded the presence of prostitutes; to expel the latter from Abilene would
serve to discourage the cattle trade. His plan was to establish a separate

[58] "Touring Kansas and Colorado in 1871: the Journal of George C. Anderson,
Part One," *Kansas Historical Quarterly*, 22:215–216 (Autumn, 1956).
[59] Abilene *Chronicle*, May 18, 25, 1871.
[60] Gross to Edwards, April 13, 1922.
[61] Stuart Henry, *Conquering Our Great American Plains* (New York, 1930),
277–278.
[62] *Abilene Minute Book*, 67; Abilene *Chronicle*, June 1, 1871.
[63] *Ibid.*, June 15, 1871.

brothel district, where prostitutes might be segregated from "respectable" Abilene but might still be available.[64] On June 16, therefore, the city council passed a resolution appointing a committee "to cause the removal from the limits of the city proper of all bawdy houses or houses of ill fame and to relocate the same upon some uninhabited portion of the City Commons." [65]

Editor Wilson furiously refused to accept this measure, and mounted a moral crusade of savage proportions against the mayor. The new district, located on the southeast outskirts of town, was branded "McCoy's Addition" by the paper, and the insinuation was made that McCoy supported Abilene vice because of his own depraved physical lusts. On July 27 the crest of the anti-McCoy assault was reached as the paper printed a letter openly charging the mayor with being a regular patron of his addition. "On last Saturday night," alleged the anonymous writer,

> he was seen there with two harlots at once on his lap, one on each knee. I suppose that in this way he is trying to carry out his plan of making houses of ill-fame "respectable." Why don't the city council have enough backbone to turn out such a worse than beastly mayor? Every respectable citizen must despise such conduct.[66]

As an old resident later testified, the establishment of McCoy's Addition "did not fully satisfy good people & some always Howled but it helped some, & matters got quieter —" [67]

Despite this antiseptic measure, Abilene was experiencing a moral upheaval resulting in a self-conscious social division of the village. This interesting phenomenon was reflected everywhere. For example, Stuart Henry, T. C.'s younger brother, remembered the grade school's two antagonistic gangs of boys. "One," he recalled, "was known as bad, the other good, in emulation of the factions trying for mastery in the town." [68] Even the physical configuration of the town reflected the division between that which was considered civilized and moral, and that which was alien and immoral. As a correspondent for the Topeka *State Record* observed at precisely this time,

> . . . Abilene is divided by the railroad into two sections. . . . The north side is literary[,] religious and commercial, and possesses our friend Wilson's *Chronicle*, the churches, the banks, and several large stores of various description; the south side of the road is the Abilene of "story and song," and posesses the large hotels, the saloons, and

[64] Gross to Edwards, April 13, 1922.

[65] *Abilene Minute Book*, 71; *Abilene Ordinance Book*, 56. The brothel district consisted of 40 acres leased by the city in Fisher's Addition to Abilene. See Roenigk, *Pioneer History*, 38.

[66] "A Citizen" in Abilene *Chronicle*, July 27, 1871.

[67] Gross to Edwards, April 13, 1922.

[68] Stuart Henry, *Conquering Our Plains*, 277.

the places where the "dealers in cardboard, bone and ivory" most do
congregate. When you are on the north side of the track you are in
Kansas, and hear sober and profitable conversation on the subject of
the weather, the price of land and the crops; when you cross to the
south side you are in Texas. . . .[69]

Even the cowboys, asserted one resident of 1871, recognized the difference
and became temporarily subdued when crossing to the north side of the
tracks to visit the post office.[70]

The citizens of the two halves of town still occasionally clashed, however, as for example when the school program was held in the community's only theater, located in "Texan" Abilene south of the tracks. The
Texans attended the program in numbers, soon became bored, and threatened to spoil it with their restless conversation until lumberman The-
ophilus Little lost his temper and roughed up a pair of them. The theater
quieted considerably after this outburst, but Little and his family had to
be escorted home afterwards by Marshal Hickok.[71]

Yet, the economic structure of the town did not conform to the moral
dichotomy. Both permanent residents and transients alike purchased quantities of hardware, clothing and groceries, and there were many "respectable" businessmen who were getting rich off the cattle trade. Thomas C.
McInerney, for example, kept 10 to 20 employees busy manufacturing
Lone Star-spangled cowboy boots which the Texans bought at fancy
prices.[72] An index of how lucrative a source this transient consumer
group had become is seen in the improvement in cowhands' wages. Driving up the trail for the first time in 1868, E. P. Byler drew only $30 per
month, experienced men in his outfit receiving an extra $10. In 1870, his
second drive, Byler drew $75 per month. Bill Jackman, an inexperienced
hand that same year, drew $100 per month.[73] The following year another
inexperienced hand earned wages of $150 per month.[74] Thus by 1871
each herd driven to Abilene brought with it several cowboys, each with
around three months' pay — perhaps $500 — burning a hole in his pocket.
Much of that money was spent in Abilene. Cowboy Lake Porter returned
to Texas after the 1871 season with a suit of clothes, a pair of new boots
and just $2.50 in his pocket to show for five months' work. Some of the
cattle-owners were even bigger spenders. John James Haynes and John
Putnam sold a herd in Abilene that year at a surprising profit. "We found

[69] Topeka *Kansas State Record*, Aug. 5, 1871. A writer in the Junction City
Weekly Union, Aug. 19, 1871, copied the observation or independently made a
similar one.
[70] Roenigk, *Pioneer History*, 38.
[71] *Dickinson Historical Sketches*, 2:130–132.
[72] Edwards, *Early Days in Abilene*, 8.
[73] Hunter, *Trail Drivers*, 779, 781, 853.
[74] John Wesley Hardin, *The Life of John Wesley Hardin* (Seguin, Texas,
1896), 34.

ourselves in possession of $8,000," recalled Haynes, "and had started out without a dollar. But any old trail driver who found himself rich in Abilene, Kansas, in 1871, knows the rest." [75]

It was hard to argue with profits. Throughout that summer the *Chronicle* brutally hammered at Joe McCoy, the father of Abilene's cattle trade, and Abilene vice, its indispensable service industry. The cattle trade as such was carefully exempted from any hint of criticism.

Beyond the outskirts of town events threatened the cattle trade more directly. The herd law's failure to pass in the April plebiscite received quick response from portions of the rural electorate favoring restrictions. In Grant Township only the pro-cattle votes of Abilene had swung the margin against the law, and the law actually carried Lamb Township, which surrounded Detroit.[76] Here angered settlers fell back on a local option substitute, an act of 1868 which provided that three-fifths of the electors in a township could require the county commissioners to impose a "night herd law" on their township. This forced drovers to keep their animals under restraint during the hours of darkness and was the next best thing to a full herd law.[77] The Grant and Lamb night herd laws were approved, and were scheduled to go into effect May 1.[78] But apparently through negotiation with certain Abilene citizens, Grant Township farmers agreed to drop the law, as did Detroit Precinct of Lamb Township.[79]

The price paid by the pro-cattle faction in Abilene for clearing these obstructions to continued prosperity was an agreement signed May 15 by representatives of a new organization, the Dickinson County Farmers' Protective Association, and an informal group of Abilene citizens. The contract defined limits within which Texas cattle were restricted that season, established a "committee of arbitration" to investigate claims by farmers who lost cattle by Spanish fever, and established a $5,000 citizens' fund out of which legitimate claims could be paid. Most important, the contract specified that the cattle trade would continue in Dickinson County after March 1, 1872, *only with the consent* of the Protective Association. Signing for Abilene were realtors T. C. Henry and C. H. Lebold, and, making it semi-official, a city councilman, G. L. Brinkman. Samuel Richards, an Abilene farm equipment dealer and president of the county agri-

[75] Hunter, *Trail Drivers*, 245, 838.

[76] *Dickinson Commissioners' Journal*, 157–159.

[77] *General Statutes of the State of Kansas*, 1868, 1001–1002.

[78] *Dickinson Commissioners' Journal*, 164, 166.

[79] The deduction that Grant Township and Detroit Precinct of Lamb Township agreed subsequently to drop their laws is made in the absence of information possibly contained in the missing April issues of the *Chronicle*. No Grant and Lamb township herd laws were published in surviving issues of the paper, but the June 8, 1871, *Chronicle* published a notice for Upper Chapman Creek Precinct of Lamb Township. At the same meeting at which Grant and Lamb citizens were granted night herd laws, citizens of Newbern Township also asked for a night herd law, but their request was denied "on account of informality in petition."

cultural society, James Bell, a prominent farmer, and a second farmer signed for the Protective Association. Henry, Abilene liveryman Ed Gaylord, and Bell were chosen as the committee of arbitration.[80]

This body commenced hearings the first week of June, and on June 13 announced that it found $4,040 in Spanish fever claims legitimate. Several prominent persons were claiming cattle losses. Among them were James Bell himself, Abilene justice of the peace E. Barber, former county probate judge Cyrus Kilgore, and county commissioner C. Kohler.[81]

The Abilene *Chronicle* hailed this voluntary arrangement as a "satisfactory" assurance "that the cattle trade will be continued at Abilene without molestation or hindrance." [82] It did not satisfy many settlers, however, perhaps because it did not cover destruction of crops by trampling. For the new upland settler, who perhaps owned few if any cattle, this was the major threat. Watson A. Cleveland, settling in north Dickinson County that spring, tried to raise a corn crop but the Texas cattle being held on vacant lands around his claim trampled it into the ground. "No fence would stop them," recalled his daughter.[83] Any momentary negligence on the part of herders invited disaster, as when cowboy George W. Saunders and his partner discovered the herd they were guarding had broken into a patch of young corn, had pawed and trampled it badly and had crushed 20 chickens to death.[84] But aggravating this was the deliberate orneriness of many Texans. When Almon C. Dixon of the Buckeye Colony intercepted a herd of longhorns approaching his claim, he requested the two cowboys in attendance to guide them around his 40-acre meadow. The cowboys advised him "to go to hell," and insolently bedded the herd down right in the meadow, causing Dixon serious loss, as hay was a valuable crop.[85]

Chapman Creek Precinct of Lamb Township, Lincoln Township (including Solomon City) and Sherman Township in the north all requested and received night herd laws to impose damages for trampling.[86] Even so, although it never broke into the columns of the *Chronicle*, the situation out in the rural uplands teetered dangerously on the brink of bloodshed that summer. For example, William S. Brewer, farming near the south border of the county attempted to head off a herd hungrily approaching his patch of sod corn. He asked the herd boss to divert them. "Oh, certainly, certainly," the Texan mumbled, riding on and paying no attention. Losing his temper, Brewer ran for a rifle, but some Mexican cowboys he had befriended luckily grasped what was about to happen and intercepted

---

[80] Abilene *Chronicle*, May 18, 25, 1871.

[81] *Ibid.*, June 15, 1871.

[82] *Ibid.*, May 18, 1871.

[83] Abilene *Reflector*, Nov. 20, 1953.

[84] Hunter, *Trail Drivers*, 436.

[85] *Dickinson Historical Sketches*, 1:60.

[86] *Dickinson Commissioners' Journal*, 175–176, 179; Abilene *Chronicle*, June 8, July 27, 1871. See also ftn. 79 above.

the cattle.[87] Elsewhere in the county, S. L. Graham had a small field of corn planted, but the Texans paid no mind either to his fencing or his requests. When he protested destruction of his corn too strongly, they threatened to burn him out. Finally, the owner of a nearby herd rode over and said he was going to kill Graham. Though unarmed, Graham moved in close as the Texan started to draw his revolver. But then the latter relented and said he would spare Graham because he was a husband and father.[88]

Much more serious was the incident at Jacob Schopp's claim. He also had a few acres of corn which were invaded and nearly destroyed one day by a herd of longhorns and Texas cow-ponies. Angered, Schopp captured two of the ponies and held them for damages. A platoon of cowboys threatened his life, but Schopp and a friend levelled at them with a carbine and cocked six-shooter and dared them to draw. The Texans finally paid Schopp $50 damages and commended his grit.[89]

The many incidents that must have taken place that summer went unpublicized. Livestock losses by disease, however, did not go without notice. "Many cattle are dying in this county with what is commonly called the Spanish fever," the *Chronicle* announced in mid-September, and the Farmers' Protective Association was called together on September 16 for the first time since spring. The topic of discussion was protection of "rights and property," apparently concerned with Spanish fever rather than trampling.[90] Elaborate preparations were subsequently made by the association, reflected in the proclamation addressed "To the Farmers, Citizens & Stock Men of Dickinson Co." —

> All who are opposed to the Texas Cattle trade, and [who] are determined to resist every effort put forth for its continuation in our county, feeling that it impedes the development of our agricultural resources, and brings nothing but taxation and crime upon us, are requested to elect delegates to meet at the court house in the city of Abilene,
>
> On Wednesday, October 25, '71
>
> At 11 o'clock in the forenoon, to take such steps as shall be deemed necessary to free our county of this nuisance.
>
> Each school district in the county will send three delegates to the county meeting. The delegates will come prepared with full reports of stock killed in their several districts by Spanish Fever.[91]

The handwriting now was on the wall for anyone to see. Mayor McCoy had already read it and entered into an agreement to design, construct and promote the Atchison, Topeka & Santa Fe Railroad stockyard at New-

---

[87] *Dickinson Historical Sketches*, 2:170.
[88] *Chapman Advertiser*, May 12, 1932.
[89] *Dickinson Historical Sketches*, 1:193.
[90] Abilene *Chronicle*, Sept. 14, 1871.
[91] *Ibid.*, Sept. 28, 1871.

ton, obviously on the assumption that this point would inherit Abilene's cattle trade should the latter reject it.[92] Many Texans stopped their herds at Newton that summer, some at least under the impression that settlers had so filled Dickinson that there was no room left for grazing there.[93]

Whether or not Newton and other more convenient points would naturally have inherited the cattle trade in 1872, the fact remains that a strong anti-cattle movement in Dickinson County threatened to expel it regardless. This movement had two distinct currents. The first was the anti-vice activity of urban Abilene; the second was the anti-cattle movement in the county at large. By the late summer of 1871 these were converging. One of the best illustrations of this was a letter to the *Chronicle* in November from "A Taxpayer" which attacked J. A. Gauthie, an Abilene councilman. Gauthie was presented as (1) in favor of the continuation of vice in Abilene, allegedly having been a patron of McCoy's Addition all summer, and (2) in favor of encouraging the Abilene cattle trade, twice that fall allegedly having led mobs to intimidate juries hearing farmers' damage suits against cattlemen.[94]

Many new rural settlers that year must have responded sympathetically to the equation of cattle with vice. The new "Iowa Colony" of immigrants, for instance, consisted mostly of members of a religious sect.[95] Another major settlement that season was that of the "Chicago Prohibition Colony," also led by a minister.[96] The only occupational group, rural or urban, with a total commitment to the cattle trade was its Abilene service industries. As time passed, the other supporters of the cattle trade had to assume the burden of being associated with the disreputable elements of the latter group. In short, the cattle trade question was becoming defined in moral as well as economic terms by almost everyone.

Yet, there continued to be a broad economic argument against the cattle trade to which all Dickinson taxpayers, whether rural or urban, could subscribe. In July, for example, a postscript to the published report of county treasurer J. B. Shane stated that but for "thousands of dollars . . . thrown away" on criminal prosecutions the county would be $6,000 ahead. As Editor Wilson commented to this, "Here is a fact for the taxpayers to ponder. — Nearly every one of the criminals was a non-resident, and only in the county for temporary purposes." [97]

Indicative of the growing momentum of the anti-cattle crusade was emergence of its leadership. T. C. Henry, J. B. Shane, and S. A. Bur-

[92] McCoy, *Historic Sketches*, 228–229; *Kansas Daily Commonwealth*, Aug. 15, 1871.

[93] Hunter, *Trail Drivers*, 785.

[94] Abilene *Chronicle*, Nov. 2, 1871.

[95] *Ibid.*, Feb. 9, 16, 1871.

[96] *Ibid.*, Feb. 16, 1871; Lawrence *Republican Daily Journal*, Feb. 21, 1871; Roenigk, *Pioneer History*, 33–34.

[97] Abilene *Chronicle*, July 27, 1871.

roughs, of the realty firm of Shane & Henry, were not prominently featured in the summer's agitation against the cattle trade, but certain clues indicate their involvement. Henry, who issued the first public demand for cattle trade abolition in 1870, was one of the negotiators of the cattle restrictions in May, 1871. At the end of July the *Chronicle* cited Henry and Shane as being among the very few to speak out publicly against local vice.[98] Shane, as county treasurer, publicized the distressing tax statistics. Burroughs by this date was practically the only city official who had not, in the words of Editor Wilson, "betrayed the confidence of the respectable people of the city." [99] At the October 25 meeting of the Farmers' Protective Association these three were openly agitating against the cattle trade. Burroughs gave the major address, an earnest denunciation of the evils resulting from the trade, and followed this with a resolution that the best way to stop it was to enforce Kansas laws already on the books. The resolution was carried. T. C. Henry then motioned that a committee of five be appointed "to prepare resolutions and present a plan of organization which shall embrace the whole county and concentrate the opposition to this trade, and make it most efficient and powerful." This carried, and Burrough was among the five appointees. Also carried was another resolution establishing a county-wide committee to gather statistics on the total cost of the cattle trade to the public of Dickinson in 1871, apparently including both Spanish fever and trampling losses. Burroughs and Henry were among the men appointed from Abilene.[100]

It was Henry, finally, who composed the terse notice to Texas cattlemen that first appeared in the *Chronicle* of February 8, 1872.[101] The product of over a year's agitation, it read as follows:

> Circular. — We the undersigned members of the Farmers' Protective Association and Officers and Citizens of Dickinson county, Kansas, most respectfully request all who have contemplated driving Texas Cattle to Abilene the coming season to seek some other point for shipment, as the inhabitants of Dickinson will no longer submit to the evils of the trade.

Following this declaration were the names of 52 Dickinson County male citizens. The first three names were those of Shane, Henry and Burroughs. The issues of February 15, February 22, and March 14 repeated the circular under the explicit headline, "TO CATTLE DROVERS." Copies were also mailed to Texas. In the final printing a total of 366 names fol-

[98] *Ibid.*

[99] *Ibid.*, Aug. 24, 1871.

[100] *Ibid.*, Nov. 2, 1871. Burroughs obviously referred to a Kansas statute of 1867 which allowed summer driving of Texas cattle only into the underpopulated southwest quarter of the state. See *Laws of Kansas*, 1867, 263–267. Needless to say, this statute was widely disregarded.

[101] "Two City Marshals," *Transactions of the Kansas State Historical Society*, 9:532 (1905–1906).

lowed those of all the county officers, the list extending an entire column of the newspaper. These were probably not all the signers, as Henry later claimed a majority of the citizens of the county added their names to the circular.[102]

A clincher to this formal discouragement of the Texas cattle trade was "An Act to provide for the regulation of the running at large of animals" by the Kansas legislature, approved February 24. This new law brusquely repealed all conflicting acts or parts thereof, and provided that "The boards of county commissioners . . . shall have power at any session after the taking effect of this act, to direct by an order what animals shall not be allowed to run at large within the bounds of their county." Neither petition nor plebiscite for this herd law was required.[103] Thus, county commissioners were given virtually dictatorial powers.

As the names of all three Dickinson commissioners were planted beneath the anti-cattle circular, there was never any doubt that a herd law was in store for Dickinson County. On March 20, in special session, the commissioners imposed a herd law and agreed to let the citizens at large ratify or reverse their action. If the majority voted against it, the law would be repealed.[104] The number of qualified voters in Dickinson in 1871 was 1,167.[105] On April 2, 1872, a total of 1,094 citizens — nearly the entire electorate — cast ballots on the herd law. The law was sustained by a vote of 780 to 314. Only the three precincts of Union Township, in the Lyon's Creek watershed in the southeast quarter of the county, reported majorities against it.[106] "The herd law," wrote a resident of that area a few years later, "was ordered in force by the board of county commissioners, much to the annoyance and against the wish of the settlers on Lyon's Creek." [107] These apparently were farmers who had successfully adjusted to the consumer market in Abilene. The rather strong pro-cattle vote on Turkey Creek and lower Chapman Creek may also reflect this. Most heavily anti-cattle were the newly-settled upland precincts like Buckeye. The three urban centers also went anti-cattle — by a somewhat slender 118 to 85 margin at Abilene, by a solid 74 to 27 at Detroit and in a landslide, 104 to one, at Solomon City. As a matter of fact, the total urban vote was almost three to one against the trade, whereas the rural total was something less than two-and-one-half to one.[108]

[102] *Ibid.* Henry probably exaggerated as to the numbers who signed the circular; however, the *Chronicle* appears to have printed only a portion of the final list, i.e., as much of it as would fill one column.

[103] *Laws of Kansas,* 1872, 384–385.

[104] *Dickinson Commissioners' Journal,* 202.

[105] Abilene *Chronicle,* April 18, 1872.

[106] *Dickinson Commissioners' Journal,* 206–214. The *Journal* mistakenly notes the victory of the herd law by a 602-vote margin.

[107] A. D. Blanchett in *Dickinson County Chronicle,* Oct. 13, 1876.

[108] *Dickinson Commissioners' Journal,* 206–214.

In conclusion, the examination of the decline and fall of Abilene as a cattle-trade center indicates that social conflict attending the trade cannot be explained merely in terms of conflicts and coalitions between broad economic groups. To impose farm or business blocs upon Abilene and vicinity in this period, for example, is manifestly incorrect because these groups were themselves divided on the issue at hand. The rural voting statistics and other surviving information suggest that recent settlers, moving into the upland cattle-grazing grounds, opposed the trade, as did certain more affluent established farmers long entrenched in the bottomlands. Also against the cattle trade were the citizens of Detroit and Solomon City, in habitual insurgency against Abilene's political and economic hegemony in Dickinson County.

Exactly how significant was the part played by leadership in the expulsion of the cattle trade? Writing a year or two after the event, Joe McCoy himself described it as paramount —

> The trade was driven away by the schemes and concerted actions of a trio of office seekers [apparently Lebold, Augustine and Wilson] . . . affiliated with certain county officers [apparently Henry, Shane and Burroughs], . . . [who] formed a ring, or clique, which, with consummate presumption, undertook to manipulate all public matters, even assuming to dictate who should and who should not have public offices, or in any manner have ought to say about matters of a public nature.

This clique, charged McCoy, published the circular to Texas cattlemen in order "to cater to certain farmers who had suffered small grievances from the presence of the cattle trade and thus secure political strength," as well as to be "bought off" by the cattle drovers.[109]

Although Stuart Henry termed his brother, T. C. Henry, as primarily responsible for the defeat of the cattle trade, the altruistic motives he assigns him should command the same skepticism as that attending McCoy's allegation of extortion.[110] The elder Henry came close to supporting McCoy's delineation of a power clique when in later years he rather cynically described his Abilene career. Wrote Henry:

> . . . I purchased quite a tract of land, adjoining the town . . . [and] became a farmer. . . . I soon "caught on," however. Within two years I captured a county office and became a real-estate broker. My two partners were both county officers, and all together, including some deputyships, we held about four-fifths of what there was of

[109] McCoy, *Historic Sketches*, 229–231.

[110] Stuart Henry, *Conquering Our Plains*, 306–307. Henry's entire description of his elder brother's activities is cloaked in romanticism. James C. Malin, *Winter Wheat in the Golden Belt of Kansas* (Lawrence, 1944), 35–36, demolishes his contention that T. C. Henry, in an heroic effort to save Dickinson County from "impending bankruptcy," covertly introduced winter wheat into Kansas.

them in sight. Having successfully organized what the envious termed "the court-house ring," we gained a second term. Meantime I was steadily adding to my land holdings. By 1872 I had bought out my partners and my competitors, gaining practically a monopoly of the real-estate business in Dickinson county.[111]

It seems clear, in short, that men with real estate interests were those who prodded, marshalled and finally led the anti-cattle movement in Dickinson County. Their final thrust was the circular to drovers early in 1872, with the simultaneous passage of new herd law provisions a coincidental but welcome finisher. Local anti-cattle sentiment, whether resultant from propaganda, individual experience, or just predisposition, was in any event sufficiently aroused to ratify the speculators' coup. Whether a crusade not blessed with these leaders could have succeeded with such spectacular dispatch is doubtful. A similar movement in nearby Ellsworth County, for example, dragged on for five traumatic years, testimony to its failure to attract sustained, dynamic leadership. In any case, Dickinson's anti-cattle crusade was more than simply a spontaneous grass-roots upsurge against entrenched social or economic evil. The cattle trade, to the bitter end, had its partisans as well as its enemies. The last days of "Texan" Abilene, therefore, are less to be understood in terms of corporate community action than in the complex politics of community conflict.*

[111] T. C. Henry, "Story of a Wheat Field," 503. The term "Court House Ring" actually came to be applied to the entire Henry-Wilson-Lebold group. See G. W. Hurd in *Dickinson County Chronicle*, Aug. 4, 1876.

* Editor's note: The author, in developing the themes presented here into a full-length treatment of the Kansas cattle towns, subsequently discovered that Abilene's moral criticism of the cattle trade had been informed by a local liquor prohibition movement of some strength — but about which Editor V. P. Wilson all but refused to comment in his newspaper. For a more complete account of the moral and economic attack on Abilene's cattle trade, which also corrects this error of omission, see Robert R. Dykstra, *The Cattle Towns* (New York, 1968), 257–263, 294–307, 382.

Some Parameters of Populism

WALTER T. K. NUGENT

Walter T. K. Nugent, a historian at Indiana University, has written widely on the late nineteenth-century Populists. In the following essay, he utilizes some of the techniques of quantitative analysis to isolate and measure the socio-economic characteristics of particular Populist groups. His purpose is to test whether their ideology truly reflected the nature of their condition. A primary reliance upon rhetoric as a clue to contemporary actuality is risky. It is a flimsy and deceptive foundation for projecting or understanding the motivation of persons or groups at a given time; indeed, historians often find rhetoric wholly unrelated to actual positions or conditions. For example, an analysis of a congressman's voting record on a particular issue can bear little relation to his speeches on the floor of Congress or in his constituency. Historians have varied widely in their approach to the Populists' motivation. Some have seen them as genuine "agrarian radicals," laboring with very real grievances against both personal and impersonal forces. Others have argued that the Populists were no more economically hard-pressed than other groups in society, but that instead they irrationally lashed out against conditions and changes that did not square with their mistaken and idyllic notions of a nation dominated by yeoman farmers. These historians see Populism as essentially a cranky and seamy episode in the history of American reform movements. Nugent's analysis is one of the first attempts to bring some measure of precision to the problem of the Populists' economic condition. To resolve this question as he suggests is to take a long step toward understanding the significant shift in political behavior by those people who became Populists in the 1890's.

Why did people become Populists? Was it chiefly for the reasons that the Populists themselves gave — that they were a victimized economic

Reprinted by permission of the author from *Agricultural History*, XL (October 1966), pp. 255–270.

class? Did Populist rhetoric about money, land, and transportation have any correspondence to actual economic conditions and events? Or were the Populists agitated because of status problems and, hence, liable to be criticized (as they since have been) as neurotic, stubbornly disdainful of reality, and a mucker group recklessly trying to upset the homely but happy applecart of American politics and society?

According to some historians, the Populists overdrew their problems. Things were grim indeed, but the violent protest reflected in Populist rhetoric had no firm base in reality. Populism was an aberration, rather than a chapter, in American liberal reform. However, other writers have maintained that here were sufficient economic grounds for Populist political protest. This study confirms the latter view and refines it at a number of points.

One hastens to admit that some of the people who jumped upon the broad bandwagon of Populism were, to put it gently, not the sort whom one would like to see in a position of high elective trust. Reform then, as before and since, had its lunatic fringe. But the mass of Populists claimed that their new allegiance resulted from certain economic facts of life. Did these problems oppress those who became Populists more than other people? To answer that question, this study focuses on the mortgage question, the easiest of the leading Populist issues to use for comparing Populists with non-Populists. In addition, it points up certain other social and economic differences and similarities between Populists and their neighbors. With these in mind, other Populist complaints (money and transportation) become more comprehensible, although the differing impact of these problems on Populists and non-Populists is difficult to discover because of source limitations.

This study utilized quantitative methods almost exclusively. When one asks whether the economic problems of which the Populists complained really existed, he may find through studying "normal," i.e., qualitative source materials, that they probably did. A skeptic's immediate rejoinder, however, is that, if these conditions affected Populists in a certain area, did they not also affect others who lived there? "Qualitative" sources leave the question begged; they can not satisfactorily show why many people, probably subject to the same conditions as the Populists, behaved so differently. Populist politicians and editors *said* they were in worse shape, but that proves nothing. A more adequate answer, if one can be found at all, may emerge by comparing the economic condition of groups of Populists to that of non-Populists, and some of their social characteristics, insofar as such things can be measured. The "null hypothesis" that socio-economic conditions and rhetoric would be unrelated and even, perhaps, contradictory was assumed at the outset, but this did not prove to be the case. Not only was this null hypothesis not borne out, but, on the contrary, political rhetoric and socio-economic conditions did appear to match.

What follows, then, is an attempt to answer the following questions. Did Populists and non-Populists, in the same time and place, differ significantly, and if so to what degree, and to what degree of certainty, in their social, economic, and cultural characteristics and conditions? If differences did exist, were they the differences implied in the political rhetoric of the time? More succinctly: were the Populists' calamity howls justified by actual conditions? If they were, then presumably these conditions related somehow to the serious shift in political behavior undertaken by most of the people who became Populists around 1890. If conditions did not support rhetoric, then some very different sort of hypothesis about why people became Populists (for example, a socio-psychological one) would be justified.

For answering these questions, the ideal comparison (because it would eliminate so many variables) would be that of a group of rank-and-file Republicans-who-became-Populists with a group of Republicans-who-remained-Republicans, in the same specific places over the same time period. The available sources were too spotty to permit this. Instead, it was possible to compare a limited number of Populists, whatever their previous political behavior, with groups of Republicans and Democrats.[1] Aside from this unavoidable impurity in the samples, it was possible to compare sizable sample groups along fairly narrow lines and smaller samples rather broadly.

I selected for comparison political groups in one Great Plains state in which Populists abounded, namely, Kansas. Two pairs of groups lent themselves to this. The first pair were Republican and Populist state legislators, members of the Kansas House elected in 1890 and the Senate elected in 1892. The second pair were candidates on the Republican, Democratic, and Populist tickets for county offices in nine Kansas counties from 1889 through 1892. These groups represented the best compromise between the typical but anonymous rank-and-file voter, on the one hand, and the thoroughly documented but atypical high official (Governor, Congressman), on the other.

Profiles of legislators came from what passed at that time for legislative

---

[1] The Republicanism of the first group prior to the emergence of the People's Party was considerable anyway, since the bulk of midwestern Populists were ex-Republicans. The statewide proportion of Republicans voting (for Secretary of State, the office best indicating party regularity, see Burton E. Lyman, "Voting Behavior of Kansas Counties 1862–1936 as Measured by Pluralities for Governor and Secretary of State" [unpublished Master's thesis, University of Kansas, 1937]) through the 1880's was between 54 per cent and 61 per cent of the total electorate. The Democrats and the leading third party, usually Greenback or Union Labor, took most of the rest. There were simply not enough Democrats and consistent third-party men to constitute wholly or even in great part the enormous Populist voting body.

blue books, whose data were apparently compiled from questionnaires filled in by the legislators themselves. Other sources, such as newspapers, added further information, but less reliably and consistently. Although the number of legislators was only 169, the sources permitted comparisons as to seven characteristics: age, birthplace, Civil War service, religious affiliation, occupation, maximum education, and previous political experience. The Populists' former party labels also emerged from the analysis.[2]

The second pair of groups, the candidates for county office, were compared according to data from two different types of sources and in two different ways. The nine counties from which they came represented about 8 per cent of the whole number of counties and, therefore, roughly the same percentage of county office candidates in the state for the period.[3] The counties were not selected by a scientific random drawing, but they should be practically equivalent to a random sample, since the universe of Kansas counties exhibiting Populist activity was not large.

Local newspapers yielded the names, and very little else, of persons who ran for county office on the three major tickets in 1889 through 1892. Duplication and other reasons eliminated a few individuals, leaving a sample of 334, which includes roughly one of every twelve candidates for county office on major party tickets in Kansas during the formative years of Kansas Populism. If the central third of the state is defined as the core area of Populism, and since eight of the nine counties lie there, the group represents about every fourth candidate from that key region plus a scattering from outside. Thus defined, the sample is about 25 per cent of the universe of county office candidates, although, as a sample of the total electorate, it is obviously quite small.[4] The first comparison of these two groups is an attempt to examine the validity of Populist complaints about mortgages. Registers of Deeds' records provided all of the real estate transactions of these 334 persons from mid-1886, before the peak of the Kansas land boom of the 1880's, to mid-1893, when the formative years of Populism and the first half of the decade-long depression were over. Only a very few actual transaction instruments were examined, since to examine them all would have been prohibitive in time and funds. Consequently, the amounts of mortgages, purchases, and other transactions were not compared. But Registers' alphabetical indexes of transactions indicated who

[2] No Senate was elected in 1890, and biographical sketches of the 1892 House apparently were not published, owing probably to the many disputed elections of that year and the subsequent "Legislative War of 1893."

[3] The counties were Atchison, in the northeastern part of the state, and Barton, Dickinson, Ellis, Ellsworth, Mitchell, Riley, Saline, and Washington, all in the north-central part.

[4] A note on deviations: Verbal and mathematical probability statements appearing in this article (in some cases not noted) amply allow for a possible sampling error of this size.

granted a deed or a mortgage, to whom it was granted, what type of legal instrument was involved (warranty, quitclaim, tax, or sheriff's deeds in cases of purchases or sales), a description of the property, and the date of the transaction.

Populist and non-Populist county office candidates were compared in a second way. Many of these people were listed in the Kansas *Census of 1885*. A search located 210 or roughly 60 per cent of the original group, who then could be compared according to age, Civil War service, occupation, birthplace, last place of residence before emigrating to Kansas, and, if they were farmers, the size, value, and land use of their resident property.

In summary, the method of this study consisted simply in comparing Populist and non-Populist state legislators and candidates for county office according to such of their social, economic, and "cultural" characteristics as were recorded in certain types of sources. The question is not whether these differences caused Populist political behavior, but whether they tallied with Populist rhetoric.

Comparisons of Populist and non-Populist state legislators according to their socio-cultural characteristics showed that here the two groups resembled each other more than they differed.[5]

In the first category of comparison, chronological age, Populists and Republicans differed very little. The average (mean) age of the 109 reporting Populists (adjusted as of 1890) was 46.63 years; the mean age of the 44 reporting Republicans (similarly adjusted) was 45.43 years. Contrary to one recent author's impression, the Populists can not be said to have been a party of old men, absolutely or relatively.

Comparisons of legislators' places of birth revealed some variations. Conclusions drawn from these figures must be somewhat tentative, but the least uncertain ones seem to be these: a Populist legislator, compared to a Republican, was more likely to have been New England-born. The Populist was considerably less likely to have been a native of New York, Pennsylvania, or one of the other Middle Atlantic states, and a little more likely to have been born in the Old Northwest, particularly in Ohio. There appears to have been an equal chance that he was from either the old or the new South, the trans-Mississippi West, or a state on the Pacific coast. He was almost twice as likely to have been born outside the United States as the non-Populist.

Service for the Union in the Civil War is the third category — an interesting one because Republican editors in the Midwest at that time were

---

[5] In the seven categories of comparison permitted by consistently available sources, nearly all of the 169 legislators reported data. Among the House members elected in 1890 and Senators elected in 1892, the five Populists and one Republican who were elected to both bodies are included only once.

still prone, in season and out, to wave the bloody shirt. Appomattox preceded the first Populist campaign by only thirty-five years, Democrats were still Copperheads to some Republicans, and the younger generation of Republicans vigorously shouted the rallying cries of the Federal cause that their father had so recently bequeathed them. Republican campaign appeals to the "old soldiers" were not inappropriate, nor were they, in many cases, insincere. What is interesting is that so many Populists may also have legitimately listened to them (and probably listened again after 1896, with better results for Republicanism), but in 1890 and for the next few years Populists ignored the familiar call. Among the legislators, about two out of seven Populists were Union veterans compared to about three out of eight Republicans. The barrenness of the bloody shirt as an issue in 1890 may underscore the seriousness of the economic situation. No one vouchsafed that he had been a Confederate.

Some differences in religious affiliation, the fourth category, did exist. The sample is not large, since about half the legislators, irrespective of party, did not report any religious affiliation at all. There is no easy way of knowing whether they were modest, embarrassed, considered it nobody's business, were afraid of their constituents, or were heathen. The data show that, of those reporting, the Populists included (in percentages) somewhat fewer Baptists, many fewer Presbyterians, more Methodists and Roman Catholics, noticeably more United Brethren, and very roughly equal numbers in other denominations. The Republicans had, perhaps, a slight status edge.

By far the most striking difference between the two party groups was in occupation. There was a decided rural-urban split. About one out of four Republicans was a merchant, manufacturer, physician, editor, loan man, or banker. Not one Populist fell into any of those categories. Another quarter of the Republicans were lawyers, compared to about one-twentieth of the Populists. Thus, half of the Republicans, compared to only a scattering of Populists, were engaged in occupations normally urban. In two occupational categories that could have been either rural or urban — skilled labor and the ministry — neither party predominated. In contrast, more than seven out of eight Populist legislators were farmers, compared to less than half the Republicans. No serious shift occurred in either party in this pattern between 1890 and 1892. Such an occupational divergence suggests that Republicans probably outstripped Populists in average net worth, although there is no certain proof of this, and it should not be strained into a contention that the Populists were a rural proletariat.

As for maximum education, the Republicans apparently had an edge, though a slim one. About two-fifths of the Populists and one-fourth of the Republicans attended or completed common schools only. An equal percentage of each group, about one-fifth, claimed an academy education. A few more Republicans, about two-sevenths of them as against one-fifth of the Populists, attended or completed college. The Republicans, somewhat more commonly, had some professional training (28 per cent against 17 per cent), but this reflects little more than the greater proportion of lawyers among the Republicans. At any rate, the image of the unlettered and bucolic Populist hurling solecisms at a waistcoated Republican of polished periods arose more from Republican editorials and speeches and perhaps also from Populists anxious to propagate a homespun, man-of-the people image, than from any very significant differences in educational achievement. Considering their heavily rural background, the Populists were reasonably well educated.

The seventh category revealed Populist legislators to have had considerably less previous political experience than their Republican counterparts. Again, it would be an exaggeration to say that the Populists were thoroughly inexperienced. Of the Republicans, 45 per cent had held county office before, and more than another fourth had been state legislators or had had even more experience (such as statewide office). In contrast, of the total number of Populists, about one out of five had had experience limited to the township level, another 15 per cent had held county office, and less than 10 per cent had held legislative seats or statewide office before. Less than half of the Populists reported political experience at some level compared to more than two-thirds of the Republicans. No doubt this is another, more obscure way of stating their heavier rural concentration.

The same body of sources that provided data for the previous comparisons also indicated, in nearly all cases, the former party affiliation of these Populists legislators. If such affiliations were a reflection of the "old party" distribution among the rank-and-file, then the composition of the People's Party did not deviate greatly from statewide political groupings of a few years earlier. The People's Party drew from all parties, somewhat according to the size of those parties. Among the legislators there were more third-party men (Greenbackers and Union Laborites), fewer Democrats, and about the same percentage of Republicans as in the state elections through the 1880's. The notable fact, in view of much that has been said and written about Midwestern Populists, is the close correspondence, not the divergence, of the legislators' former political homes to the party divisions of the years immediately preceding. This was not a party of dissidents and Democrats, but a party the majority of whom were ex-Republicans. About four out of seven of the Populist legislators had been Republicans until a short time before. About one-fifth had been Democrats and just under another one-fifth had been chronic third-party adherents. About 6 per cent classed themselves as "independents" by which they may have meant that they too were third-party men, rather than ticket-splitting or fence-sitting "independents" in the more modern sense. Not only these figures but also election returns throughout the 1880's and 1890's support the contention that Populism drew the bulk of its strength from the Republican Party. It had to, as far as voters were concerned; there were not enough of other kinds to make up the vast body of Populists. As I have stated elsewhere, such a degree of former Republicanism endowed the Populist electorate with a consistent unsteadiness, since a slackening of hard times made Republican appeals to "come back home" more attractive.

In all of these comparisons of Republican and Populist state legislators, one difference stands out markedly — rural-urban cleavage. Populists and Republicans were much alike: they were about the same age; many from each party had served the Union cause; they differed in some (but not many) respects as to their birthplaces; they went to much the same churches; they had attended or avoided schools about equally; and they shared a common culture. What distinguished them was that Populists had held political office much less often, and the great majority of them were active farmers. Whether the same social and cultural characteristics obtained among the rank-and-file mass of Populist and Republican voters, the sources do not say. It seems sensible to assume that they did.

Comparisons of Populist and non-Populist county office candidates concerned not only socio-cultural characteristics, which paralleled those just described, but also the mortgage question, about which the Populists complained mightily. Here the differences between the groups outran the similarities.

The sample was of 352 people (334 after certain eliminations [6]) who undertook a total of 1,448 bona fide, separate transactions [7] classifiable

[6] Those eliminated included women, in some counties candidates for school superintendent, whose property dealings, because of their youth or for other reasons, were nonexistent or were recorded in the name of a father or brother; persons whose names could too easily lead to confusion, such as "James Smith," or in Scandinavian areas, "A. Anderson," and the like. Excluding such people left a group of 334 persons, of whom 161 (48.20 per cent) were Republicans, 39 (11.6 per cent) were Democrats, and 134 (40.11 per cent) were Populists. The real estate transactions of these people were sought in the nine Registers of Deeds offices in their home counties, principally in the alphabetical general indexes of deeds and of mortgages, both "direct" (grantor to grantee) or "inverted" (grantee to grantor). In a few cases, actual mortgages, deeds, or other instruments were consulted; like the indexes, these are accessible public records.

[7] Certain types of transactions were arbitrarily omitted too. These included exchanges of property between two persons with the same surname, since these may have been family matters not obviously or primarily the result of general economic conditions; any transactions executed by an individual in an official as distinct from a personal capacity, such as sales recorded as sheriff's deeds by a sheriff, or tax deeds executed by a county clerk (this was of course fairly common in cases of incumbents, mostly Republicans); such instruments as bonds, bills of sale, assignments, and powers of attorney, unless the transaction involved was not other-

into four types: purchases of land; loans of money for real estate purposes; sales of land; and borrowings of money on real estate, i.e., mortgages. These transactions were recorded officially in nearly every case as warranty deeds, quitclaim deeds, and mortgages, with a sprinkling of patents and other forms of transfers. The precise acreage and dollars involved in these transactions would be very interesting and could be compiled easily if time, money, and researchers were available. Still, the indexes alone reveal that the two political groups (Populists and non-Populists) behaved quite differently.

The first difference is a rural-urban split, confirming what was already noticed among the legislators. The 334 persons may be segregated into those who had no dealings of any sort, those whose dealings were in farm land only, those who dealt only in town lots, and those who had dealings in both farm land and town lots. The Populists, compared to the Republicans, included larger percentages of people who had no dealings at all and of those who dealt in farm land only; Populists, moreover, dealt less frequently than Republicans in town lots alone or in a mixture of town and farm properties. Interestingly, the few Democrats included in the sample showed an even greater urban emphasis than the Republicans, having dealt more frequently in both town lots and farm parcels and less frequently in farm land only. With regard to urban real estate dealings, which in the mid-1880's meant involvement in the town lot boom, Democrats were the heaviest plungers (on a percentage basis), with Republicans not far behind, and Populists a distant third. Likewise, Democrats more often combined rural and urban operations than either of the other groups, with Republicans a close second, and Populists again third. To generalize a bit more broadly, it seems that the Democrats participated more than anyone else, man for man, in the land boom of the 1880's, especially the town lot part of it. Furthermore, Republicans and Democrats may have helped to create and sustain the boom in farm property in the late 1880's much more than did Populists. If these generalizations truly reflect what happened, it is quite likely that the Populists were unwilling victims, not only of the bust, but of the boom in farm property in those years. Apparently, neither boom nor bust was primarily of their making. These simple figures of rural and urban transactions leave no clue as to why this may have been so. Were the Populists less anxious to risk what capital they had, or was it that they simply had less to risk?

Both reasons probably operated. Other data, this time concerning the relative participation of the three groups in buying, loaning, selling, and borrowing, show that a lack of speculative spirit, at least as compared to

---

wise recorded; deeds to cemetery lots in all cases; and, since they would have severely complicated the data collecting, any transactions a person may have undertaken outside his home county. These probably occurred more or less frequently in cases of persons who lived near a county line.

the Republicans, seems to have played a part. Most critical is the fact that, although the involvement of Populists in mortgages was very little different from that of Democrats and Republicans, Populists dealt much less often in other ways (purchases, loans, or sales) than the others did. Populists, Democrats, and Republicans mortgaged land about equally often, man for man; if one stops comparing at this point, then, of course, the Populist complaint rings hollow. But, if one considers the Populists' total involvement in real estate transactions (which probably reflects their general financial position rather closely), they were in deep mortgage trouble compared to the adherents of the old parties.

This relative lack of involvement in other forms of transactions may also largely exonerate them from the charge of having been improvident during the boom period. Some writers, particularly contemporary ones, have suggested that, if the Populists were, in fact, in worse trouble during the bust, it was through their own negligence, since they overextended themselves during the boom. The interpretation of quantitative data is as prone to subjectivity at a juncture such as this as any other kind of data, but at least one interpretation, which these figures seem to support, is that the financial squeeze in which the Populists found themselves in 1889 and afterward not only was real, but could well be blamed on others. In short, someone else's chickens came home to roost on them.

To express a few of these relationships more precisely: the mean number of purchases per man from 1886 to 1893 was somewhat fewer for Populists than for the others. The mean number of loans made was highest by Republicans, about two-thirds as high by Populists, and half as high by Democrats. Sales of land — and perhaps this is the most interesting figure — were made by Populists about half as often as by Republicans and considerably less frequently than by Democrats. But the mean number of borrowings, i.e., mortgages, was the same for members of all three groups.

Considering purchases and loans together, Populists made those types of transactions considerably less often than Republicans and Democrats, which may indicate no more than that they had less liquid capital. When that fact is connected with the even greater difference in sales, however, it underscores the conclusion that the Populists, even though less well capitalized, hung on to their land with a greater tenacity than anyone else. If what is termed metaphorically "the yeoman farmer" means a farmer of high stability and attachment to a given piece of property, then the Populists may have indeed been more "yeoman-like" than others.

Median averages point up these differences even more sharply than mean averages, since medians minimize the distortion thrown into almost every county group by the few individuals, almost all of them Republicans, who were professional money lenders or land agents. The Populists again (man for man) bought land less frequently, loaned money for land purchases less frequently (this time, even less frequently than Democrats), and sold land much less frequently; median borrowings were about the same from group to group. Probability statements, using the chi-square method, support these mean variations.

Perhaps the best way in which the point may be made is by expressing differing ratios of combined mean purchases, loans, and sales to mean borrowing for the three groups. Purchases, loans, and (in boom times, at least) sales can be called forms of entrepreneurship in land. Mortgages are also entrepreneurial, when granted for improvement or extension of holdings. They are, however, an entrepreneurial tactic more suited to people of limited capital; of course, they may also be indicators of stress. If this is so, these ratios reveal the Populists to have been not only persons of more limited capital, but of a weaker entrepreneurial thrust as well. The combined mean of purchases, loans, and sales was much smaller for Populists than for Democrats and smaller still than for Republicans and would be much less in almost any sample, according to probability statements. But the mean of borrowings was about the same for each group. Consequently, the ratio of purchases, loans, and sales to borrowings was more than twice as high for Republicans, and nearly as high as that for Democrats, as for Populists. On the average, then, a Republican undertook slightly less than four other transactions per mortgage, while a Populist undertook less than two other transactions per mortgage. For each transaction that he made, a Populist was twice as likely to be mortgaging his land as a Republican was.

The Populist was apparently a man of lower capital and of lower speculative energy than a Republican. Although the Populists and Republicans mortgaged land about equally often, the Populist did so far more often than the Republican did, in terms of his total participation in the real estate market. Mortgage distress was not only real, but particularly severe, for the Populists.

Grouping these transactions into five chronological periods,[8] in order to determine to what extent a business cycle of some sort might have operated, brought out some further points. The first period was one of boom conditions, running from mid-1886 into the fall of 1887, at which time crop failures of that year and the results of the disastrous winter of 1886–1887 began to have effect.[9] The other four periods included the next six years and were years of bust or depression.

[8] Period I ran from July 1, 1886 to September 30, 1887 (five quarters); period II from October 1, 1887 to December 31, 1888 (five quarters); period III was the calendar year (four quarters) of 1889; period IV the calendar year 1890; period V ran from January 1, 1891 through June 30, 1893 (ten quarters).

[9] Fred A. Shannon, *The Farmers' Last Frontier* (New York: Farrar & Rinehart, Inc., 1945), 307, dates the end of the Great Plains boom in the early fall of 1887, when these crop and livestock difficulties appeared; then "the inhabitants became

The shift from boom to bust was, of course, the most pervasive business trend of the whole seven-year period. It affected all three political groups profoundly. In all counties, all four major forms of real estate transactions were frequent and heavy in 1886 and 1887, but thereafter fell off for an extended time. In several counties the deeds and mortgages executed in the two years from 1886 to 1888 (midyear to midyear) were about equivalent to all of those executed for the next dozen years or more. From the peak of the boom in 1886–1887, all forms of transactions declined precipitously until a very slight upturn occurred in 1891. The most difficult years for everyone seem to have been 1889 and (especially) 1890, also the year of the first statewide Populist campaign. Loans of money for real estate purposes were notably infrequent in 1890, but became more common therafter. The frequency of mortgages, however, steadily declined from first to last.

Since outside (mostly loan company) sources of money, together with local ones, constituted the total available supply, the sources of credit tended to dry up through the whole period. Did the demand for credit dry up as well? Here again the question of mortgage motives arises: Were the Populists simply undercapitalized or were they not interested in mortgaging? At this point, the figures leave room for the latter possibility, but support the former more strongly. Some Populists, perhaps a great many, must not have been hard hit, in the sense that their mortgages were "of the calamity class," since the rate of their purchases and lendings significantly exceeded their seven-year average only *after* the bust was well under way. Moreover, and this is surprising too, mortgaging by Populists (as a percentage of all their transactions during the period) was well above their seven-year average *before* and shortly after the bust began and noticeably below their average after the depression was well under way. Republicans and Democrats, on the contrary, did more mortgaging (as a percentage of their total transactions) after the depression started. Populist mortgages occurred more often in prosperous times, and they were probably entered into to a large extent for purposes of improvement, rather than to alleviate distress. This suggests that a lack of capital beset the Populists, both before the bust when borrowing seemed the best way to get ahead and after the bust when they were probably considered poor credit risks.

Transactions of other kinds fluctuated as well as mortgages. In terms of purchases, sales, and loans, Populists did not participate as much in the boom as the others did and were perhaps less tightly pinched and more active, in terms of their respective seven-year means, than the Republicans

---

panicky and began dumping their speculative holdings on the market." This is supported by the author's impressions of the number and kinds of land transactions undertaken in the nine counties under study.

in the ensuing depression period. Contrariwise, as just pointed out, they were more active mortgagors during the boom and early bust than the others. Populist-Republican differences were not extreme, but totals of loans indicate that local Republicans possessed or were willing to risk larger financial reserves in the months immediately following the bust, though those same people were decidedly unable or unwilling to loan money for land by 1890. Such money, incidentally, constituted a large part of the local money market; this market, therefore, may have remained fluid for some months after outside sources of capital, such as loan companies, dried up. The Populists, conversely, did very little of their more limited lending in 1888 and 1889, but were in a better position or of a better mind to do so in 1890 and thereafter.

Figures on sales tend to confirm this pattern. The Populists did less of their selling than the Republicans did of theirs up to 1891 and later. This seems to mean that some Populists held out until 1891 and then were forced to sell, while Democrats were earlier and heavier sellers. The composite pattern of buying, lending, and selling of land supports the contention that the Populists were not as well prepared as others for a long period of money stringency and reduced income. It also suggests, however, a lower degree of entrepreneurship, since they sold land less frequently during the boom and less often in the early "panicky" stages of the depression than at other times.

Relating these trends to mortgage trends, where party differences were more notable, the pieces come together as follows. Populist mortgaging was well above their seven-year average during the boom and early bust and well below it later, especially after 1890, while the Republican trend was just the opposite — below average before the bust and in its early stages and heavier as time went on. This alone may indicate that the Populists were simply poorer credit risks, had less collateral, or for other reasons were unable to dredge up the funds needed for economic survival. Purchase and sales figures also indicate that Populists had considerably less initial capital than the Republicans, but show further that Populists were better able to hang on through the early part of the depression, until bad times were three or more years old. They were probably not wealthy to begin with, borrowed (largely for improvement or expansion purposes) in 1886, 1887, and 1888, when funds were available at least from local sources, fought to survive in 1889 and 1890, and then in 1891 and afterward either succumbed or began to pull out of trouble. The Populist was less able or less willing to speculate — probably both. His real property involvement was probably with a single or a very few pieces of land, constituting his principal or sole real assets. He fought with considerable success to maintain these assets, although he was very hard pressed to do so. His economic enterprise was noticeably more precarious than the Repub-

licans', but he did not sell or mortgage his assets until absolutely necessary, with the exception that he did some mortgaging, probably for
improvement or expansion, whenever the pre-1889 money market permitted.

Many of these same people can be compared also as to their social characteristics. The same group of county office candidates sought in county
land records, originally 352 persons, were sought also in the 1885 Kansas
census.[10] Of these, 210 or 59.7 per cent were found, and of these 106
reported farm property. For a group of 106 Republicans, 20 Democrats,
and 84 Populists, the census yielded the following information.

Again, as in the case of legislators, no significant age difference existed
between Republicans and Populists: in 1885 the former averaged 39.10
years of age, the latter 40.89 years. Second, Union military service appears
to have been, for this group, slightly more common among the Populists:
20.2 per cent of the Populists as compared to 18.9 per cent of the Republicans were Federal veterans. Since this source was apparently used to
support pension claims, it should be fairly complete.

Occupational comparisons for this group revealed the same very decided rural-urban cleavage as the legislators did. Republicans included a
far greater number of merchants, manufacturers, bankers, loan agents, surveyors, and skilled laborers than did Populists. Republicans outnumbered
Populists also, but less decisively, in the categories of medicine, law, and
journalism. The two groups were about equally favored with ministers.
Again, however, farming was the main occupation of Populists, while
Republican farmers were much more scarce.

Differences in birthplace occurred for these groups, and they were usually the same differences that the comparison of legislators showed. One

10 This census consists of several hundred bound volumes of manuscript book-
lets gathered and certified by township and county officials. Although it probably
includes a considerable number of inaccuracies and omissions, it is an invaluable
(because unique) source on hundreds of thousands of people contemporaneously
recorded as to several of their more obvious social and economic characteristics.
The local assessors varied considerably as to their literacy, their penmanship, their
thoroughness, and probably also in the frequency with which they depended upon
their memories rather than actual interviews of the persons entered. Greatest
fidelity probably occurred in their entries of land holdings and land use, since
these data were related to tax assessments; accuracy was greatest where dollars
were involved. In general, a substantial, though not complete, level of confidence
may be attached to these sources. Failure of the 1885 census to mention a sizable
number of people sought for indicates, very probably, some lack of thoroughness
by the census takers, but no doubt many of the people simply had moved after the
spring of 1885, when the census was taken. It is interesting, incidentally, that the
rate of absence varied from party to party: Democrats were considerably harder to
locate than Republicans or Populists, which implies that they were less stable
residentially. The census volumes are in the Kansas State Historical Society,
Topeka.

discrepancy — New England birth — appeared between the two sets of groups compared (Populists were much more often Yankee among the legislators, Republicans more frequently Yankee among county office candidates), but the two comparisons generally matched otherwise. Among the county office candidates, Republicans edged Populists in Middle Atlantic and Old Northwest nativity. Populists, on the other hand, more frequently were natives of the upper Mississippi Valley or Missouri Valley and the Old Southwest. In these comparisons, therefore, Populists seem to have come more often from recently settled states, Republicans from older ones. As with the legislators, immigrants occurred more frequently among the Populists. The Populist tendency to include the foreign-born, less pronounced among these people than among the legislators, approached but did not quite reach statistical significance. The Republicans in this group were foreign-born in 10.9 per cent of the cases, the Populists in 17.9 per cent; the federal census of 1890 gave the percentage of foreign-born residents of Kansas as about 10.4 per cent.

Again, the Populists do not seem to have been a party of old men; they seem to have been about as active in the Civil War as Republicans had been; they were very heavily rural in contrast to the usually urban-based Republicans; their places of birth and previous out-of-state residence varied, but not according to a systematic pattern; and immigrants were more common among them.

The census included no educational or political data, but it was a unique source of comparative property-holding and land use information. Rural-urban cleavage was extremely significant statistically, confirming observations already noted. The most important fact, in the context of everything that has already been said, is that the size and value of a residential farm did not differ greatly according to the political affiliation of the man who operated it. The average acreage of a Republican farm, either mean or median, was only slightly larger than that of a Populist.[11] The assessed valuation of these farms did not vary significantly according to party affiliation, nor did the value of the equipment on them. These were the farms of residence; for Populists one would guess that they were probably their main or only properties.

If this is so, it would indicate that Populists were probably not as well capitalized as the Republicans, in terms of total net worth, but it would support a contention that the farms they operated and from which they derived the bulk of their income were competitive commercial enterprises. The safe conclusion seems to be this: the Populists may have been generally less wealthy and more sensitive to hard times, but to call them a

---

[11] At least this was so regarding the means, after one Republican sheep baron, with the very untypical holdings of 11,000 acres valued at $225,000, was omitted from the computations.

"have-not" group in relation to their neighbors would be a gross over-simplification.

The commercial uses to which these farms were put also appears in the census. The most interesting point is that both Populist and Republican land use involved a diversity of crops and stock, but principally was concerned with winter wheat, beef cattle, and corn-hog production. Some of the secondary literature on Populism gives the impression that the Populists were wheat farmers, and other people raised some other crop, probably corn. Stretched just a bit, this becomes the notion that wheat was a radical crop, corn a conservative one. The gradual westward movement after the Civil War of the wheat-growing region was matched, of course, by a gradual westward migration of agrarian radicalism. Everyone knows that Populism flourished several hundred miles to the west of the Granger strongholds of twenty years earlier. It is certainly true that Midwestern Populism was very strong in states which were the principal wheat-growing states and that it fared badly in staple corn states, e.g., far better in Kansas and Nebraska than in Iowa or Illinois. But it does not follow that Populists were wheat growers and other people corn-hog producers. Kansas was not wholly a wheat state and included many corn-hog farms, especially in the central and eastern areas of the state. It still does. This sample, in fact, included more corn-hog farms than wheat farms, and there were apparently just about as many winter wheat or beef cattle producers among Republicans as among Populists. Populists, however, more often engaged in corn-hog production. The difference does not reach statistical significance, but it is considerable. If Populists, the great majority of them farmers, were affected peculiarly by one commodity market more than Republicans were, it was apparently the corn market.

Certain speculations arise from this, and perhaps they are worth noting without trying to answer them conclusively. For example, one wonders whether the Populist farm was more diversified and, if so, whether for subsistence or commercial reasons and whether the Populist farmer was, on the average, generally slower to adopt new crops, new techniques, and new commercial possibilities. Was he slower than the Republican to convert from corn to wheat? And, to raise an earlier question, was it because of a lack of the necessary capital or of the necessary entrepreneurship? Was he hostile to new ways or unable to pay for them?

Land use figures do suggest that a Populist was commercially competitive with regard to the farm on which he lived. The size of his holding, its value, and probably even the value of his equipment and stock were about average. If Republicans weathered economic storms better and complained of them less, it was probably because of larger capitalization or net worth, not because of the general aspects of Great Plains agriculture at that time. If such statements are generally true for the country in the late nineteenth century, they not only underscore the old view that agriculture was declining relative to manufacturing as a mode of capitalist enterprise, in spite of new technology and the new cultivation of vast regions, particularly in the 1870's and 1880's, but they also suggest that the "family farm" was already in decay as an economic proposition before the end of the nineteenth century.

Before undertaking this study, it seemed to me anomalous that the Populists seemed in so many ways to resemble their Republican neighbors, yet behaved so differently as political animals. Were they like the Republicans (which would suggest that their behavior was not very rational), or were they unlike the Republicans? The only hypothesis that seemed to fit was that they were like and unlike the Republicans at the same time, but this answer obviously raised many other questions requiring somewhat refined answers. The analyses of quantitative data just described seem to support not only the idea of simultaneous similarity and dissimilarity, but to indicate where these lay.

To put it very crudely, the Populists seem to have resembled the Republicans in most major discoverable sociological ways and in some economic ways, but their economic situation was more precarious. The generalization is very rough and slurs many qualifications already indicated. Finally and generally, however, the conclusion must be that there was a realistic economic basis to the Populist land issue and, by extension, to money and transportation too, since people already harder pressed would have greater difficulty with the high freight rates and scarce currency and credit that afflicted the section at large. Populists were harder pressed. Tight conditions with regard to mortgages, farm income, and freight costs were more severely felt by those whose capital was less extensive and whose enterprise was more marginal to begin with.

Another conclusion, though a more tentative one, is this. If one defines "yeoman-like" farming as a kind that reflects a desire to own, operate, and remain on a given parcel and commercially oriented farming as characterized by greater transiency and speculativeness, then the Populists actually did lean more to the "yeoman" type. Their "yeoman myth" rhetoric was by no means self-delusive or unthinking. The Populist self-image as a yeoman farmer, to the extent that it did exist, derived from a real mirror of events, though one often cloudy and distorted, and not solely from imagination and folk tales. Perhaps it is also well to remember that "yeoman" and "commercial" agrarianism have a polarity that exists only in logic. Tension and aggression would have resulted only if the two were in psychic conflict. But the Populists were not aware of the distinction, nor subject to the psychic stress that might have resulted. To the degree that the polarity applies at all, the Populists themselves were situated at some point on a continuum between the two, nearer the yeoman end than the Republicans, and there they perched harmoniously.

Populists, then, resembled Republicans sociologically, differed from them economically, and were more "yeoman-like"; in short, they were scratching where they itched. These are the main conclusions. It should be remembered that Populist political rhetoric did not correspond perfectly, sometimes not even approximately, to economic, social, or political realities. It is impossible to measure the difference precisely; these data establish no "coefficient of inaccuracy" or "standard deviation" of rhetoric from reality. That rhetoric came from many pens and many throats. Some of it was mild, some sharp and pungent, some of it reeked. It should also be remembered that, while variations in economic conditions and to a lesser extent in social background did in fact exist, very few were black and white. Enough exceptions have already appeared to forbid one from concluding that Populists were wholly unlike Republicans economically, or wholly like them socially, or that, therefore, Populism attracted its membership entirely as a result of economic distresses affecting them in particular. Populist behavior was a chosen response to economic distress. It was not determined by this distress.

One can support with more confidence the interpretation that Populism was primarily a political response to economic trouble, both real and felt. It was not a case study in class struggle, nor a group (one hundred thousand-plus strong) of walking ideologues, nor a group of one-gallus mudsills fighting established society and the progressive trends within it, nor a group of neurotic malcontents trying to throttle their equally hard-pressed but saner neighbors. It was, instead, a momentarily very large and diverse group of people, seeking by a handy means to preserve themselves against such inimical forces in their society as were threatening, in very concrete ways, their personal arrangements and, therefore, their view of life.

American Business Interests and the Open Door in China

CHARLES S. CAMPBELL, JR.

*There are two distinct approaches to the history of American
foreign policy. Some historians focus on the ideas of policy-
makers and the intricacies of formal diplomatic exchanges.
Others, however, define foreign policy as an extension of
domestic political and economic conditions. The following
essay by Charles S. Campbell, Jr., a professor of history at
Claremont Graduate School, falls in the latter category. A
number of writers, including George Kennan, have pointed
out the fascinating interplay between Secretary of State John
Hay, W. W. Rockhill, an American diplomat, and Alfred
Hippisley, an Englishman serving in the Chinese Customs
Service, to explain the origins of the "Open Door" policy for
China. They have argued that the policy was designed to
prevent a few European nations from carving all of China
into exclusive spheres of interest, and not from an altruistic
concern for China. Campbell concentrates on the domestic
pressures, particularly the activities of key commercial groups
that sought to influence changes in official policy in order to
gain governmental support for their China ventures. He
analyzes their interests and goals, and then traces their activities, including private contacts among diplomats and public
lobbying. In sum, Campbell offers a careful case study por-
traying the operations of a special interest group in the development of foreign policy.*

One of the basic aims of American foreign policy has been to maintain the
right of all countries to trade with China on an equal basis. The first
formal declaration of this aim came with the sending of the Open Door
notes in September, 1899. The origin of these notes has received much
attention from historians in recent years, and certain aspects of their
origin, particularly the part played by W. W. Rockhill and the English-

Reprinted with the permission of the *Journal of Asian Studies* from the *Far
Eastern Quarterly*, I (1949), pp. 43–58.

man, Alfred Hippisley, have become very well known.[1] At least one aspect, however, has been entirely overlooked: namely, that special business interests in the United States were concerned over the possible loss of the Chinese market; were eager to have the government take just the sort of action which it did take; and were active in bringing pressure to bear on the government. It is the thesis of this article that they were partly responsible for the sending of the notes and, consequently, for America's Open Door policy.

It should be emphatically stated, however, that this article does not pretend to give a complete account of the origins of the Open Door policy. Not only does the author not believe that such an account can be given merely in terms of business pressure on Washington, but the article does not even consider business in general; it is limited almost exclusively to two groups of special interests, which might, indeed, be called one, so closely did they overlap. The almost complete absence of reference to many of the well-known aspects of the origin of the policy does not mean that the author considers these factors unimportant, but simply that he is confining himself to what has not been elaborated elsewhere. Numerous writers have attempted to give a rounded account of the matter; a very few have gone deeply into the part played by business; [2] but no writer has dealt specifically with the special interests here under consideration. Yet the influence of these interests appears to have been so great that any complete history of the origins of the Open Door policy should include some mention of them.

One of these special interests was the American-China Development Company, a corporation founded in 1895 for the purpose of getting railroad concessions in China.[3] Its sixty shares of stock were held by forty-nine shareholders, of whom the best known were the following: the Carnegie Steel Company; Thomas C. Platt, Senator from New York; Levi P. Morton, vice-president of the United States under President Harrison; Frederick P. Olcott, president of the Central Trust Company of New York; John I. Waterbury, president of the Manhattan Trust Company; James Stillman, president of the National City Bank; George F. Baker, president of the First National Bank of New York; Charles Coster, member of J. P. Morgan and Company; Jacob Schiff, member of Kuhn, Loeb, and Company; E. H. Harriman, chairman of the executive committee of

[1] See A. L. P. Dennis, *Adventures in American Diplomacy, 1896–1906* (New York, 1928), chap. 8; and A. Whitney Griswold, *The Far Eastern Policy of the United States* (New York, 1938), chap. 2 and the Appendix.

[2] Especially A. Vagts, *Deutschland und die Vereinigten Staaten in der Weltpolitik* (New York, 1935); and J. W. Pratt, *Expansionists of 1898; the Acquisition of Hawaii and the Spanish Islands* (Baltimore, 1936).

[3] Department of State, Miscellaneous Letters, May, 1898, part 1.

the Union Pacific Railway; and G. R. Hegeman, president of the Metropolitan Life Insurance Company. Three officials of the Development Company were also important shareholders: A. W. Bash, its representative in China; General William Barclay Parsons, its chief engineer; and Clarence Cary, its legal adviser. With seven shares of stock, Cary was the company's chief shareholder.[4]

Shortly after the formation of the American-China Development Company, Bash was sent to China to try to get a concession. In May, 1895, he called on Charles Denby, the American minister in Peking, and asked for his assistance.[5] Since Denby had for years been trying to persuade Americans to do business in China, he was anxious to do what he could for Bash; but in view of the State Department's traditional caution about supporting private business interests, he thought it prudent to ask for instructions from Washington.[6]

About this time Richard Olney became Secretary of State. As an advocate of more vigorous support for American enterprise in foreign countries than most of his predecessors, it is not surprising to find him advising Denby "to employ all proper methods for the extension of American commercial interests." [7] It was perhaps as a result of this note that Bash secured shortly afterwards a preliminary contract for a railway concession between Peking and Hankow. But Bash was not empowered to conclude the contract; it was, therefore, necessary to wait until authorized agents of the company should arrive in China. When the agents, one of whom was Clarence Cary, did arrive, they found the Chinese refusing to continue negotiations. Accordingly, they complained to Denby. The minister called on the Chinese foreign office and told the officials that it would be "a breach of good faith" not to go through with the contract. Taking a strong line, he succeeded in persuading the Chinese to resume negotiations.[8]

Meanwhile Olney had been succeeded by John Sherman, a man who did not believe in government support for such ventures as the Development Company. When the new Secretary of State read Denby's official report about the above incident, he was not pleased. "You should be cautious," he warned the minister, "in giving what might be understood as this Government's indorsement of the financial standing of the persons seeking contracts with that of China." [9] It is not wholly surprising,

---

[4] *Ibid.*, July 1899, part 2. Some of Cary's shares were held for Vanderbilt interests; similarly Stillman represented Rockefeller interests as well as his own.

[5] Vagts, *op. cit.*, vol. 2, p. 962.

[6] Denby to Gresham, May 10, 1895, *ibid.*, p. 963.

[7] Olney to Denby, Dec. 19, 1896, *Papers Relating to the Foreign Relations of the United States, 1897* (Washington, 1898), p. 56. This letter, of course, was not in response to Denby's letter to Gresham mentioned above.

[8] Denby to Olney, Jan. 10, 1897, *ibid.*, pp. 57–59.

[9] Sherman to Denby, Mar. 8, 1897, *ibid.*, pp. 59–60.

therefore, that two months later a Belgian syndicate, instead of the American-China Development Company, was awarded the contract.

Despite the turn of events the Americans continued their efforts to obtain a concession somewhere in China; but the year closed with no success to report. Did the officials and the powerful shareholders of the Development Company know of Sherman's warning to Denby? Whether they did or not, they must have found little to their liking in the negative policy of the State Department under its new Secretary; and some of them took part in the organized attempt, as will be noted in what follows, to persuade the government to adopt a different policy.

A second group of special interests was the American exporters of cotton goods. Cotton goods were America's chief export to China, and that country provided by far the largest market for American cotton mills. In 1899 this country exported $24,852,691 worth of cotton goods, of which almost half, $10,290,981, went to China alone. No other country came close to this, the second largest importer taking only about one-fourth as much.[10]

At that time England was the leading exporter of cotton goods to China, the United States was second, and far in the rear were Japan and the Netherlands. Although the annual value of the American exports was only about half that of the English, it had increased over 120 per cent from 1887 to 1897; while English exports had declined almost 14 per cent.[11] Americans attached considerable importance to this rapid growth of exports. They believed that the United States was capturing the Chinese market and that it was a market well worth acquiring. Even those with little or no business in China were impressed, for they had great hopes for the future. In those times, as still today, China was considered in wide circles to be potentially the greatest market in the world.[12]

We have, then, in the case of cotton, an American industry vitally concerned with the Chinese market. As many members of the industry were almost altogether dependent on that market, anything which the government might do to preserve it would be to their direct interest. The same, of course, was true of the American-China Development Company. The men connected with this company, along with the cotton exporters, were those who had the greatest financial interest in China, and it was they who were most active in bringing pressure to bear on the American government. Of course, business anxiety over the Chinese market was by no means limited to these two groups, but as they had so much more at stake than any other group, it would be misleading not to give them special treatment.

[10] These figures have been compiled from *Commercial Relations of the United States*, 1899, vol. 12.

[11] *Consular Reports* (Washington, 1899), vol. 59, chart following p. 560.

[12] Many statements about the future of the Chinese market can be found in business journals of the period.

The first step taken by these special interests occurred at the beginning of 1898. At that time considerable anxiety arose out of developments in China. The previous March, France had made the island of Hainan a sphere of influence; in November, German troops had landed at Kiaochow; and shortly afterwards a Russian fleet had dropped anchor at Port Arthur. It looked to many businessmen as though something which they had been fearing for several years — the partition of China — might be on the verge of realization. The threat to Port Arthur was particularly disturbing to Americans, for it was a key city of Manchuria, which, together with the adjoining provinces of China proper, was the chief market for American cotton goods. It was widely expected that, should Russia get control, discriminatory tariffs would be introduced, and an important market would be lost to the United States.[13]

Business opinion was also aroused by the attitude of the State Department. Despite what seemed to be so obviously a dangerous situation in China, responsible officials were giving no sign of alarm; in fact, they seemed almost to welcome the situation. Interviewed by the Philadelphia *Press*, Secretary Sherman stated that he did not see any likelihood of partition — at least, not for some time. Even if China should be partitioned, he said, "the powers would gladly seize the opportunity to trade with us. Our commercial interests would not suffer, as far as I can see, in the least — quite the contrary." [14]

This expression of opinion was most disturbing to those with financial interests in China. In an article which he wrote apparently just after Sherman's statement, Clarence Cary, back from his unsuccessful trip to China in behalf of the American-China Development Company, denounced what he termed the Secretary's "quaint and dangerous view that the interests of the citizens of the United States are not threatened by a possible partition of China." [15] In a similar vein, the New York *Journal of Commerce and Commercial Bulletin*, a newspaper which often expressed the point of view of many cotton exporters, spoke in a strongly worded editorial of the "generally admitted necessity of prompting the Administration to give notice to the world that the United States will suffer no interference with the commercial rights it now possesses in China." [16]

This combination of encroachment on Chinese soil and evidence of

[13] American cotton exporters had just had an object-lesson of what to expect. In 1896 Russia's ally, France, annexed the island of Madagascar and the next year introduced a tariff favoring French products. The United States had been the leading supplier of cotton to Madagascar, but after the new tariff her exports dropped from $431,688 in 1897 to $245 in 1899, while French cotton exports rose correspondingly. See *Commercial Relations*, 1900, vol. 1, p. 294.

[14] Philadelphia *Press*, Jan. 4, 1898.

[15] Clarence Cary, "China's Complications and American Trade," *Forum*, vol. 25 (1898), p. 25.

[16] *Journal of Commerce and Commercial Bulletin*, Jan. 4, 1898.

what they took to be disinterestedness on the part of the State Department so alarmed some of those with financial interests in China that they determined to take action. On January 6, 1898, three days after Sherman's statement to the *Press*, they held a meeting in the office of Clarence Cary in New York City. At the meeting a "Committee on American Interests in China" was founded. It was instructed to confer, first with the New York Chamber of Commerce, and then, if it should seem desirable, with other commercial organizations throughout the country, regarding "the methods to be adopted to conserve the rights of citizens of the United States in the Chinese Empire." [17]

There were five members of the Committee: Clarence Cary, Everett Frazer, S. D. Brewster, John Foord, and E. L. Zalinski. Cary has been mentioned before; Frazer was the head of an American firm in Shanghai; Brewster, a partner in one of the large firms handling the export of cotton to China; Foord, a contributing editor of the *Journal of Commerce and Commercial Bulletin*; and Zalinski, a member of the Bethlehem Iron Company. It should be noted that men connected both with the American-China Development Company and with the cotton interests were on the committee. The committee became the channel through which men like Cary, interested in China as a field of investment, and others, anxious to preserve a market for their cotton, could and did attempt to divert the government from the negative attitude characteristic of it while Sherman was Secretary of State. Through it they were able to organize and coordinate their efforts to bring about a new policy.

Just a week after its founding the committee submitted to the New York Chamber of Commerce a petition signed by a large number of important firms. The petition urged the chamber to take such action as would direct the attention of the government to the threatening situation in China and would ensure "that the important commercial interests of the United States" be safeguarded.[18] As a result of the petition the chamber adopted the following memorial on February 3 and forwarded it to President McKinley the same day:

> That there are important changes now going on in the relations of European powers to the Empire of China . . . affecting the privileges enjoyed under existing treaty rights by American citizens trading in and with China. That the trade of the United States to China is now rapidly increasing, and is destined, with the further opening of that country, to assume large proportions unless arbitrarily debarred by the action of foreign governments. . . . That, in view of the changes threatening to future trade development of the United States in China, the Chamber of Commerce . . . respectfully

[17] The American Asiatic Association, 1899 (unpublished pamphlet), p. 10.
[18] *Ibid.*, pp. 10–11; Chamber of Commerce of the State of New York, *Annual Report, 1897–1898*, p. 74.

and earnestly urge that such proper steps be taken as will commend themselves to your wisdom for the prompt and energetic defence of the existing treaty rights of our citizens in China, and for the preservation and protection of their important commercial interests in that Empire.[19]

Secretary Sherman, to whom the President had referred the memorial, informed the New York Chamber that the matter was being given the "most careful consideration." [20] As a matter of fact, the same day that he wrote to the chamber he instructed the ambassador in Berlin to inform the authorities in that country of "the interest which this Government must necessarily feel in conserving and expanding the volume of trade which it has built up with China." [21] If, as seems probable, this step was in part the result of the above memorial, it was the first success of the special interests in influencing the policy of the government.

During the first four months of 1898 there were several further developments which originated in the Committee on American Interests in China. The committee had communicated with the commercial organizations of Philadelphia, Boston, San Francisco, and Cleveland, as well as with that of New York, and during this period all except the Cleveland Chamber sent to Washington memorials similar to the one quoted above.[22] Not quite so directly attributable to the committee were memorials received by the government from the chambers of Commerce of Baltimore and Seattle.[23] That they were inspired, at least indirectly, by the Committee on American Interests is evident in the fact that they were almost identical in wording with the memorial from the New York Chamber. It might also be mentioned that a number of American businessmen in China sent a telegram to the New York body, endorsing its memorial and stating that "immediate action" was necessary for the protection of American interests.[24] This message was forwarded to the State Department.

[19] New York Chamber of Commerce to McKinley, Feb. 3, 1898, Miscellaneous Letters, Feb., 1898, part 1. Chamber of Commerce of the State of New York, *Annual Report, 1897–1898*, p. 75.

[20] Sherman to Orr, Feb. 11, 1898, Department of State, Domestic Letters, vol. 225, pp. 386–87.

[21] Sherman to White, Feb. 11, 1898, Instructions, Germany, vol. 20, pp. 371–73.

[22] Philadelphia Board of Trade to McKinley, Feb. 25, 1898, Miscellaneous Letters, Feb., 1898, part 3. Chamber of Commerce of San Francisco to McKinley, Mar. 8, 1898, *ibid.*, Mar., 1898, part 2. Boston Chamber of Commerce to McKinley, Mar. 30, 1898, *ibid.*

[23] Baltimore Chamber of Commerce to Sherman, Mar. 17, 1898, *ibid.* Seattle Chamber of Commerce to McKinley, Apr. 14, 1898, *ibid.*, Apr. 1898, part 2.

[24] New York Chamber of Commerce to Day, Mar. 16, 1898, *ibid.*, Mar., 1898, part 2. Apparently without any direct connection with the Committee on American Interests were similar resolutions sent to the government by the China and

The adoption of these memorials of early 1898 is doubtless to be attributed not only to the Committee on American Interests but also to events taking place in China during these same months. In February, China was forced to promise Great Britain that the rich Yangtze provinces would never be alienated to another power. This came as something of a shock to Americans, for Britain was commonly regarded as one of the bulwarks of the Open Door in China. Two months later a similar agreement regarding some of the southern provinces was made with France. Most alarming of all were the settlements with Germany and Russia in March — settlements which wound up the Kiaochow and Port Arthur affairs, the beginnings of which have been referred to. Germany succeeded in obtaining a ninety-nine-year lease of the land around Kiaochow Bay, along with extensive economic rights in Shantung province. Russia, after an acute crisis which almost led to war with Great Britain, secured a twenty-five-year lease of the southern tip of the Liaotung peninsula, with the right of building a railway to its principal city, Port Arthur. A more direct threat to the North China market could hardly have been imagined.

Despite both the ominous developments in the Far East and the memorials urging action, the State Department was not pursuing a forceful line.[25] Apart from the mild warning to Germany mentioned above, the only positive step taken during the first part of 1898 was the sending of a telegram by the Secretary of State to Ambassador Hitchcock in St. Petersburg. Hitchcock was instructed to sound out Russia's intentions and to inform the Russian government that the United States was anxious to "maintain open trade in China." [26] Although it was not at all the strong kind of move desired by the special interests, this *démarche* represented a further step in the evolution of the State Department away from the extreme indifference of Sherman earlier in the year. Together with the telegram to Germany it suggests that the memorials originating in the Committee on American Interests were having some effect in Washington.

Not only the government, but also the public in general, was becoming more conscious of the China market; and here too, part of the change must be attributed to the Committee on American Interests in China. Since the memorials inspired by it had been widely discussed in the press, they had reached a larger audience than government circles, and they had

---

Japan Trading Company and by the New England Shoe and Leather Association. See *ibid.* and Domestic Letters, vol. 227, pp. 474–75.

[25] The State Department also received a request for support from another source. On March 8, 1898, a memorandum was received from Great Britain, asking for the "co-operation of the United States in opposing action by foreign Powers which may tend to restrict freedom of commerce of all nations in China." The American government refused to commit itself. See Dennis, *op. cit.*, pp. 170–71.

[26] Sherman to Hitchcock, Mar. 16, 1898, Instructions, Russia, vol. 18.

not been without effect on public opinion. Evidence for this is to be found in an article by John Foord, stating that because of the memorials the whole question of American business interests in China "began to assume a position of national prominence." [27] As a member of the Committee on American Interests and as an editor of the *Journal of Commerce*, Foord, it would seem, was in a position to assess the situation accurately.

The war with Spain, which began in April, 1898, brought with it a rising tide of imperialistic sentiment in the United States.[28] Caught up in this tide and modified by it was the American attitude toward the complex situation in China. To be sure, there was no widespread thought of China as a possible colony, or even of a sphere-of-influence there, but, as Professor Pratt has shown,[29] the foothold which the triumph at Manila Bay gave us in the Philippines was considered by many to be important chiefly because it might help us to hold open the door in the Far East. Then too the fact that America seemed to be suddenly growing up into a great power probably had the effect of making Americans more insistent that treaty rights, including those in China, be upheld.[30]

During the war one of the most important developments in the history of the origins of the Open Door policy took place. The Committee on American Interests had come to the decision that a more permanent form of organization was needed, and to meet that need the committee was transformed in June, 1898, into the American Asiatic Association. The association had the same general aim as its predecessor. As stated in its constitution, this was "to secure the advantage of sustained watchfulness and readiness for action . . . in respect of . . . Asiatic trade, as well as in matters of legislation, or treaties affecting the same." [31] All the members of the original committee became members of the Asiatic Association, and four of them became leading officials. Everett Frazer was the president; S. D. Brewster, the vice-president; John Foord, the secretary; and Clarence Cary, a member of the executive committee.[32]

[27] John Foord, "The Genesis of the Open Door," *Asia: Journal of the American Asiatic Association*, vol. 2 (1901–1903), p. 122.

[28] For accounts of the imperialistic sentiment at the turn of the century see F. R. Dulles, *Americans in the Pacific; a Century of Expansion* (Boston and New York, 1932); Pratt, *op. cit.*; F. H. Harrington, "The Anti-Imperialist Movement in the United States, 1898–1900," *Mississippi Valley Historical Review*, vol. 22 (Sept., 1935), pp. 211–30; A. K. Weinberg, *Manifest Destiny; a Study in Nationalist Expansionism in American History* (Baltimore, 1935).

[29] Pratt, *op. cit.*, pp. 267–71.

[30] Events transpiring in China at the time also helped keep up public interest in that country. Japan secured a pledge from China not to alienate the valuable province of Fukien to any other country; Kwangchow Wan was leased to France; Kowloon and Weihaiwei were leased to Great Britain.

[31] *Asia*, vol. 1 (1898–1901), p. 45.

[32] The American Asiatic Association, 1899, *op. cit.*, p. 2.

The reader will have noticed how often the names of two of these officials, Clarence Cary and John Foord, have occurred in the above pages. Both of them were intimately associated with the campaign to influence the policy of the government. Consider the strategic position of each: Cary, counsel for the American-China Development Company and member of the executive committee of the American Asiatic Association; Foord, secretary of the Asiatic Association, editor of its magazine, *Asia*, and contributing editor of the *Journal of Commerce*. Although these men were influential only in indirect ways, it is entirely possible that they had as much to do with the sending of the September notes as had such well-known figures as W. W. Rockhill and Alfred Hippisley.

Four days after its founding the Association had just under fifty members. Among them were the General Electric Company; the Guaranty Trust Company; the New York Central and Hudson River Railroad Company; Charles Denby; W. W. Rockhill; Calvin Brice and W. D. Washburn, both officials of the American-China Development Company; and a large number of men in the cotton business.[33]

In order to reach as wide an audience as possible, the association undertook the publication of a periodical entitled *Asia: Journal of the American Asiatic Association*, the editor of which, as has been said, was John Foord. But propaganda by the association did not become particularly widespread at this time; for, like its predecessor, the association devoted its attention chiefly to the State Department.

The American Asiatic Association was the principal channel through which the special interests made their influence felt in Washington and in the country at large. It was strongly supported by the *Journal of Commerce and Commercial Bulletin*, which devoted an extraordinary amount of editorial and news space to questions of the Chinese market and consistently advocated energetic action by the government to safeguard that market. Co-operation between the association and the journal was doubtless facilitated by the fact that John Foord occupied an important position in each of these guardians of American interests in the Far East.

The founding of the Asiatic Association was the chief event concerned with the origins of the Open Door policy which took place during the war with Spain. However, a few other developments of the same time, though of comparatively minor importance, may also be mentioned.

Perhaps the outstanding of these was a recommendation to Congress by Sherman's successor in the State Department, William R. Day, that a trade commission be sent to China to investigate possibilities for greater exports to that part of the world.[34] Although Congress took no action at

---

[33] Miscellaneous Letters, June, 1898, part 2. For the complete list of members at a later date see The American Asiatic Association, 1900 (unpublished pamphlet), pp. 27–32.

[34] *House Doc.* 536, 55th Cong., 2nd Sess.

the time, the incident has some significance as marking a further step in the evolution of the government toward the point of view of the special interests.

Also of significance was the appointment of John Hay to the position of Secretary of State. In view of the memorials of the early part of the year and such a further indication of the opinion of influential business-men as the establishment of the Asiatic Association, it is quite possible that Hay's well-known propensity for the Open Door in China was one of the reasons for his appointment. Hardly had he assumed office when the new Secretary showed that his Far Eastern policy was going to be stronger than that of his two predecessors. Perhaps as a result of a memorial from one of the American establishments in China, stating that there was a "probability of serious interference [by Russia] with America's important trade in cotton . . . unless immediate steps are taken in Pekin to insist that our treaty rights with China be maintained," [35] Hay ordered two gunboats to proceed to North China. The New York Chamber of Commerce, incidentally, expressed its "high appreciation" of the act.[36] For the time being, however, nothing further came of the Russian threat.

The last event we need mention which occurred during the war was the annual message to Congress of President McKinley. Repeating Day's recommendation of a trade commission, the President stated that the United States was not an "indifferent spectator" of what was going on in China but that it would preserve its "large interests in that quarter by all means appropriate to the constant policy of our Government." [37] This strong declaration was naturally hailed with delight by those with business interests in China.

When the war with Spain formally came to an end early in 1899 with the ratification of the peace treaty by the Senate,[38] the government was able to turn its attention from military matters to such peacetime considerations as trade with China. In January it received an important memorial. Coming from a large number of cotton manufacturers, the memorial stated that the Chinese market would be lost to American cotton exporters "unless a vigorous policy is pursued on the part of the . . . Government"; it requested that the American diplomatic repre-

[35] J. S. Fearon to C. N. Bliss, Sept. 24, 1898, Miscellaneous Letters, Sept., 1898, part 2. Bliss referred the letter to the State Department.

· [36] New York Chamber of Commerce to Hay, Oct. 10, 1898, *ibid.*, Oct., 1898, part 1.

[37] *Papers Relating to the Foreign Relations of the United States, 1898* (Washington, 1901), p. lxxii.

[38] It might perhaps be more realistic to treat the war as having ended with the armistice of August 12, 1898, although the United States did not ratify the peace treaty until February 6, 1899. Nevertheless, it has seemed better to include events of the last months of 1898 in the section dealing with the war, although events of January, 1899, have not been included in it.

sentatives at Peking and St. Petersburg "be instructed to give special attention to the subject." [39] This memorial seems to have impressed Secretary Hay even more than the memorial of the preceding January had impressed Sherman. Referring to the "high character and standing of the signers," he ordered the envoys to give the "special attention" requested of them; [40] and about a month later, apparently afraid he had not been sufficiently emphatic, he wrote a second time to the ambassador to Russia, asking him to continue "to act energetically in the sense desired by the numerous and influential signers of the petition." [41]

Another episode of early 1899 worth mentioning was the Asiatic Association's strong support of a protest by the United States against an attempt by France to extend her concession in Shanghai. The association wrote to McKinley and Hay, urging that "all available means" be used "towards preserving for the world's commerce an 'open door' in the Far East." [42] In sharp contrast with this was the association's viewpoint regarding an attempt to obtain an extension of the combined British and American concession. Negotiations with China had been going on for some time but without success. Angered and alarmed, the association informed Secretary Hay of "the necessity of . . . vigorous action . . . in order to obtain a definite solution." [43] Sending a copy of this letter to the minister to China, Hay instructed him to devote his efforts to obtaining the extension.[44] Two months later China gave way.

In March the campaign for the Open Door took a more decisive turn. It became known at that time that Italy was endeavoring to secure from the Chinese government a lease of Sanmen Bay, a bay located not far from Shanghai, the center of foreign business in China. Fears of partition once again rose quickly to the surface. There was widespread suspicion that Italy had the backing of Great Britain; if true, it would mean that the only remaining great power opposed to the partition of China was the United States.

[39] To the Secretary of State, Jan. 3, 1899, Miscellaneous Letters, Jan., 1899, part 1.

[40] Hay to Pierce, Feb. 2, 1899, Instructions, Russia, vol. 18, p. 156, no. 213. Hay to Conger, Feb. 2, 1899, Instructions, China, vol. 5, p. 644, no. 126.

[41] Hay to Tower, Mar. 10, 1899, Instructions, Russia, vol. 18, pp. 171–72, no. 14.

[42] Foord to Hay, Jan. 7, 1899, Miscellaneous Letters, Jan. 1899, part 1.

[43] Foord and Brewster to Hay, Mar. 23, 1899, *ibid*., Mar., 1899.

[44] Hay to Conger, Apr. 3, 1899, Instructions, China, vol. 5, pp. 660–61, no. 155. Another episode of early 1899 which should perhaps be mentioned was the visit of Lord Charles Beresford to the United States. Beresford was a member of Parliament who was anxious to have the United States co-operate with Great Britain in maintaining the Open Door. While in America Beresford addressed the Asiatic Association and, in consequence of a petition (signed by officials of the Association among others), spoke to the New York Chamber of Commerce as well. For an account of his trip in the United States see his book, *The Break-up of China* (New York and London, 1899), chap. 29.

The situation disturbed the American Asiatic Association to an extent which might seem surprising today. Today we know that the Sanmen Bay affair turned out to be a comparatively insignificant incident. But to those who lived at the time of the crisis itself this knowledge was lacking, and to them, fearful as they were that it would take very little indeed to start off the process of dismembering China, the spring of 1899 was a time of grave anxiety. So disturbing was the situation to the officials of the Asiatic Association that they held a series of meetings in order to discuss the possibility of a fundamental modification of the policy they had been pursuing.

As has been shown, this policy was to concentrate on the Department of State. True, there had been a certain amount of propaganda directed at the public in general through the periodical, *Asia: Journal of the American Asiatic Association*, and true it is also that this propaganda had been meeting with some success. As early as January the *Journal of Commerce*, that close observer of anything pertaining to the Open Door, had pointed to the "new attitude of this country towards its commercial interests in China" and had stated that it was "partly the result of the American Asiatic Association." [45] Nevertheless, greater success had been gained with the State Department. Secretary Sherman and Secretary Day had moved closer to the viewpoint of businessmen who were eager to see the Chinese market safeguarded. John Hay had not once failed to carry out any formal request regarding Far Eastern policy, and, indeed, the department under Hay had shown itself so willing to co-operate that there could be no doubt about its desire to maintain the Open Door in China.

Because of these facts the *Journal of Commerce* and the Asiatic Association appear to have realized that pressure upon the State Department had become much less necessary than before. But this did not suggest to them that their usefulness was at an end. For although it was clear that many of the high officials in Washington were convinced that the Chinese market was of considerable value to the United States, it was equally clear that the general public was not convinced. Consequently, what had become desirable in place of so much attention to the State Department was, as the journal said, "education of the people, the press, and the politicians by those who see the vital necessity of the Chinese market" — in short, "active propaganda in the country at large." [46] The Asiatic Association, as a faithful ally of the journal, came to the same conclusion. At the series of meetings which its officials were holding it was decided to embark upon "a campaign of public education in regard to the magnitude

---

[45] *Journal of Commerce and Commercial Bulletin*, Jan. 24, 1899.

[46] *Ibid.*, Mar. 18, 1899. One wonders if John Foord, as editor of the journal, did not write these words and then, as secretary of the Asiatic Association, help launch the propaganda campaign described below.

of the commercial interests of the United States in China." [47] A committee to take charge of the campaign was appointed.

The writer has not been able to discover many details about the ensuing campaign. It is known that it was carried on in the press — the *Journal of Commerce* presumably being the chief organ — and in publications of the association itself. It is also known that by the end of 1899 the association had at its disposal a fund for propaganda purposes amounting to several thousand dollars and that among the contributors to this fund were many of the exporters of cotton goods.[48] Not much additional material, however, is available.

Did the campaign have any success in persuading the public of the importance of the market in China? No conclusive answer can be given to this question; for not only is it foolish to make too definite claims about the effects of any bit of propaganda, no matter how much one may know of its nature, but also we have here a propaganda campaign concerning which relatively little is known.

It is worth while, however, to point out that both the American Asiatic Association and the *Journal of Commerce* were convinced that their propaganda did have very considerable success. The statement of the journal in January, 1899, regarding the influence of the Asiatic Association in moulding public opinion has been mentioned above. Ten months later, in November, the propaganda of the Association had had more time to make itself felt. At that time the *Journal of Commerce* reported that "there has never been a more remarkable advance of public sentiment in this country than that which has taken place . . . in regard to the responsibilities to be faced by our Government in the Far East." [49] The journal boasted that "to the stage of public education which has been reached on this subject [the necessity of the Open Door to the United States] this journal may fairly claim to have largely contributed." [50] The vice-president of the Asiatic Association said that the work of his organization would "take its place in history as part of one of the most memorable chapters in the annals of the American people. . . . You have only to compare," he said, "the state of public sentiment which we found existing in regard to the responsibilities of our country in Eastern Asia with the feeling which exists on that subject to-day to appreciate what the influence of the Association has been." [51]

Moreover, at least one contemporary observer supported their claims.

[47] Minute-Book of the American Asiatic Association, 1898–1919, p. 17, meeting of Mar. 2, 1899; *ibid.*, p. 19, meeting of Mar. 17, 1899.

[48] For information regarding the campaign see The American Asiatic Association, 1900, *op. cit.*, p. 19. For a complete list of contributors to the propaganda fund see *Asia*, vol. 1, p. 58 and p. 108.

[49] *Journal of Commerce and Commercial Bulletin*, Nov. 11, 1899.

[50] *Ibid.*, Jan. 27, 1900.

[51] *Asia*, vol. 2, p. 5.

James S. Fearon, one of the leading exporters of cotton to China and for years chairman of the Shanghai Muncipal Council — presumably a man whose opinions regarding American relations with China are worthy of respect — stated that much of the credit for the changed attitude of the American people toward the Chinese market was due to the American Asiatic Association and to the *Journal of Commerce*.[52]

The propaganda campaign was the outstanding feature of the months just before the sending of the Open Door notes, but this period was also marked by further pressure brought to bear on the State Department by the special interests. Although they initiated no more memorials at this time, the officials of the Asiatic Association are known to have corresponded with Secretary Hay and to have called upon him frequently regarding the country's Far Eastern policy.[53]

The activity of the special interests during these months of 1899 was of such a nature as to make it extremely difficult to evaluate its significance. It is, of course, quite understandable that no records exist stating explicitly whether or not the administration was influenced by the propaganda campaign, and it is equally understandable that Secretary Hay never wrote anything which would enable us to judge whether or not his thinking was affected by the letters from the officials of the Asiatic Association and by the visits these men paid him. It is far easier to trace the effects of the memorials of 1898 than of the propaganda and informal contacts of 1899.

But it would be a great mistake to overlook the possibility that these later activities too were of considerable importance. It may well have been that the *Journal of Commerce* and the Asiatic Association were quite correct in their belief that the propaganda campaign was successful. If it was successful, if it did in fact make the public more conscious of America's stake in the Far East, it doubtless made it easier for the administration to take action designed to preserve the Chinese market. As for the letters and visits from the Asiatic Association to Hay, it is highly probable that such frequent reminders of the desires of certain businessmen had at least the effect of bolstering up the Secretary's own inclinations with respect to China. At any rate, it is clear that these activities of the special interests during the spring and summer of 1899 must have, along with the memorials of 1898, a place in any complete history of the origins of the Open Door policy.

On September 6, 1899, the first group of Open Door notes was dispatched. This was just the kind of step for which the special interests had been hoping and for which they had been working. To the cotton exporters the notes meant that their market appeared to be far more secure; [54] and

[52] *Journal of Commerce and Commercial Bulletin*, Feb. 20, 1900.

[53] *Asia*, vol. 1, p. 73.

[54] References to the cordial reception given the Open Door notes can be found in many business journals. See also the *Literary Digest*, vol. 19 (Nov., 1899),

to the American-China Development Company they meant that there was much to be hoped for from a grateful China — and, indeed, a few months later the company at last secured the contract which it had so long been seeking.[55]

The sending of these notes resulted from a great many factors, one of which was the organized attempt of certain business interests, particularly the men connected with the American China Development Company and the cotton exporters, to persuade the government to take just such a step. It has been shown how these interests, fearful lest the turn of events in China should result in financial loss to themselves, took measures designed to persuade the government to safeguard the Chinese market. First of all, they established the Committee on American Interests in China; later on, when this proved to be too weak an organization, they transformed it into the American Asiatic Association. This association, consistently supported by the *Journal of Commerce and Commercial Bulletin*, was influential in persuading the administration (and very possibly the general public as well) that a particular line of policy would be of benefit to the nation as a whole. In these facts lies part of the explanation for the formulation of America's Open Door policy.

---

p. 607; *Proceedings of the Thirtieth Annual Meeting of the National Board of Trade*, Jan., 1900, p. 290; *Proceedings of the Fifth Annual Convention of the National Association of Manufacturers of the United States of America*, Apr., 1900, pp. 113–14.

[55] See W. W. Rockhill, *Treaties and Conventions With or Concerning China and Korea, 1894–1904, Together With Various State Papers and Documents Affecting Foreign Interests* (Washington, 1904), pp. 259–77. It is interesting to come across Alfred Hippisley's remark to his friend, W. W. Rockhill: "China can hardly decline to do so [conclude the contract with the Development Company] much longer in view of what American diplomacy is doing for her" (Papers of W. W. Rockhill, Nov. 4, 1899).

The Politics of
Reform in Municipal
Government in the
Progressive Era

SAMUEL P. HAYS

*The ideology of the Progressive Era, like that of Populism, has
been an uncertain touchstone for historical analysis. In this
essay, Samuel P. Hays, a historian who has pioneered in the
application of statistical and social science techniques, devises
another test for measuring the reality of ideology. Whereas
Walter Nugent's study of Populism explored the conditions
and motives of the actors, Hays's weighs rhetoric against patterns of behavior. He tests, and finds wanting, the widespread
assumption that the Progressive Movement was middle-class
in nature, and that it sought a diffusion of power and authority. Concentrating on the politics of municipal reform,
one of the most important areas of activity during the period,
Hays seeks to understand "who distinctively were involved in
reform and why." On the basis of his findings, Hays challenges the traditional liberal interpretation of Progressivism as
essentially involving the democratization and decentralization
of political power and decision-making. The reforms usually
cited in support of this thesis — direct election of public officials, the initiative, referendum, and recall — provided at best,
Hays writes, "only an occasional and often incidental process
of decision-making." Much more significant for the period
and in the long run, were the innovations and changes that
centralized power and decision-making in the hands of smaller
groups. Hays's study thus questions the very idea of a "Progressive Era"; the "reformers" of this period were much like
any other special interest group that desired change out of
self-interest.*

In order to achieve a more complete understanding of social change in the
Progressive Era, historians must now undertake a deeper analysis of the

Reprinted by permission of the author and publisher from *Pacific Northwest
Quarterly*, LV (October 1964), pp. 157–169.

practices of economic, political, and social groups. Political ideology alone is no longer satisfactory evidence to describe social patterns because generalizations based upon it, which tend to divide political groups into the moral and the immoral, the rational and the irrational, the efficient and the inefficient, do not square with political practice. Behind this contemporary rhetoric concerning the nature of reform lay patterns of political behavior which were at variance with it. Since an extensive gap separated ideology and practice, we can no longer take the former as an accurate description of the latter, but must reconstruct social behavior from other types of evidence.

Reform in urban government provides one of the most striking examples of this problem of analysis. The demand for change in municipal affairs, whether in terms of over-all reform, such as the commission and city-manager plans, or of more piecemeal modifications, such as the development of city-wide school boards, deeply involved reform ideology. Reformers loudly proclaimed a new structure of municipal government as more moral, more rational, and more efficient and, because it was so, self-evidently more desirable. But precisely because of this emphasis, there seemed to be no need to analyze the political forces behind change. Because the goals of reform were good, its causes were obvious; rather than being the product of particular people and particular ideas in particular situations, they were deeply imbedded in the universal impulses and truths of "progress." Consequently, historians have rarely tried to determine precisely who the municipal reformers were or what they did, but instead have relied on reform ideology as an accurate description of reform practice.

The reform ideology which became the basis of historical analysis is well known. It appears in classic form in Lincoln Steffens' *Shame of the Cities*. The urban political struggle of the Progressive Era, so the argument goes, involved a conflict between public impulses for "good government" against a corrupt alliance of "machine politicians" and "special interests."

During the rapid urbanization of the late 19th century, the latter had been free to aggrandize themselves, especially through franchise grants, at the expense of the public. Their power lay primarily in their ability to manipulate the political process, by bribery and corruption, for their own ends. Against such arrangements there gradually arose a public protest, a demand by the public for honest government, for officials who would act for the public rather than for themselves. To accomplish their goals, reformers sought basic modifications in the political system, both in the structure of government and in the manner of selecting public officials. These changes, successful in city after city, enabled the "public interest" to triumph.[1]

[1] See, for example, Clifford W. Patton, *Battle for Municipal Reform* (Wash-

Recently, George Mowry, Alfred Chandler, Jr., and Richard Hofstadter have modified this analysis by emphasizing the fact that the impulse for reform did not come from the working class.[2] This might have been suspected from the rather strained efforts of National Municipal League writers in the "Era of Reform" to go out of their way to demonstrate working-class support for commission and city-manager governments.[3] We now know that they clutched at straws, and often erroneously, in order to prove to themselves as well as to the public that municipal reform was a mass movement.

The Mowry-Chandler-Hofstadter writings have further modified older views by asserting that reform in general and municipal reform in particular sprang from a distinctively middle-class movement. This has now become the prevailing view. Its popularity is surprising not only because it is based upon faulty logic and extremely limited evidence, but also because it, too, emphasizes the analysis of ideology rather than practice and fails to contribute much to the understanding of who distinctively were involved in reform and why.

Ostensibly, the "middle-class" theory of reform is based upon a new type of behavioral evidence, the collective biography, in studies by Mowry of California Progressive party leaders, by Chandler of a nationwide group of that party's leading figures, and by Hofstadter of four professions — ministers, lawyers, teachers, editors. These studies demonstrate the middle-class nature of reform, but they fail to determine if reformers were distinctively middle class, specifically if they differed from their opponents. One study of 300 political leaders in the state of Iowa, for example, discovered that Progressive party, Old Guard, and Cummins Republicans were all substantially alike, the Progressives differing only in that they were slightly younger than the others and had less political experience.[4] If its opponents were also middle class, then one cannot describe Progres-

---

ington, D.C., 1940), and Frank Mann Stewart, A *Half-Century of Municipal Reform* (Berkeley, 1950).

[2] George E. Mowry, *The California Progressives* (Berkeley and Los Angeles, 1951), 86–104; Richard Hofstadter, *The Age of Reform* (New York, 1955), 131–269; Alfred D. Chandler, Jr., "The Origins of Progressive Leadership," in Elting Morrison *et al.*, eds., *Letters of Theodore Roosevelt* (Cambridge, 1951–54), VIII, Appendix III, 1462–64.

[3] Harry A. Toulmin, *The City Manager* (New York, 1915), 156–68; Clinton R. Woodruff, *City Government by Commission* (New York, 1911), 243–53.

[4] Eli Daniel Potts, "A Comparative Study of the Leadership of Republican Factions in Iowa, 1904–1914," M.A. thesis (State University of Iowa, 1956). Another satisfactory comparative analysis is contained in William T. Kerr, Jr., "The Progressives of Washington, 1910–12," *Pacific Northwest Quarterly*, Vol. 55 (1964), 16–27.

sive reform as a phenomenon, the special nature of which can be explained in terms of middle-class characteristics. One cannot explain the distinctive behavior of people in terms of characteristics which are not distinctive to them.

Hofstadter's evidence concerning professional men fails in yet another way to determine the peculiar characteristics of reformers. For he describes ministers, lawyers, teachers, and editors without determining who within these professions became reformers and who did not. Two analytical distinctions might be made. Ministers involved in municipal reform, it appears, came not from all segments of religion, but peculiarly from upper-class churches. They enjoyed the highest prestige and salaries in the religious community and had no reason to feel a loss of "status," as Hofstadter argues. Their role in reform arose from the class character of their religious organizations rather than from the mere fact of their occupation as ministers.[5] Professional men involved in reform (many of whom — engineers, architects, and doctors — Hofstadter did not examine at all) seem to have come especially from the more advanced segments of their professions, from those who sought to apply their specialized knowledge to a wider range of public affairs.[6] Their role in reform is related not to their attempt to defend earlier patterns of culture, but to the working out of the inner dynamics of professionalization in modern society.

The weakness of the "middle-class" theory of reform stems from the fact that it rests primarily upon ideological evidence, not on a thoroughgoing description of political practice. Although the studies of Mowry, Chandler, and Hofstadter ostensibly derive from behavioral evidence, they actually derive largely from the extensive expressions of middle-ground ideological position, of the reformers' own descriptions of their contemporary society, and of their expressed fears of both the lower and the upper classes, of the fright of being ground between the millstones of labor and capital.[7]

Such evidence, though it accurately portrays what people thought, does not accurately describe what they did. The great majority of Americans look upon themselves as "middle class" and subscribe to a middle-ground ideology, even though in practice they belong to a great variety of distinct social classes. Such ideologies are not rationalizations or deliberate attempts to deceive. They are natural phenomena of human behavior. But the historian should be especially sensitive to their role so that he will not

[5] Based upon a study of eleven ministers involved in municipal reform in Pittsburgh, who represented exclusively the upper-class Presbyterian and Episcopal churches.

[6] Based upon a study of professional men involved in municipal reform in Pittsburgh, comprising eighty-three doctors, twelve architects, twenty-five educators, and thirteen engineers.

[7] See especially Mowry, *The California Progressives*.

take evidence of political ideology as an accurate representation of political practice.

In the following account I will summarize evidence in both secondary and primary works concerning the political practices in which municipal reformers were involved. Such an analysis logically can be broken down into three parts, each one corresponding to a step in the traditional argument. First, what was the source of reform? Did it lie in the general public rather than in particular groups? Was it middle class, working class, or perhaps of other composition? Second, what was the reform target of attack? Were reformers primarily interested in ousting the corrupt individual, the political or business leader who made private arrangements at the expense of the public, or were they interested in something else? Third, what political innovations did reformers bring about? Did they seek to expand popular participation in the governmental process?

There is now sufficient evidence to determine the validity of these specific elements of the more general argument. Some of it has been available for several decades; some has appeared more recently; some is presented here for the first time. All of it adds up to the conclusion that reform in municipal government involved a political development far different from what we have assumed in the past.

Available evidence indicates that the source of support for reform in municipal government did not come from the lower or middle classes, but from the upper class. The leading business groups in each city and professional men closely allied with them initiated and dominated municipal movements. Leonard White, in his study of the city manager published in 1927, wrote:

> The opposition to bad government usually comes to a head in the local chamber of commerce. Business men finally acquire the conviction that the growth of their city is being seriously impaired by the failures of city officials to perform their duties efficiently. Looking about for a remedy, they are captivated by the resemblance of the city-manager plan to their corporate form of business organization.[8]

In the 1930's White directed a number of studies of the origin of city-manager government. The resulting reports invariably begin with such statements as, "the Chamber of Commerce spearheaded the movement," or commission government in this city was a "businessmen's government."[9] Of thirty-two cases of city-manager government in Oklahoma

[8] Leonard White, The City Manager (Chicago, 1927), ix–x.
[9] Harold A. Stone et al., City Manager Government in Nine Cities (Chicago, 1940); Frederick C. Mosher et al., City Manager Government in Seven Cities (Chicago, 1940); Harold A. Stone et al., City Manager Government in the United States (Chicago, 1940). Cities covered by these studies include: Austin,

examined by Jewell C. Phillips, twenty-nine were initiated either by chambers of commerce or by community committees dominated by businessmen.[10] More recently James Weinstein has presented almost irrefutable evidence that the business community, represented largely by chambers of commerce, was the overwhelming force behind both commission and city-manager movements.[11]

Dominant elements of the business community played a prominent role in another crucial aspect of municipal reform: the Municipal Research Bureau movement.[12] Especially in the larger cities, where they had less success in shaping the structure of government, reformers established centers to conduct research in municipal affairs as a springboard for influence.

The first such organization, the Bureau of Municipal Research of New York City, was founded in 1906; it was financed largely through the efforts of Andrew Carnegie and John D. Rockefeller. An investment banker provided the crucial support in Philadelphia, where a Bureau was founded in 1908. A group of wealthy Chicagoans in 1910 established the Bureau of Public Efficiency, a research agency. John H. Patterson of the National Cash Register Company, the leading figure in Dayton municipal reform, financed the Dayton Bureau, founded in 1912. And George Eastman was the driving force behind both the Bureau of Municipal Research and city-manager government in Rochester. In smaller cities data about city government was collected by interested individuals in a more informal way or by chambers of commerce, but in larger cities the task required special support, and prominent businessmen supplied it.

The character of municipal reform is demonstrated more precisely by a brief examination of the movements in Des Moines and Pittsburgh. The Des Moines Commercial Club inaugurated and carefully controlled the drive for the commission form of government.[13] In January, 1906, the Club held a so-called "mass meeting" of business and professional men to secure an enabling act from the state legislature. P. C. Kenyon, president of the Club, selected a Committee of 300, composed principally of business and professional men, to draw up a specific proposal. After the legislature approved their plan, the same committee managed the campaign

---

Texas; Charlotte, North Carolina; Dallas, Texas; Dayton, Ohio; Fredericksburg, Virginia; Jackson, Michigan; Janesville, Wisconsin; Kingsport, Tennessee; Lynchburg, Virginia; Rochester, New York; San Diego, California.

[10] Jewell Cass Phillips, *Operation of the Council-Manager Plan of Government in Oklahoma Cities* (Philadelphia, 1935), 31–39.

[11] James Weinstein, "Organized Business and the City Commission and Manager Movements," *Journal of Southern History,* XXVIII (1962), 166–82.

[12] Norman N. Gill, *Municipal Research Bureaus* (Washington, D.C., 1944).

[13] This account of the movement for commission government in Des Moines is derived from items in the Des Moines *Register* during the years from 1905 through 1908.

which persuaded the electorate to accept the commission form of government by a narrow margin in June, 1907.

In this election the lower-income wards of the city opposed the change, the upper-income wards supported it strongly, and the middle-income wards were more evenly divided. In order to control the new government, the Committee of 300, now expanded to 530, sought to determine the nomination and election of the five new commissioners, and to this end they selected an avowedly businessman's slate. Their plans backfired when the voters swept into office a slate of anticommission candidates who now controlled the new commission government.

Proponents of the commission form of government in Des Moines spoke frequently in the name of the "people." But their more explicit statements emphasized their intent that the new plan be a "business system" of government, run by businessmen. The slate of candidates for commissioner endorsed by advocates of the plan was known as the "businessman's ticket." J. W. Hill, president of the committees of 300 and 530, bluntly declared: "The professional politician must be ousted and in his place capable business men chosen to conduct the affairs of the city." I. M. Earle, general counsel of the Bankers Life Association and a prominent figure in the movement, put the point more precisely: "When the plan was adopted it was the intention to get businessmen to run it."

Although reformers used the ideology of popular government, they in no sense meant that all segments of society should be involved equally in municipal decision-making. They meant that their concept of the city's welfare would be best achieved if the business community controlled city government. As one businessman told a labor audience, the businessman's slate represented labor "better than you do yourself."

The composition of the municipal reform movement in Pittsburgh demonstrates its upper-class and professional as well as its business sources.[14] Here the two principal reform organizations were the Civic Club and the Voters' League. The 745 members of these two organizations came primarily from the upper class. Sixty-five per cent appeared in upper-class directories which contained the names of only 2 per cent of the city's families. Furthermore, many who were not listed in these directories lived in upper-class areas. These reformers, it should be stressed, comprised not an old but a new upper class. Few came from earlier industrial and mercantile families. Most of them had risen to social position from wealth

---

[14] Biographical data constitutes the main source of evidence for this study of Pittsburgh reform leaders. It was found in city directories, social registers, directories of corporate directors, biographical compilations, reports of boards of education, settlement houses, welfare organizations, and similar types of material. Especially valuable was the clipping file maintained at the Carnegie Library of Pittsburgh.

created after 1870 in the iron, steel, electrical equipment, and other industries, and they lived in the newer rather than the older fashionable areas.

Almost half (48 per cent) of the reformers were professional men: doctors, lawyers, ministers, directors of libraries and museums, engineers, architects, private and public school teachers, and college professors. Some of these belonged to the upper class as well, especially the lawyers, ministers, and private school teachers. But for the most part their interest in reform stemmed from the inherent dynamics of their professions rather than from their class connections. They came from the more advanced segments of their organizations, from those in the forefront of the acquisition and application of knowledge. They were not the older professional men, seeking to preserve the past against change; they were in the vanguard of professional life, actively seeking to apply expertise more widely to public affairs.

Pittsburgh reformers included a large segment of businessmen; 52 per cent were bankers and corporation officials or their wives. Among them were the presidents of fourteen large banks and officials of Westinghouse, Pittsburgh Plate Glass, U.S. Steel and its component parts (such as Carnegie Steel, American Bridge, and National Tube), Jones and Laughlin, lesser steel companies (such as Crucible, Pittsburgh, Superior, Lockhart, and H. K. Porter), the H. J. Heinz Company, and the Pittsburgh Coal Company, as well as officials of the Pennsylvania Railroad and the Pittsburgh and Lake Erie. These men were not small businessmen; they directed the most powerful banking and industrial organizations of the city. They represented not the old business community, but industries which had developed and grown primarily within the past fifty years and which had come to dominate the city's economic life.

These business, professional, and upper-class groups who dominated municipal reform movements were all involved in the rationalization and systematization of modern life; they wished a reform of government which would be more consistent with the objectives inherent in those developments. The most important single feature of their perspective was the rapid expansion of the geographical scope of affairs which they wished to influence and manipulate, a scope which was no longer limited and narrow, no longer within the confines of pedestrian communities, but was now broad and city-wide, covering the whole range of activities of the metropolitan area.

The migration of the upper class from central to outlying areas created a geograhical distance between its residential communities and its economic institutions. To protect the latter required involvement both in local ward affairs and in the larger city government as well. Moreover, upper-class cultural institutions, such as museums, libraries, and symphony orchestras, required an active interest in the larger municipal context from which these institutions drew much of their clientele.

Professional groups, broadening the scope of affairs which they sought to study, measure, or manipulate, also sought to influence the public health, the educational system, or the physical arrangements of the entire city. Their concerns were limitless, not bounded by geography, but as expansive as the professional imagination. Finally, the new industrial community greatly broadened its perspective in governmental affairs because of its recognition of the way in which factors throughout the city affected business growth. The increasing size and scope of industry, the greater stake in more varied and geographically dispersed facets of city life, the effect of floods on many business concerns, the need to promote traffic flows to and from work for both blue-collar and managerial employees — all contributed to this larger interest. The geographically larger private perspectives of upper-class, professional, and business groups gave rise to a geographically larger public perspective.

These reformers were dissatisfied with existing systems of municipal government. They did not oppose corruption per se — although there was plenty of that. They objected to the structure of government which enabled local and particularistic interests to dominate. Prior to the reforms of the Progressive Era, city government consisted primarily of confederations of local wards, each of which was represented on the city's legislative body. Each ward frequently had its own elementary schools and ward-elected school boards which administered them.

These particularistic interests were the focus of a decentralized political life. City councilmen were local leaders. They spoke for their local areas, the economic interests of their inhabitants, their residential concerns, their educational, recreational, and religious interests — i.e., for those aspects of community life which mattered most to those they represented. They rolled logs in the city council to provide streets, sewers, and other public works for their local areas. They defended the community's cultural practices, its distinctive languages or national customs, its liberal attitude toward liquor, and its saloons and dance halls which served as centers of community life. One observer described this process of representation in Seattle:

> The residents of the hill-tops and the suburbs may not fully appreciate the faithfulness of certain downtown ward councilmen to the interests of their constituents. . . . The people of a state would rise in arms against a senator or representative in Congress who deliberately misrepresented their wishes and imperilled their interests, though he might plead a higher regard for national good. Yet people in other parts of the city seem to forget that under the old system the ward

elected councilmen with the idea of procuring service of special benefit to that ward.[15]

In short, pre-reform officials spoke for their constituencies, inevitably their own wards which had elected them, rather than for other sections or groups of the city.

The ward system of government especially gave representation in city affairs to lower- and middle-class groups. Most elected ward officials were from these groups, and they, in turn, constituted the major opposition to reforms in municipal government. In Pittsburgh, for example, immediately prior to the changes in both the city council and the school board in 1911 in which city-wide representation replaced ward representation, only 24 per cent of the 387 members of those bodies represented the same managerial, professional, and banker occupations which dominated the membership of the Civic Club and the Voters' League. The great majority (67 per cent) were small businessmen — grocers, saloonkeepers, livery-stable proprietors, owners of small hotels, druggists — white-collar workers such as clerks and bookkeepers, and skilled and unskilled workmen.[16]

This decentralized system of urban growth and the institutions which arose from it reformers now opposed. Social, professional, and economic life had developed not only in the local wards in a small community context, but also on a larger scale had become highly integrated and organized, giving rise to a superstructure of social organization which lay far above that of ward life and which was sharply divorced from it in both personal contacts and perspective.

By the late 19th century, those involved in these larger institutions found that the decentralized system of political life limited their larger objectives. The movement for reform in municipal government, therefore, constituted an attempt by upper-class, advanced professional, and large business groups to take formal political power from the previously dominant lower- and middle-class elements so that they might advance their own conceptions of desirable public policy. These two groups came from entirely different urban worlds, and the political system fashioned by one was no longer acceptable to the other.

Lower- and middle-class groups not only dominated the pre-reform governments, but vigorously opposed reform. It is significant that none of the occupational groups among them, for example, small businessmen or white-collar workers, skilled or unskilled artisans, had important representation in reform organizations thus far examined. The case studies of city-manager government undertaken in the 1930's under the direction of

[15] *Town Crier* (Seattle), Feb. 18, 1911, p. 13.
[16] Information derived from same sources as cited in footnote 14.

Leonard White detailed in city after city the particular opposition of labor. In their analysis of Jackson, Michigan, the authors of these studies wrote:

> The *Square Deal*, oldest Labor paper in the state, has been consistently against manager government, perhaps largely because labor has felt that with a decentralized government elected on a ward basis it was more likely to have some voice and to receive its share of privileges.[17]

In Janesville, Wisconsin, the small shopkeepers and workingmen on the west and south sides, heavily Catholic and often Irish, opposed the commission plan in 1911 and in 1912 and the city-manager plan when adopted in 1923.[18] "In Dallas there is hardly a trace of class consciousness in the Marxian sense," one investigator declared, "yet in city elections the division has been to a great extent along class lines." [19] The commission and city-manager elections were no exceptions. To these authors it seemed a logical reaction, rather than an embarrassing fact that had to be swept away, that workingmen should have opposed municipal reform.[20]

In Des Moines working-class representatives, who in previous years might have been council members, were conspicuously absent from the "businessman's slate." Workingmen acceptable to reformers could not be found. A workingman's slate of candidates, therefore, appeared to challenge the reform slate. Organized labor, and especially the mineworkers, took the lead; one of their number, Wesley Ash, a deputy sheriff and union member, made "an astonishing run" in the primary, coming in second among a field of more than twenty candidates.[21] In fact, the strength of anticommission candidates in the primary so alarmed reformers that they frantically sought to appease labor.

The day before the final election they modified their platform to pledge both an eight-hour day and an "American standard of wages." They attempted to persuade the voters that their slate consisted of men who represented labor because they had "begun at the bottom of the ladder and made a good climb toward success by their own unaided efforts." [22] But their tactics failed. In the election on March 30, 1908, voters swept into office the entire "opposition" slate. The business and professional community had succeeded in changing the form of government, but not in securing its control. A cartoon in the leading reform newspaper illustrated their

---

[17] Stone *et al.*, *Nine Cities*, 212.

[18] *Ibid.*, 3–13.

[19] *Ibid.*, 329.

[20] Stone *et al.*, *City Manager Government*, 26, 237–41, for analysis of opposition to city-manager government.

[21] Des Moines *Register and Leader*, March 17, 1908.

[22] *Ibid.*, March 30, March 28, 1908.

disappointment; John Q. Public sat dejectedly and muttered, "Aw, What's the Use?"

The most visible opposition to reform and the most readily available target of reform attack was the so-called "machine," for through the "machine" many different ward communities as well as lower- and middle-income groups joined effectively to influence the central city government. Their private occupational and social life did not naturally involve these groups in larger city-wide activities in the same way as the upper class was involved; hence they lacked access to privately organized economic and social power on which they could construct political power. The "machine" filled this organizational gap.

Yet it should never be forgotten that the social and economic institutions in the wards themselves provided the "machine's" sustaining support and gave it larger significance. When reformers attacked the "machine" as the most visible institutional element of the ward system, they attacked the entire ward form of political organization and the political power of lower- and middle-income groups which lay behind it.

Reformers often gave the impression that they opposed merely the corrupt politician and his "machine." But in a more fundamental way they looked upon the deficiencies of pre-reform political leaders in terms not of their personal shortcomings, but of the limitations inherent in their occupational, institutional, and class positions. In 1911 the Voters' League of Pittsburgh wrote in its pamphlet analyzing the qualifications of candidates that "a man's occupation ought to give a strong indication of his qualifications for membership on a school board." [23] Certain occupations inherently disqualified a man from serving:

> Employment as ordinary laborer and in the lowest class of mill work would naturally lead to the conclusion that such men did not have sufficient education or business training to act as school directors. . . . Objection might also be made to small shopkeepers, clerks, workmen at many trades, who by lack of educational advantages and business training, could not, no matter how honest, be expected to administer properly the affairs of an educational system, requiring special knowledge, and where millions are spent each year.

These, of course, were precisely the groups which did dominate Pittsburgh government prior to reform. The League deplored the fact that school boards contained only a small number of "men prominent throughout the city in business life . . . in professional occupations . . . holding positions as managers, secretaries, auditors, superintendents and foremen" and exhorted these classes to participate more actively as candidates for office.

[23] Voters' Civil League of Allegheny County, "Bulletin of the Voters' Civic League of Allegheny County Concerning the Public School System of Pittsburgh," Feb. 14, 1911, pp. 2–3.

Reformers, therefore, wished not simply to replace bad men with good; they proposed to change the occupational and class origins of decision-makers. Toward this end they sought innovations in the formal machinery of government which would concentrate political power by sharply centralizing the processes of decision-making rather than distribute it through more popular participation in public affairs. According to the liberal view of the Progressive Era, the major political innovations of reform involved the equalization of political power through the primary, the direct election of public officials, and the initiative, referendum, and recall. These measures played a large role in the political ideology of the time and were frequently incorporated into new municipal charters. But they provided at best only an occasional and often incidental process of decision-making. Far more important in continuous, sustained, day-to-day processes of government were those innovations which centralized decision-making in the hands of fewer and fewer people.

The systematization of municipal government took place on both the executive and the legislative levels. The strong-mayor and city-manager types became the most widely used examples of the former. In the first decade of the 20th century, the commission plan had considerable appeal, but its distribution of administrative responsibility among five people gave rise to a demand for a form with more centralized executive power; consequently, the city-manager or the commission-manager variant often replaced it.[24]

A far more pervasive and significant change, however, lay in the centralization of the system of representation, the shift from ward to city-wide election of councils and school boards. Governing bodies so selected, reformers argued, would give less attention to local and particularistic matters and more to affairs of city-wide scope. This shift, an invariable feature of both commission and city-manager plans, was often adopted by itself. In Pittsburgh, for example, the new charter of 1911 provided as the major innovation that a council of twenty-seven, each member elected from a separate ward, be replaced by a council of nine, each elected by the city as a whole.

Cities displayed wide variations in this innovation. Some regrouped wards into larger units but kept the principle of areas of representation smaller than the entire city. Some combined a majority of councilmen elected by wards with additional ones elected at large. All such innovations, however, constituted steps toward the centralization of the system of representation.

[24] In the decade 1911 to 1920, 43 per cent of the municipal charters adopted in eleven home-rule states involved the commission form and 35 per cent the city-manager form; in the following decade the figures stood at 6 per cent and 71 per cent respectively. The adoption of city-manager charters reached a peak in the years 1918 through 1923 and declined sharply after 1933. See Leonard D. White, "The Future of Public Administration," *Public Management*, XV (1933), 12.

Liberal historians have not appreciated the extent to which municipal reform in the Progressive Era involved a debate over the system of representation. The ward form of representation was universally condemned on the grounds that it gave too much influence to the separate units and not enough attention to the larger problems of the city. Harry A. Toulmin, whose book, *The City Manager*, was published by the National Municipal League, stated the case:

> The spirit of sectionalism had dominated the political life of every city. Ward pitted against ward, alderman against alderman, and legislation only effected by "log-rolling" extravagant measures into operation, mulcting the city, but gratifying the greed of constituents, has too long stung the conscience of decent citizenship. This constant treaty-making of factionalism has been no less than a curse. The city manager plan proposes the commendable thing of abolishing wards. The plan is not unique in this for it has been common to many forms of commission government. . . .[25]

Such a system should be supplanted, the argument usually went, with city-wide representation in which elected officials could consider the city "as a unit." "The new officers are elected," wrote Toulmin, "each to represent all the people. Their duties are so defined that they must administer the corporate business in its entirety, not as a hodge-podge of associated localities."

Behind the debate over the method of representation, however, lay a debate over who should be represented, over whose views of public policy should prevail. Many reform leaders often explicitly, if not implicitly, expressed fear that lower- and middle-income groups had too much influence in decision-making. One Galveston leader, for example, complained about the movement for initiative, referendum, and recall:

> We have in our city a very large number of negroes employed on the docks; we also have a very large number of unskilled white laborers; this city also has more barrooms, according to its population, than any other city in Texas. Under these circumstances it would be extremely difficult to maintain a satisfactory city government where all ordinances must be submitted back to the voters of the city for their ratification and approval.[26]

[25] Toulmin, *The City Manager*, 42.
[26] Woodruff, *City Government*, 315. The Galveston commission plan did not contain provisions for the initiative, referendum, or recall, and Galveston commercial groups which had fathered the commission plan opposed movements to include them. In 1911 Governor Colquitt of Texas vetoed a charter bill for Texarkana because it contained such provisions; he maintained that they were "undemocratic" and unnecesasry to the success of commission government. *Ibid.*, 314–15.

At the National Municipal League convention of 1907, Rear Admiral F. E. Chadwick (USN Ret.), a leader in the Newport, Rhode Island, movement for municipal reform, spoke to this question even more directly:

> Our present system has excluded in large degree the representation of those who have the city's well-being most at heart. It has brought, in municipalities . . . a government established by the least educated, the least interested class of citizens.
>
> It stands to reason that a man paying $5,000 taxes in a town is more interested in the well-being and development of his town than the man who pays no taxes. . . . It equally stands to reason that the man of the $5,000 tax should be assured a representation in the committee which lays the tax and spends the money which he contributes. . . . Shall we be truly democratic and give the property owner a fair show or shall we develop a tyranny of ignorance which shall crush him.[27]

Municipal reformers thus debated frequently the question of who should be represented as well as the question of what method of representation should be employed.

That these two questions were intimately connected was revealed in other reform proposals for representation, proposals which were rarely taken seriously. One suggestion was that a class system of representation be substituted for ward representation. For example, in 1908 one of the prominent candidates for commissioner in Des Moines proposed that the city council be composed of representatives of five classes: educational and ministerial organizations, manufacturers and jobbers, public utility corporations, retail merchants including liquor men, and the Des Moines Trades and Labor Assembly. Such a system would have greatly reduced the influence in the council of both middle- and lower-class groups. The proposal revealed the basic problem confronting business and professional leaders: how to reduce the influence in government of the majority of voters among middle- and lower-income groups.[28]

A growing imbalance between population and representation sharpened the desire of reformers to change from ward to city-wide elections. Despite shifts in population within most cities, neither ward district lines nor the apportionment of city council and school board seats changed frequently. Consequently, older areas of the city, with wards that were small in geographical size and held declining populations (usually lower and middle class in composition), continued to be overrepresented, and newer upper-class areas, where population was growing, became increasingly underrepresented. This intensified the reformers' conviction that the structure

[27] *Ibid.*, 207–208.
[28] Des Moines *Register and Leader*, Jan. 15, 1908.

of government must be changed to give them the voice they needed to
make their views on public policy prevail.[29]

It is not insignificant that in some cities (by no means a majority)
municipal reform came about outside of the urban electoral process. The
original commission government in Galveston was appointed rather than
elected. "The failure of previous attempts to secure an efficient city government through the local electorate made the business men of Galveston
willing to put the conduct of the city's affairs in the hands of a commission dominated by state-appointed officials." [30] Only in 1903 did the
courts force Galveston to elect the members of the commission, an innovation which one writer described as "an abandonment of the commission idea," and which led to the decline of the influence of the business
community in the commission government.[31]

In 1911 Pittsburgh voters were not permitted to approve either the
new city charter or the new school board plan, both of which provided
for city-wide representation; they were a result of state legislative enactment. The governor appointed the first members of the new city council,
but thereafter they were elected. The judges of the court of common
pleas, however, and not the voters, selected members of the new school
board.

The composition of the new city council and new school board in
Pittsburgh, both of which were inaugurated in 1911, revealed the degree
to which the shift from ward to city-wide representation produced a
change in group representation.[32] Members of the upper class, the advanced professional men, and the large business groups dominated both.
Of the fifteen members of the Pittsburgh Board of Education appointed
in 1911 and the nine members of the new city council, none were small
businessmen or white-collar workers. Each body contained only one person who could remotely be classified as a blue-collar worker; each of these
men filled a position specifically but unofficially designed as reserved for a
"representative of labor," and each was an official of the Amalgamated
Association of Iron, Steel, and Tin Workers. Six of the nine members of
the new city council were prominent businessmen, and all six were listed
in upper-class directories. Two others were doctors closely associated with
the upper class in both professional and social life. The fifteen members
of the Board of Education included ten businessmen with city-wide interests, one doctor associated with the upper class, and three women previously active in upper-class public welfare.

29 Voters' Civic League of Allegheny County, "Report on the Voters' League
in the Redistricting of the Wards of the City of Pittsburgh" (Pittsburgh, n.d.).
30 Horace E. Deming, "The Government of American Cities," in Woodruff,
City Government, 167.
31 *Ibid.*, 168.
32 Information derived from same sources as cited in footnote 14.

Lower- and middle-class elements felt that the new city governments did not represent them.[33] The studies carried out under the direction of Leonard White contain numerous expressions of the way in which the change in the structure of government produced not only a change in the geographical scope of representation, but also in the groups represented. "It is not the policies of the manager or the council they oppose," one researcher declared, "as much as the lack of representation for their economic level and social groups." [34] And another wrote:

> There had been nothing unapproachable about the old ward alder-men. Every voter had a neighbor on the common council who was interested in serving him. The new councilmen, however, made an unfavorable impression on the less well-to-do voters. . . . Election at large made a change that, however desirable in other ways, left the voters in the poorer wards with a feeling that they had been deprived of their share of political importance.[35]

The success of the drive for centralization of administration and representation varied with the size of the city. In the smaller cities, business, professional, and elite groups could easily exercise a dominant influence. Their close ties readily enabled them to shape informal political power which they could transform into formal political power. After the mid-1890's the widespread organization of chambers of commerce provided a base for political action to reform municipal government, resulting in a host of small-city commission and city-manager innovations. In the larger, more heterogeneous cities, whose sub-communities were more dispersed, such community-wide action was extremely difficult. Few commission or city-manager proposals materialized here. Mayors became stronger, and steps were taken toward centralization of representation, but the ward system or some modified version usually persisted. Reformers in large cities often had to rest content with their Municipal Research Bureaus through which they could exert political influence from outside the municipal government.

A central element in the analysis of municipal reform in the Progressive Era is governmental corruption. Should it be understood in moral or political terms? Was it a product of evil men or of particular socio-political circumstances? Reform historians have adopted the former view. Selfish and evil men arose to take advantage of a political arrangement whereby

[33] W. R. Hopkins, city manager of Cleveland, indicated the degree to which the new type of government was more responsive to the business community: "It is undoubtedly easier for a city manager to insist upon acting in accordance with the business interests of the city than it is for a mayor to do the same thing." Quoted in White, *The City Manager*, 13.

[34] Stone *et al.*, *Nine Cities*, 20.

[35] *Ibid.*, 225.

unsystematic government offered many opportunities for personal gain at public expense. The system thrived until the "better elements," "men of intelligence and civic responsibility," or "right-thinking people" ousted the culprits and fashioned a political force which produced decisions in the "public interest." In this scheme of things, corruption in public affairs grew out of individual personal failings and a deficient governmental structure which could not hold those predispositions in check, rather than from the peculiar nature of social forces. The contestants involved were morally defined: evil men who must be driven from power, and good men who must be activated politically to secure control of municipal affairs.

Public corruption, however, involves political even more than moral considerations. It arises more out of the particular distribution of political power than of personal morality. For corruption is a device to exercise control and influence outside the legal channels of decision-making when those channels are not readily responsive. Most generally, corruption stems from an inconsistency between control of the instruments of formal governmental power and the exercise of informal influence in the community. If powerful groups are denied access to formal power in legitimate ways, they seek access through procedures which the community considers illegitimate. Corrupt government, therefore, does not reflect the genius of evil men, but rather the lack of acceptable means for those who exercise power in the private community to wield the same influence in governmental affairs. It can be understood in the Progressive Era not simply by the preponderance of evil men over good, but by the peculiar nature of the distribution of political power.

The political corruption of the "Era of Reform" arose from the inaccessibility of municipal government to those who were rising in power and influence. Municipal government in the United States developed in the 19th century within a context of universal manhood suffrage which decentralized political control. Because all men, whatever their economic, social, or cultural conditions, could vote, leaders who reflected a wide variety of community interests and who represented the views of people of every circumstance arose to guide and direct municipal affairs. Since the majority of urban voters were workingmen or immigrants, the views of those groups carried great and often decisive weight in governmental affairs. Thus, as Herbert Gutman has shown, during strikes in the 1870's city officials were usually friendly to workingmen and refused to use police power to protect strikebreakers.[36]

Ward representation on city councils was an integral part of grass-roots influence, for it enabled diverse urban communities, invariably identified

[36] Herbert Gutman, "An Iron Workers' Strike in the Ohio Valley, 1873–74," *Ohio Historical Quarterly*, LXVIII (1959), 353–70; "Trouble on the Railroads, 1873–1874: Prelude to the 1877 Crisis," *Labor History*, II (Spring, 1961), 215–36.

with particular geographical areas of the city, to express their views more clearly through councilmen peculiarly receptive to their concerns. There was a direct, reciprocal flow of power between wards and the center of city affairs in which voters felt a relatively close connection with public matters and city leaders gave special attention to their needs.

Within this political system the community's business leaders grew in influence and power as industrialism advanced, only to find that their economic position did not readily admit them to the formal machinery of government. Thus, during strikes, they had to rely on either their own private police, Pinkertons, or the state militia to enforce their use of strikebreakers. They frequently found that city officials did not accept their views of what was best for the city and what direction municipal policies should take. They had developed a common outlook, closely related to their economic activities, that the city's economic expansion should become the prime concern of municipal government, and yet they found that this view had to compete with even more influential views of public policy. They found that political tendencies which arose from universal manhood suffrage and ward representation were not always friendly to their political conceptions and goals and had produced a political system over which they had little control, despite the fact that their economic ventures were the core of the city's prosperity and the hope for future urban growth.

Under such circumstances, businessmen sought other methods of influencing municipal affairs. They did not restrict themselves to the channels of popular election and representation, but frequently applied direct influence — if not verbal persuasion, then bribery and corruption. Thereby arose the graft which Lincoln Steffens recounted in his *Shame of the Cities*. Utilities were only the largest of those business groups and individuals who requested special favors, and the franchises they sought were only the most sensational of the prizes which included such items as favorable tax assessments and rates, the vacating of streets wanted for factory expansion, or permission to operate amid antiliquor and other laws regulating personal behavior. The relationships between business and formal government became a maze of accommodations, a set of political arrangements which grew up because effective power had few legitimate means of accomplishing its ends.

Steffens and subsequent liberal historians, however, misread the significance of these arrangements, emphasizing their personal rather than their more fundamental institutional elements. To them corruption involved personal arrangements between powerful business leaders and powerful "machine" politicians. Just as they did not fully appreciate the significance of the search for political influence by the rising business community as a whole, so they did not see fully the role of the "ward politician." They stressed the argument that the political leader manipulated voters to his own personal ends, that he used constituents rather than reflected their views.

A different approach is now taking root, namely, that the urban political organization was an integral part of community life, expressing its needs and its goals. As Oscar Handlin has said, for example, the "machine" not only fulfilled specific wants, but provided one of the few avenues to success and public recognition available to the immigrant.[37] The political leader's arrangements with businessmen, therefore, were not simply personal agreements between conniving individuals; they were far-reaching accommodations between powerful sets of institutions in industrial America.

These accommodations, however, proved to be burdensome and unsatisfactory to the business community and to the upper third of socioeconomic groups in general. They were expensive; they were wasteful; they were uncertain. Toward the end of the 19th century, therefore, business and professional men sought more direct control over municipal government in order to exercise political influence more effectively. They realized their goals in the early 20th century in the new commission and city-manager forms of government and in the shift from ward to city-wide representation.

These innovations did not always accomplish the objectives that the business community desired because other forces could and often did adjust to the change in governmental structure and reëstablish their influence. But businessmen hoped that reform would enable them to increase their political power, and most frequently it did. In most cases the innovations which were introduced between 1901, when Galveston adopted a commission form of government, and the Great Depression, and especially the city-manager form which reached a height of popularity in the mid-1920's, served as vehicles whereby business and professional leaders moved directly into the inner circles of government, brought into one political system their own power and the formal machinery of government, and dominated municipal affairs for two decades.

Municipal reform in the early 20th century involves a paradox: the ideology of an extension of political control and the practice of its concentration. While reformers maintained that their movement rested on a wave of popular demands, called their gatherings of business and professional leaders "mass meetings," described their reforms as "part of a world-wide trend toward popular government," and proclaimed an ideology of a popular upheaval against a selfish few, they were in practice shaping the structure of municipal government so that political power would no longer be broadly distributed, but would in fact be more centralized in the hands of a relatively small segment of the population. The paradox became even sharper when new city charters included provisions for the initiative,

37 Oscar Handlin, *The Uprooted* (Boston, 1951), 209–17.

referendum, and recall. How does the historian cope with this paradox? Does it represent deliberate deception or simply political strategy? Or does it reflect a phenomenon which should be understood rather than explained away?

The expansion of popular involvement in decision-making was frequently a political tactic, not a political system to be established permanently, but a device to secure immediate political victory. The prohibitionist advocacy of the referendum, one of the most extensive sources of support for such a measure, came from the belief that the referendum would provide the opportunity to outlaw liquor more rapidly. The Anti-Saloon League, therefore, urged local option. But the League was not consistent. Towns which were wet, when faced with a county-wide local-option decision to outlaw liquor, demanded town or township local option to reinstate it. The League objected to this as not the proper application of the referendum idea.

Again, "Progressive" reformers often espoused the direct primary when fighting for nominations for their candidates within the party, but once in control they often became cool to it because it might result in their own defeat. By the same token, many municipal reformers attached the initiative, referendum, and recall to municipal charters often as a device to appease voters who opposed the centralization of representation and executive authority. But, by requiring a high percentage of voters to sign petitions — often 25 to 30 per cent — these innovations could be and were rendered relatively harmless.

More fundamentally, however, the distinction between ideology and practice in municipal reform arose from the different roles which each played. The ideology of democratization of decision-making was negative rather than positive; it served as an instrument of attack against the existing political system rather than as a guide to alternative action. Those who wished to destroy the "machine" and to eliminate party competition in local government widely utilized the theory that these political instruments thwarted public impulses, and thereby shaped the tone of their attack.

But there is little evidence that the ideology represented a faith in a purely democratic system of decision-making or that reformers actually wished, in practice, to substitute direct democracy as a continuing system of sustained decision-making in place of the old. It was used to destroy the political institutions of the lower and middle classes and the political power which those institutions gave rise to, rather than to provide a clear-cut guide for alternative action.[38]

[38] Clinton Rodgers Woodruff of the National Municipal League even argued that the initiative, referendum, and recall were rarely used. "Their value lies in their existence rather than in their use." Woodruff, *City Government*, 314. It seems apparent that the most widely used of these devices, the referendum, was

The guide to alternative action lay in the model of the business enterprise. In describing new conditions which they wished to create, reformers drew on the analogy of the "efficient business enterprise," criticizing current practices with the argument that "no business could conduct its affairs that way and remain in business," and calling upon business practices as the guides to improvement. As one student remarked:

> The folklore of the business elite came by gradual transition to be the symbols of governmental reformers. Efficiency, system, orderliness, budgets, economy, saving, were all injected into the efforts of reformers who sought to remodel municipal government in terms of the great impersonality of corporate enterprise.[39]

Clinton Rodgers Woodruff of the National Muncipal League explained that the commission form was "a simple, direct, businesslike way of administering the business affairs of the city . . . an application to city administration of that type of business organization which has been so common and so successful in the field of commerce and industry." [40] The centralization of decision-making which developed in the business corporation was now applied in municipal reform.

The model of the efficient business enterprise, then, rather than the New England town meeting, provided the positive inspiration for the municipal reformer. In giving concrete shape to this model in the strong-mayor, commission, and city-manager plans, reformers engaged in the elaboration of the processes of rationalization and systematization inherent in modern science and technology. For in many areas of society, industrialization brought a gradual shift upward in the location of decision-making and the geographical extension of the scope of the area affected by decisions.

Experts in business, in government, and in the professions measured, studied, analyzed, and manipulated ever wider realms of human life, and devices which they used to control such affairs constituted the most fundamental and far-reaching innovations in decision-making in modern America, whether in formal government or in the informal exercise of power in private life. Reformers in the Progressive Era played a major role in shaping this new system. While they expressed an ideology of restoring a previous order, they in fact helped to bring forth a system drastically new.[41]

---

popularized by legislative bodies when they could not agree or did not want to take responsibility for a decision and sought to pass that responsibility to the general public, rather than because of a faith in the wisdom of popular will.

[39] J. B. Shannon, "County Consolidation," *Annals of the American Academy of Political and Social Science,* Vol. 207 (January, 1940), 168.

[40] Woodruff, *City Government,* 29–30.

[41] Several recent studies emphasize various aspects of this movement. See, for example, Loren Baritz, *Servants of Power* (Middletown, 1960); Raymond E.

The drama of reform lay in the competition for supremacy between two systems of decision-making. One system, based upon ward representation and growing out of the practices and ideas of representative government, involved wide latitude for the expression of grass-roots impulses and their involvement in the political process. The other grew out of the rationalization of life which came with science and technology, in which decisions arose from expert analysis and flowed from fewer and smaller centers outward to the rest of society. Those who espoused the former looked with fear upon the loss of influence which the latter involved, and those who espoused the latter looked only with disdain upon the wastefulness and inefficiency of the former.

The Progressive Era witnessed rapid strides toward a more centralized system and a relative decline for a more decentralized system. This development constituted an accommodation of forces outside the business community to the political trends within business and professional life rather than vice versa. It involved a tendency for the decision-making processes inherent in science and technology to prevail over those inherent in representative government.

Reformers in the Progressive Era and liberal historians since then misread the nature of the movement to change municipal government because they concentrated upon dramatic and sensational episodes and ignored the analysis of more fundamental political structure, of the persistent relationships of influence and power which grew out of the community's social, ideological, economic, and cultural activities. The reconstruction of these patterns of human relationships and of the changes in them is the historian's most crucial task, for they constitute the central context of historical development. History consists not of erratic and spasmodic fluctuations, of a series of random thoughts and actions, but of patterns of activity and change in which people hold thoughts and actions in common and in which there are close connections between sequences of events. These contexts give rise to a structure of human relationships which pervade all areas of life; for the political historian the most important of these is the structure of the distribution of power and influence.

The structure of political relationships, however, cannot be adequately understood if we concentrate on evidence concerning ideology rather than practice. For it is becoming increasingly clear that ideological evidence is no safe guide to the understanding of practice, that what people thought and said about their society is not necessarily an accurate representation of what they did. The current task of the historian of the Progressive Era is to quit taking the reformers' own description of political practice at its

Callahan, *Education and the Cult of Efficiency* (Chicago, 1962); Samuel P. Hays, *Conservation and the Gospel of Efficiency* (Cambridge, 1959); Dwight Waldo, *The Administrative State* (New York, 1948), 3–61.

face value and to utilize a wide variety of new types of evidence to reconstruct political practice in its own terms. This is not to argue that ideology is either important or unimportant. It is merely to state that ideological evidence is not appropriate to the discovery of the nature of political practice.

Only by maintaining this clear distinction can the historian successfully investigate the structure of political life in the Progressive Era. And only then can he begin to cope with the most fundamental problem of all: the relationship between political ideology and political practice. For each of these facets of political life must be understood in its own terms, through its own historical record. Each involves a distinct set of historical phenomena. The relationship between them for the Progressive Era is not now clear; it has not been investigated. But it cannot be explored until the conceptual distinction is made clear and evidence tapped which is pertinent to each. Because the nature of political practice has so long been distorted by the use of ideological evidence, the most pressing task is for its investigation through new types of evidence appropriate to it. The reconstruction of the movement for municipal reform can constitute a major step forward toward that goal.

Law and Social Change in the Progressive Era: The Law of Industrial Accidents

LAWRENCE M. FRIEDMAN
AND JACK LADINSKY

Hays's essay examines the relationship between political reform and social change. The following study, written by a law professor and a sociologist respectively, aims at clarifying the concept of social change and linking its relationship to the role of law. While their essay is a detailed case study of the development of the workmen's compensation system, their concepts, drawn from the legal and sociological disciplines, are useful for tracing the impact of social change upon law and legal institutions. In addition, Friedman and Ladinsky shed more light on the character of reform in the early twentieth century. The abolition of the "fellow-servant" rule for industrial accidents was hardly a triumph of "progressive" over "reactionary" forces, of labor over capital, of good over evil. Such judgments of behavior, they properly note, generally amount to "premature moral assessments." These are labels that historians (and others) often are quick to apply; but they are "based on perceptions of conditions, [and are] not terms referring to conditions themselves." Changes in the law of industrial accidents, like most reforms, occurred when the existing situation proved intolerable to divergent, affected groups. Legal change, then, is usually conditioned by "group bargains" on terms satisfactory to most parties.

Sociologists recognize, in a general way, the essential role of legal institutions in the social order.[1] They concede, as well, the responsiveness of law to social change and have made important explorations of the interrelations involved.[2] Nevertheless, the role law plays in initiating — or reflecting — social change has never been fully explicated, either in theory or through research. The evolution of American industrial accident law from tort principles to compensation systems is an appropriate subject for a case-study on this subject. It is a topic that has been carefully treated by legal scholars,[3] and it is also recognized by sociologists to be a significant instance of social change.[4] This essay, using concepts drawn from both legal and sociological disciplines, aims at clarifying the concept of social change and illustrating its relationship to change in the law.

I. The Concept of Social Change

Social change has been defined as "any nonrepetitive alteration in the established modes of behavior in . . . society." [5] Social change is change

Reprinted by permission of the authors and publisher from *Columbia Law Review*, LXVII (January 1967), pp. 50–82, with a change of title and minor revisions approved by the authors.

[1] See, e.g., T. Parsons, *Structure and Process in Modern Society*, 190–92 (1960).

[2] See, e.g., J. Willard Hurst, *Law and Social Process in United States History* (1960).

[3] See generally C. Auerbach, L. Garrison, W. Hurst and S. Mermin, *The Legal Process* (1961) [hereinafter cited as Auerbach].

[4] See, e.g., W. Ogburn, *Social Change With Respect to Culture and Original Nature*, 213–36 (Viking ed. 1950).

[5] R. Freedman, A. Hawley, W. Landecker and H. Miner, *Principles of Sociology*, 312 (1st ed. 1952) [hereinafter cited as Freedman].

in the way people relate to each other, not change in values or in technology. Major alterations in values or technology will, of course, almost invariably be followed by changes in social relations — but they are not in themselves social change. Thus, although the change from tort law to workmen's compensation presupposed a high level of technology and certain attitudes toward the life and health of factory workers, it was not in itself a change in values or technology but in the patterning of behavior.

Social change may be revolutionary, but it normally comes about in a more-or-less orderly manner, out of the conscious and unconscious attempts of people to solve social problems through collective action. It is purposive and rational; although social actions have unanticipated consequences and often arise out of unconscious motivations, nonetheless social change at the conscious level involves definition of a state of affairs as a "problem" and an attempt to solve that problem by the rational use of effective means. The *problem* defined collectively in this instance was the number of injuries caused to workmen by trains, mine hazards, and factory machinery. It is clear that the number of accidents increased over the course of the century, but it is not self-evident that this objective fact necessarily gave rise to a correspondent subjective sense of a problem that had to be solved in a particular way. To understand the process of social change, one must know how and why that subjective sense evolved. This requires knowledge of how and why various segments of society perceived situations — whether they identified and defined a set of facts or a state of affairs as raising or not raising problems.[6] It also requires an understanding of what were considered appropriate and rational means for solving that problem. The perspective of a particular period, in turn, sets limits to the way a people collectively defines problems and the means available for their solution.[7]

This essay deals with behavior at the societal level. At that level, social change necessarily means changes in powers, duties, and rights; it will normally be reflected both in custom and law, in formal authority relations and informal ones. In mature societies, law will be an important indicator of social change; it is institutional cause and institutional effect at the same time, and a part of the broader pattern of collective perceptions and behavior in the resolution of social problems. The essay will therefore also deal with the way in which legal systems respond to their society — the social impact on law, modified and monitored by the institutional habits of the legal system.

In legal terms, this is the story of the rise and fall of a *rule*, the fellow-

[6] A "collective problem solving" approach to the study of social change is set forth in detail by Guy E. Swanson, in Freedman, 554–621.

[7] Thus, for example, the problem of sickness and feebleness of the aged can be "solved" by euthanasia, prayer, medicare, socialized medicine, or left alone — depending on the society.

servant rule, as the legal system's operating mechanism for allocating (or refusing to allocate) compensation for industrial injuries. It is an exploration of how the rule originated, how it changed, how and when it was overthrown.

II. Development of the Law of Industrial Accidents

A. *Background of the Fellow-Servant Rule*. At the dawn of the industrial revolution, the common law of torts afforded a remedy, as it still does, for those who had suffered injuries at the hands of others. If a man injured another by direct action — by striking him, or slandering him, or by trespassing on his property — the victim could sue for his damages. Similarly, the victim of certain kinds of negligent behavior had a remedy at law. But tort law was not highly developed. Negligence in particular did not loom large in the reports and it was not prominently discussed in books of theory or practice.[8] Indeed, no treatise on tort law appeared in America until Francis Hilliard's in 1859;[9] the first English treatise came out in 1860.[10] By this time, the field was rapidly developing. A third edition of Hilliard's book was published in 1866, only seven years after the first edition. The explosive growth of tort law was directly related to the rapidity of industrial development. The staple source of tort litigation was and is the impact of machines — railroad engines, then factory machines, then automobiles — on the human body. During the industrial revolution, the size of the factory labor force increased, the use of machinery in the production of goods became more widespread, and such accidents were inevitably more frequent. In Hilliard's pioneer treatise, railroads already played a major role in tort litigation — a role which he ascribed to their "great multiplication and constant activity; their necessary inter-

---

[8] Blackstone's *Commentaries* has virtually no discussion of negligence. In early 19th-century America, tort law (and particularly the law of negligence) remained fairly obscure. Dane's *Abridgment* — an eight-volume compendium of British and American law — has a short, miscellaneous chapter on negligence: cases "which cannot be brought conveniently under more particular heads." 3 N. Dane, *A General Abridgment and Digest of American Law*, 31 (1824). These include some commercial and maritime instances ("If the owner of a ship, in the care of a pilot, through *negligence* and want of skill, sinks the ship of another, this owner is liable," *id*. at 35); and some cases of negligence in the practice of a trade or profession ("if a register of deeds neglects to record a deed as he ought to do, this action lies against him for his negligence," *id*. at 32). Under this latter heading comes one of the very few examples of personal injury — a doctor's negligent practice of his art. *Id*. at 32. (Another example had to do with the negligent owner of a dog or other animal, *id*. at 33.) But, in general, personal injury cases are rare in Dane; and the shadow of the industrial revolution has not yet fallen on this corner of the law.

[9] F. Hilliard, *The Law of Torts* (1st ed. 1859); see C. Warren, *History of the American Bar*, 450 (1911).

[10] C. Addison, *Wrongs and Their Remedies* (1st ed. 1860).

ference, in the act of construction, with the rights of property . . . the large number and various offices of their agents and servants; and the dangers, many of them of an entirely novel character, incident to their mode of operation. . . ." [11]

In theory, at least, recovery for industrial accidents might have been assimilated into the existing system of tort law. The fundamental principles were broad and simple. If a factory worker was injured through the negligence of another person — including his employer — an action for damages would lie. Although as a practical matter, servants did not usually sue their master nor workers their employers, in principle they had the right to do so.

In principle, too, a worker might have had an action against his employer for any injury caused by the negligence of any other employee. The doctrine of *respondeat superior* was familiar and fundamental law. A principal was liable for the negligent acts of his agent. As Blackstone put it:

> he who does a thing by the agency of another, does it himself . . . .
> If an innkeeper's servants rob his guests, the master is bound to
> restitution. . . . So likewise if the drawer at a tavern sells a man
> bad wine, whereby his health is injured, he may bring an action
> against the master.[12]

Conceivably, then, one member of an industrial work force might sue his employer for injuries caused by the negligence of a fellow worker. A definitive body of doctrine was slow to develop, however. When it did, it rejected the broad principle of *respondeat superior* and took instead the form of the so-called fellow-servant rule. Under this rule, a servant (employee) could not sue his master (employer) for injuries caused by the negligence of another employee. The consequences of this doctrine were far reaching. An employee retained the right to sue the employer for injuries, provided they were caused by the employer's personal misconduct. But the factory system and corporate ownership of industry made this right virtually meaningless. The factory owner was likely to be a "soulless" legal entity; even if the owner was an individual entrepreneur, he was unlikely to concern himself physically with factory operations. In work accidents, then, legal fault would be ascribed to fellow employees, if anyone. But fellow employees were men without wealth or insurance. The fellow-servant rule was an instrument capable of relieving employers from almost all the legal consequences of industrial injuries. Moreover, the doctrine left an injured worker without any effective recourse but an empty action against his co-worker.

When labor developed a collective voice, it was bound to decry the rule

[11] 2 F. Hilliard, *The Law of Torts*, 339 (3d ed. 1866).
[12] 1 W. Blackstone, *Commentaries*, *429–30.

as infamous,[13] as a deliberate instrument of oppression — a sign that law served the interests of the rich and propertied, and denied the legitimate claims of the poor and the weak. The rule charged the "blood of the workingman" not to the state, the employer, or the consumer, but to the working man himself.[14] Conventionally, then, the fellow-servant rule is explained as a deliberate or half-deliberate rejection of a well-settled principle of law in order to encourage enterprise by forcing workmen to bear the costs of industrial injury. And the overthrow of the rule is taken as a sign of a conquest by progressive forces.

It is neither possible nor desirable to avoid passing judgment on human behavior; but one's understanding of social processes can sometimes be hindered by premature moral assessments. The history of industrial accident law is much too complicated to be viewed as merely a struggle of capital against labor, with law as a handmaid of the rich, or as a struggle of good against evil. From the standpoint of social change, good and evil are social labels based on *perceptions* of conditions, not terms referring to conditions in themselves. Social change comes about when people decide that a situation is evil and must be altered, even if they were satisfied or unaware of the problem before. In order, then, to understand the legal reaction to the problem of industrial accidents, one must understand how the problem was perceived within the legal system and by that portion of society whose views influenced the law.

B. *Birth and Acceptance of the Rule.* The origin of the fellow-servant rule is usually ascribed to Lord Abinger's opinion in *Priestley* v. *Fowler*,[15] decided in 1837. Yet the case on its facts did not pose the question of the industrial accident, as later generations would understand it; rather, it concerned the employment relationships of tradesmen. The defendant, a butcher, instructed the plaintiff, his servant, to deliver goods which had been loaded on a van by another employee. The van, which had been overloaded, broke down, and plaintiff fractured his thigh in the accident. Lord Abinger, in his rather diffuse and unperceptive opinion, reached his holding that the servant had no cause of action by arguing from analogies drawn neither from industry nor from trade:

> If the master be liable to the servant in this action, the principle
> of that liability will . . . carry us to an alarming extent . . . . The

---

[13] And Labor was not alone. "Lord Abinger planted it, Baron Alderson watered it, and the devil gave it increase," said the Secretary for Ireland in a famous remark to the House of Commons in 1897. Quoted in W. Dodd, *Administration of Workmen's Compensation*, 5 n.7 (1936). Lord Abinger wrote the decision in *Priestley* v. *Fowler*, 150 Eng. R. 1030 (Ex. 1837); Baron Alderson in *Hutchinson v. York, N. and B. Ry.*, 155 Eng. R. 150 (Ex. 1850).

[14] The slogan "The cost of the product should bear the blood of the working man" has been attributed to Lloyd George; it expresses the theory that the price of the commodity should include all costs, including that of industrial accidents. See W. Prosser, *Torts*, 554–55 and n.3 (3d ed. 1964).

[15] 150 Eng. R. 1030 (Ex. 1837).

> footman . . . may have an action against his master for a defect in
> the carriage owing to the negligence of the coachmaker. . . . The
> master . . . would be liable to the servant for the negligence of
> the chambermaid, for putting him into a damp bed; . . . for the
> negligence of the cook in not properly cleaning the copper vessels
> used in the kitchen. . . .[16]

These and similar passages in the opinion suggest that Abinger was worried about the disruptive effects of a master's liability upon his household staff. These considerations were perhaps irrelevant to the case at hand, the facts of which did not deal with the household of a nobleman, great landowner, or rich merchant; *a fortiori* the decision itself did not concern relationships within an industrial establishment. Certainly the opinion made extension of the rule to the factory setting somewhat easier to enunciate and formulate technically. But it did not justify the existence of an industrial fellow-servant rule. The case might have been totally forgotten — or overruled — had not the onrush of the industrial revolution put the question again and again to courts, each time more forcefully. *Priestley* v. *Fowler* and the doctrine of *respondeat superior* each stood for a broad principle. Whether the one or the other (or neither) would find a place in the law relative to industrial accidents depended upon needs felt and expressed by legal institutions in response to societal demands. Had there been no *Priestley* v. *Fowler*, it would have been necessary — and hardly difficult — to invent one.

In the United States, the leading case on the follow-servant situation was *Farwell* v. *Boston and Worcester Railroad Corp.*,[17] decided by Massachusetts' highest court in 1842. The case arose out of a true industrial accident in a rapidly developing industrial state. Farwell was an engineer who lost a hand when his train ran off the track due to a switchman's negligence. As Chief Justice Shaw, writing for the court, saw it, the problem of *Farwell* was how best to apportion the risks of railroad accidents. In his view, it was superficial to analyze the problem according to the tort concepts of fault and negligence. His opinion spoke the language of contract, and employed the stern logic of nineteenth-century economic thought. Some occupations are more dangerous than others. Other things being equal, a worker will choose the least dangerous occupation available. Hence, to get workers an employer will have to pay an additional wage for dangerous work. The market, therefore, has already made an adjustment

---

[16] *Id.* at 1032.

[17] 45 Mass. (4 Met.) 49 (1842). *Murray* v. *South Carolina R.R.*, 26 S.C.L. (1 McMul.) 385 (1841), was decided a year earlier and came to the same result. But *Farwell* is the better known case, the one usually cited and quoted. In England, Baron Alderson extended *Priestley* to a railroad accident situation in *Hutchinson v. York, N. and B. Ry.*, 155 Eng. R. 150 (Ex. 1849). The House of Lords, in *Barton's Hill Coal Co.* v. *Reid*, 111 Rev. R. 896 (1858), held the rule applicable in Scotland as well as in England. Lord Cranworth cited *Farwell* with great praise as a "very able and elaborate judgment." *Id.* at 906.

in the wage rate to compensate for the possibility of accident, and a cost somewhat similar to an insurance cost has been allocated to the company. As Shaw put it, "he who engages in the employment of another for the performance of specified duties and services, for compensation, takes upon himself the natural and ordinary risks and perils incident to the performance of such services, and *in legal presumption, the compensation is adjusted accordingly.*" [18] The worker, therefore, has assumed the risk of injury — for a price. The "implied contract of employment" between the worker and employer did not require the employer to bear any additional costs of injury (except for those caused by the employer's personal negligence).

In *Priestley* v. *Fowler* too, counsel had argued in terms of implied contract.[19] But Lord Abinger had not framed his logic accordingly. Shaw did, and his opinion had great influence on subsequent judicial reasoning. The facts of the case were appropriate and timely, and Shaw saw the issue in clear economic terms. His decision helped convert the rules and concepts of the status-bound law of master and servant to the economic needs of the period, as he understood them.[20]

Shaw's opinion makes extreme assumptions about behavior, justified only by a philosophy of economic individualism.[21] Partly because of this, it has a certain heartlessness of tone. A disabled worker without resources was likely to be pauperized if he had no realistic right to damages. Unless his family could help him, he would have to fall back upon poor relief, the

---

[18] *Farwell* v. *Boston and* W.R.R., 45 Mass. (4 Met.) 49, 57 (1842) (emphasis added).

[19] 150 Eng. R. 1030, 1031 (Ex. 1837).

[20] The same impulse motivated Timothy Walker, who introduced his discussion of master and servant in his text on American law with these words:

> The title of *master and servant*, at the head of a lecture, does not sound very harmoniously to republican ears. . . . But the legal relation of master and servant must exist, to a greater or less extent, wherever civilization furnishes work to be done, and the difference of condition makes some persons employers, and others laborers. In fact, we understand by the relation of master and servant, nothing more or less than that of *employer* and *employed*. It is, therefore, a relation created by contract, express or implied, and might properly be treated under the head of contracts; but custom has placed it among the personal relations, and I shall so treat it.

T. Walker, *Introduction to American Law,* § 114, at 275 (6th ed. 1837).

[21] "[*Farwell* represents] the individualistic tendency of the common law, which took it for granted that an employee was free to contract and was not bound to risk life or limb in any particular employment . . . ." W. Dodd, *supra* note 13, at 7. "[T]he leading employers' liability cases, from which the whole subsequent juristic development received its tone and direction, were decided at the very moment when the *laissez faire* movement in economic and political thought reached its culmination." E. Downey, *History of Work Accident Indemnity in Iowa,* 13 (1912). See also F. Bohlen, *Studies in the Law of Torts,* 461–65 (1926).

costs of which were borne by the public through taxation. The railroads and other industrial employers paid a share as taxpayers and, in addition, a kind of insurance cost as part of their wage rate — but no more. Additional damages had to be borne by the worker; if he could not bear them, society generally would pay the welfare costs. Thus the opinion expresses a preference for charging the welfare cost of industrial accidents to the public generally, rather than to the particular enterprise involved.

It is not surprising that such a preference was expressed. Shaw's generation placed an extremely high value on economic growth. As Willard Hurst has noted, that generation was thoroughly convinced it was "socially desirable that there be broad opportunity for the release of creative human energy," particularly in the "realm of the economy." [22] The establishment of a functioning railroad net was an essential element in economic growth. Furthermore, Shaw's resolution of the *Farwell* case is cruel only insofar as society makes no other provision for the victims of accidents — that is, if social insurance and public assistance are inadequate, degrading, or unfair. In a society with a just and workable system of state medical insurance and disability pensions, the *Farwell* solution would be neither inhumane nor inappropriate, even today. Indeed, it could be argued that the broader social responsibility is preferable to one which taxes a particular industry for the claims of its workers. Whether the one side or the other is correct, in economic or political terms, is not here relevant.

Of course, from today's viewpoint, the word "inadequate" is too weak a judgment on what passed for public relief in the early nineteenth century. Social insurance was unknown. Local poor relief was cruel, sporadic, and pinchpenny. Institutions for the helpless were indescribably filthy and heartless. Villages sometimes shunted paupers from place to place, to avoid the burden of paying for them. Moreover, the whole system was shot through with what strikes us today as an inordinate fear of the spread of idleness and a perverse notion that pauperism generally arose out of the moral failings of the poor. The most that can be said is that the system usually made a minimum commitment to keeping the poor alive. [23]

But our condemnation of nineteenth-century welfare administration is based on a certain amount of hindsight. Social welfare is looked upon today as a task of government, and government can lay claim to far greater resources to accomplish welfare goals. In Shaw's day, private charity was assigned a higher place in the relief of misery. Probably most people would

[22] J. Willard Hurst, *Law and the Conditions of Freedom in the Nineteenth-Century United States*, 5–6, *passim* (1956).
[23] See, e.g., D. Schneider and A. Deutsch, *The History of Public Welfare in New York State, 1609–1866*, at 211–30 (1938). For a vivid description of early nineteenth-century poor relief administration, see M. Rosenheim, "Vagrancy Concepts in Welfare Law," 54 *Calif. L. Rev.*, 511, 528–30 (1966).

have agreed then that the disabled and wretched poor ought not to starve. Where private philanthropy failed, local poor relief stepped in. It was the most miserable sort of minimum, but its deficiencies were not apparent to the average middle- or upper-class citizen who seldom gave the matter a second thought — just as today the inadequacies of mental hospitals and prisons are only vaguely known and rarely given a second thought by most Americans. Poor relief was not *perceived* as a major social problem in the most literal sense. Furthermore, in Shaw's day certain kinds of crises and risks had to be accepted as inevitable, far more than they would be accepted today. High mortality rates from disease threatened all classes of society. Business entrepreneurs ran heavy risks; business failure was common and could be avoided only by great skill and good fortune. The instability of the monetary system threatened an entrepreneur with sudden, unpredictable, and uninsurable ruin. At the onset of the great business panic of 1857, for example, banks failed by the score; currency turned to ashes, and chain reactions of default were set off by distant collapse or defalcation.[24] Hardly any businessman was safe or immune. Furthermore, imprisonment for debt was still a living memory when Shaw wrote; the present national bankruptcy system did not exist, and local insolvency laws were chaotic and unpredictable.[25] Men like Shaw, the bearers of power and influence, might have conceded that the misfortunes of factory workers were real, but insecurity of economic position cursed the lot of all but the very rich. The problem was one of *general* insecurity.

Shaw and his generation placed their hopes of salvation on rapid economic growth.[26] Perhaps they were anxious to see that the tort system of

[24] See B. Hammond, *Banks and Politics in America* (1957).

[25] For a discussion of legal and political aspects of the short-lived national bankruptcy acts before 1898, see C. Warren, *Bankruptcy in United States History* (1935).

[26] It is generally assumed that the "considerations of policy" invoked by Shaw in the Farwell case were those in favor of the promotion of railroad and industrial expansion. Charles Warren . . . observed that railroads began to operate only 8 years before the Farwell decision, and quoted an 1883 writer to the effect that the decision was "a species of protective tariff for the encouragement of infant railway industries." The United States Supreme Court has said that the "assumption of risk" doctrine was "a judicially created rule . . . developed in response to the general impulse of common law courts . . . to insulate the employer as much as possible from bearing the 'human overhead' which is an inevitable part of the cost — to someone — of the doing of industrialized business." "The general purpose behind this development in the common law," the Court continued, "seems to have been to give maximum freedom to expanding industry." *Tiller v. Atlantic Coast Line Railroad,* 318 U.S. 54, 58–59 (1943). Auerbach, 84–85; see W. Dodd, *supra* note 13, at 7; E. Downey, *supra* note 21, at 15; E. Freund, *Standards of American Legislation,* 21 (1917); A. Brodie, "The Adequacy of Workmen's Compensation as Social Insurance: A Review of Developments and Proposals," 1963 *Wis. L. Rev.,* 57, 58.

accident compensation did not add to the problems of new industry. Few people imagined that accidents would become so numerous as to create severe economic and social dislocations. On the contrary, rash extension of certain principles of tort law to industrial accidents might upset social progress by imposing extreme costs on business in its economic infancy. The 1840's and 1850's were a period of massive economic development in New England and the Midwest, a period of "take-off" (perhaps) into self-sustaining economic growth.[27] Textiles, and then iron, spearheaded the industrial revolution; westward expansion and the railroads created new markets. Communities and states made a social contribution to the construction of railroads through cash subsidies, stock subscriptions, and tax exemptions. The courts, using the fellow-servant doctrine and the concepts of assumption of risk and contributory negligence,[28] socialized the accident costs of building the roads. That these solutions represented the collective, if uneasy, consensus of those with authority and responsibility is supported by the fact that every court of the country, with but one transient exception,[29] reached the same conclusion in the years immediately following *Farwell*. Moreover, the fellow-servant rule was not abolished by any legislature in these early years. Although legislative inaction is not a necessary sign of acquiescence, it at least indicates lack of a major feeling of revulsion.

C. *Weakening the Rule.* A general pattern may be discerned which is common to the judicial history of many rules of law. The courts enunciate a rule, intending to "solve" a social problem — that is, they seek to lay down a stable and clear-cut principle by which men can govern their conduct or, alternatively, by which the legal system can govern men. If the rule comports with some kind of social consensus, it will in fact work a solution — that is, it will go unchallenged, or, if challenged, will prevail. Challenges will not usually continue, since the small chance of overturning the rule is not worth the cost of litigation. If, however, the rule is weakened — if courts engraft exceptions to it, for example — then fresh challenges probing new weaknesses will be encouraged. Even if the rule

[27] The 1840's were marked by rail and manufacturing development in the East. The 1850's brought heavy foreign capital inflow and the railroad push into the Midwest. W. Rostow, *The Stages of Economic Growth*, 38 (1960).

[28] For these doctrines see W. Prosser, *supra* note 14, at 426–28, 450. Both are essentially 19th-century doctrines — indeed, Prosser feels assumption of risk "received its greatest impetus" from *Priestley* v. *Fowler*. *Id.* at 450 and n.3. On the significance in American law of the doctrine of contributory negligence, see the important article by Wex Malone, "The Formative Era of Contributory Negligence," 41 *Ill. L. Rev.*, 151 (1946).

[29] Wisconsin, in *Charmberlain* v. *Milwaukee and M.R.R.*, 11 Wis. 248 (1860), rejected the fellow-servant rule, but one year later, in *Moseley* v. *Chamberlain*, 18 Wis. 700 (1861), the court reversed itself and adopted the rule which was "sustained by the almost unanimous judgments of all the courts both of England and this country . . . [an] unbroken current of judicial opinion." *Id.* at 736.

retains *some* support, it will no longer be efficient and clear-cut. Ultimately, the rule may no longer serve *anybody's* purposes. At this point, a fresh (perhaps wholly new) "solution" will be attempted.

The history of the fellow-servant rule rather neatly fits this scheme. Shaw wrote his *Farwell* opinion in 1842. During the latter part of the century, judges began to reject his reasoning. The "tendency in nearly all jurisdictions," said a Connecticut court in 1885, was to "limit rather than enlarge" the range of the fellow-servant rule.[30] A Missouri judge in 1891 candidly expressed the change in attitude:

> In the progress of society, and the general substitution of ideal and invisible masters and employers for the actual and visible ones of former times, in the forms of corporations engaged in varied, detached and widespread operations . . . it has been seen and felt that the universal application of the [fellow-servant] rule often resulted in hardship and injustice. Accordingly, the tendency of the more modern authorities appears to be in the direction of such a modification and limitation of the rule as shall eventually devolve upon the employer under these circumstances a due and just share of the responsibility for the lives and limbs of the persons in its employ.[31]

The rule was strong medicine, and it depended for its efficacy upon continued, relatively certain, and unswerving legal loyalty. Ideally, if the rule were strong and commanded nearly total respect from the various agencies of law, it would eliminate much of the mass of litigation that might otherwise arise. Undoubtedly, it did prevent countless thousands of law suits; but it did not succeed in choking off industrial accident litigation. For example, industrial accident litigation dominated the docket of the Wisconsin Supreme Court at the beginning of the age of workmen's compensation; far more cases arose under that heading than under any other single field of law.[32] Undoubtedly, this appellate case-load was merely the visible portion of a vast iceberg of litigation. Thus, the rule did not command the respect required for efficient operation and hence, in the long run, survival.

One reason for the continued litigation may have been simply the great number of accidents that occurred. At the dawn of the industrial revolution, when Shaw wrote, the human consequences of that technological change were unforeseeable. In particular, the toll it would take of human life was unknown. But by the last quarter of the nineteenth century, the number of industrial accidents had grown enormously. After 1900, it is

[30] *Ziegler* v. *Danbury and N.R.R.,* 52 Conn. 543, 556 (1885).
[31] *Parker* v. *Hannibal and St. J.R.R.,* 109 Mo. 362, 397 (1891) (Thomas, J., dissenting).
[32] Unpublished survey and classification of all Wisconsin Supreme Court cases 1905–1915, by Robert Friebert and Lawrence M. Friedman.

estimated, 35,000 deaths and 2,000,000 injuries occurred every year in the United States. One quarter of the injuries produced disabilities lasting more than one week.[33] The railway injury rate doubled in the seventeen years between 1889 and 1906.[34]

In addition to the sheer number of accidents, other reasons for the increasing number of challenges to the rule in the later nineteenth century are apparent. If the injury resulted in death or permanent disability, it broke off the employment relationship; the plaintiff or his family thereafter had nothing to lose except the costs of suit. The development of the contingent fee system provided the poor man with the means to hire a lawyer. This system came into being, in the words of an investigating committee of the New York State Bar:

> shortly after the beginning of that which we now call the age of machinery. With the advent of steam and the vast variety of machines for its application to the service of mankind, came a multitude of casualties. This resulted in . . . a class of litigants, whose litigation theretofore had only involved controversies in small transactions . . . calling for the services of inexpensive lawyers. In the new era . . . the poor man found himself pitted . . . against corporations entrenched in wealth and power. . . . Thus resulted a great crop of litigation by the poor against the powerful. . . .[35]

The contingent fee system was no more than a mechanism, however. A losing plaintiff's lawyer receives no fee; that is the essence of the system. The fact is that plaintiffs won many of their lawsuits; in so doing, they not only weakened the fellow-servant rule, but they encouraged still more

[33] E. Downey, *supra* note 21, at 1–2, gives these estimates based on *U.S. Bureau of Labor Bull.* No. 78, at 458.

[34] Accidents were about 2.5 per 100 railway employees in 1889 and 5 per 100 in 1906. Calculated from ICC figures reported in [1909–1910] *Wis. Bureau of Labor and Industrial Statistics Fourteenth Biennial Rep.*, 99 (1911).

Railroads had been the earliest major source of industrial accidents, and most of the leading American and English fellow-servant cases arose out of railroad accidents. Railroads accounted for more serious industrial accidents than any other form of enterprise in the middle of the 19th century. But in the late 19th century, mining, manufacturing, and processing industries contributed their share to industrial injury and death. For example, close to 80 per cent of the employer liability cases that reached the Wisconsin Supreme Court before 1890 related to railroad accidents; from 1890 to 1907 less than 30 per cent were railroad cases. [1907–1908] *Wis. Bureau of Labor and Industrial Statistics Thirteenth Biennial Rep.*, 26 (1909). In 1907–1908, manufacturing injuries and deaths were more than double those of the railroads. [1909–1910] *Wis. Bureau of Labor and Industrial Statistics Fourteenth Biennial Rep.*, 79 (1911).

[35] Report of Committee on Contingent Fees, 31 *Proceedings of the N.Y. St. B. Ass'n*, 99, 100–01 (1908). The elite of the bar always looked with suspicion upon the contingent fee. But the system was a source of livelihood to many members of the bar, and it suited the American proposition that justice was classless and open to all.

plaintiffs to try their hand, still more attorneys to make a living from personal injury work. In trial courts, the pressure of particular cases — the "hard" cases in which the plight of the plaintiff was pitiful or dramatic — tempted judges and juries to find for the little man and against the corporate defendant. In Shaw's generation, many leading appellate judges shared his view of the role of the judge; they took it as their duty to lay down grand legal principles to govern whole segments of the economic order. Thus, individual hardship cases had to be ignored for the sake of higher duty. But this was not the exclusive judicial style, even in the appellate courts. And in personal injury cases, lower court judges and juries were especially prone to tailor justice to the case at hand. For example, in Wisconsin, of 307 personal injury cases involving workers that appeared before the state supreme court up to 1907, nearly two-thirds had been decided in favor of the worker in the lower courts. In the state supreme court, however, only two-fifths were decided for the worker.[36] Other states undoubtedly had similar experiences. Whether for reasons of sympathy with individual plaintiffs, or with the working class in general, courts and juries often circumvented the formal dictates of the doctrines of the common law.

Some weakening of the doctrine took place by means of the control exercised by trial court judge and jury over findings of fact. But sympathy for injured workers manifested itself also in changes in doctrine. On the appellate court level, a number of mitigations of the fellow-servant rule developed near the end of the nineteenth century. For example, it had always been conceded that the employer was liable if he was personally responsible (through his own negligence) for his worker's injury. Thus, in a Massachusetts case, a stable owner gave directions to his employee, who was driving a wagon, that caused an accident and injury to the driver (or so the jury found). The employer was held liable.[37] Out of this simple proposition grew the so-called vice-principal rule, which allowed an employee to sue his employer where the negligent employee occupied a supervisory position such that he could more properly be said to be an alter ego of the principal than a mere fellow-servant. This was a substantial weakening of the fellow-servant doctrine. Yet some states never accepted the vice-principal rule; in those that did, it too spawned a bewildering multiplicity of decisions, sub-rules, and sub-sub-rules. "The decisions on the subject, indeed, are conflicting to a degree which, it may safely be affirmed, is without a parallel in any department of jurisprudence." [38] This statement appeared in a treatise, written on the eve of workmen's

---

[36] [1907–1908] *Wis. Bureau of Labor and Industrial Statistics Thirteenth Biennial Rep.*, 85–86 (1909).

[37] *Haley* v. *Case*, 142 Mass. 316, 7 N.E. 877 (1886). In *Priestley* v. *Fowler* itself the same point was made.

[38] 4 C. Labatt, *Master and Servant*, 4143 (1913).

compensation, which devoted no fewer than 524 pages to a discussion of the ramifications of the vice-principal rule.

There were scores of other "exceptions" to the fellow-servant rule, enunciated in one or more states. Some of them were of great importance. In general, an employer was said to have certain duties that were not "delegable"; these he must do or have done, and a failure to perform them laid him open to liability for personal injuries. Among these was the duty to furnish a safe place to work, safe tools, and safe appliances. Litigation on these points was enormous, and here too the cases cannot readily be summed up or even explained. In *Wedgwood* v. *Chicago and Northwestern Railway Co.*[39] the plaintiff, a brakeman, was injured by a "large and long bolt, out of place, and which unnecessarily, carelessly and unskillfully projected beyond the frame, beam or brakehead, in the way of the brakeman going to couple the cars." [40] The trial court threw the case out, but the Wisconsin Supreme Court reversed:

> It is true, the defendant . . . is a railroad corporation, and can only act through officers or agents. But this does not relieve it from responsibility for the negligence of its officers and agents whose duty it is to provide safe and suitable machinery for its road which its employees are to operate.[41]

So phrased, of course, the exception comes close to swallowing the rule. Had the courts been so inclined, they might have eliminated the fellow-servant rule without admitting it, simply by expanding the safe place and safe tool rules. They were never quite willing to go that far, and the safe tool doctrine was itself subject to numerous exceptions. In some jurisdictions, for example, the so-called "simple tool" rule applied:

> Tools of ordinary and everyday use, which are simple in structure and requiring no skill in handling — such as hammers and axes — not obviously defective, do not impose a liability upon employer[s] for injuries resulting from such defects.[42]

Doctrinal complexity and vacillation in the upper courts, coupled with jury freedom in the lower courts, meant that by the end of the century the fellow-servant rule had lost much of its reason for existence: it was no longer an efficient cost-allocating doctrine. Even though the exceptions did not go the length of obliterating the rule, and even though many (perhaps most) injured workers who had a possible cause of action did not or could not recover, the instability and unpredictability of operation of the common law rule was a significant fact.

[39] 41 Wis. 478 (1877).
[40] *Id.* at 479.
[41] *Id.* at 483.
[42] *Dunn* v. *Southern Ry.*, 151 N.C. 313, 315, 66 S.E. 134–35 (1909); see 3 C. Labatt, *supra* note 38, at 2476–84.

The numerous judge-made exceptions reflected a good deal of uncertainty about underlying social policy. The same uncertainty was reflected in another sphere of legal activity — the legislature. Though the rule was not formally abrogated, it was weakened by statute in a number of jurisdictions. Liability statutes, as will be seen, were rudimentary and in many ways ineffective. This was partly because of genuine uncertainty about the proper attitude to take toward industrial accident costs — an uncertainty reflected in the cases as well. The early nineteenth century cannot be uncritically described as a period that accepted without question business values and practices. Rather, it accepted the ideal of economic growth, which certain kinds of enterprise seemed to hinder. Thus in the age of Jackson, as is well known, popular feeling ran high against financial institutions, chiefly the chartered banks. Banks were believed to have far too much economic power; they corrupted both the currency and the government. They were a "clog upon the industry of this country." [43] But many a good judge, who decried the soulless corporation (meaning chiefly the moneyed kind) in the best Jacksonian tradition, may at the same time have upheld the fellow-servant rule. One did not, in other words, necessarily identify the interests of the common man with industrial liability for personal injuries.

Later on, the railroads replaced the banks as popular bogeymen. By the 1850's some of the fear of excessive economic power was transferred to them. Disregard for safety was one more black mark against the railroads; farmers, small businessmen, and the emerging railroad unions might use the safety argument to enlist widespread support for general regulation of railroads, but the essential thrust of the movement was economic. The railroads were feared and hated because of their power over access to the market. They became "monopolistic" as the small local lines were gradually amalgamated into large groupings controlled by "robber barons." Interstate railroad nets were no longer subject to local political control — if anything, they controlled local politics, or so it plausibly appeared to much of the public. Farmers organized and fought back against what they identified as their economic enemy. It is not coincidental that the earliest derogations from the strictness of the fellow-servant rule applied *only* to railroads. For example, the first statutory modification, passed in Georgia in 1856, allowed railroad employees to recover for injuries caused by the acts of fellow-servants, provided they themselves were free from negligence. [44] A similar act was passed in Iowa in 1862. [45] Other statutes were passed in Wyoming (1869) [46] and Kansas (1874). [47] The chronology

[43] T. Sedgwick, Jr., "What is a Monopoly?" (1865), quoted in *Social Theories of Jacksonian Democracy*, 220, 231 (Blau ed. 1954).
[44] No. 103, [1855] Ga. Acts 155.
[45] Ch. 169, § 7, [1862] Iowa Laws 198.
[46] Ch. 65, [1869] Wyo. Terr. Laws 433.
[47] Ch. 93, § 1, [1874] Kan. Laws 143.

suggests — though direct evidence is lacking — that some of these statutes were connected with the general revolt of farmers against the power of the railroad companies, a revolt associated with the Granger movement, which achieved its maximum power in the 1870's.[48] Wisconsin in 1875 abolished the fellow-servant rule for railroads; in 1880, however, when more conservative forces regained control of the legislature, the act was repealed.[49]

The Granger revolt, and similar movements, were not without lessons for the railroad companies. Despite the fall of Granger legislatures, the legal and economic position of the railroads was permanently altered. Great masses of people had come to accept the notion that the power of the railroads was a threat to farmers and a threat to the independence and stability of democratic institutions. Out of the ashes of ineffective and impermanent state regulation of railroads arose what ultimately became a stronger and more systematic program of regulation, grounded in federal power over the national economy.

The Interstate Commerce Commission was created in 1887,[50] chiefly to outlaw discrimination in freight rates and other practices deemed harmful to railroad users. The original legislation had nothing to say about railroad accidents and safety. But this did not long remain the case. The railroads had become unpopular defendants relatively early in American legal history. By 1911, twenty-five states had laws modifying or abrogating the fellow-servant doctrine for railroads.[51] Railroad accident law reached a state of maturity earlier than the law of industrial accidents generally; safety controls were imposed on the roads, and the common law tort system was greatly modified by removal of the employer's most effective defense. The Interstate Commerce Commission called a conference of state regulatory authorities in 1889; the safety problem was discussed, and the Commission was urged to investigate the problem and recommend legislation.[52] In 1893, Congress required interstate railroads to equip themselves with safety appliances, and provided that any employee injured "by any locomotive, car, or train in use" without such appliances would not "be deemed . . . to have assumed the risk thereby occasioned." [53]

---

[48] See generally R. Hunt, *Law and Locomotives* (1958).

[49] Ch. 173, [1875] Wis. Laws 293 (*repealed,* Ch. 232, [1880] Wis. Laws 270). A new act, somewhat narrower than that of 1875, was passed in 1889. Ch. 348, [1889] Wis. Laws 487.

[50] Interstate Commerce Act § 11, 24 Stat. 379 (1887). As much as workmen's compensation, the development of utility regulation was a kind of compromise among interests. Under public regulation, companies gain freedom from local political harassment and uncontrolled competition; they are virtually guaranteed a "fair" but limited return on investment. In exchange, they agree to accept supervision and regulation by the general government.

[51] 1 A. Larson, *Workmen's Compensation,* § 4.50, at 30 (1965).

[52] 1 I. Sharfman, *The Interstate Commerce Commission,* 246 n.4 (1931).

[53] Safety Appliance Act, 27 Stat. 531–32 (1893) (now 45 U.S.C. § 7 (1964).

The Federal Employers' Liability Act of 1908 [54] went much further; it abolished the fellow-servant rule for railroads and greatly reduced the strength of contributory negligence and assumption of risk as defenses. Once the employers had been stripped of these potent weapons, the relative probability of recovery by injured railroad employees was high enough so that workmen's compensation never seemed as essential for the railroads as for industry generally. The highly modified FELA tort system survives (in amended form) to this day for the railroads.[55] It is an anachronism, but one which apparently grants some modest satisfaction to both sides. Labor and management both express discontent with FELA, but neither side has been so firmly in favor of a change to workmen's compensation as to make it a major issue.[56]

FELA shows one of many possible outcomes of the decline in efficacy of the fellow-servant rule. Under it, the rule was eliminated, and the law turned to a "pure" tort system — pure in the sense that the proclivities of juries were not interfered with by doctrines designed to limit the chances of a worker's recovery. But the railroads were a special case. Aside from the special history of regulation, the interstate character of the major railroads made them subject to national safety standards and control by a single national authority. For other industrial employers, the FELA route was not taken; instead, workmen's compensation acts were passed. In either case, however, the fellow-servant rule was abolished, or virtually so. Either course reflects, we can assume, some kind of general agreement that the costs of the rule outweighed its benefits.

D. Rising Pressures for Change. The common law doctrines were designed to preserve a certain economic balance in the community. When the courts and legislatures created numerous exceptions, the rules lost much of their efficiency as a limitation on the liability of businessmen. The rules prevented many plaintiffs from recovering, but not all; a few plaintiffs recovered large verdicts. There were costs of settlements, costs of liability insurance, costs of administration, legal fees and the salaries of staff lawyers. These costs rose steadily, at the very time when American business, especially big business, was striving to rationalize and bureaucratize its operations. It was desirable to be able to predict costs and insure against fluctuating, unpredictable risks. The costs of industrial accident liability were not easily predictable, partly because legal consequences of

---

[54] 35 Stat. 65 (1908).

[55] The 1908 act was limited to railroad employees injured while engaged in interstate commerce. A 1906 act [Act of June 22, 1906, ch. 3073, 34 Stat. 232] had been declared invalid by the Supreme Court in the Employers Liability Cases, 207 U.S. 463 (1908), because it applied to employees not engaged in interstate commerce. The 1908 act was liberalized in 1910 and in 1939. See 45 U.S.C. §§ 51–60 (1964). See generally V. Miller, "FELA Revisited," 6 *Catholic U.L. Rev.* 158 (1957).

[56] Arguments by supporters and opponents of FELA are reviewed in H. Somers and A. Somers, *Workmen's Compensation*, 320–25 (1954).

accidents were not predictable. Insurance, though available, was expensive.

In addition, industry faced a serious problem of labor unrest. Workers and their unions were dissatisfied with many aspects of factory life. The lack of compensation for industrial accidents was one obvious weakness. Relatively few injured workers received compensation. Under primitive state employers' liability statutes, the issue of liability and the amount awarded still depended upon court rulings and jury verdicts. Furthermore, the employer and the insurance carrier might contest a claim or otherwise delay settlement in hopes of bringing the employee to terms. The New York Employers' Liability Commission, in 1910, reported that delay ran from six months to six years.

> The injured workman is driven to accept whatever his employer or an insurance company chooses to give him or take his chance in a lawsuit. Half of the time his lawsuit is doomed to failure because he has been hurt by some trade risk or lacks proof for his case. At best he has a right to retain a lawyer, spend two months on the pleadings, watch his case from six months to two years on a calendar and then undergo the lottery of a jury trial, with a technical system of law and rules of evidence, and beyond that appeals and perhaps reversals on questions that do not go to the merits. . . . If he wins, he wins months after his most urgent need is over.[57]

When an employee did recover, the amount was usually small. The New York Commission found that of forty-eight fatal cases studied in Manhattan, eighteen families received no compensation; only four received over $2,000; most received less than $500. The deceased workers had averaged $15.22 a week in wages; only eight families recovered as much as three times their average yearly earnings.[58] The same inadequacies turned up in Wisconsin in 1907. Of fifty-one fatal injuries studied, thirty-four received settlements under $500; only eight received over $1,000.[59]

Litigation costs consumed much of whatever was recovered. It was estimated that, in 1907, "of every $100 paid out by [employers in New York] on account of work accidents but $56 reached the injured workmen and their dependents." And even this figure was unrepresentative because it included voluntary payments by employers. "A fairer test of employers' liability is afforded by the $192,538 paid by these same employers as a result of law suits or to avoid law suits, whereof only $80,888, or 42 per cent, reached the beneficiaries." [60] A large fraction of the disbursed payments, about one-third, went to attorneys who accepted the cases on a contingent basis.[61]

[57] Quoted in W. Dodd, *supra* note 13, at 23–24.
[58] *Id.* at 19.
[59] *Id.* at 20–21.
[60] E. Downey, *supra* note 21, at 83.
[61] See W. Dodd, *supra* note 13, at 22–23.

These figures on the inadequacy of recoveries are usually cited to show how little the workers received for their pains. But what did these figures mean to employers? Assuming that employers, as rational men, were anxious to pay as little compensation as was necessary to preserve industrial peace and maintain a healthy workforce, the better course might be to pay a higher *net* amount direct to employees. Employers had little or nothing to gain from their big payments to insurance companies, lawyers, and court officials. Perhaps at some unmeasurable point of time, the existing tort system crossed an invisible line and thereafter, purely in economic terms, represented on balance a net loss to the industrial establishment. From that point on, the success of a movement for change in the system was certain, provided that businessmen could be convinced that indeed their self-interest lay in the direction of reform and that a change in compensation systems did not drag with it other unknowable and harmful consequences.

As on many issues of reform, the legal profession did not speak with one voice. Certainly, many lawyers and judges were dissatisfied with the status quo. Judges complained about the burdens imposed on the court system by masses of personal injury suits; many felt frustrated by the chaotic state of the law, and others were bothered by their felt inability to do justice to injured workmen. One writer noted in 1912:

> [A]mendatory legislation in scores of separate jurisdictions have made employers' liability one of the most involved and intricate branches of the law, have multiplied definitions more recondite and distinctions more elusive than those of the marginal utility theory, and have given rise to conflicts of decisions that are the despair of jurists.[62]

Some influential judges despaired of piecemeal improvements and played an active role in working for a compensation system. In a 1911 opinion, Chief Justice J. B. Winslow of Wisconsin wrote:

> No part of my labor on this bench has brought such heartweariness to me as that ever increasing part devoted to the consideration of personal injury actions brought by employees against their employers. The appeal to the emotions is so strong in these cases, the results to life and limb and human happiness so distressing, that the attempt to honestly administer cold, hard rules of law . . . make[s] drafts upon the heart and nerves which no man can appreciate who has not been obliged to meet the situation himself . . . . These rules are archaic and unfitted to modern industrial conditions . . . .
> When [the faithful laborer] . . . has yielded up life, or limb, or health in the service of that marvelous industrialism which is our boast, shall not the great public . . . be charged with the duty of securing from want the laborer himself, if he survive, as well as his

[62] E. Downey, *supra* note 21, at 17.

helpless and dependent ones? Shall these latter alone pay the fearful price of the luxuries and comforts which modern machinery brings within the reach of all?

These are burning and difficult questions with which the courts cannot deal, because their duty is to administer the law as it is, not to change it; but they are well within the province of the legislative arm of the government.[63]

Justice Roujet D. Marshall propagandized for workmen's compensation in his judicial opinions.[64] He claimed in his autobiography "to have been largely the exciting cause of the establishment of the workmen's compensation law" in Wisconsin.[65] He also wrote part of the governor's message to the 1909 legislature appealing for a workmen's compensation statute, and he helped induce the Republican Party to back a workmen's compensation plan in its 1910 platform.[66] Legal writers and law teachers also spoke out against the common law and in favor of a compensation system. Roscoe Pound voiced a common opinion in 1907:

> [I]t is coming to be well understood by all who have studied the circumstances of modern industrial employment that the supposed contributory negligence of employees is in effect a result of the mechanical conditions imposed on them by the nature of their employment, and that by reason of these conditions the individual vigilance and responsibility contemplated by the common law are impossible in practice.[67]

In 1911, when the New York Court of Appeals unanimously declared the nation's first workmen's compensation statute unconstitutional,[68] Dean Pound and thirteen other "experts in political and Constitutional law" issued a lengthy statement in an influential New York City weekly newspaper, *The Outlook*, which the editors summarized as demonstrating that

[63] *Driscoll* v. *Allis-Chalmers Co.*, 144 Wis. 451, 468–69, 129 N.W. 401, 408–09 (1911); see *Monte* v. *Wausau Paper Mills Co.*, 132 Wis. 205, 209, 111 N.W. 1114, 1115 (1907), (Winslow, C.J.).

[64] See, e.g., *Houg* v. *Girard Lumber Co.*, 144 Wis. 337, 352, 129 N.W. 633, 639 (1911) (separate opinion); *Monaghan* v. *Northwestern Fuel Co.*, 140 Wis. 457, 466, 122 N.W. 1066, 1070 (1909) (dissenting opinion).

[65] 2 *Autobiography of Roujet D. Marshall*, 53 (Glasier ed. 1931).

[66] *Id.* at 239–46.

[67] R. Pound, "The Need of a Sociological Jurisprudence," 19 *Green Bag*, 607, 614 (1907). The entire April 1906 issue of *The Green Bag* was devoted to employers' liability and workmen's compensation. See, particularly, R. Newcomb, "The Abuse of Personal Injury Litigation," 18 *Green Bag*, 196, 199–200 (1906). See also F. Walton, "Workmen's Compensation and the Theory of Professional Risk," 11 *Colum. L. Rev.*, 36 (1911); E. Wambaugh, "Workmen's Compensation Acts: Their Theory and Their Constitutionality," 25 *Harv. L. Rev.*, 129 (1911).

[68] *Ives* v. *South Buffalo Ry.*, 201 N.Y. 271, 94 N.E. 431 (1911), *declaring unconstitutional* Ch. 674, [1910] N.Y. Laws 1945.

the "decision of the Court of Appeals of the State of New York is not in accordance with the best legal authorities in the United States." [69]

When considerations of politics were added to those of business economics and industrial peace, it was not surprising to find that businessmen gradually withdrew their veto against workmen's compensation statutes. They began to say that a reformed system was inevitable — and even desirable. A guaranteed, insurable cost — one which could be computed in advance on the basis of accident experience — would, in the long run, cost business less than the existing system. [70] In 1910, the president of the National Association of Manufacturers (NAM) appointed a committee to study the possibility of compensating injured workmen without time-consuming and expensive litigation, and the convention that year heard a speaker tell them that no one was satisfied with the present state of the law — that the employers' liability system was "antagonistic to harmonious relations between employers and wage workers." [71] By 1911 the NAM appeared convinced that a compensation system was inevitable and that prudence dictated that business play a positive role in shaping the design of the law — otherwise the law would be "settled for us by the demagogue, and agitator and the socialist with a vengeance." [72] Business would benefit economically and politically from a compensation system, but only if certain conditions were present. Business, therefore, had an interest in pressing for a specific kind of program, and turned its attention to the details of the new system. For example, it was imperative that the new system be in fact as actuarially predictable as business demanded; it was important that the costs of the program be fair and equal in their impact upon particular industries, so that no competitive advantage or disadvantage flowed from the scheme. Consequently the old tort actions had to be eliminated, along with the old defenses of the company. In exchange for certainty of recovery by the worker, the companies were prepared to demand certainty and predictability of loss — that is, limitation of recovery.

---

[69] "The Workmen's Compensation Act: Its Constitutionality Affirmed," 98 *The Outlook*, 709–11 (1911). Lyman Abbott, editor of *The Outlook*, and his contributing editor, Theodore Roosevelt, wrote frequently about employers' liability and compensation statutes. See especially the issue of April 29, 1911, 97 *The Outlook*, 955–60 (1911).

Roosevelt, as President, had stated as early as 1907 that "it is neither just, expedient, nor humane; it is revolting to judgment and sentiment alike that the financial burden of accidents occurring because of the necessary exigencies of their daily occupation should be thrust upon those sufferers who were least able to bear it. . . ." E. Downey, *supra* note 21, at 277 n.540.

[70] For a comparison of the cost efficiency of the two systems, see generally W. Dodd, *Administration of Workmen's Compensation*, 737–83 (1936).

[71] *National Association of Manufacturers, Proceedings of the Fifteenth Annual Convention*, 280 (1910).

[72] *National Association of Manufacturers, Proceedings of the Sixteenth Annual Convention*, 106 (1911) (remarks of Mr. Schwedtman).

The jury's caprice had to be dispensed with. In short, when workmen's compensation became law, as a solution to the industrial accident problem, it did so on terms acceptable to industry. Other pressures were there to be sure, but when workmen's compensation was enacted, businessmen had come to look on it as a positive benefit rather than as a threat to their sector of the economy.

E. *The Emergence of Workmen's Compensation Statutes.* The change of the businessman's, the judge's, and the general public's attitudes toward industrial injuries was accelerated by the availability of fresh information on the extent of accidents and their cost to both management and workers. By 1900, industrial accidents and the shortcomings of the fellow-servant rule were widely perceived as *problems* that had to be solved. After 1900, state legislatures began to look for a "solution" by setting up commissions to gather statistics, to investigate possible new systems, and to recommend legislation.[73] The commissions held public hearings and called upon employers, labor, insurance companies, and lawyers to express their opinions and propose changes. A number of commissions collected statistics on industrial accidents, costs of insurance, and amounts disbursed to injured workmen. By 1916, many states and the federal government had received more-or-less extensive public reports from these investigating bodies.[74] The reports included studies of industrial accident cases in the major industries, traced the legal history of the cases, and looked into the plight of the injured workmen and their families.

From the information collected, the commissions were able to calculate the costs of workmen's compensation systems and compare them with costs under employers' liability. Most of the commissions concluded that a compensation system would be no more expensive than the existing method,[75] and most of them recommended adoption, in one form or another, of workmen's compensation. In spite of wide variations in the systems proposed, there was agreement on one point: workmen's compensation must fix liability upon the employer regardless of fault.

Between 1910 and 1920 the method of compensating employees in-

[73] For example, in 1907, Illinois required employers to report their employees' accidents to the State's Bureau of Labor Statistics. [1907] Ill. Laws 308.

[74] See W. Dodd, *supra* note 70, at 18.

[75] For example, the Wisconsin Bureau of Labor and Industrial Statistics argued, on the basis of cost estimates in 1908, that:

> Employers' liability insurance costs now in Wisconsin from 12 cents per $100 of wages in knitting mills to at least $9.00 in some building operations — an average of 50 or 60 cents. But it is very probable that this expense would be increased in the near future by weakening the defense of the employer in the courts. . . . The cost of the present system would be sufficient to inaugurate a general system of compensation if properly administered.

[1907–1908] *Wis. Bureau of Labor and Industrial Statistics Thirteenth Biennial Rep.* (1909), quoted in Auerbach, 588.

jured on the job was fundamentally altered in the United States. In brief, workmen's compensation statutes eliminated (or tried to eliminate) the process of fixing civil liability for industrial accidents through litigation in common law courts. Under the statutes, compensation was based on statutory schedules, and the responsibility for initial determination of employee claims was taken from the courts and given to an administrative agency. Finally, the statutes abolished the fellow-servant rule and the defenses of assumption of risk and contributory negligence. Wisconsin's law, passed in 1911, was the first general compensation act to survive a court test.[76] Mississippi, the last state in the Union to adopt a compensation law, did so in 1948.[77]

Compensation systems varied from state to state, but they had many features in common. The original Wisconsin law was representative of the earlier group of statutes. It set up a voluntary system — a response to the fact that New York's courts had held a compulsory scheme unconstitutional on due process grounds.[78] Wisconsin abolished the fellow-servant rule and the defense of assumption of risk for employers of four or more employees. In turn, the compensation scheme, for employers who elected to come under it, was made the "exclusive remedy" for an employee injured accidentally on the job. The element of "fault" or "negligence" was eliminated, and the mere fact of injury at work "proximately caused by accident," and not the result of "wilful misconduct," made the employer liable to pay compensation but exempt from ordinary tort liability.[79] The state aimed to make it expensive for employers to stay out of the system. Any employer who did so was liable to suit by injured employees and the employer was denied the common law defenses.

The compensation plans strictly limited the employee's amount of recovery. In Wisconsin, for example, if an accident caused "partial disability," the worker was to receive 65 per cent of his weekly loss in wages during the period of disability, not to exceed four times his average annual earnings.[80] The statutes, therefore, were compensatory, not punitive, and the measure of compensation was, subject to strict limitations, the loss of earning power of the worker. In the original Wisconsin act, death benefits were also payable to dependents of the worker. If the worker who died left "no person dependent upon him for support," the death benefit was limited to "the reasonable expense of his burial, not exceeding $100." [81] Neither death nor injury as such gave rise to a right to compensation — only the fact of economic loss to someone, either the worker himself or his family. The Wisconsin act authorized employers to buy annuities from

[76] *Borgnis* v. *Falk Co.*, 147 Wis. 327, 133 N.W. 209 (1911).
[77] Ch. 354, [1948] Miss. Laws 507.
[78] *Ives* v. *South Buffalo Ry.*, 201 N.Y. 271, 94 N.E. 431 (1911).
[79] Ch. 50, § 1, [1911] Wis. Laws 43, 44.
[80] Ch. 50, § 1, [1911] Wis. Laws 46.
[81] Ch. 50, § 1, [1911] Wis. Laws 48.

private insurance companies to cover projected losses. Most states later made insurance or self-insurance compulsory. Some states have socialized compensation insurance, but most allow the purchase of private policies.[82]

In essence, then, workmen's compensation was designed to replace a highly unsatisfactory system with a rational, actuarial one. It should not be viewed as the replacement of a fault-oriented compensation system with one unconcerned with fault. It should not be viewed as a victory of employees over employers. In its initial stages, the fellow-servant rule was not concerned with fault, either, but with establishing a clear-cut, workable, and predictable rule, one which substantively placed much of the risk (if not all) on the worker. Industrial accidents were not seen as a social problem — at most as an economic problem. As value perceptions changed, the rule weakened; it developed exceptions and lost its efficiency. The exceptions and counter-exceptions can be looked at as a series of brief, ad hoc, and unstable compromises between the clashing interests of labor and management. When both sides became convinced that the game was mutually unprofitable, a compensation system became possible. But this system was itself a compromise: an attempt at a new, workable, and predictable mode of handling accident liability which neatly balanced the interests of labor and management.

III. The Law of Industrial Accidents and Social Theory: Three Aspects of Social Change

This case study, devoted to the rise and fall of the fellow-servant rule, utilizes and supports a view of social change as a complex chain of group bargains — economic in the sense of a continuous exchange of perceived equivalents, though not economic in the sense of crude money bargains. It also provides a useful setting for evaluating three additional popular explanations of the origin or rate of social change. First, the apparently slow development of workmen's compensation is the classic example of what Ogburn called "cultural lag." Second, since German and English statutes were enacted prior to the American laws, the establishment of compensation schemes in America can be viewed as a case of cross-cultural influence. Third, the active role of particular participants (in Wisconsin, for example, Judge Marshall and John R. Commons) may substantiate the theory which advances the causal influence of "great men" in the process of social change. A thorough examination of these theories is not contemplated here. Students both of law and of sociology, however, may profit from a brief discussion of these theories in the context of the social change embodied in workmen's compensation statutes.

A. *The Concept of Cultural Lag.* The problem of "fair and efficient incidence of industrial accident costs," in the words of Willard Hurst,

---

[82] See A. Reede, *Adequacy of Workmen's Compensation*, 231–38 (1947); H. Somers and A. Somers, *supra* note 56, at 93–142.

"followed a fumbling course in courts and legislature for fifty years before the first broad-scale direction [leading to workmen's compensation] was applied." [83] In a famous book written in 1922, the sociologist William Fielding Ogburn used the example of workmen's compensation and the fifty-year period of fumbling to verify his "hypothesis of cultural lag." [84] "Where one part of culture changes first," said Ogburn, "through some discovery or invention, and occasions changes in some part of culture dependent upon it, there frequently is a delay . . . . The extent of this lag will vary . . . but may exist for . . . years, during which time there may be said to be a maladjustment." [85] In the case of workmen's compensation, the lag period was from the time when industrial accidents became numerous until the time when workmen's compensation laws were passed, "about a half-century, from 1850–70 to 1915." During this period, "the old adaptive culture, the common law of employers' liability, hung over after the material conditions had changed." [86]

The concept of cultural lag is still widely used, in social science and out — particularly since its popularization by Stuart Chase in *The Proper Study of Mankind*.[87] And the notion that law fails to adjust promptly to the call for change is commonly voiced. In popular parlance, this or that aspect of the law is often said to "lag behind the times." This idea is so pervasive that it deserves comment quite apart from its present status in sociological thought.

The lesson of industrial accident law, as here described, may be quite the opposite of the lesson that Ogburn drew. In a purely objective (non-teleological) sense, social processes — and the legal system — cannot aptly be described through use of the idea of lag. When, in the face of changed technology and new problems, a social arrangement stubbornly persists, there are *social* reasons why this is so; there are explanations why no change or slow change occurs. The legal system is a part of the total culture; it is not a self-operating machine. The rate of response to a call for change is slow or fast in the law depending upon who issues the call and who (if anybody) resists it. "Progress" or "catching up" is not inevitable or predictable. Legal change, like social change, is a change in behavior of individuals and groups in interaction. The rate of change depends upon

[83] J. Willard Hurst, *Law and Social Process in United States History*, 69 (1960).

[84] W. Ogburn, *Social Change With Respect to Culture and Original Nature*, 200 (Viking ed. 1950). See generally *id.* at 199–280. In the book cultural lag was offered as a hypothesis; in later writing Ogburn referred to it as a theory.

[85] *Id.* at 201.

[86] *Id.* at 236.

[87] See S. Chase, The Proper Study of Mankind, 115–17 (1st ed. 1948). For other applications of cultural lag, see H. Hart, "Social Theory and Social Change," in *Symposium on Sociological Theory*, 196, 219–25 (Gross ed. 1959). See generally H. Hart, "The Hypothesis of Cultural Lag: A Present Day View," in *Technology and Social Change*, 417–34 (Allen ed. 1957).

the kind of interaction. To say that institutions lag is usually to say no more than they are slow to make changes of a particular type. But why are they slow? Often the answer rests on the fact that these institutions are controlled by or respond to groups or individuals who are opposed to the specific change. This is lag only if we feel we can confidently state that these groups or individuals are wrong as to their own self-interest as well as that of society. Of course, people *are* often wrong about their own self-interest; they can be and are short-sighted, ignorant, maladroit. But ignorance of this kind exists among progressives as well as among conservatives — among those who want change as well as among those who oppose it. Resistance to change is "lag" only if there is only one "true" definition of a problem — and one "true" solution.

There were important reasons why fifty years elapsed before workmen's compensation became part of the law. Under the impact of industrial conditions Americans were changing their views about individual security and social welfare. Dean Pound has remarked that the twentieth century accepts the idea of insuring those unable to bear economic loss, at the expense of the nearest person at hand who can bear the loss. This conception was relatively unknown and unacceptable to judges of the nineteenth century.[88] The fellow-servant rule could not be replaced until economic affluence, business conditions, and the state of safety technology made feasible a more social solution. Labor unions of the mid-nineteenth century did not call for a compensation plan; they were concerned with more basic (and practical) issues such as wages and hours. Note the form that the argument for workmen's compensation took, after 1900, in the following quotation; few Americans reasoned this way fifty years earlier.

> [S]uppose you carry an accident policy and are negligent in stepping from a street car. Do you not expect the insurance company to pay? If you negligently overturn a lamp and your house burns, do you not expect the fire insurance company to pay? That is what insurance is for—to guard against the slips and mistakes that are characteristics of human nature. . . .
>
> Before granting a pension do we ask whether a man used due care in dodging the bullets, or do we plead that he voluntarily assumed the risk? Then why, when a man courageously volunteers to do the dangerous work in transportation, mining, building, etc., should it seem wrong to grant him or his dependents compensation in case of accidents? [89]

Social insurance, as much as private insurance, requires standardization and rationalization of business, predictability of risk, and reliability and

[88] R. Pound, "The Economic Interpretation and the Law of Torts," 53 *Harv. L. Rev.*, 365, 376 (1940).

[89] [1907–1908] *Wis. Bureau of Industrial and Labor Statistics Thirteenth Bienniel Rep.* (1909), quoted in Auerbach, 586.

financial responsibility of economic institutions. These were present in 1909, but not in 1850.

Prior to workmen's compensation, the legal system reflected existing conflicts of value quite clearly; the manifold exceptions to the fellow-servant rule and the primitive liability statutes bear witness to this fact. These were not symptoms of "lag"; rather, they were a measure of the constant adjustments that inevitably take place within a legal system that is not insulated from the larger society but an integral part of it. To be sure, the courts frequently reflected values of the business community and so did the legislatures, but populist expressions can easily be found in the work of judges, legislatures, and juries. In the absence of a sophisticated measuring-rod of past public opinion — and sophisticated concepts of the role of public opinion in nineteenth-century society — who is to say that the legal system "lagged" behind some hypothetical general will of the public or some hypothetically correct solution?

The concept of lag may also be employed in the criticism of the courts' use of judicial review to retard the efficacy of social welfare legislation. In 1911, the New York Court of Appeals declared the state's compulsory workmen's compensation act unconstitutional. As a result of this holding, the state constitution had to be amended — two years later — before workmen's compensation was legally possible in New York.[90] Because of the New York experience, six states also amended their constitutions and others enacted voluntary plans. The issue was not finally settled until 1917, when the United States Supreme Court held both compulsory and elective plans to be constitutional.[91] But it adds little to an understanding of social process to describe this delay in terms of the concept of cultural lag. Courts do not act on their own initiative. Each case of judicial review was instigated by a litigant who represented a group in society which was fighting for its interests as it perceived them; these were current, real interests, not interests of sentiment or inertia. This is completely apart from consideration of what social interests the courts thought they were serving in deciding these cases — interests which hindsight condemns as futile or wrong, but which were living issues and interests of the day.

Conflicts of value also arose in the legislatures when they began to consider compensation laws. The Massachusetts investigating commission of 1903 reported a workmen's compensation bill to the legislature, but the bill was killed in committee on the ground that Massachusetts could not afford to increase the production costs of commodities manufactured in the state.[92] Once more, the emergence of compensation depended upon

[90] N.Y. Const. art. 1, § 19, was added in 1913; the new compensation law it authorized was enacted the same year. See Ch. 816, [1913] N.Y. Laws 2277.

[91] *New York Cent. R.R.* v. *White*, 243 U.S. 188 (1917); *Hawkins* v. *Bleakly*, 243 U.S. 210 (1917). In *Mountain Timber Co.* v. *Washington*, 243 U.S. 219 (1917), the Court also held an exclusive state insurance fund to be constitutional.

[92] R. Warner, "Employers' Liability as an Industrial Problem," 18 *Green Bag*, 185, 192 (1906).

a perception of inevitability — which could cancel the business detriment to particular states which enacted compensation laws — and of general economic gain from the new system. It is not enough to sense that a social problem exists. Rational collective action demands relatively precise and detailed information about the problem, and clear placement of responsibility for proposing and implementing a solution. For many years legislatures simply did not consider it their responsibility to do anything about industrial injuries. Since they did not view accidents as a major social problem, and since state legislatures were weak political structures, they were content at first to leave accidents to tort law and the courts.[93] Moreover, state agencies were not delegated the task of collecting information on the nature and extent of industrial accidents until relatively late. The Wisconsin legislature created a Bureau of Labor and Industrial Statistics in 1883, but did not provide for the collection of data on industrial accidents until 1905.[94] When a need for accident legislation was perceived, individual legislators, under pressure of constituencies, began to introduce work accident indemnity bills. Some were inadequately drafted; most were poorly understood. In order to appraise potential legislation, investigating commissions were created to collect information, weigh the costs and report back alternative solutions.

What appears to some as an era of "lag" was actually a period in which issues were collectively defined and alternative solutions posed, and during which interest groups bargained for favorable formulations of law. It was a period of "false starts" — unstable compromise formulations by decision makers armed with few facts, lacking organizational machinery, and facing great, often contradictory, demands from many publics. There was no easy and suitable solution, in the light of the problem and the alignment of powers. Indeed, workmen's compensation — which today appears to be a stable solution — was only a compromise, an answer acceptable to enough people and interest groups to endure over a reasonably long period of time.

Part of what is later called "lag," then, is this period of false starts — the inadequate compromises by decision makers faced with contradictory interest groups pressing inconsistent solutions. There may not be a "solution" in light of the alignment of interests and powers with respect to the problem at any given point in time. Perhaps only a compromise "solution" is possible. What later appears to be the final answer is in fact itself a compromise — one which is stable over some significant period of time. Sociologically, that is what a "solution" to a problem is: nothing more than a stable compromise acceptable to enough people and interest groups to maintain itself over a significant period of time. Theoretically, of

[93] "Laying the personal injury burdens of production upon the things produced . . . should have been efficiently recognized long ago, and would have been had the lawmaking power appreciated that it is its province, not that of the courts, to cure infirmity in the law." *Borgnis* v. *Falk Co.*, 147 Wis. 327, 370, 133 N.W. 209, 223 (1911) (Marshall, J., concurring).

[94] Ch. 416, §§1, 4, [1905] Wis. Laws 680, 682.

course, total victory by one competing interest and total defeat of another is possible. But in a functioning democratic society, total victories and defeats are uncommon. Total defeat would mean that a losing group was so utterly powerless that it could exert no bargaining pressure whatsover; total victory similarly would imply unlimited power. In the struggle over industrial accident legislation, none of the interests could be so described. Different perceptions of the problem, based at least in part on different economic and social stakes, led to different views of existing and potential law. When these views collided, compromises were hammered out. Workmen's compensation took form not because it was (or is) perfect, but because it represented a solution acceptable enough to enough interests to outweigh the costs of additional struggle and bargaining. If there was "lag" in the process, it consisted of acquiescence in presently acceptable solutions which turned out not to be adequate or stable in the long run. "Lag" therefore at most means present-minded pragmatism rather than long-term rational planning.[95]

B. *Cross-Cultural Borrowing.* The adoption of workmen's compensation in America does represent an instance of what can be called conscious cross-cultural borrowing. Workmen's compensation was not an American innovation; there were numerous European antecedents. Switzerland passed a workmen's compensation act in 1881; Germany followed in 1884 with a more inclusive scheme. By 1900 compensation laws had spread to most European countries. In 1891 the United States Bureau of Labor commissioned John Graham Brooks to study and appraise the German system. His report, published in 1893, was widely distributed and successfully exposed some American opinion-leaders to the existence of the European programs.[96] Most of the state investigating commissions

---

[95] Other instances of supposed cultural lag can be analyzed in similar terms. For example, Ogburn used exploitation of the forests and the tardy rise of conservation laws as another illustration of the lag. See W. Ogburn, *supra* note 84, at 203–10. Professor Hurst's elaborate study of law and the Wisconsin lumber industry demonstrates that the legal system supported the exploitation of the forests of Wisconsin in the 19th century; the public did not and would not consider the ultimate social costs of destroying the forests. "Common opinion through the lumber era considered that the public interest *had no greater concern* than the increase of the productive capacity of the general economy." J. Willard Hurst, *Law and Economic Growth,* 261 (1964) (emphasis added). "[T]he dominant attention of nineteenth-century policy was upon promotional rather than regulative use of law." *Id.* The crucial problem was how to develop and settle the continent, not how to conserve or reforest. Certainly no one was concerned with playgrounds for unborn urban masses. People backed demands arising out of immediate interests: the development of stable, economically prosperous communities. Courts reflected these attitudes. Blindness to future needs for natural resources did not result from evil intentions or from a yielding to the "pine barons"; the law reflected "prevailing community values," seeking concrete solutions to problems concretely and currently perceived. *Id.*

[96] See 1 A. Larson, *Workmen's Compensation,* § 5.20 (1964).

also inquired into the European experience, and a number of early bills were modeled after the German and British systems.

Though workmen's compensation can therefore be viewed as an example of cross-cultural borrowing, care must be exercised in employing the concept. Successful legal solutions to social problems are often borrowed across state and national lines but this borrowing must not be confused with the actual "influence" of one legal system over another. "Influence" carries with it an implication of power or, at the least, of cultural dominance. The forces that led to a demand for workmen's compensation were entirely domestic, as this study has argued. The fact that European solutions to similar problems were studied and, to an extent, adopted here shows not dominance but an attempt to economize time, skill, and effort by borrowing an appropriate model. It would be quite wrong to detect European legal "influence" in this process. The existence of the European compensation plans was not a cause of similar American statutes. Rather, the interest shown in the foreign experiences was a response to American dissatisfaction with existing industrial accident law.[97] Similarly, the current drive for an American *ombudsman* is not an example of the "influence" of Scandinavian law. A foreign model here sharpens discussion and provides a ready-made plan. Yet the felt need for such an officer has domestic origins.

C. *Great Men and Social Change*. Sociologists are fond of pointing out the inaccuracy of the "great-man theory of history," which holds that particular persons play irreplaceably decisive roles in determining the path of social change. The influence of single individuals, they say, is hardly as critical as historians would have us believe.[98] The role of outstanding persons in bringing about workmen's compensation acts seems on one level quite clear. In Wisconsin, Roujet Marshall excoriated the existing system from the bench; off the bench he was a vigorous champion of the new law and, indeed, helped draft it. John R. Commons worked tirelessly for passage of the act, and served on the first Industrial Commission whose obligation it was to administer the law.[99] His writings and teachings helped mobilize informed public opinion and virtually created a lobby of academicians for workmen's compensation. Political figures, businessmen, union leaders, and others played active roles in the passage of the law. It is quite tempting to say that the Wisconsin law would be unthinkable but for the work of Marshall, or Commons, or LaFollette and the

---

[97] Of course, cross-cultural borrowing of legal institutions presupposes a certain level of world interchange of culture. At the time workmen's compensation was adopted, American intellectuals were in close communication with Europe, and academics were in particular infatuated with things German. African or Asiatic models — had they existed — most likely would have been ignored. America was disposed to learn from Englishmen and Germans, not from Chinese or Bantus.

[98] See, e.g., Freedman, 83 (rev. ed. 1956).

[99] See 2 J. Commons, *Institutional Economics*, 854 (1934).

Progressive tradition in the state, or the craftsmanship of Wisconsin's pioneering legislative reference service under the skilled leadership of Charles McCarthy.[100] Reformers and academicians served as important middlemen in mediating between interest groups and working out compromises. Their arguments legitimated the act; their zeal enlisted support of middle-class neutrals. They were willing to do the spadework of research, drafting, and propagandizing necessary for a viable law. In the passage of many other welfare and reform laws, outstanding personalities can be found who played dominant roles in creating and leading public opinion — for example, Lawrence Veiller for the New York tenement housing law of 1901,[101] Harvey Wiley for the Federal Food and Drug Act.[102]

The great-man hypothesis is not susceptible of proof or disproof. But the course of events underlying workmen's compensation at least suggests that social scientists are properly suspicious of placing too much reliance on a great-man view. If the view here expressed is correct, then economic, social, political and legal forces made workmen's compensation . . . virtually inevitable by the end of the nineteenth century. Outstanding men may be necessary in general for the implementation of social change; someone must take the lead in creating the intellectual basis for a change in perception. Nonetheless, when a certain pattern of demand exists in society, more than one person may be capable of filling that role. Particular individuals are normally not indispensable. The need is for talent — men with extraordinary ability, perseverance, and personal influence, men who can surmount barriers and accomplish significant results. Obviously, the absence of outstanding persons interested in a particular cause can delay problem solving or lead to inept, shoddy administration. The appearance of truly exceptional persons at the proper moment in history is undoubtedly not automatic. But talent, if not genius, may well be a constant in society; and the social order determines whether and in what direction existing talent will be exerted.

Thus, it would be foolish to deny that specific individuals exert great influence upon the development of social events, and equally foolish to conclude that other persons could not have done the job as well (or better) if given the opportunity. "Great men," however, must be in the right place, which means that society must have properly provided for the training and initiative of outstanding persons and for their recruitment into critical offices when needed. In difficult times, great businessmen, political leaders, musicians, or physicists will emerge. "Great men" appear "when the time is ripe" — but only insofar as society has created the conditions for a pool of creative manpower dedicated to the particular line of endeavor in which their greatness lies. . . .

[100] On McCarthy, see J. Commons, *Myself*, 107–11 (1934).
[101] See generally R. Lubove, *The Progressives and the Slums* (1962).
[102] See O. Anderson, Jr., *The Health of a Nation* (1958).

A Study in Nativis
The American Red
Scare of 1919–20

STANLEY COBEN

In recent years psychologists and anthropologists have directed much attention to the subject of nativism and cults. The historian, Stanley Coben, has applied some of their findings and concepts to a specific American phenomenon — the eruption of nativism and the "Red Scare" following the First World War. Coben's essay, with its careful application of social science symmetry to historical complexity, is an example of interdisciplinary scholarship. Historians long have been interested in the periodic nativistic outbreaks that have plagued the American past. But they have generally failed to account adequately for societal vulnerability to hysteria. Most explanations have been within the context of intellectual history, and usually interpreted these events as the triumph of the mindless, unreasoning masses over the wise and rational elements of society. But as Coben illustrates for the Red Scare period, severe social and economic dislocations, coupled with a fear of radicalism as a threat to cultural stability, can tell us a good deal more about irrational behavior in society, and how and why various groups are so affected. His model for 1919–20 might be applied profitably to similar outbreaks, such as the anti-Jacobin crusade of the 1790's, the Know-Nothing movement of the 1850's, and the anti-communist crusade since 1945.

At a victory loan pageant in the District of Columbia on May 6, 1919, a man refused to rise for the playing of "The Star-Spangled Banner." As soon as the national anthem was completed an enraged sailor fired three shots into the unpatriotic spectator's back. When the man fell, the *Washington Post* reported, "the crowd burst into cheering and handclapping." In February of the same year, a jury in Hammond, Indiana, took two minutes to acquit the assassin of an alien who yelled, "To Hell with the

Reprinted with permission from the *Political Science Quarterly*, LXXIX (March 1964), pp. 52–75.

United States." Early in 1920, a clothing store salesman in Waterbury, Connecticut, was sentenced to six months in jail for having remarked to a customer that Lenin was "the brainiest," or "one of the brainiest" of the world's political leaders.[1] Dramatic episodes like these, or the better known Centralia Massacre, Palmer Raids, or May Day riots, were not everyday occurrences, even at the height of the Red Scare. But the fanatical one hundred per cent Americanism reflected by the Washington crowd, the Hammond jury, and the Waterbury judge pervaded a large part of our society between early 1919 and mid-1920.

Recently, social scientists have produced illuminating evidence about the causes of eruptions like that of 1919–20. They have attempted to identify experimentally the individuals most responsive to nativistic appeals, to explain their susceptibility, and to propose general theories of nativistic and related movements. These studies suggest a fuller, more coherent picture of nativistic upheavals and their causes than we now possess, and they provide the framework for this attempt to reinterpret the Red Scare.

Psychological experiments indicate that a great many Americans — at least several million — are always ready to participate in a "red scare." These people permanently hold attitudes which characterized the nativists of 1919–20: hostility toward certain minority groups, especially radicals and recent immigrants, fanatical patriotism, and a belief that internal enemies seriously threaten national security.[2]

In one of the most comprehensive of these experiments, psychologists Nancy C. Morse and Floyd H. Allport tested seven hypotheses about the causes of prejudice and found that one, national involvement or patriotism, proved to be "by far the most important factor" associated with prejudice. Other widely held theories about prejudice — status rivalry, frustration-

[1] *Washington Post*, May 7, 1919; Mark Sullivan, *Our Times, The United States 1900–1925* (New York, 1935), VI, 169; *The Nation*, CX (April 17, 1920), 510–11. The most complete account of the Red Scare is Robert K. Murray, *Red Scare, A Study in National Hysteria* (Minneapolis, 1955). But see the critical review of Murray's book by John M. Blum in *Mississippi Valley Historical Review*, XLII (1955), 145. Blum comments that Murray failed to explain "the susceptibility of the American people and of their elite to the 'national hysteria.' . . . About hysteria, after all, psychology and social psychology in particular have had considerable to say." John Higham places the postwar movement in historical perspective in his superb *Strangers in the Land, Patterns of American Nativism, 1860–1925* (New Brunswick, 1955), especially Chaps. 8 and 9.

[2] On the incidence of prejudice against minorities in the United States, see Gordon W. Allport and Bernard M. Kramer, "Some Roots of Prejudice," *Journal of Psychology*, XXII (1946), 9–39; Morris Janowitz and Dwaine Marvick, "Authoritarianism and Political Behavior," *Public Opinion Quarterly*, XVII (1953), 185–201; Bruno Bettelheim and Morris Janowitz, *Dynamics of Prejudice, A Psychological and Sociological Study of Veterans* (New York, 1950), 16, 26, and *passim*.

aggression, and scapegoat hypotheses, for example — were found to be of only secondary importance.[3] Summarizing the results of this and a number of other psychological experiments, Gordon W. Allport, a pioneer in the scientific study of prejudice, concluded that in a large proportion of cases the prejudiced person is attempting to defend himself against severe inner turmoil by enforcing order in his external life. Any disturbance in the social *status quo* threatens the precarious psychic equilibrium of this type of individual, who, according to Allport, seeks "an island of institutional safety and security. The nation is the island he selects. . . . It has the definiteness he needs."

Allport pointed out that many apprehensive and frustrated people are not especially prejudiced. What is important, he found,

> is the way fear and frustration are handled. The institutionalistic way — especially the nationalistic — seems to be the nub of the matter. What happens is that the prejudiced person defines "nation" to fit his needs. The nation is first of all a protection (the chief protection) of him as an individual. It is his in-group. He sees no contradiction in ruling out of its beneficent orbit those whom he regards as threatening intruders and enemies (namely, American minorities). What is more, the nation stands for the status quo. It is a conservative agent; within it are all the devices for safe living that he approves. His nationalism is a form of conservatism.[4]

Substantial evidence, then, suggests that millions of Americans are both extraordinarily fearful of social change and prejudiced against those minority groups which they perceive as "threatening intruders." Societal disruption, especially if it can easily be connected with the "intruders," not only will intensify the hostility of highly prejudiced individuals, but also will provoke many others, whose antagonism in more stable times had been mild or incipient, into the extreme group.

A number of anthropologists have come to conclusions about the roots of nativism which complement these psychological studies. Since the late nineteenth century, anthropologists have been studying the religious and

[3] Nancy C. Morse and F. H. Allport, "The Causation of Anti-Semitism: An Investigation of Seven Hypotheses," *Journal of Psychology*, XXXIV (1952), 197–233. For further experimental evidence indicating that prejudiced individuals are no more anxious, neurotic, or intolerant of ambiguity than those with more "liberal" attitudes, Anthony Davids, "Some Personality and Intellectual Correlates to Intolerance of Ambiguity," *Journal of Abnormal and Social Psychology*, LI (1955), 415–20; Ross Stagner and Clyde S. Congdon, "Another Failure to Demonstrate Displacement of Aggression," *Journal of Abnormal and Social Psychology*, LI (1955), 695–96; Dean Peabody, "Attitude Content and Agreement Set in Scales of Authoritarianism, Dogmatism, Anti-Semitism and Economic Conservatism," *Journal of Abnormal and Social Psychology*, LXIII (1961), 1–11.

[4] Gordon W. Allport, *The Nature of Prejudice* (Cambridge, 1955), 406; see Boyd C. Shafer, *Nationalism, Myth and Reality* (New York, 1955), 181.

nativistic cults of American Indian tribes and of Melanesian and Papuan groups in the South Pacific. Recently, several anthropologists have attempted to synthesize their findings and have shown striking parallels in the cultural conditions out of which these movements arose.[5] In every case, severe societal disruption preceded the outbreak of widespread nativistic cult behavior. According to Anthony F. C. Wallace, who has gone farthest toward constructing a general theory of cult formation, when the disruption has proceeded so far that many members of a society find it difficult or impossible to fulfill their physical and psychological needs, or to relieve severe anxiety through the ordinary culturally approved methods, the society will be susceptible to what Wallace has termed a "revitalization movement." This is a convulsive attempt to change or revivify important cultural beliefs and values, and frequently to eliminate alien influences. Such movements promise and often provide participants with better means of dealing with their changed circumstances, thus reducing their very high level of internal stress.[6]

[5] See, especially, the works of Anthony F. C. Wallace: "Revitalization Movements," *American Anthropologist*, LVIII (1956), 264–81; "Handsome Lake and the Great Revival in the West," *American Quarterly*, IV (1952), 149–65; "Stress and Rapid Personality Change," *International Record of Medicine and General Practice Clinics*, CLXIX (1956), 761–73; "New Religions Among the Delaware Indians, 1600–1900," *Southwest Journal of Anthropology*, XII (1956), 1–21. Also, Michael M. Ames, "Reaction to Stress: A Comparative Study of Nativism," *Davidson Journal of Anthropology*, III (1957), 16–30; C. S. Belshaw, "The Significance of Modern Cults in Melanesian Development," *Australian Outlook*, IV (1950), 116–25; Raymond Firth, "The Theory of 'Cargo' Cults: A Note on Tikopia," *Man*, LV (1955), 130–32; Lawrence Krader, "A Nativistic Movement in Western Siberia," *American Anthropologist*, LVIII (1956), 282–92; Ralph Linton, "Nativistic Movements," *American Anthropologist*, XLV (1943), 220–43; Margaret Mead, *New Lives for Old* (New York, 1956); Peter Worsley, *The Trumpet Shall Sound* (London, 1957). Several sociologists and psychologists have come to conclusions about the causes of these movements that are similar in important respects to Wallace's, although less comprehensive. See Leon Festinger, *A Theory of Cognitive Dissonance* (New York, 1957); Hadley Cantril, *The Psychology of Social Movements* (New York, 1941), especially pp. 3–4, Chaps. 5, 8, and 9; Hans H. Toch, "Crisis Situations and Ideological Revaluation," *Public Opinion Quarterly*, XIX (1955), 53–67.

[6] Wallace, "Revitalization Movements." For a recent verification of Wallace's theories see Thomas Rhys Williams, "The Form of a North Borneo Nativistic Behavior," *American Anthropologist*, LXV (1963), 543–51. On the psychological results of socially caused stress, Wallace, "Stress and Rapid Personality Change"; William Caudill, *Effects of Social and Cultural Systems in Reactions to Stress*, Social Science Research Council Pamphlet No. 14 (New York, 1958); Caudill "Cultural Perspectives on Stress," Army Medical Service Graduate School, *Symposium on Stress* (Washington, D. C., 1953); Hans Selye, *The Stress of Life* (New York, 1956); Roland Fischer and Neil Agnew, "A Hierarchy of Stressors," *Journal of Mental Science*, CI (1955), 383–86; Daniel H. Funkenstein, Stanley H. King, and Margaret E. Drolette, *Mastery of Stress* (Cambridge, 1957); M. Basowitz *et al.*, *Anxiety and Stress: An Interdisciplinary Study of a Life Situation* (New York, 1955).

American Indian tribes, for example, experienced a series of such convulsions as the tide of white settlers rolled west. The Indians were pushed onto reservations and provided with Indian agents, missionaries, and physicians, who took over many of the functions hitherto assumed by chiefs and medicine men. Indian craftsmen (and craftswomen) were replaced by dealers in the white man's implements. Most hunters and warriors also lost their vocations and consequently their self-respect. What an anthropologist wrote of one tribe was true of many others: "From cultural maturity as Pawnees they were reduced to cultural infancy as civilized men." [7]

One of the last major religious upheavals among the Indians was the Ghost Dance cult which spread from Nevada through Oregon and northern California in the eighteen-seventies, and a similar movement among the Rocky Mountain and western plains Indians about 1890. Although cult beliefs varied somewhat from tribe to tribe, converts generally were persuaded that if they followed certain prescribed rituals, including the dance, they would soon return to their old ways of living. Even their dead relatives would be restored to life. Most Indians were too conscious of their military weakness to challenge their white masters directly. Ghost Dancers among the Dakota Sioux, however, influenced by the militant proselyter Sitting Bull, became convinced that true believers could not be harmed by the white man's bullets and that Sioux warriors would drive the intruders from Indian lands. Their dreams were rudely smashed at the massacre of Wounded Knee Creek in December 1890.[8]

The Boxer movement in China, 1898 to 1900, resembled in many respects the Indian Ghost Dance cults; however, the Boxers, more numerous and perhaps less demoralized than the Indians, aimed more directly at removing foreign influences from their land. The movement erupted first in Shantung province where foreigners, especially Japanese, British, and Germans, were most aggressive. A flood of the Yellow River had recently deprived about a million people in the province of food and shelter. Banditry was rampant, organized government ineffective. The Boxer

---

[7] Alexander Lesser, *The Pawnee Ghost Dance Hand Game. A Study of Cultural Change* (New York, 1933), 44.

[8] Cora DuBois, *The 1870 Ghost Dance*, Anthropological Records, III (Berkeley, 1946); Leslie Spier, *The Ghost Dance of 1870 Among the Klamath of Oregon*, University of Washington Publications in Anthropology, II (Seattle, 1927); Lesser, *Ghost Dance*; A. L. Kroeber, *Handbook of the Indians of California*, Bureau of American Ethnology Bulletin 78 (Washington, D.C., 1925). Anthropologists recently have argued about the origins of the Ghost Dance cults. Both sides agree, however, that whatever their origins, the cults took the form they did because of intolerable cultural conditions caused largely by white encroachments. David F. Aberle, "The Prophet Dance and Reactions to White Contact," *Southwest Journal of Anthropology*, XV (1959), 74–83; Leslie Spier, Wayne Suttles, and Melville Herskovits, "Comment on Aberle's Thesis of Deprivation," *Southwest Journal of Anthropology*, XV (1959), 84–88.

movement, based on the belief that these tragic conditions were due almost entirely to the "foreign devils" and their agents, determined to drive the enemy out of China. Boxers went into action carrying charms and chanting incantations supposed to make them invulnerable to the foreigners' bullets. The first object of the Boxers' nativistic fury were Chinese who had converted to Christianity, the intruders' religion. The patriots then attacked railroad and telegraph lines, leading symbols of foreign influence. Finally, the Boxers turned against the foreigners themselves, slaughtering many. Not until after the Boxers carried on a two-month siege of the foreign community in Peking did American, European, and Japanese armies crush the movement.[9]

Other revitalization attempts proved more successful than the Boxers or Ghost Dancers. The Gaiwiio movement, for example, helped the Iroquois Indians of western New York State to retain their identity as a culture while adjusting successfully to an encroaching white civilization during the first decade of the nineteenth century. The movement implanted a new moral code among the Indians, enjoining sobriety and family stability and encouraging acceptance of Western technology, while revivifying cohesive Indian traditions.[10]

Dominant as well as conquered peoples, Ralph Linton has pointed out, undergo nativistic movements. Dominant groups, he observed, are sometimes threatened "not only by foreign invasion or domestic revolt but also by the invidious process of assimilation which might, in the long run, destroy their distinctive powers and privileges." Under such circumstances, Linton concluded, "the frustrations which motivate nativistic movements in inferior or dominated groups" are "replaced by anxieties which produce very much the same [nativistic] result" in dominant groups.[11]

Communist "brainwashers" have consciously attempted to achieve results comparable to those obtained by prophets of movements like the Ghost Dance cult and the Boxers. They create intolerable stress within individuals, not through rapid societal change, but by intentional physical debilitation and continual accusations, cross-examinations, and use of other anxiety-provoking techniques. Then they offer their prisoners an

[9] The best account of the Boxer movement is Chester C. Tan, *The Boxer Catastrophe* (New York, 1955). Also, George N. Steiger, *China and the Occident, the Origin and Development of the Boxer Movement* (New Haven, 1927); Peter Fleming, *The Siege at Peking* (New York, 1959).

[10] Wallace, "Handsome Lake." Wallace compared the Gaiwiio with a Chinese attempt to accommodate their society to Western civilization in "Stress and Rapid Personality Change." For a successful movement in the South Pacific see Mead, *New Lives for Old*.

[11] Linton, 237. Also, Carroll L. Riley and John Hobgood, "A Recent Nativistic Movement Among the Southern Tepehuan Indians," *Southern Journal of Anthropology*, XV (1959), 355–60.

escape from the induced psychological torment: conversion to the new gospel.[12]

The similarity in the mental processes involved in "brainwashing" and in the formation of nativistic movements becomes even clearer upon examination of the Chinese Communist attempt to establish their doctrines in mainland China. Again, the Communists intentionally have created conditions like those out of which nativistic cults have arisen more spontaneously in other societies. In addition to the stress which ordinarily would accompany rapid industrialization of an economically backward society, the Chinese leaders have provoked additional anxiety through the systematic use of group confessions and denunciations and have intentionally disrupted family life. Hostility toward the American enemy has been purposely aroused and used to unify the masses, as well as to justify the repression of millions of alleged internal enemies. The whole population has been continually urged to repent their sins and to adopt wholeheartedly the Communist gospel, which has a strong nativistic component. As a psychologist has remarked, to a large extent the Chinese Communists provide both the disease and the cure.[13]

The ferocious outbreak of nativism in the United States after World War I was not consciously planned or provoked by any individual or group, although some Americans took advantage of the movement once it started. Rather, the Red Scare, like the Gaiwiio and Boxer movements described above, was brought on largely by a number of severe social and economic dislocations which threatened the national equilibrium. The full extent and the shocking effects of these disturbances of 1919 have not yet been adequately described. Runaway prices, a brief but sharp stock market crash and business depression, revolutions throughout Europe, widespread fear of domestic revolt, bomb explosions, and an outpouring of radical literature were distressing enough. These sudden difficulties, moreover, served to exaggerate the disruptive effects already produced by the social and intellectual ravages of the World War and the preceding reform era, and by the arrival, before the war, of millions of new immigrants. This added stress intensified the hostility of Americans strongly antagonistic to minority groups, and brought new converts to blatant nativism from among those who ordinarily were not overtly hostile toward radicals or recent immigrants.

[12] Robert J. Lifton, "Thought Reform in Western Civilians in Chinese Communist Prisons," *Psychiatry*, XIX (1956), 173–95; Edgar H. Schein, "The Chinese Indoctrination Program for Prisoners of War, A Study of Attempted Brainwashing," *Psychiatry*, XIX (1956), 149–72.

[13] Edgar H. Schein, with Inge Schneier and Curtis H. Bark, *Coercive Persuasion* (New York, 1961); William Sargent, *Battle for the Mind* (New York, 1957), 150–65; Robert J. Lifton, *Thought Reform and the Psychology of Totalism* (New York, 1961); R. L. Walker, *China Under Communism* (London, 1946).

Citizens who joined the crusade for one hundred per cent American-ism sought, primarily, a unifying force which would halt the apparent dis-integration of their culture. The movement, they felt, would eliminate those foreign influences which the one hundred per centers believed were the major causes of their anxiety.

Many of the postwar sources of stress were also present during World War I, and the Red Scare, as John Higham has observed, was partly an exaggeration of wartime passions.[14] In 1917–18 German-Americans served as the object of almost all our nativistic fervor; they were the threatening intruders who refused to become good citizens. "They used America," a patriotic author declared in 1918 of two million German-Americans, "they never loved her. They clung to their old language, their old customs, and cared nothing for ours. . . . As a class they were clannish beyond all other races coming here." [15] Fear of subversion by German agents was almost as extravagant in 1917–18 as anxiety about "reds" in the postwar period. Attorney General Thomas Watt Gregory reported to a friend in May 1918 that "we not infrequently receive as many as fifteen hundred letters in a single day suggesting disloyalty and the making of investiga-tions." [16]

Opposition to the war by radical groups helped smooth the transition among American nativists from hatred of everything German to fear of radical revolution. The two groups of enemies were associated also for other reasons. High government officials declared after the war that Ger-man leaders planned and subsidized the Bolshevik Revolution.[17] When bombs blasted homes and public buildings in nine cities in June 1919, the director of the Justice Department's Bureau of Investigation asserted that the bombers were "connected with Russian bolshevism, aided by Hun money." [18] In November 1919, a year after the armistice, a popular maga-zine warned of "the Russo-German movement that is now trying to dominate America. . . ." [19]

Even the wartime hostility toward German-Americans, however, is more

[14] Higham, 222.

[15] Emerson Hough, The Web (Chicago, 1919), 23. Hough was a rabid one hundred per center during the Red Scare also.

[16] T. W. Gregory to R. E. Vinson, May 13, 1918, Papers of Thomas Watt Gregory (Library of Congress, Washington, D.C.).

[17] Subcommittee of Senate Committee on the Judiciary, Hearings, Brewing and Liquor Interests and German and Bolshevik Propaganda, 66th Congress, 1st Session, 1919, 2669 ff.; The New York Times, July 7, August 11 and 29, Septem-ber 15–21, 1918.

[18] Washington Post, July 3, 1919. Bureau Director William J. Flynn pro-duced no evidence to back this assertion. Later he claimed to have conclusive proof that the bombers were Italian anarchists. Flynn to Attorney General Harry Daugherty, April 4, 1922, Department of Justice Records, File 202600, Sect. 5 (National Archives, Washington, D.C.).

[19] Saturday Evening Post, CXCII (November 1, 1919), 28. For similar as-sertions in other publications, Meno Lovenstein, American Opinion of Soviet Russia (Washington, D.C., 1941), Chap. 1, passim.

understandable when seen in the light of recent anthropological and psychological studies. World War I disturbed Americans not only because of the real threat posed by enemy armies and a foreign ideology. For many citizens it had the further effect of shattering an already weakened intellectual tradition. When the European governments decided to fight, they provided shocking evidence that man was not, as most educated members of Western society had believed, a rational creature progressing steadily, if slowly, toward control of his environment. When the great powers declared war in 1914, many Americans as well as many Europeans were stunned. The *New York Times* proclaimed a common theme — European civilization had collapsed: The supposedly advanced nations, declared the *Times*, "have reverted to the condition of savage tribes roaming the forests and falling upon each other in a fury of blood and carnage to achieve the ambitious designs of chieftains clad in skins and drunk with mead." [20] Franz Alexander, director for twenty-five years of the Chicago Institute of Psychoanalysis, recently recalled his response to the outbreak of the World War:

> The first impact of this news is [sic] unforgettable. It was the sudden intuitive realization that a chapter of history had ended. . . . Since then, I have discussed this matter with some of my contemporaries and heard about it a great deal in my early postwar psychoanalytic treatments of patients. To my amazement, the others who went through the same events had quite a similar reaction. . . . It was an immediate vivid and prophetic realization that something irrevocable of immense importance had happened in history.[21]

Americans were jolted by new blows to their equilibrium after entering the war. Four million men were drafted away from familiar surroundings and some of them experienced the terrible carnage of trench warfare. Great numbers of women left home to work in war industries or to replace men in other jobs. Negroes flocked to Northern industrial areas by the hundreds of thousands, and their first mass migration from the South created violent racial antagonism in Northern cities.

During the war, also, Americans sanctioned a degree of government control over the economy which deviated sharply from traditional economic individualism. Again, fears aroused before the war were aggravated, for the reform legislation of the Progressive era had tended to increase

---

20 Quoted in William E. Leuchtenburg, *The Perils of Prosperity, 1914–32* (Chicago, 1958), 13. There is no comprehensive study of the effects of the war on the American mind. For brief treatments. Henry F. May, *The End of American Innocence* (New York, 1959), 361–67; Merle Curti, *The Growth of American Thought* (New York, 1951), 687–705; Ralph Henry Gabriel, *The Course of American Democratic Thought* (New York, 1956), 387, 404; André Siegfried, *America Comes of Age* (New York, 1927), 3; Walter Lord, *The Good Years, From 1900 to the First World War* (New York, 1960), 339–41.

21 Franz Alexander, *The Western Mind in Transition* (New York, 1960), 73–74. Also see William Barrett, *Irrational Man* (Garden City, N.Y., 1961), 32–33.

government intervention, and many citizens were further perturbed by demands that the federal government enforce even higher standards of economic and social morality. By 1919, therefore, some prewar progressives as well as conservatives feared the gradual disappearance of highly valued individual opportunity and responsibility. Their fears were fed by strong postwar calls for continued large-scale government controls — extension of federal operation of railroads and of the Food Administration, for example.

The prime threat to these long-held individualistic values, however, and the most powerful immediate stimulus to the revitalistic response, came from Russia. There the Bolshevik conquerors proclaimed their intention of exporting Marxist ideology. If millions of Americans were disturbed in 1919 by the specter of communism, the underlying reason was not fear of foreign invasion — Russia, after all, was still a backward nation recently badly defeated by German armies. The real threat was the potential spread of communist ideas. These, the one hundred per centers realized with horror, possessed a genuine appeal for reformers and for the economically underprivileged, and if accepted they would complete the transformation of America.

A clear picture of the Bolshevik tyranny was not yet available; therefore, as after the French Revolution, those who feared the newly successful ideology turned to fight the revolutionary ideals. So the *Saturday Evening Post* declared editorially in November 1919 that "History will see our present state of mind as one with that preceding the burning of witches, the children's crusade, the great tulip craze and other examples of softening of the world brain." The *Post* referred not to the Red Scare or the impending Palmer Raids, but to the spread of communist ideology. Its editorial concluded: "The need of the country is not more idealism, but more pragmatism; not communism, but common sense." [22] One of the most powerful patriotic groups, the National Security League, called upon members early in 1919 to "teach 'Americanism.' This means the fighting of Bolshevism . . . by the creation of well defined National Ideals." Members "must preach Americanism and instil the idealism of America's Wars, and that American spirit of service which believes in giving as well as getting." [23] New York attorney, author, and educator Henry Waters Taft warned a Carnegie Hall audience late in 1919 that Americans must battle "a propaganada which is tending to undermine our most cherished social and political institutions and is having the effect of producing widespread unrest among the poor and the ignorant, especially those of foreign birth." [24]

[22] *Saturday Evening Post*, CXCII (November 1, 1919), 28.
[23] National Security League, *Future Work* (New York, 1919), 6.
[24] Henry Waters Taft, *Aspects of Bolshevism and Americanism, Address before the League for Political Education at Carnegie Hall, New York, December 6, 1919* (New York, 1919), 21.

When the war ended Americans also confronted the disturbing possibility, pointed up in 1919 by the struggle over the League of Nations, that Europe's struggles would continue to be their own. These factors combined to make the First World War a traumatic experience for millions of citizens. As Senator James Reed of Missouri observed in August 1919, "This country is still suffering from shell shock. Hardly anyone is in a normal state of mind. . . . A great storm has swept over the intellectual world and its ravages and disturbances still exist." [25]

The wartime "shell shock" left many Americans extraordinarily susceptible to psychological stress caused by postwar social and economic turbulence. Most important for the course of the Red Scare, many of these disturbances had their greatest effect on individuals already antagonistic toward minorities. First of all, there was some real evidence of danger to the nation in 1919, and the nation provided the chief emotional support for many Americans who responded easily to charges of an alien radical menace. Violence flared throughout Europe after the war and revolt lifted radicals to power in several Eastern and Central European nations. Combined with the earlier Bolshevik triumph in Russia these revolutions made Americans look more anxiously at radicals here. Domestic radicals encouraged these fears; they became unduly optimistic about their own chances of success and boasted openly of their coming triumph. Scores of new foreign language anarchist and communist journals, most of them written by and for Southern and Eastern European immigrants, commenced publication, and the established radical press became more exuberant. These periodicals never tired of assuring readers in 1919 that "the United States seems to be on the verge of a revolutionary crisis." [26] American newspapers and magazines reprinted selections from radical speeches, pamphlets, and periodicals so their readers could see what dangerous ideas were abroad in the land.[27] Several mysterious bomb explosions and bombing attempts, reported in bold front page headlines in newspapers across the country, frightened the public in 1919. To many

[25] U.S., *Congressional Record*, 66th Congress, 1st Session, August 15, 1919, 3892.

[26] Robert E. Park, *The Immigrant Press and Its Control* (New York, 1922), 214, 230–38, 241–45; R. E. Park and Herbert A. Miller, *Old World Traits Transplanted* (New York, 1921), 99–101; Daniel Bell, "The Background and Development of Marxian Socialism in the United States," in Donald Drew Egbert and Stow Persons, *Socialism in American Life* (Princeton, 1952), I, 334; Lovenstein, 7–50; Leuchtenburg, 67–68; Murray, 33–36.

[27] The Justice Department distributed pamphlets containing such material to all American newspapers and magazines; *Red Radicalism, as Described by Its Own Leaders* (Washington, D.C., 1920); National Popular Government League, *To the American People, Report Upon the Illegal Practices of the Department of Justice* (Washington, D.C., 1920), 64–66. The staunchly anti-radical *New York Times* published translations from a large sample of foreign language radical newspapers on June 8, 1919.

citizens these seemed part of an organized campaign of terror carried on by alien radicals intending to bring down the federal government. The great strikes of 1919 and early 1920 aroused similar fears.[28]

Actually American radical organizations in 1919 were disorganized and poverty-stricken. The Communists were inept, almost without contact with American workers and not yet dominated or subsidized by Moscow. The IWW was shorn of its effective leaders, distrusted by labor, and generally declining in influence and power. Violent anarchists were isolated in a handful of tiny, unconnected local organizations.[29] One or two of these anarchist groups probably carried out the "bomb conspiracy" of 1919; but the extent of the "conspiracy" can be judged from the fact that the bombs killed a total of two men during the year, a night watchman and one of the bomb throwers, and seriously wounded one person, a maid in the home of a Georgia senator.[30]

Nevertheless, prophesies of national disaster abounded in 1919, even among high government officials. Secretary of State Robert Lansing confided to his diary that we were in real peril of social revolution. Attorney General A. Mitchell Palmer advised the House Appropriations Committee that "on a certain day, which we have been advised of," radicals would attempt "to rise up and destroy the Government at one fell swoop." Senator Charles Thomas of Colorado warned that "the country is on the verge of a volcanic upheaval." And Senator Miles Poindexter of Washington declared, "There is real danger that the government will fall." [31] A West Virginia wholesaler, with offices throughout the state, informed the Justice Department in October 1919 that "there is hardly a respectable citizen of my acquaintance who does not believe that we are on the verge of armed conflict in this country." William G. McAdoo was told by a trusted

---

[28] Murray, Chaps. 5, 7–10. Asked by a congressional committee a few weeks after the spate of bombings in June 1919 whether there was real evidence of an organized effort to destroy the federal government, Assistant Attorney General Francis P. Garvan replied, "Certainly." Garvan was in charge of federal prosecution of radicals. *Washington Post*, June 27, 1919.

[29] Theodore Draper, *The Roots of American Communism* (New York, 1957), 198–200, 302, 312–14; David J. Saposs, *Left Wing Unionism, A Study in Policies and Tactics* (New York, 1926), 49–50, 152–57; Selig Perlman and Philip Taft (eds.), *Labor Movements* in John R. Commons (ed.), *History of Labour in the United States 1896–1932*, IV (New York, 1935), 621, 431–32; Jerome Davis, *The Russian Immigrant* (New York, 1922), 114–18; Kate Holladay Claghorn, *The Immigrant's Day in Court* (New York, 1923), 363–73; John S. Gambs, *The Decline of the I.W.W.* (New York, 1932), 133; Murray, 107–10.

[30] *The New York Times*, May 1, June 3, 4, 1919.

[31] "The Spread of Bolshevism in the United States," private memorandum, dated July 26, 1919, Papers of Robert Lansing (Liberty of Congress, Washington, D.C.); "One Point of View of the Murders at Centralia, Washington," private memorandum, dated November 13, 1919, Lansing Papers; U.S., *Congressional Record*, 66th Congress, 1st Session, October 14, 1919, 6869; *Washington Post*, February 16, 1919; New York *World*, June 19, 1919.

friend that "Chicago, which has always been a very liberal minded place, seems to me to have gone mad on the question of the 'Reds.' " Delegates to the Farmers National Congress in November 1919 pledged that farmers would assist the government in meeting the threat of revolution.[32]

The slight evidence of danger from radical organizations aroused such wild fear only because Americans had already encountered other threats to cultural stability. However, the dislocations caused by the war and the menace of communism alone would not have produced such a vehement nativistic response. Other postwar challenges to the social and economic order made the crucial difference.

Of considerable importance was the skyrocketing cost of living. Retail prices more than doubled between 1915 and 1920, and the price rise began gathering momentum in the spring of 1919.[33] During the summer of 1919 the dominant political issue in America was not the League of Nations; not even the "red menace" or the threat of a series of major strikes disturbed the public as much as did the climbing cost of living. The Washington Post early in August 1919 called rising prices, "the burning domestic issue. . . ." Democratic National Chairman Homer Cummings, after a trip around the country, told President Woodrow Wilson that more Americans were worried about prices than about any other public issue and that they demanded government action. When Wilson decided to address Congress on the question the Philadelphia Public Ledger observed that the administration had "come rather tardily to a realization of what is uppermost in the minds of the American people." [34]

Then the wave of postwar strikes — there were 3,600 of them in 1919 involving over 4,000,000 workers [35] — reached a climax in the fall of 1919. A national steel strike began in September and nationwide coal and rail walkouts were scheduled for November 1. Unions gained in membership and power during the war, and in 1919 labor leaders were under strong pressure to help workers catch up to or go ahead of mounting living costs.

[32] Henry Barham to Palmer, October 27, 1919, Justice Department Records, File 202600; unidentified correspondent to McAdoo, February 10, 1920, McAdoo Papers (Library of Congress, Washington, D.C.); A. P. Sanders to Palmer, November 12, 1919, Justice Department Records, File 202600; The New York Times, October 31, 1919.

[33] U.S. Bureau of the Census, Historical Statistics of the United States, Colonial Times to 1952, A Statistical Abstract Supplement (Washington, D.C., 1960), 91 92, 126; U.S. Department of Labor, Bureau of Labor Statistics, Bulletin Number 300, Retail Prices 1913 to December, 1920 (Washington, D.C., 1922), 4; Daniel J. Ahearn, Jr., The Wages of Farm and Factory Laborers 1914–1944 (New York, 1945), 227.

[34] Washington Post, August 1, 4, 1919; The New York Times, July 30, August 1, 1919; Philadelphia Public Ledger, August 5, 1919.

[35] Florence Peterson, Strikes in the United States, 1880–1936, U. S. Department of Labor Bulletin Number 651 (Washington, D.C., 1938), 21. More employees engaged in strikes in 1919 than the total over the ten-year period 1923–32.

Nevertheless, influential government officials attributed the walkouts to radical activities. Early in 1919, Secretary of Labor William B. Wilson declared in a public speech that recent major strikes in Seattle, Butte, Montana, and Lawrence, Massachusetts, had been instituted by the Bolsheviks and the IWW for the sole purpose of bringing about a nationwide revolution in the United States.[36] During the steel strike of early fall, 1919, a Senate investigating committee reported that "behind this strike there is massed a considerable element of I.W.W.'s, anarchists, revolutionists, and Russian soviets. . . ."[37] In April 1920 the head of the Justice Department's General Intelligence Division, J. Edgar Hoover, declared in a public hearing that at least fifty per cent of the influence behind the recent series of strikes was traceable directly to communist agents.[38]

Furthermore, the nation suffered a sharp economic depression in late 1918 and early 1919, caused largely by sudden cancellations of war orders. Returning servicemen found it difficult to obtain jobs during this period, which coincided with the beginning of the Red Scare. The former soldiers had been uprooted from their homes and told that they were engaged in a patriotic crusade. Now they came back to find "reds" criticizing their country and threatening the government with violence, Negroes holding good jobs in the big cities, prices terribly high, and workers who had not served in the armed forces striking for higher wages.[39] A delegate won prolonged applause from the 1919 American Legion Convention when he denounced radical aliens, exclaiming, "Now that the war is over and they are in lucrative positions while our boys haven't a job, we've got to send those scamps to hell." The major part of the mobs which invaded meeting halls of immigrant organizations and broke up radical parades, especially during the first half of 1919, was comprised of men in uniform.[40]

A variety of other circumstances combined to add even more force to the postwar nativistic movement. Long before the new immigrants were seen as potential revolutionists they became the objects of widespread hostility. The peak of immigration from Southern and Eastern Europe occurred in the fifteen years before the war; during that period almost ten

[36] *Washington Post*, February 21, 1919. As late as April 1920, Secretary Wilson agreed with Palmer during a Cabinet meeting that the nationwide rail walkout had been caused by Communists and the IWW. Entry in Josephus Daniels' Diary for April 14, 1920, Papers of Josephus Daniels (Library of Congress, Washington, D.C.).

[37] U.S. Senate, Committee on Education and Labor, *Report, Investigation of Strike in Steel Industry*, 66th Congress, 1st Session, 1919, 14.

[38] *The New York Times*, April 25, 1920, 23.

[39] George Soule, *Prosperity Decade, From War to Depression: 1917–1929* (New York, 1947), 81–84; Murray, 125, 182–83.

[40] *Proceedings and Committees, Caucus of the American Legion* (St. Louis, 1919), 117; *The New York Times*, May 2, 1919; *Washington Post*, May 2, 1919. Ex-servicemen also played major roles in the great Negro-white race riots of mid-1919. *Washington Post*, July 20–23, 28–31.

million immigrants from those areas entered the country. Before the anxious eyes of members of all classes of Americans, the newcomers crowded the cities and began to disturb the economic and social order.[41] Even without other postwar disturbances a nativistic movement of some strength could have been predicted when the wartime solidarity against the German enemy began to wear off in 1919.

In addition, not only were the European revolutions most successful in Eastern and to a lesser extent in Southern Europe, but aliens from these areas predominated in American radical organizations. At least ninety per cent of the members of the two American Communist parties formed in 1919 were born in Eastern Europe. The anarchist groups whose literature and bombs captured the imagination of the American public in 1919 were composed almost entirely of Italian, Spanish, and Slavic aliens. Justice Department announcements and statements by politicians and the press stressed the predominance of recent immigrants in radical organizations.[42] Smoldering prejudice against new immigrants and identification of these immigrants with European as well as American radical movements, combined with other sources of postwar stress to create one of the most frenzied and one of the most widespread nativistic movements in the nation's history.

The result, akin to the movements incited by the Chinese Boxers or the Indian Ghost Dancers, was called Americanism or one hundred per cent Americanism.[43] Its objective was to end the apparent erosion of American values and the disintegration of American culture. By reaffirming those beliefs, customs, symbols, and traditions felt to be the foundation of our way of life, by enforcing conformity among the population, and by purging the nation of dangerous foreigners, the one hundred per centers expected to heal societal divisions and to tighten defenses against cultural change.

Panegyrics celebrating our history and institutions were delivered regularly in almost every American school, church, and public hall in 1919 and 1920. Many of these fervent addresses went far beyond the usual patriotic declarations. Audiences were usually urged to join a crusade to protect our hallowed institutions. Typical of the more moderate statements was Columbia University President Nicholas Murray Butler's in-

[41] *Historical Statistics of the United States*, 56. On the causes of American hostility to recent immigrants see John Higham's probing and provocative essay "Another Look at Nativism," *Catholic Historical Review*, XLIV (1958), 147–58. Higham stresses status conflicts, but does not explain why some competitors on the crowded social ladder were much more antagonistic to the new immigrants than were others.

[42] Draper, 189–90; *Annual Report of the Attorney General for 1920* (Washington, D.C., 1920), 177; Higham, *Strangers in the Land*, 226–27.

[43] The word "Americanism" was used by the nativists of the eighteen-forties and eighteen-fifties. During World War I, the stronger phrase "100 per cent Americanism" was invented to suit the belligerent drive for universal conformity.

sistence in April 1919 that "America will be saved, not by those who have only contempt and despite for her founders and her history, but by those who look with respect and reverence upon the great series of happenings extending from the voyage of the Mayflower. . . ." [44]

What one historian has called "a riot of biographies of American heroes — statesmen, cowboys, and pioneers" [45] appeared in this brief period. Immigrants as well as citizens produced many autobiographical testimonials to the superiority of American institutions. These patriotic tendencies in our literature were as short-lived as the Red Scare, and have been concealed by "debunking" biographies of folk heroes and skeptical autobiographies so common later in the nineteen-twenties. An anusual number of motion pictures about our early history were turned out immediately after the war and the reconstruction of colonial Wililamsburg and of Longfellow's Wayside Inn was begun. With great fanfare, Secretary of State Lansing placed the original documents of the Constitution and the Declaration of Independence on display in January 1920, and the State Department distributed movies of this ceremony to almost every town and city in the United States.[46] Organizations like the National Security League, the Association for Constitutional Government, the Sons and the Daughters of the American Revolution, the Colonial Dames of America, with the cooperation of the American Bar Association and many state Bar Associations, organized Constitution Day celebrations and distributed huge numbers of pamphlets on the subject throughout the country.

The American flag became a sacred symbol. Legionaires demanded that citizens "Run the Reds out from the land whose flag they sully." [47] Men suspected of radical leanings were forced to kiss the stars and stripes. A Brooklyn truck driver decided in June 1919 that it was unpatriotic to obey a New York City law obliging him to fly a red cloth on lumber which projected from his vehicle. Instead he used as a danger signal a small American flag. A policeman, infuriated at the sight of the stars and stripes flying from a lumber pile, arrested the driver on a charge of disorderly conduct. Despite the Brooklyn patriot's insistence that he meant no offense to the flag, he was reprimanded and fined by the court.[48]

Recent immigrants, especially, were called upon to show evidence of

[44] Horace M. Kallen, *Culture and Democracy in the United States* (New York, 1924), Chap. 3, 154–155; Edward G. Hartman, *The Movement to Americanize the Immigrant* (New York, 1948), Chap. 9; Nicholas Murray Butler, *Is America Worth Saving? An Address Delivered Before the Commercial Club of Cincinnati, Ohio, April 19, 1919* (New York, 1919), 20.

[45] Emerson Hunsberger Loucks, *The Ku Klux Klan in Pennsylvania* (New York, 1936), 163.

[46] Kallen, Chap. 3, 154–55; Division of Foreign Intelligence, "Memorandum about Constitution Ceremonies," January 19, 1920, Lansing Papers; *The New York Times*, January 18, 1920.

[47] *American Legion Weekly*, I (November 14, 1919), 12.

[48] Sullivan, VI, 118; New York *World*, June 22, 1919.

real conversion. Great pressure was brought to bear upon the foreign-born to learn English and to forget their native tongues. As Senator William S. Kenyon of Iowa declared in October 1919, "The time has come to make this a one-language nation." [49] An editorial in the *American Legion Weekly* took a further step and insisted that the one language must be called "American. Why even in Mexico they do not stand for calling the language the Spanish language." [50]

Immigrants were also expected to adopt our customs and to snuff out remnants of Old World cultures. Genteel prewar and wartime movements to speed up assimilation took on a "frightened and feverish aspect." [51] Welcoming members of an Americanization conference called by his department, Secretary of the Interior Franklin K. Lane exclaimed in May 1919, "You have been gathered together as crusaders in a great cause. . . . There is no other question of such importance before the American people as the solidifying and strengthening of true American sentiment." A Harvard University official told the conference that "The Americanization movement . . . gives men a new and holy religion. . . . It challenges each one of us to a renewed consecration and devotion to the welfare, of the nation." [52] The National Security League boasted, in 1919, of establishing one thousand study groups to teach teachers how to inculcate "Americanism" in their foreign-born students.[53] A critic of the prevailing mood protested against "one of our best advertised American mottoes, 'One country, one language, one flag,'" which, he complained, had become the basis for a fervent nationwide program.[54]

As the postwar movement for one hundred per cent Americanism gathered momentum, the deportation of alien nonconformists became increasingly its most compelling objective. Asked to suggest a remedy for the nationwide upsurge in radical activity, the Mayor of Gary, Indiana, replied, "Deportation is the answer, deportation of these leaders who talk treason in America and deportation of those who agree with them and

[49] *The New York Times,* October 14, 1919.
[50] *American Legion Weekly,* I (November 14, 1919), 12.
[51] Higham, *Strangers in the Land,* 225.
[52] United States Department of the Interior, Bureau of Education, *Organization Conference, Proceedings* (Washington, D.C., 1919), 293, 345–50.
[53] National Security League, 4.
[54] *Addresses and Proceedings of the Knights of Columbus Educational Convention* (New Haven, 1919), 71. Again note the family resemblance between the attempt to protect America through absolute conformity in 1919–20 and the more drastic, centrally-planned Chinese Communist efforts at national indoctrination. A student of Chinese "coercive persuasion" described the "elaborate unanimity rituals like parades, . . . 'spontaneous' mass demonstrations and society-wide campaigns, the extensive proselytizing among the 'heretics' or the 'infidels,' the purges, programs of re-education, and other repressive measures aimed at deviants." In China, also, past national glory is invoked as evidence of present and future greatness. Schein *et al.,* 62; Lifton, *Thought Reform and the Psychology of Totalism; Walker, China Under Communism.*

work with them." "We must remake America," a popular author averred, "We must purify the source of America's population and keep it pure. . . . We must insist that there shall be an American loyalty, brooking no amendment or qualification." [55] As Higham noted, "In 1919, the clamor of 100 per centers for applying deportation as a purgative arose to an hysterical howl. . . . Through repression and deportation on the one hand and speedy total assimilation on the other, 100 per centers hoped to eradicate discontent and purify the nation." [56]

Politicians quickly sensed the possibilities of the popular frenzy for Americanism. Mayor Ole Hanson of Seattle, Governor Calvin Coolidge of Massachusetts, and General Leonard Wood became the early heroes of the movement.[57] The man in the best political position to take advantage of the popular feeling, however, was Attorney General A. Mitchell Palmer.[58] In 1919, especially after the President's physical collapse, only Palmer had the authority, staff, and money necessary to arrest and deport huge numbers of radical aliens. The most virulent phase of the movement for one hundred per cent Americanism came early in 1920, when Palmer's agents rounded up for deportation over six thousand aliens and prepared to arrest thousands more suspected of membership in radical organizations. Most of these aliens were taken without warrants, many were detained for unjustifiably long periods of time, and some suffered incredible hardships. Almost all, however, were eventually released.[59]

After Palmer decided that he could ride the postwar fears into the presidency, he set out calculatingly to become the symbol of one hundred per cent Americanism. The Palmer raids, his anti-labor activities, and his frequent pious professions of patriotism during the campaign were all part of this effort. Palmer was introduced by a political associate to the Democratic party's annual Jackson Day dinner in January 1920 as "an American whose Americanism cannot be misunderstood." In a speech delivered in Georgia shortly before the primary election (in which Palmer won control of the state's delegation to the Democratic National Convention), the Attorney General asserted: "I am myself an American and I love to preach my doctrine before undiluted one hundred per cent Americans, because my platform is, in a word, undiluted Americanism and undying loyalty to the republic." The same theme dominated the address made by Palmer's old friend, John H. Bigelow of Hazleton, Pennsylvania, when

[55] Emerson Hough, "Round Our Town," *Saturday Evening Post*, CXCII (February 21, 1920), 102; Hough, *The Web*, 456.

[56] *Higham, Strangers in the Land*, 227, 255.

[57] Murray, 62–65, 147–48, 159–60.

[58] For a full discussion of Palmer's role, Stanley Coben, *A Mitchell Palmer: Politician* (New York, 1963).

[59] Coben, *Palmer*, Chaps. 11, 12; Claghorn, Chap. 10; Constantine Panunzio, *The Deportation Cases of 1919–1920* (New York, 1920); Zechariah Chafee, Jr., *Free Speech in the United States* (Cambridge, 1941), 204–17; Murray, Chap. 13.

he placed Palmer's name in nomination at the 1920 National Convention. Proclaimed Bigelow: "No party could survive today that did not write into its platform the magic word 'Americanism.' . . . The Attorney-General of the United States has not merely professed, but he has proved his true Americanism. . . . Behind him I see a solid phalanx of true Americanism that knows no divided allegiance." [60]

Unfortunately for political candidates like Palmer and Wood, most of the social and economic disturbances which had activated the movement they sought to lead gradually disappeared during the first half of 1920. The European revolutions were put down; by 1920 communism seemed to have been isolated in Russia. Bombings ceased abruptly after June 1919, and fear of new outrages gradually abated. Prices of food and clothing began to recede during the spring. Labor strife almost vanished from our major industries after a brief railroad walkout in April. Prosperity returned after mid-1919 and by early 1920 business activity and employment levels exceeded their wartime peaks.[61] At the same time, it became clear that the Senate would not pass Wilson's peace treaty and that America was free to turn its back on the responsibilities of world leadership. The problems associated with the new immigrants remained; so did the disillusionment with Europe and with many old intellectual ideals. Nativism did not disappear from the American scene; but the frenzied attempts to revitalize the culture did peter out in 1920. The handful of unintimidated men, especially Assistant Secretary of Labor Louis F. Post, who had used the safeguards provided by American law to protect many victims of the Red Scare, found increasing public support. On the other hand, politicians like Palmer, Wood, and Hanson were left high and dry, proclaiming the need for one hundred per cent Americanism to an audience which no longer urgently cared.

It is ironic that in 1920 the Russian leaders of the Comintern finally took charge of the American Communist movement, provided funds and leadership, and ordered the Communist factions to unite and participate actively in labor organizations and strikes. These facts were reported in the American press.[62] Thus a potentially serious foreign threat to national security appeared just as the Red Scare evaporated, providing a final illustration of the fact that the frenzied one hundred per centers of 1919–20 were affected less by the "red menace" than by a series of social and economic dislocations.

[60] Coben, *Palmer*, Chap. 13; *The New York Times*, January 9, 1920; Atlanta *Constitution*, April 7, 1920; *Official Report of the Proceedings of the Democratic National Convention, 1920* (Indianapolis, 1920), 113–14. Palmer also launched a highly publicized campaign to hold down soaring prices in 1919–20, by fixing retail prices and bringing suits against profiteers and hoarders.

[61] Bell, 334; Soule, 83–88; *Seventh Annual Report of the Federal Reserve Board for the Year 1920* (Washington, D.C., 1920), 7.

[62] Draper, 244, 267–68; New York *World*, March 29, 1920.

Although the Red Scare died out in 1920, its effects lingered. Hostility toward immigrants, mobilized in 1919–20, remained strong enough to force congressional passage of restrictive immigration laws. Some of the die-hard one hundred per centers found a temporary home in the Klu Klux Klan until that organization withered away during the mid-twenties. As its most lasting accomplishments, the movement for one hundred per cent Americanism fostered a spirit of conformity in the country, a satisfaction with the *status quo*, and the equation of reform ideologies with foreign enemies. Revitalization movements have helped many societies adapt successfully to new conditions. The movement associated with the American Red Scare, however, had no such effect. True, it unified the culture against the threats faced in 1919–20; but the basic problems — a damaged value system, an unrestrained business cycle, a hostile Russia, and communism — were left for future generations of Americans to deal with in their own fashion.

MODERN
POLITICAL
TRENDS

II

Neither Ideology Nor Utopia: The New Deal in Retrospect

HEINZ EULAU

*There have been numerous attempts to describe the character
and workings of the New Deal. Stanford political scientist
Heinz Eulau examines and rejects many of these approaches
in the following essay. He contends that the New Deal was
not an ideology, not a chiliastic faith, not a crusade, not an
experiment, not a revolt of the masses, and not a charisma.
Eulau instead views the New Deal from the perspective of a
political scientist's model of a "mature" political system. His
model combines the classic version of the non-ideological,
compromise-prone nature of American politics with psychological concepts of maturity. A mature politics, Eulau writes,
"involves adjustment, compromise, integration." The New
Deal was really evidence of national political maturity, that is,
an "ability to solve . . . problems through politics rather
than through ideology or violence." While Eulau finds virtue in the non-ideological and compromising character of the
New Deal, it is just those qualities that more recently have
provoked a harsh, critical judgment by younger historians.
They find that the adjustments and compromises of the New
Deal resulted in lost or neglected opportunities to effect more
meaningful and humane change. For them, the 1930's involved a crisis of the political, social, and economic systems in
the United States that was inadequately handled and never
really resolved. The conflict between Eulau and the critics of
the New Deal poses a larger question for American politics:
Must the system function with "group bargains" and compromises for divergent interests at the cost of minimizing reform
or change?*

The New Deal of Franklin D. Roosevelt, just as the New Freedom of
Woodrow Wilson before, and the Fair Deal of Harry Truman later, had
its quota of ideologues, but was not an ideology; it had its following of

Reprinted by permission of the author and publisher from the *Antioch Review*,
XIX (Winter 1959–1960), pp. 523–537.

true believers, but was not a chiliastic faith; it produced far-ranging reforms, but was not a crusade; it was rich in inventions, but was not an experiment; it mobilized huge majorities, but was not a revolt of the masses; it generated forceful national leadership, but was not a charismatic surrender. It is possible to see the New Deal as the fulfillment of the promise of American life — Herbert Croly's dream in the years before the First World War; or as an exercise in instrumental pragmatism which John Dewey had celebrated in the years following that war. But if it was the realization of the liberal promise or the application of the pragmatic philosophy, it was so by way of improvisation rather than design. All of these elements were present, but they do not express the dynamics of the New Deal. If it was anything, the New Deal between 1932 and 1940 was, simply and foremost, evidence of the viability of democratic politics in an age of crisis.

Ardently defended by its admirers, and bitterly denounced by its enemies, the New Deal came to make a lasting impression on the American experience — an impression, I venture to say, which in the long run can only be compared with the birth of the nation itself and the fratricidal blood-letting of the Civil War. The New Deal fascinated and continues to fascinate the national consciousness, not only because it was an intense and dramatic political episode, but also because it was, like the birth of the United States and the Civil War, a national event. By comparison, the earlier New Freedom and the later Fair Deal were merely incidents — the former a pale prospectus, the latter a faded postscript, to the politically most exciting period in American history.

Not an Ideology

Though the New Deal was non-ideological, this does not mean that it was anti-ideological. In fact, it was shot through with ideologies, or utopias, whichever emphasis one may prefer. Total planners and piecemeal planners, budget-balancers and deficit-spenders, trust-regulators and trust-busters, protectionists and free traders, "sound money" proponents and inflationists — all vied with each other under the hospitable tent that was the New Deal. Wall Street bankers, Midwest farmers, Harvard economists, Columbia lawyers, labor intellectuals, old-time progressives, new liberals, social workers — men of the Right, Left, and Middle — supplied ideas and programs, if not panaceas. Theories were welcome as they had never been welcome before; and never before, or thereafter, did so many blueprints of a better order reach the citadel of influence. Ideas were, indeed, the true coins of the realm.

But, for precisely these reasons, there was little of the ideological in the New Deal — if by ideology one means a coherent and consistent set of beliefs, values, opinions, and aspirations. To attempt to construct out of the welter of these beliefs and values, opinions and aspirations an internally congruent system of thought is to do violence to history and to the meaning of the New Deal. Not that such attempts have not been made, or will not be made in the future. But they can be made only at the risk of great distortion. For the New Deal was an ideologically much too elusive phenomenon to be squeezed into the convenient categories of ideological analysis. In fact, insofar as it responded to ideological pressures at all, the New Deal was engaged in a continuous effort to disengage itself from ideological commitments.

The difficulty of ideological analysis is that it cannot easily free itself from the Aristotelian mode of thinking, with its neat and even aesthetically satisfying dichotomies. This is the mode of thought which pitches liberty against security, private property against public ownership, national regulation against decentralization, monopoly against competition. Granted, the New Deal emphasized the positive role of national government and strong federal action. But, granted too, the consequences of such action, as in the federal grants-in-aid programs, were an enormous expansion and strengthening of both state and municipal activities. Granted, the Tennessee Valley Authority represented as "socialist" an undertaking as had ever been devised in the United States. But, granted too, one of its consequences was the flowering of private enterprise in an area where previously it had great trouble flowering. Granted, the New Deal promoted social and economic security in manifold ways. But, granted too, it did not do so at the expense of liberty: there was hardly a period in American history in which public discussion of public issues and the freedom to speak freely had been practiced with as much abandon as under the New Deal. The New Deal simply defies ideological classification.

All this does not mean that the New Deal was not anchored in a cultural milieu of attitudes and predispositions which was congenial to its operation. This milieu was the liberal tradition in America. As Louis Hartz has suggested, in one sense the whole American political tradition is liberal. In this perspective, the New Deal, non-ideological though it was, was clearly an indication, if not a vindication, of liberalism. Without this tradition, there would have been no New Deal. But, in the American context, the liberal tradition as such has rarely been experienced as an ideology. Rather, it appears as a cultural fact which, like the air we breathe, is so close, so natural, so much a part of our daily life that we fail to notice it. The liberal tradition explains, I suspect, why its many contradictions and inconsistencies were "built in" New Deal programs, plans, and policies. For liberalism, unlike other isms, has never been a set of dogmas, but a state of mind. It represents an attitude which insists on questioning self-evident propositions, partly to find out what evidence there is to support them, partly to discover possible alternatives. It follows that liberalism is not bound to any particular social or economic system. No wonder that so many different ideologues, theoreticians, administrators, and politicians could find the New Deal a congenial environment in which to work. Indeed, they shaped that environment. And the New Deal reflected, in varying degrees and at varying times, the varying enthusiasm and different approaches to the national problems.

Not a Faith

That the New Deal gave new hope to millions, that it brought new confidence into government, that it ultimately became a testament of national courage, there is little doubt. Where there had been drift, the New Deal offered mastery. Just as Hoover's "we are at the end of our string" had symbolized the old order, Roosevelt's "firm belief that the only thing we have to fear is fear itself" symbolized the new approach. But at no time did the New Deal assume that man does not live by bread alone. It generated fresh expectations in the hearts of people who had recently experienced little but misery, and a new spirit came about the land. But it was a hope and a spirit nourished not by promises and good intentions, but by governmental action. The New Deal was a reconfirmation of the old American assumption that action is its own reward. What the New Deal articulated was not a faith in a better morrow, but a call for action now.

And the people were captivated, not because they were asked to be true believers, but because action gave them a new sense of dignity. The dole had given them the minimum means of subsistence, and charity had made them loathe a humility to which they were not accustomed. Now they found their way into public works, conservation corps, rural settlements, and, as the economy began to grind again, back into jobs in industry, transportation, and commerce. They were grateful. But even if the New Deal had tried to take the role of the savior, it is doubtful that it could have saved many souls. What generated the new spirit that made the thirties so exciting was not government action alone. True, the government played a role it had never played in the lives of Americans before. But what sustained the popular drive and confidence that came with the New Deal was the old faith that man can control his destiny — given the conditions that make action and self-help possible.

Much nonsense has been written to the effect that the New Deal made of Americans unthinking and faithful dependents of a "welfare state," so-called — a people which has lost initiative and entrusts its fate to the benevolence of an all-powerful government. The welfare state, it is alleged, is the new dispensation — man's reward on this earth for conformity and compliance based on faith and political suicide. But the New Deal was not a sacred mission; it was a most secular, indeed profane, manifestation of modern man's quest for security — not the security that comes from an anticipation of heavenly bliss, but the secrurity that comes from an ability to make this earth one's home.

The New Deal, then, was not an "escape from freedom," a surrender of the intellectual faculties. Rather than calling for faith, it was an enormous educational effort. Perhaps never before in the history of the republic was it necessary to re-educate the preferences and redirect the energies of the people. Whatever one may wish to call it — propaganda or education — the American people were exposed to a flow of information about the activities of the government unexcelled in the past. And the people responded. There was new understanding of the difficulties besetting the nation, a new tolerance of innovations, and a new commitment to creative intelligence in politics. Rarely has there been so much knowledgeable participation of the people in public affairs. Letters poured into Washington, and the newspaper columns reflected popular interest. Rather than escaping from freedom, people once more had a genuine sense of being part of the governmental enterprise. Not submission to authority, but a lively feeling of one's efficacy, one's ability to influence the course of events, characterized the popular response. It has sometimes been said that if the New Deal had wanted to assume totalitarian forms, it could have done so without much difficulty — for people were ready to accept almost anything that would give them a better deal. Nothing could be further from reality. The New Deal was what it was and became what it became precisely because it did not promise a millennium, but confronted the American people with the harsh realities of the present, first at home, and then abroad.

Not a Crusade

To think of the New Deal as a unified program, a plan, or a policy is as mistaken as to think of it as a movement or a crusade. There were many programs and policies, and there was more than a movement. What made the New Deal the phenomenon it was — a new deal in American life, a fresh start — was not a zest for reform, but the need to respond to national problems as they were dictated by the exigencies of the moment, not as they may have been preconceived by reformers. Whatever preferences for reform may have motivated individual New Dealers as they found themselves in the seats of power and influence after the politically lean years of normalcy, the task at hand was to revive the economy, not to translate long-cherished proposals for reform into reality.

Reforms, of course, there were. Some were successful and became permanent features of American life. Industrial violence, long the scourge of labor-management relations, gave way to the peaceful method of collective bargaining. Unemployment and old-age insurance programs remedied long-standing ills among the socially and economically most disadvantaged sector of the population. Securities legislation brought discipline and responsibility into the disorderly state of banking and investment practices. But other reforms were doomed to failure. Rural resettlement was a temporary stop-gap and fell victim to its own idealism. The National

Resources Planning Board never got off the ground. Other programs were conceived as self-liquidating and were liquidated, though some of them, like the Civilian Conservation Corps or Public Works Administration, left a rich heritage of national accomplishment. Still other programs represented *ad hoc* inventions to cope with pressing problems which had hardly been envisaged by the reformers. They were, in fact, determined efforts by the government to maintain the *status quo*. Programs such as agricultural adjustment or bank deposit insurance were acts not so much of reform as of preservation.

The one attempt made to conduct a crusade — the National Recovery Administration under Hugh Johnson — resembled more an Alice-in-Wonderland grotesque than a viable governmental structure and policy. NRA had important successes — abolishing child labor, setting maximum hours and minimum wages, removing unfair trade practices, and so forth — which, once re-enacted after NRA's demise, became monuments of social progress. But, on the whole, NRA was a fiasco because it tried to do too much in too little time within a single institutional setting which, at its roots, sought to reconcile business regulation by business itself with protection of free-market mechanisms by the government. The effort led to an atmosphere of histrionics much at variance with that kind of earnestness that is the hallmark of reform. The Blue Eagle campaign was more a circus, really, than a crusade, and few tears were shed when the whole enterprise was declared unconstitutional.

It is only in the perspective of history that the New Deal can possibly be conceived as a political or social movement. But even in this perspective, it was only a new phase, a most intensive phase, perhaps, forced by the great depression to heroic exertion, in the long-range national development which is the promise of American life. It was directly related — not only in ideas it shared, but also in some of its older personnel — to both the Square Deal and the New Freedom, to the historical trend to achieve Jeffersonian ends by Hamiltonian means. That the Square Deal had been Republican and the New Freedom Democratic made the national character of the New Deal all the more poignant. Of all the movements, so-called, in American history, the New Deal was truly national in scope, liberal in purpose, and effective in action.

Not an Experiment

The New Deal has come to be cited as the prize exhibit of the success of the experimental method in the making of public policy and the development of administrative techniques. The New Deal's willingness and capacity to chart new social and political paths is seen as an expression of John Dewey's philosophy of instrumentalism. But this interpretation represents a tendency to over-intellectualize the political process. It is more often in the nature of an apologia than of analysis. By calling anything new an "experiment," success of the experiment is heralded as proof of the uses of experimentation, while failure is explained away as inconsequential. The analogy between social efforts to create new alternatives and scientific experimentation ignores more than it explains. In fact, when the metaphor becomes a myth, it may be detrimental to a genuine understanding of the New Deal.

Roosevelt himself gave credence to the experimental metaphor when he declared that what the country needed was "bold, persistent experimentation." Yet one may doubt that his call for experimentation was intended to make experimental pragmatism into political formula. His notion hardly included the scientist's image of the carefully designed and controlled experiment. As he suggested, "it is common sense to take a method and try it; if it fails, admit it frankly and try another. But above all, try something." But an experiment is the very opposite of common sense. Quite clearly, Roosevelt's accent was less on the nature of the method used than on the injunction to "try something." Roosevelt was prepared to try things, not to test theoretical propositions or to follow hunches — his mind was much too untheoretical for that — but to meet urgent social needs and pressures. Indeed, many potential New Deal proposals never left the drafting boards, not because they might not have worked, but because they were politically unfeasible. And not a few others were prematurely terminated long before their success or failure could have been demonstrated.

Though the New Deal was not an experiment or a series of experiments, it was admittedly an experience in social inventiveness. There was, again in Roosevelt's words, no room for "foolish traditions." Innovation, not experiment, was the trade-mark of the New Deal. The proliferation of administrative agencies came with the suspicion that the old-line departments would not or could not aggressively pursue the new policies; balancing the budget no longer meant what it had traditionally meant — social values defied accounting in terms of dollars and cents, and it was the national economy, not the government budget, that was thought to be at stake; an agriculture of abundance was to be realized paradoxically, through promoting programs of scarcity, like killing pigs and plowing under the crops which could not be marketed at adequate prices; and on the political front, from Roosevelt's personal appearance at the 1932 Chicago convention to his breaking of the two-term tradition eight years later, the New Deal defied conventions. Yet, it is interesting to note that in politics proper this proved most difficult, as the ill-fated "court-packing plan" or the President's aborted attempt to influence the 1938 Democratic primaries demonstrated.

But, paradoxically too, the New Deal with all its inventions was in the great American political and social tradition. For that tradition meant innovation: free public lands, free religious worship, free public education, a chance at economic betterment and social mobility, a broad democratic franchise, and many other social gains had at first been innovations — inventions which at one time had made the difference between the Old World and the New. The New Deal was in the mainstream of that tradition, but again with a difference.

Not a Revolt

Easy comparison can be made between the New Deal's success in mobilizing great electoral majorities and the plebiscitary mirages performed by totalitarian regimes. Both, it has been claimed, represented that revolt of the masses which José Ortega y Gasset had so somberly described only a few years earlier. Increased popular participation in the most far-reaching decision a national community can make — the election of its government — has been said to be a sign not of social health, but of social tension; an index of cleavage rather than consensus; evidence of despair rather than creative involvement.

Whatever the veracity of this argument in regard to totalitarian mass behavior, it lacks relevance to the New Deal as a political event. The New Deal elections were not plebiscites, but hard-fought, free battles of the ballot. Even in the landslide election of 1936, almost seventeen million people, or about 38 per cent of the total electorate, voted for the Republican candidate. In spite of the personal attractiveness of the Democratic candidate, few campaigns in twentieth-century America have been as genuinely democratic as the early New Deal elections. Although the press was predominantly anti-New Deal, rarely has there been so much discussion of the real issues facing the nation. What moved the New Deal majorities was not a sense of revolt, but a renewed spirit of confidence in the willingness and ability of the government to carry out the popular mandate.

In organizing its electoral majorities, the New Deal restructured the political map. Its political techniques were anything but the contrived plebiscitarian technology of mass manipulation. That the New Deal succeeded in harnessing to its wagon the forces of labor, the young as well as the old, the socially underprivileged ethnic groups, farmers as well as urbanites, former Republicans as well as former Socialists, was not the result of hidden persuasion or silent threat, but of its sensitivity to popular needs and demands. In doing so, the New Deal was an almost perfect system of political feedback. Rarely in a modern democracy has the politics of democracy been equally conducive to the strengthening of democracy as a viable political system.

Had the New Deal been an ideology, a faith, or a crusade, it might have been otherwise. But because it was none of these things, the New Deal could engage in its support the great electoral majorities which it needed in order to cope forcefully with the tasks of the nation. Nevertheless, impressive as the New Deal majorities were, it would be to simplify the situation if one elevated the New Deal into a flowering of the majoritarian principle as a "general will." The New Deal majority was, above all, a product of the political process as it had developed its particular flavor in the American culture. In the abstract, one might say that the majority demanded "something be done," or that it approved of what was done. Yet, that something was invariably done, sooner or later, does not mean that the majority, so-called, was agreed on what should be done, or that it endorsed what was done for the same reasons. To assume that the New Deal majorities were united in purposes and goals is not only naive, but incorrect. The New Deal majorities were, in reality, only evidence of the complex processes of group adjustment and compromise that had preceded the electoral majorities; proof that these processes were reasonably efficient in generating the electoral power that was needed to continue the processes of adjustment and compromise. Like all American majorities, the New Deal majorities were the products of a salient coalition politics, only more so. No ideological or militant politics, no revolt of the masses, could have been equally successful — at least not in a free democracy.

Not a Charisma

If ever the right man came to occupy the right office at the right time, Franklin D. Roosevelt was that man. Indeed, so close was the contemporary identification of New Deal and FDR, and so close does it continue to be in the perspective of history, that it is difficult to think of the one without the other. Both FDR's most devoted supporters and his most vociferous critics, as well as the historians of whatever persuasion, are agreed that it was the President who symbolized the New Deal. But to acknowledge that FDR was the chief architect of the New Deal, its most convincing spokesman, its forceful leader and also its most tangible target, is not to imply that he was a charismatic personality. Undoubtedly, there were people who ascribed to him the qualities of charisma — infallibility, omniscience, omnipotence. And some of his most bitter opponents were equally intent on seeing in him the very incarnation of the charismatic opportunist. But neither orientation is correct. FDR was unduly loved by some and unduly hated by others, but to the vast majority of the American people he was Mr. President — the legally chosen head of a government whose function it was to represent and execute the power of the nation in time of crisis. This role FDR was superbly fitted and able to carry out.

While it is facile to interpret the New Deal in terms of the President's role and personality, one wonders what FDR would have been like as chief executive without the New Deal? Was it because FDR was not an ideologue, a reformer, or a prophet that the New Deal was not an ideology, a faith, or a crusade for reform? Or was it because the New Deal was none of these things that FDR came to play the role he did? A categorical answer is impossible. The President's personality and the character of the New Deal, if it is permissible to speak of character, were admirably blended to produce the kind of strong governmental leadership which the nation required in the moment of crisis. But this makes it all the more necessary not to exaggerate, yet also not to minimize, the role of the President in the total configuration of the New Deal. Because the tendency to exaggerate has probably been the dominant one, it seems desirable to point to some less frequently noticed features of the New Deal's personnel.

While Roosevelt never allowed the impression to prevail that he was not boss and master of the situation, his effectiveness as a leader did not derive from an unqualified loyalty that he may have been able to exact from his "subordinates." Rather, it derived from his ability to allow his lieutenants enough free-wheeling initiative to work out programs and policies — and it was one of his favorite images to see himself as the quarterback who was merely called upon to call the signals. The forceful leadership provided by the New Deal was not just Roosevelt's, but truly the product of teamwork. Leadership under the New Deal was both concentrated, in the White House, and decentralized, in the many departments and agencies of the federal government, most of them headed by able men who themselves were leaders, not henchmen or yes-men.

Moreover, the spirit of leadership under the New Deal was not only pervasive in the executive branch, but also in the legislative branch, and, after the mandate of 1936, in the judicial branch as well. There has been a tendency to neglect the part played by Congress in providing political leadership. There were the "Hundred Days," it is true, when the new Congress had little choice but to go along with the President's "must" programs. But the New Deal Congresses were not simply "rubber-stamp" legislatures. They included men of vision, wisdom, and sagacity, progressives who often succeeded in moving the White House in directions in which it would not have moved on its own initiative. Similarly, once the Supreme Court — or rather two of its members, including the Chief Justice — had realized that it could not set itself up against the wishes of the great majority of the people and the popular President, it produced decisions which themselves were important ingredients of New Deal policies.

It is in this larger context of "collective leadership" shared by all the branches of the federal government that the President's role must be located. Economic policies and social programs came from many sources — braintrusters, interest groups, administrators, Congressmen, and Justices. It was Roosevelt's genius that he could pick men with ideas, and it was his glory that he encouraged ideas; it was his skill that he could articulate both popular needs and governmental responses; it was his confidence that he could transmit similar confidence to his associates; it was his power that he could humor, persuade, and, if necessary, threaten those who sat on the sidelines; it was his personality that he could make charm and courage instruments of government; above all, it was his spirit that he could convey his own idealism to the people as well as those who worked with him and for him.

But Roosevelt was not an ideologue — for he did not work with theoretical preconceptions, but with presuppositions. He was not a prophet — for his faith was terrestrial, not celestial. He was not a crusader — for he did not do many things he might have done by way of reform. He was not an agitator — for he was not driven by frustration, but committed to the proposition that common problems are best solved by common efforts. He was not a charismatic leader — for his own self-image as a politician forbade a charismatic image to be held by others. Roosevelt was a politician who saw that the business of government was politics, and who came to the business of government as a politician.

A Mature Politics

If the New Deal was not an ideology, a faith, a crusade, an experiment, a revolt, or a charisma, what was it? In retrospect, what makes the New Deal so memorable, so significant an event in the history of the United States is that it is both a symbol and evidence of the nation's political maturity: its ability to solve its problems through politics rather than through ideology or violence. Politicians though they were, the Founding Fathers essentially distrusted politics. Whatever their real commitments, they believed in the cult of reason and natural law. In the Civil War, ideological intransigence — Lincoln, who came too late and passed away too early, excepted — underlined the poverty of politics, so largely responsible for both the violence and its unfortunate aftermath. By way of contrast, the New Deal was neither distrustful of politics nor poor in political strategies. If a commitment there was, it was a commitment to a mature politics.

A mature politics cannot afford to be either ideological or utopian. Ideologists and utopians are essentially apolitical. They are, in many respects, like children who are preoccupied almost exclusively with what they want when they want it, for whom their little selves are the center of the cosmos. Preoccupied with their own diagnoses and therapies, ideologists and utopians are, paradoxically, "thoughtless" in the literal sense of the word — blind to the needs of others and unconcerned with the consequences of their self-centered aspirations for others. Responsibility is a concept alien to both children and ideologues alike. Maturity, on the other hand, is the capacity to respond to others without making the demands of the self the sole criterion of perception or behavior. Real and necessary as the demands of the mature person are, maturity involves recognition of the legitimate interests of others. A mature politics involves adjustment, compromise, integration. It can never be a purely ideological politics which exaggerates the importance of the self at the expense of the other, or which may even mean the destruction of the other.

The New Deal was a politics of maturity in this sense, for it brought to the problems it faced political, not ideological, solutions. This is often not understood by its ideological critics or ideological defenders. The very debate which the New Deal aroused, and continues to arouse, is the best evidence. The New Deal is "incomprehensible" to the ideologues of the Right and Left because it was so unideological, because it was not a "scheme" but a "deal" so different from the political solitaire which the ideologue likes to play. The New Deal was a search for acceptable solutions to problems rather than an imposition of preconceived solutions on problems. The ideologues and theoreticians were necessary to the New Deal, vital in its growth and development, but they could not be its conductors. Some were disgusted, others despaired, unable to fathom the rationale of a program which was no program and had no rationale that fitted their ideological preconceptions. Those who stayed with the New Deal — men as different in their interest as Harold Ickes, the old progressive, or Jesse Jones, the financier, or Henry Wallace, the Republican farmer — served the New Deal for what it was: not a return to an ideological yesteryear, or a road to a utopian tomorrow, but a political enterprise which harnessed political forces in the spirit of political maturity.

It was not so much a characteristic of the New Deal's political maturity that many ideas and interests found expression in the hurly-burly of politics, but that politics took these ideas and interests seriously, that it encouraged their expression, that it took it for granted that these ideas and interests would clash, and that it was ready to give, but also to take away. The New Deal represented, on the level of national politics, a tough-mindedness that allowed for little ideological self-indulgence. Ideological thinking, however camouflaged, is tender-minded because it is self-indulgent. But in politics self-indulgence means bargaining from a position of weakness rather than strength. It represents an escape from a politics of maturity, not a recognition of the potentialities as well as limitations of political life. The New Deal was politically tough and mature, for it accepted the limits of the possible.

Too much emphasis has been placed on the role of the "brain trust" and the intellectuals who joined the New Deal. That they played an enormous and desirable role in orienting the public policies of the New Deal cannot be denied. But to assume that they operated with the single-mindedness of an idealized high command is to ignore the great diversity of backgrounds and opinions that they brought to bear on the common effort. Rarely did New Deal measures represent a clear-cut ideological preference. Programs were proposed, adjustments were made, compromises were negotiated, and the new syntheses only remotely resembled the original proposals. The New Deal was a governmental process which reflected the necessities and obstacles of a mature democratic politics.

Only when the shadow of war had become a spectre worse than depression, and when the New Deal had remedied much of what sickened American life, did politics give way to defense and apologia as well as to surrender of the political imagination. There appeared the bandwagon mentality — what Morris Cohen has called "the vile habit of thinking that the latest is always the best" — and the convenient belief that present trends will continue indefinitely into the future. It was then that the New Deal tended to become an affair of pronunciamento and magic formula. But this, in fact, meant the end of the New Deal. Yet it is against this later phase that the New Deal can be best assessed — as a flowering of sensitivity to the paradoxes, ambiguities, complications, compromises, and adventures of politics. To live with these characteristics, not only to tolerate them but to thrive on them, was the mark of that political maturity which distinguished the New Deal as a national event.

Modern Capitalism and the Uncertain Role of Public Power

ANDREW SHONFIELD

In no other country is old-style capitalism defended as vigorously as in the United States, according to British writer and economist Andrew Shonfield. But the history of American economic development and current practice amply demonstrate that the correlation between an ideology of absolute free enterprise and practice is about nil. Throughout much of the nineteenth century, American governments actively intervened to aid, stimulate, regulate, and even share profits with, private enterprise. In the twentieth century, the federal government has exercised tighter regulatory powers over business activities and the marketplace than have the more socialist-oriented nations. Yet governmental intervention in the American economy is exercised primarily in a judicial, or arbitrative, manner; the essential function is supervisory, and not policy-making. Why has the United States lagged behind the general movement in Western civilization toward a larger governmental role in central economic planning? Why have the most basic decisions such as production and pricing remained largely under private authority? Why has public authority in the United States deliberately been weakened by division of power? Shonfield's inquiry is directed toward these questions. Basically, he focuses on whether there has been little need for central direction because of economic success and abundant riches, or whether there is some more deep-seated impediment, such as a pluralist notion of power. Shonfield directs much of his attention to the basic conflict within the New Deal between the advocates of a corporate, centrally directed economy, and the proponents of a competitive, but publicly supervised, economy. The resolution and consequences of that struggle, he believes, largely explain the nature and role of public power today.

. . . The United States is indeed one of the few places left in the world where "capitalism" is generally thought to be an OK word. Elsewhere even a politician of the far Right, abusing socialism and the welfare state, will normally hesitate to base his appeal to popular sentiment on a call for the reassertion of good old capitalist principles. And if he did have the impulse to do so, his election manager would almost certainly suggest the use of some more discreet euphemism. The label attracts an approbrium, not only in Europe but also in most of the underdeveloped countries, which Americans sometimes find puzzling. Newspaper articles have been written suggesting that perhaps the name of the thing ought to be changed, in order to give others a fair chance to appreciate it without prejudice.

But there is something more than a semantic eccentricity dividing the common ideology of the United States from that of the rest of the world. Among the Americans there is a general commitment to the view, shared by both political parties, of the natural predominance of private enterprise in the economic sphere and of the subordinate role of public initiative in any situation other than a manifest national emergency. The West Europeans, who have no such assumptions — for even the Right in Europe tends to believe in the abiding place of active paternalistic government — have in consequence been spared the awful doctrinal wrestling, in which Americans tend to engage whenever any bit of the economic field has to be divided afresh between the public and private sectors. The commandments which issue forth after the struggle is over carry a portentous and urgent note. It is plain that something more serious than mere political decision is being exercised.

Thus the current policy directive of the U.S. Bureau of the Budget [1] to all Federal Offices and Agencies on the use of government-owned production facilities introduces the rules with the resounding preamble: "Because the private enterprise system is basic to the American economy. . . ." It goes on to warn any civil servant who proposes to use public enterprise for the "provision of a product or service" that "the burden of proof lies on the agency which determines that an exception to the general policy is required." Nor must the civil servant imagine, if he comes across a piece of public enterprise which is already in operation, that he has no duty to put matters right. "The existence of the government-owned capital assets is not in itself an adequate justification for the government to provide its own goods or services. The need for continued government ownership or operation must be fully substantiated." Finally, he may be tempted to believe that his obligations have been met, once private enterprise has been brought in to take charge of and operate the publicly owned undertaking. Nothing of the kind. "Even the operation of a government-owned facility by a private organization through contractual arrangement does not automatically assure that the government is not competing with private enterprise. This type of arrangement could act as a barrier to the development and growth of competitive commercial sources and procurement through ordinary business channels."

All the evidence suggests that these regulations are very strictly obeyed. The hostility to public initiative has deep roots in American traditional mythology. Yet that does not mean that in practice private enterprise has it entirely its own way. Indeed, coming from Europe and observing the behaviour of people in industry and commerce, one may well be struck by the way in which it seems to be accepted that it is part of the lot of businessmen to be pushed around intermittently by one Federal agency or another. The Securities and Exchange Commission in Washington has established standards for comprehensive and frequent reporting of the affairs of companies whose shares are publicly quoted which are far more stringent than anything in Europe. Even Britain, which is probably more advanced than any Continental country in the requirements of company reporting, is not nearly so demanding as the U.S. Federal authorities. This type of government supervision is sometimes defended on traditional grounds, as belonging to the same order of ideas as those which have made the American anti-trust laws tougher than anywhere else. Making the market function properly means, if it is a stock market, that investors

---

[1] "Criteria of Commercial-Industrial Activities of Government," *Bureau of the Budget Bulletin*, 60–62, quoted in Joint Economic Committee of Congress Hearings, Sub-Committee on Defense Procurement, Mar.–Apr. 1963.

must be given a lot of relevant information of guaranteed accuracy. How else can firms compete on level terms for the public's money? The foreign businessman in the United States may remark wryly that the belief in the beneficent power of the market place leads the American Government to impose a number of obligations on companies, which they manage to escape in other countries where competitive capitalism is less well-regarded. These obligations apply particularly to statements of fact which a firm puts out — not merely in its company accounts, but also in the form of advertising and the labelling of its products. Except perhaps in Sweden, labels are nowhere so closely regulated as in the United States.

There are besides some controls which interfere directly with the decisions of private enterprise about how much it is to produce. The most notorious example is the restrictions, which have operated since the early 1950s, on the acreage which American farmers are allowed to employ in the production of cereals, of cotton, of tobacco and a variety of other crops. Areas to be cultivated for particular purposes are fixed farm by farm, and are subject to inspection by officials who have grown increasingly anxious, as surpluses have mounted, to check on anyone who is inclined to cheat. On occasion the inspection has taken on features of a military exercise, with the government men engaging in surprise aerial reconnaissance over suspicious fields of corn. Even so, the great flood of produce coming off American farms has not been checked.

By the early 1960s it had become evident that the real trouble was not the farmer's traditional capacity for deceiving inspectors from outside the parish, but rather his new-found ability to draw more and more output from less land. The Government did not shrink from drawing the inference: the controls would have to be made tougher and more direct. It proclaimed the need for "supply management": farmers who had previously been told merely how much land they could devote to what, were now to have the actual quantities of each commodity to be produced laid down for them. The first attempt to introduce this system failed. In 1963 the Government's proposals were defeated in the annual wheat referendum, a procedure which up to that point had regularly produced a majority of the farmers' votes for the controls that the Government required over their productive efforts, in return for a guaranteed price for their products. There is little doubt, however, that in the long run some form of still closer control over the amounts which the American farmer is allowed to produce will be established. Even now, it is hard to argue that the 2½ million independent farmers working on their own account in the United States enjoy much entrepreneurial freedom, compared for example with most of the people who work the land in Western Europe. That is not to say that the West Europeans will be able to avoid facing the same problem for long. But the Americans must have the credit for pioneering the *dirigiste* solutions.

That the authorities should have had the confidence to go to the farmer in 1963 in the expectation that he would voluntarily accept their scheme for a still more advanced kind of dragooning indicates a set of assumptions derived from a well-established relationship of close government tutelage. The relationship is not peculiar to farming. Indeed an even more niggling control is exercised over the output of producers in the oil industry. It has been in operation since the early 1930s. The glut of oil at that time and the collapse of prices caused by the competitive struggle for markets led first of all to direct regulation of output in the early days of the New Deal, and later to the Inter-State Oil Compact, under which the individual states agreed to impose strict limits on the amounts which they would allow to be sold. Under the present system the power to regulate domestic supplies in the United States is in effect delegated to a single state-run public authority operating out of Texas, whose writ is obeyed by the governments of other states.

The Texas Railroad Commission, which controls the area with the largest volume of production, announces its figures of "allowable production" each month and the output of other oil-producing states is then fixed in relation to this. . . . Within the production quota of any state there is not much room for competition among individual firms; enforcement of the rationing rule is ensured by the big refineries which reject crude oil that has not been officially authorized. Evasion is made still more difficult by a Federal law which prohibits the transport across state boundaries of "hot oil" produced outside the allotted quotas. Evidently rugged individualism, even of the Texas variety, finds it possible to operate inside very tight limits indeed without feeling tamed in the process. No one seems to want to fight the Railroad Commission, let alone abolish it. The explanation presumably lies in the power of the myth; it is hard to think of any other. And the myth is buttressed by what seems to be a native histrionic ability; a lot of people positively want to act out the part of their national stereotypes, once the public relations men, the schoolmasters, and the journalists have established it clearly by iteration. Thus, by contrast, British business, which nowhere has to suffer the kind of detailed control over what is to be produced, and when, that is exemplified in the United States oil industry,[2] is widely convinced that it is subject to extremes of government regulation that no American would tolerate. The ordinary British businessman, too, seems to be ready to act out a part — the national stereotype of *un*enterprise, resting on the belief that circumstances make it barely worth while trying.

[2] Adolf Berle, in *The American Economic Republic* (London: Sidgwick, 1963), pp. 157–8, cites the American sugar industry as another example of a well-established system of detailed government control over individual producers. The sugar factories are allotted production quotas on the basis of an annual estimate, made in Washington, of the volume of U.S. consumption during the forthcoming year.

Tradition of Public Enterprise

I do not intend to imply that the sole difference between American and British entrepreneurial behaviour is the influence of two different and arbitrarily chosen mythical structures. There is a great deal of historical fact behind the myth. But the point that has to be established first, before analysing the real nature of the relationship between the private and public sectors in the United States, is that the conventional view of a business community with a zero margin of tolerance for public intervention is false. Historically, American capitalism in its formative period was much readier to accept intervention by public authority than British capitalism. The doctrines of *laissez-faire* bit very deep into the social and political life of England for a century and more. The constant effort to push back governmental authority of any kind from entrenched positions which it occupied in the economic process became the preoccupation of several generations of reformers. In nineteenth-century America the attitudes towards public authority did not — at any rate until the last quarter of the century — acquire the ferocious doctrinal consistency which they assumed early on among the English. The reasons are not far to seek. After all, public authority, in a territory with a vast amount of rich land being steadily opened up and a frontier constantly threatening to get out of control, had a much more obvious part to play than in a settled island where people were used to operating within well-defined social as well as physical limits.

But it was not simply that American conditions imposed the need for more active use of governmental power in order to keep the peace. The characteristic role of government in the United States during the first half of the nineteenth century, in sharp contrast to what was happening in Britain, was its emergence as an entrepreneur on a large scale, either on its own independent account or, more commonly, in partnership with private interests. Railways, canals, and banks were all treated as proper spheres for public enterprise. In the first two, several state governments were exceedingly active, at a time when in Britain private enterprise owned and ran virtually all public transport. The argument for the use of public funds was forthrightly stated in the legislative address of the Whig Party of New York State in 1838. "We hold it to be wisest . . . ," it said, "to apply the means of the state boldly and liberally to aid those great public works of railroads and canals which are beyond the means of unassisted private enterprise." [3] It is somewhat ironical that today the United States is the only advanced country of the Western world in which the railways are stubbornly preserved, against considerable odds, almost as

---

[3] Quoted in Lee Benson, *The Concept of Jacksonian Democracy* (N.J.: Princeton UP, 1961), p. 103. The author remarks that the Jeffersonian doctrine of non-interventionist liberal government was at this time "for the most part ignored in practice by all state governments."

a kind of museum piece of private enterprise. Everywhere else the state has taken over the service — for the very reasons which were recognized in New York in the dawn of American capitalism.

In his profound study of the development of economic policy in Pennsylvania during this period,[4] Louis Hartz mentions a total of over 150 "mixed corporations," in which the state government and private enterprise were partners, shown in the official records of the year 1844. He observes that the political pressure behind this remarkable movement to involve the state in business enterprise came from "the mercantile group" centred on Philadelphia; these early American businessmen regarded government as a natural partner in their efforts to compete with the trading and transport services provided by their rivals, the merchants of Baltimore and New York. The relationship between public and private enterprise at this stage of American history seems indeed to be guided by many of the underlying assumptions of the traditional French approach.

It is a widely believed legend in the United States that Andrew Jackson's Presidency (1829–37) marked the decisive rejection of the older forms of tutelary government and the assertion of the typically American principle of free enterprise at any cost. All this is somehow symbolized in Jackson's struggle against the privileges of the United States Bank, culminating in his veto on the renewal of its charter in 1832. "Free banking" was one of the popular slogans of the time. So was the demand for payments in specie, instead of banknotes. It is hard to make any serious economic sense of either; both belong in the category of primitive money magic, which has somehow to be exorcized before modern capitalism can develop efficient institutions. One of the consequences of the confused Jacksonian ideas on currency and banking was to delay the establishment of a central banking system in the United States until 1914,[5] long after the leading European nations had fully equipped themselves with this essential piece of machinery.

Jackson was the first of the great populist leaders who seem to be so readily spawned by the American political system. His political notions had neither the consistency nor the narrowness which his subsequent admirers have sometimes attributed to them. In some ways, Jacksonian democracy served to reinforce the movement for active government, in the form of public welfare services, which already existed.[6] Its opposition was not to the use of public power in the economic system, but only to any reinforcement of central power wielded through the Federal authority. State and municipal government were at liberty to expand. The fear was

[4] *Economic Policy and Democratic Thought: Pennsylvania 1776–1860* (Cambridge, Mass.: Harvard UP, 1948). See pp. 290–1.

[5] The year of the founding of the Federal Reserve system.

[6] See Arthur Schlesinger, Jr., *The Age of Jackson* (London: Eyre & Spottiswoode, 1946).

only of the potential Leviathan in Washington; the American principle of preserving individual freedom by dividing up public authority into separate pieces was not threatened by the vigorous growth of rival governmental power away from the centre. On the contrary, the theorists of pluralistic government were often inclined, and still are sometimes, to talk of the state in relation to the Federal authority as if it were a precise analogue of the heroic private individual standing against the overweening pretensions of arbitrary government power. It is the image of David being armed with more powerful weapons for his future struggle against Goliath.

At times the degree of tutelage which state governments arrogated to themselves in Jacksonian America appears so extreme that it suggests the direct inspiration of Colbert, rather than anything that belongs to the Anglo-Saxon tradition. Colbert would surely have approved of the systematic regulation of the standards of quality of all exported goods, instituted by the government of Pennsylvania in the 1830s.[7] The Pennsylvanians were in fierce competition with the state of New York and afraid that they might lose business to their aggressive neighbour unless they made a special effort to maintain the reputation of their goods. Their views were reflected in the report of a committee of the state's House of Representatives in 1833 which says: "If the article . . . forms an important item of export a well-regulated inspection is productive of benefit by preventing the exportation of inferior descriptions of the same article and thus giving it a character in foreign markets." Two years after this a law was passed which went a stage farther. After bringing all the existing inspection measures into a systematic code, it proceeded to fix detailed regulations for each individual commodity, covering the dimensions of containers, the methods of packing, and the brand marks to be put on goods.[8] The mood which prompted this active use of the public power to improve the performance of private enterprise lasted into the middle years of the century. As late as 1853 the Chief Justice of the state, in delivering judgment in a case brought by a citizen, who argued that the investment of public funds by the Pennsylvanian government was unconstitutional, declared with a feeling of confidence which reverberates through the words a century afterwards:

> It is a grave error to suppose that the duty of the state stops with the establishment of those institutions which are necessary to the existence of government: such as those for the administration of justice, preservation of the peace, and the protection of the country from foreign enemies. . . . To aid, encourage, and stimulate commerce, domestic and foreign, is a duty of the sovereign as plain and as universally recognised as any other.[9]

[7] See Hartz, *Economic Policy*.

[8] *Ibid.*, pp. 204 ff. The regulations covered a wide variety of goods ranging from flour and fish to tobacco, potash and gunpowder.

[9] Judgment in the Sharpless case (*ibid.*, p. 122).

The Reversal of the Late Nineteenth Century

Yet a couple of decades later the Pennsylvania Supreme Court judgment would have been thought to reflect a highly eccentric view of the role of government. By then business, and above all big business, seemed to have made a successful take-over bid for all the economic power that was worth having. In the last quarter of the nineteenth century, at just about the time that Britain was beginning to turn slowly away from some of the excesses of the old doctrine, the exponents of an extreme version of *laissez-faire* came to dominate the public life of the United States. The philosophy stamped itself on the country through the agency of the courts even more than through the conventional political process. Judges have at various crucial periods of American history — including most recently during the Civil Rights movement of the early 1960s — acted as conscious agents of a political trend. The task of interpreting the constitution in a system where the Federal Government's room for manoeuvre is in normal times constricted by the "separation of powers" sometimes gives the Supreme Court the initiative in the nation's politics.

What happened to change the balance between public and private initiatives so violently during the third quarter of the nineteenth century? Part of the explanation is possibly the shift in the alignment of the political parties during and after the Civil War, with the earlier exponents of active interventionist government, in the northern states, absorbed into a Republican Party which was now dominated by the big business interests.[10] But there were in addition two economic factors which helped to sharpen the reaction against all forms of public enterprise at this stage. The first was simply that there was no longer any lack of private risk capital on a sufficient scale to finance large enterprises, particularly in the field of public transport. Private investors were now eager to engage in this lucrative business. Secondly, and probably more important in terms of national politics, the management of too many public enterprises had been thoroughly inefficient. It was widely felt that some means had to be found to curb the multifarious initiatives of state governments like that of Pennsylvania, which had ended with the waste of the taxpayer's money. They also, incidentally, destroyed the credit standing of states which too often failed, through mismanagement, to meet their obligations to those who had lent them money.

The essential trouble was that state legislatures tended to regard the management of a public enterprise as merely an extension of the conventional political process. It was not so much that the managers were corrupt as that they were committed to an amateur's view of the needs of management. As was the established practice with elected political representatives in an egalitarian democracy of the American type, managers

---

[10] See Schlesinger, *Jackson*, pp. 505 ff.

were also appointed for short periods and subject to political rotation. Only in this way, it was felt, could their exercise of power be checked. They were treated as if they were no more than passive agents of the committees of the state legislature who had to make the real decisions. Thus, while the state governments embarked on public enterprise and public regulation of industry with a vigour that is reminiscent of the traditional French approach to economic policy, they entirely failed to equip themselves with a core of professional administrators of French quality. Indeed, the whole notion of a professional public officer, acting on behalf of the state rather than of the politicians who happened to make up the government of the day, was alien to the spirit of nineteenth-century American democracy. It is hardly surprising in these circumstances that public enterprise came to be regarded as inherently inferior, in its level of efficiency, to private enterprise.

J. W. Hurst points out [11] that the public authorities continued to exercise an important influence on economic development even after the popular reaction in the third quarter of the nineteenth century which forced the state governments to divest themselves of their business interests. But now government lent its power to private corporations which were developing public utilities. It did this in a variety of ways, but most blatantly by giving them the right of "eminent domain," which meant that they could compulsorily acquire any land needed for their operations.[12] These "delegated powers of legal compulsion" assisted the rapid growth of certain fortunate businesses which were able to claim that they were fulfilling a public purpose; they were one of the factors in the build-up of the massive concentration of power in corporate hands during the 1880s and 1890s.

Direct public enterprise was not immediately extinguished in all its forms. For a while municipal authorities were able to find a hole through the net which had closed on the economic ventures previously run by state governments. But the courts gradually introduced a restrictive set of criteria which made it unconstitutional to use tax money for anything other than an essential "public purpose." The decision on what constituted a proper "public purpose" depended in the last resort on the judge's view of the relationship between public and private responsibilities. And in the late nineteenth century fashionable judicial doctrine in the United States squeezed the former almost to vanishing point.

Debate on American History

It is possible to regard the extremist version of the private enterprise doctrine in the late nineteenth century, from which so many of the simple and certain formulae of the popular political debate in mid-twentieth

---

[11] See *Law and the Conditions of Freedom* (Madison: Wisconsin UP, 1956).
[12] *Ibid.*, pp. 63 ff.

century America seem to derive, as no more than a temporary distortion of the straight limb of the continuing American liberal tradition. Some eminent historians have argued this way. Affirmative government, which intervenes in the economic affairs of a nation on the basis of a long view of its collective interest, is, it is claimed, of the essence of this tradition. It was only a shabby manoeuvre of the big businessmen who captured the Republican Party after the Civil War which made it appear otherwise. As Arthur Schlesinger, Jr., puts it,[13] they were able to use the "Jeffersonian myth" that any strong government was of its nature bad, "to defeat Jefferson's essential purposes."

Whatever President Jefferson's true intentions, the myth continues to have a powerful influence in the politics of contemporary America. At any rate the words used in the political debate seem to refer to concepts implying a suspicion of public power as such, which strike a bizarre note on the average European ear today. Are the American historians right who say that all this verbiage conceals, rather than expresses, the underlying reality of American political history? The point has some practical importance, because . . . the United States has so far appeared as the outstanding laggard in the general movement of the Western world towards the eager acceptance of a vastly enlarged role for the central government in economic affairs. The question is whether the apparent lag is due to special circumstances — notably that the United States is so much richer than the rest of us and has been under less urgent political compulsion to reform itself than Western Europe in the past couple of decades — or whether there is some more deep-seated impediment in the American system to the adoption of the new order.

One version of the evolution of public economic power in the United States sees it as a dialectical process in three distinct phases. J. W. Hurst, the legal historian, describes them as follows: "Over the first three-quarters of the [nineteenth] century we used law to help determine priorities among competing uses of our scarce working capital," [14] next there was an interlude lasting into the early years of this century during which private business power was unnaturally inflated at the expense of public authority; then came a "familiar pendulum movement of policy during the twentieth century," which reversed the movement. "The depression of the 1930s," he concludes, "enormously strengthened but did not initiate this swing back towards promotional use of public finance." Arthur Schlesinger, Jr., marks out the various stages on the voyage from precedent to

13 *Jackson*, p. 518.
14 Hurst (*Law and the Conditions of Freedom*, p. 53) distinguishes four types of investment decisions in which government actively intervened. "Listed in descending order" according to degree of priority attached to them by public opinion, they were: "the allocation of capital to transport, to the development of commercial agriculture, to the fostering of credit facilities, and the encouragement of industry."

precedent during the twentieth century in these terms: "Slowly the liberal tradition was overhauled. . . . The Hamiltonian progressivism of Theodore Roosevelt ushered in a period of energetic government. Woodrow Wilson understood even more plainly the need for executive vigor and government action. Franklin D. Roosevelt carried out these tendencies more decisively than Wilson, and the New Deal achieved the emancipation of liberalism from this aspect of the Jeffersonian myth." [15]

On this view the New Deal was not a sharp break with American tradition but simply a continuation, at a somewhat accelerated pace, of a process which went back to the start of the twentieth century and affected Republican and Democratic governments alike. Schlesinger's comment was written in 1941. Many American liberals at that stage thought that the antipathy to positive government had finally been overcome as a result of the experience of the New Deal. Adolf Berle, who is perhaps the most abiding spokesman of New Deal radicalism, untiring in his series of attempts to adapt its principles to changing conditions during the subsequent two and a half decades, wrote in 1940 about the future of public enterprise in the American system: "I am pretty clear . . . that, within ten years, we shall be forced into a vast expansion of direct production of one sort or another. . . . The Tennessee Valley Authority may well prove to be the great example. . . ." [16] Berle envisaged a further development of New Deal policies in the private sector too. Private ownership could not simply be left to the unpredictable and often perverse guidance of market forces; there had to be central control — "some sort of cartel formation or other organisation of industry." He singled out three categories which especially required public supervision. They were first of all industries where, for technical reasons, the average size of the single unit of production was large, for example steel; secondly, those where market forces tended to result in damaging fluctuations in output (e.g., the automobile industry) or in long-term depletion of a natural resource (e.g., oil); and thirdly, those whose products ought, for reasons of social welfare, to be supplied in a "reasonably continuous . . . even flow" to consumers.[17]

All this reads rather like a blueprint for modern capitalist planning, with a slightly more radical twist, on the French model. Indeed, there were many elements in the early New Deal which pointed, at a time when few of the European politicians of either the Right or the Left were ready for it, in the direction which much of Western Europe has taken since the

[15] *Jackson*, p. 520.

[16] *New Directions in the New World* (New York: Harper, 1940), p. 95.

[17] See also *Power Without Property* (London: Sidgwick, 1960), where Berle has shifted the emphasis away from public ownership — in the light of twenty years of further experience — but the basic techniques of the regulation of private enterprise to secure a public purpose, developed by the New Deal, are vigorously recommended for the treatment of postwar American economic problems.

war. The special virtue of the American reformers was their refusal to accept the simple dichotomy between socialism and capitalism which then dominated European political thinking. The New Dealers — or at any rate the leading group which stayed the course and occupied a political position a very little left of centre, close to that of Franklin Roosevelt himself — perceived the future as a new mixture of public and private initiatives, with the public side very much reinforced but still operating in the framework of a predominantly capitalist system.

Considering the opportunities for radical experiment offered by twenty years of uninterrupted Democratic administration from 1933 to 1952, it is surprising how little follow-through there was from this original impulse into the postwar world. By the 1950s the typical view of the liberal establishment in the United States had probably moved closer to that of Professor Eugene Rostow, former Dean of the Yale University Law School and another highly sophisticated lawyer-economist, in an American tradition of which Berle himself was a notable product. In *Planning for Freedom* [18] Rostow felt able to assert, after surveying the experience of American business fluctuation and economic growth during the 1940s and 1950s, that the United States system was of its nature opposed to "collectivism" in any form. Whatever measures the government might have to take in order to keep the flow of money and the flow of goods moving in step inside a market economy did "not require any change in the prevailing pattern of power distribution." Private enterprise in something very close to its traditional form was in his view a necessary condition for the survival of the American democratic system — ". . . competitive capitalism is a characteristic expression of the American culture . . . [U.S.] policy is always to avoid concentrations of authority . . . Capitalism stands with federalism, the separation of powers, the disestablishment of religion, the antitrust tradition, the autonomy of educational bodies . . . in expressing a deep suspicion of authority. Americans are committed pluralists." Here then is the antithesis, intransigently put, to the concentration of economic authority and the centralized planning of the use of resources, which have become the characteristic instruments of dynamic postwar capitalism elsewhere in the Western world.

Two Doctrines of the New Deal

The paradox is that the Americans who, in the 1930s, acted as the precursors of the new capitalism, seemed to stall in their course just when the system was coming to fruition in the Western world — showing its full powers to provide the great gifts of economic growth, full employment, and social welfare. Why was the original momentum of the New Deal halted? In order to answer the question it is necessary, briefly, to take a closer look at the New Deal itself.

[18] (New Haven, Conn.: Yale UP, 1959), p. 43.

Among the great variety of political impulses which went to make the heroic period of New Deal reforms (roughly the years 1933 and 1934) there are two major themes which constantly recur. They both appear, at first, to be accommodated in a natural ideological coalition; but once Washington has managed to cope with the immediate economic crisis, they come to be seen increasingly by their supporters as alternative and essentially conflicting policies. Arthur Schlesinger, in his history of *The Age of Roosevelt*,[19] has subtly delineated the gradual emergence of these distinct lines of thought, out of what started off by being little more than a couple of ragbags of ideas. One may be broadly described as the corporatist view. This envisaged an entirely new relationship between government and business, collaborating actively with one another in the pursuit of agreed economic objectives. The principle of competitive enterprise in pursuit of maximum profits was regarded as superseded; in its place there was a vision of organized industries in which the producers shared out their task on a rational basis. The other view emphasized supervision rather than collaboration: public supervision, of an essential judicial character, of the activities of private enterprise. Its purpose was to ensure that certain clearly stated business rules were obeyed, rather than to exact any active help from private enterprise in the objectives of public policy. It was expected that public aid in various forms would be required from time to time, in order to make some businesses function properly; but this was regarded as an underpinning for market forces, not as a means of replacing them by some alternative device.

During the emergency phase of the rescue operation in 1933, the supporters of the second view found themselves compelled to accept government intervention on the grand scale; private enterprise was so much flotsam which had to be salvaged in any way possible. But after a short while the battle between the two groups was joined around the issue of the National Recovery Administration. The NRA was given powers to compel industry to reorganize itself, fix prices, allot quotas of production, and so on. General Hugh Johnson, its head, saw it as the instrument for bringing together under one co-ordinated control the work of all the economic departments and agencies of government. Public authority would speak with a single voice and be spoken to in turn by the single corporate voice of each industry.

The inspiration of European corporatist ideas, which were fashionable at the time, is apparent. Indeed, Johnson explicitly recognized the fact when in his farewell speech he invoked "the shining name of Mussolini." [20] He was not referring to the doctrine of the one-party state or approving of the characteristic forms of Fascist violence. His concern was with the "corporations," the autonomous organizations governing the

[19] (Boston: Houghton, 1959).
[20] Schlesinger, *Roosevelt*, II, p. 153.

various sectors of the national economic life, which figured so prominently in the theory — though less in the practice — of Italian Fascism of the 1920s. Not by any means all of the enthusiastic supporters of the NRA were prepared to go as far as this. Johnson was an ebullient character who enjoyed pushing matters to extremes. But he expressed a view widely held at the time, when he insisted that the traditional form of American competitive enterprise was outmoded and must be deliberately replaced by something else. He eventually demanded of President Roosevelt "a clean-cut decision" between the established theory of American capitalism, based on anti-trust and the encouragement of small business enterprise, on the one side, and the NRA on the other. "You can't escape the issues," he said. "Cooperation or competition." [21]

Somehow or other, and not for the last time, the President did manage to escape from some seemingly ineluctable choice. He selected the pieces of policy which suited his immediate purposes, and never worried if they appeared to make a grossly inconsistent pattern. Thus, in the other major arena of the economic depression where the Government's policies were being deployed, in agriculture, they involved thorough-going controls over the output of each individual producer and over the prices of commodities. The state stepped in as an active partner here, and itself bought up the amounts necessary to maintain prices at the desired levels. The managed agricultural system of contemporary America is a permanent monument to the interventionist school of the New Deal, which believed that the era of the competitive market had gone. It is tempting to speculate about what might have happened if the methods used by the Agricultural Adjustment Administration, with the backing of Henry Wallace, the radical Secretary for Agriculture,[22] had been effectively applied to American industry.

But the industrialists recovered their nerve far more quickly than the farmers. Industry had been badly shaken by the collapse of the markets for its goods and the failure of the financial system in the early 1930s. But unlike the farmers, it did not have to face a long crisis of over-production. As soon as the Government had done what was necessary to make the banks function again and had put some money back into people's pockets, business morale perked up. Businessmen were soon ready to launch an attack on a Government which simply assumed its right to interfere, and when they resisted, bullied them. The counter-offensive against the New Deal reached a climax with the campaign against the NRA. In 1935 it was finally abolished, after the Supreme Court had declared it unconstitutional. It was potentially an instrument for centralized economic planning of the modern type. It was also the symbol of the rejection of old-style capitalism, which was the central theme of the first phase of the New

[21] *Ibid.*, p. 171.
[22] Vice-President of the U.S., 1941-5.

Deal. Schlesinger lists "the tenets of the First New Deal" as follows — "that the technological revolution had rendered bigness inevitable; that competition could no longer be relied on to protect social interests; that large units were an opportunity to be seized rather than a danger to be fought; and that the formula for stability in the new society must be combination and co-operation under enlarged federal authority." [23]

It is remarkable how soon this wave of new ideas, seemingly so powerful, was reversed. All the evidence suggests that the decisive change came round about 1935. There was no particular event that can be blamed for it, though the revulsion against some of the excesses and inefficiencies of the NRA,[24] culminating in the Supreme Court's ruling against it, certainly played an important part. It was, of course, unreasonable to expect that a new and highly experimental enterprise of this kind, which had been plunged suddenly into the task of writing codes of detailed commercial regulations and good conduct for 546 industries,[25] would function smoothly. It was bound to make a lot of mistakes. The enormously ambitious venture of devising a substitute, in the form of a new system of collaboration between public and private power, to replace the classical rules of competition could not possibly have succeeded without being given, first of all, time to correct errors and secondly, the support of an unequivocal political decision. Neither was forthcoming.

The New Deal's Permanent Legacy

In the second half of the 1930s the United States seems to have reverted contentedly to the familiar course — seeking out the remedies for the deficiencies of capitalism by regulating the behaviour of individual capitalists. The emphasis is once again all on trust-busting, on sustaining the little man in his struggle against the power of big business, on making competition work. Policy was still bent on reinforcing the exercise of public authority in the economic system; but the authority was judicial rather than administrative. It aimed at an arm's length relationship with private enterprise, not at the kind of active huddle which General Johnson had envisaged in the NRA.

Not that there was any lack of radical spirit in the design of these reforms. One example, the Securities and Exchange Commission, set up to regulate the behaviour of companies which issue shares or bonds, will serve to illustrate the use of the judicial approach to bring about significant institutional change of a kind which has not yet been compassed else-

---

[23] *Roosevelt*, p. 179.

[24] It is to be observed that some of the most radical supporters of the original New Deal, those who favoured the most active government intervention in the private sector, had also meanwhile turned against the NRA, which they saw increasingly as a device for giving business the effective power to administer itself.

[25] See E. F. Goldman, *Rendezvous with Destiny; a History of Modern American Reform* (New York: Vintage, 1956), p. 272.

where. Established in the first phase of the New Deal, when the tide seemed to be running strongly in favour of the corporatist doctrines, it was regarded as a contemptibly cautious effort by the advanced reformers. Yet thirty years after the SEC was set up, Western Europe is still groping for some means of matching the public supervision of the activities of private enterprise management which it secured in the United States. All directors and officers of companies whose shares are publicly traded are forced, as one member of the official committee inquiring into British company law in 1961 (the Jenkins Committee) put it, "to operate as if in a goldfish bowl." [26] They have to report to the Commission every one of their share transactions, within ten days of the end of the month in which it took place, and these are then set out in a regular monthly publication issued by the Government printing office. Also included in this compilation are the dealings and holdings of any person who owns 10 per cent or more of the shares of a public company. According to M. F. Cohen, a senior official of the SEC who gave evidence to the Jenkins Committee, there were in 1961 approximately 40,000 people who were subject to the reporting rule.[27] Professor Gower, a lawyer on the Committee, remarked wistfully: "If rules similar to these were adopted in Britain it would undoubtedly be a potent sanction against abuse of inside information." There was no sign however that any British Government of the early 1960s, whether of the Right or the Left, was prepared to contemplate any reform of company law as radical as this.

Yet at the time when the SEC legislation was being introduced in the United States in the early 1930s, it was dismissed by Professor W. O. Douglas (later Justice Douglas of the Supreme Court) as "a nineteenth century piece of legislation." Moreover it was, he said, "wholly antithetical to the programme of control envisaged in the New Deal and to the whole economy under which we are living." [28] He was, of course, expressing the views of the interventionist school of reformers, and on this view of what the New Deal was about he was justified in his strictures. It only became clear later on, particularly after 1935, that the New Deal — or the bits of it which lasted — was really about something else. Even when there was active intervention by the Government in the running of the economy, it never amounted to Douglas's "programme of control." Above all, there

[26] Memo. by Professor L. C. D. Gower, *Minutes of Evidence, Company Law Committee*, 10 Feb. 1961.

[27] *Minutes of Evidence*, 23 Mar. 1961. The reporting requirement is especially important, because if the persons concerned are shown to have taken a short-term profit on dealings in the shares of their company ("short-term" is defined as being a six-months' period) they can be forced by law to surrender the whole of the sum to the company. As Professor Loss, another American witness, told the Jenkins Committee, section 16(b) of the 1934 Act, which deals with the recovery of profits, "is probably the most cordially disliked single section in the entire SEC armoury by those it affects."

[28] Quoted in Schlesinger, *Roosevelt*, II, 445.

was no serious attempt to co-ordinate the various activities of the Government in the economic sphere into a coherent policy endowed with purpose and direction. Each section of the Government concentrated more or less independently on its own sphere of influence.

It is worth insisting that if there had been the urge towards positive government and economic planning on the part of the Roosevelt Administration, the opportunities for securing co-ordinated action were not lacking. The NRA was not a unique chance, which had to be passed up because of the Supreme Court's action against it. We have already seen how the Government's intervention in the agricultural field opened the way to a permanent and profound change in the organization of American farming. This happened in spite of the fact that the official crop controls operated by the agricultural agency were also declared to be unconstitutional by the Supreme Court at the time of the NRA case in 1935. Some of the New Deal radicals had seen equally rich opportunities in another of the great adminstrative agencies whose task was to salvage the economy — the Reconstruction Finance Corporation. In the face of the collapse of American banking and the desperate shortage of capital of any kind, the RFC had almost unlimited power to control the direction of national investment. Adolf Berle, who was a leading official of the Corporation at the time, urged that the power should be used. The RFC could determine not only investment policies, but also the dividends distributed by the banks to their shareholders, their employment of staff and even the salaries paid to their employees. "As long as additional capital is needed through the Reconstruction Finance Corporation," he pointed out, "just so long there must be acquiescence in the views which it happens to express." [29]

It is to be observed that it was precisely through its control over the key institutions for the provision of credit that the French state forged its most potent instrument of economic planning in the postwar period. There was no inherent reason why the RFC should not have been used in the same way. Berle in fact wanted to use the Federal Government's control over the sources of credit to establish a chain of banks whose task it would be to seek out opportunities for new investment promising a social return, as well as a profit to the borrower. In such a scheme the state would of course have been doing more than providing the wherewithal to sustain a prosperous level of business and employment; it would also have been seeking out agents for its own economic policies. Characteristically the chief aim — as with the postwar European planners — would have been to speed up industrial innovation. "Outside of the large corporations," Berle said, "men who have ideas for new enterprise cannot expect to find much assistance in the commercial banking system." [30]

[29] *Ibid.*, p. 432.
[30] *Ibid.*

In the event, the spirit of experiment in the RFC was held under close restraint. Although the New Deal introduced major reforms into the American financial system, they were of quite a different character. Thus laws were passed to regulate the proportion of bank credit that might be used for a purchase of shares in the stock exchange. It is worth noting that there is still no such official control over stock market "margin requirements" in Britain and several other European countries. In the United States changes in the minimum cash margin have come to be used nowadays as a regulator of the flow of speculative credit, and form part of the general apparatus of business cycle policy. The central bank also tightened its control over the minimum reserves to be held by commercial banks. Under the Banking Act of 1935 the Federal Reserve Board was given the authority to change bank reserve requirements as an instrument of credit policy. But the most novel feature of the reforms was the device providing government insurance for all bank deposits. This was a peculiarly American arrangement, using public authority to underwrite the finances of the banks — the end effect being to assist them in obtaining deposits from the public more easily and on better terms than would otherwise have been possible. Like the Government's parallel scheme for the insurance of house mortgage loans, it provides, at small public cost, the means of making money flow into enterprises for which bankers, acting unaided, would not have been able to provide the funds. The Government guarantee against default mobilizes extra money for commercial transactions of which the state approves, but without any active state participation in commerce. Thus it stands ready both to regulate and to buttress the system, although always from the outside.

All this contrasts sharply with the failure to achieve even the minimum rationalization of the grossly inefficient structure of American banking either during the New Deal or after. Sir Denis Brogan has suggested [31] that the reason why nothing was done about this was the irrational prejudice of the old-line Democrats on all matters connected with currency and credit. No doubt that played a part; but if the only difficulty had been the traditional ideological stance of the party, means would surely have been sought, and quite probably found, to overcome it — as happened over other equally explosive issues. The remarkable fact is that no serious attempt was made to change the power structure of American banking, to regroup the banks so as to increase their combined lending capacity or to convert them into a more flexible instrument of public policy. This was done in Western Europe by far less radical governments than Roosevelt's during the 1930s. The independent, under-capitalized, small town bank was, and still is, a hallowed institution — with an honoured and ancient place in the folklore of American free enterprise — and it has to be kept in active business, even if that means stopping the large banks from set-

[31] *New Cambridge Modern History*, XII, 169.

ting up branches in places where they might be dangerously efficient competitors.

Roosevelt and the Fragmentation of Government

Eric Goldman [32] tells the story of a conversation in 1933 between Raymond Moley, senior member of the New Deal Brains Trust, and Roosevelt on the evening when the President was about to deliver a "fireside chat" on the radio about the establishment of the NRA. Moley, who had drafted the text of the speech, had put in a passage explaining that this institution, together with the AAA [33] to look after agriculture, were to be the instruments of a new era of national planning. He was anxious to impress on the President the "enormous step" that he was taking when he turned his back on the old ideals of free market capitalism. Did he really approve of planning? Roosevelt replied: "I never felt surer of anything in my life."

Yet when it came to the point, Roosevelt's instinct was profoundly hostile to the change in the method of government which was necessary to convert "national planning" from an attractive abstract idea into a reality. To a large extent planning in a capitalist context, as we have come to know it since the war, is a matter of tightening the hierarchical structure of government, compelling all departments to put all the decisions which have significant long-term consequences into a single intellectual framework, determined at the highest level of administration. New lines of authority are established, and at each level of power there is a more precise definition of the area in which choice and local initiative are allowed. Planning thus requires a high degree of explicitness in the relations between the different departments of government and a clear division of responsibilities.

But Roosevelt always preferred to conduct his operations in a kind of extended twilight zone where responsibilities were blurred. Schlesinger describes the results: "His favourite technique was to keep grants of authority incomplete, jurisdiction uncertain, charters overlapping. The result of this competitive theory of administration was often confusion and exasperation on the operating level. . . ." [34] All this was designed to keep the initiative firmly in the President's hands; the constant likelihood of jurisdictional disputes required his presence as final arbiter. Richard Neustadt in his analysis of the different methods of governing of modern Presidents [35] contrasts with Roosevelt's technique the hierarchical system of administration employed by President Eisenhower — to the disad-

---

[32] *Rendezvous with Destiny*, p. 265.

[33] Agricultural Adjustment Administration — an innocuous-sounding name for a revolutionary device of a highly *dirigiste* character.

[34] *Roosevelt*, II, 528.

[35] *Presidential Power* (New York: Wiley, 1960), pp. 158 ff.

vantage of the latter. The task of the head of the executive in the United States, in Neustadt's view, is an unremitting process of bargaining among competing centres of power. The President must constantly manoeuvre for advantage; he is lost if he imagines, like Eisenhower, that his job is to establish a series of chains of command and then to ensure that a consistent set of orders is sent down them.

No doubt Eisenhower overdid the analogy between the White House and a military staff headquarters. However, other soldier Presidents, notably in contemporary France, seem to be more efficient both in thinking out orders and in getting them obeyed than he was. It may be that Eisenhower's real deficiency lay in his lack of understanding, and even more in his absence of any liking for politics, rather than in his failure to keep everyone guessing about the nature of their true responsibility, in the Roosevelt manner.

Indeed, it is arguable that Roosevelt's penchant for the role of bargainer-in-chief, his evident delight in the exercise of a kind of administrative athleticism, caused him to miss an opportunity which another President, endowed with less political virtuosity, might have seized. The opportunity was the sudden expansion of the small and not very professional American civil service into an enormous administrative apparatus of the modern type. Before 1933 the Federal administrative service was small and tended to be treated as a very subordinate element in the national life. It was a recognized patriotic purpose to keep it puny and somewhat depressed. With the coming of the New Deal it was hurried into a drastic change of role, pushed into the centre of the stage, and told to take charge of the plot. The number of Federal officials multiplied several times over during the New Deal. A spate of legislation endowed these men and women with extended new powers; as the Federal Government found itself compelled to engage in a mass of fresh activities, the area of administrative discretion left to officials was greatly enlarged. It is hard to avoid the reflection that if the head of such a government had been seriously concerned with the formulation of a coherent social and economic policy, he would have insisted on a clear pattern of relationships between the disparate organs of authority on which the reform depended. If the commitment to national planning meant anything, it implied at least this.

That Roosevelt preferred the blurred and uncertain lines of demarcation to a more conventional administrative system may have been partly temperamental. There is a story in The White House Papers about the President's astonishment and admiration when he was told by Robert Sherwood (the author of the book) that he had had to leave Washington for a few days in order to sack one of his subordinate officials in the Office of War Information, of which Sherwood was the head. "And did you fire him?" asked Roosevelt. When Sherwood said yes, he wanted to know more. "How did you do it?" he asked. It became apparent from Roosevelt's unaffected curiosity about the detail of the incident that he himself found it almost impossible to sack anyone.[36] His preferred method was not to remove a man who had failed from his job, but to deflate the job, leave the same man in it, and invent a new post alongside it with more authority to be filled by someone else.

This was of course marvellously designed to exacerbate the process which Theodore Roosevelt had described back in 1910 as "the over-division of governmental powers." [37] The elder Roosevelt had become convinced by that time — when he was launching his break-away reform movement outside the established two-party structure of U.S. politics [38] — that this was one of the peculiar deficiencies of the American system: it was responsible, he argued, for the "impotence" of the Government in the pursuit of positive and coherent policies designed to serve the public interest. The evidence suggests that he really did possess some of the impulses of a planner to which his nephew, a quarter of a century later, laid not very convincing claim. However, it would not be fair to blame Franklin Roosevelt's temperament solely for this enlarged obstacle to coherent government in the United States in the second half of the twentieth century. He was in fact only allowing himself to be moved along by a powerful and abiding undercurrent of American political life, and acting out the process with an American politician's characteristic zest. He was responding to a national instinct to break up government into many small parts, an instinct which seems at times to be guided by some eccentric model of a system of administration in which a lot of independent bodies engage in furious competition with one another — the nearest thing in fact to a market place. It is fashionable to praise Franklin Roosevelt for his lightness and skill in manoeuvring over the muddy terrain of American government. It is less usual to recall that he left it a lot muddier than he found it.

American political analysts of the Neustadt school seem at times to imply that the fragmentation of government, the presidential manoeuvring and generally the huge impediment to the execution of coherent public policy, are essentially the consequence of the separation of powers.[39] But this is only true because Americans have been inclined to interpret the doctrine of separation in an extreme sense. This has something to do with the national culture, not with the constitutional doctrine. In France,

[36] *The White House Papers of Harry L. Hopkins* (London: Eyre & Spottis-woode, 1949), I, 72.

[37] Quoted by Goldman, *Rendezvous with Destiny*, p. 162.

[38] The Bull Moose Party, hived off from the Republicans.

[39] Neustadt (*Presidential Power*, p. 191) does at the same time make some interesting practical suggestions for mitigating the divisions in American government, e.g., by reforming the electoral process, so that President and Congress are both elected at the same time and serve for the same period.

where constitutions express at least an equal devotion to the separation of powers — which is after all by way of being a French idea [40] — the opposite trend operates. Independent public agencies may be created and their independence protected by laws; yet somehow they all seem to end up centralizing the important decisions in a small circle of offices in Paris.

The Federal Agencies

Thus the advance of public regulation and public welfare activity since the early 1930s, which is the common experience of the Western world, has had a noticeably different outcome in the United States from anywhere else. The difference is not simply a matter of the relative importance of governmental activities in the U.S. economy. Public consumption of goods and services, by all forms of government, although not as large as in many West European countries, still amounts to over one-fifth of the GNP [41] — a respectable *masse de manoeuvre* in conducting the nation's economic policy. Of course, the division of powers between the individual states and the Federal authority creates special problems for the conduct of a coherent domestic policy. But federalism by itself hardly accounts for the extraordinary propensity to fragment authority at the very centre of the life of the nation.

In order to see just how far the United States deviates from the techniques of government in other Western societies, where the general trend is to use the aggregation of public power in order to create a coherent force whose significance will be greater than the sum of its individual parts, it is necessary to examine the detail of the curious disorder which seems to have been deliberately organized at the heart of the American administrative process. There are altogether over eighty different government departments and agencies which report direct to the President of the United States. They are not grouped in any hierarchy which would permit the President to restrict his dealings to a smaller number of intermediaries who would make reports and carry back the government's decisions to the agency chiefs. Each of them has the right of access to the man at the top and is determined to use it. It is almost inconceivable that a coherent policy could emerge out of an administrative welter of this kind. Its effect under any but the strongest President is to turn the offices of the Government into a loose confederation of more or less hostile bodies competing with one another for more money and more power.

The competition for money is perhaps the one salutary aspect of the situation. It means that the agencies are constantly forced to refer to the Bureau of the Budget for permission to spend more. The Budget Bureau has, indeed, over recent years come to be the chief instrument for the

[40] Partly derived from a not very accurate interpretation by Montesquieu of English 18th-century practice.
[41] 1963 figures.

co-ordination of government available to the President. It is not only the sole authority for the spending of money; it has also been given the job of formulating the whole of the Government's legislative programme for each session of Congress. In theory this task is merely one of bringing together the bits and pieces of legislation proposed by all the various government departments and then presenting the result in a tidy form to the President for his approval. This is in line with the fiction that the Director of the Budget Bureau is a rather subordinate member of the government apparatus, without even a place in the Cabinet. (Franklin Roosevelt himself was sufficiently caught up in this illusion of the "non-political" character of the Budget Bureau to offer at one stage to make the post of Director a career civil servant appointment.) In fact, the job of "legislative reference" performed by the Director, when he decides which bills shall take precedence in the queue of government business and which shall go to the bottom or be left out altogether, is the closest that any member of an American Government gets to the power exercised by the Leader of the House of Commons in Britain. The difference is that in America he still has to wait on the pleasure of the Chairman of the Rules Committee before a government bill is allowed to go before Congress and be voted on. The U.S. Budget Director also has some of the power that normally goes with the U.K. head of the civil service; he is supposed to ensure that official business gets done and to sort out jurisdictional disputes about the boundaries of authority between competing government agencies. It is freely admitted inside the Bureau of the Budget that it is much easier in practice to work out the most complex legislative programme than to compel a couple of government departments with overlapping spheres of influence to agree on which of them shall do what.

The most striking example of free-wheeling government is provided by the Federal Agencies, which regulate a host of basic economic activities including railroads, oil and electric power, air travel and shipping, radio and television. An examination of these agencies provides an insight into the mood and atmosphere in which the American Administration conducts its affairs, and points to the obstacles that would have to be overcome before this style of doing business could accommodate a set of coherent policies. The system originated with the belated effort to assert the public interest in the management and the fixing of rates on the American railroads in the 1880s. Congress was loth to hand this power over to the Department of the Interior, which had up till then been responsible for railway matters, because this would have strengthened the power of the executive and ultimately of the President.[42] On the other

[42] The President of the day, Grover Cleveland, happened to be a former railroad lawyer (see Mark S. Massel, in *Administrative Regulation, Law and Contemporary Problems* [Duke Univ., Spring 1961], to which I am indebted for much of what follows on the subject of the regulatory agencies).

hand, Congress realized that it could not itself directly hand down the stream of decisions which would be necessary to ensure the effective supervision of the railways. It therefore set up in 1887 an independent executive agency, the Inter-State Commerce Commission, which was not subject to any government department or indeed to the President's own orders. This was regarded as a triumph for the legislature in its constant struggle to curb the power of the central government, which was firmly established by then as the chief menace to the freedom of the individual citizen. Since the area of government regulation could not be prevented from growing, in view of the way that private enterprise, not in railways only but also in other spheres, impinged increasingly on the public interest, the best solution was to break it up. It was a new variety of the traditional pluralist formula: if you can't lick it, atomize it.

Moreover the legislators came to see the independent Federal Agency as a special instrument for the assertion of its own power — an "arm of Congress," it was called, inside the executive. The formula was used increasingly during the twentieth century as the range of activities which had to be regulated or promoted by the Federal Government widened — banking and credit through the Federal Reserve Board, business practices through the Federal Trade Commission, the stock exchange through the Securities and Exchange Commission, right through to the establishment of the Atomic Energy Commission, after the last war. In fact the decision whether to place some new governmental activity inside an existing department under the control of the President or whether to float it off in a separate agency was pretty haphazard. However it was necessary to create some doctrine which would provide the theoretical framework for this curiously separate piece of government. One of the things which all the agencies appeared to have in common was that they interfered, more or less, with private business. They could be treated as a set of regrettable exceptions to the principle of *laissez-faire* capitalism — itself, in the national myth, the guarantor of the freedom of the individual from oppression by the Government. Here was the justification for picking out this one sphere of activity for Congress's special attention.

Nor was this all. Because the typical work of the Federal Agency involved it in relations which could either help or hinder private enterprise — sometimes make or break it — its primary role was thought to be a judicial one.[43] Characteristically, its function as an instrument of positive

43 E.g., Massel (*ibid.*, p. 193) estimates that "a television licence in a town of moderate size can be worth between $3 and $4 million." No payment is made for this franchise. The trouble, and the public expense and finally the enormous delays incurred through the insistence on the full judicial treatment, designed to ensure "equal opportunity" for all contenders, have been described by Newton N. Minow, Chairman of the Federal Communications Commission, 1961–3:

"When an applicant seeks a television license, he fills out the prescribed application forms and the regulatory processing begins. If it is a desirable channel, then,

government, which ought at its best to secure the public good with the minimum of friction, was underplayed; all the emphasis was on its appearance in the guise of a judge between competing private interests. Professor M. H. Bernstein sums up the historical process which led to this curious device as follows: "The inability to come to terms with the political character of regulation has been glorified as an honourable escape from politics, and it has sanctified the drive towards further judicialisation of administrative regulation." [44]

The judicial rot, once it set in, went deep. In the effort to establish a consistent doctrine for the regulatory agencies, the lawyers have tried to isolate and heighten the judicial element in the process. More and more the trend has been to hive off the "judges" (who are usually the most senior people) from the rest of the staff, whose business is to promulgate administrative laws governing the activities which fall within the agency's responsibility. For example, the five Commissioners who are in charge of the Federal Trade Commission are not allowed to consult their own staff of economists and accountants when they are reviewing a case. This is because their impartiality as judges might be reduced through receiving advice from someone engaged in the formulation of long-term policy for the Government.

The result of this kind of attitude is that the people with ultimate authority in the field of policy tend to abdicate it to the junior officials, in order to keep their own minds clear and their hearts pure for the vital judicial process. Like some tireless primitive organism exclusively concerned with reproduction, these agencies divide themselves again into yet more parts, each with an independent body and soul. It has to be understood that, in the American context, it is the judicial role which attracts high public esteem. Lesser people merely make policy — and, if they value a quiet life, they make as little of it as possible, at any rate overtly. For once a Federal Agency lays down a general rule governing some ac-

---

wholly apart from the massive influence the broadcaster will have upon his viewers, the license is also worth millions of dollars. Willing contenders compete vigorously for the prize. The contest will cost the applicant many hundreds of thousands of dollars and the government invests a staggering sum of man-hours and dollars to determine the winners.

"To make the choice, the FCC follows a course prescribed by law. There will be a hearing on the public record before a trained Examiner, followed by appeals and arguments to the Commission, followed by appeals and arguments to the courts. The transcript will run into thousands of pages with hundreds of charts and exhibits. While I served at the Commission, we sometimes heard cases that had begun as long as five, ten, and even fifteen years earlier. Once, while testifying in Congress, I was asked about the status of a specific case, and upon checking I discovered that it had begun when I was in the army in India during World War II. It is still pending" (*The Mazes of Modern Government* [Santa Barbara, Calif.: Center for the Study of Democratic Institutions, 1964]).

[44] See *Administrative Regulation* (Duke University, Spring 1961), p. 330.

tivity which it is supposed to supervise, Congress is tempted to question it. It is, after all, a piece of rival legislation. But so long as the agencies stick to the business of case-by-case judgement, the legislators will be less inclined to feel that they ought to argue about the outcome of a judicial ritual. Thus a large slice of American government is farmed out in pieces to a number of individuals who neither know nor are expected to care about the long-range purposes of the President and his administration. It is the principle of *anti-planning* deliberately elevated into a way of life.

The central government can from time to time make its influence felt through the Bureau of the Budget. All Federal Agencies need some legislation at some stage, in order to cope with their tasks; their place in the queue depends on the goodwill of the Director of the Budget Bureau. But if a majority on some Federal Commission decides to oppose the Government's policies, the President cannot get rid of them. Commissioners cannot be prevented from serving out their full term of office, which is usually about five years. It is only when that is over that the President can bring in his own men to conduct the policies that he desires. It may take more than one presidential term to alter the composition of a Federal Agency sufficiently to provide a majority for some new policy. That may sometimes be too long to wait, not only for the President, but also for some of his appointees.[45]

Government by Bargaining — with Exceptions

It may be thought that the independent Federal Agencies are an offbeat and eccentric manifestation of a certain riotous pluralism in U.S. public life. On the contrary, their aims and ideals pervade the whole system of American government. Each Bureau within a government department aims to secure the maximum freedom of manoeuvre, and generally thinks of itself as being connected with the Cabinet minister who is officially in charge of the department only by the loosest rein. Some of the subordinate offices of government, like the Bureau of Land Reclamation (Department of the Interior) or the Corps of Engineers (Army), are notorious for the way in which they have built up their autonomous power by peddling their influence both outside and inside Congress. A mere Cabinet minister would think twice before ordering them to perform some action which conflicted with the ideas of the Bureau chiefs. Each Bureau takes pains to organize its own "constituency" of people who are dependent on its goodwill and interested in maintaining its independent power. The civil contractors behind the Bureau of Land Reclamation, for example, are known to be a formidable lot with an extensive influence in Congress. They

---

[45] For example, Newton Minow, the radical Chairman of the FCC, appointed by Kennedy in 1961, was able to make little impression on his fellow Commissioners, largely hard-line Republican nominees left over from the Eisenhower régime, and retired after two years.

could, if they were crossed, make life very awkward for a minister when he came on the unavoidable trip to Capitol Hill to ask a Congressional Committee for support on some task for which he needed legislative authority. There is no secret made about the process of mutual back-scratching; it is accepted in Washington as the natural way of life of a society in which power is dispersed. Chairmen of powerful Congressional Committees will make it quite clear to a high officer of state appointed by the President that he will not get his way on A unless he makes a deal on B, even though it has no apparent connexion with the case.

Bargaining is the essence of government. So everyone tries to have something to bargain with. Autonomy inside and influence outside the executive are recognized as the two main instruments. It is regarded as normal for a subordinate organ of government to seek to strengthen both. Congress for its part encourages the process openly: it is its special con-tribution in the fight against "big government." Thus the budget of a department is broken down and allocated in advance to the subordinate Bureaus; the heads of these Bureaus are then asked to come before the Congressional Committees and justify their claims for funds or explain how the money already spent has been used.

This constant stimulus to rivalry is applied to the armed forces too, and shows up in competition for funds between different branches of the same service — e.g., in the Navy Department between the sailors in the Bureau of Ships (BuShips) and the airmen in the Bureau of Aeronautics (BuAer) over a project like the Polaris missile. The planners of Polaris, when they started the project in 1956, wisely decided to bypass these jurisdictional disputes by setting up an entirely new office, the Special Projects Office, inside the Navy Department with the right to draw peo-ple in from any arm of the service. Only in this way was it possible to overcome the natural inertia of service departments, which have been graphically described as "holding companies" for a number of government Bureaus, each with its own separate and diverse interest. As Samuel Hunt-ington puts it: "The Services become holding companies serving a variety of purposes rather than integrated companies devoted to a unifying goal." [46]

Congress is constantly seeking new levers of power to insert in the hid-den interstices of government. One such device which proved especially efficient was the ruling, which Congress imposed on President Truman in 1949, that the individual members of the Joint Chiefs of Staff were to be empowered to speak to any Congressional Committee freely in their own personal capacity, without any commitment to the official line of policy adopted by the government. Since the members of the JCS are put there with the expectation that they will represent the interests, as well as express

[46] *The Common Defense: Strategic Programs in National Politics* (New York: Columbia UP, 1961).

the expertise, of each of the armed services, it is a well established forum for bargaining. Congress was able to ensure that the bargaining would not be confined within the walls of the Defense Department, but would be extended into a richer and more dramatic argument on Capitol Hill. This changed after Robert McNamara appeared in Washington in 1961 as Secretary of Defense in the new Democratic Administration, and seriously set about the task of converting the U.S. military effort into a coherent enterprise. But until then the arrangements with Congress had provided much aid and comfort to each of the services in their struggle to counter the threat of a co-ordinated U.S. defence policy.

When public power is systematically fragmented, its ability to control the over-mighty subject tends to be weakened. In the American context there is also the effect of a species of officially sponsored inferiority complex in regard to any form of public enterprise; it is clearly expressed in the directive of the Bureau of the Budget quoted at the beginning of this chapter. The underlying doctrine of that directive is: anything the public sector can do, the private can do better. Its explicit reference is admittedly confined to the production of goods and services — this is where the private alternative must invariably be preferred — but it would be reasonable to expect that some of the distrust for public initiative would spill over into other activities of the state. That perhaps explains why it is a commonly heard complaint that the officials of some Federal Agency are acting as the representatives and spokesmen for the people whom they are supposed to supervise. In a competitive system of government, where effective administrative power often is drawn from sources outside the official machine, an official may easily come to regard it as part of his normal function to seek the goodwill of his "constituency."

But this is by no means the consistent pattern of official behaviour when it is called upon to regulate the affairs of private industry. We have already observed that some government controls over the activities of private enterprise in the United States are unusually fierce, by the standards of other countries. The Food and Drug Administration since the reforms of 1962 has introduced rules requiring positive proof of the efficacy claimed for any medicinal preparation, which are extremely stringent. And actions like the seizure of three different "anti-wrinkle" preparations by officials of the FDA in the summer of 1964 [47] suggest that the officials who have been armed with these extra powers are not inhibited about using them promptly. They demanded scientific evidence, which was very hard to come by, that wrinkles were actually removed as a result of the treatment proposed. In the same spirit the Federal Trade Commission in 1964 ordered tobacco manufacturers "to disclose clearly and prominently" on all packets of cigarettes that "cigarette smoking is dangerous

[47] See *The Economist*, 6 June 1964.

to health and may cause death from cancer and other diseases." [48] This was regarded by the tobacco companies as far harsher treatment than anything that had been meted out to them in other countries which prided themselves on their systems of social welfare and protection.

It might be argued that hazards to health and use of drugs have an emotional significance which put them in a class apart. But officials from other departments have at times been equally aggressive in their behaviour towards private enterprise, when they conceived that it was not abiding by the rules of the game. One outstanding case, which occurred during the militant pro-business crusade at the beginning of the Eisenhower régime in the early 1950s, concerned the use of a chemical called AD-X2, which when added to a battery was supposed to make it last longer. The Bureau of Standards tried some tests and decided that the chemical did not in fact add anything to the life of batteries. The Post Office then refused permission for the use of the U.S. mail service for the transmission of advertisements for this product. This is a powerful sanction which has been used in other cases to prevent the propagation of falsehood by advertisers. The Secretary of Commerce, Sinclair Weeks, was furious and tried to sack the head of the Bureau of Standards. His testimony to a Congressional Committee which was investigating the affair in 1953 reads like the apotheosis of the spirit of private enterprise. "I am not a man of science . . . ," he said, "but as a practical man, I think that the National Bureau of Standards has not been sufficiently objective because they discount entirely the play of the market place." But Congress upheld the Bureau of Standards, and in the end both the Secretary of Commerce and the makers of AD-X2 had to admit defeat. [49]

It is not claimed that this case is typical. But what it shows is that when a government office possesses an established status, like the Bureau of Standards, and is also supported by Congress, it can exercise effective power. It is, after all, unusual even in the most advanced welfare states for the Post Office to take responsibility for the scientific veracity of advertising claims made on behalf of some not very important consumer product. The significant point, however, is that all these examples are concerned with matters where government intervention can be justified ultimately

---

[48] Quoted in *Financial Times*, 25 June 1964. The regulation was due to come into force in 1965.

[49] F. C. Newman and S. S. Surrey, eds., *U.S. Legislation: Cases and Materials* (Englewood Cliffs, N.J.: Prentice Hall, 1955). The chairman of the FTC giving evidence before the Commerce Committee in 1964 in the cigarette labelling case explained the wide-ranging principles guiding his intervention in the market place as follows: "The Commission has the authority to proceed against any actual or potential deception in the sale . . . of any product in commerce. . . . Such deception may result either from a direct statement concerning a product or a failure to disclose any material facts relating to such product" (see *Financial Times*, 25 June 1964).

by reference to some simple true-or-false criterion. Public authority is seen, once again, to be active and confident once it appears in a judge's robe.

Judicial Instruments for Political Ends

Yet in practice the line between the judicial and the policy decision is often a blurred one. Perhaps the outstanding example of the deliberate employment of the judicial process to develop the content and extend the range of official policy is the behaviour of the Anti-Trust Division of the Department of Justice. There can be no doubt about the aggressive ideological spirit in which the 300 lawyers on the payroll of the Division set about their task. They do not conceive it to be their duty merely to uncover the individual wrong-doer and bring him to justice. As a senior member of the Division, G. B. Spivack, put it, these officials have other functions "as well as imposing punishment or obtaining relief in a particular situation" — notably they must help to create "a social environment in which businessmen are induced to conduct their businesses in accordance with not only the letter but also the spirit of the Anti-Trust laws." [50] Again, when the Anti-Trust Division lawyers are engaged in litigation, they should not be exclusively concerned with the merits of the particular case; they "should consider how valuable a conviction based on particular evidence and particular issues might be on subsequent damage suits in determining their trial strategy and tactics." [51]

When the methods actually employed by these lawyers are examined at closer hand, it becomes clear that their power over American industry extends much further than the identification and suppression of monopolistic practices. Through the Justice Department's "consent orders" — that is an arrangement whereby the authorities consent to certain business practices which have been questioned, but on condition that the business concerned obeys a number of specific instructions in the conduct of its future policy — the government engages increasingly in detailed interventions which influence the structure of whole industries. These consent orders are in fact the result of what Mark S. Massel has called "shirt sleeve negotiations" between the Anti-Trust Division and the individual management concerned, a bargain on business conduct in return for a promise to be left alone.[52] Moreover, the legal action and the court case are often used merely as a device to put an official stamp on a decision whose essentials have already been agreed in private. "The Anti-Trust Division," Massel says, "frequently formulates the complaint after it has negotiated the

[50] British Inst. of Internat. and Comparative Law, Conference on Comparative Aspects of Anti-Trust Law in the U.S., the U.K. and the E.E.C., *Report*, Suppl. 6, 1963.

[51] *Ibid.*

[52] *Administrative Regulation.* Massel estimates that "between 85 and 90 per cent of the consent decrees of recent years have been negotiated in this manner" (p. 192).

consent decree." [53] Matters which have been subjected to official supervision in this way include the disposal of patents (an order that certain firms must be given the opportunity of acquiring them), the future behaviour of a business under examination towards firms which are dependent on it, either as suppliers or customers, and even the manner in which a concern is to conduct the affairs of its sales department. A notable instance of the latter was the case of International Business Machines [54] which was directed to dispose of fewer of its data-processing machines under rental agreements and to increase its proportion of outright sales. This was specifically intended to loosen the company's established hold on the goodwill of its rental customers. By the early 1960s there had in fact been a noticeable shift in the composition of IBM's sales, with a diminished, though still large, proportion of rented machines. [55]

The special character of the American anti-trust operations becomes very clear when one tries to transpose them into some other national context. It is hard to imagine a British judge being called upon to decide not the question of ascertainable fact about the existence or not of monopolistic conditions in a given market, but whether a particular merger between two firms *was likely at some future date* to create conditions in an industry which would weaken the competitive process in it. The conclusion reached must depend on such factors as the judge's interpretation of an underlying historical trend. Is this an industry, he must ask himself, where technological developments or the possible management success of particular firms or the financial backing at their disposal will probably lead to certain changes in ownership over the next ten or twenty years? Thus in the crucial Brown Shoe case in 1962 the Supreme Court refused to allow a large but by no means dominant shoe manufacturing firm, Brown — the third largest in the industry — to buy out a firm of footwear retailers, Kinney, who were responsible for less than 2 per cent of retail sales, on the ground that by tying up this retail outlet the scope for Brown's competitors would be diminished. The essential point was that the Court came to the conclusion that, on the evidence available, there was in this industry a trend towards vertical integration by the larger manufacturers which threatened in the long run to create a situation in which a few big firms dominated the market.

Now, it was suggested that this particular firm, Brown, producing less than 10 per cent of the output of the footwear industry, would be able, by itself, to have a significant effect on competition. It could not therefore be held to have transgressed any regulation laid down by public authority. Yet

---

[53] *Ibid.*

[54] The decision was issued in a consent order of 25 Jan. 1956.

[55] This was assisted by the independent decision of the Department of Defense in the early 1960s, to buy its computers, on grounds of economy, instead of renting them as it had done in the past.

the firm was penalized by having this important commercial transaction declared illegal, because of a judgement about the probable future behaviour of other persons whom it could not in any case control. As one American lawyer has remarked, this kind of doctrine "requires the Federal courts to make economic judgements of a kind that would seem entirely non-judicial to most civilian [i.e., exponents of Roman civil law] and British observers." [56] Such judgements would also be regarded in Britain as intolerably unfair to the individual firm which found that a normal commercial transaction had become illegal because it affected some long-range objective of public policy concerning the future structure of an industry. This is an essential point of principle. In the traditional British system there is no place for the use of the courts to further some evolving purpose of public administration. In America there is.[57]

Moreover, the purpose itself is frequently subject to considerable intellectual confusion. It is not clear on what principle vertical mergers, like Brown Shoe, should be treated more strictly than horizontal mergers (i.e., those within the same branch of industry or trade). A recent judgement suggests that the barrier to acquisition applies in the latter case only when the new business resulting from the combination accounts for 30 per cent or more of the sales in its market.[58] Then there is the problem of what are termed "conglomerate mergers" — unions between firms of significant size in industries which are not related at all to one another. These have become a matter of particular concern to the Anti-Trust Division in recent years. It does not like them. It feels that these powerful and diversified industrial groups, which have "deep pockets" out of which to finance the operations of their individual member companies, place any new entrant to an "industry affected by a conglomerate merger" at an unfair disadvantage. But there is no clear doctrine in sight which will allow businesses contemplating a deal to predict how their case will be treated. The only safe thing to do is to get permission in advance, by persuading the authorities that the arrangement will, in some sense, positively serve the public interest. To succeed a firm must, in fact, be able to offer its collaboration in the pursuit of some objective of policy which transcends the mere making of extra profits.

Observing the aggressive interventionist spirit of public power in this instance and the readiness with which private enterprise is guided by official directives, based on a good deal of administrative discretion, one is led to ask whether the obstacles to positive centralized government in the

[56] H. M. Blake, "Mergers and U.S. Anti-Trust Law," *Internat. and Comparative Law Q.*, Suppl. 6 (1963), p. 88.

[57] G. B. Spivack (*ibid.*, p. 49) says that it is a principle "clearly established that the court may not only prohibit otherwise lawful activity and direct action not otherwise required by law, but may also reorganise corporate structures."

[58] *Ibid.* See *U.S.* v. *Philadelphia National Bank*, 1963.

United States are, after all, as great as the earlier argument seemed to suggest. If the trust-busters can do it, why not those in charge of social welfare or bodies concerned with economic planning? The answer seems to be that anti-trust in the United States is a unique case; it is best understood when it is treated as a form of national religion. Moreover, unlike the other, merely theological religions in the United States, the propagation of this one doctrine by public means is entirely constitutional. Indeed the whole American way of life is believed to depend on it: it is the only firm guarantee of pluralism, the only defence against overwhelming private power. Public authority having been deliberately weakened by division, private power must be kept divided too.

Private Governments
and the Constitution

ARTHUR S. MILLER

Shonfield's essay emphasized the diffusion of power within the formal structure of government. In the following selection, Arthur S. Miller, Professor of Law at George Washington University, explores the power exercised by private groups and organizations. By "private governments," Miller means the corporate organizations of business, labor, agriculture, and education, which have amassed great independent power and influence in the last three decades. The present facts of power and power relationships, Miller argues, demand rethinking and a modification of traditional constitutional law and theory. The constitutional system must recognize, he writes, the role of private groups that perform essentially governmental functions. The American Constitution, and the law that results from its interpretation, deal only, and minimally, with the governmental apparatus that exerts formal control over social and economic affairs. Miller's inquiry focuses on the non-official centers of power that are not inhibited by traditional guarantees against unrestrained or irresponsible use of their power. Since this essay was published, the Supreme Court has enlarged significantly the zone of officiality. More and more purportedly "private" action is now subject to the terms of the Constitution. For example, the Court has extended constitutional guarantees against certain aspects of private racial discrimination, such as the refusal to sell a house to a Negro. There also have been notable legislative actions, such as the Civil Rights Acts of 1964 and 1968, that prohibit various forms of discrimination by private concerns. What other areas of private power can, or should, be subjected to increased public authority?

The Exercise of Power

For the purposes of this study the United States can be thought of as a combination of a Social Service or Welfare State, which we have become during the past two decades, and a Garrison State, which we have in some measure approximated since the end of World War II. An appropriate label for this combination is the "Security State," a name derived from the apparent character of Americans today, which reflects the demands of of the individual for economic and psychic security subsumed under the notion of the social-service or welfare principle of government and the demands of people generally for national security or self-preservation.

An examination of the way power is exercised in this Security State is indispensable to an understanding of the important decision and of those who make it. Power is the key concept in the American decision-making process and in the study of constitutional law. Although its meaning is not a settled one in the social sciences, let us adopt this definition here: Power is the ability or capacity to make decisions affecting the values of others, the ability or capacity to impose deprivations and to bestow rewards so as to control the behavior of others.

This definition does not necessarily imply that a person who has power must also have the ability to exercise actual physical coercion over others. The sanctions through which decisions are enforced are usually more subtle than that. They include those of a psychological and economic nature, as well as physical controls, and they can be direct or indirect. We are not interested in the myriad of routine and trivial decisions resulting from exercises of power between individuals. Our interest lies in decisions that result in social control imposed on a relatively broad base.

The Security State is the institutionalization of a society whose aim is to further the primordial value of security, individual and national, domestic and external. (That the two are intimately connected is obvious, but often forgotten. They are separated here for purposes of analysis, but they are actually the two sides of a single coin.)

The domestic aspect of the Security State — which carries the label of "Welfare State" or "Social Service State" — has as a primary function the

Reprinted by permission of the author. Published by *Fund for the Republic* (Santa Barbara, Calif., 1959).

realization of economic well-being for its inhabitants, as A. C. Pigou has said, "by stimulating production, improving the allocation of real income, and combating large inter-temporal fluctuations." To a large extent, this entails the view that government has an affirmative role to play by widening the opportunity for individual income security and at the same time providing income security for those who cannot achieve it on their own.

The concept of the Garrison State — external security — is not nearly as well known or as extensively used as the Welfare State label. According to Harold Lasswell, a Garrison State is one "in which the specialists on violence are the most powerful group in society." This formulation focuses on the decision-maker. But if the decision rather than the decision-maker is emphasized, the Garrison State can be defined as one in which considerations of physical security influence or control a wide range of decisions.

The medium through which security is maintained is the military. The "specialists on violence," however, do not perforce create the policy; they articulate it. Again, government has an affirmative role to play: that of creating the conditions that will enhance the preservation of the nation as an entity. And another refinement on Lasswell's statement appears necessary: a Garrison State should be carefully distinguished from a "Garrison-Police State," which is a Garrison State accompanied by important measures severely restricting individual freedoms. A Garrison State need not be authoritarian, but may well become so. It is, in fact, one of the pressing constitutional problems today to find means of furthering the goals both of national security and of individual freedom at one and the same time.

Wide diffusion of power has always been a striking fact of the American political and economic arena. The American ideal has been to have as broad a base in decision-making as possible. In economics, this has called for a laissez-faire role for government and the use of the market as a medium through which the numberless decisions of individual participants are sifted. In politics, and thus of course in constitutional law, the idea of the State as umpire, rather than participant, has been traditional. The fears of the Founding Fathers were directed at the possible excesses of *official* wielders of power only. This reflected the absence of any power centers rivaling and competing with the State, but even if other loci of power did exist, the frontier was always available as a safety valve and an escape for the discontented. (It is significant that the growth of other centers of power coincided in time roughly with the close of the American frontier.)

The ideal of broadly based decision-making is still prevalent, in the American myth at least, but in practice it has been greatly modified. Power has long been centralized in the sense that some national (although unofficial) institution did often exercise effective control over important decisions. For example, the direction and intensity of investment depended largely upon the desires of a relatively small group of men operating in the New York money market. Today, in addition to the rise of the State to a position of great influence, other groups have come along to challenge the dominance of the propertied and financial aristocracy.

Who actually exercises power in the United States today? We may be able to find the answer by analyzing the two fundamental concepts of constitutional law — federalism and separation of powers — in the light of today rather than in the light of tradition. The analysis of these two concepts postulates (1) that the federal system is of two types, formal and functional, and (2) that the separation-of-powers doctrine, so important to the Founding Fathers, is changing in content. It also assumes that the American constitutional system today displays at least the following characteristics:

1. Power (as formal authority) is divided spatially (the federal system) and functionally (separation of powers).

2. The *formal* allocation of power in the Constitution relates only to political decisions. The other important decisions, of which those of an economic nature are of particular significance, are not dealt with in express terms.

3. The twentieth century has witnessed the growth of large semi-autonomous economic organizations, called by Peter Drucker the "industrial enterprise" and by Adolf Berle the "corporate concentrate," which are the basic units of economic federalism The name used here for these organizations is the "factory community."

4. While orthodox theory and constitutional doctrine presupposed only two entities — the State and the individual person — it is now widely believed that the isolated individual does not exist as such and that he is significant only as a member of a group. In addition to the large corporate enterprise, which includes both the managerial class and the labor union, the new groups include farm organizations, veterans' associations, and charitable foundations, among others.

5. Assuming that real power is formal authority conjoined with effective control, it can be said that no *one* person or *one* group, however large or comprehensive — including the State — exercises real power over any area of decision. Real power is diffused, shared by a congeries of groups including the State, which is probably merely the most powerful, but not necessarily the dominant, group.

6. Given this wide dispersion of power, it is important to have an arbiter among the power-wielders. Relative priorities must be assigned to the various demands, and hierarchies among the groups must be determined. This may well be the major role that the State plays in the American system today.

7. During the nineteenth and early twentieth centuries, when the negative "watchguard" theory of governmental action prevailed, the United

States Supreme Court was the principal organ of State power. Umpiring the system of formal federalism and providing "a nexus between our fundamental law and our fundamental economic institutions," it formulated final policy in matters relating to political economy. Today, the Supreme Court apparently shares control of this job with Congress and the bureaucracy.

8. The urgent problems for constitutional law and theory today are the relationship of the State and the individual to the other centers of power within the nation, and the relationship of the United States to the remainder of the world.

The Federal System. Perhaps the most noteworthy feature of the formal organization of power under the United States Constitution is its division into a federal system. Federalism as practiced in America has captured the imagination of several other nations, particularly those with large land areas like Australia, Canada, and India, and of those people who dream about and work for the political integration of Western Europe.

Originally, when the functions of government were considered to be strictly limited, American federalism assumed that the jobs of the State could be pigeonholed and kept distinct from each other. But in recent decades the role of the State has moved from the negative to the affirmative, and the initial conception of the federal system has accordingly undergone marked alterations. Not the least of these is the apparent necessity for one of the two governments — national or state — to be dominant.

Whatever the intention of the framers of the Constitution, the two governments were roughly coequal in relative power during the formative years of the nation. Even though a series of early decisions by the Supreme Court sanctioned broadly conceived exercise of national power, the central government was exceedingly reluctant to intervene in social and economic affairs. The federal system could correctly be viewed as dual federalism. The first real shift in this attitude came with the Civil War, but it was not until the late nineteenth century that national intervention of a non-emergency nature took place in individual activities. Since 1900, although the myth still indicates otherwise, the structure of formal federalism has been greatly altered. Dual federalism has become "national federalism" or, better, "national cooperative federalism." The national government is now the dominant government in the federal system, and there has been a concurrent alteration in the traditional content of the doctrine of separation of powers.

The reasons for the fundamental alteration in formal federalism are not difficult to locate. They include the industrialization and urbanization of American society, the growth of rapid transportation and communication, the impact of two world wars and the great depression of the 1930's, the advent of the federal income tax with the result that the bulk of the tax dollar flows to the national treasury, and the lack of fiscal independence of state governments, with their consequent inability to fulfill the demands of their constituents and still remain financially viable. All these factors have coalesced to bring about the demise of dual federalism and the establishment of the new model of formal federalism.

Formal Federalism Today. Law follows society and cannot run contrary to the main impulses and beliefs of society. Even the Supreme Court recognized this in the late 1930's. Reluctant at first, refusing to believe that changes in American society meant inevitable changes in all law, even constitutional law, the Court in a series of landmark decisions finally recognized the unifying forces of American society. The turning point came with NLRB v. *Jones and Laughlin Steel Corp.*, but the leading cases setting out the new type of federalism were those that upheld the Social Security Act. Coming shortly after *Jones and Laughlin*, they gave final constitutional approval to the outlines of cooperative federalism. The trickle of decisions became a stream and then a flood. The result is that today the federal grant-in-aid is the principal means of financing the *new* activities of state governments. State taxation systems still take care of the traditional functions of state and local governments, but anything new — and this includes some old but greatly expanded activities — is, by and large, involved with a federal grant or a federal subsidy.

The implications of this change are clear. States today operate, in general, less as practically autonomous units than as administrative districts for centrally established policies. They are not quite hollow political shells, but their once great power has been vitiated by the movement of history. They have "housekeeping" duties, but little real concern with important decisions. When new problems arise, eyes turn to Washington, not to the state capital. It is undoubtedly accurate to say that states exercise a great deal of control over individuals — in fact, much more today than they did during the nineteenth century — but mostly in relatively minor or purely local matters.

In areas of major public concern the decision-making process has been nationalized. We are apparently unwilling to tolerate fragmentation of policy in those areas. We also apparently believe that the broad problems of government — social service domestically, national security externally — are beyond the effective powers of the individual states. Our demands can be satisfied only through the promulgation of uniform national policies. The national government, thus, must be the chief policy-making organ of formal government.

Harold Laski noted this basic alteration in formal federalism twenty years ago. "The Federal form . . . ," he said in 1939, "is unsuitable to the stage of economic and social development that America has reached. . . . I infer . . . that the epoch of federalism is over." Later, Karl Loewenstein stated: "Experience . . . demonstrates that, whatever strength of tradition and emotional values of political theory federalism is still imbued with, the economic imperatives of the technological state require unified if not uniform economic policies throughout the entire territory and do not brook that kind of economic fragmentation which goes with effective member-state sovereignties."

This view is still by no means widely accepted. Many people appear to find continuing elements of strength in federalism. But if this is so, the strength is displayed in far different ways from what it was historically. Federalism, in its former sense of true dual government, is no longer possible in the age of the Security State. The formal structure will doubtless remain, but only as a façade behind which the great changes that have taken place are hidden.

These fundamental changes in formal federalism are only part of the picture. In addition, and probably of far greater importance, there is the concurrent growth of "functional federalism"; in other words, the system of "private governments" that exist within the United States of America.

Functional Federalism. Orthodox constitutional theory and doctrine, as we have said, recognize only two entities: government and the individual person. Nothing intermediate is envisaged. The Constitution limits government in favor of individuals, a notion based on the unstated assumption that individuals live and act as autonomous units. Not even the political party is mentioned in the Constitution, and it is only through a sometimes disputed construction that such "artificial persons" as the corporation are included within the scope of the constitutional individual.

But it has become widely recognized in the past few decades that the completely autonomous, "isolated" individual does not exist as such. The Protestant Ethic of the eighteenth century — which extolled the sacredness of property, decried the spiritually debilitating effects of security, and asserted the supreme virtues of hard work, thrift, and independence — has been replaced by what William H. Whyte, Jr., calls the "Social Ethic":

> . . . By Social Ethic I mean that contemporary body of thought which makes morally legitimate the pressures of society against the individual. Its major propositions are three: a belief in the group as the source of creativity; a belief in "belongingness" as the ultimate need of the individual; and a belief in the application of science to achieve the belongingness.

The group is an apparatus for the escape from anomy by individuals beset with feelings of isolation, of nothingness, of rootlessness and purposelessness. It also enables them to increase and strengthen their freedom and liberty. This seeming paradox is explained by the theory that, through union, persons may accomplish objectives they would be unable to achieve as individuals and may also be able to oppose the coercive tactics of other and stronger individuals or associations. For society as a whole, the groups perform urgent business as agencies of social control. Operating in reality as arms of the State, they may validly be viewed as recipients of delegated power from the State. This is not new; it has apparently always been so in history. Compare the following statements, the first by Charles Merriam, the second by Charles Beard:

> . . . As Aristotle said centuries ago, the isolated individual could not exist except as a stone hand. The lone individual does not figure either in family relations, in neighborhood relations, in state relations, in social relations, or in the higher values of religion. Nowhere is he left without guiding social groups, personalities, and principles.

> . . . This great fact stands out clearly, that through the centuries — down until our own day — group interests were recognized as forming the very essence of politics both in theory and practice.

John Dewey maintained that the individual achieves his meaning only in his relations with others — in associational activity. Earl Latham begins his seminal study on politics with the statement that "*the* chief social values cherished by individuals in modern society are realized through groups." Peter Drucker provides an economic basis for William Whyte's notion of the Social Ethic by stating that it is "the organization rather than the individual which is productive in an industrial system." And John R. Commons put it even more tersely: "This is an age of collective action."

These are the philosophers, the political scientists, the sociologists. Legal theorists, in large part, have lagged behind. Most of them have doggedly continued to assume that Maine's dictum about the movement of progressive societies from status to contract is still valid, even though increased sanction and approval have been accorded in law to group and associational activities. While speaking in the symbols of individualism, for example, the Supreme Court has by indirection created a constitutional law of freedom of association. And Congress has legislated so as to legitimize organizational behavior, as in its labor legislation. It is now time for constitutional theorists to recognize an entity intermediate between the individual and the State. This is the group — the basic unit of functional federalism, the wielder of effective control over large parts of the American power system.

Commons observed that "the 'modern state,' or 'political power,' . . . is increasingly focused upon the delegation of power to administrative commissions whose members are officials of government, while the 'new economic state,' or 'economic power,' is the corresponding delegation of power to private corporations whose officials are the boards of directors." This is exercising power in the sense of making the countless decisions necessary to carry out a policy that has been established by superior authority. It is a system of administered capitalism, to use Adolf Berle's concept, or of the "delegated power of command," to quote Karl Renner, with attention focused on the organs to which the State has entrusted the performance of some of its essential functions. These are the organs with economic power — the large corporate enterprises or factory community. They are probably the most important of the groups in American society. They are the functional units of economic federalism and the basic units of a system of private governments.

Clearly, the State does not exercise a monopoly of power. Pluralism is the operative political fact of American society, the American brand of collectivism. The pluralism, in addition, can probably be thought of as the pluralism of elites — the leaders of the groups which make up society and exercise sovereignty. The factory community is the most important of these groups, and its impact on the allocation of resources, the level and distribution of income, the rate of economic development, and the price system demonstrates its essentially governmental character. As Adolf Berle has pointed out, "The modern corporation plainly lies in that no-man's land where economics, law, and political science converge; and it is an important and durable institution in the twentieth century." And further: "The corporation is now, essentially, a non-statist political institution, and its directors are in the same boat with public officeholders."

The factory community is the hub around which the economy revolves. The individual does not exist as an important entity in the economic picture — and perhaps not even in the political picture. The American system is one of giants, and will continue to be so despite the anti-trust laws.

Of course, the units of this system are not as clearly defined as are the units of political federalism. They are not geographically delimited; they are far more amorphous. But their importance can be discerned in the decisions that they make. As decision-makers in a decentralized system of decision-making, they tend to be far more viable and autonomous than the states, which by and large follow the lead of central authority. And they raise real problems about their relationship to the government — problems of control, problems of how their power should be limited. Before taking up that question, however, we should mention some accompanying changes which have taken place within government.

Separation of Powers. Massive changes have taken place, and will probably continue to take place, in the way decisions are made within government. The Constitution set up a governmental system, but "the hard logic of events" has necessitated major departures from the original model. The 1789 model of a tripartite division of governmental powers has been giving way to what approaches a bipartite division and what threatens to become even more streamlined. Both the judiciary and the legislature have waned in their positions of relative power, as the power of the executive has expanded. These changes can be summed up in four propositions:

1. The role of the Supreme Court in the national government has undergone a marked change in the past twenty years. The thrust of its

power is more in interpretation of the legislative and executive will than as an aristocratic censor through constitutional construction.

2. The bureaucracy has taken on a much more important position in the power hierarchy than it held historically. It can rightly be termed a fourth branch of government.

3. It has proved necessary for basic policy decisions to be made by institutions outside the constitutional allocation of governmental powers.

4. The executive — that is, the President and his immediate office — has taken an increasingly important role in the formulation of State policy.

The growth of the executive and of the bureaucracy has coincided with the rise of the Security State; within them is located the nerve center of the American State today. The vast bulk of routine decisions are made administratively, including many of very great importance to individuals immediately and directly affected. Operating on broad delegations of authority from Congress, the administrators have a high degree of flexibility (not always used) and only nominal supervision from other branches of government. Supreme Court deference to the legislature has also meant deference to the creatures of Congress, which are the administrative agency and the government department. Some restraints exist in the threat of judicial review, but it is a fact of modern life that only a microscopic number of administrative decisions are reviewed by the federal courts. Fewer are overturned. The pattern is not as clear in the relation of Congress to the bureaucracy, but it seems to be true that congressional supervision of administrative decisions is nominal at best, and non-existent in many instances. As for the President, it can be said that his is not a position of dominance over the bureaucracy, but that he exercises "great influence" over some of the decisions it makes.

Whatever the framers visualized as the office of the Presidency, the Chief Executive seems to be emerging as the strongest of the traditional branches of government. As Corwin has put it, "taken by and large, the history of the Presidency is a history of aggrandizement, but the story is a highly discontinuous one." Try as some have done to avoid the tasks of governing and of leadership, today's problems do not allow it. We can even agree with Justice Black's poorly conceived opinion in the steel seizure case and say that only Congress can set policy; but this still does not eliminate the need for the President to point the way to required policies and to work to get them enacted. The schoolboy version of government, with three watertight compartments, is no longer enough. The government has to take affirmative steps to meet a continuing series of crises, and under our constitutional system only the President can furnish the leadership that these affirmative steps demand.

Separation of powers and the formal structure of policy-making within the national government have been supplanted by an institutionalized, informal system which cuts across the executive, administrative, and legislative branches. The picture is blurred and difficult to get into focus, but my contention is that the really important decisions made within the government are taken by a relatively small group of men: the President and his closest advisers; the leaders of Congress, particularly the Senate; and the administrators directly interested in the decision to be made. This can, I think, be called decision-making by a high-level committee with a shifting membership. Were the connotations not so invidious, such a committee might well be called a supra-constitutional *camarilla* or *junta*. To some extent, this group has been given a legal basis in the creation of the National Security Council.

A strong case can be made for the proposition that government by *junta* is a cardinal fact of mid-twentieth-century America. But even if that is granted, it must immediately be added that this emphatically does not mean that the group of men can, or does, act without regard for the demands of the people generally. These decision-makers take into account not only what in fact the "people" generally are demanding but also what, in their judgment, the "people" will go along with. The will of the "people" can be considered to be a myth, but the national government is not free to issue a decree at will. Furthermore, as de Tocqueville observed, "when the central government . . . has issued a decree, it must entrust the execution of its will to agents over whom it frequently has no control and whom it cannot perpetually direct."

Government in a Pluralistic Society. Our discussion of the role the State plays in the decision-making process takes two avenues: first, the position of government as one of the groups in society; and, second, the role of each of the units of government. These should be examined concurrently, in order to see the interplay which takes place. The following propositions will be ventured.

1. The State is but one of the many groups that make up the pluralistic nature of American society. It must share power with other groups, the most important of which is the factory community.

2. However, there may be what Wolfgang Friedmann has called a "reserve function" of the State, which enables it, during times of emergency, to be the dominant group.

3. Policies are made through a complex process of group interaction, often but not necessarily resulting in official sanction being given by the State.

4. Policies enunciated by the national government tend to represent a consensus of the groups most affected by such policies.

5. The organs of government have specialized functions to perform in the process of group interaction, functions which complement each other and together make up the role of the State in national decision-making.

A few years ago, Friedmann tells us, advocates of pluralism "pleaded for more recognition of the social groups within the State . . . in mitigation of the legal and ideological glorification of the State. A generation later, the question must be raised in all seriousness whether the 'over-mighty subjects' of our time — the giant corporations, both of a commercial and non-commercial character, the labor unions, the trade associations, farmers' organizations, veterans' legions, and some other highly organized groups — have taken over the substance of sovereignty." Just what is the relationship of the State to these other groups in society?

The formation and establishment of important policies in the United States appear to require the reaching of a consensus among the groups most affected, beneficially or adversely, by those policies. As a result, policies tend to become those sanctioned by the lowest common denominator among interest groups, those that strike a balance between pleasing the most people and offending the fewest. Put in another way, this means that the State is not all-powerful: it cannot operate as it wishes; it cannot fail to take into serious consideration the demands and wishes of our organizational society. National decision-making in final analysis is an amalgam of the aspirations of the State watered down by the influence of the units of neo-feudalism. Government today is a countervailing force in American society, a force which "establishes the norms of permissible behavior in group relations and enforces these norms."

Early in American history the dominant groups were the mercantile and the aristocratic land-holding classes (except for an occasional displacement, as in the administration of President Jackson, by the farmers and artisans). The Constitution itself has been thought of as the product of the pressures brought by those early dominant classes. Whether it was or not, certainly the pattern of official decision-making during the first century of American constitutional history clearly favored the aristocratic landholders. Astute use of the interstate commerce clause by Chief Justice John Marshall cut away any likelihood of adverse state regulation; at the same time, the national government showed no inclination to enact affirmative commercial regulations.

After the Civil War, other groups arose to challenge the political supremacy of the business ruling-class. The Granger movement, the Populist movement, the trade-union movement, all reflected a growing ferment in politics and a growing participation in local decision-making by formerly dormant groups. By 1900 the dominant position of the business leadership had been threatened and breached. More and more the other groups demanded an opportunity to make their weight felt in decisions. They soon found that their balloting power gave them control of the state and even the national legislatures. The trend toward social equality prophesied by de Tocqueville was coming true. For a number of years the business leadership was able to invoke the power of the federal judiciary to stave off the impact of most of the decisions made by the new combinations of power, but even this bastion crumbled during the 1930's. The result is a congeries of groups, none of which can normally impose its will on the remainder of society but all of which operate or stop or water down things conceivably inimical to their interests. Thus, a group is often able to veto a proposed policy, even though it cannot insist that its own wishes become policy. The net result is a process whereby policies are made after a consensus is reached among the interested groups of the polity.

Power on the national level, therefore, should be viewed in terms of issues, not in terms of dominant decision-makers. In the group process, leaders of the various groups bargain among themselves to reach temporary accords on particular issues. This bargaining must take place in order for decisions to be made. If there was basic agreement, there would be no need to bargain; on the other hand, if the groups and their leaders agreed on nothing, no bargaining could take place. There must at least be agreement on fundamental goals, on the ends sought; the bargaining has to be over the means to achieve those ends. "Leaders bargain because they disagree and expect that further agreement is possible and will be profitable — and the profit sought may accrue not merely to the individual self but to the group, an alliance of groups, a region, a nation, unborn generations, 'the public interest.' " Bargaining in turn creates the need for the "decision-broker" — the person who can bring disparate groups together. In the United States, the key bargainer is often the politician. He juggles conflicting interests, creates alliances, and effects the compromise among seemingly irreconcilable views. Franklin D. Roosevelt was one of these; Senator Lyndon Johnson, the current majority leader in the Senate, is one today.

Within the State itself, each of the branches of government has its own specialized role to play in this bargaining process. The *legislature* operates as an arbiter of the group struggle, notes the emergence of a successful compromise or conquest, and enacts a statute which in effect ratifies the result. As an official group, the Congress has drives and demands of its own, but essentially its purpose is to recognize when an equilibrium is reached in the group struggle and then to place its stamp of approval on that equilibrium. To a marked extent, this is Calhoun's doctrine of the concurrent majority in action: No important group is forced to accept legislation unfavorable to it in the particulars in which it is most vitally interested.

Furthermore, Congress at times operates to correct outrageous decisions made by the private legislative process of the factory community. In doing this, Congress and the Supreme Court often act in concert, complementing each other. Congress, however, is the dominant member of the duo. For example, the anti-trust laws are really used by Congress to try to establish and enforce norms of corporate behavior; the fundamental problem dealt with is that of the distribution of power in the community. The broad policy statement is established by Congress, which then leaves it up to the Court to make necessary refinements and applications to particular situations. In other areas where the exercise of private power becomes sufficiently obnoxious, Congress can and does step in to redress the balance of power and, at times, to try to protect individual liberty. This "taming of feudal institutions" is also done by the Supreme Court acting alone, without prior legislative guidance. Such activity by the State is necessary, for, as Robert Hale has pointed out:

> . . . as far as individual liberty is concerned, it is just as important that legislative bodies should be able to protect persons from oppression at the hands of private groups which exercise power indistinguishable from that exercised by government as it is that the courts should be able to protect them from oppression by officials whose power is more generally recognized as governmental.

The role of the *bureaucracy* is to see that the basic ground rules established by Congress are obeyed. This is carried out by applying the general rules to an infinitely detailed number of particular instances. Another primary function of the bureaucracy is to represent the unofficial groups, whose activities they are set up to regulate, in the governmental decision-making process. This does not mean, as is often averred, that a regulatory commission necessarily becomes the captive of the activity it regulates, but it does mean that the regulators tend to espouse the cause of the regulated when conflicts with other group interests arise. Finally, in conjunction with the executive, the bureaucracy exists to further the public, as distinguished from group, interest — the interests of all of the people of the nation. Whether it does or not is the subject of much controversy.

Ostensibly superior to the bureaucracy is the *federal court system*, which operates to check the administrators and to see that they adhere to the statutory rules and to constitutional mandate. Actually, however, judicial control of the administrative agency is nominal at best. Great deference is paid to a mysterious quality called expertise which administrators are reputed to have. Of course, this is just a confession on the part of the courts and judges that they do not know much about modern business affairs in an industrial civilization. The Supreme Court itself has been quick to point out its own shortcomings in the complex area of regulation and governmental control.

Even so, the judiciary's role is not minor. It does effect a nexus between fundamental economic institutions and the fundamental law. But the flow of decisions in administrative law during the past twenty years indicates a judicial desire to leave the routine process of governmental decision-making to the bureaucracy, subject only to tenuous judicial restraints. Thus, the role of the Supreme Court is to bring about, through the

medium of statutory interpretation, group adherence to nationally prescribed legislative policies and, through the medium of constitutional
interpretation, adherence to constitutional norms. While it is no doubt
true that the Court's decisions on personal liberties really relate to the
liberties of groups, the necessary corollary is that the groups are made
responsible for adhering to the fundamental prescriptions of the Constitution. Hence, the Supreme Court has a dual role to play: on the one hand,
it operates as an arm of the legislature to put legislative policy into operation; on the other, by enlarging the zone of officiality it seeks to prevent
the excessive use of arbitrary power by private law-making groups. This
second function is just now in its formative stages; but it is the direction
of future judicial law-making.

This entails bringing within the scope of governmental action, and
thus within the reach of the proscriptions of the Constitution, the activities of private groups that have been invested with governing functions. In
effect, the Court "public-izes" the system of private governments. First,
by according a high degree of deference to Congress, the Court has legiti-
mized governmental participation on a broad scope in the affairs of
society. As a result, much of what was formerly beyond public control has
now been "politicized"; and "in the mass societies of the twentieth century, politics and public affairs have come to impinge ever more closely on
the life of the common man."

The second method by which the Supreme Court enlarges the zone of
officiality is perhaps more important. Whenever any organization or
group performs a function of a sufficiently important public nature, it can
be said to be performing a governmental function and thus should have its
actions considered against the broad provisions of the Constitution. In
the racial covenant cases, the white primary cases, and the company town
cases, the Court "has shown that the concept of private action must yield
to a conception of state action where public functions are being performed. . . ." With the continuing "pluralizing" of American society and
the increasing recognition of the governmental power of private groups,
it can be forecast with some certainty that the trend of the Court in
"public-izing" private groups will continue. It should become the important constitutional law development of the mid-twentieth century.

If this outline so far is valid, the *President and his executive advisers*
have a dual role as the chief decision-brokers, operating as titular and
actual head of the "government by committee" and as the principal exponent of the national interest, as distinguished from sectional or group
interests. In both of these, the President has had to transcend what the
Constitution apparently says and, today at least, to adopt a theory of office
that is far more than what Chief Justice Fred Vinson once castigated as
the "messenger-boy" concept of the Presidency.

With Congress by and large made up of spokesmen for lesser interests and with the judiciary unable to perform affirmatively, the President has been forced to take an aggressive posture in order to get the urgent business of governing done. As guardian of the over-all national interest, he attempts with varying degrees of success to get the various group interests to agree to compromises and to resolutions of current problems.

With regard to the "private" centers of power, two questions of crucial importance to American constitutionalism today are:

1. To what extent should an individual be able to invoke the Constitution upon arbitrary action taken by groups which vitally affect his values?

2. To what extent can truly *national* decisions be made, decisions which can be called in the national interest, or in Lippmann's Public Interest?

The first of these questions fits into the traditional mold of constitutional law and requires only a slight change of focus of the present flow of decisions in constitutional construction. If the factory community is a "private" government, to put it another way, should it not be treated as such under the Constitution?

The second question is different in focus; rather than striking down certain behavior, it deals with the problem of attaining a certain type of behavior in an affirmative way. It is a political problem, of the first order of magnitude, and it strikes at the heart of the American Constitution.

Limiting Private Power

If the factory community is taken as the model of private groups, it can be seen that the power it exercises is of two types. On the one hand, there are the decisions it makes relating to the direction and intensity of investment, the nature of economic development, and other similar economic factors. On the other, there are decisions which *directly* affect an individual in his value position. The first group may be considered by some as constituting a situation that demands some sort of public, or at least eternal, control. A delineation of possible control techniques has, in fact, recently been suggested by Wolfgang Friedmann. They run from total socialization through mixed public and private enterprises, cooperatives, mixed companies, capital and labor partnerships, public regulation by commission, and anti-trust legislation to other similar social restraints. While all of these raise at least peripheral constitutional questions, not one calls for the application of constitutional precepts to the decisions of the factory community. Indeed, in this aspect of the group decision-making process it is difficult to see how the Constitution could be validly applied. Control, if it should be imposed, would not be through the medium of resort to a basic higher law.

It is in the second category of decisions — those taken by the factory community (and other groups) that directly affect the value position of individuals — that the question arises whether the Constitution can and should be applied to private exercises of power. "The Constitution," it is often said, "runs against governments only." Is it now time to recognize the dimension of private governments?

As a beginning, we can set out the following propositions:

1. The Constitution was framed on the theory that limitations should exist on the formal exercise of power in government but not on control exercised unofficially.

2. The essential problem of individual liberty, however, is one of freedom from arbitrary restraints and restrictions, wherever and however imposed.

3. The Constitution should be so construed as to apply to arbitrary applications of power against individuals by centers of private government.

4. The main flow of group decisions in the factory community would not be thrown into litigation or controversy by such a constitutional construction, but only those which directly and substantially affect an individual.

5. It would take only a slight modification of present constitutional doctrine to effect such a constitutional construction.

The discussion can properly begin with a quotation from Wolfgang Friedmann, one used to underscore the proposition that the factory community should be recognized as a private government:

> One paramount conclusion emerges from the various representative analyses that have been sketched out above — and they apply to all industrialized democracies of our time, with differences only of degree rather than substance. *The corporate organizations of business and labor have long ceased to be private phenomena.* That they have a direct and decisive impact on the social, economic, and political life of the nation is no longer a matter of argument. It is an undeniable fact of daily experience. The challenge to the contemporary lawyer is to translate the social transformation of these organizations from private associations to public organisms into legal terms.

Hobbes once likened private associations to "worms in the entrails of man" and sought ways to minimize their influence. Madison, in *The Federalist Papers*, dealt extensively with them. The problem is not to attempt the impossible and eliminate them but to insure that their excesses are curbed. One way of doing this, insofar as individuals are concerned, is through application of the basic limitations of the Constitution to certain group decisions: *Governing power, wherever located, should be subject to the fundamental constitutional limitation of due process of law.* This proposition, as it is worded, eliminates the great majority of group decisions — those which do not impinge directly on an individual — as well as the *non-arbitrary* uses of power. It assumes that groups such as the factory community have responsibilities as well as rights under the Constitution, and one of them is not to act arbitrarily toward certain individuals.

Let us suppose two different situations in order to see how the proposition would operate. First, take the situation where an employee of a factory community is discharged from his job for the announced reason that his loyalty to the United States is in question. Should he be accorded "due process of law"? Would it make any difference if the enterprise is one which has a number of federal contracts, as distinguished from an enterprise depending entirely on non-governmental business? The second factual situation involves a member of an ethnic group, say a Negro, who is denied employment because of his race. Should he be able to contest that decision on constitutional grounds? If so, under what theory should he proceed?

The basic proposition should be able to cover both of these situations. The factory worker discharged for loyalty reasons should be afforded "procedural due process of law"; the Negro denied employment should be granted rights under a theory of equal protection of the laws, or, possibly, a theory of "substantive due process." For both, the constitutional problem is essentially the same: that of persuading the United States Supreme Court to recognize that the factory community performs some governmental functions.

The historical trend of judicial decision-making has been to bring more and more activity within the reach of the limitations of the Constitution. Since 1789, moreover, more and more governmental activity has been made subject to due process and similar limitations. The next logical step would be to draw private governments into the tent of state action. This is not a particularly startling proposition, for a number of recent cases have shown that "the concept of private action must yield to a conception of state action where public functions are being performed. . . ." State courts in Kansas and California have reached similar decisions. Compare the following statements of the United States Supreme Court and the California Supreme Court:

> [If the Railway Labor Act confers an exclusive bargaining power on a union] . . . without any commensurate statutory duty toward its members, constitutional questions arise. For the representative is clothed with power not unlike that of a legislature which is subject to constitutional limitations on its power to deny, restrict, destroy or discriminate against the rights of those for whom it legislates and which is also under an affirmative constitutional duty equally to protect those rights. (*Steele* v. *Louisville and Nashville R.R.*)

> . . . Where a union has . . . attained a monopoly of the supply of labor by means of closed shop agreements and other forms of collective labor action, such a union occupies a quasi public position similar to that of a public service business and it has certain corre-

sponding obligations. It may no longer claim the same freedom from legal restraint enjoyed by golf clubs or fraternal associations. Its asserted right to choose its own members does not merely relate to social relations; it affects the fundamental right to work for a living. (*James* v. *Marinship Corp.*, 1944)

What is true of a labor union is certainly true of the factory community of which the union is a part. For the employee who is threatened with discharge, or is in fact discharged, from the community, a compelling case can be built that this should not be done in an arbitrary way. The employee should get "his day in court," so to speak; he should have due process of law. His capacity to earn a living, perhaps the most important value he has, is directly affected. If we go a step further and find that the enterprise for which he works is the recipient of federal contracts, the employee should be able to invoke the due-process clause of the fifth amendment (in addition to his possible use of the due-process clause of the fourteenth amendment). The employer can be considered to be an agent of the federal government, clothed with the protection of that government, and therefore subject to the same constitutional limitations as the federal government.

The same arguments would appear to be equally applicable to the Negro. He is not yet a member of the community to which he has applied for a job, and not yet subject to its governing power, but he is being subjected to arbitrary power. Whether the attack on that power is based on equal-protection grounds (as an unreasonable classification) or on due-process grounds (substantive due process), the problem would again be to convince the Supreme Court that the factory community was a form of state action. And if the particular enterprise that refused the job was a federal contractor, there would seem to be no insuperable reason why the Negro could not invoke the fifth amendment's due-process clause.

These are the type of decisions made by the factory community, whether by corporate management or union management, that should be subject to constitutional proscriptions. The great bulk of decisions, if controlled at all, would have to be met with other techniques — probably legislation by Congress or by the growth of countervailing power centers.

The Problem of Consensus

"There can be no grosser mistake," observed Sir Henry Maine in 1886, than the impression that "Democracy differs from Monarchy in essence. . . . The tests of success in the performance of the necessary and natural duties of a government are precisely the same in both cases." Those "necessary and natural duties of government" are, as Walter Lippmann has pointed out, the defense and advancement abroad of the vital interests of the nation, and order, security, and solvency at home. Can the American constitutional democracy insure the making of the hard decisions — those that assert a national or "public" interest against private inclination and against what is easy and popular? Or is there a Gresham's law of politics in which the soft decisions tend to triumph over the hard ones? These are tough questions, which go to the heart of American constitutionalism.

The following propositions can be ventured as a point of departure:

1. The Constitution is largely a charter for the resolution of purely domestic matters. Although war is mentioned, the framers obviously considered international peace to be the normal state of affairs. Problems of war and application of the Constitution during times of war are not mentioned; problems of "cold war" did not even enter the minds of the Founding Fathers.

2. The original constitutional theory of limited government, particularly that of the centralized authority, requires revamping. The notion that that government is best which governs least is no longer tenable. The essential negativism of the Constitution toward government requires alteration in the light of the affirmative duties of the State today.

3. The "national" or "public" interest must have an authoritative spokesman. But in the constitutional system as it exists today there is no one, not even the President, who can speak so as to enforce this interest.

4. Pluralistic society, to be successful, requires not only a common agreement on the values to be sought but also a common willingness to forego group advantage for the general good.

The problem is greater than that of attaining consensus in the national decision-making process: The consensus so reached must reflect more than the normal bargaining and compromises, it must in some way transcend parochial interests and reach the over-all public interest. One illustration, drawn from the penumbral area where constitutional and international law meet and merge, should indicate the nature of the problem.

A cardinal point of post-World War II American economic policy toward other nations has been summed up in the phrase, "Trade, Not Aid." Apparently, this means the re-creation of a system of multilateral world trade carried out with minimal, if any, national barriers. Most of the effort so far has been toward implementing GATT or the General Agreement on Tariffs and Trade. Although both President Truman and President Eisenhower, together with the majority of informed commentators, have tried valiantly to make American participation in GATT more meaningful, all the efforts have foundered on the shoals of domestic group interests. The International Trade Organization became a dead letter, and, thus far at least, the Organization for Trade Cooperation appears likely to meet a similar fate. The point is that what the President and many others thought was in the *national* interest has had to give way to parochial interests which fear the impact of an expanded world trade.

Another facet of the same problem is shown in the question of the importation of Japanese textiles. Efforts by the State Department to retain the Japanese orientation toward the United States included a recognition that Japan must trade to live. This led to the limited importation of textiles, but this was met with outraged cries from domestic manufacturers. As a result, the amount of textiles allowed to be imported was severely reduced. Again, the parochial interest was served at the expense of what was apparently the national interest. This was another failure of leadership, brought about by national governmental officials registering the popular will, or at any rate the will of certain private groups.

The international result of this type of domestic activity may well be a diminution of the power position of the United States vis-à-vis Soviet Russia. It raises the question of whether the State can in fact draw on a "reserve function" in such parochial circumstances. In times of outright, widely recognized emergency there is no doubt that the State is able to transcend, although temporarily, special group interests. War is an illustration, the depression of the 1930's perhaps another — at least in the early days of Roosevelt's first term. On the other hand, during "normal" times it seems equally clear that the State cannot draw on its reserve function. This is not a black-and-white proposition. In our apparent position of quasi-emergency, the State can enforce certain minimal demands such as selective service and high taxes to pay for high defense expenditures. But the tougher decisions, those that vitally affect important group interests, cannot be made.

The challenge in this is to find the legal — that is, the constitutional — basis for a decision-making process that would be reasonably calculated to further the national interest. This is a greater challenge than that of dealing with the growth of corporate centers of power, for it calls for the preservation of the democratic values imbedded in the Constitution while simultaneously devising means to transcend the shortcomings of mass democracy. It is no exaggeration to say that the American constitutional system will prosper or founder according to the manner in which this challenge is met.

Conclusion

Some of the essentials of a contemporary statement of constitutional law and theory have been set out here. It is a brief sketch for a new, or at least a somewhat different, look at American constitutionalism from a legal standpoint. Perhaps enough has been said to indicate that the massive changes in American society and in the doctrine of the Constitution require rethinking the basic premises of the constitutional system. A modernized study of constitutional law should inquire into those who wield

CHARLES E. GILBERT   291

power in fact as well as those who have the official authority to make decisions. The inhabitants of the Security State need a theory that will serve the dual purpose of placing proper restraints on the exercise of power and of providing for the making of true "public interest" decisions. The study of constitutional law today should include not only what governments can and cannot do, but also what they *must* do.

National Political
Alignments and
the Politics of
Large Cities

CHARLES E. GILBERT

Since the 1920's, national politics has become steadily "urbanized," and the city vote has held a decisive balance of power in a number of recent elections. In 1960, for example, John F. Kennedy ran poorly throughout much of New York and Pennsylvania, yet by carrying New York City and Philadelphia, he received the large electoral votes of those states. In addition, urban interests and programs naturally have dominated an increasingly large part of the rhetoric of national politics as electoral success has come to be equated with an intelligible appeal to urban voters. In this essay, Charles E. Gilbert, a political scientist, examines some aspects of the relationship between urban and presidential politics and the role of local party organizations. Among other things, he refines our understanding of national political postures as a key determinant of the party preferences that influence local politics. Since the New Deal era, the national Democratic party has tended to identify most successfully with urban groups and their problems, and, in turn, Democrats have dominated local elections. According to Gilbert's findings, it would take a large change in national political affiliations in the cities to reverse Democratic supremacy in local politics. And recent presidential elections offer little indication that the Republican party has made any significant impact on urban groups.

Big city politics and presidential politics are commonly thought to be closely related, but the details of the relationship are obscure. Here an attempt is made to illuminate them by historical and comparative analysis of elections in large, northern partisan cities.[1] Many of our larger cities, mostly west of the Mississippi, hold nonpartisan local elections; and they figure in the discussion only occasionally and for comparative purposes.[2]

There are several common propositions about the inter-relation of national and big city politics. One is that our national politics was progressively "urbanized" in the nineteen-twenties and thirties; that issues and programs of interest to urban "minorities" came to the fore in this period and significantly altered both the subject matter and structure of national politics. An allied proposition is that Democratic strength in presidential elections came critically to be based on the large cities. A more specific form of this thesis asserts that Democratic presidential victories have depended upon the efforts of party "machines" or "organizations" in the large cities; that is, that more than the personal party preferences of city dwellers is involved. A final proposition amounts to the converse of the foregoing: that local Democratic electoral dominance and/or organization control in our large cities is largely a function of party preferences based on *national* politics.

These propositions may all be true; they are not necessarily inconsistent, especially if long-run and short-run effects are distinguished. In this article the relations between presidential and municipal elections are examined first in the "long run," which is taken as the period since the advent of the New Deal; and the level of Democratic dominance in most of our large northern cities is examined historically to try to identify the major influences at work. Within this span the years before and after 1944 (when Democratic presidential margins began seriously to decline) are taken as "short-run" periods. It cannot be claimed that these "long-run" and "short-run" periods are typical of others, since they were probably unique. The dating of the periods, or of the long run and short run, must be rather arbitrary; but it is hoped that the periods are appropriate for the purposes of this discussion. The main purpose is examination of the

Reprinted with permission from the *Political Science Quarterly*, LXXIX (March 1964), pp. 25–51.

[1] The principal cities in the analysis are listed in Table 1 below. This discussion is drawn from a broader study of twenty-four of our largest cities based primarily upon election returns and newspaper reports of campaigns and elections, supplemented by the available periodical and monographic literature. All cities of 500,000 or more by the 1950 Census (save Washington) were included, plus seven cities of 300,000–500,000 selected on regional considerations and for availability of data.

[2] Actually, four large cities that are formally nonpartisan in some or all local elections, but which are *de facto* more-or-less partisan, are included in this discussion: Chicago, Cincinnati, Cleveland, and Kansas City.

propositions set out above. The conclusions do not overturn what seem to be the accepted views; but they do suggest some qualifications and distinctions — they force one to refine the propositions. Finally, it is hoped that the historical and comparative discussion below will be worthwhile for its own sake, since the electoral behavior of our large cities has not received much of this kind of treatment and our published knowledge of it is fragmentary.[3]

I

This section contains a brief review of political changes in the large partisan cities since the nineteen-twenties. City election returns in presidential and local elections are set out in Table 1 for reference during the discussion.

The growth of urban Democratic alignments in national politics in the twenties and thirties is well known,[4] as is the increasing importance of Democratic city pluralities in presidential elections.[5] More partisan cities could be described as *locally* competitive in the twenties and thirties than can be so described today; and no partisan cities have become *more* closely competitive in general elections despite the oft-remarked erosion of the bases of "machine" politics since that time. All of the cities that have become less competitive since the nineteen-thirties have tended in a *Democratic* direction; and, in contrast to the period of the nineteen-twenties, none of the partisan large cities today is normally Republican, and only one or two are closely contested with any frequency.[6]

It thus appears that, in the long run, local electoral behavior in the partisan cities has been heavily influenced by national electoral behavior and attitudes — that "party identifications" primarily rooted in national politics have resulted in Democratic dominance locally and have reduced the incidence of local party competition.

While the foregoing statement of the basic national-local relationship is probably correct, the review that follows reveals some qualifications and

[3] Newspaper and periodical reports of campaigns and elections have been read from 1920, where they are available. Neither "hard" data nor election chronicles are as available for the prewar as for the postwar period; and there is less material for some cities than for others. Every effort has been made to collect data and accounts relevant to *crucial* elections or episodes.

[4] See Samuel Lubell, *The Future of American Politics* (New York, 1952), especially Chaps. 1–3.

[5] See Samuel Eldersveld, "The Influence of Metropolitan Party Pluralities in Presidential Elections since 1920," *American Political Science Review*, XLIII (1949), 1189.

[6] Cincinnati today is Republican both nationally and locally; but it is a formally (if not effectively) nonpartisan city, and prior to the demise of Proportional Representation in 1957 was very closely contested. The local Charter party often held majorities in Cincinnati's city council.

TABLE 1   Democratic Percentages in Presidential and Local Elections[a]

Cities	1928		1932		1936		1940		1944		1948		1952		1956		1960	
	P	L	P	L	P	L	P	L	P	L	P	L	P	L	P	L	P	L
Baltimore	48.3	69.0	67.0	64.0	68.3	56.2	64.0	42.5	59.2	57.2	53.3	64.6	51.7	55.7	44.1	67.9	63.9	49.0
Buffalo[b]	46.6	47.5	48.2	54.6	58.3	50.3	54.5	50.2	55.6	42.9	56.8	44.9	49.6	50.8	42.3	50.0	64.9	41.5
Chicago	46.9	58.3	57.1	70.8	66.9	56.2	56.5	54.7	61.4	58.7	58.6	56.1	54.4	54.9	48.7	71.4	63.6	55.6
Cincinnati[c]	42.7		50.9		59.2	51.0	49.9	46.0	49.7	52.1	48.3	47.6	43.2	48.6	37.5	60.0	50.4	
	63.7		54.3		56.0		40.0		45.0		52.8		51.4		49.7			
Cleveland	46.1	53.3	52.8	45.0	76.5	43.2	69.9	57.6	67.9	67.0	61.8	61.5	59.9	59.9	54.6	69.5	70.9	73.8
Indianapolis	40.1	62.5	52.1	54.7	59.0	51.8	49.6	47.5	48.6	53.2	48.3	44.4	41.2	56.1	40.8	57.4	47.0	
Kansas City	43.3	58.2	67.5	63.4	74.3	61.2	57.6	38.9	55.0	44.9	61.2	44.9	51.9	33.3	53.1	57.1	55.7	49.0
New York[d]	62.1	61.0	71.4	27.0	75.4	40.0	44.0	46.0	33.9	57.0	43.5	36.0	54.4	46.0	50.9	68.0	62.8	51.1
			52.0				61.2				51.1							
											49.0							
Philadelphia	39.7	7.8	44.0	46.5	62.1	48.0	60.0	44.9	58.9	43.8	49.6	58.1	58.4	59.3	57.0	65.6	68.1	
Pittsburgh	42.7		55.5	59.2	70.7	57.0	61.6	50.8	60.8	53.1	60.1	61.4	56.1	62.6	52.3	64.3	67.0	66.6
St. Louis	52.2	48.3	64.7	52.6	67.0	58.8	58.1	44.6	60.4	33.3	64.3	54.4	62.0	63.7	60.9	76.8	66.6	62.9

a Local elections are city-wide elections, for mayor in most cases except in Cincinnati.

b Buffalo Democratic percentage is of two-party vote; minor party votes have sometimes resulted in winners without absolute majorities.

c In Cincinnati, percentage is non-Republican vote — combination of Charter party, independents, and Democratic since 1957.

d New York City percentage is for Democratic candidate against all others.

complications of it. A summary statement here will add point and clarity to the narrative:

(1) Despite the trend in presidential voting, *local* Democratic electoral dominance was long delayed in some large cities, indicating the independent role of local conditions.

(2) There were significant differences in the strength and effectiveness of political organization from one city to another which affected the timing of party turnover.

(3) Another important local condition was municipal corruption and its exposure; party turnover was often the immediate result of public scandal.

(4) The Depression (entirely apart from the New Deal) had a serious effect on city political organizations, *both* Republican and Democratic; dominant Democratic organizations in such cities as Baltimore and New York were shaken severely and never fully recovered. In such cities, as one would expect, competition was most effective and organization control least effective in city-wide elections, where city councils were elected by districts.

(5) There was a sharp recession in local Democratic strength in some large cities in the late thirties and early forties coincident with a decline in Democratic margins in national elections.

(6) In the period since 1944, Democratic local electoral strength has been consolidated in most large cities and has become quite impervious to short-run trends in presidential elections. Local politics in large partisan cities are, generally speaking, less competitive than they were in the prewar period.

(7) The history under examination here can therefore be divided into two periods, roughly prewar and postwar, with the years of World War II a very broad dividing line. The differences between these periods are discussed in Section II; and the party organizational differences indicated above are examined in Section III.

That the long-run relation between presidential and city politics has been dominated by the presidential — that is, by national party identifications — is indicated by a brief review of long-run local change in the large partisan cities since the nineteen-twenties. Only two northern partisan cities in Table 1 — Baltimore and New York — may be said to have been dominantly Democratic in the nineteen-thirties.[7] After a local Republican

---

[7] Baltimore elected a Republican mayor twice between World War I and the Depression, and from 1927–31 had a Republican mayor and a council evenly divided between the two parties. The council was normally heavily Democratic, and the two Republican mayoral victories were at least partly creditable to Democratic organizational sabotage of a non-"organization" candidate who won the primary (1919) and to reaction against a Catholic Democratic candidate (1927). Since 1926 more than 60 per cent of Baltimore's voters have regularly been registered as Democrats.

threat in the late twenties and Hoover's capture of the city by a bare 10,000 votes in 1928, Baltimore went more solidly Democratic than ever in the thirties, though the Democratic party was subject to more serious and persistent factionalism than it was before the Depression and New Deal.[8] Although the Republicans elected a mayor in 1943 against a four-term incumbent, they carried but one councilman after 1931, and none at all after 1939. When, in 1963, the same Republican, McKeldin, again won the mayoralty with heavy newspaper support and factional Democratic defections from a much criticized nominee, the Council, elected by districts, remained wholly Democratic.

In New York, Mayor LaGuardia's success in city-wide elections cannot be credited to conventional Republicanism: the Depression, the Seabury investigations, LaGuardia's social-economic liberalism and support of President Roosevelt, Roosevelt's support of LaGuardia, La Guardia's successful promotion of "Fusion" and later reliance on the American Labor party, his personal qualities and calculated appeal to minority groups were all elements of electoral success. Throughout his administration the City Council remained Democratic though the Fusion forces controlled the Board of Estimates after 1937. In the postwar period New York again went solidly Democratic, though not always "organization" Democratic at the city-wide level; and, in fact, organization "control" appeared to be weakening despite the continued strength of Democratic voting.[9]

Two other partisan cities in Table 1 — Chicago and Pittsburgh — were relatively competitive and regularly Republican, respectively, in the nineteen-twenties. Hoover narrowly carried both in 1928. Chicago, after a close and factionalized party balance in the twenties, went Democratic in 1931 in response to the Depression, and the uninterrupted Democratic dominance of the city since 1931 is well known.[10] Pittsburgh, after a lengthy period of Republican hegemony, elected a Democratic mayor and and council majority in 1933.[11] Democratic dominance rapidly increased;

[8] The reasons for this are discussed in Edwin Rothman, "Factional Machine Politics: William Curran and the Baltimore City Democratic Organization, 1929–1946" (unpublished Ph.D. dissertation, The Johns Hopkins University, 1946).

[9] Compare W. Sayre and H. Kaufman, *Governing New York City* (New York, 1960), 180–202, for a detailed discussion of the strengths and weaknesses of New York's Democratic organization in city elections; and F. Shaw, *History of the New York City Legislature* (New York, 1954) on the City Council in the LaGuardia period.

[10] Chicago's city council was Democratic throughout the nineteen-twenties save for an evenly divided council, 1929–31, indicating the strength of the Democratic organization in the wards. Both Republicans and Democrats elected mayors in the nineteen-twenties. For a discussion relating the 1931 election to the Depression, see H. Gosnell, *Machine Politics* (Chicago, 1937), Chap. 1.

[11] Republican control of Pittsburgh in the nineteen-twenties was tight and effectively unchallenged, as it had been for years. In 1933, however, indictment of the Republican mayor for malfeasance and the developing disaffection of an independent Republican group (which beat the organization in the 1931 primary) probably contributed to the Republican defeat.

by 1936 the Democrats held a registration majority for the first time since the Civil War, and since 1939 no Republican has held elective city office in Pittsburgh (despite close elections in the late thirties and early forties).

Four cities in Table 1 seemed safely Republican in the twenties, consistently returned Democratic presidential majorities from 1928 or 1932 (1936 in the case of Philadelphia) until at least 1948, but, while they became more closely competitive or even leaned Democratic in local elections in the thirties, Democratic dominance was delayed until the postwar period. Then it came by gradual drift (in Buffalo and Cleveland) or by dramatic reversals (in Philadelphia and St. Louis). The apparent reasons for this behavior will be discussed shortly.

Finally, there are two of our partisan large cities which are not dominantly Democratic today. Cincinnati (which is formally but not effectively nonpartisan) was closely contested by Republicans and the local Charterites until the end of Proportional Representation in 1957; it is now at least leaning Republican locally and might better be described as Republican-prone. It went Democratic presidentially in 1932 and 1936 but not thereafter until it barely did so in 1960.[12] True, Cincinnati is formally a nonpartisan city, and the Democrats merged in the mid-twenties with the local Charter party; but the long-run maintenance of this merger (up to 1957) at least suggests that the ephemeral trend to Democratic presidential voting in Cincinnati did not involve changing personal party identifications or enable the local Democrats, on their own, to challenge effectively the strong Republican organization and tradition.[13] Indianapolis has had more-or-less competitive local politics since 1929. Safely Republican in the twenties, it was governed by Democrats in the thirties; but election margins were not lopsided throughout the thirties, and there

[12] Like most other large cities, Cincinnati was subject to the falling-off of urban Republican electoral strength in 1928 (though not throughout the twenties) described in Eldersveld; but Cincinnati's Republican presidential margins in the early twenties were far more lopsided than those of most large cities.

[13] On Cincinnati politics, see R. Straetz, PR Politics in Cincinnati (New York, 1958). I have been unable to ascertain whether the Cincinnati Democrats seriously considered striking out on their own locally in the early thirties. Kansas City is similar to Cincinnati in that formally nonpartisan elections have made possible the creation of a local party to compete with the established political organization; but in this case the Democrats were in power in the nineteen-twenties and thirties down to 1939, when the Reform party ousted the organization (or congeries of organizations) and remained in power to 1959. A number of Democrats participated in the Reform party just as reforming Republicans worked in Cincinnati's Charter party. The Kansas City history may seem an exception to the argument being developed here; but the effect of nonpartisan elections, the factionalism of the local Democratic party together with its excesses, and its temporary return to power in 1959 appear to disqualify it as a serious exception. See A. T. Brown, The Politics of Reform: Kansas City's Municipal Government, 1925–1950 (Kansas City, Community Studies, Inc., 1958); M. Mulligan, Missouri Waltz (New York, 1948); and W. Reddig, Tom's Town (New York, 1947).

has been rather regular party alternation since 1943 although the city might be said to be leaning Democratic today.[14] Like Cincinnati, Indianapolis went Republican for president throughout the twenties and narrowly Democratic in 1932 and 1936, but it has since been consistently Republican in presidential elections.

Thus, to sum up, the two cities not now dominantly Democratic in local elections are the only two not carried by the Democrats in presidential elections after 1936; that is, they are the two with the strongest tradition of Republican presidential voting. Both cities became *competitive* both presidentially and locally (though local competition in Cincinnati probably depended upon formal nonpartisanship, PR, and the local party device). Two cities (Baltimore and New York) were already normally Democratic both presidentially and locally in the twenties. Despite the LaGuardia phenomenon, it may be said that both remained dominantly Democratic locally after 1932, and that Baltimore became more so after a Republican threat at the end of the twenties. Two cities (Pittsburgh and Chicago) were Republican or roughly competitive in the twenties, and both quickly became dominantly Democratic locally. One — Chicago — was already competitive with strong (often warring) Democratic organizations in the wards, but the Republicans were gaining in the late twenties. In Pittsburgh the rapid shift to Democratic dominance seems to have been aided by a rift in the Republican organization, its more-or-less discrediting through the public discovery of corruption in 1933, and a local tradition of (often factional) machine politics.[15] Organized labor also played an active, auxiliary role in Pittsburgh.

Finally, four cities — formerly Republican nationally and locally — began to go Democratic for president in 1928, 1932, or 1936, and became, on the whole, competitive and *more* Democratic locally but not *dominantly* Democratic. In each city certain local factors conditioned and delayed the impact of presidential politics upon city politics. Buffalo and Cleveland have in common the lack of a modern tradition of cohesive, city-wide party organization. The formal nonpartisanship of Cleveland city elections favors insurgency and independence in primary elec-

[14] The politics of this city and of the state of Indiana have historically been competitive. Indianapolis seemed safely Republican in the nineteen-twenties, although the role of the Ku Klux Klan in the Republican party may, in the end, have alienated more voters than it attracted. The election of a Democratic city government in 1929 followed the conviction of the Republican mayor and state governor of bribery and political corruption and the interim appointment of a Democratic mayor by the Republican city council in 1927.

[15] In its heyday the Pittsburgh Republican party was recurrently threatened with factionalism until, in 1925, Secretary of the Treasury Mellon dictated a "harmony ticket." The minority Democrats were similarly factionalized, and remained so until the postwar period. Many Pittsburgh professional politicians are reported to have changed parties in the thirties.

tions; and the vigorous nationality politics of each city makes organization discipline difficult and occasions frequent crossing of party lines.[16] In Cleveland, the nonpartisan primary, the personality and reputation of Harold Burton, continued Republican control of the Negro vote in the "machine wards," and serious Democratic divisions in which the majority faction lacked New Deal and labor support all helped elect Republican mayors and council majorities through the nineteen-thirties.[17] The gradual growth of Democratic electoral dominance began in 1941 after Burton's withdrawal and the advent of Frank Lausche, an independent Democrat with strong ethnic appeal; but city-wide organization control has never been achieved.[18]

In Buffalo the Democrats narrowly won control of the Council in 1931 and the mayoralty in 1933 and retained them in close elections through the thirties, but the Republicans regained control in the early forties. In the nineteen-fifties demographic movements and council redistricting resulted in Democratic city control despite Republican presidential majorities, but city-wide electoral margins have remained close.[19] Nationality has perversely and pervasively affected Buffalo's politics: the Republican recovery of the forties was partly based on their turning to the Polish bloc for candidates and on Italian foreign policy resentments; and the large Polish vote went Republican for president in the fifties on foreign policy issues. But Buffalo's history of persistent insurgency and disregard of primary election outcomes dates back at least to World War I; it appears that nationality identifications have reinforced an antecedent condition of

[16] On the volatile, anti-organization tradition in Cleveland politics, see R. L. Maher, "Cleveland: A Study in Political Paradoxes," in R. S. Allen (ed.), *Our Fair City* (New York, 1947). Party lines and affiliations are patent in Cleveland elections, and the city cannot be called effectively nonpartisan. Buffalo held nonpartisan elections during most of the nineteen-twenties; its nonpartisanship was no more effective than Cleveland's, though it seems similarly to have favored insurgency.

[17] Democratic factionalism (partially based on the "organization's" failure to support Roosevelt at the 1932 convention) led to defeat of the incumbent Democratic mayor in 1933. In 1935 Harold Burton eliminated the Republican organization incumbent in the primary and won the general election in an "anti-machine" campaign in which he also promised to deal more firmly with organized labor and city finances. By the late thirties Democratic organization and opposition were negligible; and Burton's general election opponent in 1939 was another Republican, supported by organized labor and the vestigial Democratic "machine."

[18] The recent Mayor Celebrezze, capitalizing on his own national origin and his appeal to the "cosmopolitan" vote (the Cleveland *Plain Dealer's* term), eliminated the Democratic organization's well-qualified candidate in the 1953 primary and went on to win.

[19] In 1961 a Republican won the mayoralty when the larger Democratic vote was divided between two candidates of different nationality backgrounds. The winner, Koval, had long held city office and had closely contested the mayoralty in the past.

party infirmity which has also been favored by a one-term limit for mayors and at-large councilmen.[20]

Philadelphia entered the Depression with a Republican organization at least as dominant as that of Pittsburgh. This organization survived the New Deal in the wards and divisions; but the city leadership was shaken, and control of the party changed hands in 1934 and again in the early forties. The party was unable to deliver presidential majorities after 1932; mayoral elections in 1935 and 1939 were hard fought and narrowly won, and the Democrats prevailed in the off-year elections of 1933 and 1937; but the Republicans recovered in the early forties.[21] Late in the forties, as the Democratic organization continued to build, a series of city scandals broke which, reminiscent of Pittsburgh, brought about a party reversal in 1951. The quick trend to local Democratic dominance seems to have resulted from the tradition of Democratic presidential voting since 1936 and the strength of the minority Democratic organization which this made possible, as well as from prolonged malversation and peculation in city government.[22]

In St. Louis, too, corruption and scandal played a role. Republican in the twenties (though in closely contested elections), the city went Democratic for mayor and council in 1933 and lopsidedly so in 1937, and it seemed on its way to Democratic dominance under the influence of heavy presidential majorities. But the Missouri "governorship steal" of 1940–41, together with the local excesses of the Democratic organization, gave the Republicans an opportunity; they won the mayoralty and council control

[20] The importance of minor parties and occasional insurgent factions in Buffalo elections probably reflects and reinforces this tradition, though it is also conditioned by the New York election law. In the early years of this century Buffalo city elections were formally, if rather ineffectively, nonpartisan; this, too, may have fostered a tradition of insurgency.

[21] The 1934 change should probably be attributed to the decline and demise of William Vare as well as the ascendancy of Roosevelt, though there had always been factionalism in the local Republican organization. See J. Salter, "The End of Vare," *Political Science Quarterly*, L (1935), 215; and J. Reichley, *The Art of Government* (New York, 1959), Chap. 1. The 1935 primary was an "open" primary, won by a long-time opponent of the organization (who had won the controllership in 1933 as a *Democrat*). As Mayor, Wilson again turned Democratic and persistently feuded with the Republican city council up to his death. All this the Republican organization survived, together with the virtual bankruptcy of the city and its major services by 1940 and a general reputation for thoroughgoing corruption.

[22] The Roosevelt victories (and temporary Democratic control of the state) stimulated Democratic organization under new leadership. John P. Kelly, the principal organizer and mayoral candidate in 1935, had been a Republican, as had several other leaders. In 1935 the Democratic organization was described as modeled after the Vare machine and just as strongly controlled. *The New York Times*, September 15, 1935, Sect. 2, 1. After 1951 many professionals switched sides. The transition to Democratic control is described in Reichley.

in 1941 and again (by landslides) in 1944 and 1945.[23] Negro defection over insufficient "recognition" contributed to the Democratic decline. The postwar Democratic recovery began in 1949, and seems traceable in part to Republican factionalism and another Negro realignment. Democratic electoral dominance of St. Louis rapidly increased after 1949, although the Democratic organization suffered from factionalism and some hard-fought primaries, and a majority of the city's wards were weakly organized.[24]

This brief and selective history seems to support the general proposition that party identifications mainly oriented to presidential elections have led the way to *local* Democratic dominance, and that in this sense national politics have come to dominate the politics of the large partisan cities in the long run. Two further aspects of the post-World War I history support the proposition in this qualified, long-run form. One is the fact that several of our large partisan cities were somewhat more competitive in the twenties than they are today, despite the then Republican dominance in national elections. In Buffalo, Indianapolis, and St. Louis city-wide elections were occasionally close and Republican control was not secure; and the same comments apply to Democratic control in Baltimore and Chicago. One reason for this seems to have been the rise of disturbing and distinctively "urban" issues in city politics in the twenties — chiefly ethnic and religious competition and conflict, together with the prohibition issue in some cities. It has been argued that the "nationalization" of these issues resulted in the big city trend into the Democratic column in national elections that had set in by 1928.[25] Thus, we might expect to find a significant association between the proportion of ethnic and religious minorities in the urban population and the Democratic percentage of the presidential vote, though there are many other influences to be allowed for.[26] Table 2 shows, for twenty large northern cities, the Census figures for percentage of foreign-born white population in the Census years 1900–30; the average for those four years; the percentage non-white in 1930; and the mean Democratic percentage of the presidential vote, 1928–40.

[23] On the "governorship steal," see C. F. Hurd, "St. Louis: Boundary-Bound," in Allen, 237 and *passim*.

[24] On the factional and fragmentary character of political organization in St. Louis in the nineteen fifties, see R. H. Salisbury, "St. Louis Politics: Relationships Among Interests, Parties, and Governmental Structure," *Western Political Quarterly*, XIII (1960), 498.

[25] See Lubell, Chap. 3.

[26] The degree and directness of association between the proportion of urban minorities and percentage of Democratic presidential voting would presumably be affected by such things as local and state political traditions and political organization, and by differences and rivalries among the minorities themselves, *inter alia*.

TABLE 2   Census Data for Selected Cities

	I Percentage foreign-born white				II Average foreign-born white	III Percentage Negro 1930	IV Mean Democratic percentage for president 1928–1940	V Mean Democratic percentage for president 1956–1960	VI Percentage "minority" by 1960 census [a]
City	1900	1910	1920	1930					
New York	36.6	40.4	35.4	33.1	36.4	4.7	67.5	56.9	63.3
Boston	35.1	35.8	31.9	29.4	34.1	2.6	67.4	64.1	55.3
Chicago	34.4	35.7	29.8	24.9	31.2	6.2	57.4	56.2	59.5
Cleveland	32.5	34.9	30.1	25.5	30.8	8.0	61.3	62.8	59.8
Detroit	33.7	33.6	29.1	25.5	30.5	7.7	57.1	66.4	61.4
San Francisco	30.4	31.3	27.1	24.2	28.3	1.3	63.2	53.1	61.9
Milwaukee	31.1	29.8	24.1	18.9	26.0	1.3	69.8	54.6	38.9
Buffalo	29.5	27.9	24.0	20.6	25.5	2.4	51.9	53.6	48.9
Minneapolis	30.0	31.3	27.1	24.2	24.8	1.0	54.2	50.5	34.9
Seattle	23.1	25.6	23.4	20.2	23.0	0.6	55.2	46.5	17.8
Pittsburgh	26.3	26.3	20.4	16.3	22.3	8.2	57.6	59.7	47.1
Philadelphia	22.6	24.6	21.8	18.9	22.0	11.3	51.5	62.6	55.8
Portland	19.6	21.1	18.2	16.0	18.7	0.5	57.0	48.6	31.1
Los Angeles	17.4	18.9	15.9	14.7	17.5	3.1	55.3	52.6	49.4
Denver	18.9	18.2	14.1	10.9	15.5	2.5	52.5	51.1	25.6
St. Louis	19.2	18.2	13.3	9.8	15.1	11.4	60.5	63.8	42.9
Cincinnati	17.7	15.6	10.7	7.7	12.9	10.6	50.7	44.0	33.7
Baltimore	13.3	13.7	11.4	9.2	11.9	17.7	62.0	54.0	49.8
Kansas City	11.1	10.1	7.9	6.1	8.8	9.6	60.7	54.4	28.6
Indianapolis	10.0	8.4	5.4	3.8	6.9	12.1	50.2	43.9	27.1

[a] Foreign-born; persons of mixed or foreign-born parentage; and non-white persons.

Inspection of the table suggests that percentage foreign-born, or of foreign derivation, *was* associated in some degree with Democratic presidential voting. In statistical terms, the association is strengthened when the mean foreign-born white percentage, 1900–30, is combined with the percentage non-white in 1930; but the correlation is still not especially strong.[27] Statistics apart, the association is probably strengthened by Samuel Lubell's argument that higher birth rates prevailed, in that period, among immigrant families and urban low-income groups than among native and upper-income groups. In considering the correlation coefficient, one might also allow for North European (generally non-Democratically disposed) immigration in Minneapolis, Milwaukee, and the Pacific Northwest, and for the delaying effects of local leadership and political organization on Negro party identification in such cities as Cleveland, Philadelphia, and St. Louis.[28] Today it is often argued that recent metropolitan migration patterns have probably reduced politically relevant demographic diversity and thus diminished electoral competition in many large cities.[29] Striking increases have occurred in many large cities in the non-white proportion of the population; and the "ethnic" or "foreign stock" component has more than held its own, though it is hard to measure beyond the second generation. This is the most dramatic change, for measures of population diversity or concentration in the lower ranges of education,

[27] The coefficient of correlation between columns II and IV is .44; that between the sum of columns II and III, on the one hand, and column IV, on the other, is .51. The coefficient of correlation between column II and the percentage non-white population *in 1950*, on the one hand, and the average Democratic percentage of the presidential vote, *1944–60*, is .65; but that between column II alone and the presidential percentage, 1944–60, is only .18.

[28] See Lubell, Chaps. 3 and 5, and the data on urban birth rates in W. Thompson and P. K. Whelpton, *Population Trends in the U.S.* (New York, 1933), Chap. 8. In Cleveland the predominantly Negro wards remained Republican throughout the nineteen-thirties, despite serious Democratic efforts to reverse their allegiance and recurrent pre-election rumors that a switch was coming. The Republican organization was strongly based on these wards, which finally went Democratic in 1943 (the second election of Mayor Lausche). In Philadelphia many Negroes changed their vote to Democratic in the early thirties and returned to the Republican fold in the election of 1939. (See especially *The New York Times* for November 9, 1939.) In St. Louis the Republican Negro vote was wavering for local reasons in the late twenties, the Negro wards went decisively Democratic in 1933, shifted back to the Republicans (again, largely for local reasons) in 1941, and went Democratic again in 1949 and subsequently; that is, the "Negro vote" was with the majority on each occasion and was clearly an important influence. Insufficient recognition by patronage is said to have been one important local factor in the shift against the Democrats in 1941. See especially *St. Louis Post-Dispatch*, April 2, 1941, and the fictional treatment by Fanny Cook, *Mrs. Palmer's Honey* (New York, 1945).

[29] See Lubell; and E. C. Banfield, "The Politics of Metropolitan Integration," *Midwest Journal of Political Science*, I (1957), 77, and references there cited, for related discussions.

occupation, and income show relatively little change over the period.[30] On these indicators of class and status, big city populations have not increased in homogeneity; but "minority group" members are typically the majority in large cities today and, to date, have strongly tended to be Democratic in their party identification.[31]

A second aspect of this history suggests that our general proposition must be limited to the long run. In the instances where Democratic electoral dominance was *quickly* achieved in local elections, corruption had discredited Republican machines and/or minority Democratic organizations were already rather strong. The Depression and the political and programmatic efforts of the New Deal severely shook most big city party organizations, Republican and Democratic; and some Republican organizations recovered in the nineteen-thirties while some Democratic organizations did not. Thus, the character of local political organization was of some independent importance in the short run.

It may be useful to distinguish between electoral dominance and organization control, the former resting on party identification, the latter on techniques ranging from social and economic sanctions to the *quid pro quo* to suasion based upon purely personal influence in the precincts. The distinction is not as clear practically as it is conceptually, for many votes must be determined by some combination of electoral dominance and organizational control, and each could be seen as reinforcing the other. Few city political organizations have escaped recurrent factionalism or ineffectiveness. Nonetheless, the distinction between electoral dominance and organization control does lead to two important points. (1) In the cities under examination here Republican organizations have ultimately lost local control after continued Democratic presidential majorities (even though their own atrophy or excess immediately accounted for their downfall). (2) Some cities display marked Democratic electoral dominance in the absence of strong organization control, but the reverse is not the case. Together, these points seem further to support the proposition that the influence of national politics was decisive in the long run. They are further examined in Section III below.

[30] The data are not reproduced here. Census classifications of occupations and education were scaled and means and standard deviations were computed as well as proportions in the lower classifications. For income, the semi-interquartile range was computed as well as proportions below and above certain arbitrarily chosen extremes. The general conclusion must be that, by these socialeconomic indicators, there has been little change in diversity within the big city populations; but the increase in non-white and "ethnic" has been pronounced. "Ethnic" here is the Census usage: the foreign-born and those of foreign-born or mixed parentage.

[31] For the twenty cities considered here the coefficient of correlation between percentage of population "ethnic" and non-white, on the one hand, and the mean Democratic percentage of the presidential vote, 1956–60, on the other hand, is .5986.

II

What has already been said about the long-run relations between presidential and local voting indicates that the short-run relation will not normally be a close one. There are two illustrations of this in the history reviewed above. One is that, in the late thirties or early forties, several large cities experienced Republican recoveries, notably Buffalo, Indianapolis, and St. Louis. In Pittsburgh the Republicans briefly challenged the Democrats before finally succumbing; in Philadelphia the Democratic threat of the nineteen-thirties subsided; in Kansas City the Democrats lost to the forces of reform allied with Republicans; and in Baltimore the Republicans elected a mayor. This occurred in a period of decline in Democratic presidential and congressional margins from their 1934–36 highs, but local conditions seem also to have been important in most cases. Local conditions were evidently of great importance in St. Louis, especially the exposure of Democratic organizational excesses and the reversal of Negro voting noted above. In Philadelphia, local and national electoral trends moved in opposite directions. The local conditions, including formal nonpartisanship, affecting Kansas City are well known. Democratic factionalism played an important role in Pittsburgh and Baltimore, and in Baltimore the Democratic reversal was confined to a controversial four-term mayor, while the City Council was unaffected. Trends in party preferences related to national politics must certainly have assisted these local Republican revivals, but it seems doubtful that this alone was controlling. Buffalo and Indianapolis displayed no dramatic short-run change since neither city had ceased to be competitive nationally or locally, and in Buffalo the Democratic party was chronically plagued with factionalism and by minor parties.

A much more striking instance of local electoral independence is that of the Eisenhower elections of the nineteen-fifties and, more broadly, the entire postwar period. In this period Democratic electoral dominance of most large cities was remarkably stable in local elections. Reference to Table 1 will reveal the short-run independence of local and presidential elections. While the Democratic presidential trend is generally downward through the 1956 election and then is sharply reversed in 1960, there is no corresponding trend in mayoral elections in the partisan cities. In those cities that might be said to have "lagged" in converting to Democratic dominance locally (Philadelphia, St. Louis, and, less markedly, Buffalo and Indianapolis) the Democratic trend in mayoral elections is generally upward throughout the period; but in the other partisan cities there is no discernible trend or pattern. In general the mayoral vote is somewhat more variable than the presidential vote, though the variances of the two sets of series do not differ systematically. Democratic mayor margins are not consistently higher or lower than presidential margins, but there was a tendency toward the end of the period for the local Democratic margins to exceed the presidential as the latter fell off in the Eisenhower elections. All this suggests that local elections in the partisan cities are, within the limits resulting from long-run party identifications, quite independent of short-run national changes. To put the same point another way: short-run national trends have evidently not disturbed the long-run bases of local Democratic dominance.[32]

Two related factors help explain the short-run local independence. One is the fact that all of the partisan large cities hold local elections in non-presidential years.[33] Although ticket-splitting was common in the Eisenhower elections, it seems probable that the staggering of elections aided the local Democrats.[34] Similarly, the lower turnout in local elections may have favored the Democratic "organization" vote over the Republican vote since, even in the weakly organized cities, the dominant Democratic party is usually better organized than is the Republican minority.[35]

There is, in fact, a bare indication in the election data that party organization makes a difference in local turnout, though the case is far from conclusive. Table 3 shows turnout data for large cities classified as partisan, doubtful, and nonpartisan (the "doubtful" cities are formally nonpartisan, but party lines are salient in local elections). No cities are included that hold municipal elections concurrently with contests for "higher" jurisdictions, and the one-party cities of the South are omitted. The turnout figures are means for mayoral elections over the postwar period. It is clear from the table that factors other than partisanship-nonpartisanship are at work; but there is some tendency for turnout in partisan cities to exceed that in nonpartisan cities, and to be highest in those partisan cities characterized by tight party organization control, of which control of primaries is the principal test.[36] The tendency is less

---

[32] See Angus Campbell, *et al.*, *The American Voter* (New York, 1960), Chap. 6 and the same authors' "Stability and Change in 1960: A Reinstating Election," *American Political Science Review*, LX (1961), 273–74, for evidence that the distribution of party identifications in the country at large did not change much during the Eisenhower administrations. It seems reasonable to assume, in light of the Survey Research Center data, that this was true for the population of large cities apart from demographic change.

[33] This is true of most large cities and of all the partisan cities in Table 1. Indeed, each of these cities *now holds* municipal elections in odd-numbered years, free of the immediate influences of both state and national elections.

[34] On ticket-splitting in the Eisenhower elections, see Campbell, *et al.*, *The American Voter*. On the "insulating" effect on state politics of off-year state elections, see V. O. Key, *American State Politics* (New York, 1956), Chap. 2.

[35] Here, and for purposes of the discussion following, turnout is computed as a percentage of the population twenty-one years of age and older, rather than as a percentage of registered voters. For inter-censal years some interpolations are involved.

[36] Buffalo is the chief exception, in terms of party organization, in Table 3; but elections have been competitive there. Use of medians rather than means does not significantly change the ranking in Table 3.

TABLE 3

Selected Partisan and Nonpartisan Cities Ranked by Mean Election Turnouts in Mayoral Elections, 1944–1960

Partisan	Doubtful	Nonpartisan
Chicago (51.5)		
Pittsburgh (50.5)		
Philadelphia (49.8)		
Buffalo (49.1)		
	Cincinnati (49.0)	
		Boston (47.0)
		San Francisco (46.3)
New York (42.3)		
Indianapolis (41.4)		
		Seattle (39.8)
		Minneapolis (37.0)
		Denver (36.7)
	Cleveland (34.8)	
		Detroit (33.8)
Baltimore (31.5)		
		Los Angeles (31.3)
St. Louis (30.4)		
	Kansas City (29.9)	

marked in presidential elections, and it appears from Table 3 that some broadly regional factors are also at work. The differences between the two groups of partisan and nonpartisan cities are not statistically significant.[37] The turnout data are not very reliable but it does appear that partisanship marginally increases turnout in local elections. This, in turn, may indicate that if an "organization" vote exists — and if the majority party may be assumed to enjoy organizational superiority — then off-year elections favor the dominant local party.

This tenuous line of argument is not, however, necessary to the main point: that, in the short run, local elections in the partisan cities show some independence of presidential trends to the recent advantage of the dominant Democratic party. Off-year elections and majority organizational superiority (which varies greatly among the cities) are probably part of the explanation, but it seems likely that persisting party identifications,

[37] The test was made in terms of Student's "t" at the 5 per cent level. If means for all mayoral *elections* in the two groups, rather than individual city means, are used the difference is significant, though not dramatically so, at the 1 per cent level: $T = 3.2$; N (partisan elections) $= 32$; Np (nonpartisan elections) $= 39$. This is so although there is no difference in mean electoral margins of the two groups, so that close elections are evidently not influencing the result.

more stable respecting local than national elections, are at least of equal
if not of isolable importance.

III

The question discussed in the preceding section can be turned around:
How important are big city political organizations in presidential elections? It is often alleged either that city "machines" deliver the presidential vote, or, less commonly, that they depend upon it for local control.
The role of our large cities in presidential elections was explored by
Eldersveld (see n. 5 above) in 1949 and no attempt is made here to
extend that analysis. Instead, some suggestions in the available data are
brought to bear on the question of the importance of city political
"machines" or organizations in presidential elections.

The partisan large cities appear to vary considerably as respects the
cohesiveness and effectiveness of their party organizations. By cohesiveness
is meant freedom from tendencies to factionalism, either regional or city-
wide; and by effectiveness is meant the organization's demonstrated ability
to win primaries and its *reputed* effectiveness in general elections as reported by newspapers and political scientists. Three broad types of party
structure can be defined: those exhibiting high cohesiveness and effectiveness; those in which the majority party contains two or more continuing
factions, each of which may be relatively "effective" in its own bailiwick;
and those that are weakly organized and reported to be relatively ineffective at the ward or precinct level. Of the cities under discussion here, those
that are most party-competitive do not have party organizations of the
first type; but neither do all of the most dominantly Democratic cities. It
thus appears that differences in cohesiveness and effectiveness of local party
organization are not systematically associated with the size of Democratic
presidential pluralities or with the degree of *local* Democratic electoral
dominance; in most cities these outcomes appear primarily to depend
upon cultural and socio-economic determinants of party identification.
This general conclusion may be defended and detailed in several ways:

(1)   Of the *nonpartisan* large cities, two, Boston and Detroit, have
been as Democratic in presidential elections as any of the *partisan* large
cities.[38] Another nonpartisan city, Milwaukee, has regularly produced
Democratic presidential margins close to those of its neighbor, the
strongly organized city of Chicago. These cities differ in degree and nature
of nonpartisanship; local elections in Detroit are normally quite effectively
nonpartisan; those in Milwaukee are somewhat less so, in the sense that
candidates have had partisan identities though the party organizations

[38] Generally in the postwar period the large cities west of the Mississippi have
been closely competitive and frequently Republican in presidential elections. These
are *all* nonpartisan cities, and the difference seems to lie largely in regional and
demographic factors rather than in partisan *versus* nonpartisan elections.

have not openly intervened in elections; and in Boston nearly all candidates are Democrats and have sometimes represented party factions, though the Democratic party has recently tried to maintain its own neutrality among the contenders.[39] Each of these cities is reported to have an effective Democratic party organization for state and national elections, but none of these organizations depends on *local* patronage, and those in Detroit and Milwaukee have little in common with the classical urban "machine." Local control, then, is evidently not requisite to electoral success in presidential elections, at least in cities where *neither* side can accomplish control.

(2) In fact, the variance in the Democratic percentage of the presidential vote, 1944–60, has been no greater in the nonpartisan than in the partisan large cities; but it is true that several nonpartisan cities west of the Mississippi have been more Republican in presidential elections than have any of the partisan cities. From this one *might* conclude that party organization served to reinforce and maintain Democratic voter predispositions, but this conclusion would ignore the marked sectionalism evident in city voting in presidential elections since, say, 1944. It is generally true that the more effectively nonpartisan cities are located west of the Mississippi, and that degree of party organization and degree of Democratic presidential voting in cities appear to be associated; but the direction of the relationship is not at all clear, in view of what has been said above; and the association may even be spurious.

(3) Two of the large cities (Cleveland and St. Louis) where party organization is *relatively* weak — at least on the city-wide level — show very wide mean Democratic margins in Table 2 and have lately been heavily dominated by the Democratic party in local elections.[40] This indicates that Democratic dominance in either presidential elections *or* local elections does not necessarily depend upon highly cohesive and effective local organization.

(4) Variability in the presidential vote has been as great (in some cases greater) in the reputedly strongly organized cities as in cities with organizations low in cohesiveness or reported effectiveness. The variance in Democratic presidential margins, 1936–60, shows little relation to co-

---

[39] See the reports on these three cities in the series of *City Politics Reports*, edited by E. C. Banfield (mimeographed, Joint Center for Urban Studies of Harvard University and M.I.T. [Cambridge, Mass., 1960 and 1961]). The Democratic registration majority is large in each city, but especially so in Boston, where the margin is reported to be 7:1.

[40] There have been close primary election contests in both cities in the postwar period, indicating low organization effectiveness; but Republican candidates have not seriously threatened in Cleveland since 1943 and St. Louis since 1949. Party organization seems to have been declining in effectiveness in St. Louis in recent years. The possibility that Cleveland's nonpartisan primary weakens organization control was noted above.

hesiveness or reported effectiveness.[41] For instance, both Baltimore and Chicago are "safely" Democratic cities locally, as we saw in Section I; yet in neither city was the Democratic organization able to deliver a Democratic presidential majority in the election of 1956. Cleveland and St. Louis (presumably "weakly" organized cities) did deliver Democratic majorities, but they started with a higher "normal" Democratic vote. Democratic presidential majorities fell sharply in the Eisenhower years in New York and Pittsburgh; only in Philadelphia, among the reputedly well organized cities, was the variance in presidential margins minimal.[42] The 1960 election affords another interesting study; the percentage increase in the Democratic presidential margin over 1956 bears little relation to reported organization strength in the several partisan cities in Table 1.

(5) It may be that big city political organizations, even if insignificant as independent determinants of party preference, do substantially influence presidential elections by increasing the turnout, if only marginally, of those already disposed to vote Democratic. On this point, too, the evidence is mixed; but there is some support for the proposition. The available data on presidential turnout and in Table 3 above indicate that: (a) Turnout in *local* elections tends to be higher in the partisan cities than in the nonpartisan cities, but there is a strong suggestion that regional differences are involved. (b) Turnout in *partisan* local elections tends to be highest in those cities — Chicago, Philadelphia, and Pittsburgh — whose party organizations score highest on cohesiveness and effectiveness by reputation and primary election performance. (c) Among the partisan cities these same three cities stand at or close to the top in turnout in *presidential* elections (in 1948, 1952, and 1960); but so do some partisan cities — such as Buffalo — much lower in party cohesiveness. (d) Moreover, several nonpartisan cities score as high or higher in presidential election turnout as any of the partisan cities; other things equal, partisanship is not significantly related to turnout in presidential elections. (e) The more cohesive and effective city organizations (by other tests) appear to do somewhat better in *registration* than most other cities, but the data on this point are not very good.[43] It appears from all this that certain city organizations — particularly in Chicago, and probably in Philadelphia and Pittsburgh — have some effect upon turnout. They are the city organizations that stand highest in cohesiveness and effectiveness by other indications. They are located in states that, of all the parent states of the

[41] For various reasons, the period 1936–60 seems the fairest to use. The variances in margins were calculated and related by simple inspection to the reports of party "strength" taken from newspapers and such scholarly literature as was available and to organization performances in primary elections.

[42] Attention should be called to the sharp decline in Democratic presidential margins in New York and Philadelphia in 1948 (see Table 1), evidently the result of the third party vote, and indicating low organizational effectiveness on that occasion.

[43] For one thing, it is necessary to use registration *in all parties* as the datum.

cities examined here, have consistently had the closest electoral margins in state-wide elections since 1944.[44] This, taken with the prestige and patronage at stake, may provide both incentive and wherewithal for high organizational effectiveness and thus afford a partial explanation of it.

More generally, it could be argued that party organization enlarges turnout because the partisan cities are those with the larger low-status, low-income populations that are least likely to vote; that the partisan cities hold their own in presidential turnout with nonpartisan cities is thus evidence of party effectiveness. One could add that nonpartisan cities like Boston with high turnout have effective party organization for other than local elections and relatively ineffective nonpartisan local traditions. Table 4 indicates that the partisan cities tend to have higher proportions of

TABLE 4

Socio-Economic Factors and Turnout in Partisan and Nonpartisan Large Cities

	Percentage of population in white collar jobs	Median family income	Percentage family incomes <$3,000	Percentage family incomes >$10,000	Median years of school completed	Local election turnout	1960 presidential turnout
Partisan cities above median	2	3	6	2	1	6	5
Partisan cities below median	7	6	3	7	8	3	4
Nonpartisan cities above median	7	7	2	8	8	2	5
Nonpartisan cities below median	2	2	7	1	1	5	3

Note: Cincinnati and Kansas City were included in evaluation of medians but not in table. Cleveland was classified "partisan." Based on Tables 32 and 33 of the 1960 Census, *General Social and Economic Characteristics*.

[44] Means and standard deviations of contests for President and Governor were examined, and Illinois and Pennsylvania scored lowest. *State* turnout (total state vote as percentage of the state population twenty-one and older) in those states does not seem to differ systematically from that in the other states containing large cities.

low-income and low-status population than have the nonpartisan cities, while equaling nonpartisan cities in presidential turnout and surpassing them in local elections. As in several analyses above, regional factors of some sort are obviously at work; for, except for San Francisco in respect to turnout, the nonpartisan cities in the minority rows are always and only those east of the Mississippi. Nevertheless, it seems a fair conclusion from Table 4 that the partisan cities have higher electoral turnout than would be expected if their elections were held under nonpartisan conditions.

IV

The conclusions and suggestions that emerge from this account and analysis are not novel, but perhaps they will extend our understanding of the relations between national politics and big city politics. They can be briefly summarized:

(1) There was a secular trend in city Democratic voting, both national and local, underway in many cities in the nineteen-twenties, as has often been pointed out. Some of the issues involved — chiefly respecting the position of urban "minorities" — were "nationalized" by the New Deal; they became subjects of national policy and political action. This is probably a major reason why national politics are most important in the party preferences that now heavily influence city politics, although the trend to Democratic voting was in some cities as evident in local as in national elections in the nineteen-twenties. Historically the movement began with city politics at least as much as with national politics; in particular, ethnic and religious rivalries were important in several cities in the nineteen-twenties and these rivalries, as in Baltimore and Indianapolis, occasionally gave rise to bitter interparty cleavage in city campaigns and elections.

(2) The effect of the Depression on city politics was profound. Dissatisfaction with governmental performance quickly became widespread and publicly accepted, and this probably accelerated the group tensions already undermining urban political "machines" in some cities — Baltimore and New York in particular, among the largest cities. In some cities strong organizations survived or were created, but few large city organizations today avoid serious factional challenges.

(3) Scandal and corruption often have significant effects on city elections. In most instances discussed above, exposure of official corruption was abetted in its effect by Democratic national election trends, but in St. Louis and Kansas City in the nineteen-forties city scandals probably played an important role in political change. This would indicate that the minority party does have a role to play as a "gun behind the door" even where party competition is not normally close.

(4) Close and regular party competition in city elections is rare, and Democratic dominance is characteristic; but several Democratic organizations have lost city-wide elections — either primary or general — in the postwar period. There is great variety in organizational effectiveness, dependent on a variety of factors including patronage, electoral systems, social or regional factionalism, the size, distribution, and leadership of the low social rank population, and the activity and alignment of city elites, including the newspapers.

(5) Party preferences related to national politics appear to be controlling in city elections in the long run. This suggests that, other things being equal, it would take a change in group alignments respecting national politics in most large partisan cities to put the Republicans in a regularly competitive position locally.

(6) *In the short run*, city elections have not been seriously affected by changes in voter orientations to national elections for several reasons suggested in Section II above. But national politics can have an effect in the few closely competitive large cities, just as most factors are more effective under these conditions. In the long run, party organization is probably an important factor in hastening or delaying local response to national trends; a powerful organization, especially when it is undamaged by scandal, may tend to discourage minority voting simply because it seems futile; where patronage is freely available it may capture parts of the minority organization. But persistent presidential majorities seem to be controlling.

(7) There is no reason adduced above to doubt that city political organization is important in state and national elections by influencing turnout and marginally offsetting "outstate" results. Organizations tend to make the most of existing partisan predispositions. But in the long run, party preferences rather than organization control seem to be decisive in both city and national elections, and it seems doubtful from the analysis above that these preferences are primarily determined by organization dominance or control.

(8) The cities under discussion here are located outside what are commonly thought of as the South and West. That is because, in those regions, most cities are nonpartisan in law and/or in fact. In most nonpartisan cities it is especially unlikely that local "machines" are seriously affecting the presidential or local vote. There is, however, a significant regional difference in big city voting in postwar presidential elections; Republicans have done better in the West (including Cincinnati and Indianapolis) than in the East. In the light of the argument so far it seems unlikely that partisanship-nonpartisanship accounts for the difference. The demographic data in Table 2 above, together with occupational and home ownership data indicating somewhat smaller low social rank populations in several Western cities, suggest that variations in urban populations help account for the political differences, and so perhaps do

regional variations in political cultures or attitudes. It hardly seems that restricting the discussion broadly to the Northeast results in understating the importance of city political organizations.

(9) These conclusions imply skepticism about the influence of city political machines today and in the recent past in presidential elections — or, in the long run, in local elections. But they also indicate real variation in organizational effectiveness, which can best be understood by observation in depth and detail rather than, as here, in some breadth and perspective.

Decision-Making in a Democracy: The Supreme Court as a National Policy-Maker

ROBERT A. DAHL

It has been clear since John Marshall's day that the Supreme Court is, in large part, a political institution, and that the justices are usually part of the dominant political majority. They are appointed, as Robert Dahl notes in this essay, with proper "regard to their basic attitudes on fundamental questions of public policy." Yet some congressmen and newspapers invariably protest with shocked indignation against judicial appointments that are "political" in nature. The myth of the Supreme Court as a disinterested institution, wholly abstracted from competing views of public policy, lingers on. Despite a century and a half of practice to the contrary, there remains a persistent tendency to view the Court exclusively as a legal institution and to see judicial decisions as something that should be divorced from political presuppositions. Dahl, a political scientist, views the Court more realistically. Its main task, as he sees it, has been to confer legitimacy on the policies of the dominant political majority, and also "upon the basic patterns of behavior required for the operation of a democracy." But, Dahl observes, there are significant times when the Court does exercise a creative, policy-making func-

tion. For example, the dominant political coalition can be "unstable" regarding certain questions, thus giving the Court (at some risk) the opportunity to intervene and formulate policy. It can succeed, however, only if its policy conforms to certain norms accepted by influential segments of political leadership and the general public. This is a logical explanation for the making, and acceptance, of the Court's numerous decisions on Negro rights and segregation in the last fifteen years. The reapportionment decisions, which Chief Justice Earl Warren has called the most significant cases during his tenure, also can be explained in this manner. But what of the Court's recent decisions affecting the rights of accused criminals? Has the Court overstepped the proper bounds of its powers?

To consider the Supreme Court of the United States strictly as a legal institution is to underestimate its significance in the American political system. For it is also a political institution, an institution, that is to say, for arriving at decisions on controversial questions of national policy. As a political institution, the Court is highly unusual, not least because Americans are not quite willing to accept the fact that it *is* a political institution and not quite capable of denying it; so that frequently we take both positions at once. This is confusing to foreigners, amusing to logicians, and rewarding to ordinary Americans who thus manage to retain the best of both worlds.

I

A policy decision might be defined as an effective choice among alternatives about which there is, at least initially, some uncertainty. This uncertainty may arise because of inadequate information as to (a) the alternatives that are thought to be "open"; (b) the consequences that will probably ensue from choosing a given alternative; (c) the level of probability that these consequences will actually ensue; and (d) the relative value of the different alternatives, that is, an ordering of the alternatives from most preferable to least preferable, given the expected consequences and the expected probability of the consequences actually occurring. An *effective* choice is a selection of the most preferable alternative accompanied by measures to insure that the alternative selected will be acted upon.

No one, I imagine, will quarrel with the proposition that the Supreme Court, or indeed any court, must make and does make policy decisions in

Reprinted by permission of the author and publisher from *Journal of Public Law*, VI, No. 2 (1958), pp. 279–295.

this sense. But such a proposition is not really useful to the question before us. What is critical is the extent to which a court can and does make policy decisions by going outside established "legal" criteria found in precedent, statute, and constitution. Now in this respect the Supreme Court occupies a most peculiar position, for it is an essential characteristic of the institution that from time to time its members decide cases where legal criteria are not in any realistic sense adequate to the task. A distinguished associate justice of the present Court has recently described the business of the Supreme Court in these words:

> It is essentially accurate to say that the Court's preoccupation today is with the application of rather fundamental aspirations and what Judge Learned Hand calls "moods," embodied in provisions like the due process clauses, which were designed not to be precise and positive directions for rules of action. The judicial process in applying them involves a judgment . . . . that is, on the views of the direct representatives of the people in meeting the needs of society, on the views of Presidents and Governors, and by their construction of the will of legislatures the Court breathes life, feeble or strong, into the inert pages of the Constitution and the statute books.[1]

Very often, then, the cases before the Court involve alternatives about which there is severe disagreement in the society, as in the case of segregation or economic regulation; that is, the setting of the case is "political." Moreover, they are usually cases where competent students of constitutional law, including the learned justices of the Supreme Court themselves, disagree; where the words of the Constitution are general, vague, ambiguous, or not clearly applicable; where precedent may be found on both sides; and where experts differ in predicting the consequences of the various alternatives or the degree of probability that the possible consequences will actually ensue. Typically, in other words, although there may be considerable agreement as to the alternatives thought to be open [(a)], there is very serious disagreement as to questions of fact bearing on consequences and probabilities [(b) and (c)], and as to questions of value, or the way in which different alternatives are to be ordered according to criteria establishing relative preferability [(d)].

If the Court were assumed to be a "political" institution, no particular problems would arise, for it would be taken for granted that the members of the Court would resolve questions of fact and value by introducing assumptions derived from their own predispositions or those of influential clienteles and constituents. But, since much of the legitimacy of the Court's decisions rests upon the fiction that it is not a political institution but exclusively a legal one, to accept the Court as a political institution

[1] Frankfurter, "The Supreme Court in the Mirror of Justices," 105 *U. of Pa. L. Rev.* 781, 793 (1957).

would solve one set of problems at the price of creating another. Nonetheless, if it is true that the nature of the cases arriving before the Court is sometimes of the kind I have described, then the Court cannot act strictly as a legal institution. It must, that is to say, choose among controversial alternatives of public policy by appealing to at least some criteria of acceptability on questions of fact and value that cannot be found in or deduced from precedent, statute, and Constitution. It is in this sense that the Court is a national policy-maker, and it is this role that gives rise to the problem of the Court's existence in a political system ordinarily held to be democratic.

Now I take it that except for differences in emphasis and presentation, what I have said so far is today widely accepted by almost all American political scientists and by most lawyers. To anyone who believes that the Court is not, in at least some of its activities, a policy-making institution, the discussion that follows may seem irrelevant. But to anyone who holds that at least one role of the Court is as a policy-making institution in cases where strictly legal criteria are inadequate, then a serious and much debated question arises, to wit: Who gets what and why? Or in less elegant language: What groups are benefited or handicapped by the Court and how does the allocation by the Court of these rewards and penalties fit into our presumably democratic political system?

II

In determining and appraising the role of the Court, two different and conflicting criteria are sometimes employed. These are the majority criterion and the criterion of Right or Justice.

Every policy dispute can be tested, at least in principle, by the majority criterion, because (again: in principle) the dispute can be analyzed according to the numbers of people for and against the various alternatives at issue, and therefore according to the proportions of the citizens or eligible members who are for and against the alternatives. Logically speaking, except for a trivial case, every conflict within a given society must be a dispute between a majority of those eligible to participate and a minority or minorities; or else it must be a dispute between or among minorities only.[2] Within certain limits, both possibilities are independent of the number of policy alternatives at issue, and since the argument is not sig-

---

[2] Provided that the total membership of the society is an even number, it is technically possible for a dispute to occur that divides the membership into two equal parts, neither of which can be said to be either a majority or minority of the total membership. But even in the instances where the number of members is even (which should occur on the average only half the time), the probability of an exactly even split, in any group of more than a few thousand people, is so small that it may be ignored.

nificantly affected by the number of alternatives, it is convenient to assume that each policy dispute represents only two alternatives.[3]

If everyone prefers one of two alternatives, then no significant problem arises. But a case will hardly come before the Supreme Court unless at least one person prefers an alternative that is opposed by another person. Strictly speaking, then, no matter how the Court acts in determining the legality or constitutionality of one alternative or the other, the outcome of the Court's decision must either (1) accord with the preferences of a minority of citizens and run counter to the preferences of a majority; (2) accord with the preferences of a majority and run counter to the preferences of a minority; or (3) accord with the preferences of one minority and run counter to the preferences of another minority, the rest being indifferent.

In a democratic system with a more or less representative legislature, it is unnecessary to maintain a special court to secure the second class of outcomes. A case might be made out that the Court protects the rights of national majorities against local interests in federal questions, but so far as I am aware, the role of the Court as a policy-maker is not usually defended in this fashion; in what follows, therefore, I propose to pass over the ticklish question of federalism and deal only with "national" majorities and minorities. The third kind of outcome, although relevant according to other criteria, is hardly relevant to the majority criterion, and may also be passed over for the moment.

One influential view of the Court, however, is that it stands in some special way as a protection of minorities against tyranny by majorities. In the course of its 167 years, in seventy-eight cases, the Court has struck down eighty-six different provisions of federal law as unconstitutional,[4]

---

[3] Suppose the number of citizens, or members eligible to participate in collective decisions, is n. Let each member indicate his "most preferred alternative." Then it is obvious that the maximum number of most preferred alternatives is n. It is equally obvious that if the number of most preferred alternatives is more than or equal to $n/2$, then no majority is possible. But for all practical purposes those formal limitations can be ignored, for we are dealing with a large society where the number of alternatives at issue before the Supreme Court is invariably quite small. If the number of alternatives is greater than two, it is theoretically possible for preferences to be distributed so that no outcome is consistent with the majority criterion, even where all members can rank all the alternatives and where there is perfect information as to their preferences; but this difficulty does not bear on the subsequent discussion, and it is disregarded. For an examination of this problem, consult Arrow, *Social Choice and Individual Values* (1951).

[4] Actually, the matter is somewhat ambiguous. There appear to have been seventy-eight cases in which the Court has held provisions of federal law unconstitutional. Sixty-four different acts in the technical sense have been construed, and eighty-six different provisions in law have been in some respects invalidated. I rely here on the figures and the table given in Library of Congress, Legislative Reference Service, *Provisions of Federal Law Held Unconstitutional By the Supreme Court of the United States*, 95, 141–47 (1936), to which I have added

and by interpretation it has modified a good many more. It might be argued, then, that in all or in a very large number of these cases the Court was, in fact, defending the rights of some minority against a "tyrannical" majority. There are, however, some exceedingly serious difficulties with this interpretation of the Court's activities.

III

One problem, which is essentially ideological in character, is the difficulty of reconciling such an interpretation with the existence of a democratic polity, for it is not at all difficult to show by appeals to authorities as various and imposing as Aristotle, Locke, Rousseau, Jefferson, and Lincoln that the term democracy means, among other things, that the power to rule resides in popular majorities and their representatives. Moreover, from entirely reasonable and traditional definitions of popular sovereignty and political equality, the principle of majority rule can be shown to follow by logical necessity.[5] Thus to affirm that the Court supports minority preferences against majorities is to deny that popular sovereignty and political equality, at least in the traditional sense, exist in the United States; and to affirm that the Court *ought* to act in this way is to deny that popular sovereignty and political equality *ought* to prevail in this country. In a country that glories in its democratic tradition, this is not a happy state of affairs for the Court's defenders; and it is no wonder that a great deal of effort has gone into the enterprise of proving that, even if the Court consistently defends minorities against majorities, nonetheless it is a thoroughly "democratic" institution. But no amount of tampering with democratic theory can conceal the fact that a system in which the policy preferences of minorities prevail over majorities is at odds with the traditional criteria for distinguishing a democracy from other political systems.[6]

Fortunately, however, we do not need to traverse this well-worn ground; for the view of the Court as a protector of the liberties of minorities against the tyranny of majorities is beset with other difficulties that are not so much ideological as matters of fact and logic. If one wishes to be at all rigorous about the question, it is probably impossible to demonstrate that any particular Court decisions have or have not been at odds with the

---

United States v. *Lovett*, 328 U.S. 303 (1946), and *United States ex rel. Toth* v. *Quarles*, 350 U.S. 11 (1955). There are some minor discrepancies in totals (not attributable to the differences in publication dates) between this volume and *Acts of Congress Held Unconstitutional in Whole or in Part by the Supreme Court of the United States*, in Library of Congress, Legislative Reference Service, *The Constitution of the United States of America, Analysis and Interpretation* (Corwin ed., 1953). The difference is a result of classification. The latter document lists seventy-three acts held unconstitutional (to which *Toth* v. *Quarles, supra,* should be added) but different sections of the same act are sometimes counted separately.

[5] Dahl, *A Preface to Democratic Theory,* c. 2 (1956).

[6] Compare Commager, *Majority Rule and Minority Rights* (1943).

preferences of a "national majority." It is clear that unless one makes *some* assumptions as to the kind of evidence one will require for the existence of a set of minority and majority preferences in the general population, the view under consideration is incapable of being proved at all. In any strict sense, no adequate evidence exists, for scientific opinion polls are of relatively recent origin, and national elections are little more than an indication of the first preferences of a number of citizens — in the United States the number ranges between about 40 and 60 per cent of the adult population — for certain candidates for public office. I do not mean to say that there is no relation between preferences among candidates and preferences among alternative public policies, but the connection is a highly tenuous one, and on the basis of an election it is almost never possible to adduce whether a majority does or does not support one of two or more policy alternatives about which members of the political elite are divided. For the greater part of the Court's history, then, there is simply no way of establishing with any high degree of confidence whether a given alternative was or was not supported by a majority or a minority of adults or even of voters.

In the absence of relatively direct information, we are thrown back on indirect tests. The eighty-six provisions of federal law that have been declared unconstitutional were, of course, initially passed by majorities of those voting in the Senate and in the House. They also had the president's formal approval. We could, therefore, speak of a majority of those voting in the House and Senate, together with the president, as a "lawmaking majority." It is not easy to determine whether any such constellation of forces within the political elites actually coincides with the preferences of a majority of American adults or even with the preferences of a majority of that half of the adult population which, on the average, votes in congressional elections. Such evidence as we have from opinion polls suggests that Congress is not markedly out of line with public opinion, or at any rate with such public opinion as there is after one discards the anwsers of people who fall into the category, often large, labelled "no response" or "don't know." If we may, on these somewhat uncertain grounds, take a "lawmaking majority" as equivalent to a "national majority," then it is possible to test the hypothesis that the Supreme Court is shield and buckler for minorities against national majorities.

Under any reasonable assumptions about the nature of the political process, it would appear to be somewhat naive to assume that the Supreme Court either would or could play the role of Galahad. Over the whole history of the Court, on the average one new justice has been appointed every twenty-two months. Thus a president can expect to appoint about two new justices during one term of office; and if this were not enough to tip the balance on a normally divided Court, he is almost certain to succeed in two terms. Thus, Hoover had three appointments;

Roosevelt, nine; Truman, four; and Eisenhower, so far, has had four. Presidents are not famous for appointing justices hostile to their own views on public policy nor could they expect to secure confirmation of a man whose stance on key questions was flagrantly at odds with that of the dominant majority in the Senate. Justices are typically men who, prior to appointment, have engaged in public life and have committed themselves publicly on the great questions of the day. As Mr. Justice Frankfurter has recently reminded us, a surprisingly large proportion of the justices, particularly of the great justices who have left their stamp upon the decisions of the Court, have had little or no prior judicial experience.[7] Nor have the justices — certainly not the great justices — been timid men with a passion for anonymity. Indeed, it is not too much to say that if justices were appointed primarily for their "judicial" qualities without regard to their basic attitudes on fundamental questions of public policy, the Court could not play the influential role in the American political system that it does in reality play.

TABLE 1	The Interval between Appointments to the Supreme Court	
Interval in years	Percentage of total appointments	Cumulative percentage
Less than 1	21	21
1	34	55
2	18	73
3	9	82
4	8	90
5	7	97
6	2	99
------	------	------
12	1	100
Total	100	100

Note: The table excludes the six appointments made in 1789. Except for the four most recent appointments, it is based on data in the *Encyclopedia of American History*, 461–62 (Morris ed., 1953). It may be slightly inaccurate because the source shows only the year of appointment, not the month. The twelve-year interval was from 1811 to 1823.

The fact is, then, that the policy views dominant on the Court are never for long out of line with the policy views dominant among the lawmaking majorities of the United States. Consequently it would be most unrealistic to suppose that the Court would, for more than a few years at

[7] Frankfurter, *op. cit., supra* note 1, at 782–84.

most, stand against any major alternatives sought by a lawmaking majority. The judicial agonies of the New Deal will, of course, quickly come to mind; but Mr. Roosevelt's difficulties with the Court were truly exceptional. Generalizing over the whole history of the Court, the chances are about one out of five that a president will make one appointment to the Court in less than a year, better than one out of two that he will make one within two years, and three out of four that he will make one within three years. Mr. Roosevelt had unusually bad luck: he had to wait four years for his first appointment; the odds against this long an interval are four to one. With average luck, the battle with the Court would never have occurred; even as it was, although the "court-packing" proposal did formally fail, by the end of his second term Mr. Roosevelt had appointed five new justices and by 1941 Mr. Justice Roberts was the only remaining holdover from the Hoover era.

It is to be expected, then, that the Court is least likely to be successful in blocking a determined and persistent lawmaking majority on a major policy and most likely to succeed against a "weak" majority; e.g., a dead one, a transient one, a fragile one, or one weakly united upon a policy of subordinate importance.

IV

An examination of the cases in which the Court has held federal legislation unconstitutional confirms, on the whole, our expectations. Over the whole history of the Court, about half the decisions have been rendered more than four years after the legislation was passed.

Of the twenty-four laws held unconstitutional within two years, eleven were measures enacted in the early years of the New Deal. Indeed, New

TABLE 2

Percentage of Cases Held Unconstitutional Arranged by Time Intervals between Legislation and Decision

Number of years	New Deal legislation %	Other %	All legislation %
2 or less	92	19	30
3– 4	8	19	18
5– 8	0	28	24
9–12	0	13	11
13–16	0	8	6
17–20	0	1	1
21 or more	0	12	10
Total	100	100	100

Cases Holding Legislation
Unconstitutional within four
TABLE 3   Years after Enactment

Interval in years	New Deal No.	%	Other No.	%	Total No.	%
2 or less	11	29	13	34	24	63
3 to 4	1	3	13	34	14	37
Total	12	32	26	68	38	100

Deal measures comprise nearly a third of all the legislation that has ever been declared unconstitutional within four years after enactment.

It is illuminating to examine the cases where the Court has acted on legislation within four years after enactment — where the presumption is, that is to say, that the lawmaking majority is not necessarily a dead one. Of the twelve New Deal cases, two were, from a policy point of view, trivial; and two, although perhaps not trivial, were of minor importance to the New Deal program.[8] A fifth [9] involved the NRA, which was to expire within three weeks of the decision. Insofar as the unconstitutional provisions allowed "codes of fair competition" to be established by industrial groups, it is fair to say that President Roosevelt and his advisers were relieved by the Court's decision of a policy they had come to find increasingly embarrassing. In view of the tenacity with which Mr. Roosevelt held to his major program, there can hardly be any doubt that had he wanted to pursue the major policy objective involved in the NRA codes, as he did, for example, with the labor provisions, he would not have been stopped by the Court's special theory of the Constitution. As to the seven other cases,[10] it is entirely correct to say, I think, that whatever some of the eminent justices might have thought during their fleeting moments of glory, they did not succeed in interposing a barrier to the achievement of the objectives of the legislation; and in a few years most of the constitu-

[8] *Booth v. United States*, 291 U.S. 339 (1934), involved a reduction in the pay of retired judges. *Lynch v. United States*, 292 U.S. 571 (1934), repealed laws granting to veterans rights to yearly renewable term insurance; there were only twenty-nine policies outstanding in 1932. *Hopkins Federal Savings and Loan Ass'n v. Cleary*, 296 U.S. 315 (1935), granted permission to state building and loan associations to convert to federal ones on a vote of 51 per cent or more of votes cast at a legal meeting. *Ashton v. Cameron County Water Improvement District*, 298 U.S. 513 (1936), permitting municipalities to petition federal courts for bankruptcy proceedings.

[9] *Schechter Poultry Corp. v. United States*, 295 U.S. 495 (1935).

[10] *United States v. Butler*, 297 U.S. 1 (1936); *Perry v. United States*, 294 U.S. 330 (1935); *Panama Refining Co. v. Ryan*, 293 U.S. 388 (1935); *Railroad Retirement Board v. Alton R. Co.*, 295 U.S. 330 (1935); *Louisville Joint Stock Land Bank v. Radford*, 295 U.S. 555 (1935); *Rickert Rice Mills v. Fontenot*, 297 U.S. 110 (1936); *Carter v. Carter Coal Co.*, 298 U.S. 238 (1936).

tional interpretation on which the decisions rested had been unceremoniously swept under the rug.

The remainder of the thirty-eight cases where the Court has declared legislation unconstitutional within four years of enactment tend to fall into two rather distinct groups: those involving legislation that could reasonably be regarded as important *from the point of view of the lawmaking majority* and those involving minor legislation. Although the one category merges into the other, so that some legislation must be classified rather arbitrarily, probably there will be little disagreement with classifying the specific legislative provisions involved in eleven cases as essentially minor from the point of view of the lawmaking majority (however important they may have been as constitutional interpretations).[11] The specific legislative provisions involved in the remaining fifteen cases are by no means of uniform importance, but with one or two possible exceptions it seems reasonable to classify them as major policy issues from the point of view of the lawmaking majority.[12] We would expect that cases involving major legislative policy would be propelled to the Court much more rapidly than cases involving minor policy, and, as the table below shows, this is in fact what happens.

Thus a lawmaking majority with major policy objectives in mind usually has an opportunity to seek for ways of overcoming the Court's veto. It is an interesting and highly significant fact that Congress and the president do generally succeed in overcoming a hostile Court on major policy issues. It is particularly instructive to examine the cases involving major policy. In two cases involving punitive legislation enacted by Radical Republican Congresses against supporters of the Confederacy during the Civil War, the Court faced a rapidly crumbling majority whose death knell as an

[11] *United States* v. *Dewitt*, 9 Wall. (U.S.) 41 (1870); *Gordon* v. *United States*, 2 Wall. (U.S.) 561 (1865); *Monongahela Navigation Co.* v. *United States*, 148 U.S. 312 (1893); *Wong Wing* v. *United States*, 163 U.S. 228 (1896); *Fairbank* v. *United States*, 181 U.S. 283 (1901); *Rassmussen* v. *United States*, 197 U.S. 516 (1905); *Muskrat* v. *United States*, 219 U.S. 346 (1911); *Choate* v. *Trapp*, 224 U.S. 665 (1912); *Evans* v. *Gore*, 253 U.S. 245 (1920); *Untermyer* v. *Anderson*, 276 U.S. 440 (1928); *United States* v. *Lovett*, 328 U.S. 303 (1946). Note that although the specific legislation provisions held unconstitutional may have been minor, the basic legislation may have been of major policy importance.

[12] *Ex parte Garland*, 4 Wall. (U.S.) 333 (1867); *United States* v. *Klein*, 13 Wall. (U.S.) 128 (1872); *Pollock* v. *Farmers' Loan and Trust Co.*, 157 U.S. 429 (1895), rehearing granted 158 U.S. 601 (1895); *Employers' Liability Cases*, 207 U.S. 463 (1908); *Keller* v. *United States*, 213 U.S. 138 (1909); *Hammer* v. *Dagenhart*, 247 U.S. 251 (1918); *Eisner* v. *Macomber*, 252 U.S. 189 (1920); *Knickerbocker Ice Co.* v. *Stewart*, 253 U.S. 149 (1920); *United States* v. *Cohen Grocery Co.*, 255 U.S. 81 (1921); *Weeds, Inc.* v. *United States*, 255 U.S. 109 (1921); *Bailey* v. *Drexel Furniture Co.*, 259 U.S. 20 (1922); *Hill* v. *Wallace*, 259 U.S. 44 (1922); *Washington* v. *Dawson and Co.*, 264 U.S. 219 (1924); *Trusler* v. *Crooks*, 269 U.S. 475 (1926).

TABLE 4

Number of Cases Involving
Legislative Policy other than
Those Arising under New
Deal Legislation Holding
Legislation Unconstitutional
within Four Years after
Enactment

Interval in years	Major policy	Minor policy	Total
2 or less	11	2	13
3 to 4	4	9	13
Total	15	11	26

effective national force was sounded with the election of 1876.[13] Three cases are difficult to classify and I have labelled them "unclear." Of these, two were decisions made in 1921 involving a 1919 amendment to the Lever Act to control prices.[14] The legislation was important, and the provision in question was clearly struck down, but the Lever Act terminated three days after the decision and Congress did not return to the subject of price control until World War II, when it experienced no constitutional difficulties arising from these cases (which were primarily concerned with the lack of an ascertainable standard of guilt). The third case in this category successfully eliminated stock dividends from the scope of the Sixteenth Amendment, although a year later Congress enacted legislation taxing the actual income from such stock.[15]

The remaining ten cases were ultimately followed by a reversal of the actual policy results of the Court's action, although not necessarily of the specific constitutional interpretation. In four cases,[16] the policy consequences of the Court's decision were overcome in less than a year. The other six required a long struggle. Workmen's compensation for longshoremen and harbor workers was invalidated by the Court in 1920;[17] in 1922 Congress passed a new law which was, in its turn, knocked down by

13 *Ex parte Garland*, 4 Wall. (U.S.) 333 (1867); *United States* v. *Klein*, 13 Wall. (U.S.) 128 (1872).

14 *United States* v. *Cohen Grocery Co.*, 255 U.S. 81 (1921); *Weeds, Inc.* v. *United States*, 255 U.S. 109 (1921).

15 *Eisner* v. *Macomber*, 252 U.S. 189 (1920).

16 *Employers' Liability Cases*, 207 U.S. 463 (1908); *Keller* v. *United States*, 213 U.S. 138 (1909); *Trusler* v. *Crooks*, 269 U.S. 475 (1926); *Hill* v. *Wallace*, 259 U.S. 44 (1922).

17 *Knickerbocker Ice Co.* v. *Stewart*, 253 U.S. 149 (1920).

TABLE 5

Type of Congressional Action Following Supreme Court Decisions Holding Legislation Unconstitutional within Four Years after Enactment (other than New Deal Legislation)

Congressional action	Major policy	Minor policy	Total
Reverses Court's policy	10ᵃ	2ᵈ	12
Changes own policy	2ᵇ	0	2
None	0	8ᵉ	8
Unclear	3ᶜ	1ᶠ	4
Total	15	11	26

Note: For the cases in each category.

ᵃ Pollock v. Farmers' Loan and Trust Co., 157 U.S. 429 (1895); Employers' Liability Cases, 207 U.S. 463 (1908); Keller v. United States, 213 U.S. 138 (1909); Hammer v. Dagenhart, 247 U.S. 251 (1918); Bailey v. Drexel Furniture Co., 259 U.S. 20 (1922); Trusler v. Crooks, 269 U.S. 475 (1926); Hill v. Wallace, 259 U.S. 44 (1922); Knickerbocker Ice Co. v. Stewart, 253 U.S. 149 (1920); Washington v. Dawson and Co., 264 U.S. 219 (1924).

ᵇ Ex parte Garland, 4 Wall. (U.S.) 333 (1867); United States v. Klein, 13 Wall. (U.S.) 128 (1872).

ᶜ United States v. Cohen Grocery Co., 255 U.S. 81 (1921); Weeds, Inc. v. United States, 255 U.S. 109 (1921); Eisner v. Macomber, 252 U.S. 189 (1920).

ᵈ Gordon v. United States, 2 Wall. (U.S.) 561 (1865); Evans v. Gore, 253 U.S. 245 (1920).

ᵉ United States v. Dewitt, 9 Wall. (U.S.) 41 (1870); Monongahela Navigation Co. v. United States, 148 U.S. 312 (1893); Wong Wing v. United States, 163 U.S. 228 (1896); Fairbank v. United States, 181 U.S. 283 (1901); Rassmussen v. United States, 197 U.S. 516 (1905); Muskrat v. United States, 219 U.S. 346 (1911); Choate v. Trapp, 224 U.S. 665 (1912); United States v. Lovett, 328 U.S. 303 (1946).

ᶠ Untermyer v. Anderson, 276 U.S. 440 (1928).

the Court in 1924;[18] in 1927 Congress passed a third law, which was finally upheld in 1932.[19] The notorious income tax cases [20] of 1895 were first somewhat narrowed by the Court itself;[21] the Sixteenth Amendment was recommended by President Taft in 1909 and was ratified in 1913,

[18] Washington v. Dawson and Co., 264 U.S. 219 (1924).

[19] Crowell v. Benson, 285 U.S. 22 (1932).

[20] Pollock v. Farmers' Loan and Trust Co., 157 U.S. 429 (1895).

[21] Nicol v. Ames, 173 U.S. 509 (1899); Knowlton v. Moore, 178 U.S. 41 (1900); Patton v. Brady, 184 U.S. 608 (1902); Flint v. Stone Tracy Co., 220 U.S. 107 (1911).

some eighteen years after the Court's decisions. The two child labor cases represent the most effective battle ever waged by the Court against legislative policy-makers. The original legislation outlawing child labor, based on the commerce clause, was passed in 1916 as a part of Wilson's New Freedom. Like Roosevelt later, Wilson was somewhat unlucky in his Supreme Court appointments; he made only three appointments during his eight years, and one of these was wasted, from a policy point of view, on McReynolds. Had McReynolds voted "right," the subsequent struggle over the problem of child labor need not have occurred, for the decision in 1918 was by a Court divided five to four, McReynolds voting with the majority.[22] Congress moved at once to circumvent the decision by means of the tax power, but in 1922 the Court blocked that approach.[23] In 1924 Congress returned to the engagement with a constitutional amendment that was rapidly endorsed by a number of state legislatures before it began to meet so much resistance in the states remaining that the enterprise miscarried. In 1938, under a second reformist president, new legislation was passed, twenty-two years after the first; this a chastened Court accepted in 1941,[24] and thereby brought to an end a battle that had lasted a full quarter-century.

The entire record of the duel between the Court and the lawmaking majority, in cases where the Court has held legislation unconstitutional within four years after enactment, is summarized in Table 6.

TABLE 6

Type of Congressional Action after Supreme Court Decisions Holding Legislation Unconstitutional within Four Years after Enactment (Including New Deal Legislation)

Congressional action	Major policy	Minor policy	Total
Reverses Court's policy	17	2	19
None	0	12	12
Other	6*	1	7
Total	23	15	38

* In addition to the actions in Table 5 under "Changes own policy" and "Unclear," this figure includes the NRA legislation affected by the *Schechter Poultry* case.

22 *Hammer* v. *Dagenhart*, 247 U.S. 251 (1918).
23 *Bailey* v. *Drexel Furniture Co.*, 259 U.S. 20 (1922).
24 *United States* v. *Darby*, 312 U.S. 100 (1941).

Thus the application of the majority criterion seems to show the following: First, if the Court did in fact uphold minorities against national majorities, as both its supporters and critics often seem to believe, it would be an extremely anomalous institution from a democratic point of view. Second, the elaborate "democratic" rationalizations of the Court's defenders and the hostility of its "democratic" critics are largely irrelevant, for law-making majorities generally have had their way. Third, although the Court seems never to have succeeded in holding out indefinitely, in a very small number of important cases it has delayed the application of policy up to as much as twenty-five years.

V

How can we appraise decisions of the third kind just mentioned? Earlier I referred to the criterion of Right or Justice as a norm sometimes invoked to describe the role of the Court. In accordance with this norm, it might be argued that the most important policy function of the Court is to protect rights that are in some sense basic or fundamental. Thus (the argument might run) in a country where basic rights are, on the whole, respected, one should not expect more than a small number of cases where the Court has had to plant itself firmly against a lawmaking majority. But majorities may, on rare occasions, become "tyrannical"; and when they do, the Court intervenes; and although the constitutional issue may, strictly speaking, be technically open, the Constitution assumes an underlying fundamental body of rights and liberties which the Court guarantees by its decisions.

Here again, however, even without examining the actual cases, it would appear, on political grounds, somewhat unrealistic to suppose that a Court whose members are recruited in the fashion of Supreme Court justices would long hold to norms of Right or Justice substantially at odds with the rest of the political elite. Moreover, in an earlier day it was perhaps easier to believe that certain rights are so natural and self-evident that their fundamental validity is as much a matter of definite knowledge, at least to all reasonable creatures, as the color of a ripe apple. To say that this view is unlikely to find many articulate defenders today is, of course, not to disprove it; it is rather to suggest that we do not need to elaborate the case against it in this essay.

In any event the best rebuttal to the view of the Court suggested above will be found in the record of the Court's decisions. Surely the six cases referred to a moment ago, where the policy consequences of the Court's decisions were overcome only after long battles, will not appeal to many contemporary minds as evidence for the proposition under examination. A natural right to employ child labor in mills and mines? To be free of income taxes by the federal government? To employ longshoremen and harbor workers without the protection of workmen's compensation? The

Court itself did not rely upon such arguments in these cases, and it would be no credit to their opinions to reconstruct them along such lines.

So far, however, our evidence has been drawn from cases in which the Court has held legislation unconstitutional within four years after enactment. What of the other forty cases? Do we have evidence in these that the Court has protected fundamental or natural rights and liberties against the dead hand of some past tyranny by the lawmakers? The evidence is not impressive. In the entire history of the Court there is not one case arising under the First Amendment in which the Court has held federal legislation unconstitutional. If we turn from these fundamental liberties of religion, speech, press and assembly, we do find a handful of cases — something less than ten — arising under Amendments Four to Seven in which the Court has declared acts unconstitutional that might properly be regarded as involving rather basic liberties.[25] An inspection of these cases leaves the impression that, in all of them, the lawmakers and the Court were not very far apart; moreover, it is doubtful that the fundamental conditions of liberty in this country have been altered by more than a hair's breadth as a result of these decisions. However, let us give the Court its due; it is little enough.

Over against these decisions we must put the fifteen or so cases in which the Court used the protections of the Fifth, Thirteenth, Fourteenth and Fifteenth Amendments to preserve the rights and liberties of a relatively privileged group at the expense of the rights and liberties of a submerged group: chiefly slaveholders at the expense of slaves,[26] white people at the expense of colored people,[27] and property holders at the expense of wage earners and other groups.[28] These cases, unlike the relatively innocuous ones of the preceding set, all involved liberties of genuinely funda-

[25] The candidates for this category would appear to be *Boyd v. United States*, 116 U.S. 616 (1886); *Rassmussen v. United States*, 197 U.S. 516 (1905); *Wong Wing v. United States*, 163 U.S. 228 (1896); *United States v. Moreland*, 258 U.S. 433 (1922); *Kirby v. United States*, 174 U.S. 47 (1899); *United States v. Cohen Grocery Co.*, 255 U.S. 81 (1921); *Weeds, Inc. v. United States*, 255 U.S. 109 (1921); *Justices of the Supreme Court v. United States ex rel. Murray*, 9 Wall. (U.S.) 274 (1870); *United States ex rel. Toth v. Quarles*, 350 U.S. 11 (1955).

[26] *Dred Scott v. Sandford*, 19 How. (U.S.) 393 (1857).

[27] *United States v. Reese*, 92 U.S. 214 (1876); *United States v. Harris*, 106 U.S. 629 (1883); *United States v. Stanley* (*Civil Rights Cases*), 109 U.S. 3 (1883); *Baldwin v. Franks*, 120 U.S. 678 (1887); *James v. Bowman*, 190 U.S. 127 (1903); *Hodges v. United States*, 203 U.S. 1 (1906); *Butts v. Merchants and Miners Transportation Co.*, 230 U.S. 126 (1913).

[28] *Monongahela Navigation Co. v. United States*, 148 U.S. 312 (1893); *Adair v. United States*, 208 U.S. 161 (1908); *Adkins v. Children's Hospital*, 261 U.S. 525 (1923); *Nichols v. Coolidge*, 274 U.S. 531 (1927); *Untermyer v. Anderson*, 276 U.S. 440 (1928); *Heiner v. Donnan*, 285 U.S. 312 (1932); *Louisville Joint Stock Land Bank v. Radford*, 295 U.S. 555 (1935).

mental importance, where an opposite policy would have meant thoroughly basic shifts in the distribution of rights, liberties, and opportunities in the United States — where, moreover, the policies sustained by the Court's action have since been repudiated in every civilized nation of the Western world, including our own. Yet, if our earlier argument is correct, it is futile — precisely because the basic distribution of privilege *was* at issue — to suppose that the Court could have possibly acted much differently in these areas of policy from the way in which it did in fact act.

VI

Thus the role of the Court as a policy-making institution is not simple; and it is an error to suppose that its functions can be either described or appraised by means of simple concepts drawn from democratic or moral theory. It is possible, nonetheless, to derive a few general conclusions about the Court's role as a policy-making institution.

National politics in the United States, as in other stable democracies, is dominated by relatively cohesive alliances that endure for long periods of time. One recalls the Jeffersonian alliance, the Jacksonian, the extraordinarily long-lived Republican dominance of the post-Civil War years, and the New Deal alliance shaped by Franklin Roosevelt. Each is marked by a break with past policies, a period of intense struggle, followed by consolidation, and finally decay and disintegration of the alliance.

Except for short-lived transitional periods when the old alliance is disintegrating and the new one is struggling to take control of political institutions, the Supreme Court is inevitably a part of the dominant national alliance. As an element in the political leadership of the dominant alliance, the Court of course supports the major policies of the alliance. By itself, the Court is almost powerless to affect the course of national policy. In the absence of substantial agreement within the alliance, an attempt by the Court to make national policy is likely to lead to disaster, as the *Dred Scott* decision and the early New Deal cases demonstrate. Conceivably, the cases of the last three decades involving the freedom of Negroes, culminating in the now famous decision on school integration, are exceptions to this generalization; I shall have more to say about them in a moment.

The Supreme Court is not, however, simply an *agent* of the alliance. It is an essential part of the political leadership and possesses some bases of power of its own, the most important of which is the unique legitimacy attributed to its interpretations of the Constitution. This legitimacy the Court jeopardizes if it flagrantly opposes the major policies of the dominant alliance; such a course of action, as we have seen, is one in which the Court will not normally be tempted to engage.

It follows that within the somewhat narrow limits set by the basic policy goals of the dominant alliance, the Court *can* make national policy.

Its discretion, then, is not unlike that of a powerful committee chairman in Congress who cannot, generally speaking, nullify the basic policies substantially agreed on by the rest of the dominant leadership, but who can, within these limits, often determine important questions of timing, effectiveness, and subordinate policy. Thus the Court is least effective against a current lawmaking majority — and evidently least inclined to act. It is most effective when it sets the bounds of policy for officials, agencies, state governments or even regions, a task that has come to occupy a very large part of the Court's business.[29]

Few of the Court's policy decisions can be interpreted sensibly in terms of a "majority" versus a "minority." In this respect the Court is no different from the rest of the political leadership. Generally speaking, policy at the national level is the outcome of conflict, bargaining, and agreement among minorities; the process is neither minority rule nor majority rule but what might better be called *minorities* rule, where one aggregation of minorities achieves policies opposed by another aggregation.

The main objective of presidential leadership is to build a stable and dominant aggregation of minorities with a high probability of winning the presidency and one or both houses of Congress. The main task of the Court is to confer legitimacy on the fundamental policies of the successful coalition. There are times when the coalition is unstable with respect to certain key policies; at very great risk to its legitimacy powers, the Court can intervene in such cases and may even succeed in establishing policy. Probably in such cases it can succeed only if its action conforms to and reinforces a widespread set of explicit or implicit norms held by the political leadership; norms which are not strong enough or are not distributed in such a way as to insure the existence of an effective lawmaking majority but are, nonetheless, sufficiently powerful to prevent any successful attack on the legitimacy powers of the Court. This is probably the explanation for the relatively successful work of the Court in enlarging the freedom of Negroes to vote during the past three decades and in its famous school integration decisions.[30]

Yet the Court is more than this. Considered as a political system, democracy is a set of basic procedures for arriving at decisions. The opera-

[29] "Constitutional law and cases with constitutional undertones are of course still very important, with almost one-fourth of the cases in which written opinions were filed [in the two most recent terms] involving such questions. Review of administrative action . . . constitutes the largest category of the Court's work, comprising one-third of the total cases decided on the merits. The remaining . . . categories of litigation . . . all involve largely public law questions." Frankfurter, *op. cit., supra* note 1, at 793.

[30] *Rice* v. *Elmore*, 165 F.2d 387 (C.A. 4th, 1947), cert. denied 333 U.S. 875 (1948); *United States* v. *Classic*, 313 U.S. 299 (1941); *Smith* v. *Allwright*, 321 U.S. 649 (1944); *Grovey* v. *Townsend*, 295 U.S. 45 (1935); *Brown* v. *Board of Education*, 347 U.S. 483 (1954); *Bolling* v. *Sharpe*, 347 U.S. 497 (1954).

tion of these procedures presupposes the existence of certain rights, obligations, liberties and restraints; in short, certain patterns of behavior. The existence of these patterns of behavior in turn presupposes widespread agreement (particularly among the politically active and influential segments of the population) on the validity and propriety of the behavior. Although its record is by no means lacking in serious blemishes, at its best the Court operates to confer legitimacy, not simply on the particular and parochial policies of the dominant political alliance, but upon the basic patterns of behavior required for the operation of a democracy.

MODERN SOCIAL
AND ECONOMIC
TRENDS

III

Reflections on
the History of the
French and American
Labor Movements

VAL R. LORWIN

*Why have American workers, through their labor unions, se-
cured a standard of living and security unlike workers of any
other country? How can we account for the institutional power
and success of American labor unions? Val R. Lorwin, an economic historian at the University of Oregon, approaches these
questions through a comparative study of the American and
French labor union movements. He analyzes each movement
in terms of social structure, national economy, and political
posture. Perhaps a key to understanding the differing nature
and degree of success between the movements lies in an aspect
of their respective national characters. Lorwin notes Napoleon III's observation that in France, "we hardly care to make
reforms, we only make revolutions." In the United States, on
the other hand, de Tocqueville's judgment that the American
people, while loving change, despise revolution, draws into
focus an essential difference in national mood and style that
has been exemplified in their respective union activities and
goals. The American labor movement has emphasized worker
assimilation into a large national social structure, whereas the
French movement has underlined class interest and goals. In
the United States unions have worked within the system, emphasizing organizational solidity, while in France they have
concentrated on class solidarity. The American unions are job-
oriented and recognize a community of interest with employers
whereby accommodation can and must be beneficial for both
sides. In France, however, the contest with employers is
viewed as a component, a skirmish, of the larger class and revolutionary struggle. The abortive French revolution of 1968
showed that the French working class had lost little of its
revolutionary ardor. In the United States, however, organized
labor exemplified its establishment position by supporting a
war that deeply affected submerged classes both at home and
abroad.*

Jules Michelet remarked that the forms of association "must differ . . . among the different countries, according to the diversity of national genius." [1] And Denis W. Brogan once said (although he is surely one who does not merit the reproach): "Because we have studied only France, we have not understood even France." The second remark might apply to the United States, too. There has been talk of the value of comparative study of labor movements, but comparatively little application of comparative methods to labor history.[2] A comparison of the history of association in labor unions in France and the United States may therefore throw a little more light on the "national genius" of each country as well as on the behavior of each labor movement.

This paper does not aim to elucidate general laws of history or a "theory of labor." It is not comparative history in the style of Lucien Febvre's "grande dame chère à nous tous." [3] Its modest purpose is to note some of the differences and similarities in the backgrounds (the "national genius") which explain in turn differences in the development of the French and American labor movements.

"Labor movements" I shall take (in the American usage, more limited than the European) to mean labor unions; I can touch on the labor-based political movements only by reference to the unions. If in seeking the roots of unionism I refer to some of the well-known qualities of the soil of the two countries, let it not be thought that I think I have discovered America or France.

Reprinted by permission of The Economic History Association, with minor changes approved by the author from the *Journal of Economic History*, XVII (March 1957), pp. 25–44.

[1] *Le Peuple* (Paris: Costes, 1946 [first published 1846]), p. 228.

[2] See Selig Perlman, *A Theory of the Labor Movement* (New York: The Macmillan Company, 1928); Charles A. Gulick and Melvin K. Bers, "Insight and Illusion in Perlman's Theory of the Labor Movement," *Industrial and Labor Relations Review*, VI (1953), 510–31; discussion of Perlman's *Theory* in Industrial Relations Research Association, *Proceedings of the Third Annual Meeting* (Madison, Wisconsin: The Association, 1951), pp. 140–83; Walter Galenson, ed., *Comparative Labor Movements* (New York: Prentice-Hall, Inc., 1952), pp. ix–xiv; Adolf Sturmthal, *Unity and Diversity in European Labor* (Glencoe, Illinois: Free Press, 1953); Sturmthal, "National Patterns of Union Behavior," *Journal of Political Economy*, LVI (1948), 515–26; Val. R. Lorwin, "Recent Research on Western European Labor Movements," in Industrial Relations Research Association, *Proceedings of the Seventh Annual Meeting* (Madison, Wisconsin: The Association, 1955), esp. pp. 77–78; Clark Kerr and Abraham Siegel, "The Structuring of the Labor Force in Industrial Society: New Dimensions and New Questions," *Industrial and Labor Relations Review*, VIII (1955), 151–68; Clark Kerr, Frederick H. Harbison, John T. Dunlop, and Charles A. Myers, "The Labor Problem in Economic Development," *International Labour Review*, LXXI (1955), 223–35.

[3] Lucien Febvre, *Combats pour l'histoire* (Paris: Colin, 1953), p. 115, n. 2. See also pp. 136–43, 369.

Between France and the United States the differences are enough to make the studies intriguing, yet the similarities enough to make the comparisons valid and significant. There is a large literature on the labor movements of France [4] and the United States,[5] although there is no satis-

[4] Among the general works of labor history and description: Michel Collinet, *Esprit du syndicalisme* (Paris: Editions Ouvrières, 1952); Edouard Dolléans, *Histoire du mouvement ouvrier* (vols. 1 and 2; Paris: Colin, 1936, 1939); Henry W. Ehrmann, *French Labor: from Popular Front to Liberation* (New York: Oxford, 1947); Robert Goetz-Girey, *Pensée syndicale française: militants et théoriciens* (Paris: Colin, 1948); Daniel Halévy, *Essais sur le mouvement ouvrier en France* (Paris: Société Nouvelle de Librairie, 1901); Pierre Laroque, *Les relations entre patrons et ouvriers* (Paris: Aubier, 1938); Georges Lefranc, *Histoire du mouvement syndical français* (Paris: Librairie syndicale, 1937); Lefranc [under the name of Jean Montreuil], *Histoire du mouvement ouvrier en France des origines à nos jours* (Paris: Aubier, 1946), and Lefranc, *Les expériences syndicales en France de 1939 à 1950* (Paris: Aubier, 1950); Maxime Leroy, *La coutume ouvrière* (2 vols.; Paris: Giard et Brière, 1913); Lewis L. Lorwin, *Syndicalism in France* (2d ed.; New York: Columbia University Press, 1914); Val R. Lorwin, *The French Labor Movement* (Cambridge, Massachusetts: Harvard University Press, 1954); Paul Louis, *Histoire du mouvement syndical en France* (2 vols.; Paris: Valois, 1947–1948); Fernand Pelloutier, *Histoire des bourses du travail* (reissued; Paris: Costes, 1946); David J. Saposs, *The Labor Movement in Post-War France* (New York: Columbia University Press, 1931); and Georges Weill, *Histoire du mouvement social en France, 1852–1924* (Paris: Alcan, 1924).

[5] Of the extensive literature, one may list here Jack Barbash, *Labor Unions in Action* (New York: Harper & Brothers, 1948); Paul F. Brissenden, *The IWW* (New York: Columbia University Press, 1920); Neil W. Chamberlain, *The Union Challenge to Management Control* (New York: Harper & Brothers, 1948); John R. Commons and Associates, *History of Labor in the United States* (2 vols.; New York: The Macmillan Company, 1918); Walter Galenson, *Rival Unionism in the United States* (New York: American Council on Public Affairs, 1940); Samuel Gompers, *Seventy Years of Life and Labor* (2 vols.; New York: E. P. Dutton & Co., 1925); Charles O. Gregory, *Labor and the Law* (rev. ed.; New York: W. W. Norton & Company, Inc., 1949); J. B. S. Hardman, ed., *American Labor Dynamics* (New York: Harcourt, Brace & Co., 1928); Hardman and Maurice F. Neufeld, eds., *The House of Labor: Internal Operations of American Unions* (New York: Prentice-Hall, Inc., 1951); R. F. Hoxie, *Trade Unionism in the United States* (2d ed.; New York: Appleton-Century-Crofts, Inc., 1923); Industrial Relations Research Association, *Interpreting the Labor Movement* (Madison, Wisconsin: The Association, 1952); Lewis L. Lorwin, *The American Federation of Labor* (Washington: Brookings Institute, 1933); Harry A. Millis et al., *How Collective Bargaining Works* (New York: Twentieth Century Fund, 1942); Millis and Emily C. Brown, *From the Wagner Act to Taft-Hartley* (Chicago: University of Chicago Press, 1950); Millis and Royal E. Montgomery, *Organized Labor* [Vol. III of *Economics of Labor*] (New York: McGraw-Hill Book Co., 1945); Selig Perlman, *A History of the Labor Movement* (New York: The Macmillan Company, 1922); Perlman and Philip Taft, *History of Labor in the United States, 1896–1932* [Vol. IV of Commons and Associates, *History*] (New York: The Macmillan Company, 1935); David J. Saposs, *Left Wing Unionism* (New York: International, 1926); Joel Seidman, *Union Rights and Union Duties* (New York: Harcourt, Brace & Co., 1943), and Seidman, *American Labor from Defense to Reconversion* (Chicago: University of Chicago, 1953); Sumner H. Slichter,

factory history of either movement up to the most recent times, and other gaps in our knowledge are still great.

Some words of warning: the contradictions and the exceptions *within* each country and each movement give us some of the richest threads in the web of history. But if comparison is to be essayed, some crudity and seeming dogmatism must be the ransom of synthesis and brevity. In a single article one can only acknowledge the diversities that one must then shut one's eyes to.

No social movement is ever homogeneous or consistent. Individuals are a complex of contradictory sentiments and aspirations. Groups swing back and forth between patience and bursts of violence, between parochialism and class solidarity, between petty calculation and generous sacrifice, between economic and political action.

The French labor movement whose official doctrine was the revolutionary syndicalism of the Charter of Amiens numbered perhaps as many reformists as revolutionaries. The unionists of Lille or Limoges differed from those of Paris or St. Etienne; the metalworkers, from the printers or textile workers.

The American Federation of Labor that Samuel Gompers spoke for at one moment almost endorsed socialism. There has been a vast difference between the adaptation to technical change of the American building trades and that of the miners; between the internal union democracy of the dock workers and that of the auto workers; between the political actions of the carpenters and the railroad workers. Out of the same ethnic group have come both Joseph A. Ryan and George Meany; out of the same generation of the same union both William Green and John L. Lewis. The politically and socially conservative building trades-unions have sacrificed contract observance to sympathetic strikes and boycotts; the more radical garment workers, miners, and brewers have respected the sanctity of contracts.

I

France has long been less urban than the United States; more of its labor force has been self-employed; of its wage earners, many more (in proportion) have been employed in small and middle-sized establishments. Industry has occupied a smaller part of the population. This balance between argiculture and industry has been hailed as a great force for social stability. But a needlessly large population on the land has long retarded

---

The Challenge of Industrial Relations (Ithaca, New York: Cornell University Press, 1947); George W. Taylor, Government Regulation of Industrial Relations (New York: Prentice-Hall, Inc., 1948); Norman J. Ware, The Labor Movement in the United States, 1860–1895 (New York: Appleton-Century-Crofts, Inc., 1929).

agricultural development and failed to provide industry with either prosperous rural markets or an adequate labor force. A dubious social stability has been purchased by recurrent economic stagnation.

"We are in such fine equilibrium that we decline so gently that no one notices it," said an industrialist of the Nord. But Frenchmen have been complaining of a decline, not absolute, but relative to the real or fancied growth of other countries, for a century. Articulate workers have been talking of it at least since the London Exposition of 1862 and the Chicago Fair of 1893.

With some notable exceptions, French industry has set its sights relatively low. To the "force that does not hesitate at expense to acquire industrial supremacy," [6] it has preferred security of control within the firm and security against competition. By government protection, and by trade associations and cartels, it has shut out from abroad and from within France most of the liveliness of competition.

Smallness and slowness have been praised in the name of stability, in the name of quality, and in terms of the national character, to which one can always appeal in behalf of the *status quo*. We are "small folk but prudent," René P. Duchemin, the head of the National Confederation of French Production, comfortably assured his constituents in 1934. "France will always have a higher cost of production than its competitors," because of its moderation in the application of mass-production methods, "a moderation which is in the genius of the race." [7]

Nor have the banks made up for the lack of daring among industrialists. "We have no banks in France," suggested a banker. "We have only *caisses d'épargne*." While at home the banks "facilitated the contented and routine ways of French economic life," [8] they mobilized the savings of Frenchmen for placement abroad: there they sought financial safety, too, and political soundness — in such investments as the Trans-Siberian Railway.

Any industrial economy shows machinery ranging from the obsolete to the most modern, organization ranging from miserable to superb. In France business is geared to permit more of the inefficient to continue to exist. And it is the marginal firms which have frequently set the levels of prices and wages and the pace of social progress in "an old country," as

[6] The phrase is that of the porcelain decorators returning from the London Exposition of 1862. Dolléans, *Histoire du mouvement ouvrier*, II, 271–72.

[7] René P. Duchemin, *Organisation syndicale patronale en France* (Paris: Plon, 1940), pp. 172, 169. He saw this moderation saving France from the weight of the depression as compared with the United States, suffering more and saving itself only by "authoritarian methods."

[8] Herbert Feis, *Europe: The World's Banker* (New Haven: Yale University Press, 1930), p. 43.

the French National Employers Council called it, "where numerous enterprises have survived the historical reasons that created them." [9]

Typically, French business has produced restricted quantities of unstandardized articles at high margins of profit and high selling prices: "little deals but good ones," as one businessman said. This was enough for an aristocratic or a bourgeois market but hardly enough to build the domestic markets which might be a base for successful international competition. Moreover, this narrow and static concept of the market has contradicted the social implications of French political democracy. Neither as organizers of production nor as distributors of its output have French employers won the confidence of French workers. Therefore that "moderation of the race" which to M. Duchemin explained sluggish economic growth has not been apparent in working-class politics or unionism. [10]

"One of the peculiarities of our industry is that it is always about to die," sardonically observed a French glassworkers' leader in 1912. "Our employers are too routine minded, too flabby, to compete internationally. But they always use international competition as an excuse for conditions." [11]

French industry was perhaps producing more than most Frenchmen, including industrialists, said. The workers' leaders were echoing the self-denigration so articulate in the nation, and sometimes long after the criticism had been most deserved. But what counted as much as the trends of output and the actions of entrepreneurs were the popular images of industrial performance and entrepreneurial behavior.

In 1910 Victor Griffuelhes, the former secretary general of the General Confederation of Labor (the CGT or *Confédération Générale du Travail*), compared the capitalists of his own nation with those of other nations whose competition they bewailed. [12] In accents that many a productivity mission was to echo forty years later he concluded:

> Let them not din into our ears these cries of danger threatening us. Let them harness themselves in a practical way to the job of extending their influence and developing their trade; let them modify their methods of operation, their sales, and their payment of labor, and they will be able to register the terrific progress made, for example (I cite this because it is my own trade), by the shoe manufacturers of the United States.

[9] "Les causes de la disparité entre les prix français et les prix étrangers," *Bulletin du Conseil National du Patronat Français*, April 20, 1953.

[10] Temporarily moderation did make itself felt in the mid- and late 1920's, years of economic recovery and growth. The reformist CGT was then the dominant group among the minority of French workers who were organized.

[11] Charles Delzant, *Le Travail de l'enfance dans les verreries* (Paris: Temps Nouveaux, 1912), pp. 18, 3.

[12] Victor Griffuelhes, "L'Infériorité des capitalistes français," *Movement socialiste*, no. 226, December 1910, pp. 329–32.

"The development of class antagonism keeps even pace with the development of industry," said the *Communist Manifesto*.[13] Yet among the great industrial nations where people are free, the only two where most workers choose to be represented by the Communist party and Communist-controlled unions are France and Italy: the two in which capitalists have shown the least economic dynamism and in which economic development has lagged most. To complete one of the richest ironies of the history of Marxist prediction, the land of greatest capitalist development shows comparatively little class antagonism.

If history has made the United States proud, geography must make us humble — that geography which has twice blessed us, with the vast scale of a continent and its resources and with remoteness from all the explosions and plunder and most of the bloodletting of Europe's two modern wars. What is most relevant here — and what American unionism finally came to reflect — was the spirit of expansiveness in the economy and in the country's whole life, a faith in progress, a receptiveness to change. These qualities meant a vigor of production, a relative acceptance of the risks of competition — again one must ignore the exceptions — and a dynamic concept of the market which have made possible dramatic, though uneven, improvements in the levels of living. "On the reefs of roast beef and apple pie, socialistic utopias of every sort are sent to their doom," Sombart concluded.[14] More important than the day's apple pie, however, was the largeness and liveliness of American life, which gave workers confidence in the morrow's likelihood of improvement. True, the improvements were long distributed most inequitably and for years arrested or actually lost. But in general there remained a confidence in the ability of employers to perform their function that survived repeated business panics and even one panic so great it had to be called "the depression."

II

American unionism has had the inestimable advantage of being born in a land whose social landscape was not cluttered with the debris of a feudal age. It was easier for workers and their organizations to accept private property and industrial capitalism where economic inequity was not compounded by apparently hopeless social stratification. The Continental word "proletarian" has never had any popular currency in the United States. Work enjoyed respect; education was democratic by comparison with Europe; there was considerable openness of communication between workers and management in many shops. Even after the frontier's passing,

---

[13] Karl Marx, *The Communist Manifesto* (Chicago: Regnery, 1949), p. 43.
[14] Quoted by Daniel Bell, in Donald D. Egbert and Stow Persons, eds., *Socialism and American Life* (2 vols.; Princeton: Princeton University Press, 1952), I, 216.

people continued to move about the country. Geographic and social mobility reinforced each other.

Social distinctions in France have made economic inequality doubly galling. They were particularly irksome to the leaders of the unions' formative period — men who had mastered skilled trades and, often by their own efforts, much book knowledge. The heritages of a feudal society — but with its traditional aristocracy replaced by a small-minded bourgeoisie — have continued to burden social relations down to the present. In the national commission that in 1950 drew up a workingman's budget preliminary to setting a national minimum wage, some of the employers' comments on workers' needs seemed to echo from the caverns of time supposedly sealed off on the night of August 4, 1789.[15]

III

Finally, the political backgrounds. At the birth of the modern labor movement after the Commune, French workers could look back on a troubled century that, in the words of Tocqueville earlier, had "tried a little of everything without settling anything." [16] Workers had apparently done the manual labor of revolution only to be repeatedly cheated of its fruits by a wilier bourgeoisie. In subsequent years the Republic continued to live under threats, constantly and savagely denigrated from Right and from Left. The feeling that it was unjust and the impression that it was unstable fed upon each other. Revolution remained the opium of the people, always a seemingly practical possibility in a nation whose Emperor (Napoleon III) had once remarked, "We hardly care to make reforms, we only make revolutions." [17] Just as a second generation was beginning to forget the Commune, the Russian Revolution added its spell; in no country did the great twentieth-century myth make a deeper impression than in skeptical France.

In the United States, workers — like everybody else — always took the form of government as a given, immutable fact. Even when the power of the state, especially that of the courts, was used with glaring partiality against unions and against social legislation, the political remedy was seen in replacing men and tinkering with laws, not in overthrowing the Constitution. There was plenty of violence between unions and employers (and

[15] "Les Travaux de la commission supérieure des conventions collectives tendant à l'élaboration d'un budget-type," *Revue française du travail*, V (1950), 355–428; Claude Lapierre, "L'élaboration du budget-type et la fixation du salaire minimum garanti," *Droit social*, XIV (1951), 380–87; Val R. Lorwin, *The French Labor Movement*, pp. 220–21.

[16] Alexis de Tocqueville, *Oeuvres et correspondance inédites*, ed. Gustave de Beaumont (2 vols.; Paris: Michel Lévy, 1861), II, 70–71 (written in 1837).

[17] Georges Duveau, *Histoire du peuple français de 1848 à nos jours* (Paris: Nouvelle Librairie de France, 1953), p. 14.

between unions and unions). But that had nothing to do with revolution. Finally Franklin D. Roosevelt could say, "We have had our revolution without making it." No workers' movement would have made it.

IV

The American working class was long largely recruited by immigration. The labor movement has come of age, or of size, in the last twenty years, after the cut off of practically all European immigration; but the basic structure of the movement and its patterns of aspiration were already crystallized before. Immigrant workers, come from all the countries of the Old World, integrated themselves into the national life of the New World, which needed their labor (and other gifts they brought). Most were far from desiring to accentuate, by a doctrine of class struggle not native to America, the many differences that already set them off from the older groups dominant in the new country. The influence of the Catholic Church, to which so many immigrants belonged, also weighed powerfully against radicalism. A conformism to national ideals, to middle-class ideals, was the escape from the stigma of a class and ethnic ghetto to an identification with the nation, which was realized, if not by them, by their children or their grandchildren.

"I felt identified with the people of my new home," said Samuel Gompers, "and it was without a question that I accepted American customs and American institutions and the American life. To my mind the foreigner was the one who did not identify himself with American life and purposes." [18]

It is true that many immigrants, notably Germans and Jews, were socialists and for a time committed some of their unions to socialism.[19] But for all their passionate protest against social injustice,[20] they abandoned in the American environment millennial visions to organize practical improvement. "Their very habit of contemplating a great and radical

[18] Samuel Gompers, *Seventy Years of Life and Labor*, II, 151.

[19] See, for example, William Leiserson, *Adjusting Immigrant and Industry* (New York: Harper & Brothers, 1924); Egbert and Persons, *Socialism and American Life*, esp. essay by Daniel Bell; Selig Perlman, "Jewish-American Unionism, Its Birth Pangs and Contributions to the General American Labor Movement," and discussion by Henry T. David and Nathan Reich, *Publications of the American Jewish Historical Society* XLI (1952), 298–355; Jack Barbash, "Ethnic Factors in the Development of the American Labor Movement," in Industrial Relations Research Association, *Interpreting the Labor Movement*, pp. 70–82; and Abraham Menes, "The East Side: Matrix of the Jewish Labor Movement," in Theodore Friedman and Robert Gordis, eds., *Jewish Life in America* (New York: Horizon, 1955), pp. 131–54.

[20] For a vivid portrayal of abuses and protest, see the International Ladies' Garment Workers' Union film, *With These Hands* (1950).

change in the future made them see the possibility of change under what they called capitalism and the 'present order.' " [21]

The French working class was the product, first, of an internal migration of peasants and artisans. It was easier for it to affirm a class consciousness, for, despite the talk of "the two Frances" — the "working France" and the "parasitic" one — it felt itself indubitably French. The articulate French worker wished to complete the bourgeois revolution of 1789 by the social revolution. The immigrant worker in the United States wished to assimilate himself to the national ancestors who had made the American revolution of 1776.

In the last two generations the French working class has been replenished by an increased external immigration. Most of the immigrant workers have chosen the allegiance to class they have found among fellow workers rather than a dream of assimilation to the nation. The North Africans, however, have been mainly shut out from even this conformity.

V

The contrasts in behavior of the industrial elites of the two countries are responsible for much that is contrasting in the behavior of the labor movements. But cause and effect go hand in hand: workers' attitudes have helped shape employer behavior, too. French workers have had only the most modest expectations of amelioration. Modest immediate hopes have gone along with utopian dreams of apocalyptic change.

Workers everywhere have seen in technological change the menace of degradation of skills and loss of jobs. The French workers, however, have seen little else, so low has been their opinion of their employers, their society, and their own power. In the interest of immediate security of employment they have been willing to see marginal firms survive at the expense of wage scales and living standards. These attitudes have created little pressure on management for more effective performance of its functions. That unconventional French industrialist, Auguste Detoeuf, saw in Sweden, with its powerful trade-unions and vigorous employers, what was lacking in his own land. "The Swedish method," he wrote in 1938, "by pushing wages up to the maximum, obliges the industrialist to make the maximum effort, leaves him to face the normal insecurities of life, and thus assures his progress." [22]

Even before the American unions achieved mass organization, workers' expectations of relatively high wages were one of the forces moving management in the direction of increased efficiency and mechanization. "Improved Machinery Makes Men Dearer, Their Products Cheaper" was the poster which in 1903 surprised a London union leader visiting the Na-

[21] Lewis L. Lorwin, *The Women's Garment Workers* (New York: Huebsch, 1924), p. ix.
[22] Introduction to Paul Planus, *Patrons et ouvriers en Suède* (Paris: Plon, 1938), p. 8.

tional Cash Register plant at Dayton, Ohio.[23] The sign might have read, "Dearer Men Make for Improved Machinery."

Few of the American unions have themselves pushed for higher productivity, despite the illusions recently spread by some of the more exuberant Marshall Plan technical-assistance missions that have made "pilgrimages . . . to the inspired shores where productivity was revealed to man." [24] In general, technological change has been of management's making and the worker's taking. But the unions came to accept change as natural enough to make technological advances acceptable — advances that bitter experience taught them were inevitable — as long as the workers had some voice in their application in the shop and a share in the fruits. "Accept the machine — organize the workers," urged Samuel Gompers,[25] wise with his own union's utter failure in opposing cigar-making machinery. In the years of its weakness the A.F. of L. first opposed scientific management, then embraced it; [26] its opposition helped to humanize Taylorism.

Some unions vainly tried to arrest technical progress; some succeeded for a time. Others were able to control the pace of machinery installation to preserve members' jobs. The United Mine Workers, however, has made its most spectacular gains in pay and welfare benefits under conditions of increasing mechanization and shrinking employment in the last two decades. "We decided," said John L. Lewis, "that it is better to have half a million men working in the industry at good wages and high standards of living, than . . . a million working in the industry in poverty and degradation." [27] An affirmation of confidence in the union's power in the indus-

---

[23] *Mosely Industrial Commission, Reports of the Delegates* (London, 1903), p. 225, cited by Henry Pelling, "The American Economy and the Foundation of the British Labour Party," *Economic History Review*, 2d ser., VIII (1955), 13.

[24] The ironic language is that of F.-Louis Closon, director of the French Institut National de la Statistique et des Etudes Economiques, *Recensement général de la population . . . 1946, état civil et activité professionnelle . . .* (Paris: Imprimerie Nationale: 1949), p. v.

[25] Address at Cigar Makers' convention, 1923, *Cigar Makers' Official Journal*, September 1923, p. 718, reprinted in David J. Saposs, ed., *Readings in Trade Unionism* (New York: The Macmillan Company, 1927), pp. 285–88.

[26] Robert F. Hoxie, *Scientific Management and Labor* (New York: Appleton-Century-Crofts, Inc., 1915); Morris L. Cooke and Philip Murray, *Organized Labor and Production* (New York: Harper & Brothers, 1940); Sumner H. Slichter, *Union Policies and Industrial Management* (Washington: Brookings Institution, 1941); Jean T. McKelvey, *AF of L Attitudes toward Production, 1900–1932* (Ithaca, New York: Cornell University Press, 1952); Wililam Gomberg, *A Trade Union Analysis of Time Study* (2d ed., New York: Prentice-Hall, Inc., 1955), Chs. i and ii; and Milton J. Nadworny, *Scientific Management and the Unions, 1900–1932* (Cambridge, Massachusetts: Harvard University, 1955).

[27] Rex Lauck, ed., *John L. Lewis and the . . . United Mine Workers* (Washington, D.C.: UMW, 1952), p. 239. Actually both figures of employment were overstated by Mr. Lewis. Employment in all coal mines went down from a high of 785,000 in 1920 to 421,000 in 1952. *Statistical Abstract of the United States, 1954*, p. 752.

try, this was also an act of faith in economic expansion beyond the industry.

VI

The structure of unionism deeply marks its methods and its philosophy, even as it reflects its methods and philosophy. The French workers have, with a few interesting exceptions,[28] placed a low value on organization. Perhaps the weakness and decentralization of union structure are in part a reaction to the overorganization and overcentralization of the political state. At any rate, the French have achieved a combination of strong class consciousness and weak class organization in unions. They long professed to despise the stout treasuries of the British, German, and Belgian unions. But if a rich treasury might paralyze the will to action, as they correctly predicted, it did not follow that a poor or empty treasury facilitated the expression of that will.

Adequate dues, regularly paid, are an elementary but decisive form of union discipline. For fifty years the French have repeated the statement of the 1902 General Confederation of Labor, that by nature they are too impulsive and too rebellious (*"frondeur"*) to pay substantial union dues.[29] A "heroic period" cannot last forever. Unfortunately French labor has continued the habits of the "heroic period" of the youthful CGT and stressed solidarity rather than solidity of organization. Thus it has turned a source of occasional strength into a permanent weakness.

Weakness of union structure was cause as well as consequence of the philosophy of revolutionary syndicalism, France's most distinctive contribution to labor-union theory and practice. This weakness left the unions with little protection against the offensives of a strongly structured Communist party at the time of the Popular Front and again at the Liberation. In revenge, as it were, this weakness and indiscipline, which are part of the syndicalist heritage, have continued to plague the CGT under its present hard-boiled communist management.

In the labor vocabulary, the French word *"responsable"* is rich in connotation, far richer than the nearest American counterparts, "union officer" or "business agent." But "organizer," a key word in American union parlance and practice, has no French translation. Probably nearest to it is the old term *"propagandiste,"* which accents a verbal function.[30]

American unionists learned, after early failures, to place a high value on solidity of union organization. The solidity of A.F. of L. unions was

---

[28] Notably the printers, who in almost every country show a practice of solid union organization.

[29] Quoted by Maxime Leroy, *La coutume ouvrière*, I, 214.

[30] In the 1880's and 1890's Gompers spoke of what was later to be called field organizing as "lecturing." *Seventy Years of Life and Labor*, I, 327.

made possible by adequate dues, centralization of power in the union's national headquarters, a professional union leadership, and tangible job control and on-the-job benefits by collective agreement. For a long time of course, the unions possessing these attributes were to be found only among a small minority of wage earners: the skilled crafts, mostly in the building trades, the miners, and railroad men. But even the newer, more "idealistic" unions took a characteristically American attitude toward the importance of the organizational instrument.

American workers had to fight bloodier industrial battles than the French for the right of unions to exist and to function. Their political history knew nothing like the "June Days" or the Commune. But the rail strikes of 1877, the pitched battle of Homestead, the Ludlow massacre were bloodier than Fourmies and Draveil and Villeneuve-Saint-Georges. The 1919 steel strike was more brutally repressed than the French general strike of 1920. "Bloody Harlan" had no rival in the coal country of France. France had nothing like the private armies, factory arsenals, and industrial espionage services exposed by the La Follette Committee; nothing like South Chicago's "Memorial Day Massacre" as late as 1937.

In neither country could the obstacles to union organization be overcome without government aid. In both countries the change came in the mid-1930's. With the New Deal revolution in the nation's politics, the American unions seized their opportunity by launching great drives to "organize the unorganized." In two decades they lifted union membership from a mere 3,000,000 to a solid 17,000,000. The unionization drives were typical American combinations of administrative planning, salesmanship, and public relations, made possible by the financial support of some of the older unions, notably the garment workers and — chiefly — the miners.[31] Yet businesslike attributes alone were not enough; as an old organizer used to say, "You have to know the reason why; otherwise you make mistakes." The workers' desire and need for unionization showed themselves with as much spontaneity in American auto and rubber factories as in the French sit downs of the same era.

By contrast, French unionists have long called for "the unity of the working class." This has remained an appeal for an abstract goal, however, rather than an organizational effort. There has been endless debate about the relations of the competing union confederations of the minority already organized, but hardly any discussion of how to organize the majority outside the union fold. Even in these days a militant Catholic union feels obliged to preface an organizing appeal to its members: *"Union recruit-*

---

[31] An indication of the order of magnitude (if not the exact amount) of the miners' aid is given by John L. Lewis's bill to the CIO after his break with the organization. It amounted to $3,904,303 for services (organizers, clerks, attorneys, executives, etc.), plus cash loans of $1,685,000 from the CIO's founding to 1942. Saul Alinsky, *John L. Lewis* (New York: G. P. Putnam's Sons, 1949), p. 263.

ment: This barbarous word, it goes against the grain to use it. It seems more in place in the army. . . ." [32]

Constraint as well as choice helps keep American workers organized and paying their union dues. Constraint may take the form of the exclusive bargaining agency or majority rule,[33] the union hiring hall, the union shop, or even the closed shop.[34] (There is a deeper and far different compulsion when, as is sometimes the case, unions enjoying these rights are undemocratic or corrupt or both.) By and large not only workers but employers and the community accept the case for some compulsions. Because the unions are job oriented and not essentially political or religious in attachment, they can represent the interests of all the workers in a plant or office vis-à-vis management. Because industrial citizenship has not been encumbered with conflicting loyalties, it has been possible to sacrifice the rights of dissenters to effective collective bargaining.

In France, with unions of a political and religious cast, union pluralism has been almost inevitable. Exclusive representation by the majority union, in almost any place of employment, would violate the real scruples of a minority's political and religious beliefs.[35]

The Webbs believed that "the enforcement of membership" was "a universal aspiration of trade-unionism . . . on the same footing as the enforcement of citizenship." [36] In France, too, the closed shop has reared its head. CGT unions have long tried to enforce a closed shop when they felt strong enough, most notably in printing, and on the docks and in construction.[37] These are industries known in America for the closed shop.

VII

In the early years of this century the revolutionary CGT time and again debated the wisdom and the propriety of accepting government subsidies

[32] Fédération française des Syndicats du Bâtiment, etc., CFTC, *Bulletin: Vie fédérale*, August 14, 1956, p. 5.

[33] The principle of the exclusive bargaining agency is that, within any given unit of employment in which employers bargain with their employees, the union chosen by a majority of the employees concerned will represent all the employees. The scope of the bargaining unit may be anything from a single craft or shop or department within a plant to all the plants of a nationwide corporation, or a whole industry in one labor market or the nation.

[34] Although the Taft-Hartley Act bans closed shops, many continue with the assent of employers in the construction industry. The union shop and the closed shop were banned by seventeen states as of late 1956.

[35] Majority rule and the exclusive bargaining agency are not the only effective forms of collective bargaining. Pluralism is consistent with effective collective bargaining if there is sufficient consensus among the various unions on the performance of their essential functions.

[36] Sidney and Beatrice Webb, *The History of Trade Unionism* (rev. ed.; London: Longmans, Green & Co., Inc., 1920), p. 296.

[37] The closed shop was only recently specifically banned by a law of April 27, 1956. *Journal Officiel*, April 28, 1956.

for the *bourses du travail* — the local central labor bodies which were then so much of the heart of the movement. Since World War II, and even since the cold war, a communist-controlled CGT has accepted these and more substantial disguised subsidies without discussion.

Lacking firm economic organization in the face of employer hostility, French workers have made no social innovations through collective bargaining. Advance has come, by spurts, through political victories. The gains made general by legislation have minimized the incentives for workers to remain in unions once the surge of enthusiasm is over. Thus, despite their skepticism of government, the unions have remained dependent on its favor.

Not weighed down by inherited millennial ideas, the American unions have suffered less from the contrasts between portentous words and opportunistic action. "Voluntarism," the reliance on only what their economic action could get from employers, was a casualty of the depression. To be sure, union leaders hardly admitted how much government had come to determine the balance of power in labor relations, as well as the levels of workers' well-being. But, given the New Deal, they went forth and did the job of organizing the mass-production industries and creating the power with which to treat with employer power. They availed themselves of the aid of the state, whose intervention most of them used to deplore, to win initial recognition. But they did not lean on continued state support for their very existence and functioning as did the French unions. The latter, for all their affirmation of traditional independence, have come to function by grace of the state. They win recognition from the state, rather than directly from employers by the strength of employee support.[38]

American employers came to recognize the unions only under the multiple pressures of public opinion, administration policy, a reversal of Supreme Court interpretations, and — finally and essentially — worker self-organization. Theirs was one of the most rapid (although reluctant) and far-reaching adjustments to a new situation made by any elite in social history; and an adjustment which, it was soon clear, cost them neither profits nor power in society.

In France, over the same two decades, history twice refused to turn for more than a moment. The spontaneous revival of workers' hopes in 1936 almost submerged both the union apparatus and employer resist-

[38] Once recognized as "representative" nationally, a union enjoys rights of participation in economic life from the plant to the national levels. All three workers' confederations have had such recognition and therefore have exercised their rights for the past decade, even where they have had only skeletal organization and membership. On the complicated issue of "representativity," see Val R. Lorwin, *The French Labor Movement*, pp. 205–9.

The American union must at least organize sufficiently to win an election (see note 33, above) if its claims of representation are challenged by an employer, a rival union, or dissident constituents.

ance. But the favorable political climate clouded over in a single year; governmental labor policy changed drastically in two years; political dissension racked the new mass unions. After the catastrophic general strike of 1938 employer-union relations again became those of victor and vanquished, with the roles reversed and rancor on both sides. A similar sequence of events was repeated after the Liberation, except for a longer friendliness of government to labor. A revived employer movement, more powerful than ever before, has seen little incentive to work with unions weak and divided among themselves and in their major segment under communist direction, unable to offer cooperation or to match power in constructive relations.[39]

VIII

The General Confederation of Labor, which of all national union movements had been the most antipolitical and had fought off the advances of the moderate Socialist party before World War I, became, after World War II, the servant of the most exigent of political parties. The "apolitical" revolutionary syndicalists' refusal to concede the separate and legitimate reality of politics had prevented a division of labor and a mutual regard between unions and the Socialist party, such as developed in other advanced western-European countries. Their sweeping condemnation of all politics left the unionists unprepared later to discriminate appropriately between communism and the parties of the democratic Left.

While the syndicalists were attacking the French Socialist party in the name of a self-sufficient revolutionary unionism, the A.F. of L. leaders were fighting off the American Socialist party in the name of a prudent self-sufficient trade-unionism. (Incidentally, both the old CGT and the A.F. of L. belabored the hapless intellectual. The syndicalists declared him a reformist socialist climber; the A.F. of L. a meddling Marxist visionary.)

The A.F. of L. was not quite so romantic as to hold that labor-union action could be all-sufficing. Only some of the Industrial Workers of the World, inspired by the French CGT, took that view. The A.F. of L.'s nonpartisan doctrine of rewarding one's friends and defeating one's enemies could be flexible in the hands of flexible leaders. Since 1936 it has been stretched to cover sustained political organization, campaigning, and lobbying on a widened range of public business, unimagined in Gompers's time. Meanwhile, far below the surface of national politics, the local unions have long been engaged in less publicized and even less ideological business in state and local politics, usually working with the dominant

[39] Very recently innovations have been made by collective bargaining, for the first time in French history. See Val R. Lorwin, "Collective Bargaining in Post-War France," in the March 1957 *Annals of the American Academy of Political and Social Science*, ed. by John P. Windmuller; and almost any current issue of *Droit social*.

political machines to protect members' job interests as expressed in such practical determinants as licensing requirements for the skilled trades and police conduct in strikes.

The major American parties have had neither the temper nor the structure to control labor unions. They have sought to coalesce interest groups for periodic electoral victories, not to control mass organizations for the attainment of absolute power. The Communist party threat was for a few years real in the Congress of Industrial Organizations (CIO). Unlike the threat in France, it did not arise from revolutionary tradition or a separatist class consciousness or the party's spread through the whole country. It arose out of the key positions won by a number of assiduous and competent party liners who had thrown themselves into the organizing effort of the new CIO when it needed their talents and energies. Communist belief remained characteristic of a handful and not of the mass. The handful's importance, moreover, came from its effective performance in the conventional work of bread-and-butter unionism. Characteristically, organization was met by better organization — in many unions, although not all, with success for the anticommunist caucus. The CIO exorcized what remained of the threat when, in the light of worsening Soviet-American relations, Philip Murray shook off the long torpor of tolerance toward Communists in the organization.

IX

Early this century the French unions were taking a stand on all the problems of the universe, at the same time as the A.F. of L. unions developed "pure-and-simple" trade-unionism. Since the 1930's the French unions have taken on more concrete economic tasks, and the American unions have broadened the scope of their interests. But the contrasts have continued sharp. In part they spring from differences in the receptivity to general ideas. In the Latin atmosphere, the love of general ideas knows no social frontiers. More, the issues in French life have often seemed hardly susceptible to compromise. The same issues have resisted settlement generation after generation, partly because they have been faced in ideological terms, and because these ideological terms, on both Right and Left, have been so fixed. "It is too bad that, revolutionaries that we are, we are such traditionalists," recently remarked one of the most responsible free-labor leaders.[40] The unions have frightened employers by talk of workers' control of industry. Employers have repelled workers by reiterating old insistence on "authority" in the enterprise. A wage increase has seldom been demanded — and resisted — without appeal to universal principles and contending absolutes of social philosophy.

The views dominant in the American labor movement were often

[40] Robert Bothereau, Force Ouvrière, *2ᵉ Congrès Confédéral, 25–28 octobre 1950, Compte Rendu* . . . (Paris: Force Ouvrière, 1951), p. 123.

called "a philosophy of no philosophy." [41] But the A.F. of L. leaders had a view of society, even if they saw little need to state it because they were at one with their society. (They wanted employers to move over a bit and make room in that society for the unions, too, and they had their own economic outlook, one which later entered largely into American economic policy.) Pragmatic in a pragmatic society, struggling for existence in a business-minded and anti-intellectual atmosphere, the union leaders long made a virtue of their lack of what the French would call "ideological baggage." [42] They thought so little of their earlier "preamble radicalism" [43] that they did not bother to revise anachronistic radical preambles to their old constitutions.

"We have no ultimate ends," Adolph Strasser, Gompers's associate, told a Senate Committee seventy years ago.[44] The issues in American life seemed to yield to compromise, to technical solution, and to the power of organization. It was not only the friends of Gompers who took comfort from the absence of ultimate goals. Sidney Hillman, spokesman of the "New Unionism" and long a dissident outside the A.F. of L., told the 1920 convention of his Amalgamated Clothing Workers: "I have no ultimate program . . . In time of leisure — and that time is becoming more and more scarce — I indulge in dreams. But I don't permit them to become the policy of the organization." [45] And at the height of Hillman's New Deal fame a shrewd interviewer found that "abstract theories affect him like mist on the eyeglasses." [46]

Unions could be as militant for limited aims as a movement based on a doctrine of class struggle, American history showed; in a crisis workingmen could be idealistic without a proclaimed ideology of their own. American unions could the more effectively win a share of the once untouchable prerogatives of industrial ownership and management because they vowed respect — not, as in France, destruction — to private property.[47]

---

[41] For example, J. B. S. Hardman, in *American Labor Dynamics*, pp. 283–86.

[42] The term is also used by Reinhold Niebuhr, *The Irony of American History* (London: Nisbet, 1952), p. 86.

[43] The phrase is that of J. B. S. Hardman, *American Labor Dynamics*, p. 105.

[44] Strasser was the head of the Cigar Makers' International Union. The senator presiding over the committee generously reassured the witness: "I see that you are a little sensitive lest it should be thought that you are a mere theorizer. I do not look upon you in that light at all." John R. Commons and Associates, *History of Labor in the United States*, II, 309.

[45] Matthew Josephson, *Sidney Hillman* (Garden City, New York: Doubleday & Company, 1952), p. 208.

[46] Joseph Gollomb, "The Mystery of Sidney Hillman," *Jewish Digest*, February 1941, quoted in *Ibid.*, p. 439.

[47] In violation of property rights, American workers used sit-down strikes in 1936–1937 to gain union recognition. Since then they have dropped the sit down. The French unions look back with nostalgia to the 1936 sit downs, and still currently attempt sit-down strikes.

"Humanity is everywhere the same and everywhere different," as Emile Levasseur observed.[48] Labor movements have their common features, but each movement is *sui generis*.

The French unions have felt their society to be hostile and slow to change, the economy niggardly and uncertain. The American unions have seen an economy of plenty and swift change, a society offering greater rewards for work and greater equality. The French have confronted "the social problem"; the Americans have attacked specific immediate problems. French workers have seen opposite them an employer class; the Americans, an employer or employers. The French unions have set out to emancipate a class from wage bondage; the American unions to strike better bargains for their members. For the French the strike has been an episode in the class struggle, the collective agreement a truce in that struggle. For the Americans, the strike has been a test of economic strength, and the collective agreement an end in itself, although decidedly to be improved upon next time.

The Americans, forgetting past exploitation and eschewing long looks into the future, have come to see themselves as the beneficiaries of a uniquely fortunate history; French unionists, looking back, have found themselves the victims of history. The optimism of the American unions since they have been recognized by the state and by employers has helped them bolster, while modifying, the capitalist system and the polity of which they have become an integral part. The pessimism of the French unions has led them to ineffectual industrial representation, to extremist politics, and to defeats that have confirmed that pessimism. . . .

[48] Emile Levasseur, *The American Workman*, trans. by T. S. Adams (Baltimore: Johns Hopkins, 1900), p. 405.

American Productivity: Causes and Effects

J. FREDERIC DEWHURST

A *high rate of productivity is perhaps the key factor in American economic development and change. J. Frederic Dewhurst, an economist and former director of the Twentieth Century Fund, explores the sources and meaning of that fact in the following essay. While the United States is rich in natural resources and possesses abundant fertile lands, these are not, Dewhurst argues, the controlling factors for the high level of productivity. Natural wealth was present a century ago, yet productivity is substantially higher today. In other countries, too, there is not necessarily a correlation between natural wealth and productivity. Dewhurst finds the peculiar American success "in the dynamic character of American technology, centering in the application of inanimate energy and mechanical methods in all phases of American industry." Ours is, he notes, a "high energy civilization," where fewer workers make use of more machines and equipment than anywhere else. A veritable revolution in the application of technology has led to vast changes in output and consumption of goods and services in the last hundred years. In turn, the American people enjoy a standard of living that is taken for granted, yet remains "beyond the comprehension of the vast majority of the world's people." A decade after the publication of this study, however, the American people are at last moving away from self-congratulation to a realization that millions of Americans had no share in that material well-being. In the midst of mass prosperity, there has developed an awareness of the problems and, most importantly, of the very existence, of poverty.*

Nearly all Americans, as well as most informed foreigners, agree that the United States is the "richest country in the world," but there is no consensus as to whether this is due to American genius or to American good

Reprinted by permission of the American Philosophical Society from *Proceedings of the American Philosophical Society*, C (October 1956), pp. 435–438.

fortune. Whatever the reasons, it is unquestionably true that the productivity of the American economy, and the standard of living this productivity makes possible, are higher today than ever before, and far above the highest level any other country has ever been able to achieve. With less than 7 per cent of the world's land area and little more than 6 per cent of the world's population and manpower, we produce and consume in the United States more than one-third of the world's entire output of goods and services. In factory goods alone our proportion is much higher — close to one-half of the world total — and measured by national income, the American proportion is not far from 40 per cent.[1]

Thus the typical American enjoys a standard of living some six times higher than the average of the two and one-half billion people of the world, and of course many times that of the hundreds of millions who keep the world average as low as it is. The aggregate income of the 167 million Americans today probably exceeds the combined income of the six hundred million people living in Europe and Russia, and far surpasses the total income of the more than one billion inhabitants of Asia.[2]

However, income estimates for the subsistence economies of Asia are notoriously unreliable, and comparing their meager incomes with those of an advanced industrial nation may somewhat overstate real differences in well-being. Comparisons of American standards with other urban-industrial countries are more significant, and, even here, disparities are striking. Only in Canada, Australia, New Zealand, Switzerland, Sweden, Denmark, and the United Kingdom did per capita income a few years after World War II rise to as high as 60 per cent of the American average. Even in relatively advanced European countries, such as France and Italy, and in the most advanced South American countries, average income is considerably less than half what it is in the United States. In the less developed countries of Europe, such as Greece and Spain, the average is, of course, much lower.[3]

International comparisons of national income and of wages and salaries, expressed in monetary units, are never precise measures of real differences in welfare, because of difficulties in translating one currency into another and of differences from one country to another in the way people live and in the taxes they pay. Such difficulties can be partially avoided by comparing the buying power of wages for various commodities and articles of common consumption in all countries. Many such comparisons have been made, but only two can be cited.

In 1950 our Department of Labor made a careful study of the working

---

[1] Dewhurst, J. Frederic, and others, *America's Needs and Resources: A New Survey* (New York: Twentieth Century Fund, 1955), 892.

[2] *Ibid.*, 892.

[3] *Ibid.*, 892.

time required in the United States and in nineteen other countries to earn enough to buy one pound each of eight staple foodstuffs (such as flour, butter, cheese, potatoes, etc.). The results showed American workers not only far ahead of those in other countries, but in a relatively better position than before World War II. The American worker had to put in ninety-eight minutes, or a little more than one hour and a half, to earn enough to buy this eight-pound basket of food. This compared with an average of about six hours for the other nineteen countries, and more than fourteen hours for a worker in the Soviet Union. Even in Australia, which compared most favorably with the United States, more than two hours' work was required.[4]

Another postwar study made by the French economist, Jean Fourastié, shows the purchasing power of the wages paid common labor in the United States far ahead of that in twenty-eight other countries, not only for foods but for a wide range of other goods and services. About the only exception, significantly enough, was for personal services, such as haircuts and maid service, which are little affected by mechanization and in which presumably labor productivity is much the same all over the world. The cost of a man's haircut, for example, was identical in the United States, Italy, Switzerland, and Uruguay — the equivalent of one hour's earnings for common labor. But the purchase of a pair of shoes, which was more or less typical of other factory-made articles, required four hours' work in the United States, but cost from three to eight times as much in the other three countries.[5] It appears that efficient factory methods, rather than manual skill or "labor efficiency," are the predominant causes of high productivity, low prices, and a high standard of living.

These comparisons of wage-purchasing power are only indirect measures of labor productivity, but what they show is fully confirmed by other studies of output per worker and per man-hour in different industries. All of these studies make it clear that productivity and purchasing power are much higher in the United States than anywhere else in the world. The advantage enjoyed by the average American, both in what he produces and in what he can buy with his earnings, varies from some 50 or 60 per cent in the case of a few advanced countries to several hundred per cent for the relatively underdeveloped countries of Europe, and much more for many other parts of the world, where industrial and agricultural methods are so primitive and living conditions so wretched as to defy comparison with our own. Because he is able to produce so much, the typical American today takes for granted a level of material well-being beyond the comprehension of the vast majority of the world's people. Too often our high standard of living is symbolized in terms of automobiles, electric refrigera-

---

[4] *Ibid.*, 896.
[5] *Ibid.*, 897.

tors and television sets — which overlooks the fact that such American necessities as window screens, paved streets and pure water and milk are luxuries unknown to most of the rest of the world.

And, of course, the present-day American lives on a much higher material level than his parents did a generation ago, and is vastly better off than his grandparents of the nineteenth century. Average per capita national income last year was over $1,900 — which was more than a fourfold increase over 1850, when per capita income in money of today's purchasing power was about $450.

Because this great advance in material welfare accompanied a steady decline in working hours, it reflects even larger gains in hourly productivity. The 1850 worker, working long hours, turned out in each hour of work about thirty-eight cents' worth of goods — in terms of what money will buy today. By 1900 productivity had more than doubled, to eighty-four cents per man-hour, while the period since the turn of the century has brought an even larger increase — to nearly $2.50 per man-hour last year.[6] Today's worker puts in a forty-hour week, and his family enjoys a standard of living beyond the imagination of his grandparents because he can produce as much in ten minutes as his 1850 ancestors could in an hour.

Thus, labor productivity in the United States today is not only about six times the present world average, but approximately six times what it was in our own country a century ago. And there is no reason — barring the devastation of atomic war — to believe that gains in productivity and advances in the standard of living will be any less rapid in the foreseeable future than they have been in the past. There is some evidence, in fact, that technological progress is causing productivity to increase at an accelerating rate. But even the average gain in output per man-hour during the past century would give startling results if long continued. With this rate of gain for another century, we would be able to produce as much in one seven-hour day as we produce today in a forty-hour week. If this should happen, however, it seems reasonable to assume that our descendants will not be satisfied with what they can produce by working one day a week, nor will they have enough time left over to consume all they can produce by working a forty-hour week.

On the contrary, if this upward trend in our ability to produce continues, we shall continue to take part of our potential gain in the form of shorter working hours and more leisure, as we have in the past. A century ago the work-week averaged close to seventy hours and the Sabbath was in fact, as well as name, a day of rest. By 1900 we were still working a ten-hour day and a six-day week. After World War I, the work-week dropped

[6] *Ibid.*, 902; calculated for 1955 on same basis.

to forty-eight hours, but Saturday was still a work-day for most people. Only after World War II came the five-day, forty-hour work-week. These changes, together with the spread of paid vacations, have more than doubled the amount of leisure time for the average worker since the turn of the century.

During the past half-century, a little less than two-thirds of the potential increase resulting from advancing productivity has been represented by additional goods actually produced, and a little more than one-third by shorter working time and more leisure. If these proportions prevail in the near future, we can expect by 1975, if not before, not only a much higher per capita income for a larger population than at present, but a four-day work-week and a three-day weekend.

The ultimate reasons for the rapid progress and economic superiority of the United States are many and complex, and there is no complete agreement even on the immediate causes. Many foreign observers unhesitatingly attribute our higher level of productivity and well-being to an abundance of fertile land and natural resources. These are clearly significant, especially in the case of fuel and energy materials, but it is doubtful whether they are of controlling importance. After all, the United States possessed greater resources a century ago, but our productivity is vastly higher today. If natural wealth were the principal source of productivity and prosperity, it would be hard to explain how Switzerland, with meager resources, has been able to achieve a high standard of living; or why Rumania, with large oil reserves, makes little use of automotive power; or why the steam engine is a rarity in China in spite of her extensive coal deposits. On the basis of natural resources alone one would expect Bulgaria to have a higher standard of living than Denmark, Poland to be more prosperous than Holland, and Yugoslavia to be more productive than Sweden, whereas the opposite is true in each case. For that matter, Russia has a land area twice as large as ours and certainly rivals the United States in its reserves of minerals and other resources. Yet Russia until recently failed to exploit her natural wealth, and even after three decades of intensive industrialization remains a country with low productivity and a low standard of living.

The fact that we produce so much of the world's goods with such a small share of the world's manpower finds its immediate cause not so much in abundant land and resources as in the dynamic character of American technology, centering in the application of inanimate energy and mechanical methods in all phases of American industry. It is no accident that American leadership in labor productivity and in per capita income is roughly paralleled by our heavy consumption of coal, oil, and other forms of inanimate energy. Annual consumption of mineral energy in the United States is higher than in any other country — equivalent to about eight tons of coal per capita, compared with about two tons per capita in such countries as France, Netherlands, and Poland, where average income is from one-third to one-half what it is in the United States, and less than one-fifth of a ton in such poverty-stricken countries as Egypt, India, Pakistan, and Burma. Such statistical evidence merely confirms common observation that ours is a "high energy civilization," where the worker has the use of far more numerous and powerful power-driven tools and equipment — not to mention more light and heat — than his colleagues in other parts of the world or than his own predecessors.

For we have not always been a high energy civilization. In 1850 the total rated capacity of all the steam engines and other prime movers used to supplement the work performed by human beings in mining, manufacturing, transportation, and communication in the United States was 2.5 million horsepower — less than half as much as the 6 million muscular horsepower provided by horses, mules, and other work animals. By 1900 the total of mechanical horsepower had increased to 46 million, and by 1952 to 360 million, while nearly all the work animals have long since succumbed to technological unemployment. Mineral, or "mechanical," energy accounted for less than one-third of all the physical work done in the United States a century ago, for more than two-thirds in 1900, and for nearly 99 per cent today. The work done by the muscle power of animals and men dropped from two-thirds of the total in 1850 to little more than 1 per cent today.[7]

These vast changes help to explain how we have been able in a century to multiply our net output — as well as our consumption — of goods and services about thirty times, with less than a ninefold increase in the labor force and about five times as large an input of human effort, as measured by total man-hours worked. In other words, one man with today's power-driven equipment and other mechanical and chemical aids can produce as much in a forty-hour week as three men working seventy hours a week with the primitive tools of a century ago.

Of course our technology is not limited to the substitution of mechanical power for muscle power. Specialization of tasks and division of labor appear to be carried much further in American industry than in other countries. The efficiencies of mass production would not be possible without a mass market, which in turn is supported by consumer acceptance of standardized products. This simplification and standardization of products designed for a continental market would account for higher productivity in American establishments, against foreign enterprises using identical equipment in supplying their smaller national markets and their much smaller class markets.

It is easy to see how a dynamic technology, lavish capital investment, and the development of mass markets help to account for high and rising productivity. It is more difficult to understand why American progress has

[7] *Ibid.*, 912.

been so much more rapid than that of even the largest and most favored industrial nations. In part, this rapid progress is due to geographic and demographic factors — to the fact that most of our history has been characterized by a plenitude of fertile land and a chronic scarcity of labor. Denied an abundance of muscle power, American industry and agriculture have applied labor-saving methods and machinery on a scale never equaled in any other country.

Perhaps more important, however, are the human and institutional influences that help to account for the technological factors. One of these, of which foreign visitors are immediately aware, is the more receptive attitude of American industrial management, shared by American workers and consumers, toward experimentation and change, toward the substitution of new products and methods for old ones, toward progress and expansion, even at the risk of disappointment or loss. European observers — though not always American economists — are quick to attribute American dynamism to what the English economist Graham Hutton describes as "the much greater degree of competitiveness in American business" which, he concludes, "leads to a much higher average of productive efficiency, through a much higher degree of managerial competence." [8] One of the French teams brought to the United States under the ECA program observed that a "truly competitive state of mind" made American businessmen "more ready to seek ways of lowering . . . costs, and less ready to seek ways of restricting competition." [9] One of the most thoughtful English journals, *The Economist*, concludes that "The real secret of American productivity is that American society is imbued through and through with the desirability, the rightness, the morality of production." [10]

If, in truth, capitalism in America is more individualistic, competitive and dynamic than elsewhere, the explanation, as in the case of other human institutions, may be found in the people who created it. America was settled by people of every European strain. No other nation has ever been created in so short a time from the intermingling and fusion of so many racial strains and national cultures. Whether it is true, as one geneticist suggests, that this mixture of stocks is producing the same heterosis or "hybrid vigor" that results from crossing different strains of agricultural plants and animals, the character and diversity of immigration have undoubtedly contributed to American cultural and technological vigor.

Even though the heavy immigration from Europe was free and unrestricted, the immigrants were in fact a highly selected group. Since they came on their own initiative, they were self-selected on a basis that en-

---

[8] Hutton, Graham, *We Too Can Prosper* (London: George Allen & Unwin, Ltd., 1953), 98.

[9] Productivity, source of well-being, 11, The French Association for the Improvement of Productivity, 41 Quai Branly, Paris, France.

[10] "The Riddle of Prosperity," *The Economist*, 80 (July 11, 1953).

sured a larger-than-average proportion of risk-takers, of non-conformists and innovators, of those dissatisfied with things as they were and anxious to welcome change if it promised improvement. Coming to the United States, as they did, from varied backgrounds, they brought with them many different occupational skills and a knowledge of various industrial techniques. Interchange of ideas in a highly favorable environment and within a fluid society that had not acquired fixed industrial traditions helped to create an inventive and dynamic technology. Whether the Americans are hybrids or not, Yankee ingenuity is a hybrid product.

Crime as an American Way of Life

DANIEL BELL

Despite intense, periodic efforts by "reformers," crime has per-sisted as a way of life in the United States. No other country has focused as much attention and condemnation upon crime, yet nowhere else has there been such glaring failure to control it. In the following essay, Columbia sociologist Daniel Bell abandons a simple "good versus bad guys" description of crime in the United States to view it, historically and so-ciologically, as a "Coney Island mirror, caricaturing the morals and manners" of American society. He finds a functional role for crime as an institution, a role that has been under-stood inadequately. Gambling, for example, is big business and plays an important part in our mass consumption econ-omy. Organized crime also has served as a means of upward mobility for immigrant groups excluded from "normal" routes to success. Finally, organized criminal elements have had a special relation, particularly in financing, to the urban political machines. In sum, Bell sees crime as a caricatured, or "queer" ladder of social ascent. If official pronouncements are valid, then time has not justified Bell's conclusion that organized crime, as traditionally understood and as he described it, was passing away. Congressional committees, presidential commis-sions, the Justice Department, and the head of the Federal Bureau of Investigation regularly point to the growing power of organized criminal elements and the existence of a gigantic criminal conspiracy in this country. Yet the lack of proof and inaction by the government seem to lend substance to Bell's contention that we have substituted the myth of an omnipotent Mafia for a real understanding of the social significance of crime.

In the 1890's, the Reverend Dr. Charles Parkhurst, shocked at the open police protection afforded New York's bordellos, demanded a state inquiry. In the Lexow investigation that followed, the young and dashing William Travers Jerome staged a set of public hearings that created sensation after sensation. He badgered "Clubber" Williams, First Inspector of the Police Department, to account for wealth and property far greater than could have been saved on his salary; it was earned, the Clubber explained laconically, through land speculation "in Japan." Heavy-set Captain Schmittberger, the "collector" for the "Tenderloin precincts" — Broadway's fabulous concentration of hotels, theaters, restaurants, gaming houses, and saloons — related in detail how protection money was distributed among the police force. Crooks, policemen, public officials, businessmen, all paraded across the stage, each adding his chapter to a sordid story of corruption and crime. The upshot of these revelations was reform — the election of William L. Strong, a stalwart businessman, as mayor, and the naming of Theodore Roosevelt as police commissioner.

It did not last, of course, just as previous reform victories had not lasted. Yet the ritual drama was re-enacted. Twenty years ago the Seabury investigation in New York uncovered the tin-box brigade and the thirty-three little MacQuades. Jimmy Walker was ousted as Mayor and in came Fiorello La Guardia. Tom Dewey became district attorney, broke the industrial rackets, sent Lucky Luciano to jail and went to the Governor's chair in Albany. Then reform was again swallowed up in the insatiable maw of corruption until Kefauver and the young and dashing Rudolph Halley threw a new beam of light into the seemingly bottomless pit.

How explain this repetitive cycle? Obviously the simple moralistic distinction between "good guys" and "bad guys," so deep at the root of the reform impulse, bears little relation to the role of organized crime in American society. What, then, does?

II

Americans have had an extraordinary talent for compromise in politics and extremism in morality. The most shameless political deals (and "steals") have been rationalized as expedient and realistically necessary. Yet in no

Reprinted by permission of the author from the *Antioch Review*, XIII (June 1953), pp. 131–154.

other country have there been such spectacular attempts to curb human appetites and brand them as illicit, and nowhere else such glaring failures. From the start America was at one and the same time a frontier community where "everything goes," and the fair country of the Blue Laws. At the turn of the century the cleavage developed between the Big City and the small-town conscience. Crime as a growing business was fed by the revenues from prostitution, liquor and gambling that a wide-open urban society encouraged and which a middle-class Protestant ethos tried to suppress with a ferocity unmatched in any other civilized country. Catholic cultures rarely have imposed such restrictions, and have rarely suffered such excesses. Even in prim and proper Anglican England, prostitution is a commonplace of Piccadilly night life, and gambling one of the largest and most popular industries. In America the enforcement of public morals has been a continuing feature of our history.

Some truth may lie in Svend Ranulf's generalization that moral indignation is a peculiar fact of middle-class psychology and represents a disguised form of repressed envy. The larger truth lies perhaps in the brawling nature of American development and the social character of crime. Crime, in many ways, is a Coney Island mirror, caricaturing the morals and manners of a society. The jungle quality of the American business community, particularly at the turn of the century, was reflected in the mode of "business" practiced by the coarse gangster elements, most of them from new immigrant families, who were "getting ahead," just as Horatio Alger had urged. In the older, Protestant tradition the intense acquisitiveness, such as that of Daniel Drew, was rationalized by a compulsive moral fervor. But the formal obeisance of the ruthless businessman in the workaday world to the church-going pieties of the Sabbath was one that the gangster could not make. Moreover, for the young criminal, hunting in the asphalt jungle of the crowded city, it was not the businessman with his wily manipulation of numbers but the "man with the gun" who was the American hero. "No amount of commercial prosperity," once wrote Teddy Roosevelt, "can supply the lack of the heroic virtues." The American was "the hunter, cowboy, frontiersman, the soldier, the naval hero." And in the crowded slums, the gangster. He was a man with a gun, acquiring by personal merit what was denied to him by complex orderings of a stratified society. And the duel with the law was the morality play *par excellence*: the gangster, with whom ride our own illicit desires, and the prosecutor, representing final judgment and the force of the law.

Yet all this was acted out in a wider context. The desires satisfied in extra-legal fashion were more than a hunger for the "forbidden fruits" of conventional morality. They also involved, in the complex and ever shifting structure of group, class and ethnic stratification, which is the warp and woof of America's "open" society, such "normal" goals as independence through a business of one's own, and such "moral" aspirations as the desire for social advancement and social prestige. For crime, in the language of the sociologists, has a "functional" role in the society, and the urban rackets — the illicit activity organized for continuing profit rather than individual illegal acts — is one of the queer ladders of social mobility in American life. Indeed, it is not too much to say that the whole question of organized crime in America cannot be understood unless one appreciates (1) the distinctive role of organized gambling as a function of a mass consumption economy; (2) the specific role of various immigrant groups as they one after another became involved in marginal business and crime; and (3) the relation of crime to the changing character of the urban political machines.

III

As a society changes, so does, in lagging fashion, its type of crime. As American society became more "organized," as the American businessman became more "civilized" and less "buccaneering," so did the American racketeer. And just as there were important changes in the structure of business enterprise, so the "institutionalized" criminal enterprise was transformed too.

In the America of the last fifty years the main drift of society has been toward the rationalization of industry, the domestication of the crude self-made captain of industry into the respectable man of manners, and the emergence of a mass-consumption economy. The most significant transformation in the field of "institutionalized" crime was the increasing relative importance of gambling as against other kinds of illegal activity. And, as a multi-billion-dollar business, gambling underwent a transition parallel to the changes in American enterprise as a whole. This parallel was exemplified in many ways: in gambling's industrial organization (e.g., the growth of a complex technology such as the national racing wire service and the minimization of risks by such techniques as lay-off betting); in its respectability, as was evidenced in the opening of smart and popular gambling casinos in resort towns and in "satellite" adjuncts to metropolitan areas; in its functional role in a mass-consumption economy (for sheer volume of money changing hands, nothing has ever surpassed this feverish activity of fifty million American adults); in the social acceptance of the gamblers in the important status world of sport and entertainment, i.e., "café society."

In seeking to "legitimize" itself, gambling had quite often actually become a force against older and more vicious forms of illegal activity. In 1946, for example, when a Chicago mobster, Pat Manno, went down to Dallas, Texas, to take over gambling in the area for the Accardo-Guzik combine, he reassured the sheriff as to his intent as follows: "Something I'm against, that's dope peddlers, pickpockets, hired killers. That's one thing I can't stomach, and that's one thing the fellows up there — the group won't stand for, things like that. They discourage it, they even go to headquarters and ask them why they don't do something about it."

Jimmy Cannon once reported that when the gambling raids started in Chicago, the "combine" protested that, in upsetting existing stable relations, the police were only opening the way for ambitious young punks and hoodlums to start trouble. Nor is there today, as there was twenty or even forty years ago, prostitution of major organized scope in the United States. Aside from the fact that manners and morals have changed, prostitution *as an industry* doesn't pay as well as gambling. Besides, its existence threatened the tacit moral acceptance and quasi-respectability that gamblers and gambling have secured in the American way of life. It was, as any operator in the field might tell you, "bad for business."

The criminal world of the last decade, its tone set by the captains of the gambling industry, is in startling contrast to the state of affairs in the two decades before. If a Kefauver report had been written then, the main "names" would have been Lepke and Gurrah, Dutch Schultz, Jack "Legs" Diamond, Lucky Luciano, and, reaching back a little further, Arnold Rothstein, the czar of the underworld. These men (with the exception of Luciano, who was involved in narcotics and prostitution) were in the main industrial racketeers. Rothstein, it is true, had a larger function: he was, as Frank Costello became later, the financier of the underworld — the pioneer big businessman of crime, who, understanding the logic of co-ordination, sought to *organize* crime as a source of regular income. His main interest in this direction was in industrial racketeering, and his entry was through labor disputes. At one time, employers in the garment trades hired Legs Diamond and his sluggers to break strikes, and the Communists, then in control of the cloakmakers union, hired one Little Orgie to protect the pickets and beat up the scabs; only later did both sides learn that Legs Diamond and Little Orgie were working for the same man, Rothstein.

Rothstein's chief successors, Lepke Buchalter and Gurrah Shapiro, were able, in the early '30's, to dominate sections of the men's and women's clothing industries, of painting, fur dressing, flour trucking, and other fields. In a highly chaotic and cut-throat industry such as clothing, the racketeer, paradoxically, played a stabilizing role by regulating competition and fixing prices. When the NRA came in and assumed this function, the businessman found that what had once been a quasi-economic service was now pure extortion, and he began to demand police action. In other types of racketeering, such as the trucking of perishable foods and water-front loading, where the racketeers entrenched themselves as middlemen — taking up, by default, a service that neither shippers nor truckers wanted to assume — a pattern of accommodation was roughly worked out and the rackets assumed a quasi-legal veneer. On the water-front, old-time racketeers perform the necessary function of loading — but at an exorbitant

price, and this monopoly was recognized by both the union and the shippers, and tacitly by government. (See my case study "The Last of the
Business Rackets," in the June, 1951 issue of *Fortune*.)

But in the last decade and a half, industrial racketeering has not offered
much in the way of opportunity. *Like American capitalism itself, crime
shifted its emphasis from production to consumption.* The focus of crime
became the direct exploitation of the citizen as consumer, largely through
gambling. And while the protection of these huge revenues was in-
extricably linked to politics, the relation between gambling and "the
mobs" became more complicated.

IV

Although it never showed up in the gross national product, gambling in
the last decade was one of the largest industries in the United States. The
Kefauver Committee estimated it as a twenty-billion-dollar business. This
figure has been picked up and widely quoted, but in truth no one knows
what the gambling "turnover" and "take" actually is, nor how much is
bet legally (pari-mutuel, etc.) and how much illegally. In fact, the figure
cited by the committee was arbitrary and arrived at quite sloppily. As one
staff member said: "We had no real idea of the money spent. . . . The
California crime commission said twelve billion. Virgil Peterson of Chicago estimated thirty billion. We picked twenty billion as a balance between the two."

If comprehensive data are not available, we do know, from specific instances, the magnitude of many of the operations. Some indications can
be seen from these items culled at random:

— James Carroll and the M & G syndicate did a 20-million-dollar annual business in St. Louis. This was one of the two large books in the city.

— The S & G syndicate in Miami did a 26-million-dollar volume yearly;
the total for all books in the Florida resort reached 40 millions.

— Slot machines were present in 69,786 establishments in 1951 (each
paid $100 for a license to the Bureau of Internal Revenue); the usual
average is three machines to a license, which would add up to 210,000
slot machines in operation in the United States. In legalized areas, where
the betting is higher and more regular, the average gross "take" per machine is $50 a week.

— The largest policy wheel (i.e., "numbers") in Chicago's "Black
Belt" reported taxable net profits for the four-year period from 1946
through 1949, after sizable deductions for "overhead," of $3,656,968.
One of the large "white" wheels reported in 1947 a gross income of
$2,317,000 and a net profit of $205,000. One CIO official estimated that
perhaps 15 per cent of his union's lower echelon officials are involved in
the numbers racket (a steward, free to roam a plant, is in a perfect situation for organizing bets).

If one considers the amount of betting on sports alone — an estimated six billion on baseball, a billion on football pools, another billion on basketball, six billion on horse racing — then Elmo Roper's judgment that "only the food, steel, auto, chemical, and machine-tool industries have a greater volume of business" does not seem too farfetched.

While gambling has long flourished in the United States, the influx of the big mobsters into the industry — and its expansion — started in the '30's when repeal of Prohibition forced them to look about for new avenues of enterprise. Gambling, which had begun to flower under the nourishment of rising incomes, was the most lucrative field in sight. To a large extent the shift from bootlegging to gambling was a mere transfer of business operations. In the East, Frank Costello went into slot machines and the operation of a number of ritzy gambling casinos. He also became the "banker" for the Erickson "book," which "laid off" bets for other bookies. Joe Adonis, similarly, opened up a number of casinos, principally in New Jersey. Across the country, many other mobsters went into bookmaking. As other rackets diminished, and gambling, particularly horse-race betting, flourished in the '40's, a struggle erupted over the control of racing information.

Horse-race betting requires a peculiar industrial organization. The essential component is time. A bookie can operate only if he can get information on odds up to the very last minute before the race, so that he can "hedge" or "lay off" bets. With racing going on simultaneously on many tracks throughout the country, this information has to be obtained speedily and accurately. Thus, the racing wire is the nerve ganglion of race betting.

The racing-wire news service got started in the '20's through the genius of the late Moe Annenberg, who had made a fearful reputation for himself as Hearst's circulation manager in the rough-and-tumble Chicago newspaper wars. Annenberg conceived the idea of a telegraphic news service which would gather information from tracks and shoot it immediately to scratch sheets, horse parlors, and bookie joints. In some instances, track owners gave Annenberg the rights to send news from tracks; more often, the news was simply "stolen" by crews operating inside or near the tracks. So efficient did this news distribution system become, that in 1942, when a plane knocked out a vital telegraph circuit which served an Air Force field as well as the gamblers, the Continental Press managed to gets its racing wire service for gamblers resumed in fifteen minutes, while it took the Fourth Army, which was responsible for the defense of the entire West Coast, something like three hours.

Annenberg built up a nationwide racing information chain that not only distributed wire news but controlled sub-outlets as well. In 1939, harassed by the Internal Revenue Bureau on income tax, and chivvied by the Justice Department for "monopolistic" control of the wire service, the tired and aging Annenberg simply walked out of the business. He did not sell his interest, or even seek to salvage some profit; he simply gave up. Yet, like any established and thriving institution, the enterprise continued, though on a decentralized basis. James Ragen, Annenberg's operations manager, and likewise a veteran of the old Chicago circulation wars, took over the national wire service through a dummy friend and renamed it the Continental Press Service.

The salient fact is that in the operation of the Annenberg and Ragen wire service, formally illegal as many of its subsidiary operations may have been (i.e., in "stealing" news, supplying information to bookies, etc.) gangsters played no part. It was a business, illicit, true, but primarily a business. The distinction between gamblers and gangsters, as we shall see, is a relevant one.

In 1946, the Chicago mob, whose main interest was in bookmaking rather than gambling casinos, began to move in on the wire monopoly. Following repeal, the Capone lieutenants had turned, like Lepke, to labor racketeering. Murray ("The Camel") Humphries muscled in on the teamsters, the operating engineers, and the cleaning-and-dyeing, laundry, and linen-supply industries. Through a small-time punk, Willie Bioff, and union official George Browne, Capone's chief successors, Frank ("The Enforcer") Nitti and Paul Ricca, came into control of the motion-picture union and proceeded to shake down the movie industry for fabulous sums in order to "avert strikes." In 1943, when the government moved in and smashed the industrial rackets, the remaining big shots, Charley Fischetti, Jake Guzik, and Tony Accardo decided to concentrate on gambling, and in particular began a drive to take over the racing wire.

In Chicago, the Guzik-Accardo gang, controlling a sub-distributor of the racing news service, began tapping Continental's wires. In Los Angeles, the head of the local distribution agency for Continental was beaten up by hoodlums working for Mickey Cohen and Joe Sica. Out of the blue appeared a new and competitive nationwide racing information and distribution service, known as Trans-American Publishing, the money for which was advanced by the Chicago mobs and Bugsy Siegel, who, at the time, held a monopoly of the bookmaking and wire-news service in Las Vegas. Many books pulled out of Continental and bought information from the new outfit, many hedged by buying from both. At the end of a year, however, the Capone mob's wire had lost about $200,000. Ragen felt that violence would erupt and went to the Cook County district attorney and told him that his life had been threatened by his rivals. Ragen knew his competitors. In June 1946 he was killed by a blast from a shotgun.

Thereafter, the Capone mob abandoned Trans-American and got a "piece" of Continental. Through their new control of the national racing-wire monopoly, the Capone mob began to muscle in on the lucrative

Miami gambling business run by the so-called S & G syndicate. For a long time S & G's monopoly over bookmaking had been so complete that when New York gambler Frank Erickson bought a three months' bookmaking concession at the expensive Roney Plaza Hotel, for $45,000, the local police, in a highly publicized raid, swooped down on the hotel; the next year the Roney Plaza was again using local talent. The Capone group, however, was tougher. They demanded an interest in Miami bookmaking, and, when refused, began organizing a syndicate of their own, persuading some bookies at the big hotels to join them. Florida Governor Warren's crime investigator appeared — a friend, it seemed, of old Chicago dog-track operator William Johnston, who had contributed $100,000 to the Governor's campaign fund — and began raiding bookie joints, but only those that were affiliated with S & G. Then S & G, which had been buying its racing news from the local distributor of Continental Press, found its service abruptly shut off. For a few days the syndicate sought to bootleg information from New Orleans, but found itself limping along. After ten days' war of attrition, the five S & G partners found themselves with a sixth partner, who, for a token "investment" of $20,000 entered a Miami business that grossed $26,000,000 in one year.

V

While Americans made gambling illegal, they did not in their hearts think of it as wicked — even the churches benefited from the bingo and lottery crazes. So they gambled — and gamblers flourished. Against this open canvas, the indignant tones of Senator Wiley and the shocked righteousness of Senator Tobey during the Kefauver investigation rang oddly. Yet it was probably this very tone of surprise that gave the activity of the Kefauver Committee its piquant quality. Here were some Senators who seemingly did not know the facts of life, as most Americans did. Here, in the person of Senator Tobey, was the old New England Puritan conscience poking around in industrial America, in a world it had made but never seen. Here was old-fashioned moral indignation, at a time when cynicism was rampant in public life.

Commendable as such moralistic fervor was, it did not make for intelligent discrimination of fact. Throughout the Kefauver hearings, for example, there ran the presumption that all gamblers were invariably gangsters. This was true of Chicago's Accardo-Guzik combine, which in the past had its fingers in many kinds of rackets. It was not nearly so true of many of the large gamblers in America, most of whom had the feeling that they were satisfying a basic American urge for sport and looked upon their calling with no greater sense of guilt than did many bootleggers. After all, Sherman Billingsley did start out as a speakeasy proprietor, as did the Kreindlers of the "21" Club; and today the Stork Club and the former Jack and Charlie's are the most fashionable night and dining spots in America (one prominent patron of the Stork Club: J. Edgar Hoover).

The S & G syndicate in Miami, for example (led by Harold Salvey, Jules Levitt, Charles Friedman, Sam Cohen, and Edward [Eddie Luckey] Rosenbaum) was simply a master pool of some two hundred bookies that arranged for telephone service, handled "protection," acted as bankers for those who needed ready cash on hard-hit books, and, in short, functioned somewhat analogously to the large factoring corporations in the textile field or the credit companies in the auto industry. Yet to Kefauver, these S & G men were "slippery and arrogant characters. . . . Salvey, for instance, was an old-time bookie who told us he had done nothing except engage in bookmaking or finance other bookmakers for twenty years." When, as a result of committee publicity and the newly found purity of the Miami police, the S & G syndicate went out of business, it was, as the combine's lawyer told Kefauver, because the "boys" were weary of being painted "the worst monsters in the world." "It is true," Cohen acknowledged, "that they had been law violators." But they had never done anything worse than gambling, and "to fight the world isn't worth it."

Most intriguing of all were the opinions of James J. Carroll, the St. Louis "betting commissioner," who for years had been widely quoted on the sports pages of the country as setting odds on the Kentucky Derby winter book and the baseball pennant races. Senator Wiley, speaking like the prosecutor in Camus's novel, *The Stranger*, became the voice of official morality:

> SENATOR WILEY: Have you any children?
> MR. CARROLL: Yes, I have a boy.
> SENATOR WILEY: How old is he?
> MR. CARROLL: Thirty-three.
> SENATOR WILEY: Does he gamble?
> MR. CARROLL: No.
> SENATOR WILEY: Would you like to see him grow up and become a gambler, either professional or amateur?
> MR. CARROLL: No . . .
> SENATOR WILEY: All right. Is your son interested in your business?
> MR. CARROLL: No, he is a manufacturer.
> SENATOR WILEY: Why do you not get him into the business?
> MR. CARROLL: Well, psychologically a great many people are unsuited for gambling.

Retreating from this gambit, the Senator sought to pin Carroll down on his contributions to political campaigns:

> SENATOR WILEY: Now this morning I asked you whether you contributed any money for political candidates or parties, and you said not more than $200 at any one time. I presume that does not indicate the total of your contributions in any one campaign, does it?

> MR. CARROLL: Well, it might, might not, Senator. I have been an "againster" in many instances. I am a reader of *The Nation* for fifty years and they have advertisements calling for contributions for different candidates, different causes. . . . They carried an advertisement for George Norris; I contributed, I think, to that, and to the elder La Follette.

Carroll, who admitted to having been in the betting business since 1899, was the sophisticated — but not immoral! — counterpoint to moralist Wiley. Here was a man without the stigmata of the underworld or underground; he was worldly, cynical of official rhetoric, jaundiced about people's motives, he was — an "againster" who believed that "all gambling legislation originates or stems from some group or some individual seeking special interests for himself or his cause."

Asked why people gamble, Carroll distilled his experiences of fifty years with a remark that deserves a place in American social history: "I really don't know how to answer the question," he said. "I think gambling is a biological necessity for certain types. I think it is the quality that gives substance to their daydreams."

In a sense, the entire Kefauver materials, unintentionally, seem to document that remark. For what the Committee revealed time and time again was a picture of gambling as a basic institution in American life, flourishing openly and accepted widely. In many of the small towns, the gambling joint is as open as a liquor establishment. The town of Havana, in Mason County, Illinois, felt miffed when Governor Adlai Stevenson intervened against local gambling. In 1950, the town had raised $15,000 of its $50,000 by making friendly raids on the gambling houses every month and having the owners pay fines. "With the gambling fines cut off," grumbled Mayor Clarence Chester, "the next year is going to be tough."

Apart from the gamblers, there were the mobsters. But what Senator Kefauver and company failed to understand was that the mobsters, like the gamblers, and like the entire gangdom generally, were seeking to become quasi-respectable and establish a place for themselves in American life. For the mobsters, by and large, had immigrant roots, and crime, as the pattern showed, was a route of social ascent and place in American life.

VI

The mobsters were able, where they wished, to "muscle in" on the gambling business because the established gamblers were wholly vulnerable, not being able to call on the law for protection. The Senators, however, refusing to make any distinction between a gambler and a gangster, found it convenient to talk loosely of a nationwide conspiracy of "illegal" elements. Senator Kefauver asserted that a "nationwide crime syndicate does exist in the United States, despite the protestations of a strangely assorted company of criminals, self-serving politicians, plain blind fools, and others who may be honestly misguided, that there is no such combine." The Senate Committee report states the matter more dogmatically: "There is a nationwide crime syndicate known as the Mafia. . . . Its leaders are usually found in control of the most lucrative rackets in their cities. There are indications of a centralized direction and control of these rackets. . . . The Mafia is the cement that helps to bind the Costello-Adonis-Lansky syndicate of New York and the Accardo-Guzik-Fischetti syndicate of Chicago. . . . These groups have kept in touch with Luciano since his deportation from the country."

Unfortunately for a good story — and the existence of the Mafia would be a whale of a story — neither the Senate Crime Committee in its testimony, nor Kefauver in his book, presented any real evidence that the Mafia exists as a functioning organization. One finds police officials asserting before the Kefauver committee their *belief* in the Mafia; the Narcotics Bureau *thinks* that a worldwide dope ring allegedly run by Luciano is part of the Mafia; but the only other "evidence" presented — aside from the incredulous responses both of Senator Kefauver and Rudolph Halley when nearly all the Italian gangsters asserted that they didn't know about the Mafia — is that certain crimes bear "the earmarks of the Mafia."

The legend of the Mafia has been fostered in recent years largely by the peephole writing team of Jack Lait and Lee Mortimer. In their *Chicago Confidential,* they rattled off a series of names and titles that made the organization sound like a rival to an Amos and Andy Kingfish society. Few serious reporters, however, give it much credence. Burton Turkus, the Brooklyn prosecutor who broke up the "Murder, Inc." ring, denies the existence of the Mafia. Nor could Senator Kefauver even make out much of a case for his picture of a national crime syndicate. He is forced to admit that "as it exists today [it] is an elusive and furtive but nonetheless tangible thing," and that "its organization and machinations are not always easy to pinpoint." His "evidence" that many gangsters congregate at certain times of the year in such places as Hot Springs, Arkansas, in itself does not prove much; people "in the trade" usually do, and as the loquacious late Willie Moretti of New Jersey said, in explaining how he had met the late Al Capone at a race track, "Listen, well-charactered people you don't need introductions to; you just meet automatically."

Why did the Senate Crime Committee plump so hard for its theory of the Mafia and a national crime syndicate? In part, they may have been misled by their own hearsay. The Senate Committee was not in the position to do original research, and its staff, both legal and investigative, was incredibly small. Senator Kefauver had begun the investigation with the attitude that with so much smoke there must be a raging fire. But smoke can also mean a smoke screen. Mob activities is a field in which busy gossip and exaggeration flourish even more readily than in a radical political sect.

There is, as well, in the American temper, a feeling that "somewhere," "somebody" is pulling all the complicated strings to which this jumbled world dances. In politics the labor image is "Wall Street," or "Big Business"; while the business stereotype was the "New Dealers." In the field of crime, the side-of-the-mouth low-down was "Costello."

The salient reason, perhaps, why the Kefauver Committee was taken in by its own myth of an omnipotent Mafia and a despotic Costello was its failure to assimilate and understand three of the more relevant sociological facts about institutionalized crime in its relation to the political life of large urban communities in America, namely: (1) the rise of the American Italian community, as part of the inevitable process of ethnic succession, to positions of importance in politics, a process that has been occurring independently but almost simultaneously in most cities with large Italian constituencies — New York, Chicago, Kansas City, Los Angeles; (2) the fact that there are individual Italians who play prominent, often leading roles today in gambling and in the mobs; and (3) the fact that Italian gamblers and mobsters often possessed "status" within the Italian community itself and a "pull" in city politics.[1] These three items are indeed related — but not so as to form a "plot."

VII

The Italian community has achieved wealth and political influence much later and in a harder way than previous immigrant groups. Early Jewish wealth, that of the German Jews of the late nineteenth century, was made largely in banking and merchandising. To that extent, the dominant group in the Jewish community was outside of, and independent of, the urban political machines. Later Jewish wealth, among the East European immigrants, was built in the garment trades, though with some involvement with the Jewish gangster, who was typically an industrial racketeer (Arnold Rothstein, Lepke and Gurrah, etc.). Among Jewish lawyers, a small minority, such as the "Tammany lawyer" (like the protagonist of Sam Ornitz's *Haunch, Paunch* and *Jowl*), rose through politics and occasion-

[1] Toward the end of his hearings, Senator Kefauver read a telegram from an indignant citizen of Italian descent, protesting against the impression the committee had created that organized crime in America was a distinctly Italian enterprise. The Senator took the occasion to state the obvious: that there are racketeers who are Italian does not mean that Italians are racketeers. However, it may be argued that to the extent the Kefauver Committee fell for the line about crime in America being organized and controlled by the Mafia, it did foster such a misunderstanding. Perhaps this is also the place to point out that insofar as the relation of ethnic groups and ethnic problems to illicit and quasi-legal activities is piously ignored, the field is left open to the kind of vicious sensationalism practiced by Mortimer and Lait.

ally touched the fringes of crime. Most of the Jewish lawyers, by and large the communal leaders, climbed rapidly, however, in the opportunities that established and legitimate Jewish wealth provided. Irish immigrant wealth in the northern urban centers, concentrated largely in construction, trucking and the waterfront, has, to a substantial extent, been wealth accumulated in and through political alliance, e.g., favoritism in city contracts.[2] Control of the politics of the city thus has been crucial for the continuance of Irish political wealth. This alliance of Irish immigrant wealth and politics has been reciprocal; many noted Irish political figures lent their names as important window-dressing for busines corporations (Al Smith, for example, who helped form the U.S. Trucking Corporation, whose executive head for many years was William J. McCormack, the alleged "Mr. Big" of the New York waterfront) while Irish businessmen have lent their wealth to further the careers of Irish politicians. Irish mobsters have rarely achieved status in the Irish community, but have served as integral arms of the politicians, as strong-arm men on election day.

The Italians found the more obvious big city paths from rags to riches pre-empted. In part this was due to the character of the early Italian immigration. Most of them were unskilled and from rural stock. Jacob Riis could remark in the '90's, "the Italian comes in at the bottom and stays there." These dispossessed agricultural laborers found jobs as ditch-diggers, on the railroads as section hands, along the docks, in the service occupations, as shoemakers, barbers, garment workers, and stayed there. Many were fleeced by the "padrone" system, a few achieved wealth from truck farming, wine growing, and marketing produce; but this "marginal wealth" was not the source of coherent and stable political power.

Significantly, although the number of Italians in the U.S. is about a third as high as the number of Irish, and of the 30,000,000 Catholic communicants in the United States, about half are of Irish descent and a sixth of Italian, there is not one Italian bishop among the hundred Catholic bishops in this country, or one Italian archbishop among the 21 archbishops. The Irish have a virtual monopoly. This is a factor related to the politics of the American church; but the condition also is possible because there is not significant or sufficient wealth among Italian Americans to force some parity.

The children of the immigrants, the second and third generation, became wise in the ways of the urban slums. Excluded from the political ladder — in the early '30's there were almost no Italians on the city pay-

---

[2] A fact which should occasion little shock if one recalls that in the nineteenth century American railroads virtually stole 190,000,000 acres of land by bribing Congressmen, and that more recently such scandals as the Teapot Dome oil grabs during the Harding administration, consummated, as the Supreme Court said, "by means of conspiracy, fraud and bribery," reached to the very doors of the White House.

roll in top jobs, nor in books of the period can one find discussion of Italian political leaders — finding few open routes to wealth, some turned to illicit ways. In the children's court statistics of the 1930's, the largest group of delinquents were the Italian; nor were there any Italian communal or social agencies to cope with these problems. Yet it was, oddly enough, the quondam racketeer, seeking to become respectable, who provided one of the major supports for the drive to win a political voice for Italians in the power structure of the urban political machines.

This rise of the Italian political bloc was connected, at least in the major northern urban centers, to another important development which tended to make the traditional relation between the politician and the protected or tolerated illicit operator more close than it had been in the past. This is the fact that the urban political machines had to evolve new forms of fund-raising since the big business contributions, which once went heavily into municipal politcs, now — with the shift in the locus of power — go largely into national affairs. (The ensuing corruption in national politics, as recent Congressional investigations show, is no petty matter; the scruples of businessmen do not seem much superior to those of the gamblers.) One way urban political machines raised their money resembled that of the large corporations which are no longer dependent on Wall Street: by self-financing — that is, by "taxing" the large number of municipal employees who bargain collectively with City Hall for their wage increases. So the firemen's union contributed money to O'Dwyer's campaign.

A second method was taxing the gamblers. The classic example, as *Life* reported, was Jersey City, where a top lieutenant of the Hague machine spent his full time screening applicants for unofficial bookmaking licenses. If found acceptable, the applicant was given a "location," usually the house or store of a loyal precinct worker, who kicked into the machine treasury a high proportion of the large rent exacted. The one thousand bookies and their one thousand landlords in Jersey City formed the hard core of the political machine that sweated and bled to get out the votes for Hague.

A third source for the financing of these machines was the new, and often illegally earned, Italian wealth. This is well illustrated by the career of Costello and his emergence as a political power in New York. Here the ruling motive has been the search for an entrée — for oneself and one's ethnic group — into the ruling circles of the big city.

Frank Costello made his money orginally in bootlegging. After repeal, his big break came when Huey Long, desperate for ready cash to fight the old-line political machines, invited Costello to install slot machines in Louisiana. Costello did, and he flourished. Together with Dandy Phil Kastel, he also opened the Beverly Club, an elegant gambling establishment just outside New Orleans, at which have appeared some of the top entertainers in America. Subsequently, Costello invested his money in New York real estate (including 79 Wall Street, which he later sold), the Copacabana night club, and a leading brand of Scotch whiskey.

Costello's political opportunity came when a money-hungry Tammany, starved by lack of patronage from Roosevelt and La Guardia, turned to him for financial support. The Italian community in New York has for years nursed a grievance against the Irish and, to a lesser extent, the Jewish political groups for monopolizing political power. They complained about the lack of judicial jobs, the small number — usually one — of Italian Congressmen, the lack of representation on the state tickets. But the Italians lacked the means to make their ambitions a reality. Although they formed a large voting bloc, there was rarely sufficient wealth to finance political clubs. Italian immigrants, largely poor peasants from Southern Italy and Sicily, lacked the mercantile experience of the Jews, and the political experience gained in the seventy-five-year history of Irish immigration.

During the Prohibition years, the Italian racketeers had made certain political contacts in order to gain protection. Costello, always the compromiser and fixer rather than the muscle-man, was the first to establish relations with Jimmy Hines, the powerful leader of the West Side in Tammany Hall. But his rival, Lucky Luciano, suspicious of the Irish, and seeking more direct power, backed and elected Al Marinelli for district leader on the Lower West Side. Marinelli in 1932 was the only Italian leader inside Tammany Hall. Later, he was joined by Dr. Paul Sarubbi, a partner of Johnny Torrio in a large, legitimate liquor concern. Certainly, Costello and Luciano represented no "unified" move by the Italians as a whole for power; within the Italian community there are as many divisions as in any other group. What is significant is that different Italians, for different reasons, and in various fashions, were achieving influence for the first time. Marinelli became county clerk of New York and a leading power in Tammany. In 1937, after being blasted by Tom Dewey, then running for district attor·iey, as a "political ally of thieves . . . and big-shot racketeers," Marinelli was removed from office by Governor Lehman. The subsequent conviction by Dewey of Luciano and Hines, and the election of La Guardia, left most of the Tammany clubs financially weak and foundering. This was the moment Costello made his move. In a few years, by judicious financing, he controlled a block of "Italian" leaders in the Hall — as well as some Irish on the upper West Side, and some Jewish leaders on the East Side — and was able to influence the selection of a number of Italian judges. The most notable incident, revealed by a wire tap on Costello's phone, was the "Thank you, Francisco" call in 1943 by Supreme Court nominee Thomas Aurelio, who gave Costello full credit for his nomination.

It was not only Tammany that was eager to accept campaign contributions from newly rich Italians, even though some of these *nouveaux riches* had "arrived" through bootlegging and gambling. Fiorello La Guardia, the wiliest mind that Melting Pot politics has ever produced, understood in the early '30's where much of his covert support came from. (So, too, did Vito Marcantonio, an apt pupil of the master: Marcantonio has consistently made deals with the Italian leaders of Tammany Hall — in 1943 he supported Aurelio, and refused to repudiate him even when the Democratic Party formally did.) Joe Adonis, who had built a political following during the late '20's, when he ran a popular speakeasy, aided La Guardia financially to a considerable extent in 1933. "The Democrats haven't recognized the Italians," Adonis told a friend. "There is no reason for the Italians to support anybody but La Guardia; the Jews have played ball with the Democrats and haven't gotten much out of it. They know it now. They will vote for La Guardia. So will the Italians."

Adonis played his cards shrewdly. He supported La Guardia, but also a number of Democrats for local and judicial posts, and became a power in the Brooklyn area. His restaurant was frequented by Kenny Sutherland, the Coney Island Democratic leader; Irwin Steingut, the Democratic minority leader in Albany; Anthony DiGiovanni, later a Councilman; William O'Dwyer, and Jim Moran. But, in 1937, Adonis made the mistake of supporting Royal Copeland against La Guardia, and the irate Fiorello finally drove Adonis out of New York.[3]

La Guardia later turned his ire against Costello, too. Yet Costello survived and reached the peak of his influence in 1942, when he was instrumental in electing Michael Kennedy leader of Tammany Hall. Despite the Aurelio fiasco, which first brought Costello into notoriety, he still had sufficient power in the Hall to swing votes for Hugo Rogers as Tammany leader in 1945, and had a tight grip on some districts as late as 1948. In those years many a Tammany leader came hat in hand to Costello's apartment, or sought him out on the golf links, to obtain the nomination for a judicial post.

During this period, other Italian political leaders were also coming to the fore. Generoso Pope, whose Colonial Sand and Stone Company began to prosper through political contacts, became an important political figure, especially when his purchase of the two largest Italian-language dailies (later merged into one), and of a radio station, gave him almost a monopoly of channels to Italian-speaking opinion of the city. Through

[3] Adonis, and associate Willie Moretti, moved across the river to Bergen County, New Jersey, where, together with the quondam racketeer Abner, "Longie" Zwillman, he became one of the political powers in the state. Gambling flourished in Bergen County for almost a decade but after the Kefauver investigation the state was forced to act. A special inquiry in 1953 headed by Nelson Stamler, revealed that Moretti had paid $286,000 to an aide of Governor Driscoll for "protection" and that the Republican state committee had accepted a $25,000 "loan" from gambler Joseph Bozzo, an associate of Zwillman.

Generoso Pope, and through Costello, the Italians became a major political force in New York.

That the urban machines, largely Democratic, have financed their heavy campaign costs in this fashion rather than having to turn to the "moneyed interests," explains in some part why these machines were able, in part, to support the New and Fair Deals without suffering the pressures they might have been subjected to had their source of money supply been the business groups. Although he has never publicly revealed his political convictions, it is likely that Frank Costello was a fervent admirer of Franklin D. Roosevelt and his efforts to aid the common man. The basic measures of the New Deal, which most Americans today agree were necessary for the public good, would not have been possible without the support of the "corrupt" big-city machines.

VIII

There is little question that men of Italian origin appeared in most of the leading roles in the high drama of gambling and mobs, just as twenty years ago the children of East European Jews were the most prominent figures in organized crime, and before that individuals of Irish descent were similarly prominent. To some extent statistical accident and the tendency of newspapers to emphasize the few sensational figures gives a greater illusion about the domination of illicit activities by a single ethnic group than all the facts warrant. In many cities, particularly in the South and on the West Coast, the mob and gambling fraternity consisted of many other groups, and often, predominantly, native white Protestants. Yet it is clear that in the major northern urban centers there was a distinct ethnic sequence in the modes of obtaining illicit wealth, and that uniquely in the case of the recent Italian elements, the former bootleggers and gamblers provided considerable leverage for the growth of political influence as well. A substantial number of Italian judges sitting on the bench in New York today are indebted in one fashion or another to Costello; so too are many Italian district leaders — as well as some Jewish and Irish politicians. And the motive in establishing Italian political prestige in New York was generous rather than scheming for personal advantage. For Costello it was largely a case of ethnic pride. As in earlier American eras, organized illegality became a stepladder of social ascent.

To the world at large, the news and pictures of Frank Sinatra, for example, mingling with former Italian mobsters could come somewhat as a shock. Yet to Sinatra, and to many Italians, these were men who had grown up in their neighborhoods, and who were, in some instances, bywords in the community for their helpfulness and their charities. The early Italian gangsters were hoodlums — rough, unlettered, and young (Al Capone was only twenty-nine at the height of his power). Those who survived learned to adapt. By now they are men of middle age or older. They learned to dress conservatively. Their homes are in respectable suburbs. They sent their children to good schools and had sought to avoid publicity.[4] Costello even went to a psychiatrist in his efforts to overcome a painful feeling of inferiority in the world of manners.

As happens with all "new" money in American society, the rough and ready contractors, the construction people, trucking entrepreneurs, as well as racketeers, polished up their manners and sought recognition and respectability in their own ethnic as well as in the general community. The "shanty" Irish became the "lace curtain" Irish, and then moved out for wider recognition.[5] Sometimes acceptance came first in established "American" society, and this was a certificate for later recognition by the ethnic community, a process well illustrated by the belated acceptance in established Negro society of such figures as Sugar Ray Robinson and Joe Louis, as well as leading popular entertainers.

Yet, after all, the foundation of many a distinguished older American fortune was laid by sharp practices and morally reprehensible methods. The pioneers of American capitalism were not graduated from Harvard's School of Business Administration. The early settlers and founding fathers, as well as those who "won the west" and built up cattle, mining and other fortunes, often did so by shady speculations and a not inconsiderable amount of violence. They ignored, circumvented or stretched the law when it stood in the way of America's destiny, and their own — or, were themselves the law when it served their purposes. This has not prevented them and their descendants from feeling proper moral outrage when under the changed circumstances of the crowded urban environments later comers pursued equally ruthless tactics.

IX

Ironically, the social development which made possible the rise to political influence sounds, too, the knell of the Italian gangster. For it is the grow-

[4] Except at times by being overly neighborly, like Tony Accardo, who, at Yuletide 1949, in his elegant River Forest home, decorated a 40-foot tree on his lawn and beneath it set a wooden Santa and reindeer, while around the yard, on tracks, electrically operated skating figures zipped merrily around while a loud speaker poured out Christmas carols. The next Christmas, the Accardo lawn was darkened; Tony was on the lam from Kefauver.

[5] The role of ethnic pride in corralling minority group votes is one of the oldest pieces of wisdom in American politics; but what is more remarkable is the persistence of this identification through second and third generation descendants, a fact which, as Samuel Lubell noted in his *Future of American Politics*, was one of the explanatory keys to political behavior in recent elections. Although the Irish bloc as a solid Democratic bloc is beginning to crack, particularly as middle-class status impels individuals to identify more strongly with the G.O.P., the nomination in Massachusetts of Jack Kennedy for the United States Senate created a tremendous solidarity among Irish voters and Kennedy was elected over Lodge although Eisenhower swept the state.

ing number of Italians with professional training and legitimate business success that both prompts and permits the Italian group to wield increasing political influence; and increasingly it is the professionals and businessmen who provide models for Italian youth today, models that hardly existed twenty years ago. Ironically, the headlines and exposés of "crime" of the Italian "gangsters" came years after the fact. Many of the top "crime" figures long ago had forsworn violence, and even their income, in large part, was derived from legitimate investments (real estate in the case of Costello, motor haulage and auto dealer franchises in the case of Adonis) or from such quasi-legitimate but socially respectable sources as gambling casinos. Hence society's "retribution" in the jail sentences for Costello and Adonis was little more than a trumped-up morality that disguised a social hypocrisy.

Apart from these considerations, what of the larger context of crime and the American way of life? The passing of the Fair Deal signalizes, oddly, the passing of an older pattern of illicit activities. The gambling fever of the past decade and a half was part of the flush and exuberance of rising incomes, and was characteristic largely of new upper-middle class rich having a first fling at conspicuous consumption. This upper-middle class rich, a significant new stratum in American life (not rich in the nineteenth century sense of enormous wealth, but largely middle-sized businessmen and entrepreneurs of the service and luxury trades — the "tertiary economy" in Colin Clark's phrase — who by the tax laws have achieved sizable incomes often much higher than the managers of the super-giant corporations), were the chief patrons of the munificent gambling casinos. During the war decade when travel was difficult, gambling and the lush resorts provided important outlets for this social class. Now they are settling down, learning about Europe and culture. The petty gambling, the betting and bingo which relieve the tedium of small town life, or the expectation among the urban slum dwellers of winning a sizable sum by a "lucky number" or a "lucky horse" goes on. To quote Bernard Baruch: "You can't stop people from gambling on horses. And why should you prohibit a man from backing his own judgment? It's another form of personal initiative." But the lush profits are passing from gambling, as the costs of coordination rise. And in the future it is likely that gambling, like prostitution, winning tacit acceptance as a necessary fact, will continue on a decentralized, small entrepreneur basis.

But passing, too, is a political pattern, the system of political "bosses" which in its reciprocal relation provided "protection" for and was fed revenue from crime. The collapse of the "boss" system was a product of the Roosevelt era. Twenty years ago Jim Farley's task was simple; he had to work only on some key state bosses. Now there is no longer such an animal. New Jersey Democracy was once ruled by Frank Hague; now there are five or six men each top dog, for the moment, in his part of the state or faction of the party. Within the urban centers, the old Irish-dominated political machines in New York, Boston, Newark, and Chicago have fallen apart. The decentralization of the metropolitan centers, the growth of suburbs and satellite towns, the break-up of the old ecological patterns of slum and transient belts, the rise of functional groups, the increasing middle-class character of American life, all contribute to this decline.

With the rationalization and absorption of some illicit activities into the structure of the economy, the passing of an older generation that had established a hegemony over crime, the general rise of minority groups to social position, and the break-up of the urban boss system, the pattern of crime we have discussed is passing as well. Crime, of course, remains as long as passion and the desire for gain remain. But big, organized city crime, as we have known it for the past seventy-five years, was based on more than these universal motives. It was based on certain characteristics of the American economy, American ethnic groups, and American politics. The changes in all these areas means that it too, in the form we have known it, is at an end.

Small Businessmen, Political Tolerance, and Support for McCarthy

MARTIN TROW

Social scientists have offered varied explanations for the origins of McCarthyism and the nature of support for the "Radical Right" in general. There have been some attempts to link these movements to the Populist uprising of the 1890's, especially by writers who see both movements as proto-Fascist. The Populists, however, have been ably defended by other historians, who view their goals as a radicalism of the left. Perhaps the most common explanation for McCarthyism is to see it as a manifestation of "status politics," a social-psychological concept describing the projection of status anxieties and fears into the political arena. In the following essay, Martin Trow, a political scientist, presents an empirical analysis of the social sources of McCarthyism in one community. Using field research, Trow finds that McCarthy's supporters admired his aggression "against the conservative authorities and institutions — the 'big shots,' the 'stuffed shirts,' the 'bureaucrats' — against whom many of his supporters felt anger and resentment." He also finds McCarthy's supporters deeply confused and angry toward a government and a society that challenged their deepest values. Trow substantiates the general notion that McCarthyism was also a revolt against modernity. Like Coben's study of the Red Scare of 1919–1920, Trow's essay highlights the continuing vulnerability of democratic society to a leader or a movement that can manipulate the persistent fears and insecurity of large groups within the pluralistic structure of American life.

In the past few years social scientists have responded to the threat symbolized by but by no means confined to Joseph McCarthy and have made efforts to explain the variety of illiberal and repressive movements that flourished during much of the first decade following World War II. Such social scientists as Parsons, Reisman, Shils, Hofstadter, and Lipset have written books or essays on the men, sentiments, and movements that came to be known as the "radical right." [1] These writings, and especially the essays that were collected in the volume *The New American Right*,[2] show an impressively high measure of agreement on the nature of the social forces underlying such diverse popular movements as McCarthyism, the movement for the Bricker amendment, and the many organized actions against "subversion" in schools, libraries, the mass media, and elsewhere. In addition to the generally high measure of agreement (or at least convergence) in these essays, they are also, taken together, both highly per-

Reprinted by permission of the author and The University of Chicago Press from the *American Journal of Sociology*, LXIV (1959), pp. 270–281. Copyright 1959 by The University of Chicago Press.

[1] Talcott Parsons, "McCarthyism and American Social Tension: A Sociologist's View," *Yale Review*, XLIV (December, 1954), 226–45; David Riesman and Nathan Glazer, "The Intellectuals and the Discontented Classes," *Partisan Review*, XXII (Winter, 1955), 47–72; Edward A. Shils, *The Torment of Secrecy* (Glencoe, Ill.: Free Press, 1955); Richard Hofstadter, "The Pseudo-Conservative Revolt," *American Scholar*, XXIV (Winter, 1954), 9–27; S. M. Lipset, "The Radical Right: A Problem for American Democracy," *British Journal of Sociology*, VI (June, 1955), 176–209.

[2] Daniel Bell (ed.), *The New American Right* (New York: Criterion Books, 1955).

suasive and based on almost no empirical evidence at all, at least so far as their efforts to explain the popular support of these movements are concerned.

The essayists in *The New American Right* treated McCarthyism as one manifestation of the new "radical right," largely assumed its close connection with political intolerance, and discussed the nature and sources of both as part of their interpretation of the larger phenomenon. And they saw the rise of this "radical right" as largely a consequence (or manifestation) of the increasing importance during the postwar years of "status politics" — the projection of people's status anxieties and frustrations onto the political arena — and the correlative decline in the relative importance of class or "interest" politics. Moreover, say the writers, the "status politics" which underlies the rise of the "radical right" tends to flourish in prosperous times, as "interest politics" is associated with depression and economic discontent. And the essayists deal with the "radical right's" mass support chiefly by speculating on the likely locations in our society of pockets of acute status anxieties or concerns.[3] They do this job so thoroughly that they have left little room for surprise regarding the social composition of McCarthy's popular support. The essays show, and quite persuasively, how and why McCarthy got disproportionate support almost everywhere: among old Americans and among new Americans; among the upwardly mobile, the downwardly mobile, and the low status non-mobile; among Catholics, Yankee Protestants, and rural fundamentalists; among workers, small businessmen, the new middle class, and the "new rich," etc. This kind of analysis, which explains every possible or supposed appearance of the phenomenon, is, of course, in part a function of the paucity of data on the issue. But, while such an analysis precludes surprises, it also explains a good deal too much. Unless we can account for the actual distribution of support for a given issue or for a leader or spokesman of this political tendency, without finessing the crucial questions of "more or less," then our analysis loses much of its power and cogency.

A study done in Bennington, Vermont, during 1954 provided data for an intensive analysis of some of the social and social-psychological characteristics of McCarthy supporters in the general population.[4] And though

---

[3] In the absence of data, these writers also attempted to *deduce* the character and composition of McCarthy's popular following from their analyses of the movement's economic and historical context and from the ideology of the movement's more prominent spokesmen. But the mass support for a movement and the grounds on which that support is granted may differ very greatly from what we would expect on the basis of an analysis of the public pronouncements of prominent men.

[4] This study of McCarthy's support was part of a larger study of political orientations and formal and informal communications carried out under the over-all direction of Dr. Robert D. Leigh and supported by a grant from Columbia

the movement and its leader are no longer part of the American political scene, the Bennington study indicates that the social forces that made for support of McCarthy did not die with his power or his person but remain available to other illiberal and repressive men and movements of the radical right. If that is so, then the study of McCarthy's popular support not merely is of interest to the antiquarian but may shed light on one aspect of the continuing vulnerability of a mass democratic society to radical, right-wing movements.

The study, part of which is reported in this paper,[5] aimed to investigate the social characteristics of McCarthy's supporters in its sample and on this basis make some inferences regarding the social sources of his popular support.[6] At the same time we were able to look into correlates of "political tolerance," [7] explore the nature and sources of McCarthy's support

---

University. The data reported in this paper were gathered through one- to two-hour structured interviews with men living in the Bennington area. Nearly eight hundred such interviews were conducted in the area during the spring and summer of 1954, during and just after the McCarthy-Army hearings, when McCarthy was at or near the peak of his popularity and power. A national survey done in August of that year found a third of its sample giving McCarthy their support (see Charles H. Stember, "Anti-democratic Attitudes in America: A Review of Public Opinion Research" [Publication of the Bureau of Applied Social Research (New York: Columbia University, 1954) p. 52] [mimeographed]). In Bennington over half of the men we interviewed approved of McCarthy's activities, while some 40 per cent approved of his methods of investigation — that aspect of his activities which had come under sharpest criticism. Incidentally, interest in and knowledge about McCarthy were very high during the period in which these interviews were collected. In Bennington, fewer than 5 per cent of the respondents answered "Don't know" to any of the questions about McCarthy.

[5] For fuller information on this study and its methods of investigation see Martin A. Trow, "Right-Wing Radicalism and Political Intolerance: A Study of Support for McCarthy in a New England Town" (unpublished Ph.D. dissertation, Columbia University, 1957).

[6] Information on attitudes toward McCarthy was gathered through three questions in the interview: questions bearing on his activities, his methods of investigation, and the value of his investigating committee. Although these three questions could have been combined in a scale of "support for McCarthy," the decision was made to use the single question, "Just speaking of Senator McCarthy's *methods* of investigation, how do you feel about them? Do you strongly favor them, mildly favor them, mildly oppose them, or strongly oppose them?" In most of the tabulations those who favored his methods, whether strongly or mildly, were compared with those who opposed them. For the reasons this item alone was used see Trow, *op. cit.*, pp. 12–15.

[7] The measure of "political tolerance" was an index based on the three questions: "In peacetime, do you think the Socialist party should be allowed to publish newspapers in this country?" "Do you think newspapers should be allowed to criticize our form of government?" "Do you think members of the Communist party in this country should be allowed to speak on the radio?" While these three specific attitudes were highly related to one another, there was, as we might expect, least support for the right of members of the Communist party to speak on the radio and most support for the rights of newspapers

and "political tolerance" separately and simultaneously, and, by contrast and comparison, throw into bold relief the similarities and differences in the forces underlying these two different sets of sentiments.[8]

McCarthy's Support and Political Tolerance

The widespread assumption that support for McCarthy was almost always associated with political intolerance seems to gain empirical support when we observe that support for McCarthy and political intolerance were both strongly related to the amount of formal education completed. There is nothing very startling about this: we hardly need an extensive study to know that McCarthy gained much of his popular support from poorly educated, lower-class people who are, as many studies tell us, also least likely to be tolerant of unpopular political minorities and views.

But the matter becomes not quite so routine when we examine the relationship between support for McCarthy and political tolerance holding formal education constant. When we do this, the relationship between intolerance and support for McCarthy almost or wholly disappears (Table 1). On every educational level McCarthy's supporters were about as likely as his opponents to have been tolerant toward the exercise of free speech by political dissidents. In other words, while support of McCarthy and political intolerance were both related to formal education, they were very little related to each other.

The implications of this finding are many. In its simplest terms it means that, whatever the character and content of the *public* fight between McCarthy and his more prominent opponents, the sources of his support

---

to criticize our form of government. But, on further examination, it appeared that these three questions tapped a common, more basic sentiment regarding the rights of people and groups hostile to our political and economic system to make their criticisms known through the media of public communication. Political tolerance involves, at a minimum, a willingness to grant to others the right to propagate their political views. The willingness to grant this right to unpopular political minorities is the sentiment common to these three items and is the sentiment we are calling "political tolerance."

The index was constructed by assigning a score of 2 to "Yes" responses, 1 to "Yes, qualified," and 0 to "No." In these tabulations the index was dichotomized, with those having a total score of 3 or more comprising the "High" group.

Identically worded questions have been included in a number of national surveys conducted by the National Opinion Research Center in recent years and provide comparisons with the Bennington sample. For further discussion of this measure see Trow, *op. cit.*, pp. 16–17.

[8] This investigation explored the relations between support for McCarthy and political tolerance and economic class, occupation, religious identification, union membership and identification, political party preference, and attitudes toward various national and foreign policy issues. The bearing of formal education on McCarthy's support and political tolerance was analyzed separately; since it was so highly related to both these sentiments, it was controlled in the analysis of all the other relationships.

Support for McCarthy by
Political Tolerance, Holding
Formal Education
Constant *

TABLE 1

Education Political tolerance	Grade school		Some high school		High-school graduate		Some college and more	
	High	Low	High	Low	High	Low	High	Low
Favor McCarthy's methods	51	63	44	44	43	45	23	18
N	(54)	(94)	(55)	(68)	(113)	(62)	(197)	(33)

* Percentage

and popularity in the population at large appear to have had little relation to how strongly people support the principles of free speech.

The division over McCarthy in the population at large, at least in Bennington, was not a division between the supporters of and encroachers upon civil liberties. To see it that way is to overlook the very genuine elements of "radicalism" — of anticonservatism — in the McCarthy appeal. On the one hand, many of those who disapproved of McCarthy and his methods did so not out of any particular concern for the preservation of civil liberties or freedom of speech for unpopular minorities but rather out of a feeling that what is done to suppress "subversion" be done in conservative ways through regular legislative or judicial or administrative procedures. But these men, as their responses to our questions show, were often no more concerned with the preservation of freedom of speech than McCarthy himself and much less so than many of his followers. For many of these latter, the majority of them lower class, with little formal schooling, McCarthy's appeal was not that of a man *repressing* free speech but of a man *exercising* it, in what appeared to be bold and fearless ways. Moreover, much of his boldness, violence, and aggression was directed precisely against the conservative authorities and institutions — the "big shots," the "stuffed shirts," the "bureaucrats" — against whom many of his supporters felt anger and resentment. The men who opposed McCarthy, by and large, were solid, better educated, middle-class citizens who identified with the authorities and institutions which were McCarthy's chief targets of attack by the summer of 1954. Many an executive or engineer who watched McCarthy alternately patronize and bully Army Secretary Stevens felt, and not without reason, that he himself and men like him were also under attack.

Our finding that McCarthy's support and political intolerance were not strongly related to each other does not rest solely or even primarily on the one tabulation which shows that the apparent relationship disappears when education is held constant. That finding did indeed stimulate further inquiry in that same direction, but, as evidence accumulated, it became apparent in many other ways that the social forces underlying McCarthy's popular support were simply not the same as those making for political intolerance. And, like most empirical findings, this one posed a question: If support for McCarthy were not simply an expression of political intolerance, what were its social sources, and how did they differ from the social sources of political intolerance?

Before proceeding to report one part of our investigation into that question, it may be useful to summarize briefly some of its more general findings. In précis, we found that political tolerance is a norm or cluster of norms, very strongly related to cultural sophistication, or "cosmopolitanism," and thus to the level of formal education achieved — *and to very little else*. By contrast, popular support for McCarthy can best be understood as the channeling of certain dissatisfactions with aspects of the social, economic, and political orders. There are two elements present in that formulation: the presence of considerable discontent and dissatisfaction and the ways and directions in which those dissatisfactions are channeled. We found the highest levels of support for McCarthy in social classes and categories which, on one hand, show considerable hostility toward important elements in the social structure and, on the other hand, do not have their hostilities and discontents channeled into and through existing political and economic institutions. By contrast, neither the *level* of discontent nor the *channeling* of discontent appeared to have appreciable bearing on the levels of political tolerance characteristic of these same classes and social categories.

McCarthy's Support, Political Tolerance, and Occupation

Part of the evidence on which these general propositions are based bears on the relation of economic class and occupation to the sentiments in question. When we divide our sample into the two broad categories of "manual" and "non-manual" workers, the latter including both salaried and self-employed white-collar people, we find little or no difference between them in their support of MCarthy, holding formal education constant. Even when we divide the "non-manual" category into "lower-" and "upper-middle-class" categories, on the basis of income, we still find no appreciable differences in attitudes toward McCarthy within educational categories. But when we distinguish *within* the middle class between salaried and self-employed men, we found marked differences in their respective levels of support for McCarthy (Table 2).

In every educational category the small businessmen showed a distinctly higher proportion of McCarthy supporters than did the salaried men of similar education, and among those who had not been to college, the small businessmen were even more pro-McCarthy than the manual work-

*Support for McCarthy by
Occupational Group,
Holding Formal Education
Constant* *

TABLE 2

Education Occupation	Less than 4 years of high school			High-school graduate			Some college and more		
	Man.†	Sal.†	S.B.†	Man.	Sal.	S.B.	Man.	Sal.	S.B.
Favor McCarthy's methods	53	38	65	49	36	58	32	22	32
N	(188)	(53)	(52)	(59)	(78)	(38)	(35)	(124)	(44)

* Percentage
† Occupation: "Man.": manual workers; "Sal.": salaried employees, including lower and upper white collar, salaried professionals, and executives; "S.B.": small business-men, including merchants and other small proprietors. Free professionals, farmers, un-employed, and retired people are excluded.

ers. And the differences were substantial. For example, among the men who did not finish high school, two-thirds of the small businessmen sup-ported McCarthy, as compared with only half the workers who did and only a little more than a third of the salaried employees who did. Among the men who had been to college the differences by occupational group are smaller but still substantial: where one in three of these better-educated small businessmen supported McCarthy, only a little over one in five of the salaried employees with this education did.

There are a number of possible interpretations of this finding, some of which were investigated and rejected in light of the Bennington data.[9] The interpretation that gained strongest support from the data can be summarized in the hypothesis that small businessmen in our society dis-proportionately tend to develop a generalized hostility toward a complex of symbols and processes bound up with industrial capitalism: the steady growth and concentration of government, labor organizations, and busi-ness enterprises; the correlative trend toward greater rationalization of production and distribution; and the men, institutions, and ideas that sym-bolize these secular trends of modern society. These trends and their sym-bols were, we believe, McCarthy's most persuasive targets.[10] Quite apart

[9] For example, it has been suggested that small businessmen, as a result of their economic experience and interests, tend to hold extremely conservative economic views and that these views led them into the radical right and support of McCarthy. A somewhat different hypothesis suggests that small businessmen identify with, and tend to take over what they believe to be, the values of big business, which are also the values of the radical right. Neither of these hypotheses is supported by the Bennington data.

[10] For an analysis of McCarthy's ideology and rhetoric see Bell (ed.), *op. cit.*, especially the essays of Bell, Parsons, Viereck, and Lipset.

from the questions of Communists in government, and blunders or worse in foreign policy, the congruence between McCarthy's attacks on and small businessmen's hostility to the dominant characteristics and tendencies of modern society account, we believe, for much of the disproportionate support McCarthy gained from small businessmen.[11]

This hypothesis can be explored further by looking at the connections between support for McCarthy and attitudes toward the most characteristic economic institutions of our society, that is, large corporations and trade unions. A simple but serviceable typology emerges from responses to questions asking how the respondent feels about big companies and trade unions and permits us to distinguish empirically four important and easily recognizable patterns of orientations toward the dominant economic institutions in the population at large.[12] The group which expressed approval of labor unions but suspicion of the power of big companies, (I), is closest to the familiar "labor-liberals," who in this country gave their support to the labor-oriented, administrative liberalism of the New Deal and its descendants. The pro-big business, antiunion group, (IV), resembles the equally familiar "right-wing conservatives." The orientation I have called "moderate conservatism," (III), is held by people who are reconciled to the continued existence both of big companies and of trade unions; this is the dominant political orientation of both major parties today.

To the student of right-wing radicalism the most interesting of these four orientations is that which expresses hostility toward both big business and trade unions (II). At the risk of some distortion, I have called this

---

[11] The free professionals, chiefly doctors and lawyers, not shown in this table, were markedly low in their support of McCarthy; only one in five gave him his support. These professions, as Parsons has noted, have developed relatively well-institutionalized ways of dealing with rapid social change, so that "the dynamic process of which they are agents is not so disturbing to them" (Talcott Parsons, *Essays in Sociological Theory Pure and Applied* [Glencoe, Ill.: Free Press, 1949], p. 267). Nor do they experience the insecurities flowing from the progressive rationalization of economic life that the small businessmen do. They are, in this respect, more like the salaried employees, especially the managers, technicians, and salaried professionals.

[12] The two questions were: "Do you agree or disagree that: The way they are run now, labor unions do this country more harm than good," and "Big companies control too much of American business."

		Big companies control too much of American business	
		Agree	Disagree
The way they are run now, labor unions do this country more harm than good	Disagree	I	III
	Agree	II	IV

orientation "nineteenth-century liberalism." In the middle of the twentieth century the important thing about this orientation is not its intellectual content but rather its emotional tone, its diffused anger, and its generalized suspicion toward modern tendencies of all kinds. Among our respondents, this nineteenth-century liberalism appears both as a wistful nostalgia for a golden age of small farmers and businessmen and also as an expression of a strong resentment and hatred toward a world which makes no sense in terms of older ideas and which is conducted in apparent violation of old truths and values of economic and political life.[13]

If we look at the distribution of McCarthy support among the holders of these four political orientations (and we did this separately for better- and less-well-educated men), we find that there were scarcely any differences among holders of three of the four orientations in their proportions of McCarthy supporters (Table 3).

TABLE 3

McCarthy's Support by Domestic Political Orientations, Among Better- and Less-Well-Educated Men *

Education DPO†	Less than 4 years of high school				4 years of high school and more			
	I	II	III	IV	I	II	III	IV
Favor McCarthy's methods	44	67	51	51	32	50	29	32
N	(90)	(84)	(53)	(43)	(101)	(58)	(137)	(97)

* Percentage
† DPO Type I: Labor-liberal (pro-union; anti–big business)
        II: Nineteenth-century liberal (anti-union; anti–big business)
        III: Moderate conservative (pro-union; pro–big business)
        IV: Right-wing conservative (anti-union; pro–big business)

But among the poorly educated, as among the better educated, the nineteenth-century liberals gave McCarthy distinctly higher proportions of support than any of the other three orientations we examined. Among the men who had less than four years of high school, the difference between the nineteenth-century liberals and all the others in the proportions supporting McCarthy is the difference between two-thirds and a half.

[13] Much has been said about this perspective and its illiberal tendencies, most recently by Shils (*op. cit.*, pp. 98–104) and Richard Hofstadter, *The Age of Reform* (New York: Alfred A. Knopf, 1955), pp. 3–22, 60–93, and *passim*, in connection with populism. See also C. W. Mills, *White Collar* (New York: Oxford University Press, 1951), pp. 34–59, and John H. Bunzel, "The General Ideology of American Small Business," *Political Science Quarterly*, LXX (March, 1955), 87–102.

Among the better educated, the difference is between a half as compared with a third of all others who gave McCarthy their support.

There are two findings here which are perhaps of equal interest to the student of right-wing radicalism. The first — that there was little difference in the support McCarthy gained among labor-liberals, moderate conservatives, and right-wing conservatives — contradicts the widespread liberal assumption that McCarthy got much of his mass support from the traditional right-wing conservatives.[14] The other finding, with which we are chiefly concerned here, is that men holding the nineteenth-century liberal orientation toward big business and trade unions showed a markedly greater vulnerability to McCarthy's appeal. These men, as I have noted, are often angrily confused and deeply resentful of a world that continually offends their deepest values. But as important is the fact that this particular well of resentment and indignation has no effective and institutionalized channels of expression. Right-wing conservatives have substantial power in the business community and the Republican party; labor-liberals are a strong force in the trade unions, some big-city machines, and are well represented in the Democratic party; and the moderate conservatives have everything else. It is precisely the political orientation which has no institutionalized place on the political scene, little representation or leadership in the major parties, which sought that voice and place through McCarthy. And he expressed for them their fear and mistrust of bigness and of the slick and subversive ideas that come out of the cities and the big institutions to erode old ways and faiths.

It should come as no surprise to find that the small businessmen in our sample were distinctly more likely than manual workers or salaried employees to hold nineteenth-century liberal views regarding trade unions and large corporations (Table 4). Where small businessmen comprised only one-fifth of the men in these occupational categories in our sample, they contributed a third of the nineteenth-century liberals. Moreover, the small businessmen who *held* these views gave McCarthy a very high measure of support.[15] The very highest proportion of McCarthy supporters

[14] Further investigation of holders of very conservative economic attitudes supports this finding.

[15] Even those small businessmen who held other orientations gave McCarthy more support than did workers and salaried employees with the same orientations. Looked at from another perspective, nineteenth-century liberals among workers and salaried men gave McCarthy more support than did men in similar occupations holding different orientations toward big business and trade unions. Occupation and these politico-economic orientations worked independently and cumulatively in their bearing on McCarthy's support.

In this study we are primarily concerned with the relationships and forces underlying McCarthy's popular support. But our findings that support for McCarthy was not highly related to political intolerance and that McCarthy gained disproportionate support from small businessmen should not obscure the fact that *most* of McCarthy's supporters were (*a*) intolerant and (*b*) manual workers. Our findings and the latter observations, of course, do not contradict one another.

among these categories was found among the poorly educated small businessmen holding these nineteenth-century liberal attitudes; almost three out of four of these men were McCarthy supporters. Here is evidence that a generalized fear of the dominant currents and institutions of modern society was an important source of McCarthy's mass appeal, not *only* among small businessmen, but perhaps especially among a group like small businessmen whose economic and status security is continually threatened by those currents and institutions.

TABLE 4

*Domestic Political
Orientations by Occupational
Group, for Better- and
Less-Well-Educated Men* *

Education	Less than 4 years of high school			4 years of high school and more		
Occupation	Man.†	Sal.†	S.B.†	Man.	Sal.	S.B.
DPO††						
Group I	42	27	19	48	20	21
Group II	29	25	41	12	12	18
Group III	18	25	19	25	40	36
Group IV	11	23	21	15	28	25
Total	100	100	100	100	100	100
N	(180)	(52)	(52)	(87)	(191)	(80)

* Percentage
† See note to Table 2.
†† DPO:
Group I: Labor-liberals
Group II: Nineteenth-century liberals
Group III: Moderate conservatives
Group IV: Right-wing conservatives

One can hardly consider the connection between economic class and right-wing radicalism in America without thinking of the analysis of the Nazi party's mass support before Hitler took power, an analysis developed by such men as Erich Fromm, Sigmund Neumann, Karl Mannheim, Emil Lederer, and Alfred Meusal.[16] The comparison suggests itself despite, or

[16] On the social character and political orientations of the lower middle class in Germany as shaped by their insecure and continually deteriorating social and economic positions before the rise of Hitler see Erich Fromm, *Escape from Freedom* (New York: Farrar & Rinehart, 1941), pp. 211–16; Sigmund Neumann, *Permanent Revolution* (New York: Harper & Bros., 1942), p. 28; Karl Mannheim, *Man and Society in an Age of Reconstruction* (New York: Harcourt, Brace & Co., 1940), p. 102, *passim*; Emil Lederer, *The State of the Masses* (New York: W. W. Norton & Co., 1940), pp. 51–53; and Alfred Meusal, "Middle Class," *Encyclopedia of the Social Sciences* (1933), X, 407–15.

perhaps even because of, the very great differences in the historical backgrounds and in the social, political, and economic contexts of right-wing radical movements in Europe and the United States. All the observers of naziism are agreed that lower-middle-class tradesmen, shopkeepers, and artisans gave the Nazis a disproportionately large measure of their support before the Nazis took power. And they did so, these observers agree, because of their deep-seated fear of radical proletarianism, on one hand, and of the rapid rationalization of production and distribution — that is to say, the large corporation and the department store — on the other. (These fears involved their conceran with *both* material and status security.) To the small German proprietor, Hitler promised to crush radical proletarianism and control big business.

Nothing could seem further from the social scene that these writers were speaking of — societies undergoing almost continuous crisis, experiencing intense class conflicts and increasingly wide desperation and despair — than the general climate in a relatively prosperous, small New England town in 1954. The chief characteristic of Bennington's social and political climate was an absence of intense class conflict or conflict of any kind; rather there was a very considerable amount of tolerance, good humor, and the appearance of widespread optimism about the future. Similarly, nothing could seem more inappropriate to the political orientations of Benningtonians than the apocalyptic analysis applied to pre-Hitler Europe. What is perhaps surprising is that in this climate of optimism, good humor, and low-temperature politics, small businessmen in Bennington were apparently responding to the pressures of industrial capitalism in ways not wholly unlike their beleaguered cousins in the Middle Europe of twenty-five years ago, though at much lower levels of intensity.[17]

McCarthy's Support and Salaried Employees

But this comparison of the social sources of Hitler's popular support with McCarthy's shows one very striking anomaly. Students of naziism usually speak of the disproportionate support the Nazis got from the German lower middle class, in which they lump small tradesmen, artisans, and businessmen, together with lower white-collar salaried employees. The evi-

[17] This is not to identify McCarthy with Hitler, or American right-wing movements with naziism or fascism, though this is not the place to discuss the very great differences between these movements. Nor is it meant simply to equate the role of small businessmen in the mass support for those movements. Their differing historical developments and the different political situations and structures within which these movements developed heavily conditioned their actual political *consequences*. Our concern here is not with the manifold factors that affect the translation of political sentiments into action (i.e., with their consequences) but rather with the nature of those sentiments and with their location and sources in the social structure. And here, the evidence suggests, there are certain important parallels in the two situations.

dence would seem to justify their approach: Hans Gerth's study of the membership of the Nazi party in 1933 shows that both small proprietors and salaried employees were disproportionately represented in the membership of the Nazi party and to about the same degree, both groups supplying about twice the proportion of Nazi party members as compared with their representation in the population at large.[18] And the students of naziism explain Hitler's support among the salaried white-collar workers in much the same way they explain the support the Nazis got from the small proprietors: largely in terms of their status anxieties — anxieties arising especially out of the discrepancy between their precarious and deteriorating economic positions and their status claims and aspirations.[19]

By contrast, in Bennington the salaried employees not only were not as pro-McCarthy as the small businessmen but were strikingly low in the support they gave him, as indicated above. This was true not only of the better-educated managers, executives, technicians, and salaried professionals who might be expected to identify with McCarthy's high-status targets. It was also true of the less-well-educated and low-income white-collar men. Less than 30 per cent of the very large group of salaried employees gave McCarthy their approval and support, as compared with over half of all the small businessmen and merchants.

How can we account for the fact that, while the analysis of the anxieties and politics of small businessmen in pre-Hitler Germany is not irrelevant to our understanding of the political orientations of small businessmen in Bennington in 1954, the behaviors of the salaried employees in the two situations were almost diametrically opposite? The answer seems to lie in the general orientation of the two classes to modern industrial society. Salaried employees, whether in Germany or the United States, or in the new countries of the Near and Far East,[20] are in general *not* alienated from the dominant trends and institutions of modern society; these trends and developments of concentration, specialization, rationalization, and

---

[18] Hans Gerth, "The Nazi Party: Its Leadership and Composition," *American Journal of Sociology*, XLV (January, 1940), 517–41, especially Table 1.

[19] For example, see Sigmund Neumann, "Germany: Changing Patterns and Lasting Problems," in Neumann (ed.), *Modern Political Parties* (Chicago: University of Chicago Press, 1956), pp. 36–67. See also Lederer, *op. cit.*, and Hans Speier, "The Salaried Employee in Modern Society," in his *Social Order and the Risks of War* (New York: George W. Stewart, 1952), pp. 68–85.

[20] Asoka Mehta has pointed out that in the "underdeveloped areas" of Asia the Communists make their first and chief appeal not to the peasants or industrial workers but to the emerging strata of salaried employees, who respond in large numbers precisely to the promise of rapid industrialization and bureaucratization under Communist direction and to the opportunities that will be thus opened up to them (Asoka Mehta, "Can Asia Industrialize Democratically," *Dissent*, I [Spring, 1955], 152–70). See also Morris Watnick, "The Appeal of Communism to the Peoples of Underdeveloped Areas," in Bendix and Lipset (eds.), *Class, Status, and Power* (Glencoe, Ill.: Free Press, 1953), pp. 651–62.

bureaucratization have created the class of salaried employees and are its natural habitat. But, while accepting the general shape and direction of modern society, the salaried employees in Europe responded violently to short-run crises in capitalist society — to inflation, depression, mass unemployment, and their consequent insecurities of livelihood and social status. In this light it is not surprising that the general orientation of white-collar people in a booming and expanding economy such as the United States has had since World War II should be moderate, conservative, and generally complacent about the political economy and its direction. And this because of, not despite, the fact that the tendencies toward concentration and centralization are great and swift-moving. In pre-Hitler Germany the same classes turned to Hitler in great numbers as the large organizations which structured their lives and careers proved increasingly incapable of providing the material and status security they demanded. Their response was not against large organization but against the collapse of bureaucratic society and toward a man and a party which promised to revive and extend it.[21]

By contrast, small businessmen react not so much to short-run crises in the economy as to its long-range tendencies and direction of development — against the society itself rather than merely to failures of its economy. The tendencies which small businessmen fear — of concentration and centralization — proceed without interruption in depression, war, and prosperity and irrespective of the party in power; [22] thus they are *always*

[21] One study whose findings support this interpretation reports a relationship between the proportion of unemployed among white-collar workers in German cities and the Nazi vote (S. Pratt, "The Social Basis of Nazism and Communism in Urban Germany," unpublished M.A. thesis, Michigan State College, 1948).

[22] See, e.g., Kurt Mayer, "Small Business as a Social Institution," *Social Research*, XIV (September, 1947), 332–49.

Lipset and Bendix, in two articles in the *American Journal of Sociology* (January and March, 1952), point to the very high turnover of small business in this country. Using Department of Commerce figures, they observe that "even during the postwar boom of 1945–48 almost 30 per cent of the businesses in the United States were discontinued," the bulk of these, of course, being small businesses (S. M. Lipset and R. Bendix, "Social Mobility and Occupational Career Patterns. II. Social Mobility," *American Journal of Sociology*, LVII [March, 1952], 500). Translated into occupational career patterns, the high rate of business turnover reflects itself in the fact that nearly 20 per cent of their sample of Oakland, California, men who were not then proprietors had at one time owned their own businesses. And they present further data showing that many businessmen who fail fall back into the ranks of manual labor. It is probable that an awareness of these dangers constitutes a continuing threat to many small proprietors.

Rush Welter finds similar high rates of turnover among the predominantly small-and medium-sized manufacturing firms that have established themselves in Bennington (Rush Welter, "Bennington, Vermont: An Economic History" [Bennington College, 1956] [mimeographed]). Welter has no comparable data on non-manufacturing concerns, specifically the roughly 150 retail shops in the town. But these, in Bennington as elsewhere, are hard pressed by chain stores and the disaffected, though probably the acute pinch they feel in depressions makes their anxieties and angers sharper and more pointed. In this light, the small businessmen in prosperous Bennington of 1954 were not so fundamentally different in their response to the social and economic pressures of modern society from the equivalent strata in pre-Hitler Germany, or from their opposite members in the France of Poujade.

Occupation and Political Tolerance

It remains to be said, and with some emphasis, that the disproportionate support small businessmen gave to McCarthy is *not* evidence that they constitute a pool of repressive and illiberal sentiments of all kinds. On the contrary, we can see that, despite their vulnerability to a right-wing demagogue like McCarthy, small businessmen are no more politically intolerant than are salaried employees or manual workers of simliar education (Table 5). Here again we find that occupation and economic class, and all the varied discontents that flow from membership in different class and occupational groups, seem to have little bearing on political tolerance, certainly as compared with the bearing of formal education and cultural sophistication. By contrast with support of McCarthy, tolerance of dissidence appears to be almost wholly a function of the degree to which men have learned and internalized the rules of the democratic political game: in the United States this, in turn, is closely related to general political awareness and sophistication, acquired in part through formal education and through exposure to the serious political media which support those norms, rather than through economic or occupational experience.[23] Where political tolerance for the most part is a norm held and enforced in the sub-cultures of sophisticated men, most of whom have been to college, popular support for McCarthy, by contrast, seemed to have been largely the channeled expression of various kinds of socially engendered discontents.[24]

---

big mail-order houses. All in all, small proprietors earn their livelihood under conditions of considerable economic insecurity and respond to these conditions in some of the ways we have been describing in this essay.

[23] The free professionals, whom we noted were very low in their support for McCarthy, were not more politically tolerant than other men who had been to college.

[24] The kind of discontent we have been dealing with in this essay takes the form of a fearful and suspicious hostility toward the main defining features of modern society. Another kind, not discussed in this essay, is a simpler, more direct envious resentment of the status order and of high-status individuals and groups. A closer study of politically relevant discontents and their social sources also involves a study of the forces that *channel* them — that determine who become the targets and who the spokesmen for the hostilities of a given group. To identify the nature and social location of discontent is not in itself sufficient to identify its targets, for it cannot be assumed that the conditions which channel hostilities are necessarily identical with the conditions that generate them. On this see Trow, *op. cit.*, pp. 203–15.

Political Tolerance by
Occupational Group,
Holding Educational
TABLE 5   Constant *

Education	Less than 4 years of high school			High-school graduate			Some college and more		
Occupation	Man.†	Sal.†	S.B.†	Man.	Sal.	S.B.	Man.	Sal.	S.B.
High political tolerance	36	44	50	60	68	71	81	88	86
N	(181)	(52)	(46)	(55)	(78)	(35)	(36)	(120)	(43)

* Percentage
† See Table 2.

The "Radical Right" and Popular Sentiments

Our findings clearly indicate that students of public opinion on political issues might well be wary of such concepts as the "radical right" and its "pseudo-conservative" members, with all the assumptions regarding a coherent if latent structure of attitudes in the general population that those terms imply. Supporters of the "radical right" have been seen not only as having supported McCarthy but also as hostile to the New Deal, organized labor, the graduated income tax, and the United Nations, as authoritarian in character, intolerant of political non-conformists, and prejudiced against racial and religious groups. Whatever may be said or learned regarding the leaders and activists of right-wing radical movements, it is not likely that these characteristics and sentiments will be found in close association in the population at large. In this respect "radical rightism" may be like "liberalism," whose articulate representatives are usually civil libertarians, internationalists, in favor of organized labor and social welfare programs, whereas in the population at large these supposed components of "liberalism" do not tend to be found together.[25]

[25] See W. A. Kerr, "Untangling the Liberalism-Conservatism Continuum," *Journal of Social Psychology*, XXXV (1952), 111–25; G. H. Smith, "Liberalism and Level of Information," *Journal of Education Psychology*, XXXIX (February, 1948), 68–81; William McPhee, *Bibliography and Critique of Quantitative Research on Syndromes, Clusters and Factors in Social Attitudes* (New York: Bureau of Applied Social Research, Columbia University, 1954); and Robert J. Williams, "Attitude Dimensions in Public Opinion Questionnaire Material" (unpublished Ph.D. dissertation, Columbia University, 1953).

These studies report a number of distinct dimensions of "liberalism," some of which are independent, others inversely related in the general population. Our own findings, in parallel fashion, suggest at least two distinct dimensions of "radical rightism," one a general intolerance of minority groups, political, racial, and otherwise; the other a more directly *political* "radical rightism," a propensity to support movements and leaders of the McCarthy-Poujade type. These dimensions, on at least our preliminary findings, seem to be unrelated, or only slightly related, to each other in the general population.

The relationship of public opinion to the political process is devious, indirect, and complicated. If it is misleading and dangerous to deduce the structure of political power and its behavior from the distribution of political attitudes in the population at large, as political scientists warn, it is equally erroneous to deduce the nature and distribution of public opinion from the forces and ideologies that clash on high. But the distributions of sentiments on public issues and about public leaders *can* be sensitive indicators to deep-running forces in society — social forces that have heavy political consequences, though *not* necessarily through the public opinions that reveal them. If this is so, then there is a potentially rich source of new knowledge for political sociology in the secondary analysis of existing survey research data.

Assimilation in America: Theory and Reality

MILTON M. GORDON

The assimilation of divergent groups into American life has been explained by a number of theories that have been used as both descriptions of past behavior and goals for future development. Sociologist Milton M. Gordon examines the three most prominent theories of assimilation in the essay below. They are, in order, "Anglo-conformity," which has served as a curious admixture of idealist and racist notions of what Americans should be; the "melting pot," which projects the idea of Americans as a new cultural and biological composite; and finally, "cultural pluralism," which acknowledges the usefulness of differing cultural heritages in American life. Gordon's most distinctive contribution consists in marking out the practical limits of assimilation. He usefully dstinguishes between "behavioral assimilation," or acculturation, and "structural assimilation," by which he means the movement of new groups into the cliques, organizations, and activities of society. Despite a considerable degree of acculturation, structural assimilation and the movement of the new groups into primary relationships with the old have been quite limited in

practice. Instead, what Gordon labels as "structural pluralism"
has been the leading sociological fact of the American ex-
perience, and the constant barrier to an absolute assimilation.

Three ideologies or conceptual models have competed for attention on
the American scene as explanations of the way in which a nation, in the
beginning largely white, Anglo-Saxon, and Protestant, has absorbed over
41 million immigrants and their descendants from variegated sources and
welded them into the contemporary American people. These ideologies
are Anglo-conformity, the melting pot, and cultural pluralism. They have
served at various times, and often simultaneously, as explanations of what
has happened — descriptive models — and of what should happen —
goal models. Not infrequently they have been used in such a fashion that
it is difficult to tell which of these two usages the writer has had in mind.
In fact, one of the more remarkable omissions in the history of American
intellectual thought is the relative lack of close analytical attention given
to the theory of immigrant adjustment in the United States by its social
scientists.

The result has been that this field of discussion — an overridingly important one since it has significant implications for the more familiar
problems of prejudice, discrimination, and majority-minority group relations generally — has been largely preempted by laymen, representatives
of belles lettres, philosophers, and apologists of various persuasions. Even
from these sources the amount of attention devoted to ideologies of
assimilation is hardly extensive. Consequently, the work of improving intergroup relations in America is carried out by dedicated professional agencies and individuals who deal as best they can with day-to-day problems of
discriminatory behavior, but who for the most part are unable to relate
their efforts to an adequate conceptual apparatus. Such an apparatus
would, at one and the same time, accurately describe the present structure
of American society with respect to its ethnic groups (I shall use the term
"ethnic group" to refer to any racial, religious, or national-origins col-
lectivity), and allow for a considered formulation of its assimilation or
integration goals for the foreseeable future. One is reminded of Alice's
distraught question in her travels in Wonderland: "Would you tell me,
please, which way I ought to go from here?" "That depends a good deal,"
replied the Cat with irrefutable logic, "on where you want to get to."

The story of America's immigration can be quickly told for our present
purposes. The white American population at the time of the Revolution
was largely English and Protestant in origin, but had already absorbed

Reprinted by permission of *Daedalus*, Journal of the American Academy of
Arts & Sciences (Boston, Mass.), XC (Spring 1961), pp. 263–285.

substantial groups of Germans and Scotch-Irish and smaller contingents of Frenchmen, Dutchmen, Swedes, Swiss, South Irish, Poles, and a handful of migrants from other European nations. Catholics were represented in modest numbers, particularly in the middle colonies, and a small number of Jews were residents of the incipient nation. With the exception of the Quakers and a few missionaries, the colonists had generally treated the Indians and their cultures with contempt and hostility, driving them from the coastal plains and making the western frontier a bloody battleground where eternal vigilance was the price of survival.

Although the Negro at that time made up nearly one-fifth of the total population, his predominantly slave status, together with racial and cultural prejudice, barred him from serious consideration as an assimilable element of the society. And while many groups of European origin started out as determined ethnic enclaves, eventually, most historians believe, considerable ethnic intermixture within the white population took place. "People of different blood" [sic] — write two American historians about the colonial period, "English, Irish, German, Huguenot, Dutch, Swedish — mingled and intermarried with little thought of any difference." [1] In such a society, its people predominantly English, its white immigrants of other ethnic origins either English-speaking or derived largely from countries of northern and western Europe whose cultural divergences from the English were not great, and its dominant white population excluding by fiat the claims and considerations of welfare of the non-Caucasian minorities, the problem of assimilation understandably did not loom unduly large or complex.

The unfolding events of the next century and a half with increasing momentum dispelled the complacency which rested upon the relative simplicity of colonial and immediate post-Revolutionary conditions. The large-scale immigration to America of the famine-fleeing Irish, the Germans, and later the Scandinavians (along with additional Englishmen and other peoples of northern and western Europe) in the middle of the nineteenth century (the so-called "old immigration"), the emancipation of the Negro slaves and the problems created by post-Civil War reconstruction, the placing of the conquered Indian with his broken culture on government reservations, the arrival of the Oriental, first attracted by the discovery of gold and other opportunities in the West, and finally, beginning in the last quarter of the nineteenth century and continuing to the early 1920's, the swelling to proportions hitherto unimagined of the tide of immigration from the peasantries and "pales" of southern and eastern Europe — the Italians, Jews, and Slavs of the so-called "new immigration," fleeing the persecutions and industrial dislocations of the day — all these events constitute the background against which we may consider the

[1] Allan Nevins and Henry Steele Commager, *America: The Story of a Free People* (Boston: Little, Brown, 1942), p. 58.

rise of the theories of assimilation mentioned above. After a necessarily foreshortened description of each of these theories and their historical emergence, we shall suggest analytical distinctions designed to aid in clarifying the nature of the assimilation process, and then conclude by focusing on the American scene.

Anglo-Conformity

"Anglo-conformity" [2] is a broad term used to cover a variety of viewpoints about assimilation and immigration; they all assume the desirability of maintaining English institutions (as modified by the American Revolution), the English language, and English-oriented cultural patterns as dominant and standard in American life. However, bound up with this assumption are related attitudes. These may range from discredited notions about race and "Nordic" and "Aryan" racial superiority, together with the nativist political programs and exclusionist immigration policies which such notions entail, through an intermediate position of favoring immigration from northern and western Europe on amorphous, unreflective grounds ("They are more like us"), to a lack of opposition to any source of immigration, as long as these immigrants and their descendants duly adopt the standard Anglo-Saxon cultural patterns. There is by no means any necessary equation between Anglo-conformity and racist attitudes.

It is quite likely that "Anglo-conformity" in its more moderate aspects, however explicit its formulation, has been the most prevalent ideology of assimilation goals in America throughout the nation's history. As far back as colonial times, Benjamin Franklin recorded concern about the clannishness of the Germans in Pennsylvania, their slowness in learning English, and the establishment of their own native-language press.[3] Others of the founding fathers had similar reservations about large-scale immigration from Europe. In the context of their times they were unable to foresee the role such immigration was to play in creating the later greatness of the nation. They were not at all men of unthinking prejudices. The disestablishment of religion and the separation of church and state (so that no religious group — whether New England Congregationalists, Virginian Anglicans, or even all Protestants combined — could call upon the federal government for special favors or support, and so that man's religious conscience should be free) were cardinal points of the new national policy

[2] The phrase is the Coles's. See Stewart G. Cole and Mildred Wiese Cole, *Minorities and the American Promise* (New York: Harper and Brothers, 1954), ch. 6.

[3] Maurice R. Davie, *World Immigration* (New York: Macmillan, 1936), p. 36, and (cited therein) "Letter of Benjamin Franklin to Peter Collinson, 9th May, 1753, on the condition and character of the Germans in Pennsylvania," in *The Works of Benjamin Franklin, with notes and a life of the author*, by Jared Sparks (Boston, 1828), vol. 7, pp. 71–73.

they fostered. "The Government of the United States," George Washington had written to the Jewish congregation of Newport during his first term as president, "gives to bigotry no sanction, to persecution no assistance."

Political differences with ancestral England had just been written in blood; but there is no reason to suppose that these men looked upon their fledgling country as an impartial melting pot for the merging of the various cultures of Europe, or as a new "nation of nations," or as anything but a society in which, with important political modifications, Anglo-Saxon speech and institutional forms would be standard. Indeed, their newly won victory for democracy and republicanism made them especially anxious that these still precarious fruits of revolution should not be threatened by a large influx of European peoples whose life experiences had accustomed them to the bonds of despotic monarchy. Thus, although they explicitly conceived of the new United States of America as a haven for those unfortunates of Europe who were persecuted and oppressed, they had characteristic reservations about the effects of too free a policy. "My opinion, with respect to immigration," Washington wrote to John Adams in 1794, "is that except of useful mechanics and some particular descriptions of men or professions, there is no need of encouragement, while the policy or advantage of its taking place in a body (I mean the settling of them in a body) may be much questioned; for, by so doing, they retain the language, habits and principles (good or bad) which they bring with them." [4] Thomas Jefferson, whose views on race and attitudes toward slavery were notably liberal and advanced for his time, had similar doubts concerning the effects of mass immigration on American institutions, while conceding that immigrants, "if they come of themselves . . . are entitled to all the rights of citizenship." [5]

The attitudes of Americans toward foreign immigration in the first three-quarters of the nineteenth century may correctly be described as ambiguous. On the one hand, immigrants were much desired, so as to swell the population and importance of states and territories, to man the farms of expanding prairie settlement, to work the mines, build the railroads and canals, and take their place in expanding industry. This was a period in which no federal legislation of any consequence prevented the entry of aliens, and such state legislation as existed attempted to bar on an individual basis only those who were likely to become a burden on the community, such as convicts and paupers. On the other hand, the arrival in an overwhelmingly Protestant society of large numbers of poverty-

[4] *The Writings of George Washington*, collected and edited by W. C. Ford (New York: G. P. Putnam's Sons, 1889), vol. 12, p. 489.

[5] Thomas Jefferson, "Notes on Virginia, Query 8," in *The Writings of Thomas Jefferson*, ed. A. E. Bergh (Washington: The Thomas Jefferson Memorial Association, 1907), vol. 2, p. 121.

stricken Irish Catholics, who settled in groups in the slums of Eastern cities, roused dormant fears of "Popery" and Rome. Another source of anxiety was the substantial influx of Germans, who made their way to the cities and farms of the mid-West and whose different language, separate communal life, and freer ideas on temperance and sabbath observance brought them into conflict with the Anglo-Saxon bearers of the Puritan and Evangelical traditions. Fear of foreign "radicals" and suspicion of the economic demands of the occasionally aroused workingmen added fuel to the nativist fires. In their extreme form these fears resulted in the Native-American movement of the 1830's and 1840's and the "American" or "Know-Nothing" party of the 1850's, with their anti-Catholic campaigns and their demands for restrictive laws on naturalization procedures and for keeping the foreign-born out of political office. While these movements scored local political successes and their turbulences so rent the national social fabric that the patches are not yet entirely invisible, they failed to influence national legislative policy on immigration and immigrants; and their fulminations inevitably provoked the expected reactions from thoughtful observers.

The flood of newcomers to the westward expanding nation grew larger, reaching over one and two-thirds million between 1841 and 1850 and over two and one-half million in the decade before the Civil War. Throughout the entire period, quite apart from the excesses of the Know-Nothings, the predominant (though not exclusive) conception of what the ideal immigrant adjustment should be was probably summed up in a letter written in 1818 by John Quincy Adams, then Secretary of State, in answer to the inquiries of the Baron von Fürstenwaerther. If not the earliest, it is certainly the most elegant version of the sentiment, "If they don't like it here, they can go back where they came from." Adams declared: [6]

> They [immigrants to America] come to a life of independence, but to a life of labor — and, if they cannot accommodate themselves to the character, moral, political and physical, of this country with all its compensating balances of good and evil, the Atlantic is always open to them to return to the land of their nativity and their fathers. To one thing they must make up their minds, or they will be disappointed in every expectation of happiness as Americans. They must cast off the European skin, never to resume it. They must look forward to their posterity rather than backward to their ancestors; they must be sure that whatever their own feelings may be, those of their children will cling to the prejudices of this country.

The events that followed the Civil War created their own ambiguities in attitude toward the immigrant. A nation undergoing wholesale industrial expansion and not yet finished with the march of westward settlement

[6] *Niles' Weekly Register*, vol. 18, 29 April 1820, pp. 157–158; also, Marcus L. Hansen, *The Atlantic Migration, 1607–1860*, pp. 96–97.

could make good use of the never faltering waves of newcomers. But sporadic bursts of labor unrest, attributed to foreign radicals, the growth of Catholic institutions and the rise of Catholics to municipal political power, and the continuing association of immigrant settlement with urban slums revived familiar fears. The first federal selective law restricting immigration was passed in 1882, and Chinese immigration was cut off in the same year. The most significant development of all, barely recognized at first, was the change in the source of European migrants. Beginning in the 1880's, the countries of southern and eastern Europe began to be represented in substantial numbers for the first time, and in the next decade immigrants from these sources became numerically dominant. Now the notes of a new, or at least hitherto unemphasized, chord from the nativist lyre began to sound — the ugly chord, or discord, of racism. Previously vague and romantic notions of Anglo-Saxon peoplehood, combined with general ethnocentrism, rudimentary wisps of genetics, selected tidbits of evolutionary theory, and naive assumptions from an early and crude imported anthropology produced the doctrine that the English, Germans, and others of the "old immigration" constituted a superior race of tall, blonde, blue-eyed "Nordics" or "Aryans," whereas the peoples of eastern and southern Europe made up the darker Alpines or Mediterraneans — both "inferior" breeds whose presence in America threatened, either by intermixture or supplementation, the traditional American stock and culture. The obvious corollary to this doctrine was to exclude the allegedly inferior breeds; but if the new type of immigrant could not be excluded, then everything must be done to instill Anglo-Saxon virtues in these benighted creatures. Thus, one educator writing in 1909 could state: [7]

> These southern and eastern Europeans are of a very different type from the north Europeans who preceded them. Illiterate, docile, lacking in self-reliance and initiative, and not possessing the Anglo-Teutonic conceptions of law, order, and government, their coming has served to dilute tremendously our national stock, and to corrupt our civic life . . . . Everywhere these people tend to settle in groups or settlements, and to set up here their national manners, customs, and observances. Our task is to break up these groups or settlements, to assimilate and amalgamate these people as a part of our American race, and to implant in their children, so far as can be done, the Anglo-Saxon conception of righteousness, law and order, and popular government, and to awaken in them a reverence for our democratic institutions and for those things in our national life which we as a people hold to be abiding worth.

Anglo-conformity received its fullest expression in the so-called Americanization movement which gripped the nation during World War I.

[7] Ellwood P. Cubberly, *Changing Conceptions of Education* (Boston: Houghton Mifflin, 1909), pp. 15–16.

While "Americanization" in its various stages had more than one emphasis, it was essentially a consciously articulated movement to strip the immigrant of his native culture and attachments and make him over into an
American along Anglo-Saxon lines — all this to be accomplished with
great rapidity. To use an image of a later day, it was an attempt at
"pressure-cooking assimilation." It had prewar antecedents, but it was
during the height of the world conflict that federal agencies, state governments, municipalities, and a host of private organizations joined in the
effort to persuade the immigrant to learn English, take out naturalization
papers, buy war bonds, forget his former origins and culture, and give himself over to patriotic hysteria.

After the war and the "Red scare" which followed, the excesses of the
Americanization movement subsided. In its place, however, came the
restriction of immigration through federal law. Foiled at first by presidential vetoes, and later by the failure of the 1917 literacy test to halt the
immigrant tide, the proponents of restriction finally put through in the
early 1920's a series of acts culminating in the well-known national-
origins formula for immigrant quotas which went into effect in 1929.
Whatever the merits of a quantitative limit on the number of immigrants
to be admitted to the United States, the provisions of the formula, which
discriminated sharply against the countries of southern and eastern
Europe, in effect institutionalized the assumptions of the rightful dominance of Anglo-Saxon patterns in the land. Reaffirmed with only slight
modifications in the McCarran-Walter Act of 1952, these laws, then,
stand as a legal monument to the creed of Anglo-conformity and a telling
reminder that this ideological system still has numerous and powerful
adherents on the American scene.

The Melting Pot

While Anglo-conformity in various guises has probably been the most
prevalent ideology of assimilation in the American historical experience, a
competing viewpoint with more generous and idealistic overtones has had
its adherents and exponents from the eighteenth century onward. Conditions in the virgin continent, it was clear, were modifying the institutions
which the English colonists brought with them from the mother country.
Arrivals from non-English homelands such as Germany, Sweden, and
France were similarly exposed to this fresh environment. Was it not possible, then, to think of the evolving American society not as a slightly
modified England but rather as a totally new blend, culturally and bio-
logically, in which the stocks and folkways of Europe, figuratively speaking, were indiscriminately mixed in the political pot of the emerging
nation and fused by the fires of American influence and interaction into a
distinctly new type?

Such, at any rate, was the conception of the new society which motivated that eighteenth-century French-born writer and agriculturalist,

J. Hector St. John Crèvecoeur, who, after many years of American residence, published his reflections and observations in *Letters from an American Farmer*.[8] Who, he asks, is the American?

> He is either an European, or the descendant of an European, hence
> that strange mixture of blood, which you will find in no other
> country. I could point out to you a family whose grandfather was an
> Englishman, whose wife was Dutch, whose son married a French
> woman, and whose present four sons have now four wives of differ-
> ent nations. *He* is an American, who leaving behind him all his
> ancient prejudices and manners, receives new ones from the new
> mode of life he has embraced, the new government he obeys, and
> the new rank he holds. He becomes an American by being received
> in the broad lap of our great *Alma Mater*. Here individuals of all
> nations are melted into a new race of men, whose labours and
> posterity will one day cause great changes in the world.

Some observers have interpreted the open-door policy on immigration of the first three-quarters of the nineteenth century as reflecting an underlying faith in the effectiveness of the American melting pot, in the belief "that all could be absorbed and that all could contribute to an emerging national character." [9] No doubt many who observed with dismay the nativist agitation of the times felt as did Ralph Waldo Emerson that such conformity-demanding and immigrant-hating forces represented a perversion of the best American ideals. In 1845, Emerson wrote in his Journal: [10]

> I hate the narrowness of the Native American Party. It is the dog
> in the manger. It is precisely opposite to all the dictates of love and
> magnanimity; and therefore, of course, opposite to true wisdom . . . .
> Man is the most composite of all creatures . . . . Well, as in the
> old burning of the Temple at Corinth, by the melting and inter-
> mixture of silver and gold and other metals a new compound more
> precious than any, called Corinthian brass, was formed; so in this
> continent, — asylum of all nations, — the energy of Irish, Germans,
> Swedes, Poles, and Cossacks, and all the European tribes, — of the
> Africans, and of the Polynesians, — will construct a new race, a new
> religion, a new state, a new literature, which will be as vigorous as
> the new Europe which came out of the smelting-pot of the Dark
> Ages, or that which earlier emerged from the Pelasgic and Etruscan
> barbarism. *La Nature aime les croisements*.

[8] J. Hector St. John Crèvecoeur, *Letters from an American Farmer* (New York: Albert and Charles Boni, 1925; reprinted from the 1st edn., London, 1782), pp. 54–55.

[9] Oscar Handlin, ed., *Immigration as a Factor in American History* (Englewood, N.J.: Prentice-Hall, 1959), p. 146.

[10] Quoted by Stuart P. Sherman in his Introduction to *Essays and Poems of Emerson* (New York: Harcourt Brace, 1921), p. xxxiv.

Eventually, the melting-pot hypothesis found its way into historical scholarship and interpretation. While many American historians of the late nineteenth century, some fresh from graduate study at German universities, tended to adopt the view that American institutions derived in essence from Anglo-Saxon (and ultimately Teutonic) sources, others were not so sure.[11] One of these was Frederick Jackson Turner, a young historian from Wisconsin, not long emerged from his graduate training at Johns Hopkins. Turner presented a paper to the American Historical Association, meeting in Chicago in 1893. Called "The Significance of the Frontier in American History," this paper proved to be one of the most influential essays in the history of American scholarship, and its point of view, supported by Turner's subsequent writings and his teaching, pervaded the field of American historical interpretation for at least a generation. Turner's thesis was that the dominant influence in the shaping of American institutions and American democracy was not this nation's European heritage in any of its forms, nor the forces emanating from the eastern seaboard cities, but rather the experiences created by a moving and variegated western frontier. Among the many effects attributed to the frontier environment and the challenges it presented was that it acted as a solvent for the national heritages and the separatist tendencies of the many nationality groups which had joined the trek westward, including the Germans and Scotch-Irish of the eighteenth century and the Scandinavians and Germans of the nineteenth. "The frontier," asserted Turner, "promoted the formation of a composite nationality for the American people . . . . In the crucible of the frontier the immigrants were Americanized, liberated, and fused into a mixed race, English in neither nationality nor characteristics. The process has gone on from the early days to our own." And later, in an essay on the role of the Mississippi Valley, he refers to "the tide of foreign immigration which has risen so steadily that it has made a composite American people whose amalgamation is destined to produce a new national stock." [12]

Thus far, the proponents of the melting pot idea had dealt largely with the diversity produced by the sizeable immigration from the countries of northern and western Europe alone — the "old immigration," consisting of peoples with cultures and physical appearance not greatly different from those of the Anglo-Saxon stock. Emerson, it is true, had impartially included Africans, Polynesians, and Cossacks in his conception of the mixture; but it was only in the last two decades of the nineteenth century that a large-scale influx of peoples from the countries of southern and eastern Europe imperatively posed the question of whether these uprooted

[11] See Edward N. Saveth, *American Historians and European Immigrants,* 1875–1925 (New York: Columbia University Press, 1948).
[12] Frederick Jackson Turner, *The Frontier in American History* (New York: Henry Holt, 1920), pp. 22–23, 190.

newcomers who were crowding into the large cities of the nation and the industrial sector of the economy could also be successfully "melted." Would the "urban melting pot" work as well as the "frontier melting pot" of an essentially rural society was alleged to have done?

It remained for an English-Jewish writer with strong social convictions, moved by his observation of the role of the United States as a haven for the poor and oppressed of Europe, to give utterance to the broader view of the American melting pot in a way which attracted public attention. In 1908, Israel Zangwill's drama, *The Melting Pot*, was produced in this country and became a popular success. It is a play dominated by the dream of its protagonist, a young Russian-Jewish immigrant to America, a composer, whose goal is the completion of a vast "American" symphony which will express his deeply felt conception of his adopted country as a divinely appointed crucible in which all the ethnic divisions of mankind will divest themselves of their ancient animosities and differences and become fused into one group, signifying the brotherhood of man. In the process he falls in love with a beautiful and cultured Gentile girl. The play ends with the performance of the symphony and, after numerous vicissitudes and traditional family opposition from both sides, with the approaching marriage of David Quixano and his beloved. During the course of these developments, David, in the rhetoric of the time, delivers himself of such sentiments as these: [13]

> America is God's crucible, the great Melting Pot where all the races of Europe are melting and re-forming! Here you stand, good folk, think I, when I see them at Ellis Island, here you stand in your fifty groups, with your fifty languages and histories, and your fifty blood hatreds and rivalries. But you won't be long like that, brothers, for these are the fires of God you've come to — these are the fires of God. A fig for your feuds and vendettas! Germans and Frenchmen, Irishmen and Englishmen, Jews and Russians — into the Crucible with you all! God is making the American.

Here we have a conception of a melting pot which admits of no exceptions or qualifications with regard to the ethnic stocks which will fuse in the great crucible. Englishmen, Germans, Frenchmen, Slavs, Greeks, Syrians, Jews, Gentiles, even the black and yellow races, were specifically mentioned in Zangwill's rhapsodic enumeration. And this pot patently was to boil in the great cities of America.

Thus around the turn of the century the melting-pot idea became embedded in the ideals of the age as one response to the immigrant receiving experience of the nation. Soon to be challenged by a new philosophy of group adjustment (to be discussed below) and always competing with the more pervasive adherence to Anglo-conformity, the melting-pot image,

[13] Israel Zangwill, *The Melting Pot* (New York: Macmillan, 1909), p. 37.

however, continued to draw a portion of the attention consciously directed toward this aspect of the American scene in the first half of the twentieth century. In the mid-1940's a sociologist who had carried out an investigation of intermarriage trends in New Haven, Connecticut, described a revised conception of the melting process in that city and suggested a basic modification of the theory of that process. In New Haven, Ruby Jo Reeves Kennedy [14] reported from a study of intermarriages from 1870 to 1940 that there was a distinct tendency for the British-Americans, Germans, and Scandinavians to marry among themselves — that is, within a Protestant "pool"; for the Irish, Italians, and Poles to marry among themselves — a Catholic "pool"; and for the Jews to marry other Jews. In other words, intermarriage was taking place across lines of nationality background, but there was a strong tendency for it to stay confined within one or the other of the three major religious groups, Protestants, Catholics, and Jews. Thus, declared Mrs. Kennedy, the picture in New Haven resembled a "triple melting pot" based on religious divisions, rather than a "single melting pot." Her study indicated, she stated, that "while strict endogamy is loosening, religious endogamy is persisting and the future cleavages will be among religious lines rather than along nationality lines as in the past. If this is the case, then the traditional 'single-melting-pot' idea must be abandoned, and a new conception, which we term the 'triple-melting-pot' theory of American assimilation, will take its place as the true expression of what is happening to the various nationality groups in the United States." [15] The triple melting-pot thesis was later taken up by the theologian, Will Herberg, and formed an important sociological frame of reference for his analysis of religious trends in American society, *Protestant-Catholic-Jew*.[16] But the triple melting-pot hypothesis patently takes us into the realm of a society pluralistically conceived. We turn now to the rise of an ideology which attempts to justify such a conception.

Cultural Pluralism

Probably all the non-English immigrants who came to American shores in any significant numbers from colonial times onward — settling either in the forbidding wilderness, the lonely prairie, or in some accessible urban slum — created ethnic enclaves and looked forward to the preservation of at least some of their native cultural patterns. Such a development, natural as breathing, was supported by the later accretion of friends, relatives, and

[14] Ruby Jo Reeves Kennedy, "Single or Triple Melting-Pot? Intermarriage Trends in New Haven, 1870–1940," *American Journal of Sociology*, 1944, 49: 331–339. See also her "Single or Triple Melting-Pot? Intermarriage in New Haven, 1870–1950," *ibid.*, 1952, 58: 56–59.

[15] Ruby Jo Reeves Kennedy, "Single or Triple Melting-Pot? . . . 1870–1940," p. 332 (author' italics omitted).

[16] Will Herberg, *Protestant-Catholic-Jew* (Garden City, N.Y.: Doubleday, 1955).

countrymen seeking out oases of familiarity in a strange land, by the desire of the settlers to rebuild (necessarily in miniature) a society in which they could communicate in the familiar tongue and maintain familiar institutions, and, finally, by the necessity to band together for mutual aid and mutual protection against the uncertainties of a strange and frequently hostile environment. This was as true of the "old" immigrants as of the "new." In fact, some of the liberal intellectuals who fled to America from an inhospitable political climate in Germany in the 1830's, 1840's, and 1850's looked forward to the creation of an all-German state within the union, or, even more hopefully, to the eventual formation of a separate German nation, as soon as the expected dissolution of the union under the impact of the slavery controversy should have taken place.[17] Oscar Handlin, writing of the sons of Erin in mid-nineteenth-century Boston, recent refugees from famine and economic degradation in their homeland, points out: "Unable to participate in the normal associational affairs of the community, the Irish felt obliged to erect a society within a society, to act together in their own way. In every contact therefore the group, acting apart from other sections of the community, became intensely aware of its peculiar and exclusive identity." [18] Thus cultural pluralism was a fact in American society before it became a theory — a theory with explicit relevance for the nation as a whole, and articulated and discussed in the English-speaking circles of American intellectual life.

Eventually, the cultural enclaves of the Germans (and the later arriving Scandinavians) were to decline in scope and significance as succeeding generations of their native-born attended public schools, left the farms and villages to strike out as individuals for the Americanizing city, and generally became subject to the influences of a standardizing industrial civilization. The German-American community, too, was struck a powerful blow by the accumulated passions generated by World War I — a blow from which it never fully recovered. The Irish were to be the dominant and pervasive element in the gradual emergence of a pan-Catholic group in America, but these developments would reveal themselves only in the twentieth century. In the meantime, in the last two decades of the nineteenth, the influx of immigrants from southern and eastern Europe had begun. These groups were all the more sociologically visible because the closing of the frontier, the occupational demands of an expanding industrial economy, and their own poverty made it inevitable that they

[17] Nathan Glazer, "Ethnic Groups in America: From National Culture to Ideology," in Morroe Berger, Theodore Abel, and Charles H. Page, eds., *Freedom and Control in Modern Society* (New York: D. Van Nostrand, 1954), p. 161; Marcus Lee Hansen, *The Immigrant in American History* (Cambridge: Harvard University Press, 1940), pp. 129–140; John A. Hawgood, *The Tragedy of German-America* (New York: Putnam's, 1940), *passim*.

[18] Oscar Handlin, *Boston's Immigrants* (Cambridge: Harvard University Press, 1959, rev. edn.), p. 176.

would remain in the urban areas of the nation. In the swirling fires of controversy and the steadier flame of experience created by these new events, the ideology of cultural pluralism as a philosophy for the nation was forged.

The first manifestations of an ideological counterattack against draconic Americanization came not from the beleaguered newcomers (who were, after all, more concerned with survival than with theories of adjustment), but from those idealistic members of the middle class who, in the decade or so before the turn of the century, had followed the example of their English predecessors and "settled" in the slums to "learn to sup sorrow with the poor." [19] Immediately, these workers in the "settlement houses" were forced to come to grips with the realities of immigrant life and adjustment. Not all reacted in the same way, but on the whole the settlements developed an approach to the immigrant which was sympathetic to his native cultural heritage and to his newly created ethnic institutions.[20] For one thing, their workers, necessarily in intimate contact with the lives of these often pathetic and bewildered newcomers and their daily problems, could see how unfortunate were the effects of those forces which impelled rapid Americanization in their impact on the immigrants' children, who not infrequently became alienated from their parents and the restraining influence of family authority. Were not their parents ignorant and uneducated "Hunkies," "Sheenies," or "Dagoes," as that limited portion of the American environment in which they moved defined the matter? Ethnic "self-hatred" with its debilitating psychological consequences, family disorganization, and juvenile delinquency, were not unusual results of this state of affairs. Furthermore, the immigrants themselves were adversely affected by the incessant attacks on their culture, their language, their institutions, their very conception of themselves. How were they to maintain their self-respect when all that they knew, felt, and dreamed, beyond their sheer capacity for manual labor — in other words, all that they *were* — was despised or scoffed at in America? And — unkindest cut of all — their own children had begun to adopt the contemptuous attitude of the "Americans." Jane Addams relates in a moving chapter of her *Twenty Years at Hull House* how, after coming to have some conception of the extent and depth of these problems, she created at the settlement a "Labor Museum," in which the immigrant women of the various nationalities crowded together in the slums of Chicago could illustrate their native methods of spinning and weaving, and

[19] From a letter (1883) by Samuel A. Barnett; quoted in Arthur C. Holden, *The Settlement Idea* (New York: Macmillan, 1922), p. 12.

[20] Jane Addams, *Twenty Years at Hull House* (New York: Macmillan, 1914), pp. 231–258; Arthur C. Holden, *op. cit.*, pp. 109–131, 182–189; John Higham, *Strangers in the Land* (New Brunswick, N.J.: Rutgers University Press, 1955), p. 236.

in which the relation of these earlier techniques to contemporary factory methods could be graphically shown. For the first time these peasant women were made to feel by some part of their American environment that they possessed valuable and interesting skills — that they too had something to offer — and for the first time, the daughters of these women who, after a long day's work at their dank "needletrade" sweatshops, came to Hull House to observe, began to appreciate the fact that their mothers, too, had a "culture," that this culture possessed its own merit, and that it was related to their own contemporary lives. How aptly Jane Addams concludes her chapter with the hope that "our American citizenship might be built without disturbing these foundations which were laid of old time." [21]

This appreciative view of the immigrant's cultural heritage and of its distinctive usefulness both to himself and his adopted country received additional sustenance from another source: those intellectual currents of the day which, however overborne by their currently more powerful opposites, emphasized liberalism, internationalism, and tolerance. From time to time, an occasional educator or publicist protested the demands of the "Americanizers," arguing that the immigrant, too, had an ancient and honorable culture, and that this culture had much to offer an America whose character and destiny were still in the process of formation, an America which must serve as an example of the harmonious cooperation of various heritages to a world inflamed by nationalism and war. In 1916 John Dewey, Norman Hapgood, and the young literary critic, Randolph Bourne, published articles or addresses elaborating various aspects of this theme.

The classic statement of the cultural pluralist position, however, had been made over a year before. Early in 1915 there appeared in the pages of *The Nation* two articles under the title "Democracy *versus* the Melting-Pot." Their author was Horace Kallen, a Harvard-educated philosopher with a concern for the application of philosophy to societal affairs, and, as an American Jew, himself derivative of an ethnic background which was subject to the contemporary pressures for dissolution implicit in the "Americanization," or Anglo-conformity, and the melting-pot theories. In these articles Kallen vigorously rejected the usefulness of these theories as models of what was actually transpiring in American life or as ideals for the future. Rather he was impressed by the way in which the various ethnic groups in America were coincident with particular areas and regions, and with the tendency for each group to preserve its own language, religion, communal institutions, and ancestral culture. All the while, he pointed out, the immigrant has been learning to speak English as the language of general communication, and has participated in the over-all economic and political life of the nation. These developments in which

[21] Jane Addams, *op. cit.*, p. 258.

"the United States are in the process of becoming a federal state not merely as a union of geographical and administrative unities, but also as a cooperation of cultural diversities, as a federation or commonwealth of national cultures," [22] the author argued, far from constituting a violation of historic American political principles, as the "Americanizers" claimed, actually represented the inevitable consequences of democratic ideals, since individuals are implicated in groups, and since democracy for the individual must by extension also mean democracy for his group.

The processes just described, however, as Kallen develops his argument, are far from having been thoroughly realized. They are menaced by "Americanization" programs, assumptions of Anglo-Saxon superiority, and misguided attempts to promote "racial" amalgamation. Thus America stands at a kind of cultural crossroads. It can attempt to impose by force an artificial, Anglo-Saxon oriented uniformity on its peoples, or it can consciously allow and encourage its ethnic groups to develop democratically, each emphasizing its particular cultural heritage. If the latter course is followed, as Kallen puts it at the close of his essay, then,[23]

> The outlines of a possible great and truly democratic commonwealth become discernible. Its form would be that of the federal republic; its substance a democracy of nationalities, cooperating voluntarily and autonomously through common institutions in the enterprise of self-realization through the perfection of men according to their kind. The common language of the commonwealth, the language of its great tradition, would be English, but each nationality would have for its emotional and involuntary life its own peculiar dialect or speech, its own individual and inevitable esthetic and intellectual forms. The political and economic life of the commonwealth is a single unit and serves as the foundation and background for the realization of the distinctive individuality of each *natio* that composes it and of the pooling of these in a harmony above them all. Thus "American civilization" may come to mean the perfection of the cooperative harmonies of "European civilization" — the waste, the squalor and the distress of Europe being eliminated — a multiplicity in a unity, an orchestration of mankind.

Within the next decade Kallen published more essays dealing with the theme of American multiple-group life, later collected in a volume.[24] In the introductory note to this book he used for the first time the term "cultural pluralism" to refer to his position. These essays reflect both his increasingly sharp rejection of the onslaughts on the immigrant and his culture which the coming of World War I and its attendant fears, the

[22] Horace M. Kallen, "Democracy *versus* the Melting-Pot," *The Nation*, 18 and 25 February 1915; reprinted in his *Culture and Democracy in the United States* (New York: Boni and Liveright, 1924); the quotation is on p. 116.

[23] Kallen, *Culture and Democracy* . . . , p. 124.

[24] *Op. cit.*

"Red scare," the projection of themes of racial superiority, the continued exploitation of the newcomers, and the rise of the Ku Klux Klan all served to increase in intensity, and also his emphasis on cultural pluralism as the democratic antidote to these ills. He has since published other essays elaborating or annotating the theme of cultural pluralism. Thus, for at least forty-five years, most of them spent teaching at the New School for Social Research, Kallen has been acknowledged as the originator and leading philosophical exponent of the idea of cultural pluralism.

In the late 1930's and early 1940's the late Louis Adamic, the Yugoslav immigrant who had become an American writer, took up the theme of America's multicultural heritage and the role of these groups in forging the country's national character. Borrowing Walt Whitman's phrase, he described America as "a nation of nations," and while his ultimate goal was closer to the melting-pot idea than to cultural pluralism, he saw the immediate task as that of making America conscious of what it owed to all its ethnic groups, not just to the Anglo-Saxons. The children and grand-children of immigrants of non-English origins, he was convinced, must be taught to be proud of the cultural heritage of their ancestral ethnic group and of its role in building the American nation; otherwise, they would not lose their sense of ethnic inferiority and the feeling of rootlessness he claimed to find in them.

Thus in the twentieth century, particularly since World War II, "cultural pluralism" has become a concept which has worked its way into the vocabulary and imagery of specialists in intergroup relations and leaders of ethnic communal groups. In view of this new pluralistic emphasis, some writers now prefer to speak of the "integration" of immigrants rather than of their "assimilation." [25] However, with a few exceptions,[26] no close analytical attention has been given either by social scientists or practitioners of intergroup relations to the meaning of cultural pluralism, its nature and relevance for a modern industrialized society, and its implications for problems of prejudice and discrimination — a point to which we referred at the outset of this discussion.

Conclusions

In the remaining pages I can make only a few analytical comments which I shall apply in context to the American scene, historical and current. My

[25] See W. D. Borrie *et al.*, *The Cultural Integration of Immigrants* (a survey based on the papers and proceedings of the UNESCO Conference in Havana, April 1956), Paris, UNESCO, 1959; and William S. Bernard, "The Integration of Immigrants in the United States" (mimeographed), one of the papers for this conference.

[26] See particularly Milton M. Gordon, "Social Structure and Goals in Group Relations," and Nathan Glazer, "Ethnic Groups in America; From National Culture to Ideology," both articles in Berger, Abel, and Page, *op. cit.*; S. N. Eisenstadt, *The Absorption of Immigrants* (London: Routledge and Kegan Paul, 1954); and W. D. Borrie *et al.*, *op. cit.*

view of the American situation will not be documented here, but may be considered as a series of hypotheses in which I shall attempt to outline the American assimilation process.

First of all, it must be realized that "assimilation" is a blanket term which in reality covers a multitude of subprocesses. The most crucial distinction is one often ignored — the distinction between what I have elsewhere called "behavioral assimilation" and "structural assimilation." [27] The first refers to the absorption of the cultural behavior patterns of the "host" society. (At the same time, there is frequently some modification of the cultural patterns of the immigrant-receiving country, as well.) There is a special term for this process of cultural modification or "behavioral assimilation" — namely, "acculturation." "Structural assimilation," on the other hand, refers to the entrance of the immigrants and their descendants into the social cliques, organizations, institutional activities, and general civic life of the receiving society. If this process takes place on a large enough scale, then a high frequency of intermarriage must result. A further distinction must be made between, on the one hand, those activities of the general civic life which involve earning a living, carrying out political responsibilities, and engaging in the instrumental affairs of the larger community, and, on the other hand, activities which create personal friendship patterns, frequent home intervisiting, communal worship, and communal recreation. The first type usually develops so-called "secondary relationships," which tend to be relatively impersonal and segmental; the latter type leads to "primary relationships," which are warm, intimate, and personal.

With these various distinctions in mind, we may then proceed.

Built on the base of the original immigrant "colony" but frequently extending into the life of successive generations, the characteristic ethnic group experience is this: within the ethnic group there develops a network of organizations and informal social relationships which permits and encourages the members of the ethnic group to remain within the confines of the group for all of their primary relationships and some of their secondary relationships throughout all the stages of the life cycle. From the cradle in the sectarian hospital to the child's play group, the social clique in high school, the fraternity and religious center in college, the dating group within which he searches for a spouse, the marriage partner, the neighborhood of his residence, the church affiliation and the church clubs, the men's and the women's social and service organizations, the adult clique of "marrieds," the vacation resort, and then, as the age cycle nears completion, the rest home for the elderly and, finally, the sectarian cemetery — in all these activities and relationships which are close to the core of personality and selfhood — the member of the ethnic group may

[27] Milton M. Gordon, "Social Structure and Goals in Group Relations," p. 151.

if he wishes follow a path which never takes him across the boundaries of his ethnic structural network.

The picture is made more complex by the existence of social class divisions which cut across ethnic group lines just as they do those of the white Protestant population in America. As each ethnic group which has been here for the requisite time has developed second, third, or in some cases, succeeding generations, it has produced a college-educated group which composes an upper middle class (and sometimes upper class, as well) segment of the larger groups. Such class divisions tend to restrict primary group relations even further, for although the ethnic-group member feels a general sense of identification with all the bearers of his ethnic heritage, he feels comfortable in intimate social relations only with those who also share his own class background or attainment.

In short, my point is that, while *behavioral assimilation* or acculturation has taken place in America to a considerable degree, *structural assimilation*, with some important exceptions has not been extensive.[28] The exceptions are of two types. The first brings us back to the "triple melting pot" thesis of Ruby Jo Reeves Kennedy and Will Herberg. The "nationality" ethnic groups have tended to merge within each of the three major religious groups. This has been particularly true of the Protestant and Jewish communities. Those descendants of the "old" immigration of the nineteenth century, who were Protestant (many of the Germans and all the Scandinavians), have in considerable part gradually merged into the white Protestant "subsociety." Jews of Sephardic, German, and Eastern-European origins have similarly tended to come together in their communal life. The process of absorbing the various Catholic nationalities, such as the Italians, Poles, and French Canadians, into an American Catholic community hitherto dominated by the Irish has begun, although I do not believe that it is by any means close to completion. Racial and quasi-racial groups such as the Negroes, Indians, Mexican-Americans, and Puerto Ricans still retain their separate sociological structures. The outcome of all this in contemporary American life is thus pluralism — but it is more than "triple" and it is more accurately described as *structural pluralism* than as cultural pluralism, although some of the latter also remains.

My second exception refers to the social structures which implicate intellectuals. There is no space to develop the issue here, but I would argue that there is a social world or subsociety of the intellectuals in America in which true structural intermixture among persons of various ethnic backgrounds, including the religious, has markedly taken place.

My final point deals with the reasons for these developments. If structural assimilation has been retarded in America by religious and racial

[28] See Erich Rosenthal, "Acculturation without Assimilation?" *American Journal of Sociology*, 1960, 66: 275–288.

lines, we must ask why. The answer lies in the attitudes of both the majority and the minority groups and in the way these attitudes have interacted. A saying of the current day is, "It takes two to tango." To apply the analogy, there is no good reason to believe that white Protestant America has ever extended a firm and cordial invitation to its minorities to dance. Furthermore, the attitudes of the minority-group members themselves on the matter have been divided and ambiguous. Particularly for the minority religious groups, there is a certain logic in ethnic communality, since there is a commitment to the perpetuation of the religious ideology and since structural intermixture leads to intermarriage and the possible loss to the group of the intermarried family. Let us, then, examine the situation serially for various types of minorities.

With regard to the immigrant, in his characteristic numbers and socioeconomic background, structural assimilation was out of the question. He did not want it, and he had a positive need for the comfort of his own communal institutions. The native American, moreover, whatever the implications of his public pronouncements, had no intention of opening up his primary group life to entrance by these hordes of alien newcomers. The situation was a functionally complementary standoff.

The second generation found a much more complex situation. Many believed they heard the siren call of welcome to the social cliques, clubs, and institutions of white Protestant America. After all, it was simply a matter of learning American ways, was it not? Had they not grown up as Americans, and were they not culturally different from their parents, the "greenhorns"? Or perhaps an especially eager one reasoned (like the Jewish protagonist of Myron Kaufmann's novel, *Remember Me To God*, aspiring to membership in the prestigious club system of Harvard undergraduate social life) "If only I can go the last few steps in Ivy League manners and behavior, they will surely recognize that I am one of them and take me in." But, alas, Brooks Brothers suit notwithstanding, the doors of the fraternity house, the city men's club, and the country club were slammed in the face of the immigrant's offspring. That invitation was not really there in the first place; or, to the extent it was, in Joshua Fishman's phrase, it was a " 'look me over but don't touch me' invitation to the American minority group child." [29] And so the rebuffed one returned to the homelier but dependable comfort of the communal institutions of his ancestral group. There he found his fellows of the same generation who had never stirred from the home fires. Some of these had been too timid to stray; others were ethnic ideologists committed to the group's survival; still others had never really believed in the authenticity of

[29] Joshua A. Fishman, "Childhood Indoctrination for Minority-Group Membership and the Quest for Minority-Group Biculturism in America," in Oscar Handlin, ed., *Group Life in America* (Cambridge: Harvard University Press, forthcoming).

the siren call or were simply too passive to do more than go along the familiar way. All could now join in the task that was well within the realm of the sociologically possible — the build-up of social institutions and organizations within the ethnic enclave, manned increasingly by members of the second generation and suitably separated by social class.

Those who had for a time ventured out gingerly or confidently, as the case might be, had been lured by the vision of an "American" social structure that was somehow larger than all subgroups and was ethnically neutral. Were they, too, not Americans? But they found to their dismay that at the primary group level a neutral American social structure was a mirage. What at a distance seemed to be a quasi-public edifice flying only the all-inclusive flag of American nationality turned out on closer inspection to be the clubhouse of a particular ethnic group — the white Anglo-Saxon Protestants, its operation shot through with the premises and expectations of its parental ethnicity. In these terms, the desirability of whatever invitation was grudgingly extended to those of other ethnic backgrounds could only become a considerably attenuated one.

With the racial minorities, there was not even the pretense of an invitation. Negroes, to take the most salient example, have for the most part been determinedly barred from the cliques, social clubs, and churches of white America. Consequently, with due allowance for internal class differences, they have constructed their own network of organizations and institutions, their own "social world." There are now many vested interests served by the preservation of this separate communal life, and doubtless many Negroes are psychologically comfortable in it, even though at the same time they keenly desire that discrimination in such areas as employment, education, housing, and public accommodations be eliminated. However, the ideological attachment of Negroes to their communal separation is not conspicuous. Their sense of identification with ancestral African national cultures is virtually nonexistent, although Pan-Africanism engages the interest of some intellectuals and although "black nationalist" and "black racist" fringe groups have recently made an appearance at the other end of the communal spectrum. As for their religion, they are either Protestant or Catholic (overwhelmingly the former). Thus, there are no "logical" ideological reasons for their separate communality; dual social structures are created solely by the dynamics of prejudice and discrimination, rather than being reinforced by the ideological commitments of the minority itself.

Structural assimilation, then, has turned out to be the rock on which the ships of Anglo-conformity and the melting pot have foundered. To understand that behavioral assimilation (or acculturation) without massive structural intermingling in primary relationships has been the dominant motif in the American experience of creating and developing a nation out of diverse peoples is to comprehend the most essential sociological fact of that experience. It is against the background of "structural pluralism" that strategies of strengthening intergroup harmony, reducing ethnic discrimination and prejudice, and maintaining the rights of both those who stay within and those who venture beyond their ethnic boundaries must be thoughtfully devised.

The Racial Ghettos

REPORT OF THE NATIONAL
ADVISORY COMMISSION
ON CIVIL DISORDERS

The place of racial minorities in the process of assimilation always has been a unique problem. As Milton Gordon noted in the previous essay, "there was not even the pretense of an invitation" for assimilation extended to Negroes or other racial minorities. Instead, they have been subjected to a process of economic and social isolation dissimilar from that of any other group in the American experience. It has been an almost absolute isolation imposed and maintained from above. Other immigrant groups have functioned within their own isolated communities, but always in a limited manner, and their isolation has broken down rapidly with each successive generation. The isolation of racial groups, however, has been largely physical, to the point where they have not even experienced what Gordon called the "secondary relationships" of behavioral assimilation. The result has been the creation of the racial ghetto, a static institution characterized by general conditions of violence and harshness, prompted in turn by the accumulated burdens of poverty, exploitation, unemployment, poor education — in short, the lack of social and economic opportunities. Yet the role of white Americans in the ghetto has been imperfectly understood. The recent report of the presidential commission on urban riots, however, carefully culled the historical record, and current social and economic data, to underline that role: "White institutions created [the ghetto], white institutions maintain it, and white society condones it." The following selections from that report cover the formation of the racial ghetto, urban change in the last decades, unemployment, and the social impact of poverty. Finally, the commission offers a perceptive critique on the difficulties of analogizing the immigrant and Negro experiences in the United States.

The Formation of the Racial Ghettos

Major Trends in Negro Population. Throughout the 20th century, and particularly in the last three decades, the Negro population of the United States has been steadily moving — from rural areas to urban, from South to North and West.

In 1910, 2.7 million Negroes lived in American cities — 28 per cent of the nation's Negro population of 9.8 million. Today, about 15 million Negro Americans live in metropolitan areas, or 69 per cent of the Negro population of 21.5 million. In 1910, 885,000 Negroes — 9 per cent — lived outside the South. Now, almost 10 million, about 45 per cent, live in the North or West.

These shifts in population have resulted from three basic trends:

A rapid increase in the size of the Negro population.

A continuous flow of Negroes from Southern rural areas, partly to large cities in the South, but primarily to large cities in the North and West.

An increasing concentration of Negroes in large metropolitan areas within racially segregated neighborhoods.

Taken together, these trends have produced large and constantly growing concentrations of Negro population within big cities in all parts of the nation. Because most major civil disorders of recent years occurred in predominantly Negro neighborhoods, we have examined the causes of this concentration.

The Growth Rate of the Negro Population. During the first half of this century, the white population of the United States grew at a slightly faster rate than the Negro population. Because fertility rates [1] among Negro women were more than offset by death rates among Negroes and large-scale immigration of whites from Europe, the proportion of Negroes in the country declined from 12 per cent in 1900 to 10 per cent in 1940.

By the end of World War II — and increasingly since then — major advances in medicine and medical care, together with the increasing youth

Report of the National Advisory Commission on Civil Disorders (Washington, D.C.: Government Printing Office, 1968), pp. 115–120, 123–130, 143–145, and *passim.*

[1] The "fertility rate" is the number of live births per year per 1,000 women age 15 to 44 in the group concerned.

of the Negro population resulting from higher fertility rates, caused death rates among Negroes to fall much faster than among whites. This is shown in [Table 1]. In addition, white immigration from outside the United States dropped dramatically after stringent restrictions were adopted in in the 1920's. [See Table 2.]

TABLE 1   *Death Rate/1,000 Population*

Year	Whites	Nonwhites	Ratio of nonwhite rate to white rate
1900	17.0	25.0	1.47
1940	10.4	13.8	1.33
1965	9.4	9.6	1.02

TABLE 2

20-year period	Total immigration (millions)
1901–20	14.5
1921–40	4.6
1941–60	3.6

Thus, by mid-century, both factors which had previously offset higher fertility rates among Negro women no longer were in effect.

While Negro fertility rates, after rising rapidly to 1957, have declined sharply in the past decade, white fertility rates have dropped even more, leaving Negro rates much higher in comparison. [See Table 3.]

TABLE 3   *Live Births Per 1,000 Women Aged 15–44*

Year	White	Nonwhite	Ratio of nonwhite to white
1940	77.1	102.4	1.33
1957	117.4	163.4	1.39
1965	91.4	133.9	1.46

The result is that Negro population is now growing significantly faster than white population. From 1940 to 1960, the white population rose 34.0 per cent, but the Negro population rose 46.6 per cent. From 1960 to 1966, the white population grew 7.6 per cent, whereas Negro population rose 14.4 per cent, almost twice as much.

Consequently, the proportion of Negroes in the total population has risen from 10.0 per cent in 1950 to 10.5 per cent in 1960, and 11.1 per cent in 1966.[2]

In 1950, at least one of every ten Americans was Negro; in 1966, one of nine. If this trend continues, one of every eight Americans will be Negro by 1972.

Another consequence of higher birth rates among Negroes is that the Negro population is considerably younger than the white population. In 1966, the median age among whites was 29.1 years, as compared to 21.1 among Negroes. About 35 per cent of the white population was under 18 years of age, compared with 45 per cent for Negroes. About one of every six children under five and one of every six new babies are Negro.

Negro-white fertility rates bear an interesting relationship to educational experience. Negro women with low levels of education have more children than white women with similar schooling, while Negro women with four years or more of college education have fewer children than white women similarly educated. [Table 4] illustrates this. This suggests that the difference between Negro and white fertility rates may decline in the future if Negro educational attainment compares more closely with that of whites, and if a rising proportion of members of both groups complete college.

TABLE 4

Education level attained	Number of children ever born to all women (married or unmarried) 35–39 years old, by level of education (based on 1960 census)	
	Nonwhite	White
Completed elementary school	3.0	2.8
Four years of high school	2.3	2.3
Four years of college	1.7	2.2
Five years or more of college	1.2	1.6

The Migration of Negroes from the South. The Magnitude of This Migration. In 1910, 91 per cent of the Nation's 9.8 million Negroes lived in the South. Twenty-seven per cent of American Negroes lived in cities of 2,500 persons or more, as compared to 49 per cent of the Nation's white population.

By 1966, the Negro population had increased to 21.5 million, and two significant geographic shifts had taken place. The proportion of Negroes

---

[2] These proportions are undoubtedly too low because the Census Bureau has consistently undercounted the number of Negroes in the U.S. by as much as 10 per cent.

living in the South had dropped to 55 per cent, and about 69 per cent of all Negroes lived in metropolitan areas compared to 64 per cent for whites. While the total Negro population more than doubled from 1910 to 1966, the number living in cities rose over fivefold (from 2.7 million to 14.8 million) and the number outside the South rose elevenfold (from 885,000 to 9.7 million).

Negro migration from the South began after the Civil War. By the turn of the century, sizable Negro populations lived in many large Northern cities — Philadelphia, for example, had 63,400 Negro residents in 1900. The movement of Negroes out of the rural South accelerated during World War I, when floods and boll weevils hurt farming in the South and the industrial demands of the war created thousands of new jobs for unskilled workers in the North. After the war, the shift to mechanized farming spurred the continuing movement of Negroes from rural Southern areas.

The Depression slowed this migratory flow, but World War II set it in motion again. More recently, continuing mechanization of agriculture and the expansion of industrial employment in Northern and Western cities have served to sustain the movement of Negroes out of the South, although at a slightly lower rate. [See Table 5.]

TABLE 5

Period	Net Negro out-migration from the South	Annual average rate
1910–20	454,000	45,400
1920–30	749,000	74,900
1930–40	348,000	34,800
1940–50	1,597,000	159,700
1950–60	1,457,000	145,700
1960–66	613,000	102,500

From 1960 to 1963, annual Negro out-migration actually dropped to 78,000 but then rose to over 125,000 from 1963 to 1966.

Important Characteristics of This Migration. It is useful to recall that even the latest scale of Negro migration is relatively small when compared to the earlier waves of European immigrants. A total of 8.8 million immigrants entered the United States between 1901 and 1911, and another 5.7 million arrived during the following decade. Even during the years from 1960 through 1966, the 1.8 million immigrants from abroad were almost three times the 613,000 Negroes who departed the South. In these same 6 years, California alone gained over 1.5 million new residents from internal shifts of American population.

Three major routes of Negro migration from the South have developed.

One runs north along the Atlantic Seaboard toward Boston, another north from Mississippi toward Chicago, and the third west from Texas and Louisiana toward California. Between 1955 and 1960, 50 per cent of the nonwhite migrants to the New York metropolitan area came from North Carolina, South Carolina, Virginia, Georgia, and Alabama; North Carolina alone supplied 20 per cent of all New York's nonwhite immigrants. During the same period, almost 60 per cent of the nonwhite migrants to Chicago came from Mississippi, Tennessee, Arkansas, Alabama, and Louisiana; Mississippi accounted for almost one-third. During these years, three-fourths of the nonwhite migrants to Los Angeles came from Texas, Louisiana, Mississippi, Arkansas, and Alabama.

The flow of Negroes from the South has caused the Negro population to grow more rapidly in the North and West, as indicated [in Table 6].

TABLE 6

Period	Total Negro population gains (millions)		Percentage of gain in
	North & West	South	North & West
1940–50	1.859	0.321	85.2
1950–60	2.741	1.086	71.6
1960–66	2.119	0.517	80.4

As a result, although a much higher proportion of Negroes still reside in the South, the distribution of Negroes throughout the United States is beginning to approximate that of whites, as [Tables 7 and 8] show.

TABLE 7

Percentage Distribution of the Population by Region — 1950, 1960, and 1966

	Negro			White		
	1950	1960	1966	1950	1960*	1966
United States	100	100	100	100	100	100
South	68	60	55	27	27	28
North	28	34	37	59	56	55
Northeast	13	16	17	28	26	26
Northcentral	15	18	20	31	30	29
West	4	6	8	14	16	17

* Rounds to 99.

Negroes in the North and West are now so numerous that natural increase rather than migration provides the greater part of Negro popula-

TABLE 8

Negroes as a Percentage of the Total Population in the United States and Each Region 1950, 1960, and 1966

	1950	1960	1966
United States	10	11	11
South	22	21	20
North	5	7	8
West	3	4	5

tion gains there. And even though Negro migration has continued at a high level, it comprises a constantly declining proportion of Negro growth in these regions. [See Table 9.]

TABLE 9

Period	Percentage of total North and West Negro gain from Southern in-migration
1940–50	85.9
1950–60	53.1
1960–66	28.9

In other words, we have reached the point where the Negro populations of the North and West will continue to expand significantly even if migration from the South drops substantially.

Future Migration. Despite accelerating Negro migration from the South, the Negro population there has continued to rise. [See Table 10.]

TABLE 10

Date	Negro population in the South (millions)	Change from preceding date Total	Annual average
1940	9.9	—	—
1950	10.2	321,000	32,100
1960	11.3	1,086,000	108,600
1966	11.8	517,000	86,200

Nor is it likely to halt. Negro birth rates in the South, as elsewhere, have fallen sharply since 1957, but so far this decline has been offset by the rising Negro population base remaining in the South. From 1950 to 1960, southern Negro births generated an average net increase of 254,000 per year and, from 1960 to 1966, an average of 188,000 per year. Even if

Negro birth rates continue to fall they are likely to remain high enough to support significant migration to other regions for some time to come.

The Negro population in the South is becoming increasingly urbanized. In 1950, there were 5.4 million southern rural Negroes; by 1960, 4.8 million. But this decline has been more than offset by increases in the urban population. A rising proportion of interregional migration now consists of persons moving from one city to another. From 1960 to 1966, rural Negro population in the South was far below its peak, but the annual average migration of Negroes from the South was still substantial.

These facts demonstrate that Negro migration from the South, which has maintained a high rate for the past 60 years, will continue unless economic conditions change dramatically in either the South or the North and West. This conclusion is reinforced by the fact that most Southern states in recent decades have also experienced outflows of white population. From 1950 to 1960, 11 of the 17 Southern states (including the District of Columbia) "exported" white population — as compared to 13 which "exported" Negro population. Excluding Florida's net gain by migration of 1.5 million, the other 16 Southern states together had a net loss by migration of 1.46 million whites.

The Concentration of Negro Population in Large Cities. Where Negro Urbanization Has Occurred. Statistically, the Negro population in America has become more urbanized, and more metropolitan, than the white population. According to Census Bureau estimates, almost 70 per cent of all Negroes in 1966 lived in metropolitan areas, compared to 64 per cent of all whites. In the South, more than half the Negro population now lives in cities. Rural Negroes outnumber urban Negroes in only four states: Arkansas, Mississippi, North Carolina, and South Carolina.

Basic data concerning Negro urbanization trends . . . indicate that:

> Almost all Negro population growth is occurring within metropolitan areas, primarily within central cities. From 1950 to 1966, the U.S. Negro population rose 6.5 million. Over 98 per cent of that increase took place in metropolitan areas — 86 per cent within central cities, 12 per cent in the urban fringe.
>
> The vast majority of white population growth is occurring in suburban portions of metropolitan areas. From 1950 to 1966, 77.8 per cent of the white population increase of 35.6 million took place in the suburbs. Central cities received only 2.5 per cent of this total white increase. Since 1960, white central-city population has actually declined by 1.3 million.
>
> As a result, central cities are steadily becoming more heavily Negro, while the urban fringes around them remain almost entirely white. The proportion of Negroes in all central cities rose steadily from 12 per cent in 1950, to 17 per cent in 1960, to 20 per cent in 1966. Meanwhile, metropolitan areas outside of central cities remained 95

per cent white from 1950 to 1960 and became 96 per cent white by 1966.

The Negro population is growing faster, both absolutely and relatively, in the larger metropolitan areas than in the smaller ones. From 1950 to 1966, the proportion of nonwhites in the central cities of metropolitan areas with 1 million or more persons doubled, reaching 26 per cent, as compared with 20 per cent in the central cities of metropolitan areas containing from 250,000 to 1 million persons and 12 per cent in the central cities of metropolitan areas containing under 250,000 persons.

The 12 largest central cities — New York, Chicago, Los Angeles, Philadelphia, Detroit, Baltimore, Houston, Cleveland, Washington, D.C., St. Louis, Milwaukee, and San Francisco — now contain over two-thirds of the Negro population outside the South and almost one-third of the total in the United States. All these cities have experienced rapid increases in Negro population since 1950. In six — Chicago, Detroit, Cleveland, St. Louis, Milwaukee, and San Francisco — the proportion of Negroes at least doubled. In two others — New York and Los Angeles — it probably doubled. In 1968, seven of these cities are over 30 per cent Negro, and one, Washington, D.C., is two-thirds Negro.

Factors Causing Residential Segregation in Metropolitan Areas. The early pattern of Negro settlement within each metropolitan area followed that of the immigrant groups. Migrants converged on the older sections of the central city because the lowest cost housing was located there, friends and relatives were likely to be living there, and the older neighborhoods then often had good public transportation.

But the later phases of Negro settlement and expansion in metropolitan areas diverge sharply from those typical of white immigrants. As the whites were absorbed by the larger society, many left their predominantly ethnic neighborhoods and moved to outlying areas to obtain newer housing and better schools. Some scattered randomly over the suburban area. Others established new ethnic clusters in the suburbs, but even these rarely contained solely members of a single ethnic group. As a result, most middle-class neighborhoods — both in the suburbs and within central cities — have no distinctive ethnic character, except that they are white.

Nowhere has the expansion of America's urban Negro population followed this pattern of dispersal. Thousands of Negro families have attained incomes, living standards, and cultural levels matching or surpassing those of whites who have "upgraded" themselves from distinctly ethnic neighborhoods. Yet most Negro families have remained within predominantly Negro neighborhoods, primarily because they have been effectively excluded from white residential areas.

Their exclusion has been accomplished through various discriminatory practices, some obvious and overt, others subtle and hidden. Deliberate efforts are sometimes made to discourage Negro families from purchasing or renting homes in all-white neighborhoods. Intimidation and threats of violence have ranged from throwing garbage on lawns and making threatening phone calls to burning crosses in yards and even dynamiting property. More often, real estate agents simply refuse to show homes to Negro buyers.

Many middle-class Negro families, therefore, cease looking for homes beyond all-Negro areas or nearby "changing" neighborhoods. For them, trying to move into all-white neighborhoods is not worth the psychological efforts and costs required.

Another form of discrimination just as significant is white withdrawal from, or refusal to enter, neighborhoods where large numbers of Negroes are moving or already residing. Normal population turnover causes about 20 per cent of the residents of average U.S. neighborhoods to move out every year because of income changes, job transfers, shifts in life-cycle position or deaths. This normal turnover rate is even higher in apartment areas. The refusal of whites to move into changing areas when vacancies occur there from normal turnover means that most of these vacancies are eventually occupied by Negroes. An inexorable shift toward heavy Negro occupancy results.

Once this happens, the remaining whites seek to leave, thus confirming the existing belief among whites that complete transformation of a neighborhood is inevitable once Negroes begin to enter. Since the belief itself is one of the major causes of the transformation, it becomes a self-fulfilling prophecy which inhibits the development of racially integrated neighborhoods.

As a result, Negro settlements expand almost entirely through "massive racial transition" at the edges of existing all-Negro neighborhoods, rather than by a gradual dispersion of population throughout the metropolitan area.

Two points are particularly important:

> "Massive transition" requires no panic or flight by the original white residents of a neighborhood into which Negroes begin moving. All it requires is the failure or refusal of other whites to fill the vacancies resulting from normal turnover.
>
> Thus, efforts to stop massive transition by persuading present white residents to remain will ultimately fail unless whites outside the neighborhood can be persuaded to move in.

It is obviously true that some residential separation of whites and Negroes would occur even without discriminatory practices by whites. This would result from the desires of some Negroes to live in predominantly Negro neighborhoods and from differences in meaningful social variables, such as income and educational levels. But these factors alone would not lead to the almost complete segregation of whites and Negroes which has developed in our metropolitan areas.

The Exodus of Whites from Central Cities. The process of racial transition in central-city neighborhoods has been only one factor among many others causing millions of whites to move out of central cities as the Negro populations there expanded. More basic perhaps have been the rising mobility and affluence of middle-class families and the more attractive living conditions — particularly better schools — in the suburbs.

Whatever the reason, the result is clear. In 1950, 45.5 million whites lived in central cities. If this population had grown from 1950 to 1960 at the same rate as the Nation's white population as a whole, it would have increased by 8 million. It actually rose only 2.2 million, indicating an outflow of 5.8 million.[3]

From 1960 to 1966, the white outflow appears to have been even more rapid. White population of central cities declined 1.3 million instead of rising 3.6 million — as it would if it had grown at the same rate as the entire white population. In theory, therefore, 4.9 million whites left central cities during these 6 years.

Statistics for all central cities as a group understate the relationship between Negro population growth and white outflow in individual central cities. The fact is, many cities with relatively few Negroes experienced rapid white-population growth, thereby obscuring the size of white outmigration that took place in cities having large increases in Negro population. For example, from 1950 to 1960, the 10 largest cities in the United States had a total Negro population increase of 1.6 million, or 55 per cent, while the white population there declined 1.4 million. If the two cities where the white population increased (Los Angeles and Houston) are excluded, the nonwhite population in the remaining eight rose 1.4 million, whereas their white population declined 2.1 million. If the white population in these cities had increased at only half the rate of the white population in the United States as a whole from 1950 to 1960, it would have risen by 1.4 million. Thus, these eight cities actually experienced a white outmigration of at least 3.5 million, while gaining 1.4 million nonwhites.

The Extent of Residential Segregation. The rapid expansion of all-Negro residential areas and large-scale white withdrawal have continued a pattern of residential segregation that has existed in American cities for decades. A recent study [4] reveals that this pattern is present to a high

[3] The outflow of whites may be somewhat smaller than the 5.8 million difference between these figures, because the ages of the whites in many central cities are higher than in the Nation as a whole, and therefore the population would have grown somewhat more slowly.

[4] "Negroes in Cities," Karl and Alma Taeuber, Aldine Publishing Co., Chicago (1965).

degree in every large city in America. The authors devised an index to measure the degree of residential segregation. The index indicates for each city the percentage of Negroes who would have to move from the blocks where they now live to other blocks in order to provide a perfectly proportional unsegregated distribution of population.

According to their findings, the average segregation index for 207 of the largest U.S. cities was 86.2 in 1960. This means that an average of over 86 per cent of all Negroes would have had to change blocks to create an unsegregated population distribution. Southern cities had a higher average index (90.9) than cities in the Northeast (79.2), the North Central (87.7), or the West (79.3). Only eight cities had index values below 70, whereas over 50 had values above 91.7.

The degree of residential segregation for all 207 cities has been relatively stable, averaging 85.2 in 1940, 87.3 in 1950, and 86.2 in 1960. Variations within individual regions were only slightly larger. However, a recent Census Bureau study shows that in most of the 12 large cities where special censuses were taken in the mid-1960's, the proportions of Negroes living in neighborhoods of greatest Negro concentration had increased since 1960.

Residential segregation is generally more prevalent with respect to Negroes than for any other minority group, including Puerto Ricans, Orientals, and Mexican-Americans. Moreover, it varies little between central city and suburb. This nearly universal pattern cannot be explained in terms of economic discrimination against all low-income groups. Analysis of 15 representative cities indicates that white upper- and middle-income households are far more segregated from Negro upper- and middle-income households than from white lower-income households.

In summary, the concentration of Negroes in central cities results from a combination of forces. Some of these forces, such as migration and initial settlement patterns in older neighborhoods, are similar to those which affected previous ethnic minorities. Others — particularly discrimination in employment and segregation in housing and schools — are a result of white attitudes based on race and color. These forces continue to shape the future of the central city.

Unemployment, Family Structure and Social Disorganization

Recent Economic Trends. The Negro population in our country is as diverse in income, occupation, family composition, and other variables as the white community. Nevertheless, for purposes of analysis, three major Negro economic groups can be identified.

The first and smallest group consists of middle- and upper-income individuals and households whose educational, occupational, and cultural characteristics are similar to those of middle- and upper-income white groups.

The second and largest group contains Negroes whose incomes are above the "poverty level" but who have not attained the educational, occupational, or income status typical of middle-class Americans.

The third group has very low educational, occupational, and income attainments and lives below the "poverty level."

A recent compilation of data on American Negroes by the Departments of Labor and Commerce shows that although incomes of both Negroes and whites have been rising rapidly,

> Negro incomes still remain far below those of whites. Negro median family income was only 58 per cent of the white median in 1966.
>
> Negro family income is not keeping pace with white family income growth. In constant 1965 dollars, median nonwhite income in 1947 was $2,174 lower than median white income. By 1966, the gap had grown to $3,036.
>
> The Negro upper income group is expanding rapidly and achieving sizeable income gains. In 1966, 28 per cent of all Negro families received incomes of $7,000 or more, compared with 55 per cent of white families. This was 1.6 times the proportion of Negroes receiving comparable incomes in 1960, and four times greater than the proportion receiving such incomes in 1947. Moreover, the proportion of Negroes employed in high-skill, high-status, and well-paying jobs rose faster than comparable proportions among whites from 1960 to 1966.
>
> As Negro incomes have risen, the size of the lowest income group has grown smaller, and the middle and upper groups have grown larger — both relatively and absolutely. [See Table 11.]

TABLE 11

Group	Percentage of Negro families			Percentage of white families
	1947	1960	1966	1966
$7,000 and over	7	17	28	55
$3,000 to $6,999	29	40	41	33
Under $3,000	65	44	32	13

About two-thirds of the lowest income group — or 20 per cent of all Negro families — are making no significant economic gains despite continued general prosperity. Half of these hardcore disadvantaged — more than 2 million persons — live in central-city neighborhoods. Recent special censuses in Los Angeles and Cleveland indicate that the incomes of persons living in the worst slum areas have not risen at all during this period, unemployment rates have declined only slightly, the proportion of families with female heads has increased, and housing conditions have worsened even though rents have risen.

Thus, between 2.0 and 2.5 million poor Negroes are living in disadvantaged neighborhoods of central cities in the United States. These persons comprise only slightly more than 1 per cent of the Nation's total population, but they make up about 16 to 20 per cent of the total Negro population of all central cities, and a much higher proportion in certain cities.

Unemployment and Underemployment. The Critical Significance of Employment. The capacity to obtain and hold a "good job" is the traditional test of participation in American society. Steady employment with adequate compensation provides both purchasing power and social status. It develops the capabilities, confidence, and self-esteem an individual needs to be a responsible citizen, and provides a basis for a stable family life. As Daniel P. Moynihan has written:

> The principal measure of progress toward equality will be that of employment. It is the primary source of individual or group identity. In America what you do is what you are: to do nothing is to be nothing; to do little is to be little. The equations are implacable and blunt, and ruthlessly public.
>
> For the Negro American it is already, and will continue to be, the master problem. It is the measure of white bona fides. It is the measure of Negro competence, and also of the competence of American society. Most importantly, the linkage between problems of employment and the range of social pathology that afflicts the Negro community is unmistakable. Employment not only controls the present for the Negro American but, in a most profound way, it is creating the future as well.

For residents of disadvantaged Negro neighborhoods, obtaining good jobs is vastly more difficult than for most workers in society. For decades, social, economic, and psychological disadvantages surrounding the urban Negro poor have impaired their work capacities and opportunities. The result is a cycle of failure — the employment disabilities of one generation breed those of the next.

Negro Unemployment. Unemployment rates among Negroes have declined from a post-Korean War high of 12.6 per cent in 1958 to 8.2 per cent in 1967. Among married Negro men, the unemployment rate for 1967 was down to 3.2 per cent.[5]

Notwithstanding this decline, unemployment rates for Negroes are still double those for whites in every category, including married men, as they have been throughout the postwar period. Moreover, since 1954, even during the current unprecedented period of sustained economic growth, unemployment among Negroes has been continuously above the 6 per

---

[5] Adjusted for Census Bureau undercounting.

cent "recession" level widely regarded as a sign of serious economic weakness when prevalent for the entire work force.

While the Negro unemployment rate remains high in relation to the white rate, the number of additional jobs needed to lower this to the level of white unemployment is surprisingly small. In 1967, approximately 3 million persons were unemployed during an average week, of whom about 638,000, or 21 per cent were nonwhites. When corrected for undercounting, total nonwhite unemployment was approximately 712,000 or 8 per cent of the nonwhite labor force. To reduce the unemployment rate to 3.4 per cent, the rate prevalent among whites, jobs must be found for 57.5 per cent of these unemployed persons. This amounts to nearly 409,000 jobs, or about 27 per cent of the net number of new jobs added to the economy in the year 1967 alone and only slightly more than one-half of 1 per cent of all jobs in the United States in 1967.

The Low-Status and Low-Paying Nature of Many Negro Jobs. Even more important perhaps than unemployment is the related problem of the undesirable nature of many jobs open to Negroes. Negro workers are concentrated in the lowest skilled and lowest paying occupations. These jobs often involve substandard wages, great instability and uncertainty of tenure, extremely low status in the eyes of both employer and employee, little or no chance for meaningful advancement, and unpleasant or exhausting duties. Negro men in particular are more than three times as likely as whites to be in unskilled or service jobs which pay far less than most. [See Table 12.]

This concentration in the least desirable jobs can be viewed another way by calculating the changes which would occur if Negro men were

TABLE 12

Type of occupation	Percentage of male workers in each type of occupation, 1966		Median earnings of all male civilians in each occupation, 1965
	White	Nonwhite	
Professional, technical, and managerial	27	9	$7,603*
Clerical and sales	14	9	5,532*
Craftsmen and foremen	20	12	6,270
Operatives	20	27	5,046
Service workers	6	16	3,436
Nonfarm laborers	6	20	2,410
Farmers and farm workers	7	8	1,669*

* Average of two categories from normal Census Bureau categories as combined in data presented in The Social and Economic Conditions of Negroes in the United States (BLS No. 332).

TABLE 13

Number of male nonwhite workers, 1966

Type of occupation	As actually distributed*	If distributed the same as all male workers	Difference	
			Number	Percentage
Professional, technical, and managerial	415,000	1,173,000	+758,000	+183
Clerical and sales	415,000	628,000	+213,000	+51
Craftsmen and foremen	553,000	894,000	+341,000	+62
Operatives	1,244,000	964,000	−280,000	−23
Service workers	737,000	326,000	−411,000	−56
Nonfarm laborers	922,000	340,000	−582,000	−63
Farmers and farm workers	369,000	330,000	−39,000	−11

* Estimates based upon percentages set forth in BLS No. 332, p. 41.

employed in various occupations in the same proportions as the male labor force as a whole (not solely the white labor force). [See Table 13.]

Thus, upgrading the employment of Negro men to make their occupational distribution identical with that of the labor force as a whole would have an immense impact upon the nature of their occupations. About 1.3 million nonwhite men — or 28 per cent of those employed in 1966 — would move up the employment ladder into one of the higher status and higher paying categories. The effect of such a shift upon the incomes of Negro men would be very great. Using the 1966 job distribution, the shift indicated above would produce about $4.8 billion more earned income for nonwhite men alone if they received the 1965 median income in each occupation. This would be a rise of approximately 30 per cent in the earnings actually received by all nonwhite men in 1965 (not counting any sources of income other than wages and salaries).

Of course, the kind of "instant upgrading" visualized in these calculations does not represent a practical alternative for national policy. The economy cannot drastically reduce the total number of low-status jobs it now contains, or shift large numbers of people upward in occupation in any short period. Therefore, major upgrading in the employment status of Negro men must come through a faster relative expansion of higher level jobs than lower level jobs (which has been occurring for several decades), an improvement in the skills of nonwhite workers so they can obtain a high proportion of those added better jobs, and a drastic reduction of discriminatory hiring and promotion practices in all enterprises, both private and public.

Nevertheless, this hypothetical example clearly shows that the concentration of male Negro employment at the lowest end of the occupational scale is greatly depressing the incomes of U.S. Negroes in general. In fact, this is the single most important source of poverty among Negroes. It is even more important than unemployment, as can be shown by a second hypothetical calculation. In 1966, there were about 724,000 unemployed nonwhites in the United States on the average, including adults and teen-agers, and allowing for the Census Bureau undercount of Negroes. If every one of these persons had been employed and had received the median amount earned by nonwhite males in 1966 ($3,864), this would have added a total of $2.8 billion to nonwhite income as a whole. If only enough of these persons had been employed at that wage to reduce non-white unemployment from 7.3 per cent to 3.3 per cent — the rate among whites in 1966 — then the income gain for nonwhites would have totaled about $1.5 billion. But if nonwhite unemployment remained at 7.3 per cent, and nonwhite men were upgraded so that they had the same occupa-tional distribution and incomes as all men in the labor force considered together, this would have produced about $4.8 billion in additional in-come, as noted above (using 1965 earnings for calculation). Thus the potential income gains from upgrading the male nonwhite labor force are much larger than those from reducing nonwhite unemployment.

This conclusion underlines the difficulty of improving the economic status of Negro men. It is far easier to create new jobs than either to cre-ate new jobs with relatively high status and earning power, or to upgrade existing employed or partly employed workers into such better quality employment. Yet only such upgrading will eliminate the fundamental basis of poverty and deprivation among Negro families.

Access to good-quality jobs clearly affects the willingness of Negro men actively to seek work. In riot cities surveyed by the Commission with the largest percentage of Negroes in skilled and semiskilled jobs, Negro men participated in the labor force to the same extent as, or greater than, white men. Conversely, where most Negro men were heavily concentrated in menial jobs, they participated less in the labor force than white men.

Even given similar employment, Negro workers with the same educa-tion as white workers are paid less. This disparity doubtless results to some extent from inferior training in segregated schools, and also from the fact that large numbers of Negroes are only now entering certain occupations for the first time. However, the differentials are so large and so universal at all educational levels that they clearly reflect the patterns of discrimination which characterize hiring and promotion practices in many segments of the economy. For example, in 1966, among persons who had completed high school, the median income of Negroes was only 73 per cent that of whites. Even among persons with an eighth-grade education, Negro me-dian income was only 80 per cent of white median income.

At the same time, a higher proportion of Negro women than white women participates in the labor force at nearly all ages except 16 to 19. For instance, in 1966, 55 per cent of nonwhite women from 25 to 34 years of age were employed, compared to only 38 per cent of white women in the same age group. The fact that almost half of all adult Negro women work reflects the fact that so many Negro males have unsteady and low-paying jobs. Yet even though Negro women are often better able to find work than Negro men, the unemployment rate among adult nonwhite women (20 years old and over) in 1967 was 7.1 per cent, compared to the 4.3 per cent rate among adult nonwhite men.

Unemployment rates are, of course, much higher among teenagers, both Negro and white, than among adults; in fact about one-third of all unemployed Negroes in 1967 were between 16 and 19 years old. During the first 9 months of 1967, the unemployment rate among nonwhite teenagers was 26.5 per cent; for whites, it was 10.6 per cent. About 219,300 nonwhite teenagers were unemployed.[6] About 58,300 were still in school but were actively looking for jobs.

Subemployment in Disadvantaged Negro Neighborhoods. In disadvantaged areas, employment conditions for Negroes are in a chronic state of crisis. Surveys in low-income neighborhoods of nine large cities made by the Department of Labor late in 1966 revealed that the rate of unemployment there was 9.3 per cent, compared to 7.3 per cent for Negroes generally and 3.3 per cent for whites. Moreover, a high proportion of the persons living in these areas were "underemployed," that is, they were either part-time workers looking for full-time employment, or full-time workers earning less than $3000 per year, or had dropped out of the labor force. The Department of Labor estimated that this underemployment is 2½ times greater than the number of unemployed in these areas. Therefore, the "subemployment rate," including both the unemployed and the underemployed, was about 32.7 per cent in the nine areas surveyed, or 8.8 times greater than the overall unemployment rate for all U.S. workers. Since underemployment also exists outside disadvantaged neighborhoods, comparing the full subemployment rate in these areas with the unemployment rate for the Nation as a whole is not entirely valid. However, it provides some measure of the enormous disparity between employment conditions in most of the Nation and those prevalent in disadvantaged Negro areas in our large cities.

The critical problem is to determine the actual number of those unemployed and underemployed in central-city Negro ghettos. . . . The outcome of this process is summarized in [Table 14].

Therefore, in order to bring subemployment in these areas down to a level equal to unemployment alone among whites, enough steady, reasonably paying jobs (and the training and motivation to perform them) must be provided to eliminate all underemployment and reduce unemployment by 65 per cent. For all three age groups combined, this deficit amounted to 923,000 jobs in 1967.

The Magnitude of Poverty in Disadvantaged Neighborhoods. The chronic unemployment problems in the central city, aggravated by the

[6] After adjusting for Census Bureau undercounting.

TABLE 14

Nonwhite subemployment in disadvantaged
areas of all central cities, 1967

Group	Unemploy- ment	Under- employment	Total sub- employment
Adult men	102,000	230,000	332,000
Adult women	118,000	266,000	384,000
Teenagers	98,000	220,000	318,000
Total	318,000	716,000	1,034,000

constant arrival of new unemployed migrants, is the fundamental cause of the persistent poverty in disadvantaged Negro areas.

"Poverty" in the affluent society is more than absolute deprivation. Many of the poor in the United States would be well off in other societies. Relative deprivation — inequality — is a more useful concept of poverty with respect to the Negro in America because it encompasses social and political exclusions as well as economic inequality. Because of the lack of data of this type, we have had to focus our analysis on a measure of poverty which is both economic and absolute — the Social Security Administration's "poverty level" [7] concept. It is clear, however, that broader measures of poverty would substantiate the conclusions that follow.

In 1966, there were 29.7 million persons in the United States — 15.3 per cent of the Nation's population — with incomes below the "poverty level," as defined by the Social Security Administration. Of these, 20.3 million were white (68.3 per cent), and 9.3 million nonwhite (31.7 per cent). Thus, about 11.9 per cent of the Nation's whites and 40.6 per cent of its nonwhites were poor under the Social Security definition.

The location of the Nation's poor is best shown from 1964 data as indicated by [Table 15].

TABLE 15

Percentage of those in poverty in each group living in —

Metropolitan areas

Group	In cities central	Outside central cities	Other areas	Total
Whites	23.8	21.8	54.4	100
Nonwhites	41.7	10.8	47.5	100
Total	29.4	18.4	52.2	100

Source: Social Security Administration.

[7] $3335 per year for an urban family of four.

The following facts concerning poverty are relevant to an understanding of the problems faced by people living in disadvantaged neighborhoods.[8]

In central cities 30.7 per cent of nonwhite families of two or more persons lived in poverty compared to only 8.8 per cent of whites.

Of the 10.1 million poor persons in central cities in 1964, about 4.4 million of these (43.6 per cent) were nonwhites, and 5.7 million (56.4 per cent) were whites. The poor whites were much older on the average than the poor nonwhites. The proportion of poor persons 65 years old or older was 23.2 per cent among whites, but only 6.8 per cent among nonwhites.

Poverty was more than twice as prevalent among nonwhite families with female heads than among those with male heads, 57 per cent compared to 21 per cent. In central cities, 26 per cent of all nonwhite families of two or more persons had female heads, as compared to 12 per cent of white families.

Among nonwhite families headed by a female, and having children under 6, the incidence of poverty was 81 per cent. Moreover, there were 243,000 such families living in poverty in central cities — or over 9 per cent of all nonwhite families in those cities.

Among all children living in poverty within central cities, non-whites outnumbered whites by over 400,000. The number of poor nonwhite children equalled or surpassed the number of white poor children in every age group. [See Table 16.]

TABLE 16

Number of Children Living in Poverty (Millions)

Age group	White	Nonwhite	Percentage of total nonwhite
Under 6	0.9	1.0	53
6 to 15	1.0	1.3	57
16 to 21	0.4	0.4	50
Total	2.3	2.7	54

Two stark facts emerge:

54 per cent of all poor children in central cities in 1964 were non-whites.

Of the 4.4 million nonwhites living in poverty within central cities in 1964, 52 per cent were children under 16 and 61 per cent were under 21.

Since 1964, the number of nonwhite families living in poverty within

[8] Source: Social Security Administration; based on 1964 data.

central cities has remained about the same; hence, these poverty conditions are probably still prevalent in central cities in terms of absolute numbers of persons, although the proportion of persons in poverty may have dropped slightly.[9]

The Social Impact of Employment Problems in Disadvantaged Negro Areas. Unemployment and the Family. The high rates of unemployment and underemployment in racial ghettos are evidence, in part, that many men living in these areas are seeking, but cannot obtain, jobs which will support a family. Perhaps equally important, most jobs they can get are at the low end of the occupational scale, and often lack the necessary status to sustain a worker's self-respect, or the respect of his family and friends. These same men are also constantly confronted with the message of discrimination: "You are inferior because of a trait you did not cause and cannot change." This message reinforces feelings of inadequacy arising from repeated failure to obtain and keep decent jobs.

Wives of these men are forced to work and usually produce more money. If the men stay at home without working, their inadequacies constantly confront them and tensions arise between them and their wives and children. Under these pressures, it is not surprising that many of these men flee their responsibilities as husbands and fathers, leaving home, and drifting from city to city, or adopting the style of "street corner men."

Statistical evidence tends to document this. A close correlation exists between the number of nonwhite married women separated from their husbands each year and the unemployment rate among nonwhite males 20 years old and over. Similarly, from 1948 to 1962, the number of new Aid to Families with Dependent Children cases rose and fell with the nonwhite male unemployment rate. Since 1963, however, the number of new cases — most of them Negro children — has steadily increased even though the unemployment rate among nonwhite males has declined. The impact of marital status on employment among Negroes is shown by the fact that in 1967 the proportion of married men either divorced or separated from their wives was more than twice as high among unemployed nonwhite men as among employed nonwhite men. Moreover, among those participating in the labor force, there was a higher proportion of married men with wives present than with wives absent. [See Table 17.]

[9] For the Nation as a whole, the proportion of nonwhite families living in poverty, dropped from 39 per cent to 35 per cent from 1964 to 1966 (defining "family" somewhat differently from the definition used in the data above). The number of such families declined from 1.9 million to 1.7 million. However, the number and proportion of all nonwhites living in central cities rose in the same period. As a result, the number of nonwhite families living in so-called "poverty areas" of large cities actually rose from 1,561,000 in 1960 to 1,588,000 in 1966.

TABLE 17

Unemployment Rate and
Participation in Total
Labor Force, 25 to 54-Year-
Old Nonwhite Men, by
Marital Status, March, 1967

	Unemployment rate, nonwhite	Labor force participation (per cent), nonwhite
Married, wife present	3.7	96.7
Other (separated, divorced, widowed)	8.7	77.6

Fatherless Families. The abandonment of the home by many Negro males affects a great many children growing up in the racial ghetto. As previously indicated, most American Negro families are headed by men, just like most other American families. Yet the proportion of families with female heads is much greater among Negroes than among whites at all income levels, and has been rising in recent years. [See Table 18.]

TABLE 18

Proportion of Families
of Various Types *

Date	Husband-Wife		Female head	
	White	Nonwhite	White	Nonwhite
1950	88.0	77.7	8.5	17.6
1960	88.7	73.6	8.7	22.4
1966	88.8	72.7	8.9	23.7

* In per cent.

This disparity between white and nonwhite families is far greater among the lowest income families — those most likely to reside in disadvantaged big-city neighborhoods — than among higher income families. Among families with incomes under $3,000 in 1966, the proportion with female heads was 42 per cent for Negroes but only 23 per cent for whites. In contrast, among families with incomes of $7,000 or more, 8 per cent of Negro families had female heads compared to 4 per cent of whites.

The problems of "fatherlessness" are aggravated by the tendency of the poor to have large families. The average poor, urban, nonwhite family contains 4.8 persons, as compared with 3.7 for the average poor, urban, white family. This is one of the primary factors in the poverty status of nonwhite households in large cities.

The proportion of fatherless families appears to be increasing in the poorest Negro neighborhoods. In the Hough section of Cleveland, the proportion of families with female heads rose from 23 to 32 per cent from 1960 to 1965. In the Watts section of Los Angeles it rose from 36 to 39 per cent during the same period.

The handicap imposed on children growing up without fathers, in an atmosphere of poverty and deprivation, is increased because many mothers must work to provide support. [Table 19] illustrates the disparity between the proportion of nonwhite women in the child-rearing ages who are in the labor force and the comparable proportion of white women:

TABLE 19

Age group	Percentage of women in the labor force	
	Nonwhite	White
20 to 24	55	51
25 to 34	55	38
35 to 44	61	45

With the father absent and the mother working, many ghetto children spend the bulk of their time on the streets — the streets of a crime-ridden, violence-prone, and poverty-stricken world. The image of success in this world is not that of the "solid citizen," the responsible husband and father, but rather that of the "hustler" who promotes his own interests by exploiting others. The dope sellers and the numbers runners are the "successful" men because their earnings far outstrip those men who try to climb the economic ladder in honest ways.

Young people in the ghetto are acutely conscious of a system which appears to offer rewards to those who illegally exploit others, and failure to those who struggle under traditional responsibilities. Under these circumstances, many adopt exploitation and the "hustle" as a way of life, disclaiming both work and marriage in favor of casual and temporary liaisons. This pattern reinforces itself from one generation to the next, creating a "culture of poverty" and an ingrained cynicism about society and its institutions.

The "Jungle." The culture of poverty that results from unemployment and family disorganization generates a system of ruthless, exploitative relationships within the ghetto. Prostitution, dope addiction, casual sexual affairs, and crime create an environmental jungle characterized by personal insecurity and tension. The effects of this development are stark:

> The rate of illegitimate births among nonwhite women has risen sharply in the past two decades. In 1940, 16.8 per cent of all nonwhite births were illegitimate. By 1950 this proportion was 18 per cent; by 1960, 21.6 per cent; by 1966, 26.3 per cent. In the ghettos of many large cities, illegitimacy rates exceed 50 per cent.

The rate of illegitimacy among nonwhite women is closely related to low income and high unemployment. In Washington, D.C., for example, an analysis of 1960 census tracts shows that in tracts with unemployment rates of 12 per cent or more among nonwhite men, illegitimacy was over 40 per cent. But in tracts with unemployment rates of 2.9 per cent and below among nonwhite men, reported illegitimacy was under 20 per cent. A similar contrast existed between tracts in which median nonwhite income was under $4,000 (where illegitimacy was 38 per cent) and those in which it was $8,000 and over (where illegitimacy was 12 per cent).

Narcotics addiction is also heavily concentrated in low-income Negro neighborhoods, particularly in New York City. Of the 59,720 addicts known to the U.S. Bureau of Narcotics at the end of 1966, just over 50 per cent were Negroes. Over 52 per cent of all known addicts lived within New York State, mostly in Harlem and other Negro neighborhoods. These figures undoubtedly greatly understate the actual number of persons using narcotics regularly — especially those under 21.

Not surprisingly, at every age from 6 through 19, the proportion of children from homes with both parents present who actually attend school is higher than the proportion of children from homes with only one parent or neither present.

Rates of juvenile delinquency, venereal disease, dependency upon AFDC support, and use of public assistance in general are much higher in disadvantaged Negro areas than in other parts of large cities. Data taken from New York City contrasting predominantly Negro neighborhoods with the city as a whole clearly illustrate this fact. [See Table 20.]

TABLE 20

Social Distress — Major Predominately Negro Neighborhoods in New York City and the City as a Whole

	Juvenile delinquency[a]	Venereal disease[b]	ADC[c]	Public assistance[d]
Brownsville	125.3	609.9	459.0	265.8
East New York	98.6	207.5	148.6	71.8
Bedford-Stuyvesant	115.2	771.3	337.1	197.2
Harlem	110.8	1,603.5	265.7	138.1
South Bronx	84.4	308.3	278.5	165.5
New York City	52.2	269.1	120.7	60.8

[a] Number of offenses per 1,000 persons 7–20 years (1965).

[b] Number of cases per 100,000 persons under 21 years (1964).

[c] Number of children in aid to dependent children cases per 1,000 under 18 years, using 1960 population as base (1965).

[d] Welfare assistance recipients per 1,000 persons, using 1960 population as base (1965).

In conclusion: in 1965, 1.2 million nonwhite children under 16 lived in central-city families headed by a woman under 65. The great majority of these children were growing up in poverty under conditions that make them better candidates for crime and civil disorder than for jobs providing an entry into American society. . . .

Comparing the Immigrant and Negro Experience

. . . We have surveyed the historical background of racial discrimination and traced its effects on Negro employment, on the social structure of the ghetto community and on the conditions of life that surround the urban Negro poor. Here we address a fundamental question that many white Americans are asking today: Why has the Negro been unable to escape from poverty and the ghetto like the European immigrants?

The Maturing Economy. The changing nature of the American economy is one major reason. When the European immigrants were arriving in large numbers, America was becoming an urban-industrial society. To build its major cities and industries, America needed great pools of unskilled labor. The immigrants provided the labor, gained an economic foothold and thereby enabled their children and grandchildren to move up to skilled, white-collar and professional employment.

Since World War II especially, America's urban-industrial society has matured; unskilled labor is far less essential than before, and blue-collar jobs of all kinds are decreasing in number and importance as a source of new employment. The Negroes who migrated to the great urban centers lacked the skills essential to the new economy, and the schools of the ghetto have been unable to provide the education that can qualify them for decent jobs. The Negro migrant, unlike the immigrant, found little opportunity in the city; he had arrived too late, and the unskilled labor he had to offer was no longer needed.

The Disability of Race. Racial discrimination is undoubtedly the second major reason why the Negro has been unable to escape from poverty. The structure of discrimination has persistently narrowed his opportunities and restricted his prospects. Well before the high tide of immigration from overseas, Negroes were already relegated to the poorly paid, low status occupations. Had it not been for racial discrimination, the North might well have recruited southern Negroes after the Civil War to provide the labor for building the burgeoning urban-industrial economy. Instead, northern employers looked to Europe for their sources of unskilled labor. Upon the arrival of the immigrants, the Negroes were dislodged from the few urban occupations they had dominated. Not until World War II were Negroes generally hired for industrial jobs, and by that time the decline in the need for unskilled labor had already begun. European immigrants, too, suffered from discrimination, but never was it so pervasive.

The prejudice against color in America has formed a bar to advancement unlike any other.

Entry into the Political System. Political opportunities also played an important role in enabling the European immigrants to escape from poverty. The immigrants settled for the most part in rapidly growing cities that had powerful and expanding political machines which gave them economic advantages in exchange for political support. The political machines were decentralized, and ward-level grievance machinery as well as personal representation enabled the immigrant to make his voice heard and his power felt. Since the local political organizations exercised considerable influence over public building in the cities, they provided employment in construction jobs for their immigrant voters. Ethnic groups often dominated one or more of the municipal services — police and fire protection, sanitation and even public education.

By the time the Negroes arrived, the situation had altered dramatically. The great wave of public building had virtually come to an end; reform groups were beginning to attack the political machines; the machines were no longer so powerful or so well equipped to provide jobs and other favors.

Although the political machines retained their hold over the areas settled by Negroes, the scarcity of patronage jobs made them unwilling to share with Negroes the political positions they had created in these neighborhoods. For example, Harlem was dominated by white politicians for many years after it had become a Negro ghetto; even today, New York's Lower East Side, which is now predominantly Puerto Rican, is strongly influenced by politicians of the older immigrant groups.

This pattern exists in many other American cities. Negroes are still underrepresented in city councils and in most city agencies.

Segregation played a role here too. The immigrants and their descendants, who felt threatened by the arrival of the Negro, prevented a Negro-immigration coalition that might have saved the old political machines. Reform groups, nominally more liberal on the race issue, were often dominated by businessmen and middle-class city residents who usually opposed coalition with any low-income group, white or black.

Cultural Factors. Cultural factors also made it easier for the immigrants to escape from poverty. They came to America from much poorer societies, with a low standard of living, and they came at a time when job aspirations were low. When most jobs in the American economy were unskilled, they sensed little deprivation in being forced to take the dirty and poorly paid jobs. Moreover, their families were large, and many breadwinners, some of whom never married, contributed to the total family income. As a result, family units managed to live even from the lowest paid jobs and still put some money aside for savings or investments, for example, to purchase a house or tenement or to open a store or factory. Since the immigrants spoke little English and had their own ethnic culture, they needed stores to supply them with ethnic foods and other services. Since their family structures were patriarchal, men found satisfactions in family life that helped compensate for the bad jobs they had to take and the hard work they had to endure.

Negroes came to the city under quite different circumstances. Generally relegated to jobs that others would not take, they were paid too little to be able to put money in savings for new enterprises. In addition, Negroes lacked the extended family characteristic of certain European groups; each household usually had only one or two breadwinners. Moreover, Negro men had fewer cultural incentives to work in a dirty job for the sake of the family. As a result of slavery and of long periods of male unemployment afterwards, the Negro family structure had become matriarchal; the man played a secondary and marginal role in his family. For many Negro men, then, there were few of the cultural and psychological rewards of family life; they often abandoned their homes because they felt themselves useless to their families.

Although Negro men worked as hard as the immigrants to support their families, their rewards were less. The jobs did not pay enough to enable them to support their families, for prices and living standards had risen since the immigrants had come, and the entrepreneurial opportunities that had allowed some immigrants to become independent, even rich, had vanished. Above all, Negroes suffered from segregation, which denied them access to the good jobs and the right unions and which deprived them of the opportunity to buy real estate or obtain business loans or move out of the ghetto and bring up their children in middle-class neighborhoods. Immigrants were able to leave their ghettos as soon as they had the money; segregation has denied Negroes the opportunity to live elsewhere.

The Vital Element of Time. Finally, nostalgia makes it easy to exaggerate the case of escape of the white immigrants from the ghettos. When the immigrants were immersed in poverty, they, too, lived in slums, and these neighborhoods exhibited fearfully high rates of alcoholism, desertion, illegitimacy and the other pathologies associated with poverty. Just as some Negro men desert their families when they are unemployed and their wives can get jobs, so did the men of other ethnic groups, even though time and affluence has clouded white memories of the past.

Today, whites tend to contrast their experience with poverty-stricken Negroes. The fact is, among the southern and eastern Europeans who came to America in the last great wave of immigration, those who came already urbanized were the first to escape from poverty. The others who came to America from rural background, as Negroes did, are only now, after three generations, in the final stages of escaping from poverty. Until the last 10 years or so, most of these were employed in blue-collar jobs, and only a small proportion of their children were able or willing to attend college. In other words, only the third, and in many cases only the fourth, generation has been able to achieve the kind of middle-class income and status that allows it to send its children to college. Because of favorable economic and political conditions, these ethnic groups were able to escape from lower class status to working class and lower middle-class status, but it has taken them three generations.

Negroes have been concentrated in the city for only two generations, and they have been there under much less favorable conditions. Moreover, their escape from poverty has been blocked in part by the resistance of the European ethnic groups; they have been unable to enter some unions and to move into some neighborhoods outside the ghetto because descendants of the European immigrants who control these unions and neighborhoods have not yet abandoned them for middle-class occupations and areas.

Even so, some Negroes have escaped poverty, and they have done so in only two generations; their success is less visible than that of the immigrants in many cases, for residential segregation has forced them to remain in the ghetto. Still, the proportion of nonwhites employed in white-collar, technical and professional jobs has risen from 10.2 per cent in 1950 to 20.8 per cent in 1966 and the proportion attending college has risen an equal amount. Indeed, the development of a small but steadily increasing Negro middle class while a great part of the Negro population is stagnating economically is creating a growing gap between Negro haves and have-nots.

The awareness of this gap by those left behind undoubtedly adds to the feelings of desperation and anger which breed civil disorders. Low-income Negroes realize that segregation and lack of job opportunities have made it possible for only a small proportion of all Negroes to escape poverty, and the summer disorders are at least in part a protest against being left behind and left out.

The immigrant who labored long hours at hard and often menial work had the hope of a better future, if not for himself then for his children. This was the promise of the "American dream" — the society offered to all a future that was open-ended; with hard work and perseverance, a man and his family could in time achieve not only material well-being but "position" and status.

For the Negro family in the urban ghetto, there is a different vision — the future seems to lead only to a dead end.

What the American economy of the late 19th and early 20th century was able to do to help the European immigrants escape from poverty is now largely impossible. New methods of escape must be found for the majority of today's poor.

WORLD POLICY IN THE TWENTIETH CENTURY: MYTH AND REALITY

IV

The Legend
of Isolationism
in the 1920's

WILLIAM APPLEMAN WILLIAMS

Following World War I, the United States allegedly underwent a transformation from the high tide of international involvement and a crusade to make the world safe for democracy to an utterly introspective attitude toward the rest of the world. The idea of American isolationism in the decade after the war is a persistent, popular (and, at times, academic) myth. The following essay by William Appleman Williams, a historian at the University of Wisconsin, decisively discredits the legend and sets American activities of the 1920's into the larger perspective of the nation's world role in the twentieth century. He views the decade as part of a continuous development in which patterns of national behavior differed only in degree, not kind. In short, the decade was a vital part of the continuous record of American expansionism dating back to the earliest days of the Republic. Furthermore, the United States found itself then, as always, in a conflict between "fidelity to ideals and the urge to power." Williams's essay is rooted in his basic conception that America's interest in the world is a manifestation of domestic considerations. In the 1920's the flowering of American corporatism at home was related to similar pursuits abroad, namely to establish what Secretary of State Charles Evans Hughes called a "community of ideals, interests and purposes." The attempt to integrate large areas of the world into the "American community" naturally involved an activist role for the United States, chiefly characterized by economic intervention. Yet, as Williams shows, there is an interesting, direct relationship between the insatiable desire for an accommodating community of interest in the 1920's and the early pattern of appeasement in the following decade.

The widely accepted assumption that the United States was isolationist from 1920 through 1932 is no more than a legend. Sir Francis Bacon might have classed this myth of isolation as one of his Idols of the Market-Place. An "ill and unfit choice of words," he cautioned, "leads men away into innumerable and inane controversies and fancies." [1] And certainly the application of the terms *isolation* and *isolationism* to a period and a policy that were characterized by vigorous involvement in the affairs of the world with consciousness of purpose qualifies as an "ill and unfit choice of words." Thus the purpose of this essay: on the basis of an investigation of the record to suggest that, far from isolation, the foreign relations of the United States from 1920 through 1932 were marked by express and extended involvement with — and intervention in the affairs of — other nations of the world.

It is both more accurate and more helpful to consider the twenties as contiguous with the present instead of viewing those years as a quixotic interlude of low-down jazz and lower-grade gin, fluttering flappers and Faulkner's fiction, and bootlegging millionaires and millionaire bootleggers. For in foreign policy there is far less of a sharp break between 1923 and 1953 than generally is acknowledged. A closer examination of the so-called isolationists of the twenties reveals that many of them were in fact busily engaged in extending American power. Those individuals and groups have not dramatically changed their outlook on foreign affairs. Their policies and objectives may differ with those of others (including professors), but they have never sought to isolate the United States.

This interpretation runs counter to the folklore of American foreign relations. Harvard places isolationism "in the saddle." Columbia sees "Americans retiring within their own shell." Yale judges that policy "degenerated" into isolation — among other things.[2] Others, less picturesque but equally positive, refer to a "marked increase of isolationist sentiment" and to "those years of isolationism." Another group diagnoses the populace as having "ingrained isolationism," analyzes it as "sullen and selfish" in consequence, and characterizes it as doing "its best to forget interna-

Reprinted by permission of the publisher from *Science and Society*, XVIII (Winter 1954), pp. 1–20.

[1] F. Bacon, *Novum Organum*, Headlam's translation as revised by C. P. Curtis and F. Greenslet, *The Practical Cogitator* (Boston: Houghton Mifflin Co., 1945), pp. 14–16.

[2] A. M. Schlesinger, *Paths to the Present* (New York: The Macmillan Co., 1949), pp. 69, 201; L. M. Hacker, "American International Relations," in *The United States and Its Place in World Affairs*, 1918–1943, ed. by A. Nevins and L. M. Hacker (Boston: D. C. Heath and Co., 1943), p. 166; S. F. Bemis, "The Shifting Strategy of American Defense and Diplomacy," in *Essays in History and International Relations in Honor of George Hubbard Blakeslee*, ed. by D. E. Lee and G. E. McReynolds (Worcester: Clark University, 1949), p. 9.

tional subjects." Related verdicts describe the Republican party as "predominantly isolationist" and as an organization that "fostered a policy of deliberate isolation." [3]

Most pointed of these specifications is a terse two-word summary of the diplomacy of the period: "Isolation Perfected." [4] Popularizers have transcribed this theme into a burlesque. Their articles and books convey the impression that the Secretaries of State were in semi-retirement and that the citizenry wished to do away with the Department itself.[5] Columnists and commentators have made the concept an eerie example of George Orwell's double-think. They label as isolationists the most vigorous interventionists.

The case would seem to be closed and judgment given if it were not for the ambivalence of some observers and the brief dissents filed by a few others. The scholar who used the phrase "those years of isolationism," for example, remarks elsewhere in the same book that "expansionism . . . really was long a major expression of isolationism." Another writes of the "return to an earlier policy of isolation," and on the next page notes a "shift in policy during the twenties amounting almost to a 'diplomatic revolution.' " A recent biographer states that Henry Cabot Lodge "did not propose . . . an isolationist attitude," but then proceeds to characterize the Monroe Doctrine — upon which Lodge stood in his fight against the League of Nations treaty — as a philosophy of "isolation." And in the last volume of his trilogy, the late Professor Frederick L. Paxton summed up a long review of the many diplomatic activities of the years 1919–1923 with

---

[3] In sequence, these quotations come from S. Adler, "The War-Guilt Question and American Disillusionment, 1919–1928," *The Journal of Modern History*, XXIII, No. 1 (March, 1951), p. 27; A. K. Weinberg, *Manifest Destiny. A Study of Nationalist Expansion in American History* (Baltimore: Johns Hopkins Press, 1935), p. 473; L. M. Hacker and H. S. Zahler, *The United States in the 20th Century* (New York: Appleton-Century-Crofts, Inc., 1952), pp. 278, 302; W. Wilson, quoted in Weinberg, *Manifest Destiny*, p. 473; F. D. Roosevelt, *Foreign Affairs*, VI, No. 4 (July, 1928), p. 577; W. Johnson, *The Battle Against Isolation* (Chicago: Chicago University Press, 1944), p. 132. For similar expressions see S. F. Bemis, *A Diplomatic History of the United States*, 3rd ed. (New York: Henry Holt and Co., 1950), p. 705; J. D. Hicks, *The American Nation* (Boston: Houghton Mifflin Co., 1949), p. 565; D. Perkins, *The Evolution of American Foreign Policy* (New York: Oxford University Press, 1949), p. 110; and A. Nevins, *America in World Affairs* (London: Oxford University Press, 1941), p. 80.

[4] D. F. Fleming, *The United States and World Organization, 1920–1933* (New York: Columbia University Press, 1938), title of Chapter VI.

[5] This literature is far too vast to cite, but even a perusal of *The Reader's Guide to Periodical Literature* will indicate the great volume of such material. It is vital to note, however, that the so-called disillusionment writers did not make this mistake — whatever their other errors. They criticized the policies of the time, but documented, in such journals as *The Nation*, the active character of the diplomacy.

the remark that this was a foreign policy of "avoidance rather than of action." [6]

But a few scholars, toying with the Idol of the Market-Place, have made bold to rock the image. Yet Professor Richard Van Alstyne was doing more than playing the iconoclast when he observed that the "militant manifest destiny men were the isolationists of the nineteenth century." For with this insight we can translate those who maintain that Lodge "led the movement to perpetuate the traditional policy of isolation." Perhaps William G. Carleton was even more forthright. In 1946 he pointed out that the fight over the League treaty was not between isolationists and internationalists, and added that many of the mislabeled isolationists were actually "nationalists and imperialists." Equally discerning was Charles Beard's comment in 1933 that the twenties were marked by a "return to the more aggressive ways . . . [used] to protect and advance the claims of American business enterprise." All these interpretations were based on facts that prompted another scholar to change his earlier conclusion and declare in 1953 that "the thought was all of keeping American freedom of action." [7]

[6] Quotations, in order, from Weinberg, *Manifest Destiny*, pp. 473, 454; H. U. Faulkner, *American Political and Social History*, 6th ed. (New York: Appleton-Century-Crofts, Inc., 1952), pp. 700, 701; J. A. Garraty, *Henry Cabot Lodge. A Biography* (New York: Alfred A. Knopf, 1953), pp. 348, 364–65; F. L. Paxton, *American Democracy and the World War. Postwar Years. Normalcy, 1918–1923* (Berkeley: University of California Press, 1948), p. 367. For other examples of this ambiguity see D. Perkins, *The American Approach to Foreign Policy* (Cambridge: Harvard University Press, 1952), p. 26; T. A. Bailey, *A Diplomatic History of the American People*, 4th ed. (New York: Appleton-Century-Crofts, Inc., 1950), p. 682 — where he says that the Harding Administration "retreated into what ex-President Wilson described as 'sullen and selfish isolation' "; H. J. Carman and H. C. Syrett, *A History of the American People* (New York: Alfred A. Knopf, 1952), pp. 264–65, and title of Chapter XII; S. E. Morison and H. S. Commager, *The Growth of the American Republic*, 4th ed. (New York: Oxford University Press, 1950), Volume II, p. 497; and H. B. Parkes, *The United States of America* (New York: Alfred A. Knopf, 1953).

[7] R. W. Van Alstyne, "The Significance of the Mississippi Valley in American Diplomatic History, 1686–1890," *Mississippi Valley Historical Review*, XXXVI, No. 2 (September, 1949), p. 238; L. L. Leonard, *Elements of American Foreign Policy* (New York: McGraw-Hill Book Co., Inc., 1953), p. 220; among the many others who characterize Lodge in this manner is S. Adler in his recent article on isolation, "Isolationism Since 1914," *The American Scholar*, XXI, No. 3 (Summer, 1952), p. 340; W. G. Carleton, "Isolationism and the Middle West," *Mississippi Valley Historical Review*, XXXIII, No. 3 (December, 1946), pp. 381–82; C. A. and M. R. Beard, *The Rise of American Civilization*, New Edition (Two Volumes in One. Revised and Enlarged) (New York: The Macmillan Co., 1933), pp. 681–83; and compare D. Perkins, *The American Approach to Foreign Policy*, 26, with D. Perkins, "The Department of State and Public Opinion," Chapter IX in *The Diplomats 1919–1939*, ed. by G. A. Graig and F. Gilbert (Princeton: Princeton University Press, 1953), p. 308. Interestingly enough, both Carleton and Van Alstyne addressed their remarks to meetings of the Mis-

These are perceptive comments. Additional help has recently been supplied by two other students of the period. One of these is Robert E. Osgood, who approached the problem in terms of *Ideals and Self-Interest in American Foreign Relations*.[8] Though primarily concerned with the argument that Americans should cease being naive, Osgood suggests that certain stereotypes are misleading. One might differ with his analysis of the struggle over the Treaty of Versailles, but not with his insistence that there were fundamental differences between Senators Lodge and William E. Borah — as well as between those two and President Woodrow Wilson. Osgood likewise raises questions about the reputed withdrawal of the American public. Over a thousand organizations for the study of international relations existed in 1926, to say nothing of the groups that sought constantly to make or modify foreign policy.

Osgood gives little attention to this latter aspect of foreign relations, a surprising omission on the part of a realist.[9] But the underlying assumption of his inquiry cannot be challenged. The foreign policy issue of the twenties was never isolationism. The controversy and competition were waged between those who entertained different concepts of the national interest and disagreed over the means to be employed to secure that objec-

---

sissippi Valley Historical Association, and their articles later appeared as lead articles in the *Review*. On the same program with Van Alstyne, furthermore, was Professor Richard Leopold, whose comments were of a similar nature and whose paper was also printed. This professional audience seems to have ignored their keen suggestions. Professor Weinberg's article, "The Historical Meaning of the American Doctrine of Isolation," *The American Political Science Review*, XXXIV (1940), pp. 539–47, offers certain concepts that would go far to resolve the contradictions in his earlier *Manifest Destiny*, but he did not apply the ideas to any later period. H. Feis writes of America's active foreign economic policy in *The Diplomacy of the Dollar, First Era, 1919–1932* (Baltimore: Johns Hopkins Press, 1950), but fails to note that these facts contradict the idea of isolation. The same approach is taken by G. Soule, *Prosperity Decade. From War to Depression: 1917–1929* (New York: Rinehart and Co., Inc., 1947), pp. 252–74. Far more stimulating than either Feis or Soule is S. Kuznets, "Foreign Economic Relations of the United States and Their Impact Upon the Domestic Economy," Chapter 11 in his *Economic Change* (New York: W. W. Norton and Co., 1953), pp. 296–333. See also the neglected work of A. D. Gayer and C. T. Schmidt, *American Economic Foreign Policy. Postwar History, Analysis, and Interpretation* (New York: no publisher given, 1939), especially pp. 11–17.

[8] R. E. Osgood, *Ideals and Self-Interest in America's Foreign Relations. The Great Transformation of the Twentieth Century* (Chicago: University of Chicago Press, 1953).

[9] This is strange for a realist trained in the school of Professor Hans J. Morgenthau's *Realpolitik*. For the realists emphasize the fact that the relationship between power and ideals is reciprocal. Not only do ideas fail to have consequences without power, but the sources and the nature of the power have some correlation with the character of the ideals. Thus it would seem doubly unrealistic to slight the sources of power and at the same time discuss the ideas without reference to the private as well as the public record of the groups and individuals in question.

tive. Secretary of State Charles Evans Hughes was merely more eloquent, not less explicit. "Foreign policies," he explained in 1923, "are not built upon abstractions. They are the result of practical conceptions of national interest arising from some immediate exigency or standing out vividly in historical perspective." [10]

Historian George L. Grassmuck used this old-fashioned premise of the politician as a tool with which to probe the *Sectional Biases in Congress on Foreign Policy*. Disciplining himself more rigorously in the search for primary facts than did Osgood, Grassmuck's findings prompted him to conclude that "the 'sheep and goats' technique" of historical research is eminently unproductive. From 1921 to 1933, for example, the Republicans in both houses of Congress were "more favorable to both Army and Navy measures than . . . Democrats." Eighty-five per cent of the same Republicans supported international economic measures and agreements. As for the Middle West, that much condemned section did not reveal any "extraordinary indication of a . . . tendency to withdraw." Nor was there "an intense 'isolationism' on the part of [its] legislators with regard to membership in a world organization." [11] And what opposition there was seems to have been as much the consequence of dust bowls and depression as the product of disillusioned scholars in ivory towers.

These investigations and correlations have two implications. First, the United States was neither isolated nor did it pursue a policy of isolationism from 1920 to 1933. Second, if the policy of that era, so generally accepted as the product of traditional isolationist sentiment, proves non-isolationist, then the validity and usefulness of the concept when applied to earlier or later periods may seriously be challenged.

Indeed, it would seem more probable that the central theme of American foreign relations has been the expansion of the United States. Alexander Hamilton made astute use of the phrase "no entangling alliances" during the negotiation of Jay's Treaty in 1794, but his object was a *de facto* affiliation with the British Fleet — not isolation.[12] Nor was Thomas Jefferson seeking to withdraw when he made of Monticello a counselling center for those seeking to emulate the success of the American Revolution. A century later Senator Lodge sought to revise the Treaty of Versailles and the Covenant of the League of Nations with the reservations that seemed no more than a restatement of Hamilton's remarks. Yet the maneuvers of Lodge were no more isolationist in character and purpose

[10] C. E. Hughes, "The Centenary of the Monroe Doctrine," *The Annals of the American Academy of Political and Social Science*, Supplement to Volume CXI (January, 1923), p. 7.

[11] G. L. Grassmuck, *Sectional Biases in Congress on Foreign Policy* (Baltimore: Johns Hopkins Press, 1951), pp. 32, 93, 162, 49.

[12] Hamilton to the British Minister, as quoted by S. F. Bemis, *Jay's Treaty. A Study in Commerce and Diplomacy* (New York: Macmillan and Co., 1924), p. 246.

than Hamilton's earlier action. And while surely no latter-day Jefferson, Senator Borah was anything but an isolationist in his concept of the power of economics and ideas. Borah not only favored the recognition of the Soviet Union in order to influence the development of the Bolshevik Revolution and as a check against Japanese expansion in Asia, but also argued that American economic policies were intimately connected with foreign political crises. All those men were concerned with the extension of one or more aspects of American influence, power, and authority.

Approached in this manner, the record of American foreign policy in the twenties verifies the judgments of two remarkably dissimilar students: historian Richard W. Leopold and Senator Lodge. The professor warns that the era was "more complex than most glib generalizations . . . would suggest"; and the scholastic politician concludes that, excepting wars, there "never [was] a period when the United States [was] more active and its influence more felt internationally than between 1921 and 1924." [13] The admonition about perplexity was offered as helpful advice, not as an invitation to anti-intellectualism. For, as the remarks of the Senator implied, recognition that a problem is involved does not mean that it cannot be resolved.

Paradox and complexity can often be clarified by rearranging the data around a new focal point that is common to all aspects of the apparent contradiction. The confusion of certainty and ambiguity that characterizes most accounts of American foreign policy in the twenties stems from the fact that they are centered on the issue of membership in the League of Nations. Those Americans who wanted to join are called internationalists. Opponents of that move became isolationists. But the subsequent action of most of those who fought participation in the League belies this simple classification. And the later policies of many who favored adherence to the League casts serious doubts upon the assumption that they were willing to negotiate or arbitrate questions that they defined as involving the national interest. More pertinent is an examination of why certain groups and individuals favored or disapproved of the League, coupled with a review of the programs they supported after that question was decided.

Yet such a re-study of the League fight is in itself insufficient. Equally important is a close analysis of the American reaction to the Bolshevik Revolution. Both the League Covenant and the Treaty of Versailles were written on a table shaken by that upheaval. The argument over the ratification of the combined documents was waged in a context determined as much by Nikolai Lenin's *Appeal to the Toiling, Oppressed, and Ex-*

---

13 R. W. Leopold, "The Mississippi Valley and American Foreign Policy, 1890–1941: an Assessment and an Appeal," *Mississippi Valley Historical Review*, XXXVII, No. 4 (March, 1951), p. 635; H. C. Lodge, "Foreign Relations of the United States, 1921–1924," *Foreign Affairs*, II, No. 4 (June, 1924), p. 526.

hausted Peoples of Europe and the Soviet *Declaration to the Chinese People* as by George Washington's Farewell Address.[14]

Considered within the setting of the Bolshevik Revolution, the basic question was far greater than whether or not to enter the League. At issue was what response was to be made to the domestic and international division of labor that had accompanied the Industrial Revolution. Challenges from organized urban labor, dissatisfied farmers, frightened men of property, searching intellectual critics, and colonial peoples rudely interrupted almost every meeting of the Big Four in Paris and were echoed in many Senate debates over the treaty. And those who determined American policy through the decade of the twenties were consciously concerned with the same problem.

An inquiry into this controversy over the broad question of how to end the war reveals certain divisions within American society. These groupings were composed of individuals and organizations whose position on the League of Nations was coincident with and part of their response to the Bolsheviks; or, in a wider sense, with their answer to that general unrest, described by Woodrow Wilson as a "feeling of revolt against the large vested interests which influenced the world both in the economic and the political sphere." [15] Once this breakdown has been made it is then possible to follow the ideas and actions of these various associations of influence and power through the years 1920 to 1933.

At the core of the American reaction to the League and the Bolshevik Revolution was the quandary between fidelity to ideals and the urge to power. Jefferson faced a less acute version of the same predicament in terms of whether to force citizenship on settlers west of the Mississippi who were reluctant to be absorbed in the Louisiana Purchase. A century later the anti-imperialists posed the same issue in the more sharply defined circumstances of the Spanish-American War. The League and the Bolsheviks raised the question in its most dramatic context and in unavoidable terms.

---

[14] None of the authors cited above makes this association of events central to their discussion of the League issue. Few of them even connect the two. The integration has, of course, been made: most notably by E. H. Carr, *The Soviet Impact on the Western World* (New York: The Macmillan Co., 1947); M. Dobb, *Political Economy and Capitalism. Some Essays in Economic Tradition* (New York: International Publishers, 1945), Chapter VII, and *Studies in the Development of Capitalism* (New York: International Publishers, 1947), Chapter VIII; H. J. Laski, *Reflections on the Revolution of Our Time* (New York, 1947); Sir L. Namier, *Conflicts. Studies in Contemporary History* (London: The Macmillan Co., 1942), Chapter I; and, of especial significance, H. Hoover, *American Individualism* (Garden City: Doubleday, Page and Co., 1923).

[15] W. Wilson, remarks to the Council of Ten, January 16, 1919, *Papers Relating to the Foreign Relations of the United States. Paris Peace Conference* (13 vols., Washington, D.C.), III, p. 583.

There were four broad responses to this reopening of the age-old dilemma. At one pole stood the pure idealists and pacifists, led by William Jennings Bryan. A tiny minority in themselves, they were joined, in terms of general consequences if not in action, by those Americans who were preoccupied with their own solutions to the problem. Many American business men, for example, were concerned primarily with the expansion of trade and were apathetic toward or impatient with the hullabaloo over the League.[16] Diametrically opposed to the idealists were the vigorous expansionists. All these exponents of the main chance did not insist upon an overt crusade to run the world, but they were united on Senator Lodge's proposition that the United States should dominate world politics. Association with other nations they accepted, but not equality of membership or mutuality of decision.

Caught in the middle were those Americans who declined to support either extreme. A large number of these people clustered around Woodrow Wilson, and can be called the Wilsonites. Though aware of the dangers and temptations involved, Wilson declared his intention to extend American power for the purpose of strengthening the ideals. However noble that effort, it failed for two reasons. Wilson delegated power and initiative to men and organizations that did not share his objectives, and on his own part the president ultimately "cast in his lot" with the defenders of the status quo.[17]

Led by the Sons of the Wild Jackass, the remaining group usually followed Senator Borah in foreign relations. These men had few illusions about the importance of power in human affairs or concerning the authority of the United States in international politics. Prior to the world war they supported — either positively or passively — such vigorous expansionists as Theodore Roosevelt, who led their Progressive Party. But the war and the Bolshevik Revolution jarred some of these Progressives into a closer examination of their assumptions. These reflections and new conclusions widened the breach with those of their old comrades who had moved toward a conservative position on domestic issues. Some of those earlier allies, like Senator Albert J. Beveridge, continued to agitate for an American century. Others, such as Bainbridge Colby, sided with Wilson in 1916 and went along with the president on foreign policy.

[16] See the excellent essay by J. H. Foote, "American Industrialists and Foreign Policy, 1919–1922. A Study in Attitudes," Master's Thesis, University of Wisconsin, Madison, 1947; for a typical expression see the remarks of Senator Walter E. Edge — "we wasted, practically wasted, two years of the opportunity presented to us at that time, unequaled, as I say, in the history of the world" — in National Foreign Trade Council, *Official Report of the Eighth National Foreign Trade Convention, 1921* (New York, 1921), p. 553.

[17] W. Wilson, remarks to the Big Five, February 14, 1919, *Foreign Relations. Russia, 1919* (Washington, D.C., 1957), p. 59.

But a handful had become firm anti-expansionists by 1919.[18] No attempt was made by these men to deny the power of the United States. Nor did they think that the nation could become self-sufficient and impregnable in its strength. Borah, for example, insisted that America must stand with Russia if Japan and Germany were to be checked. And Johnson constantly pointed out that the question was not whether to withdraw, but at what time and under what circumstances to use the country's influence. What these men did maintain was that any effort to run the world by establishing an American system comparable to the British Empire was both futile and un-American.

In this they agreed with Henry Adams, who debated the same issue with his brother Brooks Adams, Theodore Roosevelt, and Henry Cabot Lodge in the years after 1898. "I incline now to anti-imperialism, and very strongly to anti-militarism," Henry warned. "If we try to rule politically, we take the chances against us." By the end of the First World War another generation of expansionists tended to agree with Henry Adams about ruling politically, but planned to build and maintain a similar pattern of control through the use of America's economic might. Replying to these later expansionists, Borah and other anti-expansionists of the nineteen-twenties argued that if Washington's influence was to be effective it would have to be used to support the movements of reform and colonial nationalism rather than deployed in an effort to dam up and dominate those forces.

For these reasons they opposed Wilson's reorganization of the international banking consortium, fearing that the financiers would either influence strongly or veto — as they did — American foreign policies. With Senator Albert B. Cummins of Iowa they voted against the Wilson-approved Webb-Pomerene Act, which repealed the anti-trust laws for export associations. In the same vein they tried to prevent passage of the Edge Act, an amendment to the Federal Reserve Act that authorized for-

---

[18] C. Vevier reviewed these early expansionist sympathies of the Progressives in "The Progressives and Dollar Diplomacy," Master's Thesis, University of Wisconsin, Madison, 1949. W. E. Leuchtenburg later published a summary of his own study of the same question as "Progressivism and Imperialism: The Progressive Movement and American Foreign Policy, 1898–1916," *Mississippi Valley Historical Review*, XXXIX, No. 3 (December, 1952), pp. 483–504. It would seem, however, that Leuchtenburg missed the split within the Progressives over Wilson's foreign policy. For in note 38, page 493, he considers it "remarkable" that the Progressives fought Wilson in view of the degree to which the president "was involved with American imperialist aspirations." This writer's information on the division comes from the manuscript papers of Calvin Coolidge, William E. Borah, William Judson, Samuel N. Harper, Theodore Roosevelt, Alexander Gumberg, Raymond Robins, and Woodrow Wilson; from the materials in the National Archives; and the *Congressional Record*.

eign banking corporations.[19] Led by Borah, they bitterly attacked the Versailles Treaty because, in their view, it committed the United States to oppose colonial movements for self-government and to support an unjust and indefensible status quo. From the same perspective they criticized and fought to end intervention in Russia and the suppression of civil liberties at home.[20]

Contrary to the standard criticism of their actions, however, these anti-expansionists were not just negative die-hards. Senator Cummins maintained from the first that American loans to the allies should be considered gifts. Borah spoke out on the same issue, hammered away against armed intervention in Latin America, played a key role in securing the appointment of Dwight Morrow as Ambassador to Mexico, and sought to align the United States with, instead of against, the Chinese Revolution. On these and other issues the anti-expansionists were not always of one mind, but as in the case of the Washington Conference Treaties the majority of them were far more positive in their actions than has been acknowledged.[21]

Within this framework the key to the defeat of the League treaty was the defection from the Wilsonites of a group who declined to accept the restrictions that Article X of the League Covenant threatened to impose upon the United States. A morally binding guarantee of the "territorial integrity and existing political integrity of all members of the League" was too much for these men. First they tried to modify that limitation. Failing there, they followed Elihu Root and William Howard Taft, both

[19] See, for example, the debates on the Webb-Pomerene Act in *Congressional Record*, Volume 56, Part 1, pp. 69–71; and the votes on the same legislation, pp. 168, 186.

[20] Especially pertinent are the remarks of Borah, *Congressional Record*, V54: 1:636; V57:1:190; V58:3:3143–44; and his letter to F. Lynch, August 1, 1919, *Papers of William E. Borah*, Library of Congress, Manuscript Division, Washington, D.C. Also important are the comments of Senator Hiram Johnson, *Congressional Record*, V53:1:503, 505. Eric Goldman's penetrating study of the Progressives, *Rendezvous With Destiny. A History of Modern American Reform* (New York: Alfred A. Knopf, 1952), completely misses this development. On pp. 273–74, Goldman remarks that the "most striking deviation of American progressivism in foreign affairs from its attitudes in domestic affairs was the enthusiasm for international order in the form of the League of Nations." He proceeds, then, to argue that if the progressives had applied the same criticism to the League as they had to its laissez faire counterpart in domestic affairs "they could hardly have emerged with a favorable attitude." But the key point is that the hard core of the Progressives did exactly this and came out in opposition to the League.

[21] This paragraph is based on much the same material cited in note 18. But see, as representative, Cummins' remarks on the loans, *Congressional Record*, V55:11:757, 762; Borah on economic factors, V64:1:930–31; and the parliamentary maneuvers over the Liberian Loan, V63:1:287–88.

old time expansionists, to a new position behind Senator Lodge. Among those who abandoned Wilson on this issue were Herbert Hoover, Calvin Coolidge, Charles Evans Hughes, and Henry L. Stimson.

Not all these men were at ease with the vigorous expansionists. Stimson, for one, thought the Lodge reservations "harsh and unpleasant," and later adjusted other of his views.[22] Hoover and Hughes tried to revive their version of the League after the Republicans returned to power in 1920. But at the time all of them were more uneasy about what one writer has termed Wilson's "moral imperialism." [23] They were not eager to identify themselves with the memories of that blatant imperialism of the years 1895 to 1905, but neither did they like Article X. That proviso caught them from both sides, it illegalized changes initiated by the United States, and obligated America to restore a status quo to some aspects of which they were either indifferent or antagonistic. But least of all were they anxious to run the risk that the Wilsonian rhetoric of freedom and liberty might be taken seriously in an age of revolution. Either by choice or default they supported the idea of a community of interest among the industrialized powers of the world led by an American-British entente as against the colonial areas and the Soviet Union.

This postwar concept of the community of interest was the first generation intellectual off-spring of Herbert Croly's *Promise of American Life* and Herbert Hoover's *American Individualism*. Croly's opportunistic nationalism provided direction for Hoover's "greater mutuality of interest." The latter was to be expressed in an alliance between the government and the "great trade associations and the powerful corporations." [24] Pushed by the Croly-Hoover wing of the old Progressive Party, the idea enjoyed great prestige during the twenties. Among its most ardent exponents were Samuel Gompers and Matthew Woll of the labor movement, Owen D. Young of management, and Bernard Baruch of finance.

What emerged was an American corporatism. The avowed goals were

[22] Stimson, Diary entry of December 3, 1919, quoted in H. L. Stimson and McGeorge Bundy, *On Active Service in Peace and War* (New York: Harper and Brothers, 1948), p. 104.

[23] H. F. Cline, *The United States and Mexico* (Cambridge: Harvard University Press, 1953), p. 141.

[24] H. Croly, *The Promise of American Life* (New York: The Macmillan Co., 1909); H. Hoover, *American Individualism*, p. 43; and Hoover, quoted in Goldman, *Rendezvous With Destiny*, p. 309. Goldman makes this identification between Croly and Hoover, but does not develop it, either as corporatism or in foreign affairs. Other Americans had spoken the language of the community of interest. J. P. Morgan used it to describe his ideal in the economic realm. Brooks Adams warned Theodore Roosevelt that such coordination at the national level was necessary to insure American supremacy in the world. The Adams argument emphasized the need for an intellectual and political elite chosen from the upper classes to supervise the community of interest through control of the national government.

order, stability, and social peace. The means to those objectives were labor-management co-operation, arbitration, and the elimination of waste and inefficiency by closing out unrestrained competition. State intervention was to be firm, but moderated through the cultivation and legalization of trade associations which would, in turn, advise the national government and supply leaders for the federal bureaucracy. The ideal was union in place of diversity and conflict.[25]

Other than Hoover, the chief spokesmen of this new community of interest as applied to foreign affairs were Secretaries of State Hughes and Stimson. In the late months of 1931 Stimson was to shift his ground, but until that time he supported the principle. All three men agreed that American economic power should be used to build, strengthen, and maintain the co-operation they sought. As a condition for his entry into the cabinet, Hoover demanded — and received — a major voice in "all important economic policies of the administration." [26] With the energetic assistance of Julius Klein, lauded by the National Foreign Trade Council as the "international business go-getter of Uncle Sam," Hoover changed the Department of Commerce from an agency primarily concerned with interstate commerce to one that concentrated on foreign markets and

[25] American corporatism is a neglected field. This writer is greatly indebted to Professor Paul Farmer, University of Wisconsin, for many long discussions of the question. Farmer brought to these conversations his intimate and extended knowledge of French corporative theory and practice as it developed to and culminated in the Vichy Government. His insights into the American scene were equally penetrating. At a later date M. H. Elbow, *French Corporative Theory, 1789–1948. A Chapter in the History of Ideas* (New York: Columbia University Press, 1953), was helpful in review. Of other published material, the following were most helpful: S. D. Alinsky, *Reveille For Radicals* (Chicago: University of Chicago Press, 1946); G. A. Almond, "The Political Attitudes of Wealth," *Journal of Politics*, VII, No. 3 (August, 1945); R. A. Brady, *Business as a System of Power* (New York: Columbia University Press, 1938); R. Bendix, "Bureaucracy and the Problem of Power," *Public Administration Review*, V, No. 3 (Summer, 1945); J. A. C. Grant, "The Guild Returns to America," *Journal of Politics*, IV, Nos. 3 and 4 (August, November, 1942); W. E. Henry, "The Business Executive: the Psycho-Dynamics of a Social Role," *American Journal of Sociology*, LIV, No. 1 (January, 1949); E. J. Howenstine, "Public Works Policy in the Twenties," *Social Research*, XII (December, 1946); F. Hunter, *Community Power Structure. A Study of Decision Makers* (Chapel Hill: University of North Carolina Press, 1953); R. S. Lynd, "Power Politics and the Post War World," in *The Postwar World. The Merrick Lectures for 1944* (New York: Abingdon-Cokesbury Press, 1945); and M. Weber, *The Theory of Social and Economic Organization*, trans. by A. M. Henderson and T. Parsons, ed. by T. Parsons (New York: Oxford University Press, 1947). For a revealing glimpse of the later bi-partisan movement toward corporatism, and the consequences thereof, see *The Welfare State and the National Welfare. A Symposium on Some of the Threatening Tendencies of Our Times*, ed. by S. Glueck (Cambridge: Addison-Wesley Press, Inc., 1952); and the last chapter in Goldman, *Rendezvous With Destiny*.

[26] *The Memoirs of Herbert Hoover. The Cabinet and the Presidency, 1920–1933* (New York: The Macmillan Co., 1952), p. 36.

loans, and control of import sources.[27] Hughes and Stimson handled the political aspects of establishing a "community of ideals, interests and purposes." [28]

These men were not imperialists in the traditional sense of that much abused term. All agreed with Klein that the object was to eliminate "the old imperialistic trappings of politico-economic exploitation." They sought instead the "internationalization of business." [29] Through the use of economic power they wanted to establish a common bond, forged of similar assumptions and purposes, with both the industrialized nations and the native business community in the colonial areas of the world. Their deployment of America's material strength is unquestioned. President Calvin Coolidge reviewed their success, and indicated the political implications thereof, on Memorial Day, 1928. "Our investments and trade relations are such," he summarized, "that it is almost impossible to conceive of any conflict anywhere on earth which would not affect us injuriously." [30]

Internationalization through the avoidance of conflict was the key objective. This did not mean a negative foreign policy. Positive action was the basic theme. The transposition of corporatist principles to the area of foreign relations produced a parallel policy. American leadership and intervention would build a world community regulated by agreement among the industrialized nations. The prevention of revolution and the preservation of the sanctity of private property were vital objectives. Hughes was very clear when he formulated the idea for Latin America. "We are seeking to establish a *Pax Americana* maintained not by arms but by mutual respect and good will and the tranquillizing processes of reason." There would be, he admitted, "interpositions of a temporary character" — the Secretary did not like the connotations of the word intervention — but only to facilitate the establishment of the United States as the "exemplar of justice." [31]

Extension to the world of this pattern developed in Latin America was more involved. There were five main difficulties, four in the realm of foreign relations and one in domestic affairs. The internal problem was to establish and integrate a concert of decision between the government and

[27] *Official Report of the 18th Foreign Trade Convention, 1931* (New York, 1931), p. 287.

[28] C. E. Hughes, remarks concerning a substitute for Article X of the League Covenant, Union League Club Speech, New York, March 26, 1919.

[29] J. Klein, *Frontiers of Trade* (New York: The Century Co., 1929), pp. 40, 46.

[30] C. Coolidge, Address of May 30, 1928, *Congressional Record*, V69:10: 10729.

[31] C. E. Hughes, "Centenary of the Monroe Doctrine," *Annals*, p. 17; and Hughes, remarks to the Havana Conference, 1928.

private economic groups. Abroad the objectives were more sharply defined: circumscribe the impact of the Soviet Union, forestall and control potential resistance of colonial areas, pamper and cajole Germany and Japan into acceptance of the basic proposition, and secure from Great Britain practical recognition of the fact that Washington had become the center of Anglo-Saxon collaboration. Several examples will serve to illustrate the general outline of this diplomacy, and to indicate the friction between the office holders and the office dwellers.

Wilson's Administration left the incoming Republicans a plurality of tools designed for the purpose of extending American power. The Webb-Pomerene Law, the Edge Act, and the banking consortium were but three of the more obvious and important of these. Certain polishing and sharpening remained to be done, as exemplified by Hoover's generous interpretation of the Webb-Pomerene legislation, but this was a minor problem. Hoover and Hughes added to these implements with such laws as the one designed to give American customs officials diplomatic immunity so that they could do cost accounting surveys of foreign firms. This procedure was part of the plan to provide equal opportunity abroad, under which circumstances Secretary Hughes was confident that "American business men would take care of themselves." [32]

It was harder to deal with the British, who persisted in annoying indications that they considered themselves equal partners in the enterprise. Bainbridge Colby, Wilson's last Secretary of State, ran into the same trouble. Unless England came "to our way of thinking," Colby feared that "agreement [would] be impossible." A bit later Hughes told the British Ambassador that the time had come for London's expressions of cordial sentiment to be "translated into something definite." After many harangues about oil, access to mandated areas, and trade with Russia, it was with great relief that Stimson spoke of the United States and Great Britain "working together like two old shoes." [33]

Deep concern over revolutionary ferment produced great anxiety. Hughes quite agreed with Colby that the problem was to prevent revolutions without making martyrs of the leaders of colonial or other dissident movements. The despatches of the period are filled with such expressions as "very grave concern," "further depressed," and "deeply regret," in con-

---

[32] The story of the fight over diplomatic immunity for consular officers can be followed in Foreign Relations, 1925, pp. 211–54; the quote from Hughes is by J. Butler Wright, in Official Report of the 12th National Foreign Trade Convention, 1925 (New York, 1925), p. 165.

[33] Colby to Wright, November 5, 1920, National Archives of the United States (hereafter cited as NA), 574.D1/240b; Hughes, Memorandum of conversation with Geddes, September 20, 1921, NA, 500.A 4/190.5; Stimson, Memorandum of July 20, 1931, NA, 462.00 R 296/4594.5.

nection with revolutionary activity in China, Latin America, and Europe.[34] American foreign service personnel abroad were constantly reminded to report all indications of such unrest. This sensitivity reached a high point when one representative telegraphed as "an example of the failure to assure public safety . . . the throwing of a rock yesterday into the state hospital here." Quite in keeping with this pattern was Washington's conclusion that it would support "any provisional government which gave satisfactory evidence of an intention to re-establish constitutional order." [35]

Central to American diplomacy of the twenties was the issue of Germany and Japan. And it was in this area that the government ran into trouble with its partners, the large associations of capital. The snag was to convince the bankers of the validity of the long range view. Hoover, Hughes and Stimson all agreed that it was vital to integrate Germany and Japan into the American community. Thus Hughes opposed the French diplomacy of force on the Rhine, and for his own part initiated the Dawes Plan. But the delegation of so much authority to the financiers backfired in 1931. The depression scared the House of Morgan and it refused to extend further credits to Germany. Stimson "blew up." He angrily told the Morgan representative in Paris that this strengthened France and thereby undercut the American program. Interrupted in the midst of this argument by a trans-Atlantic phone call from Hoover, Stimson explained to the president that "if you want to help the cause you are speaking of you will not do it by calling me up, but by calling Tom Lamont." Stimson then turned back to Lamont's agent in Europe and, using "unregulated language," told the man to abandon his "narrow banking axioms." [36]

Similar difficulties faced the government in dealing with Japan and China. The main problem was to convince Japan, by persuasion, concession, and the delicate use of diplomatic force, to join the United States in an application of its Latin American policy to China. Washington argued that the era of the crude exploitation of, and the exercise of direct political sovereignty over, backward peoples was past. Instead, the interested powers should agree to develop and exercise a system of absentee authority while increasing the productive capacity and administrative efficiency of China. Japan seemed amenable to the proposal, and at the Washington Conference, Secretary Hughes went a great distance to convince Tokyo of American sincerity. Some writers, such as George Frost Kennan and Adolf

[34] Colby to Russell, August 13, 1920, NA, 333.3921 L 96/3; Hughes to Cottrell, April 9, 1923, NA, 824.51/174; Hughes to Morales, June 30, 1923, NA, 815.00/2609; same to same, May 15, 1923, NA, 815.00/2574.

[35] Kodding to Hughes. October 10, 1924, NA, 375.1123 Coleman and Delong/89; Hughes to Welles, April 10, 1924, NA, 815.00/3077a supplement.

[36] Stimson, Memorandum of talks with representatives of J. P. Morgan and Co., Paris, July 17, 1931, NA, 462.00 R 296/4587.5.

A. Berle, claim that the United States did not go far enough.[37] This is something of a mystery. For in his efforts to establish "cooperation in the Far East," as Hughes termed it, the Secretary consciously gave Japan "an extraordinarily favorable position." [38]

Perhaps what Kennan and Berle have in mind is the attitude of Thomas Lamont. In contrast to their perspective on Europe, the bankers took an extremely long range view of Asia. Accepting the implications of the Four and Nine Power Treaties, Lamont began to finance Japan's penetration of the mainland. Hughes and Stimson were trapped. They continued to think in terms of American business men taking care of themselves if given an opportunity, and thus strengthening Washington's position in the world community. Hughes wrote Morgan that he hoped the consortium would become an "important instrumentality of our 'open door' policy." [39] But the American members of the banking group refused to antagonize their Japanese and British colleagues, and so vetoed Washington's hope to finance the Chinese Eastern Railway and its efforts to support the Federal Telegraph Company in China.

In this context it is easy to sympathize with Stimson's discomfort when the Japanese Army roared across Manchuria. As he constantly reiterated to the Japanese Ambassador in Washington, Tokyo had come far along the road "of bringing itself into alignment with the methods and opinion of the Western World." [40] Stimson not only wanted to, but did in fact give Japan every chance to continue along that path. So too did President Hoover, whose concern with revolution was so great that he was inclined to view Japanese sovereignty in Manchuria as the best solution. Key men in the State Department shared the president's conclusion.[41]

Stimson's insight was not so limited. He realized that his predecessor, Secretary of State Frank B. Kellogg, had been right: the community of interest that America should seek was with the Chinese. The Secretary acknowledged his error to Senator Borah, who had argued just such a thesis since 1917. Stimson's letter to Borah of February 23, 1932, did not

[37] G. F. Kennan, *American Diplomacy, 1900–1950* (Chicago: University of Chicago Press, 1951), p. 82; A. A. Berle, Jr., review of H. Feis, *The China Tangle*, in the *New York Times*, Book Review Section, October 4, 1953.

[38] Hughes to Judge Hiscock, April 24, 1924, quoted in M. J. Pusey, *Charles Evans Hughes* (2 vols., New York: The Macmillan Co., 1951), II, p. 516; Hughes to Bell, October 22, 1924, NA, 893.51/4699; Hughes, Memorandum of conversations with Kato and Balfour, December 2, 1921, NA, 500.A4b/547.5.

[39] Hughes to Morgan, August 8, 1921, NA, 861.77/2184.

[40] Stimson, Memorandum of November 21, 1931, NA, 793.94/2865; and see Stimson, Memorandum of February 27, 1933, NA, 793.94/5953, for a clear review of his changing attitudes.

[41] This writer is greatly indebted to Professor Richard N. Current, University of Illinois, for sharing his extended knowledge of the Manchurian Crisis. Professor Current's study will be published in the spring of 1954 by Rutgers University Press.

say that America should abandon her isolationism, but rather that she had gone too far with the wrong friends. The long and painful process of America's great awakening had begun. But in the meantime President Hoover's insistence that no move should be made toward the Soviet Union, and that the non-recognition of Manchuko should be considered as a formula looking toward conciliation, had opened the door to appeasement.

The H-Bomb Decision: How to Decide Without Actually Choosing

WARNER R. SCHILLING

In the following essay political scientist Warner Schilling explores the decision-making process in the determination of foreign and military choices. His subject is President Truman's decision of January 1950 ordering the Atomic Energy Commission to determine the feasibility and the consequences of producing a thermonuclear weapon. Schilling's examination of the operation of interest groups and bureaucratic politics within government vividly demonstrates the process of compromise and integration of positions. Yet, even when the decision is "minimal," as it was with the H-bomb, the consequences seem to be the inevitable acceleration toward complete acceptance of one choice over another. Once government or governmental agencies veer in the direction of a particular policy, their commitment is almost irreversible. Thus, within a few years after Truman's decision, the United States found itself in a new strategic position without really having deliberately chosen this position. Schilling's essay also offers a useful insight into the basic conflict over national security policy within the so-called Garrison State. The debate over building the Super Bomb was conditioned by differences over long-range strategy. Military-oriented groups stressed the need for the most powerful weapons, while the opposition questioned a total dependence upon nuclear weapons and sought instead a basic review of the nation's military needs. There were only a few who opposed the further development of nuclear weapons and advocated a determined new effort to negotiate with the Soviet Union to forestall the arms race. But given the prevailing official and public conception of the American security position, such a suggestion was futile.

President Truman made his first H-bomb decision on January 31, 1950. He ordered the Atomic Energy Commission to continue its efforts to determine the technical feasibility of a thermonuclear weapon. The rate and scale of the effort were to be fixed jointly by the AEC and the Department of Defense. He also ordered the Department of State and the Department of Defense to re-examine the nation's strategic objectives and plans, both diplomatic and military, in light of the forthcoming developments to be expected in Soviet nuclear weapons capabilities. Both directives had been recommended to the President in a report submitted the same day by a special committee of the National Security Council, composed of the Secretaries of State and Defense and the Chairman of the Atomic Energy Commission.[1]

The report of the special committee and the President's subsequent decision marked the first resolution of a policy discussion that had begun in September, 1949, with the discovery that the Russians had exploded a fission bomb. This discussion had been broadly concerned with the implications of the Soviet explosion for American security and with the question of what actions the United States should undertake as a result of it. The first purpose of this article will be to contrast the content and form of the President's decision with that of the policy discussion that had preceded it. The point of this contrast will be to illustrate the "minimal" character of the decision made on January 31st. Of all the courses of action considered and debated during the preceding five months, that chosen by the President represented one which seemed to close off the least number of future alternatives, one that left the most issues still undecided. The second and third purposes of this article will be to advance an explanation for the minimal character of the decision and to indicate some of the policy consequences that followed from its having been made in this manner.

Reprinted with permission from the *Political Science Quarterly*, LXXVI (March 1961), pp. 24–46.
[1] See Harry S. Truman, *Memoirs* (New York, 1956, 2 vols.), vol. 2, p. 309.

The Policy Background

The explosion by the Russians of a fission bomb on August 26, 1949, was an event which took American policy-makers by surprise and one for which they had prepared neither specific plans nor a general strategy. The Joint Chiefs of Staff, taking what many believed to be a pessimistic view, had not expected the Soviet Union to detonate a fission weapon until 1952. Although steps had been taken prior to August, 1949, to provide for the detection of such an explosion, nowhere in the government had any formal attention been given to the question of what actions might be appropriately taken once the evidence of an explosion had been detected. The absence of forward planning can be attributed in part to the absence of any formal deadlines or pressures compelling planning groups in State, Defense, or the Commission to undertake it. It can also be attributed to the absence of any generally agreed-on body of strategic thought regarding the foreign policy implications of nuclear weapons which could have served as a point of departure and frame of reference for more specific plans.

Since the end of the Civil War, the continental security of the United States had been doubly insured. First, by virtue of its superior military potential which completely overshadowed that of the other Great Powers, the United States had no need to fear any nation. The weapons of World Wars I and II and the distribution of the people, skills, and re-sources necessary to make and use these weapons were such that no single foreign nation could conceivably mobilize enough military power from inside its own frontiers to assault successfully the American conti-nent. Secondly, by virtue of the balance of power abroad, the United States could afford to leave its potential largely unmobilized. The interests and arms of the other Great Powers were so committed one against the other that none was free to direct its strength against the United States. In time of peace these Powers did not dare turn their backs on more immediate enemies, and in time of war their hands were full fighting them. The American continent was subject to only one serious military threat: the possibility that through conquest and alliance the people, skills, and resources of the Old World might be gathered together into one hos-tile combination. Only in this event could the United States be confronted with a military potential roughly equivalent to its own. The result, if not in all instances the intent, of American intervention in World Wars I and II had been to remove this contingency from the realm of reality.

Following World War II two revolutionary changes occurred in this security position. The first was the inability of the European Powers to re-establish a balance of power on the European continent. The nations of Western Europe were in no position to prevent the Russians from achieving at their ease what had just been so painfully wrested from the hands of the Germans: an empire from the Urals to the Atlantic embracing all the peoples, skills, and resources of the Old World. The United States moved resolutely to meet this situation, both through policies designed to substitute American power for European (the Truman Doctrine, the North Atlantic Treaty) and through policies designed to restore to the Western Europeans themselves the capacity to balance the Russians (the Marshall Plan, the Mutual Defense Assistance Program).

These policies, which constituted the main burden of American security policy between 1945 and 1949, were addressed to a real and immediate problem. They were, however, essentially pre-nuclear in their rationale. The advent of nuclear weapons had not influenced the American determination to restore the European balance of power. It was, in fact, an objective which the United States would have had an even greater incentive to undertake if the fission bomb had not been developed. Nor were nuclear weapons believed to have qualitatively altered the military problem of achieving that objective. The American monopoly of the atomic bomb was seen as greatly facilitating the task of defeating the Red Army (and hence in deterring an attack by it), but in the judgment of at least two of the three services it would still be necessary to maintain sufficient ground strength on the continent to permit the mounting of the large-scale land offensive which they believed would be required in order to terminate the war.[2]

In the summer of 1949 the second revolutionary change in the American security position, that occasioned by the advent of Soviet nuclear weapons-systems, had yet to occur. This was a development destined to change completely the strategic significance of the traditional components of American security. The new weapons were so cheap and so destructive, relative to the old, that the Soviet Union would have the ability to mobilize from inside its own frontiers enough military power to accomplish what had heretofore been beyond the means of any single foreign nation: the capacity to strike a mortal blow at the American continent. The consequences were two-fold: the industrial superiority that had guaranteed victory in two World Wars was no longer the equivalent of overwhelming military potential, and the United States could no longer afford to leave its potential largely unmobilized during time of peace. Unlike the case of the Kaiser's or Hitler's Germany, the conquest of the people, skills, and resources of the Old World would not be a necessary first step in a Soviet attack on the United States. As a result, the United States would no

[2] For the rationale of the American interest in restoring the European balance of power, see Walter Millis and E. S. Duffield, editors, *The Forrestal Diaries* (New York, 1951), pp. 341, 349–351. For military doctrine regarding a war in Europe, see, e.g., General Omar Bradley, "This Way Lies Peace," *Saturday Evening Post*, vol. 220, October 15, 1949, and Walter Millis, Harvey C. Mansfield, and Harold Stein, *Arms and the State* (New York, 1958), pp. 237–245, 247–249.

longer be able to count on the unfolding of such conquest (1) to provide time for Americans to alert themselves to danger and to arm to meet it, and (2) to provide allies to preoccupy the enemy until they were ready. In fact, the import of the second revolution was to diminish that of the first. The more developed Russian transcontinental nuclear striking power, the less important would be the addition of Western Europe's people, skills, and resources for a Soviet attack on the United States and, perforce, the less significant the distribution of power on that continent for the security of the United States.

The implications of the advent of nuclear weapons for American security were stark. American policy between 1945 and 1949 had by no means been blind to these possibilities, and two major policies had been formulated to meet them. The first was the proposal made for international control of atomic energy, which by the fall of 1947 appeared to have little prospect of being accepted by the Soviet Union. The second was the development of a military doctrine to cope with the contingency of two-way nuclear war. The character of this doctrine can be seen in the report released in January, 1948, by the President's Air Policy Commission. Bluntly entitled "Survival in the Air Age," the Finletter Report called for a "new strategy" to provide victory in an atomic war if it came and, hopefully, by confronting the enemy with the "prospect of a counterattack of the utmost violence," to persuade him not to attack in the first place.

According to the Report, this strategy would require an Air Force capable of smashing the Russian cities and factories. The prospect of such a "devastating price" would make the Soviets hesitate to attack. The Air Force would also need the capability of launching a counteroffensive against the Russian air forces "at the earliest possible moment" in order "to silence the attack on the United States mainland and give us the time again to build up our industrial machine and our manpower to go on to win the war." The Soviet objective, on the other hand, would be to smash American industrial power "at the outset" and to destroy the American air defense and counterattack forces. Basically, however, what was outlined in the Finletter Report was not so much a "new strategy" as the problems and choices over which the discussion of strategy was to ponder for years thereafter. The Report took no note of the possible conflicts between a strategy designed to deter atomic attack and a strategy designed to win an atomic war. Neither did the Report confront the question of why, if the United States could achieve a counter-offensive blow of the magnitude described against Russian cities and delivery forces, the Russians could not do the same or better with their attacking blow, and, in this event, against what and with what would the United States launch its counterattack? [3]

---

[3] See *Survival in the Air Age*, A Report by the President's Air Policy Commission (Washington, 1948), pp. 6, 10, 12, 14, 20, 23–25.

These, then, were the three major postwar security policies that the United States had evolved by the eve of the Russian explosion: the effort to restore the European balance of power; the effort to secure international control of nuclear weapons; and the effort to evolve a force for two-way atomic war and a strategy to guide it. The three objectives were by no means carefully interrelated. Just as the strategy to restore the European balance of power made no provision for the time when American security would cease to turn on the stability of that balance, so the strategic doctrine outlined in the Finletter Report, while correctly anticipating that the future pivot would be the stability of the Soviet-American balance of terror, made no provision for the possibility that the United States would continue to have a political and military stake in the independence of Western Europe. As for the proposal for international control, this, if accepted, would require a substantial revision of the forces required to implement both of the other objectives. It should also be noted that each of these three policies had the potential of pointing the American response to the Russian explosion in a different direction. With the passing of the American monopoly on the atomic bomb, the defense of Western Europe might now require a larger commitment of ground forces than had heretofore been necessary. The need to prepare for two-way atomic war, on the other hand, would seem to call for the allocation of additional resources to the weapons for air attack and defense and an expansion in the size of the nuclear stockpile. Finally, the development by the Russians of their own nuclear weapons could be seen as the proper occasion to reopen and redouble the effort to secure their control by an international agency.

It was against this background of policy that discussion began in September, 1949, on the question of what should be done now that the Soviet Union had exploded an A-bomb. The major participants in this discussion came from five government institutions: the Departments of State and Defense; the Atomic Energy Commission (including a number of scientists employed in full or in part by the Commission or its subcontractors); the Office of the President; and the Joint Committee on Atomic Energy of Congress. By far the bulk of the policy discussion among these participants took place informally, and the degree and effect of the initiative exercised through these informal contacts fully support the insight of the observer who commented that the Federal Government is the last stronghold of private enterprise in the United States. Although a number of the participants had begun by December, 1949, to leak some of the subject matter of the discussion to the press, the policy discussion was for the most part closed to the general public.

The formal development of the policy discussion was tied to the bureaucratic history of a particular issue, that of whether to undertake an intensive effort to make a thermonuclear weapon. This matter was placed on the agenda of the Atomic Energy Commission on October 5th for reference to the Commission's main scientific advisory body, the General Advisory Committee. Both the report of the GAC, submitted on October 30th, and that submitted by the five Commissioners to the President on November 9th made it clear that the issue was hardly one that could be decided without reference to political and military as well as technical considerations. For this reason, and because he was well aware of the differences that were developing both between and within the major governmental bodies involved in the issue, the President referred the issue on November 10th to the previously noted special committee of the National Security Council. Under the auspices of this committee a working group was set up, composed of representatives from each of the three Executive agencies concerned: State, Defense, and the AEC. In addition to the work done jointly by this group, each agency also conducted a variety of independent studies into aspects of the problem, and the ultimate products of this activity were the recommendations submitted by the special committee to the President on January 31, 1950. It should be noted that throughout this period the Joint Committee on Atomic Energy was active in exploring the issue and voicing its views, through letters and personal visits by the Chairman to the President.

It will be the purpose of the following section to present a summary description of the issues and alternatives that were developed during the course of these proceedings. Although there will be occasional references to individual or institutional views, the purpose of the section is not to describe in any detail the positions held by particular individuals or government bodies with regard to the issues and alternatives discussed. The views of most of the individuals concerned were quite complex, and individual views within the same government bodies were by no means uniform. Many individuals and agencies took similar policy positions but for quite different reasons, and the views of some individuals and agencies changed over the time period involved. The summary is meant to delineate not individual or institutional positions but rather the range and content of the major policy proposals and considerations that were produced as a result of these five months of debate and deliberation.[4]

[4] The information in the preceding paragraphs and the sections that follow can largely be found in two published sources: Truman, *op. cit.*, vol. 2, ch. 20, and United States Atomic Energy Commission, *In the Matter of J. Robert Oppenheimer*, Transcript of Hearing before Personnel Security Board (Washington, 1954). The article also draws upon extended personal interviews during 1956–1958 with sixty-six of the participants in the events discussed. Given the character of interview data and the particular focus of this article, it is the present writer's conclusion that the best way to meet scholarly obligations to both readers and participants is by omitting citation for the points that follow. The same considerations are responsible for the fact that these pages omit reference to individuals except where stylistically infeasible. Detailed description and citation will, of course, be later available with the publication of the whole study of the H-bomb decision.

Issues and Alternatives

The discovery that the Soviet Union had exploded an A-Bomb several years before it had been expected to do so suggested to many that one response should be to step up the pace of America's own nuclear weapons program. Since plans had just been completed to provide for a major expansion in the facilities for producing fissionable material and to undertake the development of fission weapons of much larger power and varied size than those heretofore fabricated, the focus of attention turned to the prospects for making a fusion weapon. The possibility of such a weapon had first received detailed study in 1942, and it had been a continuing concern of the atomic energy program ever since. It had proved, however, a recalcitrant technical problem and, both during the war and after, work on it had been given a much lower priority than work on the development and improvement of fission weapons.

The idea, in the fall of 1949, that a greater effort to make a fusion weapon was now in order received some stimulus from what were believed at the time to be some promising new technical approaches to the problem, but the major motive for reconsidering the state of the program was provided by the Russian explosion. Those who advocated a greater effort were moved by two considerations. One was the idea that if the United States could develop a bomb with thousands of times the energy release of the Hiroshima bomb, it would be able to maintain its qualitative lead over the Soviet program and thereby minimize the political and military disadvantages of the loss of its fission monopoly. Even more compelling, in the minds of most advocates, was the possibility that if the United States did not move more energetically to explore this possibility, the Soviet Union might be the first to achieve such a capability.

This reasoning seemed so persuasive to its advocates that many did not bother to think through in much detail, especially in September and October, exactly what advantages the United States could get from such a weapon that it could not secure through its superior stockpile of fission bombs or, for that matter, just what it was that the Russians might do if they secured an H-bomb first. It seemed sufficient and obvious that in the first instance American interests would be advanced, and that in the second they could only be hurt. Nor were the advocates of a greater effort very definite during September and October with regard to the rate and scale of the effort they had in mind. The analogy of the effort made during the war to develop the A-bomb came naturally to mind, and it was in these terms that the proposal was formally placed on the agenda of the Commission.

The issue of the rate and scale of the program could not be left in such ambiguous terms. The particular thermonuclear design which most of the participants had in mind, the so-called "Super," required as one of its major components a large amount of tritium. The most feasible method of making tritium was to bombard lithium with neutrons, and neutrons which were used to make tritium would not be available to make plutonium. Accordingly, the manufacture of tritium for the Super would mean foregoing the manufacture of fission bombs. Moreover, the scientific talent of the nation, as well as its supply of neutrons, was limited. Scientists put to work on the Super would be scientists not available to work on the new fission weapons. A more intensive effort to make an H-bomb would, in short, involve costs to the nation's A-bomb program.

The discussion that developed among the participants about the costs that an expanded H-bomb program would entail for the A-bomb program proved to be one of monumental confusion and misunderstanding. The least of the difficulties was that no one knew just how much tritium the Super would require. The major difficulty was that (a) the participants were reasoning from diverse premises about the kind of effort to be made and about the value of the weapons involved, and (b) the divergent character of these premises were by no means always made clear in the arguments that were then joined.

Thus, the development of any consensus with regard to the plutonium costs involved was handicapped by the fact that some participants were thinking in terms of making only enough tritium in the Hanford reactors to support a test program, others contemplated a larger diversion of those piles in order to have a stockpile of tritium immediately on hand with which to fabricate a number of usable weapons in case the Super proved feasible, and still others were thinking in terms of building a number of new reactors for the production of the tritium stockpile, and it was not always clear whether they expected those reactors to be in operation before or after a demonstration of feasibility. The discussion of the talent costs was similarly complex. Some scientists did not see how additional talent could be put to work profitably on the problem even if it was made available. In their view the Los Alamos Laboratory was already doing about all that could be done. Others were convinced that the problem had been starved for talent all along. The development of a consensus on this point was further complicated by the fact that some thought the additional talent could be secured by bringing in scientists not then working on fission weapons, and others believed that if more people were put to work on the Super they would have to come mainly from those already engaged in fission work.

Difficult as it was for the participants to reach any common conception of what kind of expanded H-bomb program they were talking about and what kind of cost it would bring to the A-bomb program, this was only half the problem in reaching a conclusion about the rate and scale of the effort to be made. A judgment about the desirability of foregoing any given number of plutonium bombs or incurring the delay or loss of any given number of improvements in the development of fission weapons would depend on the application of some criteria for comparing the relative military utility of A-bombs and H-bombs. One of the major reservations expressed by the scientists on the GAC about the idea of embarking on a large-scale H-bomb program was the result of the application of such criteria. They were by no means confident that the Super could be delivered by air, and they thought there would be few targets for which a bomb of such large yield would be suited. They concluded that the military purposes of the United States would be much better served by the A-bombs and A-bomb developments which would otherwise have to be foregone or postponed.

Illustrative of how different participants were talking about different things is the fact that the GAC judgment cannot be directly compared to that of the Joint Chiefs of Staff. At the time of the GAC report, the Chiefs were on record before the Joint Committee as desiring an accelerated effort to develop the Super, but they had not been specific about the rate and scale of the effort they had in mind and, hence, the A-costs they were willing to incur. When the Commissioners submitted their report, guidance on this point had yet to be produced by the military, and this was one of the questions to which they urged the President to secure an answer before making his decision.

The issue of the rate and scale of the effort to be made on the H-bomb thus turned, in part, on the issue of the relative military utility of H- and A-bombs. The discussion of this issue was conditioned, in turn, by the issue of what strategic doctrine should guide American military policy. It was here, at the level of general strategy, that some of the most significant differences existed among the participants. The three issues were so interrelated, however, that the participants were not always able to distinguish against what (and even for what) they were arguing.

The GAC report is a case in point. Many of its members were by no means persuaded that the doctrine of strategic bombing was a desirable military policy. Their views were not far removed from those of the Admiral (who was also a member of the Military Liaison Committee to the AEC) who had argued before the House Armed Services Committee in October, 1949, that strategic bombing was militarily unsound, morally wrong, and not suited for achieving the kind of political conditions the United States would want to obtain at the conclusion of a war. The GAC's recommendation against the development of the H-bomb was grounded, in part, on the belief that its only utility would be for the bombing of large cities and the objection to a military doctrine which would lead to the mass slaughter of Russian men, women, and children. The point was blurred, however, by their failure to carry through and make clear that they had equivalently strong objections to the use for this purpose of the products of the expanded fission program which they did support.

Another issue of doctrine interjected into the debate related to the conditions under which the United States would use nuclear weapons. It was argued by some that a decision with regard to the H-bomb program could not be rationally made until it was first decided for what purpose the United States was accumulating nuclear weapons: for the purpose of deterrence and retaliation only, or with the intent of so incorporating them into military plans and structure that the United States would initiate their use regardless of whether they had been employed by the enemy. The point to the argument was the idea that if weapons were being accumulated for the first purpose only, given the great value which the Russians attached to their industrial plant, a limited number of fission bombs would be sufficient to serve it.

The preference for a strategy based on last-resort use and for a clear-cut rejection of the principle of first use was strong among those who had major reservations about the desirability of strategic bombing and those who doubted the capacity of the American public to conduct itself rationally in a world in which conflict with the Soviet Union would continue to be deep and basic but in which a resort to violence would become increasingly suicidal. Among the participants in the Department of Defense, however, these arguments received a different reception. There was no great interest in adopting a strategy which seemed to bind the United States to fight only on terms of the enemy's choosing, and there was determined opposition to the idea that the need for an H-bomb program turned on the making of such a choice. It was the judgment of these and other participants that for an effective performance of the task of deterrence as well as that of fighting a victorious war the armed services would need the most powerful weapons they could secure.

The idea that an over-all review of national policy and a decision with regard to these strategic issues should precede the further development of the H-bomb was energetically pressed at the NSC level by the Chairman of the AEC, David Lilienthal. One reason why he did so relates to still another issue: that of the relative utility of conventional as compared to nuclear weapons. During the NSC discussions, Lilienthal was shocked to learn just how dependent the military were on nuclear weapons, and he became convinced that what the United States needed far more than the H-bomb was a large-scale increase in conventional armaments. This conclusion was influenced in part by the prevailing military judgment that nuclear weapons alone could not win World War III, but it also reflected Lilienthal's own conviction that the foreign policy purposes of the nation would be better served by a military posture that was not so dependent on the use of large bombs against urban targets.

It was Lilienthal's contention that the decision on the Super should be delayed until an effort had first been made to review the nation's strategic doctrine and to consider the desirability of reducing the nation's dependence on large-yield nuclear weapons by increasing the size of its conventional forces. He believed that if the decision to press for the Super was made first it would prejudice the chances for a later review of that choice and greatly lessen the opportunity to secure conventional rearmament. There would be little prospect of persuading Congress and the public to support an expensive conventional rearmament program, he argued, once the Super program was announced, for most would conclude from the announcement that the security of the United States was in good shape and that the answer to the Russian A-bomb had been found.

One other major issue was raised in connection with the H-bomb debate and that was the question of its relationship to the effort to secure international control of atomic energy. The feeling was strong among many, especially the GAC and members of the Commission, that with the development of the Russian A-bomb the world had reached a crossroads in history. From this point it stood fair to continue into the mounting tensions of a nuclear arms race and perhaps, in time, into the horrors of nuclear war. The most appropriate thing to do at this time, so it seemed, was not to rush to try to make even bigger bombs but rather to make a last determined effort to reverse the direction that international politics had been taking since 1945. To those who thought in these terms the urgency of those who advocated a more intensive H-bomb program seemed both intemperate and short-sighted. To those who thought negotiation with the Russians fruitless, the insistence on delay seemed quixotic and dangerous.

The specific ideas advanced by the GAC and some of the Commissioners as to what might be done to reopen the international control negotiations or to otherwise try to move the world away from a nuclear arms race were, however, most indefinite and not very clearly stated. Some suggested that the United States increase the scale of its research on the H-bomb but not go all-out on the H-program without first reopening the international control negotiations with the Russians. Others recommended not pushing ahead at all on the H-bomb until it and the control of nuclear weapons in general had been first discussed with the Russians. (The minority annex of the GAC report suggested, in this connection, that the two Powers might agree not to make the H-bomb. Since its successful development was believed to require a test, violation of the agreement could be easily detected.) The most extreme position was that taken by the majority of the GAC, which recommended that the United States unilaterally announce that it was not going to make the weapon.

The last recommendation illustrates the interconnection among all the issues involved in the discussion. The judgment of those who made it was that the United States would not be losing much: a weapon that looked as if it would be very hard to make; one which would cost more in A-bombs than its military utility was worth; and one which if used would be employed in a manner highly repugnant to the values for which American culture was supposed to stand. It was believed that the Russians would not try very hard to make it themselves, given the cost of the weapon, the uncertainty that it could even be made, and the American example. Renunciation, so it was thought, was an opportunity for America to gain considerable moral prestige at very little cost and to make some contribution to the possible limitation of warfare in the future.

The Decision Examined and Explained

It is appropriate at this point to recall the content of the President's decision on January 31st: that an effort be made to determine the technical feasibility of a thermonuclear weapon; that the rate and scale of the effort be fixed jointly by the AEC and the Department of Defense; and that the State and Defense Departments undertake concurrently to review the nation's foreign and military policies in light of the prospective nuclear capabilities of the Soviet Union.

This decision stands in some contrast to the issues and alternatives just described. Had the President decided the issue of the rate and scale of the H-bomb program? Had he decided that the military utility of the Super would be worth the A-costs involved? Had he made a decision about the military and political desirability of strategic bombing? Had he decided whether military doctrine with regard to nuclear weapons was to be governed by the principle of first use or that of last resort? Had he decided that the nation needed bigger nuclear weapons more than it needed large-scale conventional rearmament? Had he decided not to renew negotiations with the Soviet Union on the subject of international control?

The President had decided none of these things. This is not, of course, to say that he had decided nothing at all. He had quite definitely decided that the United States would not unilaterally renounce the effort to make an H-bomb. Although a literal reading of his directive with regard to the determination of feasibility would indicate that he had ordered the AEC and Defense only to continue what they had already been doing, there was certainly an implication that they should approach the task with a greater sense of urgency than had heretofore been the case. The directive also made it evident that the President had not endorsed an intensive H-bomb program. The directive said nothing about production facilities for the Super, nor did it even specify that the determination of feasibility was to include a test program.

The President had also decided to order the re-examination of the nation's strategic plans that so many had urged. He further decided not to wait until the completion of that review before making his H-bomb choice. He had similarly decided against two other alternatives which involved a delay in his making that choice: the alternative of first exploring the possibility of international control, and the alternative of first endeavoring to secure a large increase in conventional arms.

The President did make choices, but a comparison of the choices that he made with those that he did not make reveals clearly the minimal character of his decision. It bears all the aspects of a conscious search for that course of action which would close off the least number of future alternatives, one which would avoid the most choice. Thus the President had affirmed his interest in exploring the feasibility of an H-bomb, but he had said nothing about testing a device if one were fabricated, nothing about producing a weapon if the device were ever tested, nothing about how many weapons would be produced if any were made, nothing about whether such weapons would ever be used if produced, and nothing about the purposes for which such weapons would be employed if ever used.

An explanation for the minimal character of this decision is to be found partly in the views and power of those who shaped the recommendations of the special committee of the NSC, partly in the character of the American governmental process, and partly in the perspectives with which the participants approached the problem of choice. With regard to the first factor, the decisive influence on the outcome of the H-bomb discussion proved to be that of the State Department. It was the Secretary of State who spoke with authority, so far as the President was concerned, with regard to the various foreign policy hopes and fears that had conditioned the views of many of the other participants. It was also the Secretary of State who held the balance of persuasion, so far as the President was concerned, on those issues on which the representatives of the Department of Defense and the Atomic Energy Commission were divided.

The State Department was responsible for rejecting the various alternatives which involved some approach to the Russians with regard to international control before undertaking to accelerate the American H-bomb program. It was, in the opinion of Secretary of State Dean Acheson and those who assisted him on the NSC committee, simply not a time period in which the Russians were interested in serious negotiations. All that could be expected from approaching them would be stalling tactics which might embarrass or perhaps even completely inhibit the American program while leaving the Russians free to push ahead on their own.

The State Department sided with the Secretary of Defense, Louis Johnson, in stressing the importance of not delaying in the effort to discover whether the Super could be made, although the reasoning in the two Departments was somewhat different. A number of planning groups within the Department of Defense had given careful study to the military utility of the Super, and the suggestions that it was in all probability not worth making struck them all as unsound, to say the least. (One member of the GAC was later to observe that the GAC report had the unprecedented effect of unifying the services.) If the judgments of some of the scientists were grounded on a concern for what the world would look like after an H-bomb war, and those of the military on a concern for what it would be like to have to fight an enemy who had a monopoly on such a powerful weapon, those of the State Department representatives reflected a concern for the diplomatic opportunities the Russians would gain from such a monopoly for political blackmail around the Soviet periphery. Most of Acheson's advisers took this possibility very seriously, as did the Secretary himself.

The State Department's strong interest in avoiding the possible consequences of the Russians getting the H-bomb first also led Acheson to side with Defense with regard to the alternatives of reviewing the nation's strategic plans and of securing an increase in conventional weapons before making a choice about the H-bomb program. Acheson was quite willing to undertake such a review concurrently (as was Defense), and, as the Department's work on this review in the spring of 1950 was to show, he was prepared to push hard for an increase in conventional weapons. But he wanted no delay on the H-bomb research.

Lilienthal's arguments for the priority of a conventional weapons program might plausibly have been expected to win him some allies in the Pentagon, especially in the Army. They did not, largely because they were suspect. The fact that they associated Lilienthal with many of the GAC views led most of the military representatives to discount his arguments as a device to delay the H-bomb for what were, really, other reasons. There was, moreover, a history of AEC-Defense disputes over the rôle of the AEC in determination of military requirements that made the defense representatives especially unresponsive to what was considered AEC meddling. President Truman, who had the greatest stake in not dissipating the persuasive lever that the Russian A-bomb gave him if he was later to press for a large-scale rearmament program, was not in the habit of examining the decision immediately before him for its implications for his future choices, and he, too, proved unresponsive to the argument.[5]

The character of the President's decision owes much to the coincidence of State and Defense views. It must also be attributed, however, to one of the major necessities of the American political process: the need to avert conflict by avoiding choice. The distribution of power and responsibility among government élites is normally so dispersed that a rather widespread agreement among them is necessary if any given policy is to be adopted and later implemented. Among the quasi-sovereign bodies that make up

---

[5] For Truman's decision-making style in this respect, see Richard E. Neustadt, *Presidential Power* (New York, 1960), pp. 172–173.

the Executive the opportunities to compel this agreement are limited. Agreement must be given, and it will not long be given for nothing. This condition of mutual dependence, the need, as it were, to "build a consensus" that includes one's enemies as well as one's friends, produces a strain toward agreement in the political process that is as fully characteristic of that process as the conflicts in which the participants are continually engaged.

There are many occasions when the necessary amount of coöperation can be achieved only by the device of avoiding disagreement, that is, by postponing the consideration of issues over which long and determined conflicts are certain to be waged. The H-bomb decision is a case in point. The issues which the President did *not* decide were all matters which, if he had endeavored to resolve them, would have pushed one group or another of his subordinates into passionate opposition. The President's position in the political process, however unique, is one which finds him, too, dependent upon the coöperation of others for the success of his policies, and Truman, in this instance, saw no reason to go out of his way to stir up a momentous struggle within his administration. Although he carefully read all the documents involved, from the GAC report through the NSC studies, Truman's own position on the H-bomb issue was the same in January as it had been in October when he first had heard of it. If the bomb could be made, he did not see how the nation could afford to let the Russians get it first, and he was therefore prepared to back whatever program made sense to the Departments concerned.[6]

If the President had no interest in maximizing conflict, neither had the members of the special committee. Acheson was quite aware of the gulf between Lilienthal's views and those of Johnson. Indeed, he was obliged to meet each separately, since Lilienthal's and Johnson's personal relationship had deteriorated to the point where they could not profitably meet together. He was therefore consciously searching for the common ground between them. The military representatives on the NSC working group, for their part, proved not only willing but eager to follow the lead of the State Department and back a recommendation that called for only a determination of the feasibility of the Super. The responsible officials in the Department of Defense had never been among those demanding an H-bomb program on the scale of the Manhattan District. They were determined primarily in their opposition to the views and recommendations that had been advanced by the GAC and some of the Commissioners.

[6] The analysis in these two paragraphs owes much to the stimulation of Gabriel Almond, *The American People and Foreign Policy* (New York, 1950), pp. 143–145; Neustadt, *op. cit.*, esp. ch. 3; Roger Hilsman, "The Foreign-Policy Consensus: An Interim Report," *Conflict Resolution*, December 1959; and Samuel P. Huntington, "Strategic Planning and the Political Process," *Foreign Affairs*, January 1960.

The final factor conditioning the character of the decision was the nature of the perspectives with which the participants approached the problem of choice. The influence of Truman's "one decision at a time" approach has already been noted. The perspective that the military members of the NSC working group brought to the decision was: "what needs to be decided *now?*" What needed to be decided now, in their view, was whether the government would make an urgent effort to determine the feasibility of the weapon. This would settle the immediate problem of defeating those who argued for delaying the program, for one reason or another, and those who argued that the weapon was of insufficient value to justify diverting any more neutrons and talent to pursue it. What need at this point, they reasoned, to stir up discussion regarding the production or use of the weapon. By avoiding these issues, Defense would avoid certain conflict with the AEC and possible conflict with State. Avoiding these issues would also permit the Department to present a unified front to its enemies. The Army and Navy were as persuaded as the Air Force that the nation had to have this weapon, if it was to be had, and that it should be secured before the Russians got it. But there was real potential for disagreement among the services once the issues of production and use became operational. If very large amounts of tritium were to be manufactured, the plutonium foregone might well cut into that which the Army and Navy hoped would soon be available for their use, and at this point the doctrinal issues that divided the services with regard to the relative importance of strategic bombing as compared to other approaches to victory would be certain to arise.

The perspective with which the State Department representatives approached the decision was one that worked, in this instance, to the same end as that of the military but was significantly different in its rationale. Instead of asking "what has to be decided *now,*" they asked: "what is the *least* possible that can be decided." The purpose was not so much to avoid conflict as it was to keep as many alternatives open for the future as possible, in order to be in a position to take maximum advantage of new information or changed conditions. It was with this perspective in mind that State drafted the recommendations that the special NSC committee later submitted to the President.

Of the three agencies, the perspective of the Commission representatives came closest to that of "what is the *most* that has to be decided." In fact, both State and Defense representatives had the feeling that the Commission was deliberately holding up the H-bomb program as a means of trying to force them to confront some of the major choices involved. The end result of the tactics of State and Defense, however, was to leave Lilienthal with very little to argue against or to argue for. Rate and scale? No one was urging an all-out program that would entail extremely large fission costs. Military utility? All that was being advocated was an effort to determine whether and at what expense the Super could be made; what better way to treat the question of its military value. Issues of strategic doctrine? State and Defense were to start immediately to review them, and an H-program so modest as not even to specify the conducting of a test could hardly be said to prejudice the results of such a review in advance. International control and the need for conventional weapons? Both of these matters would be given intensive study by the State-Defense review. Lilienthal could not shake the feeling that even in its minimal form the decision would prejudice the opportunity to depart from a big bomb strategy and he so argued to the end, but he had by now the feeling that there was no one at the NSC level with whom to argue.

Consequences of the Decision

One consequence of the minimal character of the President's decision was that all the issues on which he had avoided making any choice came back at him again. Thus, by the winter of 1951–1952 the disputes and dissatisfaction regarding the rate and scale of the program had reached such proportions that Air Force officials were considering setting up a weapons laboratory of their own. Similarly, in 1950 new investigations indicated that the tritium required for the Super would be much greater than that estimated at the time of the President's decision. This information, together with the concern that the Korean War might soon develop into all-out war with Russia, served in December, 1950, to reopen the discussion of the military utility of H- as compared to A-bombs and the desirability of incurring significant costs to the fission program in the effort to make it.

The State-Defense review, which became NSC-68, addressed itself boldly to the need to increase America's conventional weapon strength, but it did not really come to grips with the issues in nuclear strategy that had been raised during the H-bomb debate. Thus in December, 1951, when a group of scientists were active in urging the development and production of a large number of A-bombs for tactical use in the ground defense of Western Europe, the rationale for the proposal was in part the search for a strategy that would serve American security without requiring the bombing of cities. Their hope was that if the Red Army could be defeated through the battlefield use of A-bombs, the Strategic Air Command would be relieved of the burden of deterring a Soviet ground attack and free to exercise an option as to whether it struck the Soviet cities and initiated, thereby, an exchange that would bring bombs down on European and American cities as well. The issue of strategic bombing remains partly unsettled even today, as does the issue of last-resort use versus the principle of first use, although the terms are now "city-busting" versus "counterforce" and "second-strike" versus "first-strike" strategies. Similarly, the issue of conventional weapons versus nuclear weapons constituted a major source of debate during the whole of the Eisenhower administration.

The H-bomb decision is hardly the only occasion on which the policy process has produced a minimal decision. The continuous winnowing and worrying of the same old issues is an inevitable consequence of a political process that depends on the voluntary coöperation of independent and competing élites for the formulation and conduct of policy. Major policy changes can, for the most part, be effected only through slow and incremental change. However, as the same issues come around for the second, third, and nth time, they do so in a context slightly altered by the previous minimal choices to which they have been subjected.

The unilateral renunciation idea, for example, could hardly be advanced, after the Preident's decision, in the same form that the GAC had recommended it in October, 1949. It had to reappear in the form advanced by some other scientists in February, 1950: that the United States pledge itself not to be the first to initiate the use of H-bombs. Similarly, when the international control issue reappeared in November, 1952, with the proposal that the United States not set off its hydrogen device until it had first tried to negotiate an agreement with Russia not to test H-bombs, the conditions of the problem were not quite those that had prevailed when the same proposal was made in the minority annex of the GAC report. In place of an agreement on a device which no one even knew how to make, agreement would now have to be made with regard to a device which one side knew how to make and the other, presumably, did not.

The question might well be asked if there is not a possibility that through a sequence of minor "tactical" or minimal decisions the Government might some day find itself occupying a new "strategic" position without ever having made the major choice to get there. The answer, in a word, is yes, and again the H-bomb decision provides an illustration. On February 24, 1950, scarcely three weeks after the President's decision, the Joint Chiefs of Staff submitted a memorandum to the President requesting "an all-out devolopment of hydrogen bombs and means for their production and delivery." The Chiefs, Johnson reported, wanted to undertake quantity production of the H-bomb as soon as possible.

Once again, Truman summoned the special committee of the NSC with Sumner Pike now serving in place of Lilienthal, who had submitted his resignation in November, 1949, but had stayed on to see the H-bomb decision through. On March 1st, this committee recommended that, without prejudice to the State-Defense review which was still under way, the research program should proceed to a test stage as soon as possible and that preparations be made for the quantity production of the H-bomb without waiting for the results of the test. The President so ordered on March 10th, and construction began shortly thereafter on the Savannah River reactors.

So far as those who in the fall of 1949 had advocated an intensive

H-bomb effort were concerned, the program instituted in the spring of 1950 represented all that they had ever had in mind. The AEC and the Department of Defense had no basic policy disagreements in the design of this program. Although initially skeptical of the military need for an all-out H-bomb program, Pike believed that if a determined effort was going to be made to make an H-bomb a parallel production program should accompany it. Having alerted the Russians to the fact that the United States was urgently trying to make the bomb, it was to be expected that the Russians would move fast themselves and the United States had therefore better do the same.

So far as the Department of Defense was concerned, the memorandum of February 24th was designed to "button down" the decision of January 31st. What had to be decided *now* was the issue of production. Defense had no more interest than Pike in ending up in 1951 or 1952 with a handful of successful test devices and no plant with which to make the weapon. Neither did it want weapons without carriers, although in this respect the February memorandum was somewhat redundant since the January decision had also authorized the Air Force to undertake a carrier program. Unlike the Department of State, Defense had no interest in keeping the issues of production and use open. The orderly development of military plans and programs required a clear and early decision, not the flexibility and freedom sought by State. The February memorandum was, then, an invitation to State and the AEC to dispute now, if they wished, the decision to produce the H-bomb in quantity and to develop a capability to use it.

For the reasons noted, there was no dispute from the AEC. What of the Department of State and the idea that the decision to determine feasibility left open the decisions to test, to produce, and to use? There was no dispute from the Department of State either, despite the fact that the State-Defense review of strategic plans was not completed. Some of the State Department representatives have advanced the argument that a decision to produce the means for production was not yet a decision to produce the weapon, but this is to stretch words further than reality. A more accurate reading of the reasoning in the State Department would be that, while their responsibilities did not dispose them to push for quantity production, they saw no good reason for opposing it. In retrospect, it would seem that Lilienthal's sense of what was afoot on the 31st of January was not mistaken. The minimal decision permitted the Department of Defense to achieve its objectives in two bites and to take its possible opponents one at a time, and while the January decision might not have prejudiced the chances for an unfettered look at the H-bomb program, the March decision certainly did.

One cannot draw a straight line from January–March, 1950, to the present. The decisions here discussed are but two of the points from which one would have to plot the course of American policy from then to now. Whether the subsequent choices with regard to nuclear weapons policy were of the same order as those just described is, so far as the present writer is concerned, an unknown matter. Given, however, the propensity of the political process for minimal decisions, it would be plausible to expect that they were.

The H-bomb decision is essentially a tragic story. The GAC was "right" in sensing that the development of the H-bomb would drive twentieth-century man deeper into the box that he has been building for himself with his military technology, doctrine, foreign policy, and cultural ethos. The GAC was also "right" in asserting that it was a time to stop, look, and think. But the GAC was not alone in seeing the dimensions of the box. It was every bit as apparent to most of the advocates of the Super program. The trouble was that no one had any good ideas of how to get out of the box. Nor are they apparent today.

Basically, the H-bomb decision is a story of international rather than domestic politics. It affords a classic example of the traditional security dilemma. Both the Soviet Union and the United States would no doubt have preferred a world in which neither had the H-bomb. Each, however, wished to avoid a world in which the other had the H-bomb and it did not. Both rushed to make it, and they ended in a worse position than that in which they had begun.

Pax Americana

RONALD STEEL

An intensive reexamination of the origins of the Cold War and the international posture of the United States has gathered momentum in recent years. American motives, as well as policies, have been questioned and attacked. Some of the writing has merely resulted in a Manichaean reversal of concepts whereby the burden of dark, conspiratorial designs is thrust exclusively on American policy-makers. In the selection below, however, Ronald Steel explores the Cold War from the perspective of its consequences for the United States. Indeed, Steel concedes a good deal of idealistic motivation in American policy, albeit an idealism usually divorced from political reality. But whatever the origins and motivations for the acquisition of an American empire, its existence has had profound consequences that have dangerously imperiled America's position as a world power. Furthermore, Steel finds that contemporary American foreign policy is predicated on assumptions that no longer correspond to realities. His main thrust is to describe the limitations of American power, something which official and public opinion find difficult to comprehend and will not readily concede. Yet the agony of current American interventionist policies, such as those in Southeast Asia, make it abundantly clear, according to Steel, that "the alignment of national goals with national interest — of our desires with our needs — is the most pressing task facing American diplomacy." The world has changed, yet American diplomacy has remained frozen in a mold cast over two decades ago. To what extent, and in what ways, has ideology dominated vital interest as the motivating force in American foreign policy?

We in this country, in this generation are — by destiny rather than choice — the watchmen on the walls of world freedom.
— JOHN F. KENNEDY *
The United States, delighting in her resources, feeling that she no longer had within herself sufficient scope for her energies, wishing to help those who were in misery or bondage the world over, yielded in her turn to that taste for intervention in which the instinct for domination cloaked itself. — CHARLES DE GAULLE *

1. A Taste for Intervention

Sometimes people call me an idealist," Woodrow Wilson once said as he stumped the country trying to drum up support for the League of Nations. "Well, that's the way I know I am an American. America, my fellow citizens, . . . is the only idealistic nation in the world." Wilson, whose career is a tragic example of what happens when idealism is divorced from political realism, never spoke a truer word. America is an idealistic nation, a nation based upon the belief that the "self-evident

Reprinted by permission of The Viking Press, Inc., from Ronald Steel, *Pax Americana*, Chapters 1 and 2. Copyright © 1967 by The Viking Press, Inc.

* The quotation at the head of the chapter by John F. Kennedy is from an address prepared for delivery at Dallas, November 22, 1963; that by General de Gaulle is from his *Mémoires de Guerre*, vol. 2, *L'Unité* (Paris: Librairie Plon), pp. 97–98. (Translated in 3 volumes as *War Memoirs of Charles de Gaulle* [New York: Simon and Schuster, 1958–1960].)

truths" of the Declaration of Independence should be extended to unfortunate peoples wherever they may be.

For the first 170 years of our national existence, however, we were content to make this a principle rather than a program of action. America was, in John Quincy Adams's phrase, "the well-wisher to the freedom and independence of all," but "the champion and vindicator only of her own." With the exception of Mexico, the Philippines and a few brief adventures in the Caribbean, our national idealism did not go abroad in search of new fields to conquer. The great European war of 1914–1918 entangled us more against our will than by design. We entered it under the banner of idealism when neutrality became difficult, and we left Europe in disillusionment when power politics reared its ugly head at Versailles. Never again, we said. And never again we did, until the Japanese dragged us into a global war by the attack on Pearl Harbor.

From that time on, American idealism was transformed into a plan. The Word was given Flesh by the mating of American military power to a native idealism. For the first time in its history the nation had the ability to seek its idealistic goals by active intervention rather than merely by pious proclamation. The result was twin crusades, one in Europe, one in Asia: one to restore freedom to the West, one to bring it to the East. But the passing of one tyranny in Europe saw the rise of another; the defeat of Japan gave way to the resurgence of China. The triumph of the Second World War marked not the end of our labors, but only the beginning. It transformed a philosophical commitment to the principles of freedom and democracy into a political commitment to bring them about. American idealism was the foundation; American power was the instrument to achieve the ideals. From 1945 on, we were no longer simply the "well-wisher" to the world; we were its "champion and vindicator" as well. The moral purity of American isolationism gave way to the moral self-justification of American interventionism.

The change from the old isolationism to the new interventionism flowed almost inevitably from the Second World War. The unavoidable war against fascism revealed the bankruptcy of isolationism and destroyed the illusion that America could barricade herself from the immoralities of a corrupt world. It also provided the means for the dramatic growth of American military power which made the new policy of global interventionism possible. As a result of her participation in the war, America became not only a great world power but *the* world power. Her fleets roamed all the seas, her military bases extended around the earth's periphery, her soldiers stood guard from Berlin to Okinawa, and her alliances spanned the earth.

The Second World War threw the United States into the world arena, and the fear of communism prevented her from retreating. The old isolationism was buried and discredited. The crusade that was the war against fascism gave way to the new crusade that was the cold war against communism. Roused to a new sense of mission by the threat of Soviet communism, eager to bring her cherished values to the masses of mankind, a bit infatuated with the enormous power she possessed through the unleashing of the atom, America quickly accepted — and even came to cherish — her new sense of involvement in the fate of the world. The world of the early postwar era may not have been the One World of Wendell Willkie's dream, but America felt a unique sense of responsibility about its welfare.

A reaction to the old isolationism, the new globalism forced Americans to realize that they could no longer escape involvement in an imperfect world. But because the cold war, like the Second World War, was conceived as a moral crusade, it inflated an involvement that was essentially pragmatic into a moral mission. Since we were accustomed to victory in battle and were stronger than any nation had ever been in history, we believed that the world's problems could be resolved if only we willed hard enough and applied enough power. Convinced of the righteousness of our cause, we became intoxicated with our newly discovered responsibilities and saw them as a mandate to bring about the better world we so ardently desired. American military power, consecrated by the victory of the Second World War and reconfirmed by the development of the atomic bomb, joined forces with the power of American idealism to inaugurate a policy of global interventionism.

This policy of interventionism is not only military, although we have intervened massively throughout the world with our military power. Our intervention has also been economic and political. We have funneled nearly $120 billion of American money into foreign aid since the Second World War — to bring about changes in other countries that would reflect our ideals or advance our interests. We have intervened in the politics of other nations as well, trying to push some into new alignments, trying to remake the social structures of others, and helping to overthrow the governments of not a few. America, whether most of us realize it or not, has become the interventionist power par excellence. Whether we consider this to be commendable or deplorable, it is certainly undeniable.

For the past quarter-century the United States has — at a great financial, human, and even emotional cost — been pursuing a foreign policy designed to promulgate American values. This ambition inspired the policy of "cointainment" that followed the Second World War, and provided the rationale for a series of military involvements. Seeking universal peace and condemning war as a means for settling political grievances, America has, nonetheless, been an active belligerent in two major land wars since 1950 and the sponsor of a series of military interventions — a record unmatched by any other power. America did not enter these wars from a sense of adventure, or a quest for territorial gain, or an effort to retain distant colonies, but rather from a desire to contain communism and protect the values and boundaries of the "free world." "What America has done, and what America is doing now around the world," President Johnson declared at Catholic University a few months after he ordered the bombing of North Vietnam, "draws from deep and flowing springs of moral duty, and let none underestimate the depth of flow of those wellsprings of American purpose."

Who, indeed, would underestimate them? But to estimate them highly is not necessarily to understand them, or to find them always wise. The moral inspiration of America's involvement in foreign wars is undeniable. But it has also posed a terrible dilemma for American diplomacy, one which is rarely acknowledged openly and is often not even clearly recognized. It is the dilemma of how American ideals can be reconciled with American military actions — and, perhaps even more grave, of how American values can be made relevant to a world that seems not to want or even respect them. However deep the wellsprings of moral duty to which President Johnson refers, the means chosen to transfer these values to a recalcitrant and often unadmiring world has troubled many thoughtful Americans. The President and his advisers speak in the most noble rhetoric of the need to defend freedom wherever it may be threatened and of the indivisibility of our responsibility to protect other nations from external (and even internal) aggression. Yet the pursuit of this aspiration has frequently led others to believe that our motives may be self-justifying and tinged with hypocrisy.

The United States has become an interventionist power, indeed the world's major interventionist power, without most Americans quite realizing how it happened or its full implications. Intervention has been the dominant motif of American postwar foreign policy, but the purpose, and even the methods, of this intervention have been concealed in a miasma of rhetoric and confusion. In the belief that we were containing or repelling communism, we have involved ourselves in situations that have been morally compromising, militarily frustrating, and politically indecisive.

The commitment to intervention as a guiding principle has made it exceedingly difficult to distinguish between necessary and spurious motives for intervention — to determine which actions have a direct relation to the nation's security, and which merely represent wish-fulfillment on an international scale. In this respect it reflects a traditional weakness in American policy — a penchant for grandiose principles at the expense of a cool assessment of national interests, which has led the nation into painful involvements as a result of bold gestures carelessly made. The warning of John Quincy Adams has lately been forgotten in the intoxication of heady moral obligations, obligations which no one asked us to assume, and whose purpose we do not often understand. This is not the fault of the public but of its leaders, who are often tempted to use slogans to justify their actions, and then become prisoners of them. "American statesmen," as the historian Dexter Perkins has written,

> have believed that the best way to rally American opinion behind their purposes is to assert a moral principle. In doing so, they have often gone far beyond the boundaries of expediency. And perhaps it is fair to say that in underemphasizing security, they have helped to form a national habit which unduly subordinates the necessities of national defense to the assertion of lofty moral principles.[1]

The rhetoric of our cold-war diplomacy rests upon the indivisibility of freedom, the belief in self-determination, the necessity for collective security, and the sanctity of peaceful reform as opposed to violent change. These are not bad ambitions, but nowhere does this noble rhetoric seem to be in touch with the crass reality of the world as it is. Freedom, we have learned, is not only divisible between nations but subject to a hundred different interpretations. One man's freedom, all too often, is another man's exploitation. Self-determination can be a formula for political instability, and one which it may not always be in our interests to further. Collective security, as applied to our postwar military pacts, has never been much more than a polite word for a unilateral guarantee by the United States to protect her clients. Even this is now being shattered by the breakup of the cold-war alliances. The commitment to peaceful social change by constitutional processes has now collided with the reality of revolution and disorder throughout much of the world.

With every expansion of our commitments, there has been a corresponding expansion of our official rhetoric. Statesmen, unable to adjust our limited means to our unlimited ends, have committed us to goals beyond the capacity of the nation to carry out. They have done this not because they are knaves intent on foreign adventurism, but because they have been carried away by the force of their own rhetoric. Infused by the belief that nothing is unattainable so long as the cause is just, and fortified by reliance on America's awesome military power, they frequently confuse the desirable with the attainable. In doing so, they commit the nation to ends that cannot be achieved, and thereby breed a national frustration that nags at the roots of American democracy. "To some extent," in the words of a Senate committee dealing with problems of national security, "every postwar administration has indulged our national taste for the grand and even the grandiose." Because the source of this comment is not one which is normally unreceptive to the application of American military power, its conclusions deserve quotation at greater length:

> The idea of manifest destiny still survives. Officials make sweeping declarations of our world mission, and often verbally commit the

[1] Dexter Perkins, *The United States and Latin America* (Baton Rouge: Louisiana State University Press, 1961), p. 19.

Nation to policies and programs far beyond our capabilities. In this way expectations may be created at home and abroad that are certain to be disappointed and that may result in a squandering of our power and influence on marginal undertakings. We may also find ourselves entangled in projects that are incompatible with the real needs of other peoples, or are, in some cases, actually repugnant to them. To some extent every postwar administration has indulged our national taste for the grand and even the grandiose.

Our ability to think up desirable goals is almost limitless; our capabilities are limited. We still have much to learn about the need to balance what we would like to do with what we can do — and to establish intelligent priorities.

The "can do" philosophy accords with American folklore, but even the United States cannot do everything. In policymaking, also, the assumption tends to be made that "we can find a way." We can do a lot, but our power is limited and the first claimant on it is the American people. Accordingly, it must be rationed in accordance with a responsible ordering of national interests.[2]

The alignment of national goals with national interests — of our desires with our needs — is the most pressing task facing American diplomacy. It is a task that has become increasingly urgent with each expansion of our commitments. These commitments are to be found in a tangle of regional alliances, military pacts, verbal agreements, and even unilateral decisions. They can all, to one degree or another, be traced back to the Truman Doctrine of March 1947, when the United States made the ambiguous offer to defend threatened nations from aggression, whether direct or indirect. This led, through the back door of the European Recovery Program, to NATO, under which the United States is pledged to the defense of most of Europe and even parts of the Near East — from Spitzbergen to the Berlin Wall and beyond to the Asian borders of Turkey. From there the commitments become more vague, the situations more ambiguous, the countries themselves less crucial to American security.

From the seeds of the Truman Doctrine and the precedent of NATO came the Middle East Resolution, under which Congress gave President Eisenhower permission to protect the Arabs against communism; the CENTO and SEATO treaties that John Foster Dulles constructed to fill in the alliance gap from Iran to the Philippines; the ANZUS treaty with Australia and New Zealand; special defense arrangements with Japan and Korea; an unwritten obligation to protect India; the pledge for the defense of the entire western hemisphere under the Rio Pact; various peacekeeping functions under the United Nations; and, most recently, the Tonkin Gulf Resolution, a blank check given by Congress, allowing Presi-

[2] *Memorandum of the Subcommittee on National Security and International Operations of the Committee on Government Operations,* U.S. Senate, 89th Congress, 1st session, 1965, pp. 2–3.

dent Johnson to intervene as he sees fit in Southeast Asia. Early in 1968 the United States had 700,000 soldiers stationed in 30 countries, was a member of 4 regional defense alliances and an active participant in a fifth, had mutual defense treaties with 42 nations, was a member of 53 international organizations, and was furnishing military or economic aid to nearly 100 nations across the face of the globe. Put all this together and it leaves us, in James Reston's words, with "commitments the like of which no sovereign nation ever took on in the history of the world.

These entanglements happened more by accident than by design. The United States became involved in the defense of Western Europe because the defeat of Nazi Germany brought Stalin's armies into Central Europe. In Asia the disintegration of the Japanese Empire brought Russia into Manchuria and the United States into Japan, Okinawa, South Korea, and Taiwan. Later we advanced into Indochina when the French, despite our financial and military support, were unable to retain their Asian territories. We had no intention of virtually annexing Okinawa, of occupying South Korea, of preventing the return of Taiwan to China, of fighting in Indochina, or of remaining in Western Europe. If someone had said in 1947 that twenty years later there would be 225,000 American soldiers in Germany, 50,000 in Korea, and a half million Americans fighting in Vietnam, he would have been considered mad. Yet so accustomed are we to our global commitments that we take this remarkable situation for granted.

Although the postwar vacuums are receding — with the resurgence of China, the recovery of Japan, and the revival of Europe — our commitment remains unchanged. We are still playing the same role of guardian that we played twenty years ago, when America and Russia were the only important powers in the world. Our diplomacy has not kept pace with the changes in the world power structure, and we are engaged far beyond our ability to control events. The result has been a dangerous gap in our foreign policy between our involvements and our means — between what we would like to accomplish and what we can reasonably hope to accomplish.

In a way it could be said that our foreign policy has been a victim of its own success. In the decision to rebuild and defend Western Europe, the United States acted with wisdom, humanity, and an enlightened conception of her own interests. The military alliance with Western Europe worked successfully because there was a clear community of interests between America and her allies. When we built our bases in Europe and sent our own soldiers to man the front lines, it was in the knowledge that we agreed with our allies on the dangers they faced and on the means by which they should be met. We came not as an army of occupation or as foreign mercenaries, but as friends joined in a common cause. We turned our back on the isolationism of the 1930s, put the American frontier right up to the Brandenburg Gate in Berlin, pledged our atomic weapons to the defense of our allies, added our own soldiers as guarantors of this pledge, and accepted the risk of nuclear devastation. We took this terrible risk because we had to: because neither strategically nor culturally could we accept the loss of Western Europe to our adversaries. The goal we sought in Western Europe in the early postwar period had three qualities essential for military intervention: it was vital to our interests, it was within our means to achieve, and it had the support of those we were trying to protect.

The difficulty, however, arose when the principles underlying NATO and the Marshall Plan were applied indiscriminately throughout the world — when it was assumed that the success of the Atlantic alliance could be duplicated in countries which shared neither our traditions, nor our interests, nor even our assessment of the dangers facing them. Too often American diplomacy has been engaged in the effort to create miniature NATOs and Marshall Plans with countries that have only recently shaken off the yoke of Western rule, that are at a greatly inferior stage of economic and political development, that are as suspicious of us as they are of our adversaries, that are endemically poor and unstable, and that usually greet us as unwanted manipulators rather than as welcome friends.

If our policies were judged by a cold calculation of national interest, a good many of them might have been scrapped long ago. If the struggle with Russia were merely over geographical spheres of influence, if the cold war were nothing more than old-fashioned power politics on a global scale, our commitments could have been cut and our involvements drastically limited. But the cold war has not been simply a struggle of giants for supremacy; it has also been an ideological contest for the allegiance of mankind. Or so it has seemed to its leading participants. It is because we feel ourselves embroiled in a much greater struggle that we are involved in the sustenance and security of some hundred countries, that we have replaced the old isolationism with a sweeping policy of interventionism and are today fighting yet another land war in Asia.

We are there because we feel ourselves to be pledged to a world-wide struggle against communism, because we see ourselves as the defenders of freedom and democracy in the contest against tyranny, because we are, in President Kennedy's words, "by destiny rather than choice, the watchmen on the walls of world freedom." But this role of watchman is not, for all President Kennedy's noble rhetoric, imposed by destiny. It is imposed by ourselves and subject to whatever limitations we choose to put upon it. It can provide the excuse for our playing the role of global gendarme, or serve as a guideline for a measured calculation of the national interest. No task of global omniscience is imposed upon us that we do not choose for ourselves.

As we face the obligations of our global commitments, we are becoming aware of our inability to impose our will upon events or to structure the world into the form we believe it should take. We have the power to destroy most human life on the planet within a matter of minutes, yet we cannot win a guerrilla war against peasants in black pajamas. We are so rich that we can retain an army in Europe, fight a war in Asia, dispense billions in foreign aid, and increase our national wealth by 30 billion a year. Yet we cannot adequately deal with the decay of our cities, the pollution of our atmosphere, the disintegration of public services, the growing hostility between whites and blacks, and the inadequacy of our educational system. Nor, despite the fact that we have dispensed nearly $120 billion abroad during the past twenty years, have we been able seriously to alleviate the poverty and hopelessness in which most of the world's population lives. We have assumed the responsibility for creating Great Societies at home and abroad, but we have not been able to bring this goal into line with our interests or capacities.

As a nation we have what General de Gaulle has uncharitably labeled "a taste for intervention." Applied intelligently and with restraint, as in Western Europe after the war, this taste has done credit to our nation and served its interests. But expanded indiscriminately and without measure, it has involved us in struggles we do not understand, in areas where we are unwanted, and in ambitions which are doomed to frustration. Intervention is neither a sin nor a panacea. It is a method, and like all methods it must be directly related to the end in view. Otherwise it is likely to become an end in itself, dragging the nation down a path it never intended to follow, toward a goal it may find repugnant.

Too often our interventions have seemed to be imposed upon us by abstract theory rather than by a cold assessment of political realities. We have found ourselves involved in areas — the Congo the day before yesterday, Santo Domingo yesterday, Vietnam today, perhaps Thailand tomorrow — where our presence has sometimes exacerbated rather than alleviated the problem, and where it was not within our power to achieve a solution. Interventionism, as a principle of foreign policy, has not served us noticeably well in recent years. But it is a principle to which we are deeply committed: in NATO and its sister pacts, CENTO and SEATO; in the Alliance for Progress; in the Rio Pact and the OAS; in foreign aid; in Southeast Asia; and in any nation which may be taken over by communists, whether from the inside or the outside. It has fostered a staggering program of involvements and it could easily lead us, as it already has in Vietnam, into conflicts whose extent we cannot possibly foresee.

We are in very deep in Europe, in Korea and Japan, in Thailand and Vietnam, in Latin America, and in the entire nexus of underdeveloped countries which are tottering between various forms of authoritarianism. Whether we are in too deep for our own good, and perhaps even for the good of those we are trying to help, is the problem that this essay seeks to explore. The answer, however, will be found not here but in the attitude — in the modesty as well as in the wisdom — that we bring to this peculiarly American dilemma. And it is an American dilemma: the dilemma of how to use power — sometimes economic power in the form of tractors and dollars, sometimes raw military power in the form of soldiers and napalm — for the achievement of ends which American leaders declare to be morally desirable.

The answer to that dilemma has eluded us ever since we plunged wholeheartedly into the world arena a generation ago and acquired, in a bout of moral fervor, a string of dependencies stretching around the globe — an empire, in short. It is an accidental empire, the scope of which the world has never seen, and which we, to this day, have scarcely begun to recognize ourselves.

> *A great empire and little minds go ill together.*
>
> — EDMUND BURKE

2. The American Empire

If the British Empire, as Macaulay once said, was acquired in a fit of absent-mindedness, the American empire came into being without the intention or the knowledge of the American people. We are a people on whom the mantle of empire fits uneasily, who are not particularly adept at running colonies. Yet, by any conventional standards for judging such things, we are indeed an imperial power, possessed of an empire on which the sun truly never sets, an empire that embraces the entire western hemisphere, the world's two great oceans, and virtually all of the Eurasian land mass that is not in communist hands.

We are the strongest and most politically active nation in the world. Our impact reaches everywhere and affects everything it touches. We have the means to destroy whole societies and rebuild them, to topple governments and create others, to impede social change or to stimulate it, to protect our friends and devastate those who oppose us. We have a capacity for action, and a restless, driving compulsion to exercise it, such as the world has never seen. We have a technology that is the wonder of the world, an energy that compels us to challenge the obdurate forces of man and nature, and an affluence that could support whole nations with its waste. We also have a taunting sense of insecurity that makes it difficult for us to accept the limitations of our own remarkable power.

Although our adventure in empire-building may have begun without regard to its consequences, it could not have occurred at all had it not appealed to a deep-rooted instinct in our national character — an instinct to help those less fortunate and permit them to emulate and perhaps one day achieve the virtues of our own society. There was nothing arrogant in this attitude; indeed, it was heavily tinged with altruism. But it did rest upon the belief that it was America's role to make the world a happier, more orderly place, one more nearly reflecting our own image. We saw this as a special responsibility fate had thrust upon us. Standing alone as the defender of Europe, the guardian of Latin America, the protector of weak and dependent nations released from the bondage of colonialism, possessing the mightiest military force in history, an economy productive beyond any man had ever known, and a standard of living the envy of the world — we naturally became persuaded of the universal validity of our institutions, and of our obligation to help those threatened by disorder, aggression, and poverty.

We acquired our empire belatedly and have maintained, and even expanded, it because we found ourselves engaged in a global struggle with an ideology. When we picked up the ruins of the German and Japanese Empires in 1945, we discovered that we could not let them go without seeing them fall under the influence of our ideological adversaries. Struggling against communism, we created a counter-empire of anti-communism. This counter-empire was built upon the idealism enshrined in the charter of the United Nations, the altruism exemplified by the Marshall Plan, the cautious improvisation of the Truman Doctrine, and the military arithmetic of the NATO pact. It spread to Korea and the Congo, to Pakistan and Vietnam, and to a hundred troubled spots where inequality bred grievances, disorder, and instability. We came to see the world as a great stage on which we choreographed an inspiring design for peace, progress, and prosperity. Through American interventionism — benignly where possible, in the form of foreign aid; surgically where necessary, in the form of American soldiers — we hoped to contain the evil forces from the East and provide a measure of hope and security for the rest of mankind. We engaged in a kind of welfare imperialism, empire-building for noble ends rather than for such base motives as profit and influence. We saw ourselves engaged, as Under Secretary of State George Ball declared shortly after we began bombing North Vietnam, in "something new and unique in world history — a role of world responsibility divorced from territorial or narrow national interests." [3]

While it is true that we did not acquire our empire as spoils of war or from a desire for economic profits, "history," as Arnold Toynbee has observed,

> tells us that conquest and annexation are not the only means, or indeed the most frequent and most effective means, by which empires have been built up in the past. The history of the Roman Empire's growth, for instance, is instructive when one is considering the present-day American Empire's structure and prospects. The principal method by which Rome established her political supremacy in her world was by taking her weaker neighbors under her wing and protecting them against her and their stronger neighbors; Rome's

[3] George Ball, "The Dangers of Nostalgia," *Department of State Bulletin*, April 12, 1965, pp. 535–36.

relation with these protégées of hers was a treaty relation. Juridically they retained their previous status of sovereign independence. The most that Rome asked of them in terms of territory was the cession, here and there, of a patch of ground for the plantation of a Roman fortress to provide for the common security of Rome's allies and Rome herself.[4]

Unlike Rome, we have not consciously exploited our empire. In fact, our empire has exploited us, making enormous drains on our resources and our energies. It has not been the most efficient or the most profitable of empires. But then, unlike most empires of the past, ours was not acquired for efficiency or profit. It was acquired because we believe we have a responsibility to defend nations everywhere against communism. This is not an imperial ambition, but it has led us to use imperial methods: establishment of military garrisons around the globe, granting of subsidies to client governments and politicians, application of economic sanctions and even military force against recalcitrant states, and employment of a veritable army of colonial administrators working through such organizations as the State Department, the Agency for International Development, the United States Information Agency, and the Central Intelligence Agency. Having grown accustomed to our empire and having found it pleasing, we have come to take its institutions and its assumptions for granted. Indeed, this is the mark of a convinced imperial power: its advocates never question the virtues of empire, although they may dispute the way in which it is administered, and they do not for a moment doubt that it is in the best interests of those over whom it rules. A basically anti-colonial people, we tolerate, and even cherish, our empire because it seems so benevolent, so designed to serve those embraced by it.

But, many will ask, have we not been generous with our clients and allies, sending them vast amounts of money, and even sacrificing the lives of our own soldiers on their behalf? Of course we have. But this is the role of an imperial power. If it is to enjoy influence and command obedience, it must be prepared to distribute some of its riches throughout its empire and, when necessary, to fight rival powers for the loyalty of vulnerable client states. Empires may be acquired by accident, but they can be held together only by cash, power, and even blood. We learned this in Korea, in Berlin, and in Cuba; and we are learning it again in Vietnam. Whatever the resolution of that tragic conflict, it has once again shattered the recurrent illusion that empires can be maintained on the cheap.

Our empire has not been cheap to maintain, but we have never conceived of it as an empire. Rather, we saw it as a means of containing communism, and thereby permitting other nations to enjoy the benefits of freedom, democracy, and self-determination. This was particularly true in

[4] Arnold Toynbee, *America and the World Revolution* (London: Oxford University Press, 1962), pp. 29–30.

the vast perimeter of colonial and ex-colonial states which offered an enticing field for communist exploitation — and also for our own benevolent intervention. With the European colonial powers weakened and discredited, we were in a position to implement our long-standing sentiments of anti-colonialism. Opposed to the efforts of France, Britain, and Holland to regain control of their Asian colonies, we actively encouraged the efforts of such nationalists as Nehru, Sukarno, and Ho Chi Minh to win the independence of their countries.

However, once the war-weakened European powers finally did leave their colonies, we discovered that most of the newly independent nations had neither the resources nor the ability to stand on their own. With a very few exceptions, they were untrained for independence and unable, or unwilling, to exercise it in ways we approved of. Having proclaimed self-determination as a moral principle valid on every continent and in every country, we found ourselves saddled with the responsibility for some of its consequences. As a result, we stepped into the role left vacant by the departed European powers. In many of the new states we performed the tasks of an imperial power without enjoying the economic territorial advantages of empire. We chose politicians, paid their salaries, subsidized national budgets, equipped and trained armies, built soccer stadiums and airports, and where possible instructed the new nations in the proper principles of foreign policy. We did this with good intentions, because we really did believe in self-determination for everybody as a guiding moral principle, and because we thought it was our obligation to help the less fortunate "modernize" their societies by making them more like ours. This was our welfare imperialism, and it found its roots in our most basic and generous national instincts.

But we also plunged into the economic primitiveness and political immaturity of the new nations because we saw them as a testing-ground in the struggle between freedom and communism, the cataclysmic duel that was to determine the fate of the world. Carried away by the vocabulary of the cold war, we sought to combat communism and preserve "freedom" in whatever area, however unpromising or unlikely, the battle seemed to be joined. Confusing communism as a social doctrine with communism as a form of Soviet imperialism, we assumed that any advance of communist doctrine anywhere was an automatic gain for the Soviet Union. Thus we believed it essential to combat communism in any part of the globe, as though it were a direct threat to our security, even in cases where it was not allied to Soviet power. Our methods were foreign aid, military assistance, and, where all else failed, our own soldiers.

But while this policy was a reasonable one in Europe, where there was a real threat of a Soviet take-over and where our allies shared our feelings about the danger facing them, it was less reasonable throughout most of the ex-colonial world. There the ruling elites were worried not so much by communism as by the real or imagined "imperialism" of the Western powers. They were not particularly committed to our advocacy of free speech and democracy, having never ·experienced it themselves, and they were totally mystified by our praises of capitalism, which in their experience was associated with exploitation, bondage, and misery. Insofar as they thought about communism at all, they could not help being drawn to a doctrine to which the Western powers were opposed. Western antipathy in itself was a major recommendation.

Most of these new nations have genuinely tried to keep out of the struggles among the great powers. They are anti-colonial and suspicious of the West by training and instinct. But they also have not wanted to compromise their neutrality by too close an association with the communists. Insofar as communist doctrine has seemed to offer a solution for their problems of political authority and economic development, they have been receptive to it — as a doctrine. But where it has been allied with Soviet power, they have uniformly resisted it, because it represents a threat to their independence. Most of the new nations, therefore, have tried to tread a path between the conflicting demands of East and West.

Some of them, of course, have been led by clever men who learned to take advantage of our phobias. They found that a threat to "go communist" would usually win large infusions of American foreign-aid funds, just as a threat to "join the imperialists" would inspire Russian counter-bribes. They learned, with the agility of Ben Franklin at the court of Louis XVI, how to manipulate our obsessions, seek out sympathetic ears in Congress and the Pentagon, and conjure up terrible happenings that were about to befall them. The twin doctrines of communism and anti-communism became tools by which they could secure outside help to build up their feeble economies and gain a larger voice in world affairs.

These nations cannot really be blamed for any of this. Being poor, they naturally wanted to secure as much outside assistance as they could, and played upon the anxieties of the great powers to do so. They thus served their own interests and pursued legitimate objectives of their foreign policy. What was less natural, however, was that we permitted ourselves to be manipulated by those who had so little to offer us. We allowed this because we feared that the new nations would fall under the influence of communism. Just as they were inspired by sentiments of anti-colonialism, so we were inspired by an equally powerful anti-communism. It provided the stimulus which led the United States to a massive postwar interventionism and to the creation of an empire that rests upon the pledge to use American military power to combat communism not only as a form of imperialism, but even as a social doctrine in the underdeveloped states. The foundation of this American empire can be traced back to the threat to Europe as it existed more than twenty years ago.

The American empire came into being as a result of the Second World

War, when the struggle against Nazi Germany and imperial Japan brought us to the center of Europe and the offshore islands of Asia. With Russian troops on the Elbe and with the governments of Western Europe tottering under the strain of reconstruction, it seemed that only American power could halt the spread of communism. Consequently, the United States intervened to meet this new European danger, first with economic aid under the Marshall Plan, and then with direct military support under NATO. This was a necessary and proper response to a potential threat, although the emphasis on military over economic support has been sharply debated by historians. However, even before the Marshall Plan was announced, and two years before the NATO pact was signed, the United States laid down the guidelines for its intervention in Europe — and ultimately throughout the world — in the Truman Doctrine of March 12, 1947. Urging Congress to grant $400 million to help the Greek royalists fight the communist rebels, and to enable the Turks to defend themselves against Russia, President Truman declared: "It must be the policy of the United States to support free peoples who are resisting attempted subjugation by armed minorities or by outside pressure."

While such military aid may have been necessary to prevent Greece and Turkey from falling into the communist camp, the language in which the Truman Doctrine was cast implied a commitment far beyond the communist threat to those nations. Had it been confined to the containment of Soviet power, the Truman Doctrine would have expressed a legitimate American security interest. But by a vocabulary which pledged the United States to oppose armed minorities and outside pressure, it involved us in the containment of an ideology. In so doing, it provided the rationale for a policy of global intervention against communism, even in areas where American security was not involved. What was, as Kenneth Thompson has written, "a national and expedient act designed to replace British with American power in Central Europe, was presented as the defense of free democratic nations everywhere in the world against 'direct or indirect aggression.' It translated a concrete American interest for a limited area of the world into a general principle of worldwide validity, to be applied regardless of the limits of American interests and power." [5]

President Truman probably did not envisage the extreme ends toward which this policy would eventually be applied. While he argued that the United States could not permit communism to overturn the status quo by aggression or armed subversion, he put the emphasis on economic assistance and self-help. And he assumed that our efforts would be made in conjunction with our allies. What he did not intend, at least at the time, was unilateral American military intervention in support of client

[5] Kenneth Thompson, *Political Realism and the Crisis of World Politics: An American Approach to Foreign Policy* (Princeton: Princeton University Press, 1960), p. 124.

states threatened from within by communist-inspired insurgents. He did not suggest that the Greek civil war should be fought by American troops, nor did he seriously contemplate the bombardment of Yugoslavia, from whose territory the Greek communist rebels were being supplied. The language of the Truman Doctrine was sweeping, but its application was limited. It grew into a policy of global interventionism only with the later acknowledgment of America's imperial responsibilities.

Historically speaking, the Truman Doctrine was essentially an extension of the Monroe Doctrine across the Atlantic to non-communist Europe. Just as the Monroe Doctrine was designed to maintain the nineteenth-century balance of power between the New World and the Old, so its twentieth-century counterpart was meant to prevent communism from upsetting the political balance between East and West. Where the former used British seapower to serve the security interests of the United States, the latter used American economic and military power to protect non-communist Europe and thereby defend American interests. The implied limitations of the Truman Doctrine were, however, swept aside by the communist attack on South Korea and the resulting assumption that the Russians were prepared to resort to a policy of open aggression. The extension of the Truman Doctrine to cover the Korean war set the stage for its expansion into a general commitment to resist communism everywhere, not only by economic and military support, but by direct American military intervention where necessary. The alliances forged by Dulles were based upon this premise, and even the war in Vietnam is a logical corollary of the Truman Doctrine.

The old limitations of spheres of influence, treaty obligations, and Congressional consent are no longer relevant in cases where the President should deem it necessary to launch a military intervention. As Dean Rusk told a Senate committee: "No would-be aggressor should suppose that the absence of a defense treaty, Congressional declaration, or United States military presence grants immunity to aggression." [6] As a hands-off warning by an imperial power, this statement is eminently logical. It does, however, take us into waters a good deal deeper than those chartered by the Truman Doctrine. By indicating that the United States would not feel itself restricted even to the military treaties it has with more than forty nations, the Secretary of State implicitly removed all inhibitions upon a Presidential decision to intervene against communism wherever, whenever, and however it is deemed necessary.

Behind the warning of Secretary Rusk lies the belief that American military power is so great that the old considerations of national interest — which confined a nation's military interventions to areas deemed vital

[6] Dean Rusk, statement to the Senate Preparedness Subcommittee, *The Washington Post*, August 26, 1966.

to its security — are no longer necessary. The growth of American military power — the enormous array of weapons, the awesome nuclear deterrent, the largest peacetime standing army in our history, and an economy that dominates the world — has apparently convinced many in Washington that "the illusion of American omnipotence," in D. W. Brogan's famous phrase, may not be an illusion. The old feeling of being locked in a closet with Russia appears to have vanished and to have been replaced by the conviction that America alone has world responsibilities, that these are "unique in world history" and justify a policy of global interventionism. If this is not an illusion of omnipotence, it might at least be described as intoxication with power.

Although we consciously seek no empire, we are experiencing all the frustrations and insecurities of an imperial power. Having assumed a position of world leadership because of the abstinence of others, America has not been able to evolve a coherent concept of what she wants and what she may reasonably expect to attain in the world. She has not been able to relate her vision of a universal order on the American model to the more limited imperatives of her own national interests. She is a territorially satiated power, yet plagued by terrible insecurities over her global responsibilities and even over her own identity. America has rejected the old tradition of abstinence and isolationism without having been able to find a new tradition that can bring her interests into line with her ideals.

One of the expressions of this insecurity has been the emergence of anti-communism *as an ideology*, rather than as a reaction to the imperial policies followed by the Soviet Union and other communist powers. This counter-ideology of anti-communism has been both internal and external, reflecting our anxieties about ourselves and about our position in the world at large. As an external anxiety, anti-communism arose from the frustrations of the early postwar period and the disappointments of a terrible war which brought a terrible peace. To possess a military power unequaled in human history, to have marshaled an atomic arsenal capable of eradicating an enemy in a matter of hours, to have no conscious political ambitions other than to spread the virtues of American democracy to less fortunate peoples — to experience all this and still not be able to achieve more than stalemate in the cold war has been difficult for many Americans to accept. The transformation of adversaries into demons followed almost inevitably.

Anti-communism as an ideology was a response not only to stalemate abroad, but also to the insecurities of life at home, where traditional values had been uprooted. To those whose sense of security had been destroyed by the extreme mobility of American life, who felt threatened by the demands of racial minorities for equality, and who were humiliated by the impersonality of an increasingly bureaucratized society, ideological anti-communism served as a focal point of discontent. It could not allay these anxieties, but it could explain them in a form that was acceptable to those who saw as many enemies within the gates as they did outside. The McCarthyism and the witch-hunts of the 1950s, which so debased American intellectual life and spread a blanket of conformity over the government, were a reaction to this insecurity, acts of self-exorcism by a people tormented by demons.

Plagued by domestic anxieties and faced with external dangers that defy the traditional virtues of the American character — an ability to organize, to solve problems, to get things done by sustained energy and determination — the American people have been deeply shaken throughout the whole postwar period. They have had to accept the frustrations of stalemate with Soviet Russia and learn to live in the shadow of atomic annihilation, where the very survival of America is threatened for the first time in her history. This is a situation which, after the traumas of the 1950s, we have now learned to accept with resignation, and even with a certain equanimity. But it is one which breeds deep-rooted anxieties of the kind expressed on the radical right. These frustrations conflict with the most basic elements of Americanism as a secular faith. To challenge this faith is to commit a kind of heresy, and it is as a heretical doctrine that communism has been treated in this country. This is comprehensible only if we accept the fact that Americanism is a creed, that, as a British commentator has observed,

> America is not just a place but an idea, producing a particular kind of society. When immigrants choose to become Americans they are expected to accept the political values of this society, associated with the egalitarian and democratic traditions of the American revolution. As an immigrant country, perhaps only Israel is comparable in the demands it makes for the acceptance of an ideology as well as a territorial nationality. Consequently American patriotism is more readily identified with loyalty to traditional political values; . . . the reverence paid to the American Constitution and the basic political principles of the American revolution encourages the tendency to believe that all failures of the political system must be blamed on corruption, conspiracy or some external enemy. Communism has uniquely provided both an internal and external threat.[7]

Pampered by a continent of extraordinary riches, insulated from political responsibility in the world for longer than was healthy, her soil untouched by war for more than a century, spoiled by an economy which produces a seemingly inexhaustible wealth, flattered by an unnatural dominion over temporarily indigent allies, America has found it difficult to bring her political desires into line with her real needs. We think of solving problems rather than of living with them, and we find compro-

[7] Robert Stephens, *The Observer* (London), July 19, 1964.

mise an unnatural alternative to "victory." These attitudes are a reflection of our frontier mentality, of the cult of individualism, and of a national experience where success is usually the ultimate result of a major effort.

We have fought every war on the assumption that it was the final war that would usher in universal peace. We believed that every adversary was the architect of a global conspiracy, and that once he was overcome there would be "no more war." But every time we overcame an adversary, conflict continued, and we found ourselves confronted with a new adversary to take his place. The change of adversaries has not persuaded us to re-examine the theory, and we still remain chained to the belief in a global conspiracy (now directed from Peking) and the war to end all wars (now being decided in the jungles of Vietnam). We have become the victims of our own mythology: the myth of American omnipotence and the myth of a global communist conspiracy. In combination they have made it exceedingly difficult for us to evolve a foreign policy responsive to the real world we live in.

The decline of political ideology, the rise of a new Europe, the disintegration of the colonial system, the resurgence of China, the technological revolution, the population explosion, the break-up of the cold-war military blocs — these are the central realities of our time. Yet our diplomacy remains frozen in the posture of two decades ago and mesmerized by a ritual anti-communism that has become peripheral to the real conflict of power in today's world. We are in an age of nationalism, in which both communism and capitalism are ceasing to be ideologically significant, and in which the preoccupations of our diplomacy are often irrelevant. We are the last of the ideologues, clinging to political assumptions that have been buried by changing time and circumstance, a nation possessed of an empire it did not want, does not know how to administer, and fears to relinquish. We live in a time of dying ideologies and obsolete slogans, where much of what we have taken for granted is now outdated, and where even the political condition that has dominated our lives — the cold war — may now be over.